Volume 7

Reformed Catholic
Problem of the Forged Catholicism
Warning against Idolatry

PRACTICAL WORKS

Volume 8

Discourse on Conscience
Three Books on Cases of Conscience
Treatise Whether a Man is in Damnation or Grace
A Case of Conscience
Grain of Mustard Seed

Volume 9

True Manner of Knowing Christ Crucified
True Gain
Exhortation to Repentance: Zephaniah 2:1–2
Nature and Practice of Repentance
Combat of the Flesh and Spirit
Man's Imagination
Direction for Government of the Tongue
Damned Art of Witchcraft
Resolution to Countrymen on Prognostication

Volume 10

Treatise on How to Live Well in All Estates
Treatise on Vocations
Right Manner of Erecting and Ordering a Family
Calling of the Ministry
Manner and Method of Preaching
Christian Equity
Treatise on Dying Well

"On the broad shoulders of William Perkins, epoch-making pioneer, stood the entire school of seventeenth-century Puritan pastors and divines, yet the Puritan reprint industry has steadily bypassed him. Now, however, he begins to reappear, admirably edited, and at last this yawning gap is being filled. Profound thanks to the publisher and heartfelt praise to God have become due."

—J. I. Packer, Board of Governors' Professor of Theology,
Regent College, Vancouver, British Columbia

"Without a doubt, the Puritans were theological titans. The Puritan theological tradition did not emerge out of a vacuum. It was shaped by leaders and theologians who set the trajectory of the movement and shaped its commitments. William Perkins was one of those men. Perkins's contribution to Puritan theology is inestimable, and this new reprint of his collected works is a much-awaited addition to all who are still shaped and influenced by the Puritans and their commitment to the centrality of the grace of God found only in Jesus Christ. Even now, every true gospel minister stands in debt to Perkins, and in his shadow."

—R. Albert Mohler Jr., president, The Southern
Baptist Theological Seminary

"The list of those influenced by the ministry of William Perkins reads like a veritable Who's Who of the Puritan Brotherhood and far beyond. This reprinting of his works, so long unobtainable except by a few, is therefore a publishing event of the first magnitude."

—Sinclair B. Ferguson, Chancellor's Professor of Systematic Theology,
Reformed Theological Seminary; Teaching Fellow, Ligonier Ministries

"The father of Elizabethan Puritanism, Perkins presided over a dynasty of faith. The scope of his work is wide, yet on every topic he treats one discovers erudition and deep reflection. He was the first in an amazing line of ministers at Cambridge University's main church. A pastor to pastors, he wrote a best-seller on counseling, was a formative figure in the development of Reformed orthodoxy, and a judicious reformer within the Church of England. I am delighted to see Perkins's works made available again for a wide audience."

—Michael Horton, J. Gresham Machen Professor of Theology
and Apologetics, Westminster Seminary California

"William Perkins was a most remarkable Christian. In his relatively short life he was a great preacher, pastor, and theologian. His prolific writings were foundational to the whole English Puritan enterprise and a profound influence beyond his own time and borders. His works have become rare, and their republication must be a source of real joy and blessing to all serious Christians. Perkins is the first Puritan we should read."

—W. Robert Godfrey, president emeritus, Westminster Seminary California

"This is a welcome collection of the gospel-saturated writings of William Perkins. A faithful pastor, Puritan leader, prolific author, and lecturer, Perkins defended the doctrines of the Protestant Reformation throughout his life. Giving particular emphasis to *solus Christus* and *sola Scriptura*, these Reformed doctrines drove him as a pastor to preach the unsearchable riches of God's truth with confidence and assurance. Sadly, Perkins is unknown to the modern Christian. However, throughout the centuries, the writings, meditations, and treatises of this Puritan luminary have influenced Christians around the world. It is my hope that many will be introduced and reintroduced to the writings of this Reformed stalwart. May his zeal for gospel advance awaken a new generation of biblical preachers and teachers to herald the glory of our sovereign God in this present day."

—Steven J. Lawson, president, OnePassion Ministries, and
professor of preaching at The Master's Seminary

"Relatively few in the church's history have left a written legacy of enduring value beyond their own time. Perkins is surely among that select group. Reformation Heritage Books is to be commended for its commitment to making his *Works* available in this projected series, beginning with this volume."

—Richard B. Gaffin Jr., professor of biblical and systematic
theology emeritus, Westminster Theological Seminary

"Christians have heard about William Perkins, especially that he was an extraordinary preacher whose sermons made a deep impression on Cambridge and that they were still impacting the town in the decades that followed Perkins's death at a mere forty-four years of age in 1602. He was at the heart of the revival of truth and holy living that made the Reformation a glorious work of God. He was the outstanding Puritan theologian of his time, but most of us have not had the opportunity to study his works because of their rarity. After more than three hundred years, this ignorance is going to be ended with the remarkable appearance during the next decade of the complete works of this man of God. We are looking forward to their appearance very much. There will be sufficient gaps between their publication to ensure a sincere attempt at imbibing the truths of each volume, and then we face the challenge of translating Perkins's teaching into flesh-and-blood living."

—Geoff Thomas, pastor emeritus, Alfred Place Baptist Church,
Aberystwyth, Wales

The Works of
WILLIAM PERKINS

The Works of
WILLIAM PERKINS

VOLUME 10

Treatise on How to Live Well in All Estates
Treatise on Vocations
Right Manner of Erecting and Ordering a Family
Calling of the Ministry
Art of Prophesying
Christian Equity
Treatise on Dying Well

EDITED BY JOSEPH A. PIPA AND
J. STEPHEN YUILLE

General editors:
Joel R. Beeke and Derek W. H. Thomas

REFORMATION HERITAGE BOOKS
Grand Rapids, Michigan

The Works of William Perkins, Volume 10

Reformation Heritage Books
2965 Leonard St. NE
Grand Rapids, MI 49525
616-977-0889
orders@heritagebooks.org
www.heritagebooks.org

Printed in the United States of America
20 21 22 23 24 25/10 9 8 7 6 5 4 3 2 1

ISBN 978-1-60178-777-4 (vol. 10)
ISBN 978-1-60178-778-1 (vol. 10) epub

Library of Congress Cataloging-in-Publication Data

Perkins, William, 1558-1602.
[Works]
The works of William Perkins / edited by J. Stephen Yuille ; general editors: Joel R. Beeke and Derek W. H. Thomas.
pages cm
Includes bibliographical references and index.
ISBN 978-1-60178-360-8 (v. 1 : alk. paper) 1. Puritans. 2. Theology—Early works to 1800. I. Yuille, J. Stephen, 1968- editor. II. Beeke, Joel R., 1952- editor. III. Thomas, Derek, 1953- editor. IV. Title.
BX9315.P47 2014
230—dc23
2014037122

For additional Reformed literature, request a free book list from Reformation Heritage Books at the above regular or e-mail address.

Contents

General Preface ix
Preface to Volume 10 xi

Treatise on How to Live Well in All Estates 1
Treatise on Vocations 31
Right Manner of Erecting and Ordering a Family 109
Calling of the Ministry 195
Art of Prophesying 281
Christian Equity 357
Treatise on Dying Well 399

Scripture Index 459
Subject Index 477

General Preface

William Perkins (1558–1602), often called "the father of Puritanism," was a master preacher and teacher of Reformed, experiential theology. He left an indelible mark upon the English Puritan movement, and his writings were translated into Dutch, German, French, Hungarian, and other European languages. Today he is best known for his writings on predestination, but he also wrote prolifically on many doctrinal and practical subjects, including extended expositions of Scripture. The 1631 edition of his English *Works* filled over two thousand large pages of small print in three folio volumes.

It is puzzling why his full *Works* have not been in print since the early seventeenth century, especially given the flood of Puritan works reprinted in the mid-nineteenth and late twentieth centuries. Ian Breward did much to promote the study of Perkins, but Breward's now rare, single-volume compilation of the *Work of William Perkins* (1970) could only present samplings of Perkins's writings. We are extremely pleased that this lacuna is being filled, as it has been a dream of many years to see the writings of this Reformed theologian made accessible again to the public, including laymen, pastors, and scholars.

Reformation Heritage Books is publishing Perkins's *Works* in a newly typeset format with spelling and capitalization conformed to modern American standards. The old forms ("thou dost") are changed to the modern equivalent ("you do"), except in Scripture quotations and references to deity. Punctuation has also been modernized. However, the original words are left intact, not changed into modern synonyms, and the original word order retained even when it differs from modern syntax. Pronouns are capitalized when referring to God. Some archaic terms and obscure references are explained in the editor's footnotes.

As was common in his day, Perkins did not use quotation marks to distinguish a direct quotation from an indirect quotation, summary, or paraphrase, but simply put all citations in italics (as he also did with proper names). We have removed such italics and followed the general principle of placing citations in quotation marks even if they may not be direct and exact quotations. Perkins generally quoted the Geneva Bible, but rather than conforming his quotations to any particular translation of Scripture, we have left them in his words. Scripture references in the margins are brought into the text and enclosed in square brackets. Parenthetical Scripture references in general are abbreviated and punctuated according to the modern custom (as in Rom. 8:1), sometimes corrected, and sometimes moved to the end of the clause instead of its beginning. Other notes from the margins are placed in footnotes and labeled, "In the margin." Where multiple sets of parentheses were nested within each other, the inward parentheses have been changed to square brackets. Otherwise, square brackets indicate words added by the editor. An introduction to each volume by its editor orients the reader to its contents.

The projected *Works of William Perkins* will include ten volumes, including four volumes of biblical exposition, three volumes of doctrinal and polemical treatises, and three volumes of ethical and practical writings. A breakdown of each volume's contents may be found inside the cover of this book.

If it be asked what the center of Perkins's theology was, then we hesitate to answer, for students of historical theology know that this is a perilous question to ask regarding any person. However, we may do well to end this preface by repeating what Perkins said at the conclusion of his influential manual on preaching, "The sum of the sum: preach one Christ by Christ to the praise of Christ."

With the publication of this volume of Perkins's *Works*, we are grateful to God for the completion of this project, as well as to our editors, proofreaders, and typesetters who persevered throughout the years on these volumes as a labor of love. In some ways, we are grateful our goal of reprinting all the writings of "the father of Puritanism" in modern type has been reached, but in other ways, we will miss editing the writings of our friend, William Perkins, who has edified us in countless ways. It was an honor and privilege to read the corpus of his writings, and we pray God that many thousands will profit immeasurably from reading these ten remarkable volumes that so powerfully impacted the movement we now call Puritanism. *Soli Deo gloria!*

—Joel R. Beeke and Derek W. H. Thomas

Preface to Volume 10 of William Perkins's *Works*

The English Reformation was a lengthy process, in which the country wavered between Catholicism and Protestantism as monarchs came and went. In just twenty years, the religion of the land changed four times, but the reign of Elizabeth (1558–1603) brought a measure of stability which allowed the English Reformers to solidify the church's position. William Perkins (1558–1602) played a pivotal role in this, and his works became the standard polemic against Rome.

Despite the progress in reforming medieval teaching in the light of Scripture, Perkins was deeply dissatisfied with the spiritual condition within the Church of England. He was convinced that many of his fellow countrymen still suffered the ill-effects of the Roman Catholic dogma of implicit faith; that is to say, they still assumed that as long as they accepted some "necessary" points of religion they were good Christians. In a day (not unlike our own) in which mere assent was accepted as faith, empty profession was accepted as conversion, and dead formality was accepted as godliness, Perkins was particularly troubled by the prevalence of "civility" within the church. "If we look into the general state of our people," said he, "we shall see that religion is professed, but not obeyed; nay, obedience is counted as preciseness, and so reproached."[1]

This lack of fervency in religion was one of the chief reasons why Perkins was not so concerned about the external forms of the Church of England. Instead of expending his energy on issues related to church polity, he was determined to address what he perceived to be widespread ignorance within

1. William Perkins, *A Godly and Learned Exposition Upon Christ's Sermon in the Mount*, in *The Works of that Famous and Worthy Minister of Christ in the University of Cambridge, M. William Perkins*, 3 vols. (London: John Haviland, 1631), 3:261. As R. C. Lovelace explains, "The problem that confronts the Puritans as they look out on their decaying society and their lukewarm church is not simply to dislodge the faithful from the slough of mortal or venial sin, but radically to awaken those who are professing but not actual Christians, who are caught in a trap of carnal security." "The Anatomy of Puritan Piety: English Puritan Devotional Literature, 1600–1640," in *Christian Spirituality III*, eds. L. Dupré and D. E. Saliers (New York: Crossroad Publishing, 1989), 303.

the church. Simply put, he was adamant that the church's most pressing need was not for ecclesiastical innovation, but practical theological instruction.

This concern became the driving force behind much of Perkins's ministry. It is entirely fitting, therefore, that this final volume of his *Works* should bring together seven treatises that epitomize his practical instruction.[2] These serve to demonstrate Perkins's core conviction that the gospel touches all of life by bringing it under the rule of Scripture. For the reader's benefit, the seven treatises are here introduced under four key headings.

A God-Honoring Ministry

Like the early Reformers, Perkins believed that preaching is the principal means of grace; in short, the preacher is God's mouthpiece.[3] It was this conviction that led him to commit himself to serve as lecturer at Great St. Andrew's Church in Cambridge.[4] It was also this conviction that led him to devote much of his time and effort to preparing young men for pastoral ministry. He declared, "When we see a people without knowledge and without good guides or teachers, or when we see one stand up in the congregation unable to teach, here is a matter for mourning."[5] For Perkins, the dearth of capable preachers in England was explained in large part by a lack of adequate training. The university curriculum was void of any formal theological education; moreover, it provided no instruction in how to preach or provide pastoral care. Ian Breward remarks, "The assumption was that, since the shape of Christian faith was known and

2. The table of contents in volume 1 of this series indicates that *Death's Knell* is included in volume 10. Upon further review, however, it has been determined that this work is not properly attributed to William Perkins. It does not appear in the seventeenth-century editions of his *Works*. For a similar assessment, see Ian Green, *Print and Protestantism in Early Modern England* (Oxford: Oxford University Press, 2000), 479–80.

3. See John Calvin, *The Institutes of the Christian Religion,* 2 vols., ed. John T. McNeill, trans. Ford Lewis Battles (Philadelphia: The Westminster Press, 1960), 2:1018; and John Calvin, *Commentary on the Book of the Prophet Isaiah* (Grand Rapids: Eerdmans, 1947), 393.

4. A lecturer was appointed to work alongside the regular pastor. Technically, his ministry was supplemental. In many instances, it was a convenient way to circumvent the rules of conformity. For more on this, see William Haller, *The Rise of Puritanism* (Philadelphia: University of Pennsylvania Press, 1972), 53; and Paul S. Seaver, *The Puritan Lectureships: The Politics of Religious Dissent, 1560–1662* (Stanford: Stanford University Press, 1970).

5. William Perkins, *An Exposition of the Lord's Prayer in the Way of Catechising, Serving for Ignorant People* (London, 1592), 83. According to Ian Breward, Perkins "stood within a long tradition of complaint at this point. Tyndale had wanted all clergy to be able and conscientious preachers, but by 1583 only one sixth of the English clergy was licensed to preach. After a strenuous campaign by Whitgift to raise the standards of the clergy, there were still only 4,830 licensed to preach in 1603. There were 9,244 parishes." "Introduction," in *The Works of William Perkins,* vol. 2 of the Courtenay Library of Reformation Classics (Berkshire, England: Sutton Courtenay Press, 1970), 35.

the basic duties of the ministry well defined, any educated man could learn how to comfort the troubled, sick, and dying, play his role in local society, understand the Bible, and have a sufficient understanding of classical rhetoric and logic to preach a satisfactory sermon."[6]

The failure of the universities to equip men adequately for the ministry greatly distressed Perkins. He was not against a robust liberal arts education, but he recognized that something more was needed.[7] Since no major work had been produced by an English Protestant to meet the need for instruction in practical theology, Perkins decided to fill the void by setting out ministerial duties—particularly preaching—in detail.[8]

In *The Calling of the Ministry*,[9] Perkins turned his attention to expounding two texts of Scripture in an attempt to communicate the "duties and dignities" of the pastoral office. He begins with Job 33:23–24,[10] because it contains "a worthy description of a true minister."[11] In brief, he is known by his (1) *title*—"interpreter," (2) *rarity*—"one of a thousand," (3) *office*—"to declare unto men [God's] righteousness," (4) *blessing*—"then God will have mercy upon the sinner," and (5) *commission*—"[God] will say, Deliver him that he go not down into the pit." As Perkins elaborates on each of these marks, he emphasizes the pastor's two-fold role of speaking to people on God's behalf (preaching) and speaking to God on people's behalf (praying).[12]

Perkins then shifts his focus to Isaiah 6:5–8,[13] describing in detail the prophet's (1) vision, (2) consolation, and (3) commission. Based on Isaiah's example, Perkins affirms that when God calls a pastor, He humbles him for

---

6. Breward, "Introduction," 36.

7. Breward, "Introduction," 36.

8. Ian Breward, "William Perkins and the Ideal of the Ministry in the Elizabethan Church," *The Reformed Theological Review* 24, no. 3 (October 1965): 77–78.

9. William Perkins, *The Calling of the Ministry: Two Treatises, Describing the Duties and Dignities of that Calling*, in *The Works of that Famous and Worthy Minister of Christ in the University of Cambridge, M. William Perkins*, vol. 3 (London: John Haviland, 1631). It was published posthumously in 1605.

10. "If there be with him a messenger, an interpreter, one of a thousand to declare unto man his righteousness: Then will he have mercy on him, and will say, Deliver him, that he go not down into the pit, for I have received a reconciliation."

11. Perkins, *Calling of the Ministry*, 3:429.

12. Perkins, *Calling of the Ministry*, 3:431, 434–35, 444.

13. "Then I said, Woe is me, I am undone, for I am a man of polluted lips and dwell in the midst of a people of polluted lips: for my eyes have seen the King and Lord of hosts. Then flew one of the Seraphim unto me, with a hot coal in his hand, which he has taken from the altar with the tongs: And he touched my mouth, and said, Lo, this hath touched thy lips, and thine iniquity shall be taken away, and thy sin shall be purged. Also I heard the voice of the Lord, saying, Whom shall I send? and who shall go for Us? Then said I, Here am I, send me. And he said, Go."

"his own pollution and sinfulness" as "a preparative for grace."[14] When a pastor sees his sin and misery, he finds nothing in himself but "cause of fear and astonishment." At this point, God pours "the oil of grace and of sweet comfort" into his heart, thereby refreshing his weary soul with "the dew of His mercy."[15] For Perkins, this is a necessary step in a man's call to pastoral ministry, for he cannot preach movingly what he has not felt deeply. It is through his own experience that he learns "the true way of comforting troubled and distressed consciences."[16]

Perkins stays with the subject of pastoral ministry in *The Art of Prophesying*.[17] Initially, this title might seem strange to those who think of "prophecy" in terms of foretelling. It is important to note, therefore, that Perkins followed John Calvin and other Reformers in recognizing that passages such as Romans 12:6[18] apply the term "prophecy" to preaching.[19] Thus, he did not employ the term "prophesying" in the sense of *foretelling* but *forthtelling*. Viewing the apostolic period as unique in the history of the church, he was a cessationist when it comes to revelatory gifts. He was adamant that the nature of the Holy Spirit's work in the authors of Scripture was unique, meaning He now illumines what He then inspired; that is to say, He only works upon the foundation of the Word. For Perkins, this implied that the pastor's chief task is simply to expound what the Holy Spirit has revealed in Scripture. When he stands before his congregation, he does so "in the name and room of Christ," with the goal of calling people into a "state of grace" and preserving them therein.[20] Preaching,

14. Perkins, *Calling of the Ministry*, 3:443, 452.

15. Perkins, *Calling of the Ministry*, 3:452.

16. Perkins, *Calling of the Ministry*, 3:457. For more on this, see the "preface" in volume 8 of *The Works of William Perkins* (Grand Rapids: Reformation Heritage Books, 2019).

17. William Perkins, *The Art of Prophesying; or, A treatise concerning the sacred and only true manner and method of preaching*, in *The Works of that Famous and Worthy Minister of Christ in the University of Cambridge, M. William Perkins*, vol. 2 (London, 1631). It was first published in 1592 in Latin, and then translated into English in 1606. The translator was Thomas Tuke, who was later imprisoned for supporting Laudian ceremonialism. See Thomas Seaver, *The Puritan Lectureships: The Politics of Religious Dissent 1560–1662* (Stanford: Stanford University Press, 1970). The treatise consists of eleven chapters, covering the principles of hermeneutics, interpretation, application, and proclamation. For a thorough analysis, see Joseph A. Pipa, "William Perkins and the Development of Puritan Preaching" (PhD dissertation, Westminster Theological Seminary, 1985).

18. "Having then gifts differing according to the grace that is given to us, whether prophecy, let us prophesy according to the proportion of faith."

19. John Calvin, *Commentary on The Epistles of Paul: The Epistles to the Romans and to the Thessalonians,* eds. D. W. and T. F. Torrance (Grand Rapids: Eerdmans, 1961), 269. Also see the notes on these passages in the Geneva Bible.

20. Perkins, *Art of Prophesying*, 2:646. For a helpful discussion about urgency in Puritan preaching, see Maarten Kuivenhoven, "Condemning Coldness and Sleepy Dullness: The

therefore, is the means by which people experience God's grace from conversion to glorification.[21]

In *The Art of Prophesying*, Perkins lays out "the sacred and only method of preaching" in four succinct steps. The first is "to read the text distinctly out of the canonical Scriptures." At this point, Perkins's conviction regarding the authority and sufficiency of Scripture steps to the fore. The "canonical" Scriptures consist of the thirty-nine books of the Old Testament and the twenty-seven books of the New Testament, which constitute the "wisdom of God concerning the truth."[22] As such, they alone form the substance of preaching.[23]

The second step is "to give the sense and understanding" of the text. This is known as interpretation: "the opening of the words and sentences of the Scripture, so that one entire and natural sense may appear."[24] Perkins's process was straightforward. He encouraged preachers to consider the literary style

---

Concept of Urgency in the Preaching Models of Richard Baxter and William Perkins," in *Puritan Reformed Journal* 4, no. 2 (July 2012): 180–200.

21. For more on this, see J. Stephen Yuille, "Ready to Receive: Humbling and Softening in William Perkins's Preparation of the Heart," *Puritan Reformed Journal* 5, no. 2 (2013): 91–106; Joel R. Beeke, "The Lasting Power of Reformed Experiential Preaching," in *Puritan Reformed Spirituality* (Grand Rapids: Reformation Heritage Books, 2004), 425–43; and Paul R. Schaefer, "The Art of Prophesying by William Perkins (1558–1602)," *The Devoted Life: An Invitation to the Puritan Classics*, eds. Kelly M. Kapic and Randall C. Gleason (Downers Grove: InterVarsity Press, 2004).

22. Perkins, *Art of Prophesying*, 2:649. As Breward notes, the "discussion of inspiration and the nature of the Bible was...fundamental to Perkins's whole theology and to his understanding of the pastoral task of proclaiming the gospel." "Introduction," 38.

23. Perkins stood at an important juncture in the history of Reformed preaching, particularly as it relates to issues of reception and transmission. Until the latter half of the twentieth century, early modern preaching in England was a neglected field of study, "around which there hung an air of dusty antiquarianism." Arnold Hunt, *The Art of Hearing: English Preachers and Their Audiences, 1590–1640* (Cambridge: Cambridge University Press, 2010), 1. In the past fifty years, however, numerous publications have appeared, addressing continuity and discontinuity in early modern preaching in England. E.g., Peter McCullough, *Sermons at Court: Politics and Religion in Elizabethan and Jacobean Preaching* (Cambridge: Cambridge University Press, 1998); David Appleby, *Black Bartholomew's Day: Preaching, Polemic and Restoration Nonconformity* (Manchester: Manchester University Press, 2007). In these historical analyses, Perkins has received his fair share of attention because of his lasting legacy.

24. Perkins, *Art of Prophesying*, 2:653. Richard Muller observes that Perkins "evidences a preference for a close, literal/grammatical location of the meaning of the text coupled with, as was true of the work of his predecessors in the Reformed tradition, a strong sense of the direct theological address of the text to the church in the present." "William Perkins and the Protestant Exegetical Tradition: Interpretation, Style and Method," in *A Commentary on Hebrews 11 (1609 Edition)*, ed. John H. Augustine (New York: Pilgrim Press, 1991), 87. Muller explains Perkins's use of "scope" and "method" in exegesis—he divides each verse, explains the meaning of its parts, and then draws out the text's argument in terms of the grammatical and logical relations of the parts.

and structure of the text, and then explain specific words and phrases.[25] He also instructed preachers to ask questions of each text. How does it relate to the principal themes of Scripture? What is its context, author, audience, and purpose? What other passages of Scripture shed light on it? In all this, Perkins emphasized that the preacher's principal goal is to "open" Scripture, so that its meaning becomes evident to all.

The third step in preaching is "to collect a few and profitable points of doctrine." Perkins referred to this process as "the right cutting of the Word."[26] In simple terms, it involves deducing the main point of a passage: theological and practical. These "doctrines" are clearly stated in the text or rightly inferred from the text, and they should be reinforced with "proofs" as necessary.[27]

The fourth and final step in preaching is "to apply the doctrines rightly collected to the life and manners of men in a simple and plain speech."[28] This is where Perkins excelled by carefully dividing his audience into six categories: (1) the ignorant and unteachable; (2) the ignorant and teachable; (3) the knowledgeable and proud; (4) the knowledgeable and humble; (5) those who believe; and (6) those who have fallen. Recognizing that a typical congregation consists of people from each of these categories,[29] Perkins counseled preachers to know their people, so that they are able to "apply the doctrines" to each one through correction, admonition, and exhortation. "Thus any place of Scripture ought to be handled," wrote Perkins, "yet so as that all the doctrines be not propounded to the people, but those only which may be fitly applied to our times and to the present condition of the church. And they must not only be choice ones, but also few, lest the hearers be overcharged with their multitude."[30]

---

25. Perkins, *Art of Prophesying*, 2:653–62.

26. Perkins, *Art of Prophesying*, 2:662.

27. Perkins introduces nine arguments to aid in this work. For definitions of these, see Edward P. J. Corbett and Robert J. Connors, *Classical Rhetoric for the Modern Student,* 4th edition (Oxford: Oxford University Press, 1999), 84–112.

28. Perkins, *Art of Prophesying*, 2:664. Sinclair Ferguson explains, "Perkins also well knew that he was addressing the marred image of God, fallen minds, distorted affections, and rebellious wills. The task therefore was to address complex psychosomatic beings, marred in every dimension, by addressing the truth to the mind in order to illumine it, by moving the affections in order to heal them, and by liberating the will from its bondage as the preaching of the gospel effected faith in Christ. Perkins understood that when Paul speaks about Scripture being profitable for *correction*, he uses that language in a positive sense, that is, to transform, heal, and restore the whole person." *William Perkins: Architect of Puritanism,* eds. Joel R. Beeke and Greg Salazar (Grand Rapids: Reformation Heritage Books, 2019), 20.

29. For a helpful analysis of these categories, see Erroll Hulse, "William Perkins: Application in Preaching," in *The Pure Flame of Devotion: The History of Christian Spirituality*, ed. G. Stephen Weaver and Ian Hugh Clary (Kitchener, Ont.: Joshua Press, 2013), 177–94.

30. Perkins, *Art of Prophesying*, 2:669.

The effectiveness of Perkins's own preaching was due in large part to this last step. He had a penchant for dealing with "cases of conscience" through careful self-examination and faithful scriptural application.[31] By all accounts, he was a skilled spiritual physician, who excelled at expounding and applying God's truth to those under his pastoral care. He was committed to ensuring that his preaching was clear and direct, because he believed this was the best way to convince the judgment and embrace the affections, thereby bringing the mind into vital contact with the meaning of Scripture.

Despite his emphasis on method, Perkins was well aware that preaching was insufficient in itself to effect lasting change in others: "We preachers may cry until our lungs fly out, or be spent within us, and men are moved no more than stones."[32] There was still a missing element: unction (or, the demonstration of God's power). Such power is evident when people judge that the Holy Spirit is speaking through the preacher's words and gestures. Perkins explains, "When as the minister of the Word does in the time of preaching so behave himself, that all, even ignorant persons and unbelievers may judge, that it is not so much he who speaks, as the Spirit of God in him and by him.... This makes the ministry to be lively and powerful."[33] But how is such unction achieved? While recognizing that anointed preaching ultimately resides in the sovereign will of the Holy Spirit, Perkins maintained that He is more likely to bless a certain kind of preaching.

This preaching is marked by simplicity. A "simple" or "plain" style of preaching addresses people in a way that facilities their understanding of what is being said. A. F. Herr remarks, "The plain style is sober, simple in expression, as direct as possible, and free from ornamentation of either fantastic ideas or verbiage."[34] Perkins insisted on this "plain" style because he was persuaded that "a strange word hinders the understanding of those things that are spoken.... It draws the mind away from the purpose to some other matter."[35] Closely related to this, Perkins perceived that far too many preachers were overly concerned with the "trimmings" of their sermons and, therefore, unable to convey Christ in a living way to their people. He was deeply dissatisfied with and

31. See Ian Breward, "William Perkins and the Origins of Puritan Casuistry," *The Evangelist Quarterly* 40 (1968): 16–22; George L. Mosse, *The Holy Pretence: A Study in Christianity and Reason of State from William Perkins to John Winthrop* (Oxford: Blackwell, 1957), 48–67.

32. William Perkins, *A Faithful and Plain Exposition Upon the Two First Verses of the Second Chapter of Zephaniah*, in *The Works of that Famous and Worthy Minister of Christ in the University of Cambridge, M. William Perkins*, 3 vols. (London, 1631), 3:424. Also see *Calling of the Ministry*, 3:430.

33. Perkins, *Art of Prophesying*, 2:670.

34. A. F. Herr, *The Elizabethan Sermon* (New York: Octagon Books, 1969), 89–90.

35. Perkins, *Art of Prophesying*, 2:670.

openly critical of the "ornate" style of preaching widespread within the Church of England.[36] Herr describes this style as "florid" and "witty."[37] According to Perkins, it was weighed down with human learning, which rendered it ineffective. A pastor's aim in the pulpit should not be the demonstration of his skill, but the demonstration of God's power. It was essential for Perkins, therefore, that a preacher possess not only "the knowledge of divine things flowing in his brain but engraved on his heart and printed in his soul by the spiritual finger of God."[38]

Anointed preaching is also marked by liberty. Perkins was opposed to "memorizing" sermons because he believed it quenched freedom in preaching: "He who through fear does stumble at one word, does trouble the congregation, and confound the memory."[39] In addition to this, Perkins was convinced that memorization hinders "pronunciation, action, and the holy motions of the affections...because the mind is wholly bent on this, to wit, that the memory fainting now under her burden may not fail."[40] Perkins's method was straightforward. As he prepared each sermon, he studied and reviewed until he was familiar with the content of his message. Then, he developed a clear sermon outline accompanied by arguments and illustrations. He felt this approach allowed for liberty in expression. This liberty was facilitated by Perkins's use of voice and body. His voice was moderate when delivering doctrine, yet fervent when applying God's truth to the heart. His bodily gestures conveyed gravity. The trunk of his body was quiet, while the motions of his arms, hands, and eyes expressed "the godly affections of the heart."[41]

Finally, anointed preaching is marked by consistency. As far as Perkins was concerned, God's grace must be evident in a preacher's life. Such grace includes

---

36. The "ornate" style was chiefly concerned about "the abundant use of rhetorical devices such as repetition, heaping of examples, gradation or word-chains and schemata...innumerable quotations from the church fathers and various secular sources." Pipa, "William Perkins and the Development of Puritan Preaching," 38. For more on the styles of preaching, see Perry Miller, *The New England Mind* (New York: MacMillan, 1939); J. W. Blench, *Preaching in England in the Late Fifteenth and Sixteenth Centuries* (New York: Barnes & Noble, 1964); and Horton Davies, *The Worship of English Puritans* (Morgan, Pa.: Soli Deo Gloria, 1997).

37. Herr, *The Elizabethan Sermon*, 89–103. At the time of the Reformation, there were two main types of sermon structure: the "ancient" and the "modern." The "ancient" was the explanation and application of the text *secundum ordinem textus,* preaching through the text phrase by phrase. The "modern" was structured like most sermons today with an introduction, body, and conclusion. In the hands of the Anglo-Catholics, however, the "modern" declined into "cold and minute analysis and refinement, with little adaptation to life and need." Edwin Charles Dargan, *The Art of Preaching in the Light of its History* (New York: George H. Doran Company, 1922), 143.

38. Perkins, *Art of Prophesying*, 2:672.

39. Perkins, *Art of Prophesying*, 2:670.

40. Perkins, *Art of Prophesying*, 2:670.

41. Perkins, *Art of Prophesying*, 2:672.

a good conscience before God and man, and an inward feeling of God's truth. It also includes fear of God, love for people, constancy in life, and temperance in conduct.[42] Holiness in a preacher is absolutely necessary because God "abhors the combination of godly speech and an ungodly life."[43] Equally important, Perkins realized that "people do not see the ministry but the person of the minister" and, for this reason, there must be consistency between a pastor's words and walk. Perkins's own growth in godliness was a powerful example to all. According to one biographer, "he lived his sermons, and as his preaching was a comment on his text, so his practice was a comment on his preaching."[44]

Simplicity, liberty, and consistency are no guarantee of unction, but—in Perkins's opinion—characterize the kind of preaching that is most likely to experience the Holy Spirit's blessing. Given his theology of preaching (*simple* in approach and *supernatural* in effect), it is no surprise that Perkins gave himself wholeheartedly to it and to imparting his method to others. His approach became the standard for a generation of preachers, and it continues to exert an influence upon the pulpit down to the present day.[45]

A God-Honoring Vocation

As a pastor must be faithful in the performance of his calling, so too all believers must be faithful in their calling. Perkins takes up this theme in *A Treatise of the Vocations*.[46] His text is 1 Corinthians 7:20, where Paul declares, "Let every man abide in that same vocation wherein he was called." Perkins begins by identifying two calls in the life of every believer. The first is the "general" call to salvation in Christ, while the second is the "particular" (or, "personal") call to a specific role in the home, church, and commonwealth.[47] To be more precise,

42. Perkins, *Art of Prophesying*, 2:672.

43. Perkins, *Art of Prophesying*, 2:671.

44. Thomas Fuller, *Abel Redivivus: or the Dead Yet Speaking*, 2 vols. (London: William Tegg, 1867), 2:436.

45. This method was recommended by the Westminster Divines in the Directory for Public Worship. *The Westminster Confession* (Edinburgh: Banner of Truth, 2018), 559–63. Also see *The Larger Catechism*, 159.

46. William Perkins, *A Treatise of the Vocations, or Callings of Men, with the Sorts and Kinds of Them, and the Right Use Thereof* (Cambridge: John Legate, 1603).

47. Perkins, *Vocations*, 1. Much has been made of the Puritan concept of "calling." According to Max Weber, it is responsible for today's capitalism. *The Protestant Ethic and the Spirit of Capitalism* (New York: Scribner, 1976), 13. For similar views, see R. B. Schlatter, *The Social Ideas of Religious Leaders, 1660–1688* (New York: Octagon Books, 1971); and Christopher Hill, *Society and Puritanism in Pre-Revolutionary England* (London: Panther Books, 1969), 135–38. In short, Weber argues that the doctrine of election caused the Puritans to focus upon assurance. Given their concept of work as God-ordained, they urged "tireless labor in a calling…as the best possible means of attaining this self-assurance." *Protestant Ethic*, 77–78. This resulted in an emphasis upon "ceaseless, constant, systematic labor in a secular calling" as "the surest and most

the particular call is "a certain kind of life, imposed and ordained on man by God for the common good."[48] That being the case, each of us must (1) pursue a particular calling,[49] (2) determine that it is the best for us, (3) confirm that it is consistent with the Christian faith, (4) maintain a good reputation in it, and (5) ensure that it never takes precedent over our general calling.

Perkins proceeds to divide particular callings into two groups. The first includes all those that belong to the essence of a society. Without them, society could not exist. In the family, this includes masters, servants, husbands, wives, parents, and children; in the commonwealth, it includes magistrates and subjects; and, in the church, it includes ministers and congregants. The second group consists of all those that serve only for the good, happy, and quiet estate of a society.

Whatever our particular vocation, we are to seek to fulfill it in a God-honoring manner. This is accomplished by following God's will in (1) choosing a vocation, (2) entering a vocation, (3) continuing in a vocation, and (4) ending a vocation. Perkins claims that we should never choose a vocation in isolation, but in consultation with parents and other godly advisors. The church should confirm our choice by ensuring that it suits our gifts and abilities, contributes to the common good, and glorifies God. Of particular interest is Perkins's extensive discussion on "continuance" in vocation. Close to half of his treatise is devoted to this subject, in which he identifies common hindrances to the right use of a vocation; e.g., covetousness, injustice, ambition, envy, and impatience.[50]

Perkins's analysis affords many helpful lessons concerning the nature of work and our approach to it, but his most valuable contribution is his assertion that our "particular" callings are the principal means by which we glorify God in this world. Foundational to the Reformation was the rejection of the notion that the "sacred" refers to anything under the church's control whereas

---

visible proof of regeneration and the genuineness of faith." And this, according to Weber, "was inevitably the most powerful lever imaginable with which to bring the spread of that philosophy of life which we have here termed the 'spirit' of capitalism." *Protestant Ethic*, 116. Weber's thesis has generated a large body of literature. Some scholars question the legitimacy of his distinction between a particularly Puritan and generally Protestant work ethic. See Timothy Breen, "The Non-Existent Controversy: Puritan and Anglican Attitudes on Work and Wealth," *Church History* 35 (1966): 273–87. C. John Sommerville adopts an entirely different approach from Weber, arguing that Anglicanism (not Puritanism) stressed "worldly enterprise." "The Anti-Puritan Work Ethic," *Journal of British Studies* 20 (1981): 73.

48. Perkins, *Vocations*, 2.

49. In this section, Perkins expresses his disapproval of begging. This does not arise from any indifference on his part to the plight of the poor, but from his conviction that the act of begging is contrary to Scripture.

50. Perkins, *Vocations*, 82.

the "secular' refers to anything not under the church's control.[51] For Martin Luther, this separation between the sacred and secular was the first of "three walls" constructed by the Roman Church. Determined to tear it down, Luther declared, "It is pure invention that pope, bishop, priests, and monks are called the spiritual estate while princes, lords, artisans, and farmers are called the temporal estate. This is indeed a piece of deceit and hypocrisy."[52] In contrast to the Catholic position, the Reformers were convinced that all of life is sacred.[53] Perkins adopted this view and applied it to his particular context. He insisted that we have two callings. The first is our conversion to Christ; this is our identity. The second is our condition in life; this is the means by which we live out our identity in Christ. In sum, God has assigned and called each of us to a certain life—single or married, carpenter or electrician, government official or manual laborer, parent or child, student or retiree, etc. It is all sacred, in that we are to glorify God in whatever life He has appointed for us.[54]

Equally significant is Perkins's claim that, when we fulfill our vocation in a God-honoring manner,[55] we actually perform those "good works, which God

---

51. This division between secular and sacred has prevailed since the early church period. "In the early part of the fourth century, Eusebius propounded a doctrine of two lives: 'Two ways of life were thus given by the law of Christ to His church. The one is above nature, and beyond common human living...permanently separate from the common customary life of mankind, it devotes itself to the service of God alone.... Such then is the perfect form of the Christ life.' The other is 'more humble, more human, permits man to join in pure nuptials, and to produce children...it allows them to have minds for farming, for trade, and other more secular interests as well as for religion...a kind of secondary grade of piety is attributed to them.' This pattern shaped much of subsequent church thinking. So, for example, Augustine distinguished between an 'active life' and a 'contemplative life.' The [first] took in almost every kind of work, including studying, preaching, and teaching. The [second] was reflection and meditation upon God and His truth. While both kinds of life were good, the contemplative life was of a higher order." Paul Marshall, *A Kind of Life Imposed on Man: Vocation and Social Order from Tyndale to Locke* (Toronto: University of Toronto Press, 1996), 18–19.

52. Martin Luther, *To the Christian Nobility of the German Nation Concerning the Reform of the Christian Estate*, in *Luther's Works*, ed. H. T. Lehmann (Philadelphia: Fortress Press, 1960), 44:127.

53. P. J. Beale expresses the significance of this view as follows: "Whether his calling was an exalted or a humble one, the Puritan worker sought to glorify God by the way in which he worked, knowing that he had a Master in heaven." "Sanctifying the Outer Life," in *Aspects of Sanctification* (London: Westminster Conference, 1981), 72.

54. In other words, the dignity of work does not lie in its importance in the world's eyes, but in the manner in which it is performed. See Charles Robert Munson, "William Perkins, Theologian of Transition" (PhD dissertation, Case Western Reserve University, 1971), 7.

55. For recent scholarship on the sanctification of work, see Gene Edward Veith, Jr., ed., *God at Work: Your Christian Vocation in All of Life* (Wheaton: Crossway, 2002); Timothy Keller and Katherine Leary Alsdorf, *Every Good Endeavor* (New York: Penguin Books, 2012).

hath before ordained that we should walk in them" (Eph. 2:10).[56] This is the case because the faithful execution of our vocation contributes to the "common good"—the betterment of society as a whole. It is, therefore, the chief means by which we express our love for God and neighbor (Mark 12:30–31). All that to say, Perkins did not restrict "good works" to acts of serving the poor, helping the sick, visiting the infirm, etc., but viewed them as the natural outworking of the faithful performance of our "particular" calling.

Of great importance, therefore, is the manner in which we approach our calling. The glory of God must be our goal and the Word of God must be our rule. We have an example of what this entails in Perkins's *A Treatise of Christian Equity*.[57] His text is Philippians 4:5, where Paul commands, "Let your moderation be known unto all men. The Lord is at hand." Perkins argues that moderation is "so necessary [that] without the practice of it, no house, family, society, city, commonwealth, kingdom, or church, can stand or continue.... There can be no peace, no Christian neighborhood, no true friendship, unless one bears with another and one carries himself towards another in an even and moderate course."[58]

Perkins defines moderation (or, Christian equity) as "a rare and excellent virtue whereby men use a true mean and an equal moderation in all their affairs and dealings with men for the maintaining of justice and preservation of peace."[59] It is to be practiced publicly in courts, councils, parliaments, etc.,[60]

56. Robert Michaelsen argues that the Puritan concept of calling released the economic drives of Western society. Following the Reformers, the early Puritans developed a religious doctrine of vocation; however, the later Puritans moved to a more secular doctrine. "When the late Puritans talked about the general calling they thought chiefly of particular *acts* which might be called religious acts, rather than an overwhelming experience of the grace of God in Jesus Christ." "Changes in the Puritan Concept of Calling or Vocation," *The New England Quarterly* 26 (1953): 326. These later Puritans gave more power to the natural man by minimizing the doctrine of original sin and maximizing the role of good works in salvation. This shift led to a stress upon industry, prudence, diligence, and orderliness. "It is not a great step," claims Michaelsen, "from the blessing of industry and prudence as the best exercises for the soul to the blessing of these virtues in themselves, or the blessing of the material wealth gained by them." "Changes in the Puritan Concept of Calling or Vocation," 332. By way of critique, Michaelsen places far too much emphasis upon a perceived tendency among the Puritans to equate economic prosperity with God's favor. In actual fact, the Puritans stress God's inscrutability when it comes to economic prosperity. They are well aware that many times the unregenerate prosper while the regenerate experience adversity.

57. William Perkins, *Epieikeia; or, A Treatise of Christian Equity and Moderation* (Cambridge: John Legate, 1604).

58. Perkins, *Epieikeia*, 2–3.

59. Perkins, *Epieikeia*, 3.

60. Perkins, *Epieikeia*, 6.

and privately in our dealings with others.[61] It consists of (1) bearing weaknesses in others, (2) interpreting questionable actions in a positive light, (3) surrendering our rights, and (4) forgiving personal wrongs.[62]

When we pursue our vocation (particularly our relationships) with the glory of God and the good of our neighbor in view, it is pleasing in God's sight. This is a timely message for today's church. It is not uncommon for believers to revert to a medieval mindset whereby they divide life into the sacred and secular. Because of this, they look to certain callings (e.g., missionary or minister) as exemplifying some sort of super spirituality. In addition, they tend to view detachment from everyday life as essential to spiritual progress, assuming that release from the "mundane" roles and responsibilities of life will free them to pursue a deeper relationship with God. Such an outlook represents a severe distortion of the Christian faith. The lesson from Perkins is this: God has assigned each of us and called each of us to a "particular" life. Our responsibility is to live out our identity in Christ in our calling, seeking our neighbor's good to the glory of God.

A God-Honoring Home

One of the most important vocations is the place we occupy in our family.[63] God appoints and calls each of us to fulfill certain roles and responsibilities

61. Perkins, *Epieikeia*, 34.

62. Perkins, *Epieikeia*, 35.

63. By the end of the sixteenth century, there was considerable interest in the "right ordering of a household." By way of examples, see Richard Greenham, *A Godly Exhortation and Faithful Admonition to Virtuous Parents and Modern Matrons* (London, 1584); Henry Smith, *A Preparative to Marriage*, (London, 1591); John Dod and Robert Cleaver, *A Godly Form of Household Government* (London, 1598). There are diverse views as to what gave rise to the "Puritan" household. The historian, Christopher Hill, first wrote of the "spiritualization" of the Puritan household in 1964. As a Marxist, he was primarily interested in demonstrating how such a household served as the breeding ground for economic individualism and, therefore, the advent of capitalist values and practices. Christopher Hill, *Society and Puritanism in Pre-Revolutionary England* (1964; repr., London: Panther Books, 1969), 429–66. Whether employing Hill's exact phraseology or not, others have posited different theories as to the historical and sociological significance of the spiritual household. The German scholar of English literature, Levin Schucking, viewed it as the catalyst for the development of the close conjugal family, owing to its repudiation of celibacy and its celebration of intimacy. Levin Schucking, *The Puritan Family: A Social Study from Literary Sources* (London: Routledge & Kegan Paul, 1969). For a similar thesis, see Edmund Morgan, *The Puritan Family: Religion and Domestic Relations in Seventeenth-Century New England* (New York: Harper & Row, 1956). The feminist historian, Lyndal Roper, decried the spiritual household as responsible for reinforcing repressive patriarchal structures and subjecting children to harmful indoctrination. Lyndal Roper, *The Holy Household: Women and Morals in Reformation Augsburg* (Oxford: Clarendon Press, 1991). More recently, the church historian, Alexandra Walsham, revisited the spiritual household, theorizing that it functioned at times as a support for the political and ecclesiastical establishment, and at other times as an impetus

in the home. Perkins addresses this subject in *Oeconomie, or Household Government*.[64] Convinced that "the only rule of ordering the family is the written Word of God,"[65] he pores over Scripture for any text that might shed light on God's will for the home.[66] He immerses himself in the world of the patriarchs, the kings of Israel, and the New Testament saints, gleaning examples both to be shunned and emulated. In short, his right ordering of the family is the outworking of his biblical theology.[67] Centuries later, Perkins's treatment of the subject merits our attention for a number of reasons.

First, Perkins addresses familial challenges with pastoral sensitivity and theological clarity. He explains, for example, the difference between the "betrothal" and "consummation" stages in a marriage contract. He highlights the "essential signs" that indicate a person is "fit" for marriage. In relation to this, he spends several pages mapping out "the just and lawful distance of blood" that is necessary for people to marry. He also deals with issues of compatibility. Is there "parity or equality" in terms of age, condition, and reputation? Perkins also elaborates on the distinctive roles of parents and children in realizing a marriage contract.[68]

for clandestine resistance to authority. Alexandra Walsham, "Holy Families: The Spiritualization of the Early Modern Household Revisited," in *Religion and the Household* (Rochester: Boydell Press, 2014), 122–60.

64. William Perkins, *Oeconomie, or Household Government, A Short Survey of the Right Manner of Erecting and Ordering a Family, According to the Scriptures*, in *The Works of that Famous and Worthy Minister of Christ in the University of Cambridge, M. William Perkins*, 3 vols. (London, 1631), 3:669. Perkins's definition of "oeconomie" is derived from Proverbs 24:3, "By wisdom a house is built, and by understanding it is established." Perkins produced this treatise in the early 1590s—an interesting detail, given that he married Timothye Cradock in 1595. Did his impending union give him the necessary impetus to produce a marriage manual?

65. Perkins, *Oeconomie*, 3:669.

66. Perkins's treatise is saturated with Scripture references and inferences. Expectedly, he turns repeatedly to Genesis 1–2, Proverbs 31, 1 Corinthians 7, Ephesians 5–6, Colossians 3–4, 1 Timothy 3–4, and 1 Peter 3.

67. The historian, Margo Todd, has challenged any notion of a Puritan spiritual household, arising from Protestant theology in "Humanists, Puritans and the Spiritualized Household," *Church History* 49 (1980): 18. Todd argues that the exaltation of marriage, the creation of the family church, the rise of religious education, the practice of disciplinary duties, and the recognition of spiritual equality emerged from "classical ideas transmitted to the Puritans by humanism." "Humanists, Puritans and the Spiritualized Household," 22. Kathleen Davies also disputes the suggestion that Puritanism represents "a very different and more elevated view of family life from that presented in pre-Reformation or early Protestant views of marriage." "The sacred condition of equality—how original were Puritan doctrines of marriage?" *Social History* 2 (1977): 563. For the opposite view, see Roland Frye, "The Teachings of Classical Puritanism on Conjugal Love," *Studies in the Renaissance* 2 (1955): 149–55.

68. Perkins, *Oeconomie*, 3:672–82.

In addition to these practical issues, Perkins speaks to a number of specific "cases"—perplexing situations, many of which he undoubtedly faced as a pastor. What happens if a young woman is unwilling to marry a man to whom she was engaged as a child? What happens if a young man enters an engagement in a "furious and frantic" condition, and subsequently changes his mind? What happens if a young woman's parents arrange for her to marry an unbeliever? What happens if someone's prospective spouse becomes incapacitated? How should a spouse handle a prolonged absence that is "prejudicial" to the marriage? When is it permissible to dissolve a marriage? What should you do if your spouse deserts you? What should you do if your spouse threatens you? What should you do if your spouse requires something "intolerable" of you? What should you do if your spouse is unfaithful?[69]

In all this, Perkins demonstrates great biblical wisdom, especially as he applies Scripture to broken people in broken relationships. This realism is a missing element from many of the funeral sermons and biographical accounts of the time period, which tend to embellish domestic bliss while ignoring the messier aspects of family life. This is likely the result of apologetic intention. But Perkins provides a needed reality check—one which we would do well to heed. We tend to idolize the past, plunging ourselves into romantic idealism, but there was never an idyllic time in the past when families were free from the ravages of sinful human behavior. And there are never any easy fixes for marital and parental challenges. Perkins points us to God's Word as the only safe guide for navigating the many complexities that arise in the home.

Second, Perkins articulates a biblical view of the family, founded upon the creation narrative. As he surveys Genesis 1–2, he makes five observations concerning the marital relationship.[70] (1) "It was ordained by God in paradise, above and before all other states of life, in Adam's innocency before the fall."[71] (2) "It was instituted upon a most serious and solemn consultation among the three persons in the holy Trinity." (3) "The manner of this conjunction was excellent, for God joined our first parents, Adam and Eve, together immediately." (4) "God gave a large blessing unto the estate of marriage." (5) "Marriage was made and appointed by God Himself, to be the fountain and seminary of all other sorts and kinds of life in the commonwealth and in the church."

---

69. Perkins, *Oeconomie*, 3:682–90.

70. Perkins, *Oeconomie*, 3:671. Perkins acknowledges that the "gift of continency" is in many respects better than marriage, "yet not simply, but by accident, in regard of sundry calamities which came into the world by sin." This is how he interprets 1 Cor. 7:25–35.

71. "Marriage of itself," writes Perkins, "is a thing indifferent, and the kingdom of God stands no more in it than in meats and drinks; and yet it is a state in itself far more excellent than the conditions of single life." *Oeconomie*, 3:671.

For Perkins, therefore, the creation account is foundational to a biblical view of marriage (and the family). His second observation is particularly pertinent: "It was instituted upon a most serious and solemn consultation among the three persons in the holy Trinity." That is to say, the creation narrative stresses that the triune God made Adam and Eve in His image, and then commanded them to be fruitful. The inference is that the triune God intended for this family to mirror the relationship within the Trinity, and to be the context in which we enjoy the kind of relationship enjoyed within the Trinity. That is why the expression "they became one flesh" is so crucial. It highlights an experience of "diversity in unity" which is exclusive to the domain of marriage.

Third, Perkins affirms the "one flesh" principle as the defining feature of the relationship between husband and wife. "Marriage," says he, "is the lawful conjunction of the two married persons; that is of one man and one woman into one flesh."[72] He explains the duties of those who are thus conjoined. The first is "cohabitation": the "quiet and comfortable dwelling together in one place, for the better performance of mutual duties."[73] The second is "communion": the mutual communication of "their persons and goods" to each other, "for their mutual help, necessity, and comfort."[74] Perkins adds, "This duty consists principally in the performance of special benevolence one to another, and that not of courtesy, but of due debt.... Due benevolence must be showed with a singular and entire affection one towards another; and that three ways principally"—enjoying one another,[75] cherishing one another,[76] and rejoicing in one another.[77]

The significance of the "one flesh" principle is evident throughout Perkins's treatise. A husband is to love his wife as himself,[78] regarding his wife's estate as his own.[79] He is also to esteem his wife by "making account of her as his

72. Perkins, *Oeconomie*, 3:670. Perkins cites Gen. 2:21, Matt. 19:6, and Eph. 5:31.

73. Perkins, *Oeconomie*, 3:686.

74. Perkins, *Oeconomie*, 3:689.

75. Perkins, *Oeconomie*, 3:689. For Perkins, the "marriage bed" is that "solitary and secret society" that exists alone between husband and wife. The "right and lawful use" of the marriage bed "is indeed an essential duty of marriage."

76. Perkins, *Oeconomie*, 3:691. "This cherishing," writes Perkins, "is the performing of any duties that tend to the preserving of the lives one of another. Wherefore they are freely to communicate their goods, their counsel, their labors, each to other, for the good of themselves and theirs."

77. Perkins, *Oeconomie*, 3:691.

78. See Ephesians 5:33. As Edmund Leites remarks, "an outward fulfillment of the duties of marriage was not enough; the proper intentions and feelings toward your spouse must also exist." "The Duty to Desire: Love, Friendship, and Sexuality in Some Puritan Theories of Marriage," *Journal of Social History* 15 (1982): 383.

79. Perkins, *Oeconomie*, 3:691.

companion."[80] Perkins asserts that such "communion of married persons" is "a lively type of Christ and His church," and "a figure of the conjunction that is between Him and the faithful."[81] An appreciation of this truth is crucial. One of the principal strains upon marriage in our day is the Epicurean worldview, which ultimately posits no reality outside of the natural order. Faithfulness in marriage, therefore, is simply the result of personal and economic factors. Furthermore, marriage is merely a provisional convenience to be dissolved whenever one of the parties decides it is no longer in their interest. In sharp contrast, a concept of marriage, informed by the "one-flesh" principle, frees it from its modern-day caricature as a trap, chore, or burden. It elevates marriage into the realm of the divine, and it sets marriage apart as one of the greatest callings the world has ever known.

Fourth, Perkins emphasizes the importance of cultivating an intimate marital relationship. In his third observation concerning the institution of marriage, he affirms, "The manner of this conjunction was excellent, for God joined our first parents, Adam and Eve, together immediately." For Perkins, this joining was emotional, spiritual, and physical. For this reason, he denounces those who forbid marriage and view "due benevolence" as a sin.[82] He criticizes those "schoolmen" who teach that "the secret coming together of man and wife cannot be without sin."[83] He also criticizes the Church of Rome for prohibiting "certain parties" from marrying because "they think this secret coming together of man and wife to be filthiness."[84] Perkins makes specific mention of Syricius (334–399), "that filthy pope of Rome, who determined that marriage was the uncleanness of the flesh, and to that purpose abused the words of the

80. Perkins, *Oeconomie*, 3:691.

81. Perkins, *Oeconomie*, 3:690. See Eph. 5:23.

82. The view of celibacy as a means to spirituality entered the church at an early date. Beginning in the second century, many allowed dualistic philosophies (e.g., Gnosticism and Manichaeism) to influence their beliefs regarding sex. They held that lust taints all sexual activity. For many, this implied that virginity was superior to marriage. Without question, the most influential thinker of the time period was Augustine, who argues that sex practically paralyses all power of deliberate thought. See *City of God, A Select Library of the Nicene and Post-Nicene Fathers of the Christian Church*, ed. P. Schaff (New York: Random House, 1948), 2:14:16–21. As Henry Chadwick remarks, for Augustine, "in human nature as it now is the sexual impulse is the supreme symptom or expression of the irrational, the uncontrollable, the obsessive condition of the human psyche in its fallen condition." "The Ascetic Ideal in the History of the Church," in *Monks, Hermits and the Ascetic Tradition: Vol. 22*, ed. W. J. Sheils (Oxford: Basil Blackwell, 1985), 19. From this premise, the church of the Middle Ages acknowledged two reasons for marriage: the procreation of children and the avoidance of fornication. These notions remained prominent within the church until the Reformers departed from the accepted tradition by adding a third reason for marriage, namely, mutual society.

83. Perkins, *Oeconomie*, 3:671.

84. Perkins, *Oeconomie*, 3:689. Also see 3:671.

apostle (Rom. 8:8), affirming that they who are in the flesh, that is, in the state of matrimony, 'cannot please God.'"[85]

In contrast to the medieval tradition, Perkins affirms four "ends" of marriage.[86] (1) "The procreation of children, for the propagation and continuance of the seed and posterity of man upon the earth." (2) "The protection of a holy seed, whereby the church of God may be kept holy and chaste, and there may always be a holy company of men that may worship and serve God in the church from age to age." (3) "That after the fall of mankind, it might be a sovereign means to avoid fornication, and consequently to subdue and slake *[quench]* the burning lusts of the flesh."[87] (4) "That the parties married may thereby perform the duties of their calling in better and more comfortable manner."

In his treatment of this subject, Perkins demonstrates no antipathy toward the body. God's good gifts (including the conjugal relationship) are expressions of His kindness and are, therefore, intended for our enjoyment. The fact that God created Adam and Eve, declared that they should not be alone, and brought them together (all prior to the fall), is sufficient evidence that marriage is good.[88] Perkins was no ascetic. He had no problem with "natural" delights. "We may use these gifts of God," says he, "not sparingly alone, and for mere necessity...but also freely and liberally, for Christian delight and pleasure. For this is that liberty, which God has granted to all believers."[89] The way to holiness, therefore, is not found in abstaining from God's good gifts, but in enjoying them, echoing Paul's words: "So, whether you eat or drink, or whatever you do, do all to the glory of God" (1 Cor. 10:31).[90] Perkins believes that

85. Perkins, *Oeconomie*, 3:689.

86. Perkins, *Oeconomie*, 3:671.

87. Perkins makes it clear that the third "end" has only existed since "the fall of mankind." In other words, the need to avoid fornication only exists because sin exists. For an overview of Puritan views of sexuality, see Daniel Doriani, "The Puritans, Sex, and Pleasure," *Westminster Theological Journal* 53 (1991): 125–43; and Frye, "The Teachings of Classical Puritanism," 149–55. For the common charge of Puritan prudery, see Lyle Koehler, *A Search for* Power (Urbana: University of Illinois Press, 1980), 10; and Lawrence Stone, *The Family, Sex and Marriage in England, 1500–1800* (New York: Harper & Row, 1977), 499, 523. For the opposite view, see Leland Ryken, *Worldly Saints: The Puritans as They Really Were* (Grand Rapids: Zondervan, 1986), 43–45.

88. God's Word is the "warrant that they may lawfully do this action," whereas prayer is the means of seeking God's blessing upon the union between husband and wife. Perkins highlights three prayer requests: that it might (1) produce "a blessed seed," (2) preserve "the body in cleanness that it may be a fit temple for the Holy Ghost to dwell in," and (3) serve as "a lively type of Christ and his church." *Oeconomie*, 3:689.

89. William Perkins, *The Whole Treatise of the Cases of Conscience, Distinguished into Three Books*, in *The Works of that Famous and Worthy Minister of Christ in the University of Cambridge, M. William Perkins*, 3 vols. (London, 1632), 3:321. Also see 3:342.

90. The issue is not natural delights. They are good because God has ordained them. The issue is abuse, whereby we seek satisfaction in these things apart from God. When the fear of

godliness encompasses all of life; that is, everything is spiritual. Moreover, he believes there is a far better school for godliness than monastic isolationism—namely, the family, where we see our sinfulness and learn how to grow in Christ-likeness.[91]

Fifth, Perkins constructs a spiritual household, marked by mutual responsibilities, distinctive roles, and common purposes. He defines a household as "a natural and simple society of certain persons, having mutual relation one to another, under the private government of one."[92] There are two crucial components to this definition. The first is that the household consists of a "society of certain persons." Perkins distinguishes this "society" into three "couples."[93] The first is husband and wife. As the head of his wife, the husband is to love and honor her.[94] His chief responsibilities include leading family worship, ensuring attendance at public worship, providing for his family, and keeping order within his home. For her part, the wife is "to submit herself to her husband."[95] Her responsibilities include advising her husband and maintaining her home.

The second couple is parent and child. Parents have two principal duties. First, they are responsible for "bringing up" their children, ensuring "that they may live, and also that they may live well."[96] This applies to their physical well-being and, more importantly, their spiritual well-being. Parents are "to sow the seeds of godliness and religion in the heart of the child, so soon as it comes to the use of reason and understanding; and as it grows in years, so care must be had that it grows in knowledge and grace." Together, husband and wife exercise

---

God "tempers" our affections, the result is moderation in our use of natural delights. "Thus," says Frye, "the Puritan warnings were not concerned with any sin involved in physical love itself.... Two things were feared: lust as unstable sexual foundation for marriage in this world, and lust as idolatrous preventative of happiness in the world to come." "The Teachings of Classical Puritanism on Conjugal Love," 158. From his analysis of the primary literature, Leites concludes, "This sensuous love is not simply permitted, given the existence of a higher, holier, 'spiritual' relation between man and wife, nor is it allowed only to forward the other purposes of marriage. It is required as a constituent and intrinsic element of a good marriage. This sensual affection and delight must continue unabated, with the full intensity of youthful desire throughout the whole of married life." "The Duty to Desire," 388.

91. Martin Luther described family life as "the school for character." As quoted in Roland Bainton, *Here I Stand* (Nashville: Abingdon, 1951), 234ff.

92. Perkins, *Oeconomie*, 3:669.

93. As Edmund Morgan observes, "The order of society," for the Puritans, "consisted in certain dual relationships, most of them originating in agreements between the persons related and all arranged in a pattern of authority and subjection." *The Puritan Family*, 28. For a treatment of family relations in the Puritan era, see Helen Berry and Elizabeth Foyster, eds., *The Family in Early Modern England* (Cambridge: Cambridge University Press, 2007), 1–17.

94. Perkins, *Oeconomie*, 3:691.

95. Perkins, *Oeconomie*, 3:692.

96. Perkins, *Oeconomie*, 3:693.

authority over their children in raising them according to the tenets of God's Word. As for children, they must "yield" obedience, and "recompense" their parents by supporting them when they are old.[97]

The third couple in the household is master and servant. By servants, Perkins means employees such as domestic workers, apprentices, laborers, and shop assistants.[98] Under normal circumstances, these lived as members of their employer's family. The master is to assign labor according to the servant's strength. In addition, he is to recompense his servant by (1) giving him due sustenance while employed, (2) paying him fair wages at the end of his service, and (3) caring for him if he becomes sick during his time of employment.[99] On the other hand, a servant "is faithfully and diligently to demean himself in the affairs of his master, and to do service unto him, as unto Christ."[100]

Perkins's "three-couple" paradigm is developed from Ephesians 5:22–6:9 and Colossians 3:18–4:1. In the first text, Paul prefaces his remarks with a general exhortation: "Be subject to one another in the fear of Christ."[101] He then applies this to the three household relationships: he addresses wives before their husbands, and tells them to be subject to them; he addresses children before their parents, and tells them to obey them; and he addresses servants before their masters, and tells them to obey them. The success of these relationships is made contingent upon adherence to the first command: "Be subject to one another in the fear of Christ."

The second component to Perkins's definition of a household is that the above three couples relate to one another "under the private government of one." The head of the household exercises leadership under which his wife

---

97. Perkins, *Oeconomie*, 3:695.

98. Perkins makes it clear that there are "two sorts" of servants: (1) a "free servant" is hired for wages to complete a certain service; and (2) a "bond servant" ("commonly called a slave") is purchased for money. *Oeconomie*, 3:697. Perkins wrestles at some length over the legitimacy of slavery. He allows for it as long it is "used with moderation." Moreover, he insists that it must not be "procured and retained by force, for it is a more grievous crime to spoil a man of his liberty than of his riches." For Perkins, therefore, slavery is a voluntary practice. "Where this kind of servitude is abolished, it is not to be again received or entertained among Christians." *Oeconomie*, 3:698. Richard Baxter is very strong in his condemnation of the practice: "To go as pirates and catch up poor negroes or people of another land, that never forfeited life or liberty, and to make them slaves, and sell them, is one of the worst kinds of thievery in the world; and such persons are to be taken for the common enemies of mankind; and they that buy them and use them as beasts, for their mere commodity, and betray, or destroy, or neglect their souls, are fitter to be called incarnate devils than Christians." *A Christian Directory*, in *The Practical Works of Richard Baxter* (London: George Virtue, 1846; repr., Morgan, Pa.: Soli Deo Gloria, 2000), 1:462.

99. Perkins, *Oeconomie*, 3:696–97.

100. Perkins, *Oeconomie*, 3:697.

101. See Eph. 5:21.

performs her duties, as do his children and servants.[102] Such a view of the family is not without its detractors, but it is important to appreciate Perkins's full vision. Authority is never an end in itself, but a means to an end. It exists so that life can flourish. Such authority functions within the "one-flesh" principle, meaning it is based on self-giving, not self-serving. Such authority functions within the parameters of God's Word; thus, it is never arbitrary. Moreover, such authority functions within the context of mutuality—acting together, deciding together, working together, living together, etc. Its ultimate goal is to promote family relationships in which love is expressed in selflessness. In Perkins's estimation, when family members fulfill their roles and responsibilities within such a framework, the household becomes "a kind of paradise upon earth."[103]

Sixth, Perkins aims at the promotion of godliness through the family—the basic unity of society. In his struggle for reform, Perkins viewed the household as pivotal. Naturally, therefore, he looked to the head of the household as God's appointed instrument for effecting religious change. This governor must ensure that the members of his household are devoted to the worship of God, and employed "in some honest and profitable business, to maintain the temporal estate and life of the whole."[104] Perkins writes, "Governors of families must teach their children, and servants, and their whole household the doctrine of true religion, that they may know the true God, and walk in all His ways in doing righteousness and judgment.... But whereas they neglect their duty, falsely persuading themselves that it does not belong to them at all to instruct others, it is the cause of ignorance both in towns and families...."[105] In Perkins's worldview, the family is the basic unit of society, providing the pattern for larger communities: town, church, and commonwealth. The way to reform the church, transform the town, and alter the course of the commonwealth, therefore, is to spiritualize the household.

---

102. It is not difficult to see how quickly the principle of governance and obedience can become determinative in a marital relationship, especially if divorced from the "one flesh" principle. Likewise, it is relatively easy to infer (intended or not) intrinsic male superiority from some of Perkins's remarks.

103. Perkins, *Oeconomie*, 3:670.

104. Perkins, *Oeconomie*, 3:669–70. Perkins provides a brief description of family worship, focusing on biblical instruction and prayer in both the morning and evening. For examples of family devotional works, see Edward Dering, *Godly Private Prayers, for householders to meditate upon, and to say in their families*, 1578; John Parker, *A True Pattern of Piety, meet for all Christian householders to look upon, for the better education of their families*, 1592; Richard Jones, *A Brief and Necessary Catechism, for the benefit of all householders, their children and families*, 1583.

105. William Perkins, *An Exposition of the Symbol or Creed of the Apostles, According to the Tenor of the Scripture and the Consent of Orthodox Fathers of the Church*, in *The Works of that Famous and Worthy Minister of Christ in the University of Cambridge, M. William Perkins*, 3 vols. (London, 1608), 1:173.

A God-Honoring Life

Having worked through the above treatises, all that remains are two lesser known works which serve as bookends to the present volume. In the first, *How to Live, and That Well,*[106] Perkins considers what it means to live by faith (Hab. 2:4). At the outset, he makes it clear that the faith by which we are saved is the same faith by which we live. Such faith must be "rightly conceived and grounded in the heart."[107] This occurs when we "trust God upon His Word," "depend upon it," and "build upon it."[108] For Perkins, this is the "obedience of faith" of which Paul speaks in Romans 1:5. It is "absolute," "sincere," and "consistent"; moreover, it is focused on the "whole Word" and pursued with an "honest heart."[109] In short, when we live by faith, we possess "a distinct and settled purpose not to sin, but to do the will of God in all things."[110] Once faith is thus "conceived and grounded in the heart," it then "reigns and rules" by two actions: it "moves and makes us to attend on the calling of God, and yield subjection to Him in all His commandments"; and it "establishes and confirms them who believe in their obedience and subjection to God."[111]

Those who live by such faith (i.e., "in their obedience and subjection to God") will be prepared to die well. This is Perkins's contention in *A Salve for a Sick Man,*[112] where he unpacks Solomon's declaration: "The day of death is better than the day that one is born" (Eccl. 7:1). How can this be true? "The day [of] birth is an entrance into all woe and misery," declares Perkins, "whereas the day of death, joined with [a] godly and reformed life, is an entrance (or degree) to eternal life."[113]

Central to Perkins's view of eternal life is his belief that it consists of three "degrees."[114] The first is when we repent and believe in Christ; the second is when we die, and our body is buried in the grave while our soul is taken to heaven; and the third is when our body and soul are reunited, and we enter into eternal happiness. The day of our death is better than the day of our birth because it marks the entrance into the second degree of eternal life. At that

106. William Perkins, *How to Live, and That Well: In all estates and times, especially when helps and comforts fail*, in *The Works of that Famous and Worthy Minister of Christ in the University of Cambridge, M. William Perkins*, vol. 1 (London, 1631).

107. Perkins, *How to Live*, 1:476.

108. Perkins, *How to Live*, 1:476.

109. Perkins, *How to Live*, 1:477.

110. Perkins, *How to Live*, 1:477.

111. Perkins, *How to Live*, 1:477–78. Perkins proceeds to consider how faith is the means by which we live the "spiritual" life and "temporal" life.

112. William Perkins, *A Salve for a Sick Man; or, A Treatise Containing the Nature, Differences, and Kinds of Death, as also the Right Manner of Dying Well* (Cambridge: John Legate, 1597).

113. Perkins, *Salve*, 8.

114. Perkins, *Salve*, 8.

moment, we are free from "all miseries" in this fallen world;[115] moreover, we enter "into the presence of the everlasting God, of Christ, and of all the angels and saints in heaven."[116] "What happiness is this," declares Perkins, "to see the glory and majesty of God face to face, and to have eternal fellowship with God our Father, Christ our Redeemer, and the Holy Spirit our Comforter, and to live with the blessed saints and angels in heaven forever."[117] We will see Christ beatifically, meaning we will be like Him—conformed to His image.[118] To be conformed to His image is to love Him fully, and to love Him fully is to enjoy Him completely.[119]

With this hope before us, Perkins is convinced that we can die well. To aid in this, we must pursue various duties. The first is to meditate on death.[120] This serves to humble us, further our repentance, and cultivate contentment in every condition of life. The second is to endeavor to weaken the power of death.[121] We must recognize that death's power lies in sin. When we confess our sins, God pardons and removes them; as a result, death loses all its strength. The third duty is to enjoy "peace of conscience, derived from the death of Christ."[122]

---

115. Perkins, *Salve*, 9.

116. Perkins, *Salve*, 10.

117. Perkins, *Salve*, 10.

118. According to Perkins, the beatific vision is not a sight of the eye. There can be no sight of God's essence, because there is no "proportion" between a human eye and that which is infinite and invisible. The promise must, therefore, refer to a "sight of the mind"—"when the creature sees God, so far forth as it is capable of his knowledge." *Christ's Sermon in the Mount*, 3:15–16. In one sense, we see God already, in that we behold Him through the eyes of faith; but Perkins makes it clear that this sight is nothing in comparison to what is coming. At present, we see God "by His effects"; in the future, we will see Him "perfectly." At glorification, we will be like Christ and, therefore, able to commune with God to the fullest capacities of our souls. This will result in unparalleled delight, as our souls will rest fully in Him. For Perkins, "this seeing of God" will be "true happiness." *Christ's Sermon in the Mount*, 3:16.

119. Dewey Wallace provides the following insight into the importance of this motif among the Puritans: "Heavenly mindedness was the spiritual person's foretaste of the joys of heaven through meditation. This not only strengthened the soul for earthly trials but was one place in Puritan spirituality where the mystical element entered. The heavenly minded person was absorbed in divine things, weaned from earth, and advanced in communion with God because proleptically transported into that blessed state where the saints see God and enjoy his presence forever.... To meditate on that state, binding one's heart so closely to God that all else paled into insignificance, was the aim of the heavenly minded." *The Spirituality of Later English Puritans* (Macon: Mercer University Press, 1987), xvii.

120. Perkins, *Salve*, 15. The "four last things" (death, judgment, hell, and heaven) figure prominently in Perkins's meditative approach. John Calvin's call for meditation on "the future life" includes the same themes as the "four last things." *Institutes*, 3:9:1–6. For a detailed study of the four last things, see Robert Bolton, *The Four Last Things: Death, Judgement, Hell, and Heaven* (1633; Religious Tract Society, 1830; repr., Morgan, Pa.: Soli Deo Gloria, 1994).

121. Perkins, *Salve*, 17.

122. Perkins, *Salve*, 19.

The fourth is to accustom ourselves to dying little by little each day.[123] We do this by remembering that we have been crucified with Christ. The fifth duty is to follow Solomon's counsel: "Whatsoever thy hand findeth to do, do it with thy might; for there is no work, nor device, nor knowledge, nor wisdom, in the grave, whither thou goest" (Eccl. 9:10). These duties strengthen us to see that death "gives the soul passage to rest, life, and celestial glory, in which we shall see God as He is, perfectly know Him, and praise His name forever, keeping without intermission an eternal Sabbath."[124]

From these two treatises we learn (among other things) that true faith never remains indifferent to the things of God. The life of faith must not be confused with merely confessing a doctrinal formula, or participating in the sacraments of the church, or attending regular church services, or reciting a few prayers. Rather, the life of faith is all-encompassing, in that it makes every aspect of life subservient to the will of God as revealed in the Word of God.

Central to Perkins's understanding of the gospel stood the conviction that "true faith makes us one with Christ."[125] This union is *positional*, meaning "Christ, with all His benefits, is made ours."[126] In other words, the blessings of justification, adoption, and redemption (to name but a few) accrue to all those who are one with Christ through faith. Perkins was equally insistent that union with Christ is *transformational*. "The end of all God's grace," declared he, "is that we should be furthered in holiness of life."[127] This means that the gospel touches all of life. As evident in this volume, it shapes our relationships—both private and public; it determines how we carry out our roles and responsibilities at work and in the home; and it impacts the way we live and the way we die. In short, the gospel brings all of life within the bounds of God's Word.

—Joseph A. Pipa and J. Stephen Yuille

123. Perkins, *Salve*, 19.

124. Perkins, *Salve*, 44.

125. Perkins, *Christ's Sermon in the Mount*, 3:256.

126. William Perkins, *A Golden Chain: or, the Description of Theology, containing the order of the causes of salvation and damnation*, in *The Works of that Famous and Worthy Minister of Christ in the University of Cambridge, M. William Perkins*, 3 vols. (London, 1608), 1:83.

127. William Perkins, *A Godly and Learned Exposition upon the Whole Epistle of Jude* (London, 1606), 53.

How to Live, and That Well

In all estates and times, especially when helps and comforts fail

Printed by John Legate,
Printer to the University of Cambridge.

1601

And are to be sold at the Crown in Paul's Churchyard by Simon Waterton

To the Reader

Good Reader, if you would be saved by your faith in Christ after death, you must live by it here before death. And faith, for the time of this life, has two great uses.

The first is to cut off worldly sorrows and cares. It is the common fashion of men to multiply their cares out of measure, and thereby to make their lives most miserable. For, first of all, besides necessary labors, they take upon themselves many needless and superfluous businesses. Second, their manner is to care not only for the labors to be done, but also for the event and success of their labors, that they may always prosper and never be crossed. But this care belongs to God alone. Third, they content not themselves with their lot and condition, but seek by all means to increase their estate and to make themselves rich. Lastly, they exercise themselves not only in disposing of things present, but they forecast many matters in their heads and plot the success of things to come. Now faith, when we have done the works of our callings according to the prescript of the Word of God, (I say) makes us commend to God the blessing, success, and event thereof by prayer and assurance in His promises, not doubting but He will give us all necessary things. And if we want[1] the blessing and success we look for, yet faith makes us to renounce our own desires, and in silence to quiet our hearts in the good pleasure of God. And thus, many worldly cares are cut off.

Second, when a man, at his wits end, knows not what in the world to do, being (as it were) plunged into a sea of miseries, faith gives direction and stays the mind. For when all temporal things fail us, even to the very skin and life, faith preserves within us an affiance of the grace and mercy of God, and the hope of everlasting life. Faith shows us hidden things not to be discerned by sense and reason. Everlasting life is promised us, but we die for all that. We hear of the resurrection, but, in the meantime, we rot in our graves. We are pronounced blessed, but yet we are overwhelmed with infinite miseries. Abundance of all things is promised, but for all this we often hunger and thirst. God promises to hear us and to be present with us, but He seems often times to be

1. *Want:* lack.

deaf (as it were) to our cries. Now, then comes faith, which is the substance of things hoped for, and [it] makes us lift our minds above the whole world to apprehend the invisible and unspeakable things of God which He has revealed and promised unto us. I show these things more at large in the following small treatise. Read it at your leisure, use it for your good, and see you be a doer of them.

William Perkins

“The just man shall live by his faith” (Hab. 2:4).

In the former chapter, the prophet complains and expostulates the matter with God: why the Jews (the people of God) should be oppressed by the Chaldeans (the enemies of God). In the beginning of the second chapter, the Lord answers the prophet. And the effect of the answer is this: they shall certainly be delivered in the appointed time, but they shall not yet be delivered. Upon this answer, the prophet might haply[1] object in this manner: how then shall the afflicted Jews be able to live in the meantime? The Lord answers thus by a distinction: the unjust man puffs up himself with vain confidence, but the just man shall live by his faith. For the better understanding of the words, five things are to be explained in order.

First, what is meant by the just man? Justice mentioned in the Word is twofold: (1) the justice of the law; and (2) the justice of the gospel. The justice of the law has in it all the points and parts of justice, and all the perfection of all parts. And it was never found in any upon earth except Adam and Christ. The justice of the gospel has all the parts of true justice, but it wants the full perfection of parts, as a child has all the parts of a man in infancy, though it wants perfection of stature and tallness. And this kind of justice is nothing else but the conversion of a sinner with a purpose, will, and endeavor to please God according to all the commandments of the law. Noah [Gen. 6:9], Job [Job 1:1], Zachariah and Elizabeth [Luke 1:6] were thus just. And the just man must be taken thus in this place for one who turns to God, and by grace endeavors to please God according to the whole law of God in his place and calling.

The second point to be considered is what life is here meant. As death is here twofold (the first and the second), so is life. The first is the conjunction of the body and the soul; the second is the conjunction of the whole man with God. The first is called natural; the second [is called] spiritual (or eternal) life. And both are meant in this place. For Paul brings this very text to prove the justification of a sinner by faith [Rom. 1:17; Gal. 3:11], and justification is a part of spiritual life because it is the acceptation of a sinner to eternal life. And for

1. *Haply:* perhaps.

this cause, the prophet says, "The just man shall live," having relation not only to the time of affliction then to come, but also to eternal life.

The third point to be considered is what is the faith here meant. And it is justifying or saving faith, because we must live by the same faith whereby we are saved. And faith has its effect not only after this life, but also in this life. We must first live by it before we can be saved by it. Paul, therefore, in his own example, expounding this text, says, "And in that I live in the flesh, I live by the faith of the Son of God, who hath loved me, and given himself for me" [Gal. 2:20].

The fourth point is the construction of the words, and that is two ways. The first is thus: "The just by faith shall live," the words "by faith" being joined to the word "just." And then the sense is this: he who is just by his faith shall live (or have eternal life). The second is thus: "The just shall live by his faith," the words "by faith" being joined to the words "shall live." And then the sense is this: the just shall live by his faith while he lives in this world. I rather choose and embrace this latter construction and sense, because Paul even in this sense brings this text to prove that eternal life, and consequently justification, comes not by working according to the law but by believing, and he makes an opposition between "living by faith" and "living by works" (Gal. 3:11–12).

The fifth and last point to be considered is how a man should live by faith. Because this last point is of great moment, I will spend some time in the explaining of it. That a man may live by his faith, two things are required. The first [is] that faith is rightly conceived and grounded in the heart. The second [is] that, after it is once conceived, it reigns and rules in the heart.[2]

Requirement 1: Faith's Grounding in the Heart

That faith may be rightly conceived, two things are required.[3]

Point 1

The first is the knowledge of the Word of God, for faith stands in relation to the Word, and the Word alone is the foundation of our faith. Hereupon the Word is called the "foundation of the prophets and apostles" (Eph. 2:20). By light of natural reason, we understand that the world had a beginning and was made by God. Yet, reason cannot breed in us a certain persuasion of this point, but only the testimony of the Word of God. And, therefore, it is said: "By faith we understand that the world was ordained by God" (Heb. 11:3). And this made David say, "In God I will praise his word" (Ps. 56:4).[4]

2. This paragraph break is not in the original.
3. This paragraph break is not in the original.
4. This paragraph break is not in the original.

Furthermore, three things are to be known in the Word: (1) precepts (or commandments), because they teach obedience; (2) threatenings, because they restrain disobedience; and (3) promises, because they serve to confirm us in our obedience. Again, promises are either principal or less principal. The main or principal promise is that in which God offers and reveals righteousness and everlasting life by Christ. Within this promise is contained the grant of remission of our sins, of necessary patience, of the assistance of the Spirit of God, and of all gifts that are inseparably joined with faith. [The] less principal promises concern deliverances in temptations, safety in dangers, health, wealth, liberty, peace, etc. And these must all be understood with an exception of the cross and correction. And they shall be accomplished so far forth as they serve for God's glory and the good of them who believe. Now all these heads and points of the Word of God must be known, and that in some particular sort, so that a man may live by his faith.

Point 2

The second thing required for the right conceiving of faith is, after the Word of God is once known, to trust God upon His word, yea to depend upon it and to build upon it. This is the first and principal work of true faith, and it is called by Paul "the obedience of faith" (Rom. 1:5). And it is made the end and scope of the preaching of the gospel, and not without cause. For this is the first and principal honor of God, to believe Him upon His bare word, and thereby to make a confession of the truth of God. The devil knows this right well and, therefore, the first thing that he sought to overthrow in Adam was his faith in the word of God. And the scope of the first temptation whereby he assaulted our Savior Christ was to overthrow that faith and confidence He had in His Father. "If thou be the son of God, command that these stones be made bread" [Matt. 4:3]. "But Thou canst not do this; therefore, Thou art not the son of God."

That this obedience, which we give to God by trusting His very word, may be right obedience, it must have six conditions.[5]

First of all, it must be absolute. For we must (as it were) shut up our own eyes, and simply without any more ado trust God upon His bare and naked word, and suffer ourselves to be led by it. In natural things experience is first, and then faith comes afterward. And Thomas, following nature, desired first to feel before he would believe. But God must be trusted, though that which He says is against reason and experience. Abraham thus believed God "against all human hope" (Rom. 4:18).

5. The paragraph breaks (delineating the "six conditions") are not in the original.

The second condition is that this obedience must be sincere. For we must trust God's Word for itself because it is God's Word, all by-respects set apart. They who are as the stony ground receive God's Word and rejoice in it, and yet afterwards in time of temptation [they] go awry [Luke 8:13]. The reason is because they receive the Word and rejoice in it not properly for itself, but in respect of honor, profit, or pleasure, which they look to reap thereby. John the Baptist was a burning candle, and the Jews rejoiced in his light only in respect of the novelty of it. And, therefore, the Holy Spirit says, "they rejoiced in it but for a season" [John 5:35].

The third condition is that we must trust God not in part, but in His whole Word. And, therefore, many fail in their faith, who are content to trust Him in His promises of mercy and salvation, but list not to believe Him in His commandments and threats.

The fourth condition is that we must trust God in His Word with all our heart, that it may take deep root and be an "engrafted word" [James 1:21]. It is not sufficient for us to have a taste of the good Word of God and to receive it with joy, unless we thoroughly and soundly build and rely ourselves upon it.

The fifth condition is that this trusting of God must be with an honest heart, that is, with a heart in which there is a distinct and settled purpose not to sin, but to do the will of God in all things. The good hearers are they who receive the Word "with an honest and good heart" (Luke 8:15). Without this, no man can possibly live by faith. He who puts away his good conscience makes "shipwreck of his faith" (1 Tim. 1:19). It is godliness alone that has the promises of this life and the life to come. And none can live the life of faith but he who is a just man. After men have made some good proceedings, and do know the Word, receive it, rejoice in it, and bring forth some fruit, if the heart for all this is evil, it will cause them at length to depart from God by distrusting or by denying credence to His Word [Heb. 3:12].

The sixth condition is that the obedience of faith must be stable and consistent. The Lord says, "my soul hath no pleasure in them that withdraw themselves" (Heb. 10:38); that is, those who for a time believe God, and afterwards pull back their feet and go back from their faith.

Seeing this is the right way to conceive faith, to know the Word of God, and to trust Him upon the same Word, all such as would live by faith must have their hearts kindled with a desire to do the things before named, especially to give credence to every word of God. We may not forsake God for any creature. Now we forsake Him when we distrust Him in His Word. Again, not to believe God is very atheism, for by this means God is made a liar, and His glory and majesty are abolished. It is the greatest part of our glory to believe God, as Christ says, "He that receives his testimony, puts to his seal that God is true"

(John 3:33); that is, he gives unto God (as it were) a testimonial of His truth, and thereto puts his hand and seal. And what greater honor can there be than this, that the creature should give testimony to the Creator?

Requirement 2: Faith's Reigning in the Heart

Thus much of the conceiving of faith; now follows the reign of faith. The reign of faith is when it bears rule and sway in the heart and life. For where faith is, neither thought, will, affection, nor lust reigns there, but faith alone. It reigns by two actions.[6]

First of all, it moves and makes us to attend on the calling of God, and yield subjection to Him in all His commandments. Paul says that faith "establisheth the law" (Rom. 3:31). And one reason is because it makes us do that which the law prescribes. Again, Paul says that his weapons are spiritual and mighty, bringing every thought in subjection to God [2 Cor. 10:4–5]. Now these mighty weapons are the Word of God, preached and believed. He who is born of God cannot sin because the "seed of God" remains in him, that is, the Word mingled with faith [1 John 3:9]. Noah's faith made him build an ark at God's commandment [Heb. 11:7], [and,] after it was made, to enter into it, and not to dare to come out of it until he had warrant from God. Abraham's faith made him forsake his country and kindred at God's commandment, and go he knew not where [Gen. 12:4].[7]

And that good obedience may be performed to every commandment of God, faith works two things in us: memory and attention. Memory [is] when God's Word is laid up in the heart, that it may be drawn out to use when occasion shall be offered [Ps. 119:11]. Attention is when faith makes us seriously to consider and to believe that the commandment of God is a commandment not for form but in truth, and that it does indeed pertain to us [Acts 16:14]. We have an example of both [of] these actions of faith in Joseph, who, when he was tempted to folly by Potiphar's wife, answered, "Shall I do this wickedness, and sin against God?" (Gen. 39:9). Mark here how his mind was filled and possessed with a thought and consideration of God's commandment.

The second action of faith whereby it reigns in the heart is to establish and confirm them who believe in their obedience and subjection to God. And it does this by presenting God's promises to the mind. For by means of them it works four actions in the heart. First of all, it makes us fly unto the true God alone, to whom the promises belong. Second, it makes us to believe that God both can and will help us according to our need. Third, it makes us to hope for

6. This paragraph break is not in the original.
7. This paragraph break is not in the original.

His help, that is, for good success in prosperity and deliverance, or some mitigation of our evils in adversity, according to the tenor of His promises. Lastly, though temporal blessings fail, it makes us still to root on God for mercy and for everlasting life. And thus, at all times, it makes God to be our refuge, our castle, our rock, and [our] tower of defense.

Thus, we see generally how faith reigns.

To proceed further, the just man lives a double life, namely a spiritual life and a temporal [life], and both of them are led by faith, as I will plainly manifest.

Spiritual Life

Spiritual life, which is the beginning of eternal life, stands especially in four things: reconciliation with God, peace of conscience, joy of the Holy Spirit, and newness of life.[8]

Part 1: Reconciliation with God

Touching reconciliation with God in Christ, it is revealed, offered, and given unto us in the main promises of the gospel and in the sacraments. And it is [in] no way in this world made ours and held by us but by our faith. And in the case of our reconciliation with God, faith has two actions: one to receive it [and] the other to assure us of it.

Touching the first, faith apprehends and receives reconciliation in this manner. First of all, the Spirit of God works in men a general faith of the law and the threatenings thereof, and it is called "the spirit of bondage to fear" (Rom. 8:15) because it causes in us a sight of our sins, an apprehension of God's anger, a fear of due and deserved condemnation, [and] a despair of ourselves in respect of ourselves. This being done, the same Spirit works in us another faith called saving or justifying faith. And it apprehends or receives Christ with His benefits by certain steps and degrees, and they are especially three. (1) Upon a thorough touch and lively sense of our misery, there arises in the mind an earnest and serious meditation of the promise of mercy and benefits therein offered; and it is called the "opening" or "piercing" of the ear (Ps. 40:6). (2) Then there follows a purpose, will, desire, and endeavor to believe, upon consideration of the commandment of God that bids us to believe and apply the promise to ourselves [1 John 1:9]. And further, this will and desire shows itself by instant and serious invocation, which is nothing else but a flying from the condemning sentence of the law to the throne of grace for mercy [Heb. 4:16]. (3) After this, there follows in process of time a settling and quieting of the mind touching Christ and His benefits, upon some assurance thereof, wrought and conceived in the mind by

8. This paragraph break is not in the original.

the Spirit of God. And this third degree is called an "established thought" (Isa. 26:3). In this manner we come by degrees to receive Christ for our full reconciliation with God. For, when upon the commandment to believe, we do in any measure believe Christ to be our Christ, He is our Christ indeed, according to the tenor of the evangelical covenant. Thus, faith, apprehending Christ for our reconciliation with God, becomes a victorious conqueror and prevails against the law, Satan, hell, death, condemnation, and all our spiritual enemies [1 John 5:4]. And thus, every believer is above the law, sin, hell, death, even in this life.

The second action of faith, in the case of our reconciliation with God, is to certify and assure us in conscience thereof. And it is done by a practical syllogizing, which faith frames in the mind in this manner:

He who believes the gospel shall have all the benefits and blessing of God promised therein.

But I believe the gospel, and I believe in Christ.

Therefore, the benefits promised therein are mine.

The major (or first) part of this reason is the voice of the gospel. The minor (or second) part is the voice of the believing heart, which subjects itself in will and affection to the commandment which bids us believe in Christ. And this is the act of special faith. And we may not think that this voice of the believing heart is a false alarm. For he who truly believes has his mind and conscience supernaturally enlightened to discern that he believes. The third part (or conclusion) is the foundation of all our joy and spiritual comfort. For it contains in it the chiefest certainty of our adoption and salvation that can be had in this life, namely the certainty of faith. Whence follows in a lower degree, in the second place, the certainty that is by works. And thus, faith does certify all such as truly believe that they are the children of God.

Out of the former conclusion (or out of the certainty which is by faith) follows a full and lively certainty of the doctrine of the gospel, worthy [of] consideration in this manner. There is a threefold certainty. The first is certainty of reason (or of general faith), when a man by force of argument is convicted of the certainty of the doctrine of the Bible. This may be in the wicked and ungodly without faith in Christ. [Second,] after this, [there] follows in the elect, by a more special work of God's Spirit, faith in Christ, and the certainty of justifying or special faith expressed in the conclusion of the former syllogism. Third, after this certainty of special faith, [there] follows another experimental certainty of the truth of the Bible, which faith also concludes in this manner:

That doctrine, which assures us to be God's children, is certainly of God.

But the doctrine of the gospel, believed or mingled with our faith, assures us to be God's children.

Therefore, it is of God.

The major is granted by all. The minor is in effect the conclusion of the former syllogism, and it is known by an experience of that spiritual comfort which the godly feel in their hearts. The conclusion sets down the certainty of the Bible upon a further ground, which the wit (or learning) of man cannot attain unto without the Spirit of grace, namely upon an inward assurance of our reconciliation with God. Our Savior Christ speaks notably of this certainty: "If any man will do my Father's will (that is, believe it and subject himself to it), he shall know (namely, by that comfort which he shall feel upon his subjection) of the doctrine, whether it be of God, or whether I speak of myself" (John 7:17). And Paul says that "the spiritual man (that is, one regenerate by the Spirit of God) judgeth all things" (1 Cor. 2:15). Hence, it follows that such as desire to be settled for their religion, and such as desire to be good and profitable students in divinity, must first of all humble themselves and endeavor in their hearts truly to believe in Christ, because hence follows the best experience of the certainty, and consequently of the unspeakable excellency, of the Bible.

Thus, we see how we are to receive, hold, and enjoy our reconciliation with God in Christ by no other thing within us but by means of our faith alone. And, therefore, we must have special care that we may by the use of God's means attain to a lively faith. And for this cause, we must do two things. First, we are to labor to be convicted in conscience of the certainty of the Word. This done, we must then subject our wills to the commandment of God that bids us believe in Christ. We must bewail our unbelief. We must strive against the same, and pray unto God to confirm and increase our faith by establishing our hearts in His love.

Part 2: Peace of Conscience

The second part of spiritual life is peace of conscience, which is nothing else but a constant and stable tranquility of mind, when the conscience does not accuse but excuse, and when neither hell, death, condemnation, nor any danger is feared overmuch. This peace was in David when he said in the midst of manifold dangers: "I laid me down and slept, and rose again" (Ps. 3:5). This peace is of great excellency, for it is "the peace of God" [Phil. 4:7]; it is one part of the kingdom of God [Rom. 14:17]; it passes all understanding; [and] it is in stead of a guard to keep our hearts and minds in Christ. Now this excellent peace springs out of our faith whereby we believe our reconciliation with God. "Being justified by faith we have peace with God" (Rom. 5:1). "Trust in the Lord and ye shall be secure" (2 Chron. 20:20). Yea, as our faith is, so is our peace: no faith, no peace; lively faith, lively peace; constant faith, constant peace; faith in life, peace in life; faith in death, peace in death, so as we may say with Simeon, "Lord, now lettest thou thy servant depart in peace" (Luke 2:29).

Part 3: Joy of the Holy Spirit

The third part of spiritual life is the joy of the Holy Spirit, and that is to rejoice in God because He is our God, and in Christ because He is our Christ [Phil. 3:1]. And this kind of joy is not taken from us or abated in afflictions, but rather increased. "We rejoice in tribulations" (Rom. 5:3). "Ye endured the spoiling of your goods with joy" (Heb. 10:34). Now, our faith in the promise of life is the mother and breeder of this joy, which arises from that happy and blessed conclusion that faith frames in the mind: "I believe; therefore, the blessings of God promised in the gospel are mine." Thus says Saint Peter: "Believing ye rejoice with joy unspeakable and glorious" [1 Peter 1:8]. Again, the continuance and increase of our faith is the increase of this joy.

Part 4: Newness of Life

The last part of spiritual life is newness of life and conversation whereby we are born anew and made new creatures, not because the substance of body and soul is changed, but because the image of God is restored. Now this change, both for the whole and for the parts thereof, is by faith.[9]

Touching the whole, men (as they are new creatures) have their beginning from the Word of promise (or from Christ crucified, who is propounded in the promise), and that as the said Word (or Christ) is apprehended by faith. "Your hearts being purified by faith" (Acts 15:9). "He which hath this hope, purifieth himself" (1 John 3:3). "Your souls are purified in obeying the truth" (1 Peter 1:22). And again, "Being born anew of the immortal seed of the word" (v. 23).

The parts of newness of life are especially three: true wisdom, good affections, [and] good works. True wisdom is to advise of good things, and to use good means for the execution thereof. This wisdom arises from our faith in the Word of God. David says he "was wiser than his teachers, and wiser than the ancient," and he renders the cause thereof from the work of his faith: "for thy testimonies are ever with me, and they are my meditation" (Ps. 119:98–99). Out of the same fountain spring all good affections. The love whereby we love God comes from our faith, believing the love wherewith God loves us. The persuasion of the forgiveness of many sins in the woman who washed Christ's feet with her tears caused her to show much love to Christ [Luke 7:47]. Godly sorrow, when the heart is grieved properly for the offence of God, arises from

9. This paragraph break is not in the original.

faith apprehending and believing the mercy of God in Christ. And there is a threefold action of faith required in every good work. First, there is required an act of general faith, which is to believe that the work to be done in its kind pleases God. "Whatsoever is not of faith is sin" [Rom. 14:23]. The second is an act of justifying faith, which is to purge the heart, and to cause it to bring forth the good work to be done. "I believed, therefore I spoke" (Ps. 116:10). The third is also an act of justifying faith, and it is, when the work is done, to apprehend Christ who by His merit is to cover the defect of the work, because no work of ours can please God without remission of sin.

Thus, newness of life with all the parts thereof has its offspring from our faith. Yea, after a man is once made a new creature, faith gives him his life and sense. Faith is the eye of the mind whereby we behold Christ in the Word and sacraments. By this faith "Abraham saw the day of Christ and rejoiced" [John 8:56]. With this eye we may sufficiently behold Christ. And bodily sight in this case is not necessary for the time of this life. Therefore, Christ says, "Blessed are they which have not seen and have believed" (John 20:29). Again, faith is the hand of the soul whereby we lay hold on Christ and receive Him with all His benefits. It is the mouth of the heart whereby we feed on Christ, eating His body and drinking His blood to eternal life. It is the feet of the soul that makes us walk with God [Gen. 5:22]. Lastly, it is a means to bring us into familiarity with God. For it is an ear whereby we hear God speak to us in His Word, and it is (as it were) the tongue of the soul whereby we speak to God by invocation of His holy name.

To go yet further, spiritual life is most of all manifest in afflictions and temptations, in the bearing whereof faith reigns, and that by a threefold action.[10]

First of all, it makes us to depend on God's promises, and to trust God without limitation. (1) It does not limit God to any set time of deliverance, but leaves all to God. "He that believes, doth not make haste" (Isa. 28:16). Daniel waited seventy years for deliverance out of captivity in Babylon, and then, finding the time of deliverance to be at hand, he prayed to God for the same (Dan. 9:2). (2) Faith does not limit God to any means of deliverance. God made [a] promise to Abraham of a blessed seed. For the verifying of this promise He gave him Isaac in his old age. This done, He commanded him to offer his only son in sacrifice. [This was a] grievous cross, for by this means all hope [would be] cut off touching the promised seed. Yet, by faith Abraham still believed the promise, and that in the very offering of his son. (3) Faith does not limit God for the measure of affliction. Job says, "I will trust in God, though he kill me" (Job 13:15). It was a grievous affliction for David to be driven out of his

10. This paragraph break is not in the original.

kingdom by his own son, yet mark what he says in the flight: "If he say, I have no delight in thee, behold here I am, let him do unto me as shall seem good in his eyes" (2 Sam. 15:26).[11]

The second action of faith is to make us believe the promises of God when we feel the contrary, and in one contrary to believe another. When we feel our own sins, it makes us believe our justification. When we feel our wretchedness and misery, it makes us believe our happiness. When we feel nothing but death, it makes us believe our eternal salvation. When we apprehend God's anger and feel Him to be our enemy, it makes us to apprehend His mercy and to believe His fatherly kindness. When Christ was forsaken by God, He even then by His faith believed God to be His God.[12]

The third action of faith in afflictions is to assure us of God's presence, and to behold Him with the eyes of faith. Thus, David says, "I have set the Lord always before me: for he is at my right hand" (Ps. 16:8). Moses left Egypt and feared not the wrath of the king, because he saw Him "who is invisible" [Heb. 11:27]. When the servant of Elisha feared over much the host of the king of Syria who encompassed the town of Dothan, the prophet prays to God for him, that his eyes might be opened to see the fiery chariots of the angels of God protecting him [2 Kings 6:15]. And we likewise are to pray to God, that the eyes of our minds may be opened to believe and to acknowledge the same or the like protection. And men are to live thus by faith in the midst of their afflictions.

By what has been said, we are admonished, first of all, to acquaint ourselves with the promises of God as they are recorded in the books of the prophets and apostles; and, second, at all times to build upon them by our faith, and not to suffer ourselves to be drawn from them, though all temporal blessings of God fail us, yea health and life itself. This is to arm ourselves with a shield against all the fiery darts of the devil, and to put on a breast plate that will save the heart and life, though otherwise in temptations we are grievously maimed and foiled [Eph. 6:16; 1 Thess. 5:8].

Thus much of spiritual life.

Temporal Life

I make it manifest that our temporal life is led by faith as follows. Temporal life is preserved and maintained by an honest calling. Every calling has its labor and work, and the labor of all callings has misery and trouble for its companion and fellow, and in all these faith reigns and bears the sway in them who believe.

---

11. This paragraph break is not in the original.
12. This paragraph break is not in the original.

Part 1: Choosing Our Calling

For the first, that is for the choosing and holding of our callings with good conscience, there is required a double use of faith.[13]

For we must have a faith whereby we must be assured that our callings are good and lawful in themselves. As Paul says, "Whatsoever is not of faith, is sin."[14] For the settling of this faith, this rule must be remembered: that offices and callings which serve to preserve the good estate of any family, church, or commonwealth are lawful and of God, because these are estates ordained of God and established in the commandments of the moral law, especially in the first, fifth, and sixth commandments.[15]

Again, faith is required whereby every man must believe that the calling, in which he is, is the particular calling in which God will be served by him. For unless the conscience is settled in this, no good work can be done in any calling. And for the better establishing of the conscience, another rule must be remembered: that they who are furnished with gifts for their callings, namely aptness and willingness, and are thereunto called or set apart by men whom it concerns to call, are indeed called by God. Thus, the elders of Ephesus, having gifts to feed, and being not called immediately by God, but by men, are said to be "made overseers by the Holy Spirit."[16] And Paul says that God committed not only to himself, but also to Timothy, the ministry of reconciliation [2 Cor. 5:18], and yet Timothy was not called immediately by God, but by men [1 Tim. 4:14]. And thus, in all other offices and conditions of life, he who has gifts fit for his place, and is in good manner called thereto by them whose duty it is to call, may assure himself that he is called by God. And from this double faith and persuasion that our calling is lawful in itself, and lawful or pleasing God in respect of us, arises an assurance of the presence of God, and of His protection when we walk in the duties of our callings.

Part 2: Performing Our Calling

In the labor and work of our calling there is required a double action of faith.[17]

The first is to order our labors so that they are done in [a] good manner, that is, in obedience and to good ends, that is, to God's glory and to the good of men with whom we live. In this respect Noah is said to build an ark by faith [Heb. 11:7], and good princes to order their commonwealths, and in way of

13. This paragraph break is not in the original.
14. Rom. 14:23.
15. This paragraph break is not in the original.
16. Acts 20:28.
17. This paragraph break is not in the original.

protection to make war with their enemies. And every man of every office, calling, trade, [and] occupation, must thus do his duty by faith.[18]

The second action of faith is in our daily labors to restrain and moderate our care. Men commonly take upon them a double care: one is to do the works and labors of their callings; [and] the other is to procure a blessing and good success to their foresaid labors. But where faith in God's Word reigns, it stirs up the hearts of men only to the first care, which is in the performance of their painful labors and duties, and it restrains them from the second, causing them to leave it to God. For when men have done the duty that pertains unto them, then faith makes them without any more ado to wait on God for a blessing. To this purpose the Holy Spirit says, "Cast thy burden on the Lord and he shall nourish thee" (Ps. 55:22). Again, "Be nothing careful, but in all things let your requests be showed unto God in prayer and supplication with thanksgiving" [Phil. 4:6]. And, "Cast your care on God" [1 Peter 5:7]. Now this faith, whereby we depend on God for the success of our labors, has an infallible ground, namely, that God knows best our wants, and He will give unto us all things which He in His wisdom knows to be necessary. Christ says, "Your heavenly father knoweth that you have need of these things (that is, food and raiment)" (Matt. 6:32). Again, "He careth for you" [1 Peter 5:7]. And, "Nothing shall be wanting unto them that fear God" [Ps. 34:9]. If men would by faith build on these promises, they would not need like drudges of the world to toil and spend themselves and the best part of their days in worldly cares, as they do. For they would have a greater blessing from God with less care, if they would trust Him. And they would have far more time than they have to care for heaven and heavenly things.

Part 3: Persevering in Our Calling

Third and lastly, every calling since the fall of Adam has misery and affliction as its companion. And for the quiet bearing of the miseries of every calling, faith is of great moment. For it works patience by persuading and settling our minds in two things. The first [is] that God is well pleased with us, and that we are reconciled to God in Christ. The second [is] that all our miseries shall in the end turn to our good and everlasting salvation. And where these two persuasions take place, there is contentation in any estate.

Thus much for the meaning of the text; now follows the use.[19]

18. This paragraph break is not in the original.
19. This paragraph break is not in the original.

Use 1: Informing Our Judgment

The first and principal use concerns the information of our judgment in the main point of our salvation. For hence Paul has taught us to gather that a sinner is justified before God by his faith without the works of the law. And he disputes in this manner: if a sinner is justified by faith, he is not justified by the law; but a sinner is justified by faith; therefore, he is not justified by the law. The conclusion is propounded in Galatians 3:11. The major is confirmed in verse 12 by the divers manners of justifying: the law (says Paul) justifies by doing, not by believing, and faith justifies not by doing, but by believing. The minor is confirmed in verse 11 by the testimony of the prophet Habakkuk: "The just shall live by his faith."[20]

And whereas the papists of our time say that Paul, in this argument, disputes only against such works of the law as are done by nature, but not by grace, they err and are deceived. For he opposes not works of nature and works of grace, but works and faith, doing and believing. And the prophet says very plainly, and mark it, that the just man, who is a doer of the works of grace, is justified and lives not by his works, but by his faith. Again, where they make a double justification (one whereby a sinner is made a just man [and] the other whereby a just man is made more just), and teach that the first is by faith without works and the second [is] by faith and works, they err likewise. For not only a sinner unconverted, but the just man stands just and is still justified by his faith without his works. When Paul alleged this text, [he] knew but of one justification, whether we respect the beginning or the continuance and the accomplishment thereof.

Use 2: Reforming Our Life

Second, hence we may learn the right way of reformation of our lives. In this reformation two things are required: examination and change.

Point 1: Examination

If we examine our lives by this text, we shall find two main faults and aberrations in the lives of men.[21]

Aberration 1. The first is that they reject and put away the rule of direction that serves for the ordering of their lives. And they do this when they do not believe and trust God in His Word. And we may not think that this unbelief is a small matter because it is a mother sin of all other sins, and it is the principal law

20. This paragraph break is not in the original.
21. This paragraph break is not in the original.

of the kingdom of darkness not to believe God. Hereupon our enemy Satan endeavored by all means to imprint this lesson of unbelief in the minds of our first parents, and, having effected his purpose, he has endeavored ever since to make this sin to reign in the lives of men. It reigns commonly by seven special fruits or sins.[22]

The first is atheism, when men deny God and His Word. Atheism has two parts: Epicurism and temporizing. Epicurism is when men condemn God's commandments, threats, [and] promises, [and] care for nothing but meat, drink, and pleasures. Temporizing is when men embrace religion so far forth as they are forced by laws and times, and not otherwise. These are the common sins of our days.

The second fruit is heresy, and that is when men distrust God in some article of faith. This fruit abounds in this last age of the world, because in these times the devil has revived the heresies of the former ages.

The third fruit is apostasy, and that is when men change their faith and religion. And this change is made when the evil heart of unbelief causes them to depart from the living God [Heb. 3:12]. This has been the fault of the people of this land in the days of persecution.

The fourth fruit is hypocrisy, which is to make a show and pretense of faith, and to want the power of it in honest and godly conversation. Again, hypocrisy is nothing else but the unbelief of the heart covered over with the false appearance of faith. And it is the common sin of these times, in which a formal or ceremonial faith and ceremonial repentance bear a great sway. For men make the highest degree of profession that can be, when they come to the Lord's table, and yet afterwards [they] take to themselves liberty to live and do as they list.

The fifth fruit is carnal security, when men upon contempt of the judgments of God and threatenings of His Word, go on still in their sins, flattering and soothing themselves. Thus, the sons-in-law of Lot, when they heard of the destruction of Sodom, esteemed it but as mockery [Gen. 19:14]. Thus, the Jews made a league with hell and death, and said with[in] themselves that the scourges of God should not come to them [Isa. 28:15]. And in the last age of the world, men shall wholly addict themselves to pleasures and profits, thinking nothing of any judgment of God, till vengeance befalls them [Matt. 24:37–39].

The sixth [fruit] is willful ignorance of the will and Word of God. For the devil blinds the minds of unbelievers, so that the light of the gospel shines not unto them [2 Cor. 4:4]. This is the fault of our common people, who commonly hold an opinion that it belongs not to them to know the Word of God because

22. The paragraph breaks (delineating the "seven special fruits") are not in the original.

they are not learned (as they say) or because they have other business to think on.

The last fruit is worldliness, and that is when men mind nothing but worldly matters. And this comes from the want of faith in the providence of God [Matt. 6:30].

These are the principal fruits of unbelief whereby it may be easily discerned and descried where it is. And if any man thinks himself to have a fullness and perfection of faith, as many do, even this one thing is a sufficient argument of his unbelief. For it is the first step to faith to see in ourselves the want of faith.

Aberration 2. The second main aberration in the lives of men is that they set up false rules to order their lives by. And there are four.

The first is the light of natural reason. For many are of [the] opinion that it is sufficient to the pleasing of God if they live civilly (that is, do justice to every man) and live peaceably (hurting none). This is the blind divinity of the world, that if they carry themselves thus and thus, whatsoever their sins are, God will hold them excused. But they are far wide, for faith is required in a life acceptable to God. The light of reason will not serve the turn. Paul says, "The wisdom of the natural man is enmity to God; and he cannot discern the things of God" (1 Cor. 2:14). The Pharisees had civil justice and goodness, yet Christ says, "Except your justice exceed theirs, ye cannot enter into the kingdom of heaven" [Matt. 5:20].

The second false rule is sense, that is, seeing and feeling. Men commonly live by this. If we enjoy the good blessings of God (health, wealth, liberty, peace, honor, good report), then we can trust God. But if He withdraws His blessings, and presents Himself to us with an empty hand, we trust Him no longer, nay we murmur and despair, and without fear of God [we] use any unlawful means to relieve ourselves. Though we have His precious Word, yet we do not trust Him upon His bare and naked Word, unless withal He lays down unto us some good pawn, and makes us to feel and enjoy His good blessings. Again, if any man, who is our friend, makes [a] promise of help or deliverance in any danger, we rest content and find ourselves much eased thereby. And yet, the promises made by God in His Word of help and deliverance, though they are often read unto us, and often urged, breed not the like contentation. He who, on his deathbed, has commended his children to some trusty friend departs more quieted in mind than if he had commended them without help of friend to God their best Father. A man upon good security lends 100 pounds to another, hoping for the principal with the increase at the year's end. Yet, he dares not scarce deliver 100 pence to the poor members of Christ upon the promise and bond of God Himself, who says, "He that gives to the poor, lends to the Lord" (Prov. 19:17), and [that] He will return the said gifts with a blessing. Now all this comes to pass because men trust those whom they see rather than God whom they have never seen. Moreover, it is a property of them who do indeed believe to judge their estate by feeling. But they deceive themselves herein, for we must live by faith and not by feeling. And feeling is often deceitful, because such as finally fall away from God may have a feeling, or taste of the good Word of God and of the powers of the life to come [Heb. 6:4].

The third false rule is false faith, which is without (or against) the Word. Thus, the Turk lives by his false faith; the Jew by his; [and] the papist by his, for he believes the traditions of men as well as the Word of God, and he puts his trust not only in God, but in the creatures, namely saints and angels. Thus also, magicians, sorcerers, witches, [and] enchanters, whatsoever they do, [they do] by a satanical faith in that covenant which they have made with the devil. And such persons as ask counsel of witches and wizards, called cunning men and women, help themselves only by their false faith. For when they use charms or spells, or similar satanical ceremonies, they commonly find success and are helped of the evils that betide[23] them. And that comes to pass in this manner. In the use of the foresaid ceremonies prescribed and delivered by witches, they have a blind and erroneous faith. Upon their faith follows a satanical operation in [the] effecting of the care desired. For charms or spells, being but words, have no virtue in them to ease or help man or beast, either by creation or by any ordinance of God in His Word. And, therefore, their effect is by the power of the devil upon man's faith. Let our common people think on this, who though they much boast of their faith in Christ, yet when they are in any extremity or danger, very commonly practice this satanical faith.

The last false rule is the lust of the heart. And most men square their lives by this rule. The lust that commonly rules is threefold: lust of bodily pleasure, lust of worldly wealth, [and] lust of honor. As Saint John says, "Whatsoever is in the world is the lust of the flesh, the lust of the eye, and the pride of life" (1 John 2:16).

Point 2: Change

Thus much of the examination; now follows the change. That we may change our lives in respect of unbelief, four things are required.

Requirement 1. The first is that we must acknowledge and bewail our unbelief with the manifold fruits thereof. And we have good cause to do so. For by unbelief the devil erects his kingdom in men's hearts, and works his pleasure in

23. *Betide:* happen to.

us and upon us [Eph. 2:2]. Second, unbelief corrupts and defiles all our actions whatsoever, though otherwise they are good and lawful in themselves. Paul says that "to unbelievers all things are unclean, yea their minds and consciences are defiled" (Titus 1:15). Third, unbelief deprives us of the good blessings of God which otherwise we might enjoy. "If ye believe not, ye shall not be established," says the prophet [Isa. 7:9]. In Capernaum Christ could do no great wonders by reason of their unbelief [Mark 6:5]. Lastly, unbelief plucks down upon men the plagues and judgments of God. Moses and Aaron were barred [from] the land of Canaan for their unbelief [Num. 20:12]. A certain prince was trodden to death in the gates of Samaria because he would not believe the word of the Lord by the mouth of Elisha [2 Kings 7:12, 17]. Zechariah was dumb for a time because he would not believe the message of the angel [Luke 1:20–21]. Many at this day, when the judgments of God lie heavy on them, say presently they are forespoken, and they cry out on this or that suspected witch. But such persons are often deceived. For the great witch that does them all the hurt is the unbelief of their hearts whereby they distrust God in His Word. And this sin alone, if there were not witches in the world, is sufficient alone to provoke God to plague and punish us sundry ways, and that grievously. Therefore, let us with bitterness of heart bewail our unbelief, and the rather because it is a step to faith to acknowledge the want of faith.

Requirement 2. The second thing to be done is to make examination whether we are in conscience convicted of the certainty of the Word or not. If we are not, we must labor to be convinced, because that natural atheism whereby we doubt whether the books of the prophets and apostles are the Word of God or not hinders the certainty of faith. For the settling of the conscience in this point, these arguments may be used:

The first is a principle in nature that there is a God. If there is a God, nature can say He is to be worshipped. If He is to be worshipped, He has revealed Himself and His will to man, for otherwise He cannot be worshipped. And this revelation is to be found in the writings of the prophets and apostles, and in no other writings of men, because we find the doctrine of Scriptures to be agreeable to the very nature and majesty of God, and no other doctrine of learning whatsoever is so. For it is the most ancient, and all other religions come far short of it. It is one and the same, evermore consenting with itself without change or alteration. The apostles agree with the prophets; the prophets with Moses; and all with the first revelation made at the creation. Again, it discovers and reveals the secret thoughts of men, that no art or learning can discover [Ps. 10:6, 11, 13, 14; Luke 18:11–12; Rev. 18:7; 1 Cor. 2:14; Matt. 12:14; Ps. 7:8;

Isa. 8:15; Luke 12:45; Num. 20:12; Psalms 51; 119:11; 73:12–13; 1 Tim. 1:13]. And this argues that it was penned by Him who is the searcher of all hearts.

The second argument is a wonderful evidence of the truth, not to be found in any other writings in the world. This evidence stands especially in eight things. The first is that the writers of Scriptures fully and plainly set down their own faults, yea their chiefest faults, not sparing to shame themselves in man's reason. And this argues that they were guided by the Spirit of truth in writing. The second is that the books of Scripture contain many mysteries above the reach of man's reason, yet not against reason because we may discern a truth in them, and that by grounds and principles of reason. The third [is] that the speeches of Scripture aim not [at] a by-respect, but simply and absolutely give and ascribe all glory to God alone. The fourth is that the Scriptures contain full and perfect doctrine for the pacifying, settling, and directing of the conscience in all things. The fifth is the holiness and purity of the Law of Moses, in that it accuses and condemns all men of sin, and prescribes perfect righteousness. Herein it surpasses the laws of all countries, commonwealths, [and] kingdoms whatsoever. The sixth is the wisdom that appears in the policy or government of the commonwealth of the Jews set down by Moses. The seventh is a reconciliation of justice and mercy propounded in the gospel. For in Christ justice and mercy meet, and justice after a sort gives place to mercy. The eighth thing, wherein the evidence of this truth appears, is the consent of Scripture with itself, for doctrine agrees with history, and every part with every part. This manifold evidence of truth shows that Scripture is from the God of truth. If any say that they find no such evidence in Scripture, I answer it is their own fault. For if they would seriously read the Scriptures with prayer to God, it would appear.[24]

The third argument is the efficacy of the Word, which appears in this manner. God's Word is flatly contrary to the nature and corrupt disposition of man, and yet for all this, when preached, it convinces and condemns man of sin [Heb. 4:12; 2 Cor. 10:5]. It turns and converts them to itself, and causes them to live and die in the love and obedience thereof. It could never do this, unless it were of divine operation.[25]

The fourth argument is that the prophets and apostles wrought miracles for the ratifying and confirming of their doctrine. Now these miracles surpass the strength of nature, and were immediately from God. And, therefore, the doctrine thereby confirmed was also from God.[26]

---

24. This paragraph break is not in the original.
25. This paragraph break is not in the original.
26. This paragraph break is not in the original.

The fifth and last [argument] is that the writings of the prophets and apostles contain many prophecies or predictions of things to come, which none but God could foresee or foretell. The name of Josiah and his doings are foretold 330 years before he was born [1 Kings 13:2]. Cyrus and his doings are mentioned more than 100 years before his birth [Isa. 44:28]. Now these and the like prophecies argue that the whole doctrine is of God. By these and like arguments are all who inwardly doubt of the Word of God to settle and establish their consciences.

Requirement 3. This done, then follows the third point. And it is that we must search and inquire what is the substance and scope of the Word of God. The scope of the whole Bible is Christ with His benefits. And He is revealed, propounded, and offered unto us in the main promise of the Word, the tenor whereof is that God will give remission of sins and everlasting life to such as will believe in Christ [1 John 3:23]. To this main promise, God has added a main commandment, which bids us to believe the said promise, or to apply Christ with His benefits unto ourselves. Now then, our third duty is to subject our hearts and wills to this commandment that bids us believe in Christ. This is the subjection of faith, of which two things must be observed.

One is that this is the first subjection that we can give to God, to trust Him upon His promise for the pardon of our sins and for eternal life. And from this subjection of faith arises our subjection to the whole Word. In Christ all the promises of God are "yea and amen" [2 Cor. 1:20]. The law and the obedience of all the commandments thereof is established by faith. Without Christ no good thing can be done.

The second point is that this subjection is easy in respect of that subjection which the law requires. The perfect obedience of the law is impossible to all men except Christ, yea to such as are born anew of the Holy Spirit, though for the time of this life they desire it ever so earnestly. Yet, faith in Christ and repentance is so far forth possible to all who will and desire it that whosoever does seriously but will to believe and be converted does indeed believe and is converted, and does please God, and shall not perish eternally, although the beginning of this faith and conversion is weak, so it is in truth and not counterfeit. "If ye will and obey, ye shall eat the good things of the land" (Isa. 1:19). "Your heavenly father giveth the Holy Ghost to them that desire him" (Luke 11:13). "My yoke is easy and my burden light" (Matt. 11:30). Therefore, let us try ourselves whether we have a will to subject ourselves to the Word of God that bids us believe in Christ. Nevertheless, we may not think that this will to believe is in our power, for it is by the special mercy of God stirred up in the hearts of the elect by the operation of the Holy Spirit.

Requirement 4. The fourth and last thing in this change is that faith in Christ, or in the Word believed, must reign and rule in the heart, bringing the whole man in subjection to the whole Word of God. And faith in Christ does this because, when it is once felt in the heart, it works in us a full and settled faith of every part of the Word of God, namely of His precepts and His threats. Here then our duty is to subject ourselves by means of our faith to the whole Word, and to suffer nothing within us but it alone to bear sway. This is the will of God: "Let the word of God dwell in you plentifully" [Col. 3:16]. The good ground yields itself and gives place, so that the seed may take deep root. It is a blessed thing to have the kingdom of God erected in our hearts. Now this kingdom is erected when the Word of God keeps all the powers of body and soul in subjection. And when our faith in Christ brings our thoughts, affections, words, deeds, [and] sufferings in subjection to the Word of God, then we live by faith.

Use 3: Seeking Knowledge

The third use follows. In that we are to live by our faith, we are taught to seek for knowledge of the will and Word of God, and daily to increase in the same knowledge, especially to acquaint ourselves with the commandments of God that concern us, with His promises and threatenings. For faith is the life of our souls, and the Word is the life of faith, because it is first kindled and afterward confirmed by the hearing of God's Word. Again, the Word moderates our faith, so that we believe no more than we should, or come short in believing. The Word, therefore, that serves thus to limit our faith must be known in its several heads and points.

Use 4: Facing Danger

Fourth, hence we learn how we are to carry ourselves in [the] greatest dangers, as in the time of plague and pestilence, in the time of famine, in the time of war and bloodshed, in the time of our last and deadly sickness. We have then need of great help. And the only way is then to stay ourselves and establish our hearts by our faith on God's promises. It is the very scope of this text to teach this one point of doctrine to the Jews, being now oppressed by the Babylonians. David in danger, and Christ in the time of His passion, by their faith commend their spirits into the hands of God. Some of the martyrs and saints of God were by their faith imprisoned, some racked, [and] some stoned [Heb. 11:37]. Faith in perilous times is of great use. First, when a man is half dead, it quickens and puts life in him, as David says, "Remember the promise made to thy servant, wherein thou hast caused me to trust: it is my comfort in my trouble: for thy promise hath quickened me" (Ps. 119:49–50). Understand here the promise as it was tempered and mingled with his faith.[27]

Again, faith in the times of danger does (as it were) fence and compass us with the promises of God. This may be gathered by the opposition that is between these words and the former. "The unjust man puffs up himself," says the prophet, or builds towers of defense to himself. But the just man only believes, and that shall be to him instead of all the towers in the world. For it brings us under the presence, wing, and protection of God. It makes Him to be our safeguard and tower of defense. This doctrine is to be thought on the rather because, though we now enjoy peace and other blessings of God, yet our common sins and especially our unbelief calls down for the great and grievous judgments of God.

Use 5: Cultivating Faith

Moreover, hence we are taught that every man must have a faith of his own. "The just man shall live by his own faith," says the prophet. And for good reason: every man is a creature of God and must do his homage to God by believing in Him. And because every man has need of Christ for himself, therefore everyone must have a faith of his own to lay hold on Christ. It may be objected that sometimes the faith of others has saved men. "When Christ saw their faith, he said to the sick of the palsy, Thy sins are forgiven thee" (Mark 2:5). And, "The prayer of faith shall save the sick" (James 5:16). I answer that the faith of one man may be a means to procure health of body and other temporal blessings, yea faith unto others; yet no man can receive pardon of sins and eternal life but for himself. Therefore, when it is said in the first place, "When he saw their faith," the faith of the palsy man must not be excluded but included. And the place of James speaks only of bodily health.

Second, it may be alleged that, seeing we are justified by the justice of another, namely of Christ, we may also be justified and saved by the faith of another. I answer that the reason is not alike, because the obedience of Christ is both His and ours: His, because it is in Him; [and] ours, because it is applied unto us by God and received by our faith. And the like cannot be said of the faith of any other man.

Third it may be alleged that infants have no faith of their own. I answer, there are three opinions touching infants' faith. The first [is] that infants have actual faith wrought in them by the Holy Spirit, because it is said, "Whosoever offendeth one of these little ones that believes in me" (Matt. 18:6). But this opinion seems to be an untruth because faith presupposes understanding

27. This paragraph break is not in the original.

and knowledge, which infants want. Again, if infants received do believe when they are young, they would no doubt show it when they come to be of years. But they show none, unless they attain unto it afterwards by diligent teaching and instruction. And the place in Matthew may be understood of men of years who, if they have contrite and humbled hearts, are little ones believing in Christ. Again, children, after some years by good education and instruction, may attain to some knowledge and consequently to faith. Thus, Timothy was brought up in the Scripture as a child.

The second opinion is that all places of Scripture, entreating of faith, are to be understood of men of years, and that children are saved by some other unknown and unspeakable way without faith. I somewhat doubt of this because it is said, "Whosoever believeth not is already condemned" [Mark 16:16]. Again, "Without faith it is impossible to please God" [Heb. 11:6].

The third opinion is that children have faith after a sort, because the parents according to the tenor of the covenant, "I will be thy God, and the God of thy seed," believe for themselves and their children. And, therefore, their faith is not only theirs but also the faith of their children. Hence, it is that the Scripture says, "If the root be holy, the branches are holy" [Rom. 11:16]. And, "If ye believe, your children are holy" [1 Cor. 7:14]. According to human law, the father and his heirs are but one person, the father covenanting for himself and his children. What then should hinder that the father might not believe for his child, and the child by the parent's faith have title to the covenant and the benefits thereof? It is alleged that by this means children shall be born believers, and so be conceived and born without original sin.[28] I answer, believing parents sustain two persons: the one, whereby they are men, and thus they bring forth children having man's nature with all the corruptions of nature; [and] the other, as they are holy men and believers, and thus they bring forth infants who are not so much their children as the children of God. And infants are God's children not by virtue of their birth, but by means of [their] parents' faith, which entitles them to all the blessings of the covenant. Children proportionally sustain a double person. If they are considered in and by themselves, they are conceived and born in original sin. If they are considered as they are holy and believe by the faith which is both theirs and their parents' faith, and consequently have by this means title to Christ and His benefits, original sin is covered and remitted. If it is said that by this means all children of believing parents are the children of God, I answer that we must presume that they are all so, leaving secret judgments to God.[29]

28. In the margin: Bellar. lib. 1. de bapt. cap. 4.

29. This paragraph break is not in the original.

To this third opinion I most incline, because we are to judge that infants of believing parents, dying in their infancy, are justified. And I find no justification in Scripture without faith. And this has been the judgment of ancient fathers.[30] Of the words of the apostle, Augustine says, "How do infants believe? By the faith of the parents. If by the faith of the parents they are purged, by parents' sin they are polluted. The body of sin in the first parents begot them sinners. And the spirit of life in their latter parents did regenerate them to be believers."[31] Bernard says, "Among the nations as many as were faithful, if they were of years, we believe that they were cleansed by faith and the sacrifices, and that the parents' faith alone avails for children, yea that it is sufficient for them." Again, "It is meet and for the honor of God, that to whom age denies their own faith, grace should grant to them a benefit by the faith of another."[32]

Thus then, it is manifest that every person must have a faith of his own. Hence, we learn that the doctors of the Romish church err and are deceived when they teach that a man may rest himself in the faith of his teachers, believing in sundry things only as the church believes, though he knows not distinctly what is the faith of the church. Again, here the pope's pardons fall to [the] ground, for in vain does the pope by the power of the keys apply the meritorious works and the satisfactory sufferings of one man to another, considering every man is saved only by his own faith. The wise virgins professed that they had no more oil than served their own turn. They knew not the popish doctrine, that men might have good works enough for themselves, and an over plus for others. Hilary gathers hence "that one man's good works cannot be applied to another."[33] Jerome says, "Every man shall receive a reward for his own works, and that one man's works cannot cover another man's faults in the Day of Judgment."[34] The speech of Leo may stop the mouths of all papists. "Though the death of the saints is precious in the sight of God, yet the killing of no innocent is the reconciliation of the world. The righteous have received crowns but they have not given crowns. And the fortitude of believers ministers examples of patience, but not gifts of justice. For the deaths of them all were private or particular. Neither did any of them by his funeral discharge another man's debt, considering among the sins of men Christ our Lord is only found in whom all are crucified, dead, and buried, and rise again."[35] Paul indeed says

30. In the margin: See further Justin. q. 56. Aug. epist. 23, 57, 105. de bapt. lib. 4. cap. 2. Bern. ser. 66 in Cant.

31. In the text: Serm. 14.

32. In the text: Epist. 77.

33. In the margin: Upon Matt. 25.

34. In the margin: Ibidem.

35. In the margin: ser. 11 de passione.

to the Corinthians that he desired "to be bestowed for their souls" [2 Cor. 12:15] and that he suffers "all things for the elect" [2 Tim. 2:10]. But he speaks this in respect of his apostolic ministry, and not in respect of any works of satisfaction performed by him on the behalf of others. Again, he says, "I bear in mine own body the remainders of the sufferings of Christ" [Col. 1:24]. But these remainders are the sufferings which every man must bear for himself. For every disciple of Christ must take up his own cross, and so accomplish the sufferings of the whole mystical body.

Third, by this we learn not to rely on the gifts, suffrages, and prayers of others, but to seek for a sufficient and lively faith of our own. The foolish virgins, who supposed they might have furnished themselves with sufficient oil from the wise virgins, were utterly disappointed. Therefore, the speech of the papists is to be detested; namely "that the suffrages of the living, that is, their fasting, prayers, alms, masses, etc. do three ways help the dead: by way of merit of congruity, by way of entreaty, and by way of satisfaction."[36]

Use 6: Keeping a Good Conscience

Lastly, here we learn that faith and the justice of a good conscience must always go together. And for this cause, it is not said that man lives by faith, but the just man. Let all Protestants learn and remember this. For it is God's commandment that we should jointly keep faith and good conscience. And it is a common offence to atheists, papists, [and] worldlings, that such as pretend faith fail in the righteousness of good conscience. Some (it may be) will say that it shall suffice for them to call upon God when they are dying, and to die by faith. I answer that we must not only die and be saved, but also live in this world by our faith.

Finis

36. In the margin: Bellar. de indulg. cap. 14. pag. 85.

A Treatise on the Vocations
or
Callings of men, with the sorts and kinds of them, and the right use thereof

Written by M. W. Perkins

"The memorial of the just shall be blessed:
but the name of the wicked shall not" (Prov. 10:7).

Printed by John Legate,
Printer to the University of Cambridge.

1603

And are to be sold in Paul's Churchyard at the Sign of the
Crown by Simon Waterton

The Epistle Dedicatory

To the Worshipful, Mr. Robert Taylor, Esquire, one of the tellers in her Majesty's Exchequer, my very good friend.

Experience teaches, and it is a true conclusion propounded and proved in the Scriptures of the Old and New Testaments, that as God in the beginning by His omnipotent power established the whole frame of the heavens and the earth (Gen. 1:1), so He has in His wisdom directed them, and all things contained in them, unto one main end: the manifestation of His glory. Whereunto, though everything created by His appointment (Prov. 16:4; Rom. 11:36), according to the law of creation and the principles of its own entire nature, is (and ought to be) referred, yet among the works of God some do more principally and directly make for that purpose, as namely man, whom God has endued with the gifts of understanding and knowledge, and in whom He has engraved His own image in righteousness and true holiness. Now if the question is how man, being fallen from that integrity wherein he was created and having brought a confusion upon the whole world by the fall, should yet be fitted and framed for such an end, the answer is that God, who is able to draw light out of darkness, and to rectify things that are confounded, has in great wisdom set an order in mankind, which by certain degrees tends directly to the advancement of His own glory.[1]

In the first place, God would have man to acknowledge Him [as] his sovereign Lord, and serve Him immediately in the duties of faith and obedience. Second, it is His will that man, being made a sociable creature, apt to converse with his own kind, should do service unto Him by serving man in the duties of love. Third, He would not that men, conversing with each other, should be as wandering Rechabites, tied to no certain place or calling. And, therefore, [He] binds all men, both by special assignment unto Adam in his innocency (Gen. 3:19) and by particular commandment to him and all his posterity, to be confined within some certain state and condition of life, in the family, in the

1. This paragraph break is not in the original.

commonwealth, or in the church. Lastly, [He would] that man should use the place and office assigned unto him in a holy manner, performing the duties annexed unto it in faith and obedience, and eschewing those vices that usually attend upon it, with all care and circumspection. In this manner, God has disposed the whole estate of mankind for the accomplishment of the aforesaid end, the honor and glory of His name.

At this day two sorts of men do offend against this order. The first are such as live in the bosom of the church, and are not ranged within the compass of any calling or condition of life, wherein they might gain glory unto God or good unto men. Under these are comprehended all popish votaries, as monks, friars, etc., who have been justly condemned of ancient times for thieves and robbers because, living apart from the common societies of men, they are neither the members of any body nor maintainers of any of the three states before named.[2] And to them may be referred all wandering and straggling persons, who, having no settled place of abode, and being neither members of any civil society nor annexed to any particular church, have no personal calling wherein to live, and therefore cannot either glorify their Creator nor do the least good unto men.

The lives of these persons are so much the more odious because they are like the unprofitable drone[3] that brings nothing into the hive, and yet feeds of the honey that is brought in by the labor of others. Another sort of men are they who indeed are called unto a certain condition and trade of life, wherein they do walk and yield some benefit unto others, and yet they are greatly to be blamed in respect of their want in the right use and exercise of their callings. For though they may be skillful and expert in their kind, yet they err in the main point, in that they do not practice their personal callings in and with the general. Whereas, on the contrary, the principal scope of their lives ought to be the honoring of God in the service of men, and the rule of direction for the attainment of that end is nothing else but a constant performance of the duties of the moral law in that very calling wherein they are placed.

A remedy for these and sundry more corruptions incident unto the lives of men, as also a warning to those who offend in this kind, the author hereof (whose memory is blessed) has presented unto our view in the following discourse. Herein are handled at large, out of the Word of God, the differences and right use of all callings whatsoever.

In publishing [this work] I have thought good to make choice of your Worship to whose protection I might commend the same, and that upon these

2. In the margin: Socrates. hist. Eccl. l. 4. c. 18. Aug. de op. Monachorum.

3. *Drone:* male bee.

considerations. First, because you are and have been an ancient favorer and well-wisher to learning and learned men, whereof among the rest our college has already had very sufficient testimony, for which it does acknowledge you by the name of a loving and liberal benefactor. Second, for that (in my knowledge) you were very lovingly affected unto the author of this treatise while he lived, having always a reverent opinion of his gifts, and wishing him encouragement in all his proceedings. Beside these respects, it is my desire, by this dedication, to give unto you some testimony of a thankful mind for your love and kindness towards me. And thus, craving your acceptation hereof, I take my leave, and commend you with all your affairs to the grace and favor of God.

Your Worship's in all kindness to command,
W. P.
Cambridge, February 16, 1602

An advertisement to the reader and to all printers and publishers of M. Perkins's books

It is a speech uttered by the wise man in his Proverbs, worthy [of] your due observation (Christian reader) that he who sends a message by the hand of a fool is as he who cuts off his feet or drinks some hurtful thing (Prov. 26:6). By the fool, Solomon means anyone who undertakes a business on behalf of another without advice or due consideration either of the weight of the thing itself or of the party to whom it belongs. By the cutting off [of] the feet, [he means] the want of wit, skill, and dexterity, for the carriage and conveyance of the business in [a] good and seemly manner. And [the phrase], the drinking of a noisome thing, imports not only the grief, but also the hurt and prejudice that grows unto him whose affairs are either not at all or very ill dispatched by so foolish and witless a messenger. Now this may be gathered out of Solomon's parable: that it is a shameful disgrace unto a man to put the hand unto any work, either committed unto him by another or undertaken of his own head, and not to go through it with credit and commendation. Again, that a business unadvisedly begun and unskillfully followed is as a message sent by the hand of a fool, who must needs bewray his folly and mar the fashion of the message, which, besides the imputation of his own want of wit, makes greatly to the impeachment of the author's credit.

To these and such like footless messengers may not unfitly be compared some publishers and printers of men's works in these days. Upon a greedy desire of a little gain, [they] are willing to run into a greater inconvenience by doing manifest injury to the authors, and justly incurring the certain loss of their own credit and good name. Not to insist in generalities: it is not unknown unto you (good reader) what an open wrong has been done by this sort of men unto that worthy servant of God, the writer of this book lately deceased, in the publishing of two treatises under his name. One [is] entitled, *The Practice of Faith*; the other, *The Reformation of Covetousness.*

For first, the writers of these books have very boldly presumed to undertake this work without the knowledge or consent of the author's friends, not once considering what better copies might elsewhere be had, far more agreeable to his own style, and consequently more beneficial to the church. [This is] a plain argument that they wanted wit and common reason, either to conceive or carry a message of so great importance.

Second, to speak the best of their books, especially the latter, they are but rude and confused notes, some taken perhaps from the author's mouth, others foisted in by whole pages, which (upon my knowledge) he never delivered. [They are] all scraped up together by some hungry scribe, not upon conscience of crediting the author or furthering the reader, but in a covetous humor to get money of the printer as needy as themselves.

Third, let appeal be made unto the judgment of a reader but meanly grounded in knowledge, whether *The Reformation of Covetousness* (as they term it) is not for method, interpretation, collection, and application, in the most places, unlearnedly, imperfectly, disorderly, and ridiculously penned. I spare to point at the particulars (though it might easily have been done to the shame and disgrace of the writers) because there is hope upon this item, they may be better advised hereafter. As for the versifier, who writes before it, *In Memoriam Perkins,* whose also the epistle is, though he has subscribed to the verses only, as to the worthier work, besides that he bewrays his want of judgment in other matters, in being so willing to premise his letter to so sweet a piece of service. He may be well assured that both the name and the works of that holy man have sufficiently commended themselves unto the church of God, and therefore need not to be set forth by a man whose commendation is rather a blemish than an honor, and whose life and profession deserve neither just praise nor honest report. Now, if it seems strange unto any that men should be so shamefully overseen, discrediting themselves and dishonoring the dead, by these base and shameless enterprises, they may remember that the like injury was done unto him not many years before his death in the setting forth of an exposition upon the Lord's Prayer under his name without his consent or knowledge. And, therefore, it is no marvel that persons ill-disposed do now proclaim their folly to the world after his death, who did so palpably bewray it while he lived.

Considering, then, both the wrong offered even to the ashes of that holy man and the abuse of godly and religious people, by such ungodly and wicked practices, it was thought expedient to advertise the Christian reader, and all printers and publishers of books, that there are sundry copies in the hands of M. Perkins's assigns, some prepared for the press by himself, whereof this present treatise is one, and others hereafter to be published as occasion shall serve upon the view of some learned men here in Cambridge. Withal, wishing those who are well affected, and do desire still to enjoy the benefit of his labors, not to suffer themselves to be abused in such sort, as lately they have been by ruder copies, divulged hand over head by ignorant and unlettered persons, but rather to hearken after those which shall be set forth upon better warrant as occasion shall serve. In the meantime, use this in hand for your better directions, in the calling wherein you are placed by God, and finding good thereby give praise unto Him in your heart, who has vouchsafed to His church in these latter days so worthy an instrument of His glory.

Farewell.

The Contents

Part 1. What vocation is, where is set down:
- 1. The causes of every calling: efficient and final.
- 2. Two general rules belonging to all callings:
  - 1. Whatsoever any man does must be done by virtue of his calling and within the compass of it.
  - 2. Every man must do the duties of his calling with diligence.

Part 2. The parts and kinds of vocations, which are two:
- 1. General, whereof there are four main duties:
  - 1. Invocation.
  - 2. Furtherance of the state of the church.
  - 3. Serving one another in love.
  - 4. Walking worthy of the calling.
- 2. Personal, whereof there are five rules:
  - 1. Everyone in the church must have a personal calling to walk in.
  - 2. Every man must judge his particular calling, wherein he is, to be the best for him.
  - 3. Every man must join the practice of his personal calling with the practice of the general.
  - 4. Such as bear public callings must first reform themselves in private.
  - 5. A particular calling must give place to a general when they cannot both stand together.

    There are two sorts:
    - 1. Those that make a society.
    - 2. Those that preserve a society made.

Part 3. The right use of every particular calling, which stands in four things:

1. A good choice of a calling, whereof there are three rules:
    1. To choose an honest and a lawful calling.
    2. To choose a fit calling.
    3. He who is fitted for sundry must make choice of the best.
2. A good entrance into it, where are answered five questions:
    1. What calling had the first planters of our churches?
    2. What is to be done when entrance is made into a lawful calling with an evil mind and by evil means?
    3. Whether a man may lawfully offer himself and make means to enter into a calling or not?
    4. Whether a man may enter into two callings at once or not?
    5. Whether it is lawful to enter into two trades at once or not?
3. A good continuance in a calling, where is shown:
    1. What are the works of a calling: proper, profitable, [and] necessary. Here two questions are answered:
        1. Whether works of a calling, done by a man unlawfully entered, are nullities or not?
        2. Whether persons baptized by mass-priests are to be rebaptized?
    2. What is the right manner of doing the duties of a calling, where are required two things:
        1. Holiness, standing in a double sanctification:
            1. Of the worker.
            2. Of the works:

               by the Word, which gives direction for
               Eschewing of vices: covetousness and injustice
               Practicing of virtues: faith and love
               by Prayer
        2. Constancy in two things:
            1. Removing of impediments, as ambition, envy, and impatience.
            2. Using of helps, vacations, and changes.

Part 4. A good ending of the calling, which stands in:

1. A good resignation.
2. A good account.

“Let every man abide in that calling wherein he was called” (1 Cor. 7:20).

From verse 17 to verse 25 of this chapter, there are two questions handled. First, whether a man, being called to Christianity uncircumcised, must be circumcised after his calling? Second, whether, being a bond man when he is called, he must then leave his calling? Now the sum of the apostle’s answer to both of them is laid down in verse 20, as if he should say, “Let every man continue in that calling wherein he was called unto Christ, that is, wherein he walked and lived when it pleased God by the ministry of His gospel to call him to the profession of Christian religion.” The cause why I have chosen to speak of these words is because I mean to entreat of this point of vocation (or calling), considering few men rightly know how to live and go on in their callings so as they may please God. Therefore, to proceed in order in speaking of this point, first, I will show what vocation (or calling) is; second, I will set down the parts and kinds thereof; [and,] third, [I will set down] the holy and lawful use of every man’s particular calling.[1] All of this is in some sort touched in the words of my text.

Part 1: The Nature of Vocation

For the first, a vocation (or calling) is a certain kind of life, ordained and imposed on man by God for the common good. First of all, I say it is a certain condition (or kind) of life, that is, a certain manner (or order) of leading our lives in this world. For example, the life of a king is to spend his time in the governing of his subjects, and that is his calling. And the life of a subject is to live in obedience to the magistrate, and that is his calling. The state and condition of a minister is to lead his life in preaching the gospel and Word of God, and that is his calling. A master of a family is to lead his life in the government of his family, and that is his calling. In a word, that particular and honest manner of conversation, whereunto every man is called and set apart, is (I say) his calling.

Now in every calling we must consider two causes: first, the efficient [cause] and author thereof; [and,] second, the final and proper end.

1. Perkins has a fourth major heading: A Good Ending of a Calling.

The Efficient Cause

The author of every calling is God Himself. And, therefore, Paul says, "As God hath called every man let him walk" (1 Cor. 7:17). And, for this cause, the order and manner of living in this world is called a vocation, because every man is to live as he is called by God. For look as in a camp the general appoints to every man his place and standing, one place for the horseman and another for the foot man, and to every particular soldier likewise his office and his standing in which he is to abide against the enemy, and therein to live and die, even so it is in human societies. God is the general, appointing to every man his particular calling, and (as it were) his standing. And in that calling, He assigns unto him his particular office, in performance whereof he is to live and die. And as in a camp no soldier can depart [from] his standing without the leave of the general, no more may any man leave his calling except he receives his liberty from God. Again, there are many wheels in a clock made by the art and handiwork of man, and each one has its several motions, some turn this way, some that way, some go softly, some apace. And they are all ordered by the motion of the watch. Behold here a notable resemblance of God's special providence over mankind, which is the watch of the great world, allotting to every man his motion and calling, and in that calling his particular office and function. Therefore, it is true that I say that God Himself is the author and beginning of callings.

This overthrows the heathenish opinion of men who think that the particular condition and state of man in this life comes by chance, or by the bare will and pleasure of man himself. Second, we learn, by this which has been said, that many, persuading themselves of their callings, have for all this no calling at all. As, for example, such as live by usury, by carding and dicing, by maintaining houses of gaming, by plays and such like. For God is the author of every lawful calling, but these and all such miserable courses of living are either against the Word of God or else are not grounded thereupon. And, therefore, [they] are not callings or vocations but avocations from God and His ways.

Now as God is the author of every calling, so He has two actions therein. First, He ordains the calling itself; and, second, He imposes it on man called. And, therefore, I say [that] vocation is a certain kind of life, ordained and imposed by God.

Action 1: Ordination

For the first, God ordains a calling when He prescribes and commands the same in and by His Word. And those callings and states of life which have no warrant from God's Word are unlawful. Now God in His Word ordains callings [in] two ways: first, by commanding and prescribing them particularly, as He does the weightiest callings in the family, church, or commonwealth; [and,] second, by appointing and setting down certain laws and commandments generally, whereby we may easily gather that He does either approve or not approve of them, though they are not particularly prescribed in the Word.

Action 2: Imposition

The second action of God, which is the imposition of callings, is when He does particularly set apart any man to any particular calling. And this must be understood of all callings in the world. Now God does this [in] two ways.

First, [He does it] by Himself immediately without the help of any creature. Thus, in the beginning was Adam called and appointed to dress the Garden of Eden [Gen. 2:15]. Thus, Abraham was called from the idolatry of his forefathers, and received into the covenant of grace. Thus, Moses was called to be a prince over the Israelites, to guide them out of Egypt into the Promised Land. And thus, in the New Testament, the apostles were called to preach the gospel.

Second, God calls mediately by means, which are of two sorts: men [and] angels. By an angel, Philip, being a deacon, was called to be an evangelist [Acts 8:26]. And the set or appointed callings in church and commonwealth are ordinarily disposed by men who are in this matter the instruments of God. And, therefore, men lawfully called by them are truly called by God. Thus, the elders of Ephesus, called by the apostles and the rest of the church, are said to be called by the Holy Spirit [Acts 20:28].

And thus, we see how God is the author of every calling.

The Final Cause

I note the final cause (or end) of every calling in the last words of the description: for the common good, that is, for the benefit and good estate of mankind. In man's body there are sundry parts and members, and each has its several use and office, which it performs not for itself but for the good of the whole body, as the office of the eye is to see, the ear to hear, and the foot to go. Now all societies of men are bodies. A family is a body, and so is every particular church a body, and the commonwealth also. And there are several members in these bodies. They are men walking in several callings and offices, the execution whereof must tend to the happy and good estate of the rest, yea of all men everywhere, as much as possible. The common good of men stands in this, not only that they live, but that they live well in righteousness and holiness and consequently in true happiness. And for the attainment hereunto God has ordained and disposed all callings, and in His providence designed the persons to bear them. Here then we must in general know that he abuses his calling, whosoever he is, who against the end thereof employs it for himself, seeking wholly his own and not the common good. And that common saying, "Every man for himself and God for us all," is wicked, and is directed against the end of every calling or honest kind of life.

Thus much of the description of vocation in general. Now before I come particularly to entreat of the special kinds of callings, there are two general rules (which belong to every calling) to be learned by all.

Rule 1

The first [is] whatsoever any man enterprises (or does), either in word or deed, must be done by virtue of his calling, and he must keep himself within the compass, limits, or precincts thereof. This rule is laid down in these words of the apostle: "Let every man abide in that calling wherein he was called." The drift whereof is to bind men to their callings, and to teach them to perform all their actions by warrant thereof. It is said, "Without faith it is impossible to please God" (Heb. 11:6), and "Whatsoever is not of faith is sin."[2] Now whatsoever is not done within the compass of a calling is not of faith, because a man must first have some warrant and word from God to assure him of his calling to do this or that thing before he can do it in faith. When the two brethren, who strove about their inheritance, came to Christ, and willed Him to make agreement between them, Christ answered, "Who made me a judge or divider between you?" (Luke 12:14). [It is] as if He should say, "It is not within the compass of My calling, for I came to accomplish the work of man's redemption and not to divide inheritances." Hereby [He] gives us to understand that everything to be done must be done by warrant of some calling, and so long as men keep themselves in their callings they have a promise of protection from God. "He shall give his angels charge over thee to keep thee in all thy ways" (Ps. 91:11); that is, "so long as you keep yourself within the ways of your calling, so long shall My angels preserve you."[3]

The example of David is worthy [of] our consideration, for he, depending on the providence of God and walking in his calling, had the protection of God when Saul smote twice at him with a spear, when he was made captain of a thousand that he might be slain by the Philistines, when Michal was promised to be his wife for a hundred foreskins of the Philistines, when Saul commanded his own servants to kill him, when he smote again at him with a spear, when he sought to take him in his own house, when he followed him to Naioth in Ramah, when he was absent from the solemn feast made by Saul, when the priests of Nob were slain (85 persons) and all the inhabitants of the place, when

2. Rom. 14:23.

3. This paragraph break is not in the original.

Saul persecuted him in the desert of Mahan [1 Sam. 18–21, 25–26]. Contrariwise, when any man is without the compass of his calling, he is out of the way, and by this means he bereaves himself of the protection of the Almighty, and lies open and naked to all the punishments and plagues of God.[4]

And if we mark it well, the Word of God shows evidently to what dangers they are subject, who do anything either without or against their callings. Samson's strength lay not in his hair (as men commonly think) but because he went out of his calling by breaking the vow of a Nazarite when he gave occasion to Delilah to cut off his hair. Therefore, he lost his strength, for God promised strength but with a commandment that he should be a Nazarite to the end (Judg. 13:5). When Saul was commanded to slay the Amalekites, against his calling he spared Agag upon a foolish pity, and [he spared] the best things [1 Sam. 15:23]. And thereupon Samuel reproved him of rebellion against God, which was as the sin of witchcraft. And for this very cause he was rejected by God from being king over Israel. Jonah, being called to preach at Nineveh, went about by flight to shake off the calling of God, but when he came to the sea, he was tossed by a tempest, and cast out of the ship, and swallowed by a fish that God had prepared for this purpose. When Peter, beyond the limits of his calling, would needs warm himself at the high priest's fire, it cost him the breach of his conscience, for at the very voice of a damsel he denied Christ with cursing and banning. And the exorcists, who without sufficient calling took upon themselves to conjure evil spirits in the name of Jesus, were overcome by the same spirits, and were fain to flee away naked and wounded [Acts 19:16]. In a word, look what judgments befall men, mark well the time and circumstance thereof, it shall be found that they are cast upon them by the hand of God when they are forth of their callings which God has prescribed them to keep. Therefore, this must always be remembered and practiced carefully, that we take nothing in hand unless we have first ranked ourselves within the precincts of our callings.

Rule 2

The second general rule which must be remembered is this: every man must do the duties of his calling with diligence. And, therefore, Solomon says, "Whatsoever is in thy hand to do, do with all thy power" (Eccl. 9:10). Saint Paul bids him who rules [to] rule with diligence, and every man to wait on his office (Rom. 12:8). And Jeremiah says, "Cursed is he that doeth the work of the Lord negligently" (Jer. 48:10). That which Christ says of the work of our redemption,

4. This paragraph break is not in the original.

"It is meat and drink for me to do my Father's will" [John 4:34], the same must every man say in like sort of his particular calling.[5]

There are two reasons for this diligence. First of all, the end why God bestows His gifts upon us is that they might be employed in His service and to His glory, and that in this life. Therefore, Paul says, "Redeem the time."[6] And Christ [says], "Walk while ye have light."[7] And again, "I must do his work while it is day."[8] For we see [that] tradesmen and travelers rise early to their business lest night overtakes them. Second, to them who employ their gifts, more is given, and from them who employ them not, that which they have is taken. And labor in a calling is as precious as gold or silver. Hereupon he who maims a man and disables him to do the work of his calling, by God's law, is bound to give him the value of his labor (Ex.. 21:19). And to like purpose our people have a common saying that an occupation is as good as land, because land may be lost, but skill and labor in good occupation is profitable to the end because it will help at a need when land and all things fail.[9]

And, on the other side, we must take heed of two damnable sins that are contrary to this diligence. The first is idleness whereby the duties of our callings, and the occasions of glorifying God, are neglected or omitted. The second is slothfulness whereby they are performed slackly and carelessly. God, in the parable of the husbandman, calls them who are idle to His vineyard, saying, "Why stand ye idle all the day?" (Matt. 20:6). And the servant, who had received but one talent, is called an evil servant because he was slothful in the use of it. For so it is said: "Thou evil servant and slothful" (Matt. 25:26). Saint Paul gives this rule to the Thessalonians: "He that will not labor must not eat" [2 Thess. 3:10]; yea, he would have such a one to be noted by a letter as walking inordinately [v. 14]. And by this he shows that sloth and negligence in the duties of our callings are a disorder against that comely order which God has set in the societies of mankind both in church and commonwealth. And, indeed, idleness and sloth are the causes of many damnable sins. The idle body, and the idle brain, is the shop of the devil. If the sea moved not, [it] could not but putrefy. And if the body is not stirred and moved, [it] breeds diseases. Now the idle and slothful person is a sea of corruption. And when he is most idle, Satan is least idle, for then he is most busy to draw him to manifold sins.

Thus much of the two general rules.

5. This paragraph break is not in the original.
6. Eph. 5:16.
7. John 12:35.
8. John 9:4.
9. This paragraph break is not in the original.

Part 2: The Kinds of Vocation

Now follow the parts and kinds of vocations, and they are of two sorts: general or particular. The general calling is the calling of Christianity which is common to all who live in the church of God. The particular is that special calling which belongs to some particular men, as the calling of a magistrate, the calling of a minister, the calling of a master, father, child, servant, subject, or any other calling that is common to all. And Paul acknowledges this distinction of callings when he says, "Let every man abide in that calling wherein he was called"; that is, in that particular and personal calling, in which he was called to be a Christian. Of these two in order.

The General Calling

The general calling is that whereby a man is called out of the world to be a child of God, a member of Christ, and an heir of the kingdom of heaven. This calling belongs to everyone within the compass of the church, not any one excepted. Here I have just occasion to make a long discourse touching the calling of men to Christ and Christian religion, but I will only touch the main duties thereof, which are especially four.

Duty 1

The first is the invocation of the name of God in Christ. When Saul got letters from the high priests to persecute the church, it is said by Saint Luke that he received authority to "bind all that call upon the name of God" (Acts 9:14). Paul, writing to the church of Corinth, calls the members thereof saints, and such as call on the name of the Lord Jesus (1 Cor. 1:2). By both [of these] places the Holy Spirit would give us to understand that invocation is a main duty which every Christian man is to perform continually. And it contains both prayer and thanksgiving in the name and mediation of Jesus Christ. And, indeed, by this action a Christian is distinguished and severed from all other sorts of men in the world who pretend devotion or religion. By this it appears [that], howsoever all men desire to bear this name and take unto them this general calling, very few are indeed true and sound Christians. For not one in a hundred can rightly invocate the name of God. Though they can indeed repeat the words of prayer, yet they want the spirit of grace and supplication whereby they should ask grace in the name of Christ, and give thanks for benefits received. Thus, bearing in show the name of Christ, many want the power thereof. Nay, which is more, not to call on the name of God is made by the prophet David the note and mark of an atheist "that saith in his heart there is no God" (Ps. 14:1).

Duty 2

The second duty is, as much as we possibly can, to further the good estate of the true church of God. It is indeed principally the duty of the minister, and yet generally it appertains to all. For as in man's body, the eye by seeing, the ear by hearing, the tongue by speaking, and every part by its proper office, does further the good of the whole body, even so all who are called to be members of Christ must, as much as in them lies, procure the good of the whole mystical body of Christ. In the name of the whole church, David says, "I will procure thy wealth, and pray for the peace of Jerusalem, they shall prosper that love thee" (Ps. 122:6). And after he had humbled himself for the two grievous sins of adultery and murder, in the end he prays to God to build the walls of Jerusalem [Ps. 51:18]. For the building of the tabernacle, the Jews brought freewill offerings according to their ability. Some brought gold and precious stones, others their silver and silk, and such as had no better thing brought rams' skins and badgers' skins. Even so, in the building of God's church, His spiritual tabernacle, every Christian must bring a freewill offering. He must do something even to the utmost of his power to the building of God's church, though his service is but mean.[10]

Though men (as I have said) fondly imagine that this duty is proper to the ministers of the Word, yet the truth is it belongs not only unto them but to everyone who professes himself to be a member of the body of Christ, in which respect he must (as much as he can) procure and further the good of the whole. Here then we are to consider the means whereby this duty may be done. They are especially three.

The first is prayer not only for ourselves but for the good estate of the whole church of God on earth. To this effect Christ spoke to His disciples, when He saw the Jews like scattered sheep without a shepherd: "Pray to the Lord of the harvest, that he would thrust forth laborers into the harvest" (Matt. 9:38). And in that prayer commonly called the Lord's Prayer, we are taught to say, "Let thy kingdom come." By "kingdom" is not only meant the kingdom of glory in heaven, but the kingdom of grace which is the happy and blessed condition of God's church on earth. And, therefore, Paul bids the Thessalonians [to] pray that God's Word may have free passage and be glorified (2 Thess. 3:1).

The second means is the work of edification, which Paul enjoins the Thessalonians: "Edify one another" (1 Thess. 5:11). And Saint Jude: "Edify yourselves upon your most holy faith" (v. 20). The church of God is a temple made without hands; the foundation is Christ; and every member of Christ with all that pertain to God's election are living stones. The builders of this temple are

10. This paragraph break is not in the original.

principally pastors and teachers, and not only they but all Christian persons generally. The case stands here as it did in the building of the material temple, the principal builders whereof were such as cut and laid stones, and wrought curious works, besides whom there were many others who, though they could neither cut nor frame, yet they did further the building either by carrying burdens or making mortar. Even so, in the building of God's spiritual church, though all cannot square stones like masons, nor build as the minister does, yet all without exception, pertaining to the church of God, must put their helping hands to further this building. And this may be done [in] two ways. [The] first [is] by using all good means whereby we may draw our kindred, friends, and neighbors to the love and obedience of true religion. Paul propounds this duty to the Corinthians in his own example, saying, that he "pleased all men in all things, not seeking his own profit, but the profit of many that they might be saved" (1 Cor. 10:33). Second, this thing is done by confirming those who are called by often admonitions, exhortations, consolations, and all other like duties that serve to this end. And by these duties the meanest person in the church of God may build or edify.

Here I may justly complain of the neglect of this duty, for the case stands thus in this barren and fruitless age of the world: men are so far from duties of edification that they use all means to pull down rather than to build [up]. For he who gives himself but to learn the duties of religion, and in some sort to live accordingly, is made a sign and by-word among the common people, and also a wonder. And this shows that the practice of this duty of edification lies dead, whereto, nevertheless, we are bound by virtue of a general calling.

The third means of furthering the good of God's church is to confer the temporal blessings that God has bestowed on us, according to our ability, to the good thereof. "Honor God with thy riches," says Solomon (Prov. 3:9). And this is done especially when they are employed to the maintaining and furthering of true religion and the worship of God. There are other ends for which God has given riches, but this is the principal of all. Yet, alas, this duty is but slenderly practiced by such as carry the name of Christ. For many of the other sort spend a great part of their increase upon hawks, bulls, bears, dogs, or riotously misspend the same in sporting or gaming, and thus disable themselves to do that good they should unto the church of God. And the meaner sort nowadays spend what they get in fine apparel and good cheer, and by this means the house of God is less regarded. For every common man nowadays must be as a gentleman, and it is hard sometimes for a stranger to discern the master from the servant, and there is such excess in all degrees that now for daily attire the noblest are the plainest. To this duty I may also add that every Christian parent, by virtue of his general calling, is to dedicate some of his male children (as much as possible) to the service of the ministry, if they have gifts and inclination of nature for that calling. And in this case the example of Hannah may be a good direction for us to follow. She did beforehand consecrate Samuel her firstborn to the Lord. By this means the ministry shall be continued, God's church and religion maintained, and His gospel published from age to age to the end of the world.

Duty 3

The third general duty of Christianity [is] that every man should become a servant to his brother in all the duties of love. A Christian is the freest of all men in the world. For in that respect [that] he is the child of God in Christ, he is truly freed from hell, death, and condemnation, yea and in part from sin and Satan, and that in this life. And yet, for all this, he must be a servant unto every man. But how? By all the duties of love, as occasion shall be offered, and that for the common good of all men. Mark well the words of Paul: "Though I be free from all men, yet have I made myself servant to all, that I might win the more" (1 Cor. 9:19). If it is said [that] this duty appertains to an apostle, I answer that Paul enjoins it indifferently to every man. "Do service one to another in love" (Gal. 5:13). And, for this cause, the servants of God are said to be "trees of righteousness"[11] whose leaves serve for medicine and their fruit for meat, not for themselves but for others. Let us, therefore, in the fear of God be careful to learn this duty, for the practice of it is the special ornament of Christ's holy gospel.

Duty 4

The last general duty is set down by Saint Paul: "Walk worthy that calling whereto God hath called you" (Eph. 4:1). Again, he bids servants so to carry themselves toward their masters that they may adorn the gospel of God in all things (Titus 2:10). And he sets down in the following words how men may adorn religion by their profession, namely, by "denying ungodliness and worldly lusts," by "living soberly, righteously, and godly in this present world." In a word, this calling of Christianity is the most excellent calling in the world, and he walks worthy [of] the same who keeps a good conscience before God and is unblameable before all men.

I commend this duty to the meditation and practice of all men whatsoever. We were once baptized and therein gave up our names to God and Christ. And we are content to hear the Word, and receive the Supper of the Lord as a pledge of His mercy and love. We must, therefore, walk as they to whom the mercy

11. Isa. 61:3.

and love of God pertain. Christ pronounces a "woe to them that give offence" (Matt. 18:7). And, indeed, it would be better for any man to be as far under the earth as he is above it than by a bad and loose conversation to slander the name of God, whose professed servant he is. And as Christ says, "It were better a millstone were hanged about his neck, and he were thrown into the bottom of the sea" (Luke 17:2). And as David prays, "Lord take from me rebuke and shame, which I do fear, because thy judgments are good" (Ps. 119:39). And that we may evermore walk worthy of this calling, we first of all must depend by faith on the providence and mercy of God at all times. Second, we must daily turn unto Him by a continual renewing of our repentance. Third, we must endeavor to perform new obedience in respect of all His commandments.

Thus much of the general calling common to all men as they are Christians.

The Particular Calling

Now follows the second kind of calling, and it is personal. A personal calling is the execution of some particular office, arising from that distinction which God makes between man and man in every society.[12]

First, I say it is the execution of some particular office. For example, the calling of a magistrate is to execute the office of government over his subjects; the office of a minister is to execute the duty of teaching his people; the calling of a master is to execute the office of authority and government over his servants; the office of a physician is to put in practice the good means whereby life and health are preserved. In a word, in every estate, the practice and execution of that particular office wherein any man is placed is his personal calling.

Second, I add that it arises from that distinction which God makes between man and man in every society, to show what is the foundation and ground of all personal callings. And it is a point to be considered by us, [and] I explain it thus. In His Word, God has ordained the society of man with man, partly in the commonwealth, partly in the church, and partly in the family. And it is not the will of God that man should live and converse alone by himself. Now, for the maintaining of society, He has ordained a certain bond to link men together, which Saint Paul calls "the bond of peace, and the bond of perfection," namely love [Col. 3:14].[13] And howsoever He has ordained societies, and the bond of them all, yet He has appointed that there should still remain a distinction between man and man, not only in regard of person, but also in other respects. For the whole body is not the hand, nor the foot, nor the eye, but the hand [is] one part, the foot another, and the eye another. And howsoever in the body

12. This paragraph break is not in the original.
13. The original has the reference as Phil. 3:14.

one part is linked to another, yet there is a distinction between the members whereby it comes to pass that the hand is the hand, not the foot, and the foot [is] the foot, not the hand nor the eye. So it is in societies; there is a distinction in the members thereof and that in two respects.[14]

First, in regard of the inward gifts which God bestows on every man, giving to several men several gifts, according to His good pleasure. Paul entreats at large of this distinction in regard of inward gifts in 1 Corinthians 12. Through the whole chapter, he shows the diversity of gifts that God bestows on His church, and so proportionally in every society. Now look as the inward gifts of men are severed, so are the persons distinguished in their societies accordingly.[15]

Second, persons are distinguished by order, whereby God has appointed that in every society one person should be above or under another, not making all equal, as though the body should be all head and nothing else. But even in degree and order He has set a distinction that one should be above another [Rom. 13:7; 1 Peter 2:13–14]. And by reason of this distinction of men, partly in respect of gifts [and] partly in respect of order, come personal callings. For if all men had the same gifts, and all were in the same degree and order, then all should have one and the same calling. But in as much as God gives diversity of gifts inwardly, and distinction of order outwardly, hence proceed diversity of personal callings. And, therefore, I added that personal callings arise from that distinction which God makes between man and man in every society.

And thus, we see what is a personal calling. Now, before I come to entreat of the parts thereof, there are other general rules to be learned which concern all personal callings whatsoever.

Rule 1

Every person of every degree, state, sex, or condition, without exception, must have some personal and particular calling to walk in. This appears plainly by the whole Word of God. Adam, as soon as he was created, even in his integrity, had a personal calling assigned [to] him by God, which was to dress and keep the garden. And after Adam's fall, the Lord gives a particular commandment to him and all his posterity, which binds all men to walk in some calling, either in the church or commonwealth, saying, "In the sweat of thy brow shalt thou eat thy bread" (Gen. 3:19). Again, in the renewing of the law at Mount Sinai, the fourth commandment does not only permit labor on six days, but also enjoins the same (as I take it) to us all. For God's example is there propounded for us to follow, that as He rested the seventh day, so must also we. And consequently,

14. This paragraph break is not in the original.
15. This paragraph break is not in the original.

as He spent six days in the work of creation, so should we in our personal callings. And Saint Paul gives this rule: "Let him that stole, steal no more, but let him rather work with his hands the thing that is good, that he may have to give him that needeth" (Eph. 4:28). Christ, the head of men, lived with Joseph in the calling of a carpenter, till the time of His baptism, and hereupon it was that the Jews said, "Is not this the carpenter, the son of Mary?" (Mark 6:3).[16] And after He was baptized and was (as it were) solemnly admitted into the office of a Mediator, the work of our redemption was then His calling, in which He both lived and died. Yea, the angels of God have their particular callings, in that they do His "commandments in obeying the voice of his word" [Ps. 103:20]. And, therefore, all who descend from Adam must needs have some calling to walk in, either public or private, whether it is in the church, commonwealth, or family.

Hence, we may learn sundry points of instruction. First of all, it is a foul disorder in any commonwealth that rogues, beggars, [or] vagabonds should be suffered. For such kinds of persons commonly are of no civil society or corporation, nor of any particular church, and [they] are as rotten legs and arms that drop from the body. Again, to wander up and down from year to year to this end, to seek and procure bodily maintenance, is no calling, but the life of a beast, and consequently [it is] a condition or state of life flatly against the rule that everyone must have a particular calling. And, therefore, the statute made [by] the last parliament for the restraining of beggars and rogues is an excellent statute, and, being in substance the very law of God, is never to be repealed.[17]

Second, hereby is overthrown the condition of monks and friars who challenge to themselves that they live in a state of perfection because they live apart from the societies of men in fasting and prayer. But, contrariwise, this monkish kind of living is damnable. For besides the general duties of fasting and prayer, which appertain to all Christians, every man must have a particular and personal calling, so that he may be a good [and] profitable member of some society and body. And the ancient church condemned all monks for thieves and robbers, that besides the general duties of prayer and fasting, did not withal employ themselves in some other calling for their better maintenance.

Third, we learn by this that miserable and damnable is the state of those who, being enriched with great livings and revenues, do spend their days in eating and drinking, in sports and pastimes, not employing themselves in service for church or commonwealth. It may be haply thought that such gentlemen have happy lives, but it is far otherwise, considering everyone (rich or

16. In the margin: Justin contra Triph.
17. In the margin: Anno 39. Eliz.

poor, man or woman) is bound to have a personal calling in which they must perform some duties for the common good, according to the measure of the gifts that God has bestowed on them.

Fourth, hereby also it is required that such as we commonly call serving men should have, beside the office of waiting, some other particular calling, unless they tend on men of greater place and state. For only to wait and give attendance is not a sufficient calling, as common experience tells, for waiting servants, by reason they spend the most of their time in eating, drinking, sleeping, and gaming after dinner and supper, do prove the most unprofitable members both in church and commonwealth. For when either their good masters die or they are turned out of their office for some misdemeanor, they are fit for no calling, being unable to labor. And thus, they give themselves either to beg or steal. The waiting man of Cornelius, the centurion, was also a soldier by calling [Acts 10:7]. And it is to be wished nowadays that gentlemen would make choice of such servants that might not only tend on their persons but also tend upon some other convenient office. It is good for every man to have two strings to his bow.

Rule 2

Every man must judge that particular calling, in which God has placed him, to be the best of all callings for him. I say not simply best, but best for him. This rule is set forth unto us in the example of Paul. "I have learned," says he, "in whatsoever state I am to be content and well pleased" [Phil. 4:11]. The practice of this duty is the stay and foundation of the good estate both of church and commonwealth, for it makes every man to keep his own standing, and to employ himself painfully within his calling. But when we begin to mislike the wise disposition of God, and to think [that] other men's callings [would be] better for us than our own, then confusion and disorder follow in every society. When Absalom, a child and subject of king David, was not content with his estate, but sought his father's kingdom, and said, "O that I were judge among you!" [2 Sam. 15:4], many contentions and hurly-burlies followed in the commonwealth of the Jews all his days. And the sons of Zebedee, not contenting themselves with the calling of disciples, but being enflamed with desire of honor and dignity, sought two principal offices in Christ's kingdom, which (as they deemed) should be a civil and worldly kingdom. Hence, envy and heart-burning arose among the disciples, and further evils would have ensued unless the wisdom of our Savior Christ had cut them off.[18]

18. This paragraph break is not in the original.

The bishops of the Church of Rome, not content with their ecclesiastical estate, affected the honor of the empire, and by this means brought havoc and ruin upon the whole church. Yea, the very first family that ever was in the world felt the smart of this evil. Because he feared the loss of his primacy whereby he was to be a priest, prophet, and ruler in Adam's house after his decease, Cain slew his brother Abel [Gen. 4:5, 8]. And this may well be gathered by the words of the text where, when Cain began to be angry, the Lord said, "If thou doest well, there is remission: if not, sin lies at the door" [v. 7]. Now Cain might haply reply and say, "This is well, but my grief remains that I must lose my right and dignity." To this God answers thus in the next words: "And his appetite shall be to thee, and thou shalt rule over him," namely "if thou do well."[19]

And from time to time the greatest disorders that have fallen out in the church of God have issued from this fountain. And the same is also true in the commonwealth. Hence come treacheries, treasons, and seditions, when men, not content with their own estate and honors, seek higher places, and being disappointed [they] grow to discontentments, and so forward to all mischief. Therefore, in a word, the good estate of the church and commonwealth is when every person keeps himself to his own calling. And this will undoubtedly come to pass if we consider what are our callings and that we are placed in them by God, and therefore judge them to be the best callings of all for us.

Rule 3

Every man must join the practice of his personal calling with the practice of the general calling of Christianity before described. More plainly, every particular calling must be practiced in and with the general calling of a Christian. It is not sufficient for a man in the congregation and in common conversation to be a Christian, but he must show himself to be so in his very personal calling. For example, a magistrate must not only in general be a Christian, as every man is, but he must be a Christian magistrate in executing the office of a magistrate in bearing the sword. A master of a family must not only be a Christian abroad in the town, and in the congregation in the sight of strangers, but also in the administration and regiment of his particular family, toward wife, children, and servants. It is not enough for a woman to be virtuous openly to strangers, but her virtue must privately show itself in her subjection and obedience to her own husband. A schoolmaster must not only be a Christian in the assembly, when he hears the Word and receives the sacraments, but he must also show himself to be a Christian in the office of teaching. And every man must thus behave himself in his particular calling because the particular calling and the

19. This paragraph break is not in the original.

practice of the duties thereof, severed from the foresaid general calling, is nothing else but a practice of injustice and profaneness. And the general calling of Christianity without the practice of some particular calling is nothing else but the form of godliness without the power thereof. And, therefore, both callings must be joined as body and soul are joined in a living man.[20]

And that we may the better join both our callings together, we must consider the main end of our lives, and that is to serve God in serving men in the works of our callings. God, as He made man, so He can preserve man without the help of man. But His pleasure is that men shall be His instruments for the good [of] one another. For this cause, He has ordained the excellent offices of magistrates and ministers, and almost an infinite variety of trades of life, all tending to preserve the body, soul, or both. Thus, God manifests His fatherly care over us by the employment of men in His service according to their several vocations for our good. And there is not so much as the vassal or bondman but he must serve God by serving his master, as Paul teaches [Col. 3:24]. And by this one point we may learn two things.[21]

The first [is] that they profane their lives and callings, who employ them to get honors, pleasures, profits, worldly commodities, etc., for thus we live to another end than God has appointed, and thus we serve ourselves, and consequently neither God nor man. Some man will say perchance, What, must we not labor in our callings to maintain our families? I answer, this must be done, but this is not the scope and end of our lives. The true end of our lives is to do service to God in serving men. And for a recompense of this service, God sends His blessings on men's travails, and He allows them to take for their labors.[22]

Second, by this we learn how men of mean place and calling may comfort themselves. Let them consider that, in serving men by performance of poor and base duties, they serve God, and therefore that their service is not base in His sight. And though their reward from men is little, yet the reward at God's hand shall not be wanting. For seeing they serve God in serving men, they may justly look for reward from both. And thus, we may reap marvelous contentation in any kind of calling, though it is but to sweep the house or keep sheep, if we can thus in practice unite our callings.

By this rule any man may rightly judge of himself and others. For wheresoever these two callings are severed, whatsoever is in show, there is nothing in substance. And by this we may also discern a common fault in the lives of many men, who show themselves ready and willing to hear the Word of God; yea they approve it, receive the sacraments, and profess themselves to be members

20. This paragraph break is not in the original.
21. This paragraph break is not in the original.
22. This paragraph break is not in the original.

of Christ. And all these are good duties of the first and general calling. But go on further, and look into their particular callings, there you shall find nothing less, there is all out of order. Some are usurers, some oppressors, some engrossers, some use false weights and measures, some lying and swearing, some are loose and lascivious. It may be [that] such persons resolve themselves that all is well when they do some duties of their general calling. But whereas they neglect the performance of the said duties in their particular callings, they are far out of order, yea they lead a dangerous and lamentable course of life. For though they are endued with excellent gifts, and are able to speak well, conceive prayer, and with some reverence to hear the Word and receive the sacraments, yet if they practice not the duties of godliness within their own callings, all is but hypocrisy. And, therefore, unless they repent, the greater their gifts are, the more they shall make to their deeper condemnation at the Day of Judgment.

Again, this rule serves to teach all men the right way to reform their lives. If you would lead a life unblameable both before God and man, you must first of all bethink yourself what is your particular calling, and then proceed to practice the duties of the moral law, and all other duties of Christianity in that very calling. And if you would have signs and tokens of your election and salvation, you must fetch them from the constant practice of your two callings jointly together. Sever them in your life and you shall find no comfort, but rather shame and confusion of face, unless you repent.

Rule 4

Such as bear public callings must first reform themselves in private. When Moses went from Midian to Egypt to be a governor of the Israelites, the Lord withstood him in the way by reason of a fault in his private family, that his child was not circumcised according to the law of God. How shall he order public matters for the common good, who cannot order his own private estate?

Rule 5

A particular calling must give place to the general calling of a Christian when they cannot both stand together. For example, a servant is bound to his master to obey him, either because he is a vassal or at the least because he is hired to serve for wages. The said master (being a zealous papist) threatens his servant (being a Protestant) that unless he condescends to hear mass, he shall either burn at a stake or carry a faggot. Now the servant, seeing the malicious purpose of his master, and not finding himself able to bear the brunt of a trial, in this case he departs and withdraws himself for a time. And the question is whether he does well or not? The answer is [that] he does. And in such a case he may lawfully flee from his master. For a servant who is bound by personal calling to an earthly master is further bound by a general calling unto God. And the particular calling of any man is inferior to the general calling of a Christian. And when they cannot both stand together, the particular calling must give place, because we are bound unto God in the first place, and unto man under God, and so far forth only as we may withal keep our bond with God.

And thus much of the five general rules that are to be practiced in every particular calling.

To proceed, personal callings are of two sorts. The first sort are all such as are of the essence and foundation of any society without which the society cannot be; in the family, the calling of a master, servant, husband, wife, parents, and children; in the commonwealth, the calling of magistrates and subjects; and in the church, the calling of the minister and the people. The second sort are all such as serve only for the good, happy, and quiet estate of a society. And these are of sundry sorts. Some of them serve for the preservation of the life of man, as the calling of a husbandman, merchant, etc. Some serve for the preservation of health, as the calling of a physician, surgeon, etc. Some serve for the outward peace, as the calling of a soldier, lawyer, etc. Some serve for the clothing and attiring of the body, and they are almost so many as are the parts of the body. Some also serve for building, as the calling of a carpenter, mason, etc. In a word, look how many things are necessary for the good estate of any society, so many personal callings there are, which belong not to the defense and being of a society, but serve only for the good of the same. And all lawful personal callings may be referred to one of these kinds.

Thus much of callings in general, and of the kinds thereof.

Part 3: The Use of Vocation

The third point to be considered, which is the most principal, is this: how every man may in a good and holy manner use his calling. This still being remembered, that I speak not of extraordinary callings, or of the general calling of a Christian, but only of ordinary and personal callings. The handling of this point is of great weight and moment, for by the right use of every calling the works thereof are made good works, though otherwise they are but mean and base in themselves. Three things are required in a good work: first, it must be done in obedience; second, [it must be done] in faith; [and,] third, it must be directed to the glory of God.[23]

Now the works of every calling, when they are performed in a holy manner, are done in faith and obedience, and serve notably for God's glory, be the calling ever so base. For example, a man is by profession a shepherd, the calling

23. This paragraph break is not in the original.

is but base and mean, and the duties thereof are suitable. Yet, if there is grace to use that calling aright, the duties thereof are good works before God, being done with conscience of obedience unto God for His glory and the good of the master. The meanness of the calling does not abase the goodness of the work, for God looks not at the excellency of the work but at the heart of the worker. And the action of a shepherd in keeping sheep, performed, as I have said, in its kind, is as good a work before God as is the action of a judge in giving sentence or a magistrate in ruling or a minister in preaching. Thus then, we see there is good reason why we should search how every man is rightly to use his particular calling. In the right use of any calling, four things are to be considered and performed: (1) good choice of a calling; (2) good entrance into it; (3) good continuance therein; [and] (4) an honest and good leaving of the same.

Point 1: A Good Choice of a Calling

For the first, in the choice of our callings, we must remember and observe three particular rules.

Rule 1

We are to choose honest and lawful callings to walk in. "Let him that stole," says Paul, "steal no more; but let him rather labor, and work with his hands the thing that is good" (Eph. 4:28). Here we are warned by the Holy Spirit to make choice of such callings as are honest. Again, all the works of our callings must be done in faith, and there is no faith unless the calling is honest.

For better direction in the choice of an honest calling, this general ground must be observed: every calling that serves to uphold and maintain three several estates and societies, namely the estate of the church, the estate of the commonwealth, or the estate of the family, is grounded upon the moral law, and therefore lawful, and consequently may be had, used, and enjoyed with good conscience. On the contrary, if it is a hindrance to any of these three estates, in whole or in part, it is an unlawful calling.

Rule 2

Every man must choose a fit calling to walk in; that is, every calling must be fitted to the man, and every man [must] be fitted to his calling. This rule is as necessary as the former. For when men are out of their proper callings in any society, it is as much as if a joint were out of place in the body. Now in the choice of callings, two sorts of men must be considered: (1) men of years, and (2) children.[24]

24. This paragraph break is not in the original.

Men of years make choice of fit callings for themselves when they try, judge, and examine themselves, to what things they are apt and fit, and to what things they are not. And every man must examine himself of two things: first, touching his affection; [and,] second, touching his gifts. For his affection, he must search what mind he has to any calling, and in what calling he desires most of all to glorify God. For his gifts, he must examine for and to what calling they are most fit. Having thus tried both his affection and gifts, finding also the calling to which they tend with one consent, he may say that is his calling because he likes it best and [he] is every way the most fit for it. For example, one brought up in the schools of learning desires to know what ought to be his calling. Well, he examines his affection or desire, and finds it most of all inclined to the ministry of the gospel. He also examines his gifts, and finds both knowledge and utterance fitted for the same. Now such a one may safely say that the ministry is the calling to which he is set apart. And the like may any other man in any other calling say for himself. Yet, because many men are partial in judging their inclination and gifts, the best way for them is to use the advice and help of others who are able to give direction herein and discern better than they.

Now touching children, it is the duty of parents to make choice of fit callings for them before they apply them to any particular condition of life. And that they may the better judge aright for what callings their children are fit, they must observe two things in them: first, their inclination; [and,] second, their natural gifts.

Touching inclination, every child, even in his first years, does affect some particular calling more than another, as some are affected more with music than others, some with merchandise, some with a more liberal kind of learning, some with this, some with that. And by this the parents may judge something of their inclination and towardness. This was practiced among the Athenians, who, before they placed their children in any calling, did first bring them into a public place where instruments of all sorts were laid, and they observed with what kind of instrument they took delight, and to the like art did they afterward apply them with good success.[25] And it will not be amiss for Christians to be followers of the heathen in this or any other commendable practice.

Second, the natural gifts, which parents are to observe in their children, are either in their bodies or in their minds. And those children who excel in the gifts of the body are to be brought up in callings performed by the labor of the body, as in mechanical arts. And such as excel in the gifts of mind are to be applied to those sciences that are performed by wit and learning. The notes

25. In the margin: Nazian. in ep. ad Eudoxum.

of a child who is fit for learning are these: a love of learning, a love of labor, a love of praise, and a wit neither too quick nor too dull.[26] A fine wit in a child is like a pen-knife that will not shave a great loaf, but only serves to cut a quill.[27]

Again, mark a special difference in the gifts of the mind. There are two kinds of understanding: active and passive. The active understanding is that which not only conceives of things invented by others, but can also invent things by itself. The passive understanding is that which only conceives of things devised by others, and cannot invent but very hardly by itself. And everyone, both old and young, has one of these kinds of understanding. Now all those children who excel in this active understanding are to be set apart for the greatest callings in the church and commonwealth. Democritus, the philosopher, chose Protagoras to be his scholar because he showed wit in the artificial binding of a bundle of sticks. Athanasius, that famous bishop, was first put to learning because he was found by the seaside doing the part of a minister among the company of little children like himself, examining and baptizing them according to the solemn order used in the congregation. Origen, that famous clerk, when he was a child, used to question with his father, Leonidas, about the sense of the Scripture, and to demand of tradesmen the causes of things and the use of their tools and instruments.[28] And thus, we see in some sort how parents may judge to what calling every child is fit.

And here all parents must be warned that the neglect of this duty is a great and common sin. For the care of the most is that their children may live, nothing regarding whether they live well and do service to God in a fit calling or not. And the truth is [that] parents cannot do greater wrong to their children, and the society of men, than to apply them to unfit callings; as when a child is fit for learning, to apply him to a trade or other bodily service; contrariwise, to apply him to learning when he is most fit for a trade. For this is as much as if a man should apply his toes to feeling and not his fingers, and go on his hands and not on his feet, and to set the members of the body out of their proper places.

And this is the second duty.

Rule 3

The third duty is this: he who is fit for sundry callings must make choice of the best. Saint Paul plainly teaches this in the next verse of this chapter: "Art thou called, being a servant? Care not for it, but if thou mayest be free, choose it rather" [1 Cor. 7:21]. Here he gives this counsel, that a bond man, having liberty in his choice, must accept of it rather than continue a bond man still. Again,

---

26. In the margin: Plato l. 7. de Rep. Nazian. in Monodia. 1, 2, 3, 4.

27. This paragraph break is not in the original.

28. In the margin: Euseb. hist. l. 3.

Paul bids the Corinthians to covet spiritual gifts, but "especially that they may prophesy" [1 Cor. 14:1]. There he gives this rule, that in the choice of gifts we must labor for the best gifts, and if we are to seek after the best gifts, then proportionally we must seek for the best callings.

Here is a special rule for all young students in the universities. Such as are brought up in the schools of the prophets desire to know what particular calling is best for them because they have liberty to be schoolmasters, physicians, lawyers, or ministers of the Word of God. Saint Paul, according to this general rule, shows that a choice must be made of the best calling. And in the first place, if gifts will serve, a choice must be made of the calling of a prophet or teacher; and it must have the first place above all other academic callings.

Thus much of choice.

Point 2: A Good Entrance into a Calling

When choice is once made, we must then consider how a good entrance is to be made into the calling which we have chosen. Touching entrance many points are to be scanned. The first is in what sort and manner an entrance must be made. And the right manner is this: every man must so enter that he may truly in conscience say [that] God has placed him in this calling, be it ever so base a calling. Thus, Paul says in this chapter: "As God hath called every man so let him walk" (v. 17). And Christ our Savior never took upon Him openly the office of a Mediator, till He was baptized and therein called unto it by the voice of His Father from heaven, saying, "This is my beloved Son in whom I am well pleased." But immediately after, He began to teach and preach, and to show Himself [to be] the true Messiah, in performing the duties of a king, priest, and prophet. There is no calling upon earth, since the fall of Adam, but has crosses and calamities attending on it. But they are delayed, by sufficient comfort, when our conscience can tell us we were placed in our callings by God Himself. And when our conscience cannot say thus much, the comfort is gone.

Now that every man may certainly know himself to be called by God to this or that calling, he must have two things: (1) gifts for the calling from God; and (2) allowance from men.[29]

For the first, to those whom God calls, He gives competent and convenient gifts, as knowledge, understanding, dexterity to this or that, and such like. And thereby [He] makes them able for the performance of the duties of their callings. Contrariwise, they who enter into any calling, being utterly unable to perform the duties thereof, were never called by God.[30]

29. This paragraph break is not in the original.

30. This paragraph break is not in the original.

For the second, men are to be set apart to their particular callings by the appointment of men, whom God has left on earth as His instruments for the ordering and disposing of vocations. For God has His deputies to allot men their offices in every society [Numbers 30], as parents and masters to dispose of persons in private families, the governors of the church for ecclesiastical callings, [and] the magistrate and men of authority for civil [callings] in the commonwealth. And he who would truly say [that] God has placed him in any particular calling must also have the outward calling of men. And here it is to be remembered that trial of gifts and free election, without partiality, should be in the designment of all, especially of public callings. Thus, in the primitive church, not so much as deacons were admitted without just and sufficient trial (1 Tim. 3:10).[31]

And here sundry abuses are to be reproved. First of all, the buying and selling, the chopping and changing of civil offices, for where the calling is set to sale, there little or no trial, little or no election, takes place. And he who buys his office must say his money called him rather than God. Wherefore, such as lay up money to buy offices had best take heed beforehand, for the saying is true: "He who buys the seat must sell justice, and where justice is sold the poor is oppressed and all goes to wrack." The like is to be said of the sale of ecclesiastical livings, to which [the] cure of souls is annexed; yea, of the dispensing and giving them hand over head. Indeed, to buy or sell the livings of the church is not properly the sin of Simon, who sought to get the gift of the Holy Spirit with money, yet this buying is a grievous thing, flat against the order that God has set down touching entrance into any calling. The very heathen themselves have complained of this chopping and changing of places as of the ruins of states and commonwealths. Alexander Severus, the emperor, says, "It is necessary that he who buys must sell. I will not suffer buyers and sellers of offices. If I suffer them, it is because I cannot condemn such. For I am ashamed to punish him who buys and sells."[32] Seneca says, "This buying is the spoiling of provinces." And, "He who buys must needs sell."[33] Justinian complains that his "dominions are robbed and pillaged because men take gold for office."[34] And he straightly forbids it.

Thus much of [the] entrance in general. Now follow certain questions thereof.

---

31. This paragraph break is not in the original.
32. In the margin: Lampridius in vita Sever.
33. In the margin: De benefic. l. 1. c. 9.
34. In the margin: Novella. 8. in praetat.

Question 1

If it is (as I have said) that such as enter into any calling, especially public, must first be enabled with gifts from God, and also set apart by men after due trial and examination, here a question is to be scanned, which the papists usually propound; namely, what calling the first preachers of the gospel and planters of our church had? The answer to this question is needful, for if they had no calling, neither have we who are their followers. And I answer two things.[35]

First, they had their callings by virtue whereof they restored the gospel of Christ from the Romish church itself. For they were either priests or school doctors, as in England, Wycliffe; in Germany, Luther; in Bohemia, John Huss and Jerome of Prague; in Basil, Oecolampadius; in Italy, Peter Martyr and others. And, therefore, these with many others were ordained either in popish churches or in schools, and there by oath solemnly bound to do the duties of their callings with good conscience by confuting error and maintaining the ancient apostolic faith. Wherefore, if their calling is of any moment to stop their mouths, we say [that] the first restorers of the gospel in our times had their first callings of them. If it is said that these men were all perjured for preaching against the Church of Rome, to whose allegiance they were bound by oath, I answer that by virtue of their oaths at their ordination they were bound only to the catholic and apostolic church, and not to the present Church of Rome. For the words (the catholic and apostolic church of Rome), which now run in the tenor of the oath, were not so strictly used in former times, but are more urged now of late.

Second, I answer that many of them had callings in some sort extraordinary. I say, in some sort, distinguishing the office of teaching and the use of it. The office, which they performed, was ordinary, but the execution of this office in purging and restoring true religion, not in respect of that true order which God had set down in His Word, but in respect of the abuse of it in the Romish church, was extraordinary. I declare this in this manner: God calls men extraordinarily when He binds not Himself to ordinary laws of vocation set down in His Word. And He does this [in] three ways. First, by His own immediate voice. Abraham was thus called, and Moses in the bush, and so were all the apostles of Christ called immediately, and Paul likewise after Christ's ascension. Second, He calls extraordinarily by the ministry of creatures, as Elisha was called by Elijah (1 Kings 19), Aaron was called by Moses, and Philip was called to baptize the eunuch by the message of an angel (Acts 8:26). Third, by special instinct and extraordinary inspiration of the Spirit.[36]

35. This paragraph break is not in the original.

36. This paragraph break is not in the original.

We have examples hereof in the Word of God. By his first calling, Phillip was a deacon who went and preached the gospel in Samaria, and first began the church of God there. [He did it] not by calling from the apostles, because they were ignorant of his preaching (Acts 8:14). And we may not think that he did enterprise this work upon his own brain. And, therefore, by all likelihood, his calling was by a special instinct of the Spirit of God. Again, when the church of Jerusalem was dispersed, men came from Cyprus and Cyrene to Antioch [Acts 11:20], without any outward calling, and yet [they] preached there, no doubt by the instinct of the Holy Spirit, as appears in that the hand of God was with them. The like I say of Luther, and the rest, namely that they were stirred up by special instinct of the Spirit of God, whereby they were moved to restore the gospel to its former purity, as they did.[37]

But some will say [that] this doctrine lays open a gap to all heretics and deceivers, for they may likewise plead extraordinary instincts, and by this means seduce and deceive the people of God. I answer [that] there are certain special notes and marks whereby we may discern an extraordinary calling from the illusions of the devil, whereby he suborns[38] heretics to deceive the world.[39]

First, extraordinary calling never has place but when ordinary calling fails. There are two special times wherein God calls men extraordinarily. The first is in the founding and planting of the church, and hereupon were the apostles and evangelists called extraordinarily. The second time is when the church of God is defaced and universal apostasy takes place. For then there is no place for ordinary calling, and therefore to restore the church again to her former estate He calls men extraordinarily. We may not look for any reformation of a stew from them who live therein, unless the occasion is extraordinary. And the like is to be thought of the reformation of a heretical and apostatical church, as without doubt is the Church of Rome.

Second, we may discern of men extraordinarily called by the doctrine which they deliver, which must be the very doctrine of prophets and apostles. And he who pleads extraordinary calling, and yet brings any other doctrine, is not called by God, but is deluded by the devil. Moses has taught us to judge thus of true and false prophets, not by their miracles, but by their doctrine (Deut. 13:3). And when Christ was demanded by the Scribes and Pharisees, by what authority He did those things, He answered by demanding a like question: whether John's baptism (that is, his ministry and doctrine) were from God or not (Luke 20:4)? And if his doctrine were of God, then also his calling, and

37. This paragraph break is not in the original.

38. *Suborn:* induce or bribe.

39. The paragraph breaks (delineating the four "marks") are not in the original.

consequently the calling of Christ, because it was the office of John to testify of Him.

Third, they may be discerned by their lives and conversations. Christ has foretold that there should come false prophets in sheep's clothing, who are inwardly ravening wolves (Matt. 7:15). How then shall we know them? The answer is, by their fruits, that is, not only by their doctrine, but also by their lives, because their office is to teach not only by doctrine but also by example. Now the men whom God called to the restoring of the gospel, to them He gave with sincerity of judgment, integrity of heart and life, which the Lord in mercy joined together for the confirmation of the truth of their calling. And he who teaches wholesome doctrine, and brings forth contrary fruits, is in that regard a false prophet, though his doctrine is ever so true.

Fourth, those whom God calls extraordinarily, He does furnish with gifts above the ordinary measure of men, as namely with knowledge, zeal, wisdom, constancy, courage, and other gifts that serve for the discharge of extraordinary callings. And we find this to be true in the first ministers of the gospel, but especially in Luther, whom God notably armed with boldness and courage to withstand the whole Church of Rome. In our age, some startups have said that they were Elijah, John the Baptist, and Christ, but by this last note they have been descried. For when their gifts were examined, they have been found to come far short of the gifts of many ordinary men.

Now if we lay all these notes together, it will easily appear that the first preachers of the gospel in this last age, at the least some of them, may be said truly to have received extraordinary callings from God. For first, they preached in such a time when no face of a true church was to be seen, and a general apostasy overspread the world. Second, they renewed the very doctrine of the apostles and prophets. Third, they adorned their doctrine with godly life and conversation. And, lastly, [they] were all (or most of them) furnished in great measure with sufficient gifts of knowledge, wisdom, zeal, and courage, to manage their callings and professions. But the papists say [that] there was nothing extraordinary in them, because they could not confirm their doctrine by miracles. I answer, first, the doctrine which they taught needed not then to be confirmed with miracles, seeing it was at the first publishing thereof sufficiently confirmed by miracles wrought by the prophets and apostles. Second, I answer that extraordinary men do not always confirm their callings by miracles, as John Baptist and sundry prophets in the Old Testament who never wrought any miracles. Third, the gift of working a miracle may be given to him who is an enemy to God and His church, as the gift of prophecy may (that is greater), for both Balaam and Caiaphas prophesied, and yet [they] are professed enemies to Christ and His church. And Moses says plainly that false prophets, coming among the people, would work miracles for this end to try them (Deut. 13:2). Therefore, the working of a miracle serves not always to confirm an extraordinary calling.

Question 2

Second, it may be demanded, if entrance is made into a lawful calling with an evil mind and by evil means, what must then be done? I answer, he is not to forsake his place, but to repent of his bad entrance, and to do the duties of his calling with diligence and good conscience, waiting after this for further approbation from God and from men. When he has obtained [this approbation] in any measure, he may with good conscience proceed in his calling. For this after-approbation and acceptance (though it does not justify the bad entrance) yet it does make a supply thereof. A prince, as William the Conqueror, enters into a land or kingdom, and by war and bloodshed seeks to subdue the people and to make them subjects unto him. Now, by this bad entrance, he is no lawful king, for every lawful king is placed by God and by men who are appointed under God to set up princes over them, according to the laws and customs of several kingdoms. Yet, if the people do willingly submit themselves to this usurper, and are content to yield subjection, and the king likewise [is content] to rule them by good and wholesome laws, he is now become a lawful prince, though his entrance was but tyrannical.[40]

Upon this ground, another question is answered, touching the callings of the ministers of our church. There are some who say [that] our church is no church, our ministers [are] no minsters, yea the preachers of the gospel [are] the worst of all. The ground of their opinion is because (as they say) we have no good and lawful entrance into our callings and ministry, according to the Word of God. For answer to them, put the case that all the preachers and ministers in the Church of England were unlawfully called, yea wanted the very substance of true calling (which no man can with good conscience either speak or think), yet it is possible that there may be a true church of God among us, and lawful preachers of the Word, because they may have an after-approbation and acceptance both from God and from men. And an after-approbation makes supply of a bad entrance. Nay, further, it is evident that our ministers have approbation both from God and man. For, first of all, God enables them to teach the true and wholesome doctrine of the prophets and apostles, which is one special note to distinguish a false prophet from a true. Second, God enables them with grace to adorn their doctrine and profession with reformed lives. Third, God's hand is with them, in that He blesses their labors for the conversion of many

40. This paragraph break is not in the original.

souls unto God in all parts of this land. And by this, God does (as it were) set to His hand and seal, for the approbation of our callings.[41]

The question was among the Corinthians whether Paul was an apostle or not. And Paul himself answers that if he were not an apostle to others, yet he was to them because he was the minister of their conversion (1 Cor. 9:2). Now if this is a good reason to prove the extraordinary calling of an apostle, then no doubt it will serve much more to prove the calling of an ordinary minister.

Question 3

Third, it may be demanded whether a man, being to enter into a calling, may lawfully offer himself and make means to enter into it or not. *Answer.* Saint Paul answers this question when he says, "He that desireth the office of a bishop, desireth a worthy work" (1 Tim. 3:1). Here he gives us to understand how it is not unlawful to desire an office. It is true, indeed, [that] there are unlawful desires of places and callings, namely when they are sought upon a vain or greedy mind, for pleasure, or for lucre's sake. Yet, when they are desired (or sought for) upon conscience to discharge a duty unto God and men, there is no offence. Now, if the desire of an office is lawful, then to show the same desire by honest and lawful means is not unlawful. Therefore, men may use honest and lawful means to enter into callings meet for them [as long as] they bring sufficient gifts for the discharge thereof, and withal submit themselves to examination and election according to lawful order. As soon as God had touched the prophet Isaiah's tongue with a coal from the altar, [he] was ready to go at the call of God. And when the Lord said, "Whom shall I send?" he answered, "Here am I, send me" (Isa. 6:6–8). And after this example of this holy prophet any man may show himself willing to enter into an office, when God has furnished him with gifts, if so he may be called.[42]

Here then is a lesson for such as are brought up in the schools of the prophets. Their duty is, as soon as they are enabled to do the office of ministers, to show themselves willing and ready in godly manner to take upon them this kind of calling. And, therefore, without question, it is a fault in many that, being enabled with gifts sufficient, nevertheless do employ themselves wholly in their private studies, not showing any willingness to take upon them to discharge any ministerial calling for which they are fit. For howsoever to seek a calling in the church of God for lucre's sake is unlawful, yet to seek a calling is not simply unlawful if there is an honest mind, good means, and the glory of God is truly intended.

41. This paragraph break is not in the original.

42. This paragraph break is not in the original.

Question 4

Fourth, it may be demanded whether a man may enter into two callings at once or not. I answer by distinguishing, in some respects he may, and in some [respects] he may not. An entrance may be made into two callings in three cases.[43]

First, when God has combined two callings together by His own appointment. Thus Melchisedec, that he might be a lively figure of Christ our Savior, was a king and priest, and did the office both of a king and priest (Heb. 7:1). And the high priests, who were the successors of Aaron by God's appointment, were not only priests but civil judges also. Jehoiada, the high priest, was protector of Judah, in the nonage[44] of Jehoash, and by virtue of his protectorship slew Athaliah (that usurping queen) (2 Kings 11:15). And there is no marvel of this, because the Levites were the common lawyers, and the Scriptures were the positive laws of the Jews, and therefore none were so fit to be judges as the priests and Levites. Even as in this land, the fittest judges, in causes both civil and criminal, are lawyers who are expert in the laws of the land. In this regard, it was not so great a burden among the Jews to manage the office of a priest and to execute civil judgment.[45]

Second, two callings may be combined when the entering into them at once is not against the Word, and [is] for the common good. Eli was thus a priest by one calling, and a judge by another calling, in the kingdom of Israel. Samuel was thus a prophet and a judge. Moses was thus a prophet and a civil governor, yea a prince, for in those times both states were so corrupt that there could not be found ordinary men sufficient to discharge either calling severally.[46]

Third, two callings may be endured when, being joined, they hinder not each other or the common good. Thus, a man may lawfully be a master of a family and a merchant (or of any other trade whatsoever). We have examples hereof in the Word of God. Abraham, besides that he was a master of a great family, and in his family a prophet and priest in offering sacrifice, was by another calling a mighty prince and a great warrior. And the same may be said of the patriarchs. They were governors in their families and also princes, bearing the civil sword, as may appear in the examples of Judah. Now there were two causes why they might bear both these offices: first, the church of God was then very small, and comprised in one family; and, second, the doctrine of religion was comprised in few heads, and delivered from man to man by tradition. And in this case Saint Paul was by one calling an apostle and, at the same time,

43. This paragraph break is not in the original.
44. *Nonage:* the state or time of being under legal age.
45. This paragraph break is not in the original.
46. This paragraph break is not in the original.

by another calling [he was] a tent-maker (Acts 18:3) because of the poverty of the church of Corinth, as also because he would hereby stop the mouths of false apostles who would have accused him for making advantage of the gospel. And in like case of necessity, I doubt not but now the ministers of the gospel may take unto them other callings, always remembering this, that they are no hindrance to their principal calling nor offence to men.

Now I come to the second part of my distinction, to show that men may not enter into two distinct callings at once. And that in three cases. First, if God has disjoined these callings by His Word and commandment. Second, if the practice of the one hinders the practice of the other. Third, if the combining of them together hinders the common good. Upon these grounds, our Savior Christ, being the Doctor of the church, refused to be judge of [the] inheritance between the two brethren (Luke 12:13–14). And hereupon the apostles, being to do the duties of their own callings, refused to perform the office of deacons (Acts 6:2). Hence, I gather that in towns, corporations, and societies, care (as much as may be) is to be had that sundry offices and charges, being of themselves weighty and of divers kinds, are not laid on the shoulders of one man. For the execution of them all breeds distraction, and distraction disables the most able man in the discharge of one office. He who comes to the corn heap, the more he opens his hand to receive, the less he holds. So, he who does (as it were) enlarge himself to bear the most offices, the fewer shall he discharge.

Question 5

Furthermore, it may here be demanded whether it is lawful to enter into two trades at once or not? *Answer.* It is not unlawful [as long as] they hinder not each other nor the combining of them hinders the common good of men, and the party intends not filthy lucre but the common benefit. Nevertheless, it is inconvenient in a peopled commonwealth, for then one man shall hardly live by another. Yet, if one is not sufficient to maintain the charge of a family, a second calling may be added upon the former conditions.

Again, it may be demanded whether one may have two farms at once or not? *Answer.* Some have thought it not convenient, but the truth is [that] it may as well be demanded whether it is lawful to have two coats at once or not. For in a commonwealth all must not be equal, but some above [and] some under others in regard of wealth. And, therefore, such as have sundry farms, whether it is by inheritance or by honest purchases, may lawfully enjoy them.

And thus much of good entrance.

Point 3: A Good Continuance in a Calling

The third main point to be considered is the good continuance in a calling. This continuance consists in the constant practice of the duties and works of the same calling. And herein two points must be considered: first, what are the works of our callings which must be done, and of what note; [and,] second, in what manner they must be done.

Their Nature

For the first, the works of our callings must be qualified by three notes: first, they must be the proper works of our callings; second, they must be profitable; and, third, [they must be] necessary.[47]

Property 1

The first is Saint Paul's rule: "Live in peace" (1 Thess. 4:11). But how shall that be done? He answers, "by doing his own business." And Saint Peter gives the same rule, requiring that "no man suffer as a busybody in other men's matters" (1 Peter 4:15). In both [of these] places, the Holy Spirit teaches us that we must, first of all, search what are the proper works of our own callings, and then afterwards do them. The husbandman must attend on husbandry, and the minister on preaching, etc. By this single point, sundry faults that commonly fall out in the lives of men are opened.[48]

First, when men look at the things of others, not regarding their own matters. We have [an] example of this in our Savior Christ's words to Peter: "Peter, follow thou me" (John 21:22). Now Peter, little regarding his own duty, must (in a kind of curiosity) ask what John must do. But our Savior Christ gives him a check, and says, "If I will that he tarry till I come, what is it to thee?" And this is the common fault of the world. Men, who highly regard and slackly perform the duties of their own callings, are nevertheless very ready to talk of and inquire into the state and lives of other men. And it is meat and drink unto them. Let a good report be given out of a man, it is not regarded, but evil reports are taken up at the first rebound. They run like wildfire. And all this arises from vain curiosity, which is here condemned as the bane of all societies. These busybodies are like those who read books with [the] intent only to spy out the faults thereof. And they are like to the spider that creeps over all the garden only to gather poison. But men, who fear God, must learn to know their own business and to suffer their talk and meditation to be employed that way.

47. This paragraph break is not in the original.
48. This paragraph break is not in the original.

Second, here is condemned the curiosity of those who enter upon the duties of other men's callings. It is a dangerous sin, as I have shown heretofore by the example of Uzzah, who was slain for touching the ark, though his intent was only to keep it from falling, for he had no such calling. Fifty thousand men of Bethshemesh died for looking into the ark of God, when they had no calling to do so.[49] And [another example is of] Korah, Dathan, and Abiram, who would needs challenge unto them the calling and office of Moses.

Third, hereby is condemned the study and practice of figure-casting and judicial astrology, for thereby many (and that upon false grounds) go about to search what shall befall other men, either in life or death, things that God will not have known before they come to pass. In a word, everyone who does not the duties of his own calling diligently and with good conscience is hereby condemned.

Property 2

The second property is that the works of our callings must be profitable, not only to the doers, but to the commonwealth. The law of nature teaches this. By this second property sundry men are to be blamed.

First, the tradesman who gets his living by making foreign and fine fashions of attire, which serve for no use but to be displayed flags and banners, either of folly or pride or wantonness. For all such fashions are condemned by the Word of God, yea by the very light of nature. And, therefore, such as live by selling and making of them cannot be free from offence; nay, their offence is the greater. For if there were no inventors of vain novelties, they should not be so commonly used as they are.

Second, here the alchemist is to be reproved. He spends his time and substance in laboring to change baser metals into gold. [This is] in truth impossible [to do], for it is a kind of new creation, to turn one kind of creature into a creature of another kind, as every metal is. And that which is said (or rather dreamed) of the philosopher's stone is but a conceit, and nowhere to be found but in *Utopia*.[50] And there is no question but one day an account must be made of the good time unprofitably spent in seeking for it.

Property 3

The third condition of our actions is that they must be necessary. We must consider the nature and quality of the works of our callings. In every calling there are two kinds of works. Some are principal, without which the calling

---

49. 1 Sam. 6:19.

50. The philosopher's stone was an unknown substance, sought by alchemists, for its supposed ability to transform base metals into gold and silver.

cannot be maintained. And some [are] less principal, which give not essence to the calling. Now men must especially give themselves to practice the principal works of their callings. For example, the action of a minister in his calling is to read and to preach the Word of God. Now, reading is a work less necessary, and preaching the most principal. And for this cause, he must give himself especially to the practice thereof.[51]

In this manner we might go through the callings of all men, and note many wants therein. Magistrates, in towns and corporations, carry and draw the sword for the maintenance of peace and civil order. It is well done, for it is a work of their calling. Yet, [it is] not the principal, and they do commonly fail in this, that they use not the sword for this end, to urge men to the keeping of the commandments of the first table, to a practice of pure religion, and to the keeping of the Sabbath day. This is the main duty of the magistrate, who bears the sword especially for the good of men's souls. A master of a family is to care, not only for the bodies, but also for the souls of his household, for this is the principal duty. And most householders are faulty herein, for commonly they betake themselves to the lesser duties, and leave the principal. They care for the bodies of their wives, children, [and] servants, neglecting the means of the salvation of their souls. [This is] clean contrary to the rule in hand, which enjoins the practice of the principal duties in the first place. Therefore, all careless and ignorant masters of families are here to be warned to have special care to provide for the saving of the souls of all them who live under their government. This also shows us the faults of many students who, setting themselves apart for the work of the ministry, do first give themselves to study the fathers and ancient writers, whereas their first principal duty is to be soundly instructed in the Word of God, and to ground themselves in the main points of religion, that they may be able to know what is true, what is false, what is to be done, [and] what is not to be done, in all matters, whether they concern faith or manners. And when this good foundation is laid, then the foresaid helps may with good success be adjoined.

Again, necessary works I call those which, upon due consideration, are not only lawful in themselves and agreeable to our calling, but also expedient in the doer. For if they are inexpedient, though otherwise lawful, they are not to be done.

Before I proceed any further, here is a necessary question to be handled: whether the works and actions of a calling done by a man who enters unlawfully into that calling are nullities or not, that is, to be reputed by us as actions not done? I answer that, in things done, there are two kinds of faults: one in the

51. This paragraph break is not in the original.

work [and] another in the worker. A fault in the work is when the action itself is done amiss and it may be done amiss in substance or in circumstance. And if the fault is in the substance thereof, it is indeed a nullity, and must be reputed as not done. Second, the fault of the worker is when an action of a lawful calling is done by one who is not called lawfully. Now then, when the fault of an action is not in the work itself but in the person who works it, it is not to be reputed a nullity, neither to be reversed as nothing. For example, one called lawfully to the ministry baptizes infants in the name of the Father and of the Virgin Mary. Here is a fault in the action done, and that in the very substance of baptism, and therefore here is no baptism but rather a profanation of the ordinance of God. Now, put the case further, that baptism is administered by a man who is called, though not lawfully, I say, if there is no fault in the action, but only in the man, that baptism is not to be reputed a nullity.

This doctrine is agreed upon by the common consent of divines, as also by the laws and orders of kingdoms, as may appear plainly in particulars. Tiberius Caesar, a Roman emperor, invaded the kingdom of the Jews, and brought it into a province, and thus he was made king of the Jews, not by lawful means, but by intrusion. For all this, the actions done and the commandments given by him were the reputed commandments of a king, not reversed by any Jew, but obeyed by all. For when he gave commandment that all the world, yea the Jews, should be taxed, they yielded themselves to this commandment. Yea, righteous Joseph and Mary went to their own town to be taxed. Caiaphas was honored as the high priest among the Jews, and though his entrance was by corruption and bribery, yet notwithstanding the actions done by him in his office were not esteemed nullities, but actions done. And, therefore, our Savior Christ suffered Himself to be accused, arraigned, and judged by him. And [He] was also content to come into the temple and worship God according to the manner of the Jews, even before Caiaphas himself.

The scribes and Pharisees, who were the doctors of the Jews, had not (many of them) their calling by succession from Aaron, and for judgment were also in part heretical, holding some things against the foundation, namely justification by works, etc. And yet our Savior Christ, because they sat in Moses's chair, bids the church of the Jews, and His disciples, [to] hear them so far forth as they taught the doctrine of Moses. Whereby it is manifest that if there is no fault in the work, the defective calling of the worker does not make a nullity of the action done. For howsoever the worker sins in his unlawful entrance, and in that regard is not to be approved, yet the actions in the calling, to which he is entered, are the actions of that calling. For though he is called amiss, yet he stands in the room of one lawfully called. And we are to make [a] difference between him who is called though unlawfully and him who has no calling at all. For the actions done without calling are indeed nullities, whereas if there is any calling, though entrance is badly made, it does not make the action void. And whosoever denies this ground of truth overturns the regiment of kingdoms, churches, states, and societies whatsoever.

By what has been said, a question is resolved concerning baptism. Many of our ancestors heretofore have been baptized by mass-priests, and never received any baptism but in the Church of Rome. Now the demand is whether that baptism is sufficient or not, and whether they must be rebaptized? I answer thus: the Romish priest is no minister of God and Christ, but of antichrist, in that he offers Christ [as] a real sacrifice for the quick and the dead, wherein chiefly stands his office. Yet, because he has been (and is) designed by men to baptize, and stands in the room of a lawful minister, his action is not void. For though he is not a minister, lawfully called to baptize, yet he is not a mere private man, but he is between both, that is, one called (though amiss through ignorance and oversight of men) and consequently he is one who in the act of baptizing stands in [the] room of a right and lawful minister.

Again, it pleases some, carried more by affection than judgment, to dispute in this manner. There is no right and lawful calling allowed for ministers in the Church of England; therefore, there are no sacraments among us nor true preaching of the Word of God. Our sacraments (say they) are but sacraments in show, and the effect of all preaching with us is no better than the illusion of the devil. I answer, be it granted there is no lawful calling of ministers in the Church of England (which nevertheless to say is both false and wicked), yet this will not follow, that our sacraments are no sacraments and our preaching [is] no preaching, for though men are unlawfully called, yet their actions are the actions of ministers, if they are called at all. The preaching of a minister, unlawfully called, may be true preaching, and sacraments [may be] true sacraments, else Christ would not have said of the scribes and Pharisees, "Hear them." They were of other tribes than Levi, and came in often by bribery and like corruption. A bad entrance makes not the actions done to be void and of no effect [as long as] the doer is called to stand in the room of a right and lawful agent. And as good entrance makes not always the actions good, because where there is a good entrance into a lawful calling, there may be an after-apostasy, so, on the contrary, the defect of [a] good entrance makes not a nullity of ministerial actions.

Their Manner

Now I come to the second point touching continuance in a calling, namely in what manner the actions thereof are to be done. It is not sufficient for a man to do the proper works of his calling, but he must do them in a good and godly manner. And that a man may so do them, two things are principally required: holiness and constancy.

Requirement 1: Holiness

To do a work in holiness, the Word of God teaches that a double sanctification is required. The first [is] of the worker. The second [is] of the work and action to be done.

Sanctification of the Worker

It is necessary that the worker should be sanctified for two causes.[52]

First, because the person must first please God before the work of the person please Him. "For to the unclean, all things are unclean" (Titus 1:15); yea, not only their works but their minds and consciences are defiled. And the reason is plain: for so great is the corruption of our wicked natures that we defile whatsoever things we lay our hands unto. If men are not repentant sinners, all the actions which they do, though good works in themselves, are very sins and offences before God, in that they proceed not from an upright heart, neither are [they] done in obedience to God's commandments and to the glory of God.[53]

Second, sanctification of our persons is required because, unless we are born anew of water and the Spirit, we can look for no success or blessing upon our labors. It is the righteous man's privilege: "Whatsoever he doeth it shall prosper" (Ps. 1:3). No other man must look for this favor at God's hand. Righteous Joseph prospered in all that he did, for the Lord was with him when he was made ruler over the house of Potiphar the Egyptian (Gen. 39:2–3). And Jehoshaphat says, "Believe the Lord and his prophets, and thou shalt prosper" (2 Chron. 20:20). While the ark was in the house of Obed-Edom, he prospered, and all his house. How much more then shall he prosper, who has not only the sign of God's presence but God Himself dwelling in his heart? If it is said that in experience we find the ungodly man to prosper as well as the godly, I answer [that] the prosperity of the wicked is like to the quails which God did send to the Israelites in the wilderness, which brought a plague and destruction with them, for they died while the meat was yet in their mouths. The prosperity of the wicked serves to their deeper condemnation.

Hence, we learn that, being designed and set apart to any calling, we must first of all from our hearts turn unto God from all our sins, and use means to become new creatures. Because, unless we repent and turn to God and with constant purpose cleave unto Him, the best actions of our callings, though we

52. This paragraph break is not in the original.

53. This paragraph break is not in the original.

had no other sins, shall be sufficient to condemn us, considering no work ever pleased God till the person of the worker was accepted in His sight. The blind divinity of the world is this: that such as walk diligently about their business, live peaceably with all men, and do no man hurt, have all things to go well with them, and God will have mercy upon them. These things are indeed good and commendable, but not sufficient. For unless the person who does these things goes further, and repents him of his sins, and dies unto them by the virtue of the death of Christ, and lives unto God, all his peaceable and upright dealing will in the end prove no better than fig leaves before God. For even the best works that can be are damnable sins in the doer, unless he turns unto God, and is in Christ. In the same field, at the same time, in the same business, there is the work of the ox and the work of a man. Now, I demand which of these two is the better work? I know the answer will be the work of the man, but the truth is, unless he is renewed by the grace of God, his labor is worse than the labor of the beast, for the beast in its kind obeys God. The unrepentant sinner does not so. And thus, actions, lawful in themselves, in him become unlawful, not because they are done, but because they are done in [an] evil manner; even as the channel is faulty, not because it carries the water, but because it defiles the water.

Sanctification of the Work

The second thing required is sanctification of the work or action. This point also must be learned and practiced, for it is not sufficient to do a lawful action but it must be done in [a] holy manner. For lawful actions, unless they are sanctified, are sins, as may appear by one and the same action done by two persons. The publican and the Pharisee go together to pray [Luke 18:10]. They do one and the same action. And yet, the one is approved for his prayer, [but] the other is not, because the one (that is, the Pharisee) prayed in the pride of his heart and profaned the lawful action of prayer, [while] the publican prayed in the humility of his heart for the pardon of his sins, and his action was not only lawful in itself but also holy in the doer. And this is the point that must be learned and practiced in all the actions of our callings, that they must not only be lawful in themselves, but also holy in regard of us.

This discovers the blindness and ignorance of most men among us. [They] think it is sufficient for them if their actions (which they do) are lawful. For example, chapmen[54] think they may use their own liberty in buying and selling because bargaining is God's ordinance, and [they] think it [is] needless to regard in what manner they buy and sell. Nay, commonly they do not so much

54. *Chapman:* merchant, dealer, or seller.

as dream of this, that they are in such order to perform their actions that in their doings they may approve themselves unto God.

In the sanctification of the works of our calling two things are required: the Word and prayer (1 Tim. 4:5). For that which Paul sets down of the use of meats and drinks must be extended to all the ordinances of God whatsoever. I will speak of both these in order.[55]

Means 1: The Word

First of all, the Word of God must be our rule and square whereby we are to frame and fashion all our actions. And, according to [the] direction received thence, we must do the things we do or leave them undone. David, a king, had no doubt a wise and godly council, and he himself was a man of great wisdom, being a prophet of God, and yet he says that the "word and the laws of God are his counselors" [Ps. 119:24]. And that which the Lord commands the king, that, sitting upon his throne, he should have the book of the law before him to do all things herein [Deut. 17:19], the same must every subject likewise in his particular place and standing perform.[56]

Peter fished all night and caught nothing. In the morning Christ came and bade him cast his net into the sea. Though discouraged with bad success before, he presently says, "Lord, at thy word I will do it" (Luke 5:5). And every man should daily say thus much in his place, that he will do the works of his calling at God's commandment and according to His Word. When the people of Israel came out of Egypt, and went into Canaan (a type of the kingdom of heaven), in their whole journey they were led by a pillar of cloud in the day and by a pillar of fire in the night. When the cloud stood still, they stood still. And they were to follow it whichever way it went, forward or backward. Now look as the Israelites went to the earthly Canaan by following the pillar of fire and cloud, so much we (as it were) go blindfold, and suffer ourselves to be ruled by the Word of God in the works of our calling, though we seem in reason to go backward. We must do what it commands, and we must eschew what it forbids.[57]

Many things might be rehearsed out of God's Word for our better direction in particular actions, but I will reduce them all to two heads. For some directions serve for the eschewing of vice, and some others for the practice of virtue.[58]

55. This paragraph break is not in the original.
56. This paragraph break is not in the original.
57. This paragraph break is not in the original.
58. This paragraph break is not in the original.

Eschewing Vice

The vices to be eschewed in the works of men's callings are especially two: covetousness and injustice.

Vice 1: Covetousness

Covetousness is a notorious vice whereby almost all men apply their callings, and the works thereof, to the gathering of wealth and riches. This is one of the head and master sins of the world, and from it a sea of evils flows both into [the] church and commonwealth. There are many who have good affections, and receive the Word with joy, yet like the thorny ground they are choked with the cares of this world. Now then, considering covetousness is so vile a sin, let such as are placed in any calling take heed of it, and be careful lest it take place in their hearts and draw them to many other evils. Saint Paul says, "They that will be rich (that is, such as refer the labor of their callings to the gathering of wealth) fall into many and grievous temptations," and so consequently into damnation, and therefore he adds that "covetousness is the root of all evil" (1 Tim. 6:20).[59]

It might be objected that unbelief is the first particular sin that ever came into the world, and consequently that covetousness is not the root of all evil. I answer that unbelief is a mother sin whence all other sins arise, yet covetousness also is a root in another respect, because as the root gives sap and nourishment to all the branches, so does covetousness to every other sin whatsoever. Where it reigns, no sin dies or decays. In the body, when the spleen swells, all other parts decay and consume. Even so, when the heart swells with [a] desire of riches, all the graces of God consume and fade away. Judas, no doubt, had many good things in him. He forsook all to be a disciple of Christ. He preached the gospel to the Jews, as the rest of the disciples. He wrought miracles and cast out devils. Nay, what is more, he was one of Christ's own family and (as it were) a steward. He bore the bag and disposed of all things. And yet, at last, because he suffered this damnable sin of covetousness to prevail within his own heart, he condescended to sell his Master for thirty pieces of silver. And thus, all good things in him came to naught. For presently, upon this fact, he went and desperately hanged himself. And with such violence [he] cast himself down that his bowels gushed out. And it will fall out thus with all such as nourish this sin and give place unto it, though they are ever so furnished with knowledge, zeal, and [a] commendable life. If it is suffered to prevail, it will bring them at last to fearful and lamentable ends.[60]

59. This paragraph break is not in the original.
60. This paragraph break is not in the original.

In a common family, it is a great disorder to see the master play the servant, and the servant to do the office of the master. Much more then, it is a disorder in the church of God, which is the family of Christ, that men set their minds on the world, and make themselves servants of riches, which should rather serve them. Our Savior Christ says, "The Sabbath was made for man, and not man for the Sabbath."[61] Then, much more, riches were made for man, and not man for riches. Again, covetous and worldly desires are against the order of nature. For when we come into the world, we bring nothing with us, and while we live here, nature is content with little. And when we die, we must carry nothing with us but a coffin, or a winding-sheet. Why then should we set our minds so much on earthly things? Again, the gate to heaven is strait, and the way [is] narrow, so as we must be fain[62] to struggle and creep before we can make any entrance, and deny all that we enjoy.[63]

Now, when in the works of our calling, we intend only to get wealth, we do (as it were) set bars on heaven's gates, and load ourselves with burdens, which make us unable to pass. Therefore, special care must be had that our time and calling are not spent in gathering earthly treasures. And every man in his calling may remedy this vice, and the practice thereof, by doing these two duties: first, he must restrain his affection from the world; [and,] second, he must turn and dispose it to better things.

(1) Restraining our affections from the world. For the first, our affection is like a sea, which, being suffered to pass its banks, overflows the whole country. And, therefore, to keep our desires in compass, every man in his place and calling must labor for two things. The first [is] contentation. The Holy Spirit says, "Let not your conversation be in covetousness, but be content with that which you have" [Heb. 13:5]. This contentation is the esteeming of that particular estate wherein God has placed us to be the best of all estates for us that can be. We have a notable example of this virtue in the apostle Paul, who had learned in whatsoever state he was, therewith to be content. And, therefore, he says, "I can be abased, and I can abound, everywhere and in all things I am instructed both to be full and to be hungry, to abound and to have want" (Phil. 4:11–12). That which Paul practiced is soon said, but not so soon done. Now, that we for our parts, after his example, may be content in every estate of life, we are to perform these duties.

First, we must labor to see a particular providence of God, and to have experience hereof in all things that come to pass. All men acknowledge a

61. Mark 2:27.

62. *Fain:* willing.

63. This paragraph break is not in the original.

providence in health, wealth, and liberty, but in the contrary estates of sickness, bondage, and poverty, etc., the blind world sees no providence nor goodness of God. It shuts up all the goodness of God in health and wealth. But such as profess the knowledge of the true God must better acquaint themselves with this providence and goodness of God, and labor to feel it in sickness as well as in health, in want as in wealth, in persecution as in liberty and peace. And when we can in some good measure do this, experience of divine providence will breed and bring forth contentation. We have an example of this in Job who, in the midst of his misery, said, "The Lord giveth, and the Lord taketh away, now blessed be the name of the Lord" (Job 1:21). Let us, in these words, mark his contentation and the cause thereof, namely his persuasion that God Himself did lay that affliction upon him. Being settled in this persuasion, he gives thanks to God.

Second, we must labor to be resolved even in conscience with David that "God is our portion," that is, that God the Father is our Father, Christ Jesus our Redeemer, and the Holy Spirit our Sanctifier and Comforter. Herein we must settle our consciences, and then we may say as David said, "I have a goodly heritage" (Ps. 16:6). And we shall find our minds more settled and contented with any estate (good or bad) that befalls us by the will and appointment of God. All men are well pleased with health, liberty, [and] wealth. And if we could be able in truth to say, "The Lord is my portion," we should be as well pleased with sickness, bondage, and poverty.

And thus we are to endure ourselves to contentation. Now, for the better restraining of our affections from the world, two things must be done.[64]

First of all, we must in this life resolve ourselves to seek for no more but things that are necessary and sufficient for us and ours. For to seek for abundance is not lawful, neither does it stand with good conscience, which I prove in this manner. We may seek for that which we may pray for, but we have no warrant to pray for abundance. We have warrant to pray for things [that are] necessary and sufficient, as Agur does: "Give me neither poverty nor riches, feed me with food convenient for me" (Prov. 30:8). And Christ taught us to pray in this manner: "Give us this day our daily bread" (Matt. 6:11); that is, bread for our substances, or such bread as is sufficient to preserve our lives. And Saint Paul plainly condemns the desire of riches, that is, of things more than necessary, affirming that such as desire to be rich fall into the snares of the devil [1 Tim. 6:10].[65]

64. This paragraph break is not in the original.
65. This paragraph break is not in the original.

Some have observed twelve wonders in the manna of the Jews.[66] (1) The children of Israel were fed with it for forty years. (2) To the godly, it tasted according to everyone's desire. (3) To the ungodly, it was loathsome. (4) An omer of it sufficed all stomachs. (5) Whether men gathered more or less, they had [a] full measure, neither more nor less (that is, an omer full). (6) Two omers full before the Sabbath, [but] on other days but one omer full. (7) It fell every day but on the Sabbath. (8) It melted in the sun, and was hardened in the fire. (9) It was kept many years (unputrefied) in the ark. (10) Being preserved till the morrow, it putrefied, except on the Sabbath. (11) He who gathered least had his omer full. (12) He who gathered most had but his omer. Now, by the most of these wonders, and especially in that [the] manna (laid until the next day) putrefied, and that every Jew had his competent measure (whether his labor [was] more or less), we are taught that the seeking and desire of abundance pleases not God. The Lord commands the king by express law that he should not multiply his horses nor his silver and gold [Deut. 17:16–17]. It is not here the intent of God to bar kings from seeking for things sufficient to maintain their kingdoms, but to moderate their affections, so that they seek not for that abundance which may serve to maintain not one but two or three kingdoms. If God sends abundance of things (more than necessary) to princes, they may receive them at the hand of God, and they are to be thankful for them. But kings themselves may not seek for more than [that] which is sufficient for their estates.

Now if this is the duty of the prince, then much more is it the duty of the people and subjects in kingdoms to content themselves if they have as much as will provide them food and raiment. And they may seek lawfully for thus much. For example, a master of a family may with good conscience seek for that measure of wealth as shall in Christian wisdom be thought meet to maintain him and his family with convenient food and raiment. Having obtained thus much, a pause must be made, and he may not proceed further to enlarge his estate by seeking for that abundance that may well serve his own house, and a second, or many more families. It may be here demanded how we are to judge what is sufficient for any man? I answer [that] we must estimate sufficiency, not by the affection of covetous men, for then nothing shall ever be sufficient, but we are to proceed by the same rule in this matter as in like case of apparel. Because the Word of God has given no particular rule how every man or woman should be attired, therefore our rule must be the example and judgment of the godly, and grave men and women of our estate and order. So, likewise, for a sufficiency in things of this life, our rule must be the common judgment and practice of the

66. In the margin: Ruff. lib. 1. cap. 12.

most godly, frugal, and wise men, with whom we live. And that which they in good conscience judge sufficient and necessary for every man, according to his place and calling, that is to be esteemed sufficient. And here we must remember, not to make one rule for all men: that things sufficient for one should be sufficient for all. But every man must be measured according to his condition and degree. For as one man is above another in degree, more or less, so to one is more required for sufficiency than to another.[67]

But the covetous man may except,[68] and say [that] every gift of God may be sought for, but abundance is the blessing and gift of God, and therefore it may be sought for. I answer [that] we must distinguish [between] the blessings and gifts of God. Some of them are simply blessings, and some only in respect. Those which are simply blessings are such gifts and graces of God as are not only blessings in themselves but also in every man that has them. And such are the gifts of faith, repentance, the fear of God, [and] the love of God and man. The second kind of blessings, which are in respect, are such as are good in themselves, but not good to every person that has them. Such are riches and abundance of worldly things. Thus then, I answer [that] every blessing of God may be sought for [as long as] I know it is a blessing to me. Therefore, I may lawfully seek for faith and repentance and all such gifts of God, as are simply blessings. But we may not seek for such things as are only blessings in some respect, unless we can say they are blessings to us. A sword or a knife is a good thing in itself, and [it] has its use. But it is not good in the hand of a child or a mad man, because they may thereby hurt themselves. And so are riches good in themselves, but not for every man, and, therefore, [they are] no further to be sought than we know they are good and profitable for us.

Second, it is alleged [that] when men seek for abundance, they find it, and God would not give it them unless it were a blessing, because whatsoever is of God is good. I answer, first of all, that God, in giving abundance, to the covetous man is void of all blame. For the question is of the man's seeking and receiving, not of God's giving. Again, when God grants abundance to some who seek it, He gives a blessing, but like to the quails which He gave to the Israelites, which brought a plague with them. For God oftentimes gives temporal blessings in His wrath.[69]

Third, it may be alleged that God has made a promise to every righteous man, that he shall receive abundance [and] that "riches and treasures shall be in his house" [Ps. 112:3], and therefore he may lawfully seek for riches. I answer two ways. First, in the Word of God, "riches" is often understood [as] things

---

67. This paragraph break is not in the original.
68. *Except:* object.
69. This paragraph break is not in the original.

necessary, and not abundance. Second, if "riches" is taken for abundance, I answer that promises concerning temporal blessings must be understood with exception of the cross and chastisement, and therefore the meaning of the psalmist is that riches shall be given to the righteous unless it is the will of God to exercise and try him by want and poverty. And that this place must thus be understood appears plainly [in] Hebrews 11:37, where some are commended because they endured poverty by faith, wandering to and fro in sheep and goat skins. And when Lazarus died, he was received into Abraham's bosom, though in his lifetime he had not so much as crumbs from the rich man's table to feed his body. Now then, if the promise were absolute, every man might seek for abundance, and every believer should have it. But, seeing it is conditional, and we are uncertain whether it will please God to try us by want or not, therefore we may not seek for abundance.[70]

Fourth, it may be alleged that every man must do good to church and commonwealth, and therefore he must seek for plenty, so that he may have wherewith to do this good. I answer [that] we must indeed do good, but yet within the compass of our estates and callings, and according to our ability. For God accepts every man according to what he has, and not according to what he has not.

Lastly, it is alleged that there are examples of righteous men (as Abraham, Jacob, and Solomon) who abounded with riches. I answer [that] they got not their riches by seeking abundance. They were made rich by God's sending, not by their own seeking. And so, any man may accept abundance when it is the pleasure of God to bestow it on them while they walk in their callings. And it cannot be shown that Abraham, Jacob, or Solomon, wanting riches, sought for them. But commonly the covetous man lays plots how to get thus much for himself, and thus much for his children, so many hundreds and so many thousands. Whereas Jacob asked of God but food and raiment. Therefore, whatsoever is said to the contrary, the truth is that no man can with good conscience seek for things more than [are] necessary. And this one thing must be as a cord unto us to restrain our affections from the world: that God has given a commandment that we must seek only for things that may be in Christian wisdom esteemed necessary.

(2) Turning our affections from the world. Now, let us proceed to search how we may turn our affections from the world to better things. The way is this. As the choleric persons, who desire to restrain their hastiness, must turn it against themselves for their own sins, even so the worldling, who desires to

70. This paragraph break is not in the original.

turn his gripple[71] mind from earthly things, must set his mind on the kingdom of heaven. And, for the doing of this, two things are especially required.[72]

First, we must endeavor to have the eyes of our minds enlightened by God's Spirit, so that we may see how happy the estate is that God has prepared in His own kingdom for them who love Him. Paul prayed thus for the Ephesians, that "the eyes of their understanding might be enlightened, that they might know what the hope was of their calling, and what the riches of his glorious inheritance is in the saints" (Eph. 1:18). The beast that goes in a bare common, if once it sets [its] eye on a better pasture, will without further delay over hedge and ditch and all, till it comes into the said pasture. Now that which is in nature should much more be in them who are partakers of the grace of Christ. Therefore, although (like moles) we have our heads always rooting under the earth, yet if we do by grace but cast our eyes to the joys of heaven we cannot but turn our hearts from the love of this present world. We have a notable example of this in Moses, who, when he might have been heir to Pharaoh's daughter, refused honor, "esteeming the rebuke of Christ greater riches than the treasures of Egypt: because he had respect to the recompense of reward" [Heb. 11:26]. Thus, God in mercy opened his eyes, and made him see the happy estate of the kingdom of heaven, and thereby caused him to leave and forsake the honor and the wealth of Egypt.

Second, we must endeavor to have in our hearts a sense and feeling of the want of Christ, and to see our damnable estate in ourselves, and how greatly we stand in need of the blood of Christ to wash away our sins. Behold a notable means to make any man (though he were covetousness itself) to turn his heart from the pelf[73] of this world, and to seek wholly after spiritual and heavenly things. For the consideration of our own misery in ourselves, and a lively sense of the need we have of Christ, will make us hunger after Him and His righteousness above all things in the world.[74]

We find by experience that many are endued with good gifts of knowledge, joy in the Word of God, zeal, etc., who nevertheless in their callings are overcome with this foul sin of covetousness. And the reason is because they were never thoroughly touched with any sense or feeling of the need they had of Christ. Their hearts are dead in sin and corruption, and they never knew the vileness of their own natures, and in what extreme misery they are out of Christ. And if they might be brought to a feeling of their unworthiness, and made to hunger after Him, they would then begin to say with Saint Paul, "I

---

71. *Gripple:* greedy.
72. This paragraph break is not in the original.
73. *Pelf:* wealth, spoil, or booty.
74. This paragraph break is not in the original.

esteem all things as dung in regard of Christ" [Phil. 3:8]. And with David, "As the hart brayeth after the rivers of waters, so thirsteth my soul after thee, O Lord" [Ps. 42:1]. This is the counsel of Christ: "First seek the kingdom of God and his righteousness" (Matt. 6:33). We must in ourselves be as the wounded man who lay in the way, that Christ Jesus the true Samaritan may come by us to supple our wounds, and to pour His own precious blood into our souls. For as Mary said, "God fills the hungry with good things, but the rich he sends empty away" [Luke 1:53]. And thus, we shall be able by God's grace to turn our affections (set on the world) to heavenly things. Thus also, we [shall] see how to walk in our callings with [a] good conscience and to avoid the sin of covetousness.

Vice 2: Injustice

Now I come to the second sin: injustice, whereby men abuse their callings to the hurt and hindrance of others, either publicly or privately. We have [an] example of this in Zacchaeus, the publican, who enriched himself by forged cavillation [Luke 19:8]. Now this sin spreads itself as largely through all degrees and states of men as the former sin of covetousness, as will appear if we do but take a view of such as are the principal callings.[75]

First, to begin with emperors and princes by whom is practiced the greatest injustice that can be, as they are in the greatest callings. For many of them content not themselves with their own dominions, but encroach (either by fraud or violence) on their neighboring kingdoms, and for the increasing of their estates [they] spare not to shed rivers of blood, as, at this day, the Turk in Asia, and the Spaniard also, who seeks by all means to make himself the emperor of the western parts of the world. [The] like injustice appears in the calling of such magistrates as usually take bribes to respect men's persons in executing justice and judgment. Injustice also creeps into the chair of Moses, when the Word of God, the food of men's souls, is withheld, as also when it is corrupted, partly by the poison of men's errors [and] partly by the devices of men's brains. Injustice in the calling of the lawyer is to take larger fees than statute and conscience will allow, and to make delay of suits, yea to delay them, not from morning till night, as Jethro said to Moses, but from term to term, yea from year to year, for the increasing of their gain. In the calling of the physician, it is injustice to minister physic to the bodies of men, which is learned out of books without any experience; as also to minister physic upon the bare inspection of the urine, which by the best learned is judged to be insufficient, and often deceitful; yea, to prescribe drunkenness and fornication for the cure of some diseases; and to

75. This paragraph break is not in the original.

minister physic to absent parties upon the erecting of the figure at the time of the interrogation.[76]

In the calling of the merchant and tradesman, there are false weights and false measures, divers weights and divers measures, engrossing, mingling, changing, setting a gloss on wares by powdering, starching, blowing, dark shops, glazing, smoothing, lying, swearing, and all manner of bad dealing. In the patron, there is presentation given, but with secret condition of having his own tithes, or some other fleece out of the living. In the landlord, there is racking of rents,[77] taking immoderate fines, enclosing of grounds that have lain common time out of mind, and the cause is want of sobriety and temperance in diet and apparel. In the husbandman and corn-monger, there is exceeding injustice in hoarding up grain till the time of further advantage, and in taking whatsoever they can get for their own, though it is to the shedding of the blood of the poor. In the calling of the printer, which should serve for the special good of the church and commonwealth, there is exceeding injustice done to both by the publishing of libels and heretical books, whereby errors are spread abroad, as also by publishing unchaste, immodest, and unprofitable writings. And in the calling of the bookseller, there is like injustice, in that they sell all books, good and bad, of truth and falsehood, and that hand over head without any regard to everyone that comes. For at this day, in England, a papist may furnish himself with almost all kinds of books of his own heresy, and that in the shops of protestants. [This is a] thing to be thought upon, and that which greatly hinders the good of our church.[78]

Thus, the canker of injustice has spread itself over all estates and callings, so as we may take up the complaint of the prophet Micah: "It is hard to find a righteous man: every man lays a net for his brother, and seeketh his hurt, his blood, and utter undoing" [Micah 7:2]. This is so plain that he who has but half an eye may see it. Yet, the unjust man wants not excuses, but says, "The world is naught, and therefore they who will live in the world must do as other men do." *Answer.* This indeed is the blind reason of ungodly men. But Saint Paul gives another rule, and bids us "walk unblameably in this present world, as lights in the midst of a crooked and perverse generation" [Phil. 2:15]. And though the whole world should give themselves to the practice of injustice, yet he who is the child of God must carry himself in his calling in such manner that he may be a light to them with whom he lives.[79]

---

76. This paragraph break is not in the original.
77. "racking of rents," raising rent above a fair or normal price.
78. This paragraph break is not in the original.
79. This paragraph break is not in the original.

Others, more blind and shameless, for the maintaining of their injustice, allege the example and practice of our Savior Christ in sending for another man's ass and the colt when He went to Jerusalem [Matt. 21:3]. But who does not see the notorious abuse of this place of Scripture! For our Savior Christ did this as Lord, not only of the beast, but also of the owner. And, therefore, when He sent His disciples, at the same time He inclined the heart of the owner to be willing to let them go, showing thereby Himself to be the Lord who has the hearts of all men in His hand, and consequently the Governor of all other things.[80]

Other allegations for the defense of injustice are of no moment. Now then, we must enter into examination of all the works of our callings, and finding what stands not with equity and injustice, we are to forsake it. And the better to persuade us hereunto, these reasons may be used.[81]

First of all, it is God's commandment that every man should deal justly in the works of his calling. As Paul says to Titus: "The grace of God that bringeth salvation unto all men hath appeared, and teacheth us that we should deny ungodliness and worldly lusts, and that we should live soberly, righteously, and godly in this present world" [Titus 2:12]. Again, "Let no man defraud or oppress his brother in anything" [1 Thess. 4:6]. Now then, if we have been faulty in this kind heretofore, let us now begin to make conscience of this commandment.[82]

Second, we must consider with[in] ourselves that so long as we practice injustice in our particular calling, all our worship and service of God in prayer and thanksgiving, in hearing the Word and receiving the sacraments, is an abomination unto the Lord. Hereupon He says to the Jews: "I abhor your Sabbaths and new moons" [Isa. 1:13]. And the reason is because their hands were full of blood. Again, the Lord professes that the sacrifices offered unto Him by the Jews were as if a "man should cut off a dog's neck" [Isa. 66:3], and offer it to Him in a sacrifice, because they lived in their wickedness.[83]

Third, they who practice injustice have the curse of God to follow them. Paul says that the "unjust man shall never enter in the kingdom of God" [1 Cor. 6:9]. And Moses says that they "which use false weights are an abomination to the Lord" [Deut. 25:16]. Look then how many practices of injustice are used in any man's calling. So many bars and stops there are to keep him from the kingdom of God.[84]

---

80. This paragraph break is not in the original.
81. This paragraph break is not in the original.
82. This paragraph break is not in the original.
83. This paragraph break is not in the original.
84. This paragraph break is not in the original.

Lastly, let us mark what Saint Paul says of himself: "In all things he had a care to please God in consideration of the terror of the Lord" [2 Cor. 5:11]. And that is as if he had said, "I know in the last day I must come to the bar of God's judgment, where will be tried all the things I do. And, therefore, I do endeavor to keep a good conscience in all the works of my calling." And in the very same manner every one of us should stir up ourselves to the practice of justice, and to the avoiding of all bad dealing in our callings. For, at the last day, the bad practices of every man shall be made manifest, and we shall be judged according to what we have wrought when we lived in the flesh.

Thus much for the two vices to be avoided in every man's calling.

Practicing Virtue

The virtues which the Word of God requires of us in the practice of our callings are many, but especially two: faith and love.[85]

Virtue 1: Faith

By faith, I mean not only saving faith but another particular faith arising from it whereby we must be persuaded that our particular callings, and the works thereof, are pleasing unto God, and that He will give a blessing unto them for Christ's sake. And whatsoever is not of this faith is sin. When Noah is said to build an ark by faith [Heb. 11:7], we must not only understand justifying faith, but withal another particular faith flowing from it, whereby he was persuaded that the building of the ark was a work acceptable unto God, and that he should find a blessing therein. And without this particular faith, no man can please God in any calling. Now there is a relation between faith and the Word. Where faith is, there must be a word from God. And where the Word is not, there can be no faith. And, therefore, that the actions of our callings may be done in faith, we must have a word whereon to build our faith. And this word is twofold: (1) a word of commandment, and (2) a word of promise.[86]

The commandment is that word of God whereby the actions of every man's calling are either expressly commanded or at least approved. The promise is a particular word, either directly propounded or by just consequent to be gathered out of the Scriptures, whereby God has promised to bless the labors and works of our callings. And everyone must labor in his place for knowledge of both [of] these. The magistrate must have a commandment from God in His Word, that must authorize him to draw the sword, and a promise of blessing and protection when upon good cause he draws the sword indeed. The like

85. This paragraph break is not in the original.

86. This paragraph break is not in the original.

must the minister have for his calling, and the man of trade for his. And he who has not both a commandment and promise cannot possibly do the works of his calling in faith.

Now if any shall think this strange and hard, let them consider what is done in towns and corporations. Men of the same trade, have their wardens and masters of their companies, yea decrees and ordinances, to which they bind and conform themselves. Now if men are content to bind themselves to their own ordinances, shall they not much more yield themselves to the commandments of God, and walk in their callings according to them? Again, when men thus live by faith, having regard to God's commandments, it causes them to do their actions in obedience. And when they shall by the same faith rest upon the promise of God, it will make them cast their works on the Lord, and free them from carking and distrustful cares which pull the heart in pieces. And by this means also, they shall ease their minds when they lie under the crosses that are incident unto every calling since the fall of Adam. For in this promise shall we behold the blessing and goodness of God in the midst of our troubles. As the wood, that Moses cast into the bitter waters, made them sweet, so the promise of God, viewed by the eye of faith, sweetens the troubles and crosses of our callings.

Virtue 2: Love

The second virtue is love. Faith, which is alone in justification, goes not alone in life and conversation, but love and faith are both joined together, for faith works by love. And yet, they are not one and the same virtue, but differ in their actions. As the man, who serves a mason upon the ladder, uses both his hands (with one he stays himself [and] with the other he reaches up his burden), so every man has in his calling the use of two spiritual hands: the hand of faith and the hand of love. The hand of faith keeps him in compass, and stays the mind upon the Word of God. And the hand of love reaches out itself to others in duties of love toward God and man. And thus, faith and love differ.[87]

Now the practice of love stands in two things. First, we must refer all the works of our callings to the honor, praise, and glory of God. And here is the principal thing wherein love consists. And, therefore, Paul says notably of himself, "The love of Christ constraineth me" [2 Cor. 5:14], signifying thereby that, whereas Christ had so loved him as to shed His blood for him, that very love did constrain him to refer all that he could do to the honor and praise of Christ. Now look what Paul here says, the same must every particular man in his calling say of himself, that the love of Christ in shedding His blood for him

87. This paragraph break is not in the original.

constrains him to do all things for the honor and praise of His name. The second duty of love is to apply the works, duties, and labors of our callings, to the good of the church, commonwealth, and the place whereof we are members. Paul says thus to the Galatians: "Do service one to another by love" (Gal. 5:13). And this is done when we employ our labor for the good of our brethren. And thus, briefly we see how love is put in practice.

If we shall examine ourselves by these two points, it will appear that most men come short of their duties. For whereas it is the property of unfeigned love not to seek its own things but the good of others, the common practice of men is to employ their pains for themselves, according to the common saying, "Every man for himself and God for us all." Now we are in the evil days wherein men are lovers of themselves. The moving cause in almost every man, that causes him to do the duties of his calling, is the respect of private benefit. It is hard to find a man who labors in his calling upon love, to the glory of God, and [for] the good of his brethren.

Thus, we see how the Word of God gives direction for the holy use of our callings.

Means 2: Prayer

The second means to sanctify our callings, and the works thereof, is prayer. This prayer is that whereby we do not only pray unto God for the pardon of our sins, and for the supply of such graces as concern eternal life, but particularly for a blessing upon the labors of our callings. They must begin with prayer, and in due season end with thanksgiving. The commandment to this purpose is plain: "Whatsoever ye do in word or deed, do all in the name of the Lord Jesus, giving thanks to God" (Col. 3:17). The meaning is that, when we enterprise any business, either in speech or action, we must first call on God for His blessing, and give Him thanks in the end. David says, "Except the Lord build the house, they labor in vain that build it; and except the Lord keep the city, the watchman keeps the watch in vain" (Ps. 127:1).[88]

If Paul, before he took shipping, prayed on the shore, then much more must we do it in the main and weighty works of our callings. Parents in their families teach their children to say, "Father, I pray you, bless me. Mother, I pray you, bless me." Well, God's church is His family, and men who live therein are the children of God. He is the Father and Master of that family. Therefore, let this practice of earthly parents teach us, when we begin the actions of our callings, to go to our heavenly Father for His blessing. We must remember to practice this, and so shall we sanctify the works of our callings.

---

88. This paragraph break is not in the original.

Requirement 2: Constancy

The second thing required in doing the works of a man's calling in a good manner, and which also serves for a good continuance in the calling, is constancy. And it is nothing else but a perseverance in good duties, which is the more needful because it is no commendation for us to make choice of a good and fit calling, and to enter into it, unless we go through stitch[89] in the duties thereof. For even as the soldier in the field must not change his place wherein he is placed by the general, but must abide by it to the venturing of his life, so must the Christian continue and abide in his calling without change or alteration.[90]

There is a certain lightness in the nature of man whereby it comes to pass that many like other men's callings better than their own, and hereupon are moved upon every light occasion to alter their calling. But in the text in hand, the Holy Spirit meets with this lightness by commanding every man to continue constant in doing the duties of his particular calling: "Let every man abide in that vocation wherein he was called." And we must be careful to avoid three lets of constancy: ambition, envy, and impatience.[91]

Impediment 1: Ambition

Ambition is a vice whereby any man, thinking better of himself than he should, becomes malcontent with his particular calling, and seeks for himself a higher place and a better estate. We have an example of this ambition in our first parents, who by Satan's allurement became malcontent with that estate wherein they were created, and sought to attain to the condition of God Himself. And their sin cleaves fast to the nature of every man, and by it we are easily carried to a dislike of our condition. Thus, Absalom through ambition was moved to seek his father's kingdom, judging basely of his present estate, for out of natural self-love springs ambition.[92]

And for the better redressing of this vice in ourselves, every man must enter into consideration of his own estate. We must bethink ourselves that in respect of our bodies, we are but dust and ashes, and to dust we must return again, that in respect of the disposition of our hearts, altogether set upon sin, we are far more wretched than any other creature; and also, that of ourselves we have not any sufficiency for the doing of the least and smallest duties of the best calling in the world. For of ourselves we are not sufficient to think one good thought, much less to perform a good duty acceptable to God, in any calling whatsoever. And, therefore, we must consider with[in] ourselves that in our

89. *Stitch:* stabbing pain.
90. This paragraph break is not in the original.
91. This paragraph break is not in the original.
92. This paragraph break is not in the original.

particular callings we are but as weak instruments in the hand of the Lord, who is the principal worker and agent. These and like meditations might move us to contentation in the calling in which God has placed us.

Impediment 2: Envy

The second impediment to constancy is envy, which is a pining away of the heart when men see others placed in better callings and conditions than themselves. This is a common sin, and it is the cause of much dissention in the commonwealth. It is one of Machiavel's policies, to hold it necessary in a commonwealth that men of sundry degrees and callings should envy and malign each other. But, contrariwise, it is a manifest hindrance to constancy in good duties, and hurtful both to church and commonwealth. And for the better redressing of this fault, we are to consider that the greatest callings that are, are not ordained for the maintenance of pride and for the private benefit of men, but for the common good. Second, that such as are placed in [the] greatest callings have the greatest charges, and therefore are to yield unto God the greatest accompt.[93]

Impediment 3: Impatience

The third impediment of constancy is impatience, which is a disquietness of mind, arising from the continual troubles that are incident to all callings, especially when men are not able to bear them, nor to brook the injuries that are commonly done unto them in word or deed. This very sin makes many a man to leave his place. Such as go to sea, for their delight, make choice of fair and calm days; afterwards, being seasick, yea tossed with wind and weather, and in some danger of their lives, they wish themselves on land again, being grieved they ever came on shipboard, professing if they come to land again never to come on sea anymore. Even so, it fares with many men both in church and commonwealth. They take a liking of this or that calling. They enter into it, hoping for pleasure, wealth, and approbation of men. Now afterwards, finding themselves disappointed of their expectation, and to walk in callings with many troubles and discomforts, hereupon they become impatient, and either do indeed or greatly wish to leave their callings.[94]

Now to remedy this vice, we must resolve to go on to do the duties of our callings, to go through stitch in all crosses or calamities that may befall us [in] any way, arming ourselves with all mete and necessary patience. Thus, Christ commanded His disciples to "possess their souls with patience."[95] And Paul

93. *Accompt:* account.
94. This paragraph break is not in the original.
95. Luke 21:19.

charges the Philippians to "let their patient and equal minds be known to all men."[96] The surgeon, who is to cut his patient, goes on to lance and to work his cure, though his patient cries ever so much. So we must, in our particular callings, go on with courage and constancy to do the duties thereof for the glory of God and the good of men, though there are ever so many lets and impediments to hinder us. And as Paul says, [we must] pass through good report and bad report, through shame and rebuke.

And that we may thus constantly proceed in all good duties with all patience, we must often remember that the duties of any lawful calling, be it ever so base, are accepted and approved by God. Our Savior Christ Himself complains in this manner: "I have labored in vain, I have spent my strength in vain" (Isa. 49:4). Here we see the little success that the Head and perfect Doctor of the church had in His calling. But let us see how He does comfort Himself. Surely, [it is] thus in the following words: "But my work is with my God"; that is, howsoever men submit not themselves to My doctrine, yet My Father approves it. It was a thing that troubled Saint Paul, that his labor in the ministry did not turn to the good of all, but was to some the savor of death to death. Yet, he comforts himself with this, that it was always a sweet-smelling savor to God. And by the same consideration of God's approbation, we should arm ourselves with patience, so that we may with good conscience go on in good duties to the end.

Thus much of the three impediments of constancy.

To proceed yet further, constancy here commanded must be understood with three things: helps, vacations, [and] changes.[97]

Helps

Touching helps, the ordinance of God is for the better continuance of callings, so that customs and tribute are paid to magistrates, [and] necessary stipends, tithes, and dues [are paid] to ministers of the Word. And Moses says that all such as do the offices of their callings diligently, and for all this fall to decay, wanting the blessing of God upon their labors, must be helped by lending freely, forgiving of debts, and other like courtesies (Deut. 15:7). Let hard-hearted men think upon this, who will not in such cases lend freely, but prey on such persons till they have sucked their bones. These are the bane and plague of a commonwealth. These are those who make beggars and vagabonds. For where there is no free lending, there many a man goes to wrack.[98]

96. Phil. 4:5.

97. This paragraph break is not in the original.

98. This paragraph break is not in the original.

Vacations

Vacation is to cease from doing the duties of a particular calling for some time or space. And it has its warrant from the Word of God, which allows vacations in three respects.[99]

First, for religion's sake, which is the principal vacation of all, and it is commanded in the fourth commandment: "Remember the Sabbath day," that is, the day of rest (or of vacation) "to keep it holy." And here every man is bound in conscience before God to cease from the duties of his calling on the seventh day, which is now, in the New Testament, the Lord's Day, and so is to continue to the last judgment. And this vacation is necessary even in common reason, for without it there can be no good proceeding in religion. It is the means to begin, continue, and increase both knowledge and grace. He who has the most excellent gifts of nature shall never be able to attain to learning, unless he sets himself apart, and gives himself to study. Much more then, the knowledge of the mysteries of the kingdom of heaven cannot be obtained, unless men at some times lay aside all worldly affairs, especially on the Sabbath day. Therefore, it is for the good of families, towns, countries, and kingdoms, that the Lord's Day is kept, and consequently it stands us in hand to take the benefit of this vacation, and to use it for the increase of faith, repentance, and obedience, if we desire the salvation of our own souls. God, who is the sovereign King over all, might have enjoined us a perpetual labor from one day to another for all the days of our lives. But, tendering our good and salvation, He enjoined us to labor six days, commanding a vacation on the seventh.

The second vacation is in respect of recreation, which also has its warrant when it is lawfully used. God commands every man to labor in his calling, and to eat his own bread in the sweat of his brow. And in commanding labor, He allows the means that make us fit to labor. And, therefore, withal He admits lawful recreation because it is a necessary means to refresh either body or mind, that we may the better do the duties which pertain unto us. I have spoken of recreation elsewhere.[100] Therefore, it shall suffice now briefly to propound a caveat or two. Touching recreation these caveats must be remembered. First of all, it must be moderate, otherwise it is a means to call and draw us from our callings. Second, it must be in things lawful. Third, it must be on the days of labor, for labor is then only commanded. And, therefore, recreation which is a ceasing from labor for a time, and serves only to make us more able to continue in labor, must be on the six days and not on the Sabbath. Because we must abstain from ordinary labors of our callings on the Sabbath, we are much more

---

99. This paragraph break is not in the original.

100. Cf. Perkins, *Works*, 8:58–59.

to abstain from our accustomed recreations. For where that which is more necessary and principal is forbidden, there the less necessary is forbidden also. But labor is the more necessary and principal, and recreation serves for labor. This being so, it is a notable abuse of many to make the Lord's Day a set day of sport and pastime, which should be a day set apart for the worship of God and the increase in the duties of religion. And this is especially the fault of householders, who, having employed their servants to labor six whole days together, give them the seventh day, which is the Lord's, for recreation.

A third vacation is in time of necessity when men are disabled by reason of sickness, age, imprisonment, or any other just impediment. And the ordinance of God is that such persons as have the trembling hand (as Moses speaks in Leviticus 25:35) should be maintained with such things as are necessary to life and health by the labor of other men's callings. This thing must not be marveled at, for the goods we have are not our own, but the Lord's. We are but keepers and stewards of them. And it is God's will that the poor should have title to a part of every man's goods. And for this cause, it is a shame if they have not relief without roving, begging, or crying.

And here two questions are to be scanned, which are much spoken of and often moved.[101]

Question 1. First, whereas it is a general duty to visit our neighbors in time of sickness, it is demanded whether it is lawful at all to cease from this duty in time of plague or pestilence? I answer [that] there may be (and is) a lawful vacation from this duty, and that with good conscience for some time and upon some occasion. For, first of all, it is lawful to maintain our own lives, so it be without the hurt or hindrance of the lives of other men. Now, to fly in time of contagious pestilence is to preserve the life of some without the hurt of any. Second, in other common dangers (as in time of famine, fire, and sword), men for their safety may flee from their neighbors, and therefore by like proportion we may flee in time of contagious sickness. Third, in the church of the Jews, the leper was put apart from the society of men. And that in effect was as much as if all the Jews had withdrawn themselves from his society. And, therefore, now it is not simply unlawful to flee in time of contagious pestilence.[102]

It is alleged that to flee is a flat distrusting of God, as though He would not preserve and defend us. I answer that distrusting God is not a fault in the action of fleeing, but in those who flee. Men, who labor for meat and drink, do many times distrust the goodness of God, yet the fault is not in the labor itself, but in the parties who endure the labor. Second, it is alleged that to flee is to forsake

101. This paragraph break is not in the original.
102. This paragraph break is not in the original.

those to whom we are united in bond of neighborhood, which is unlawful. I answer [that] when the parties visited have sufficient helps appointed by the magistrate, both for their bodies and souls, then to flee is not to forsake, and in such cases, parties visited are not to desire the presence of their neighbors. It is alleged that David never fled away when the people were smitten with the plague. *Answer.* There are special reasons thereof. (1) That plague was sent by God upon a sudden. (2) David's very sin was the cause of the said plague upon the people. (3) David had no cause to flee because he then was assured that [he] himself should escape. Thus, then, the visiting of neighbors and friends, though it is a needful duty, sometimes admits vacations, in which we may with good conscience go aside and seek the safety of our own selves and those who belong unto us [as long as] necessary help is otherwise provided for the sick.

Question 2. The second question is whether the ministers of the gospel may flee in time of persecution? I answer [that] they may if they are freed from the bond of their callings whereby they are tied to their charges. Thus, Moses fled to Midian, and Paul out of Damascus, and our Savior Christ from among the Jews. Second, I add that ministers, not freed from their callings, may by the consent of their people for a time go aside for their own safety and the further good of men, till the brunt of [the] persecution is over, especially if they in particular are aimed at. When Demetrius had raised a tumult in Ephesus about Diana, and the people had caught Paul's companions, Gaius and Aristarchus, Paul, moved with zeal, would have entered into the middle of the press. But as Saint Luke says certain brethren overruled him, and would not suffer him to enter, but caused him to withdraw himself [Acts 19:31].[103]

Thus, then, it is manifest that in common dangers public callings admit their vacations in sundry cases.

Thus much of vacations; now I come to changes.

Changes

A change of a calling is a lawful going from one calling to another. It is not the apostle's meaning to bar men to divert from this or that calling, but he gives them an item to keep them from changing upon every light conceit and every sudden occasion. And that changes may lawfully be made, it appears thus. Amos, by calling, was first a herdsman, but after a prophet. The disciples were first fishermen, and after apostles. Our Savior Christ Himself was by calling a carpenter in his first and private life, till He was thirty years old. Yet, after His baptism, He showed Himself to be the Messiah and Savior of the world.

103. This paragraph break is not in the original.

Nevertheless, a change may not be made but upon urgent and weighty causes, and they are especially two: (1) private necessity, and (2) the common good.[104]

Private necessity is when men cannot maintain themselves and theirs by the callings in which they are, for then they may betake themselves to other callings. Thus, a merchant man may become a husbandman, and a husbandman a merchant. Thus, a physician may become a minister of the gospel, and Paul, an apostle, upon private necessity, returned to the calling of a tent maker, yet so as he performed his ministry when occasion was offered.

The second cause of making lawful change is the public good. Thus, a private man may become a magistrate. And it must be remembered that so often as we change, it must be to better and more excellent callings, in which we may glorify God more, and bring greater benefit to the church and commonwealth. Thus, Paul bids the Corinthians to seek for the best gifts, which might serve for the best callings [1 Cor. 14:1]. And here the fault of some is to be reproved, who, having notable gifts of nature and learning, because they would attain to worldly wealth, make themselves merchants, or factors to merchants, or serving men to great persons. Whereas for their gifts, they might do God better service in the greatest callings of the church.

And thus much of constancy.

The consideration of this, that we are bound to be constant in the duties of our particular callings, must teach us much more to be constant in the general duties of Christianity. And, therefore, let us all be careful, not only to profess the true religion for the present time, but to continue constant in this profession unto the end. Our general calling admits no vacation nor change as our particular callings do. Well then, in that we profess ourselves to be members of Christ, in these our happy days of peace, let us arm ourselves against the evil days to come, that we may be faithful to the end.

Again, in the general calling, every man is bound in all good conscience to obey God in all His commandments. Here also our constancy must appear so long as we live, that we may say with Paul, "I have finished my course, I have fought a good fight" (2 Tim. 4:7), and with Hezekiah on his death bed, "Lord, remember how I have walked before thee with an upright heart, and have done that which is acceptable in thy sight" (Isa. 38:3). God has made a most merciful promise of everlasting life, which is the comfort of all comforts, and without which the case of God's children would be of all most miserable. And this promise is made to them who continue faithful unto the end. These are they on whom God will bestow the crown of life.

And thus much for continuance in our callings.

---

104. This paragraph break is not in the original.

Point 4: A Good Ending of a Calling

The last point to be considered is the good ending thereof. And herein two things are required: (1) the resignment,[105] and (2) the account. In the parable of the rich man, the lord calls his steward, and bids him to give an account of his stewardship, for he can no longer be steward.[106] Here we see, besides the resignment of our callings, an account must be made of our doings therein. Of these two in order.[107]

Point 1: The Resignment

The resignment of a calling is nothing else but the laying down of the said calling by ceasing to put in execution the work and duties thereof. In the resignment of callings two things must be considered: (1) the time when; [and] (2) the manner how.[108]

The Time

The time is not left in our own choice, for we may not leave our callings when we please, but the prescribing thereof belongs to God, like as in the field the soldier may not leave his standing when he wills, until he has a warrant from the captain. For as the case stands in one kind of calling, so by proportion in the rest. Now, in one particular calling, namely in the office of the Levite, the entrance into it, the continuance and the ending of it, is in the will of God, who prescribes the time when he must enter, namely, at the age of thirty years, and how long he must continue, twenty years, and when he must end, namely, at fifty years [Num. 8]. And, therefore, the prescribing of particular seasons and times of laying down other callings is not altogether without the will of God. Hence, it follows that no man is to lay down the calling wherein he is placed, till he can say by some warrant in his conscience that it is the good will and pleasure of God that he shall then resign and cease to do the duties thereof any longer.

This rule has its truth in all things whatsoever, whether pertaining to the church or commonwealth. And by it we may judge on the contrary what may be thought of resignments of callings, both civil and ecclesiastical, upon no other ground but the very wills of men for the attainment of greater wealth, pleasure, and preferment.

To go yet further in this point, callings are of two sorts: changeable and perpetual. Changeable callings are such as are imposed for a season, as for a

105. *Resignment:* resignation.

106. Luke 16:2.

107. This paragraph break is not in the original.

108. This paragraph break is not in the original.

year or two or longer. And such callings are to be resigned according to the appointment of them who imposed them. But in perpetual callings the case stands otherwise, and other conditions are required. Nevertheless, there are four special times in which such kind of callings may be resigned.[109]

First, when men are utterly disabled, either by age or by any incurable disease of body or mind, or by want of gifts, then indeed, whatsoever the calling is, either public or private, civil or ecclesiastical, it may be laid down. When Moses was stricken in years, and saw the end of his days at hand, he called the whole congregation, and told them that (being a hundred and fifty years old) he was no more able to go in and out before them, that is, to do the office of a judge and prince. And, therefore, [he] resigned his office to Joshua, who judged the people in his stead [Deut. 31:2–7].

The second time of resignment is when any man is lawfully deposed for a crime or offence committed. Thus, the priests who offered sacrifice before the Lord, if they fell away to idolatry, were deposed from the office of the priest, and ever after were employed in some service in the temple [Ezek. 44:13].

The third time of resignment is the time of death, for when God calls us from this life, we then receive a discharge from our particular callings. For after this life the children of God cease from their labors, and in their death begin their perpetual and eternal Sabbath. For the time of this life, by God's commandment, we rest every seventh day, and labor in the six. But after, we shall continually without ceasing do that which now for substance we do on the Sabbath day, that is, honor, praise, and glorify the name of God in everlasting joy.

The fourth time of resignation is at the last Day of Judgment, to them who shall then be alive. That is the general time of all resignments. For, as Saint Paul says, Christ Jesus must then resign His kingdom up into His Father's hands, and put down all human rule, authority, and power (1 Cor. 15:24). For then, civil, ecclesiastical, and economic states and callings, in regard of government, must have an end. Yea, Christ Himself, in regard of the manner of His regiment, must give up His kingly office, and the execution both of His priesthood and prophetic office must then also have an end, though the virtue and fruit thereof shall abide forever. Then there shall be no more prince and people, magistrate and subject, master and servant, parents and children, but God shall be all in all to the elect.[110]

Thus we see the time of resignments; the manner follows.

109. This paragraph break is not in the original.
110. This paragraph break is not in the original.

The Manner

The manner is to resign them in and with the testimony of a good conscience, which is when our conscience bears witness that we have in the works of our callings kept ourselves unblameable, and have endeavored in all things to do the will of God. We have examples of this in the Scripture. When Samuel was no longer able to judge the people, he called the whole congregation of the Israelites, protesting unto them that he had not taken any man's ox or ass, received any bribes, or done any man wrong, but in all things kept a good conscience [1 Sam. 12:3]. And Saint Paul, when he drew near to the end of his days, says he had now fought a good fight and kept the faith, and that now it remained only that God should give him a crown of righteousness, laid up for all those who love the appearing of the Lord Jesus [2 Tim. 4:7–8].[111]

Now, in the Day of Judgment, it shall not suffice that men and women are found in the works of their callings (though that is far better than to be employed in the works of ungodliness). I say it shall not suffice, for at the last day, two shall be in the field in the works (no doubt) of their callings, yet the one shall be taken [and] the other refused; two women shall be grinding at the mill, [yet] the one shall be taken [and] the other refused. Therefore, besides the practice of a lawful calling, care must be had to keep a good conscience to the end, both before God and men.[112]

And thus much of resignments.

Point 2: The Account

The second (and last) point is the account that every man must make of the works of his calling. Now that such an account is to be made appears in the parable of the rich man. And Saint Paul says, "Every man must go to judgment, and give an account for himself" [Rom. 14:10, 12]. And Solomon tells the young man, roving in his own ways, that "for all this he shall come to judgment" [Eccl. 11:9]. Few are truly persuaded of this last and great account, because it is deferred. But we ought to be of better resolution, and prepare ourselves for it.

Touching this account, two things must be considered: (1) what is the account; [and] (2) how it is made.

Point 1

The giving of an account is nothing else but an action of the reasonable creature, especially of man, wherein he must be answerable and accountant to God for all his actions, both of his general and his particular callings. And by the law of nature, we are bound to this. Yea, if inferior officers in the commonwealth

111. This paragraph break is not in the original.

112. This paragraph break is not in the original.

become accountable to the highest magistrates for all their doings, then much more must every creature become accountable to God, his Creator, for the duties of his calling wherein he does Him homage and service.

There are four things required in this account: (1) the presentation of every man's person before God; (2) the manifestation of all the works that they have done; (3) the examination of them all; and (4) the giving and rendering to every man according to his works.[113]

For the first, the presentation of all persons before the tribunal of Christ shall be brought to pass by the power of God. For, as in the beginning, every creature had his being by the word of God, so shall it be in the Day of Judgment. God shall but speak the word, and all reasonable creatures, living and dead, though many thousands [of] years before, shall present themselves before Him to give an account of all the actions done in this life.

Second, when all men and angels are set before the presence of Christ, then every work that they have done shall be made manifest, even the most secret works of all. "God will bring every secret thing to light" (Eccl. 12:14). And if anyone thinks it strange, we must know that God has books of record, wherein all men's thoughts, words, and deeds (good or bad, secret or open) are enrolled. And Daniel speaks of these when he says that he "saw the Ancient of Days, and the books laid open" (Dan. 7:9–10). We may not imagine that these are material books, like to the registers of men, or the books of captains in the field, wherein are set down the names of their soldiers and their expenses. But by these books we must understand, first of all, the infinite knowledge and providence of God; [and,] second, the consciences of men to testify of our doings, and be as a thousand witnesses.[114]

The third thing that is done in this account is the trial of every man's work in respect of obedience or disobedience. The trial shall be made by the will of God, revealed partly in the law and partly in the gospel, which is the rule to discern good and evil works.[115]

The fourth and last action is the giving of reward to every man according to his works. He who has been a faithful servant shall hear the voice of Christ, saying unto him: "It is well done thou good and faithful servant; thou hast been faithful in a little, enter into thy master's joy" (Matt. 25:21). But he who has been unfaithful or unjust in the works of his calling shall hear the same voice of Christ, saying, "Take him, bind him hand and foot, and cast him into outer darkness" (Matt. 25:20).

And thus we see what this account shall be.

---

113. This paragraph break is not in the original.
114. This paragraph break is not in the original.
115. This paragraph break is not in the original.

Point 2
Now then, let us a little search how we may be able to make a good account before God at the last day. For the doing whereof, we must take a reckoning of ourselves in the time of our life. For in common experience we see that such as desire to make just reckonings with others do reckon first with themselves. In this reckoning, three things must be done.[116]

First, we must draw out the bill of our receipts and expenses. The bills of receipt are framed thus: we must call to remembrance what graces, blessings, and gifts we have received from God, whether temporal or spiritual. For temporal blessings, we must thoroughly bethink us of our peace, health, wealth, liberty, and good name, and all things of this kind. For things spiritual, we must consider what knowledge, faith, hope, love, and repentance God has bestowed upon us, as also what gifts we have received for the discharge of our callings, yea of all other things that we have enjoyed, we must take a just and full receipt. For they are the talents of our Lord, and He looks for a reckoning. This done, we are next to frame our bills of expenses, which are nothing else but large considerations of our own sins, calling them all to our remembrance, as much as we can, whether committed against God or man, with all the abuses of our gifts, all our ignorance, negligence, and frailties whatsoever.[117]

Tradesmen, for their temporal estates, keep books of receipts and expenses in their shops. Shall we not, then, much more do the like for our spiritual estates? Job says, "If he dispute with God, he cannot answer one word for a thousand" (Job 9:3). Whereby he insinuates thus much, that he had looked into the whole course of his life, and had found even thousands of sins in himself. When the prophet David says, "Who knoweth the errors of this life" (Ps. 19:12), he signifies that he had exercised himself in searching out his own offences and transgressions. Ezra could not have said that "his sins, and the sins of the people, were as a huge mountain" (Ezra 9:6) but that he first took a narrow account of his own life and of the lives of the people. And so every one of us must do for all the things that ever we did. The consideration of our earthly matters makes us know our worldly estate, and so will the consideration of our daily offences and our spiritual estate give us some light and knowledge how the case will stand with us when we shall appear before the great God of all the world, to give up our account.

Second, when these two bills of our accounts are made, we must consider in the next place whether we are able to make an even reckoning with God or not. Thus doing, we shall find that our reckonings will be far short of that which

116. This paragraph break is not in the original.
117. This paragraph break is not in the original.

God requires at our hands. There are few who think on these things, for men commonly persuade themselves that all shall go well with them at the Day of Judgment, and that they shall make a short and easy reckoning because God is merciful. It is hard to find men whose hearts are touched, or their eyes open to see and believe, first, that they must make an account, and, second, that they are utterly unable to do it (as Job was, who could not excuse one of a thousand of his offences before God). Let us, therefore, labor to see our uneven and scant reckonings, and to shake off that spiritual drowsiness which possesses our minds, so that we cannot so much as say, what have I done, or how stands the case between God and me?[118]

Third, when we have attained to this knowledge that we are unable to make a just reckoning with God, we must cleave to our surety Christ Jesus, the only Son of God, God and man. And for the time of this life, we must humble ourselves before God, and pray unto Him that He would accept the only satisfaction of Christ in His death and passion as a sufficient payment for all our sins and wants whatsoever. For thus we are taught to pray: "Forgive us our debts" [Matt. 6:12].[119]

And we must not only be hearers of these things, but doers also. And the better to persuade us to the practice of these three duties, let us consider that this account at the last day shall be a straight account. For as Christ says, "We must give an account of every idle word" [Matt. 12:36]. And Saint Paul says, "The law is a handwriting of condemnation" [Col. 2:14], that is, a bill of our own hand against us. For by the law we are debtors to God. And either we must fulfill the justice thereof, or else, according to the tenor of the law, undergo eternal judgment, unless we are acquitted by the obedience of a Mediator. If we think to escape this account by absenting ourselves, we are deceived. For then not so much as one man in all the world shall be wanting. Many shall then wish with all their hearts that hills and mountains would fall upon them and grind them to powder, that they might be hid from the presence of the Lord. But that will not serve. All without exception must needs come to this account, not one shall be freed.[120]

And we may not think that Christ will either not know or not remember our particular offences. We usually make fair weather with men, and keep close our doings from the eyes of the world. But the Lord will descry our most secret sins. There is no want of knowledge (or discerning) in Him. He can find out Adam, though he is in the thicket of Paradise, and descry him in the midst

118. This paragraph break is not in the original.
119. This paragraph break is not in the original.
120. This paragraph break is not in the original.

of his fig leaves. At this great day of account, every secret thing shall be made manifest. What then shall we do?[121]

Some men plead that they are no great sinners. They are no whoremongers, adulterers, blasphemers, or thieves. And, therefore, they hope to make an account good enough. But (alas) this is a fond and poor excuse, for the wages of the least sin is death. And he who breaks the law but once, and that in thought only, is guilty of eternal condemnation. And, therefore, it will not go for payment to say we are no great sinners as other men are. What then shall we say? That we have walked in our callings, and always had a good meaning, and did no man hurt, and therefore we hope that God will be merciful? This indeed is the common excuse, but it is no sufficient payment with God, for as Saint John says, "The axe is laid to the root of the tree" (Matt. 3:10). And he says not further that every tree shall stand which brings not forth bad fruit, but "every tree that bringeth not forth good fruit shall be cut down and cast into the fire." In a word, let us devise what we can, it will not serve the turn.[122]

Will you make up your reckoning with almsdeeds and good works, according to the opinion of many who look to be saved by their works? But they are no current payment in this account, because one breach of the law mars all the good works we do. And he who will be justified by works is bound to fulfill the whole law in the rigor thereof. Beside this, the best works we do, are in themselves defiled in the sight of God. What then shall we do? Shall we undergo the curse of the law? Some of a desperate mind say, "If the worst come, there is but one out of the way." But far be it from us to think or speak thus. For the curse of the law, and the wrath of God, is most horrible and eternal, without rest or ease. All the fire in the world laid together is but ice in regard of that spiritual and eternal fire of hell. Thus, then, having turned ourselves every way, and finding no help in anything, we must flee unto our Surety Christ Jesus, who was content to stand in our room upon the cross, and there to shed His blood for the redemption of our sins.

Thus, in this life, while the day of grace remains, we are to make reckoning aforehand with ourselves in our own person, never resting till we have assurance in our consciences that the books in heaven are cancelled, and that God is content to account of Christ's satisfaction as a payment for our sins. And this being done, we shall be able to make a good account before the Lord at the last Day of Judgment.

Finis.

---

121. This paragraph break is not in the original.
122. This paragraph break is not in the original.

Christian Oeconomie

or

A Short Survey of the Right Manner of Erecting and Ordering a Family, According to the Scriptures

First written in Latin by the author, M. W. Perkins, and now set forth in the vulgar tongue, for more common use and benefit, by Tho. Pickering, Bachelor of Divinity.

"Through wisdom is a house builded, and with understanding it is established. And by knowledge shall the chambers be filled with all precious and pleasant riches" (Prov. 24:3–4).

Printed by Felix Kingston,
and are to be sold by Edmund Weaver

London
1609

The Epistle Dedicatory

To the Right Honorable, Robert Lord Rich, Baron of Leez,[1] etc.

Right Honorable, among all the societies and states, whereof the whole world of mankind has existed from the first calling of Adam in Paradise unto this day, the family is the first and most ancient. For if we look into the Scriptures, the writings of Moses (which go beyond all the histories and records of men in time) do evidently declare [that] it was the will of God to sanctify that first conjunction of Adam and Eve as the root wherein man's whole posterity was virtually contained, and whence in the ages succeeding both church and commonwealth should spring and grow to their perfection. And all those nations and countries before the flood, the heads whereof lineally descended from the first two houses of Seth and Cain, had no outward form of civil government by which they were ruled, nor any visible face of a church whereto they had relation, but the whole frame of their policy (both civil and ecclesiastical) was confined within the precincts of private families. And from the flood, the house of Noah became the common mother, in which the other two states were included, and out of whose bowels they issued afterward in the multiplication of posterity, for number equal to the stars of the sky and the sands of the seashore.

Answerable to the voice of the Scripture has been the verdict of the heathen in this point. Some of the learned among them have called the family, "the first society in nature, and the ground of all the rest."[2] Some again have compared it to the beehive,[3] which we call the stock, wherein are bred many swarms, which thence do fly abroad into the world, to the raising and maintaining of other

1. Lord Rich of Rochford, Earl of Essex. He was a protector of the Puritans. He hired Robert Wright as domestic chaplain and protected him from danger as long as he lived. His son, Robert Rich, studied at Emmanuel and was very involved with Puritans in the Long Parliament. Benjamin Brook, *The Lives of the Puritans*, 3 vols. (1813; reprint, Morgan, Pa.: Soli Deo Gloria Publications, 1994), 1:239; *Dictionary of National Biography*, 22 vols. (London: Oxford University Press, 1917–1921), 16:1014.

2. In the margin: Aristot. Politic. 1.

3. In the margin: Xenoph. in Oecon.

states. Others do not unfitly resemble the same to a metropolis, or mother city,[4] which first trains up her native inhabitants, and then removes some of them to other places of abode, where they may be framed as members to live in obedience to the laws of their head.

Upon this condition of the family, being the seminary of all other societies, it follows that the holy and righteous government thereof is a direct means for the good ordering both of church and commonwealth; yea, that the laws thereof, being rightly informed and religiously observed, are available to prepare and dispose men to the keeping of order in other governments. Hence it is that the Holy Spirit, in the book of the Scriptures, has in great wisdom commended both rules for direction and examples for imitation to husbands and wives, to parents and children, to masters and servants, in every point of Christian carriage touching God and man. For this first society is (as it were) the school wherein the principles of authority and subjection are taught and learned. And look as the superior who fails in his private charge will prove incapable of public employment [1 Tim. 3:5], so the inferior (who is not framed to a course of oeconomical subjection) will hardly undergo the yoke of civil obedience.

Again, the corruption or declination of this first government must of necessity give way to the ruination of the rest. For an error in the foundation puts the body and parts of the whole building in apparent hazard. In the old world, before the flood, though all flesh had corrupted their ways [Gen. 6:12], yet the first ground of that universal overflow of sin issued out of the oeconomical state, and thence was derived into the whole earth. It was the fault of the private government of Eli, the priest, who made his sons, Hophni and Phineas, of ungracious children, ungodly churchmen [1 Sam. 2:12, 23–25]. It was the error of David in the administration and guidance of his own, which encouraged his sons, Absalom and Adonijah, upon presumption of their father's indulgence, to become ill commonwealth's men, to aspire and usurp the kingdom by plots and practices of rebellion [2 Samuel 14–15; 1 Kings 1, 5].

To forebear further matter of instance in this kind, by the due consideration of premises, I hold it a thing both necessary and behoveful for all estates, to be thoroughly informed of the right manner of erecting and ordering the private condition of the family, whereby they may be furnished with fit grounds for the common good in more public and open courses. For which end this present discourse of *Christian Oeconomie* was first contrived by the author, and now thought fit to be set forth for the instruction and edification of the multitude. As it commends itself by its shortness and perspicuity, both [of] which,

4. In the margin: Xenoph. ibid.

being applied to [the] understanding and memory, may give contentment to every well-disposed reader, so it carries a kind eminency above other treatises of this nature before published in sundry regards.

First, whereas experience teaches that the questions of conscience in matrimonial affairs are very many in number and difficult in nature, here we shall find either direct answers to some of them or at least the grounds of resolution in divers cases, warranted by the Word, in such sort as little or nothing will appear upon trial to be untouched, making for the reader's satisfaction.

Second, the main scope of the author in the several branches hereof is to make plain this truth in particular, that no family can be interested in the blessing and favor of God which is not founded in His fear, and ordered according to His revealed will. For though the heathen, in their writings of the like argument,[5] do show that nature, by her dim light, may afford some good directions to this purpose, and that merely natural men have prospered in the practice of oeconomical virtues, yet the true happiness of houses and inhabitants wholly depends upon the special grace of God, and issues out of His promise. And it is directed only "to them that fear him and walk in his ways" [Ps. 128:1]. It is godliness alone which "hath the promises of this life and the life to come" [1 Tim. 4:8]. Therefore, to dream of a blessing in any other state which is not seasoned with godliness, and ordered by direction of divine law, is but a witless presumption, considering that the family itself, from whence they grow, has no further assurance of blessedness than it has right and title in the promise.

Lastly, it contains here and there some special grounds of truth tending to the discovery of divers errors of popish doctrine in points appertaining to marriage, as namely these:

(1) This estate is free to all men, even to such as have the gift of continence. And for those who have not the power to abstain, it is expressly enjoined by God as necessary [1 Cor. 7:1–2, 8–9]. This discovers that error of absolute inhibition thereof to some sorts of men, without the least exception of ability to forebear. And in this case, though the Church of Rome prescribes a help by prayer and endeavor, where the gift is wanting, yet herein she adds two more absurdities to the former [by] imposing a necessity of containing by her law where God has given liberty by His Word, and causing to flee from that only remedy, which [He] Himself has sanctified, to another, whereunto He neither gives charge by His will nor encouragement by promise.

(2) Marriages, consummated without the free and advised consent of parents, either explicit in terms or implicit by convenience, are in the court of

5. In the margin: Aristot. Politic. Xenoph. in Oecon.

conscience mere nullities, a doctrine cleared in this book, both by Scriptures and by consent of antiquity. Wherein is challenged the Jesuits' proposition that the sole consent of the parties is sufficient, *ad matrimonium firmum ac ratum efficiendum*.[6] As also that decree of the Council of Trent, which professes a detestation of clandestine contracts, and yet with the same breath pronounces the curse of "anathema" upon them who affirm that parents may ratify or make void marriages, contracted by their children, without their allowance.[7]

(3) Matrimony, lawfully begun and consummated, is made void only by way of divorce in the case of adultery. Our Savior says so: "Whosoever shall put away his wife, except it be for fornication, etc." [Matt. 5:32]. And this liberty, granted by Christ both to dissolve and to marry again, cannot be restrained or cut off by any human ordinance, a point directly impugned by two other rules of that Council. First, that the Church of Rome errs not when she teaches (as they profess, *Juxta Evangelicam & Apostolicam doctrinam*, but in truth expressly contradictory thereunto),[8] that the knot of marriage cannot be broken because of adultery, and that neither party may undertake to be married again during the life of the other after the dismission. Second, that the vow of chastity and entering into holy orders is of force to loosen the bond of marriage. And, in this case, separation is made and allowed *de facto* by the sole authority of the pope, notwithstanding the refusal of the settled party to yield consent.

(4) The judgment and determination of causes matrimonial, as contracts and their impediments, degrees of kindred, divorces, etc., rests originally in the civil magistrate, in whose power it is to ordain and establish laws touching them, agreeable to God's Word, and to cause them to be put in execution. For this purpose, in doubtful and difficult cases, the ancient church has not absolutely rested in her own decrees, but has made recourse to the seat of justice, especially under Christian magistrates, submitting herself to their laws and constitutions in that kind.[9] Whereas the Church of Rome has determined that these causes do simply and only appertain to ecclesiastical judges, and therefore [it] has concluded marriage to be a sacrament, that the definition of cases conjugal, becoming, upon this ground, an action of a spiritual nature, might be transferred from the civil to their spiritual courts.[10] The sovereignty whereof, in these affairs, by their own constitutions, is greatly enlarged. For though they admit that political princes have some interest in them, yet they must hold it

6. In the margin: Bellarm. de Matrim. Sacram. Libr. c. 19.
7. In the margin: Concil. Trid. sess. 24. Decreto declandest. Matrim.
8. In the margin: Concil. Trid. sess. 24. can. 7.
9. In the margin: See the *Code* in sundry places. Lib. 5. tit. 4 de nuptiis, tit. 5, de incesto, etc.
10. In the margin: Council. Trid. sess. 24. can. 12.

with subordination to the authority of the church magistrate.[11] And when the rector of the province makes a law hereof, he must do it *approbante principe ecclesiatico*, by the allowance of the pope. Otherwise, his laws are mere nullities. And among their reasons of policy, this is one principal, that they might by this means raise a commodity to the See of Rome by the sale of their dispensations.

Now these points, together with the substance of this small discourse, I willingly commend unto your Lordship, desiring that under the wings of your Honorable protection, it may safely walk abroad in the world to the view and benefit of others. The true report of your ancient love of the truth, and favorable inclination to the ministers and dispensers thereof, has given me encouragement in this action. The rather, for that the argument sets in some sort your present estate, whose house God has adorned with olive plants [Ps. 128:3], a virtuous and hopeful issue, whose young years, being seasoned therein by the sweet savor of their father's virtues, may yield in time a plentiful increase of honor in this commonwealth, and consequently advance your name in themselves and their posterity. To this may be added my own desire to give some testimony of duty to your Lordship, as holding it your due to be had in honorable terms with men, whose care has been to maintain the honor of the Highest by your constant profession and practice of religion. And thus, emboldening myself upon the persuasion of your Lordship's favor and acceptance, I humbly take my leave, and commend you to the grace of God [Acts 20:32], who is able to build you up further, and give you an inheritance among them who are sanctified.

Your Lordship's to be commanded in all Christian duty,
Tho. Pickering

Finchingfield, September 26, 1609

---

11. In the margin: Bellarm. de Matrim. Sacram. cap. 32.

A Short Survey of the Right Manner of Erecting and Ordering a Family, According to the Scriptures

Chapter 1

Christian Oeconomie and the Family

Christian Oeconomie is a doctrine of the right ordering of a family.

The only rule of ordering the family is the written Word of God. By it, David resolved to govern his house, when he says, "I will walk in the uprightness of my heart in the midst of my house" (Ps. 101:2). And Solomon affirms that "through wisdom a house is builded, and with understanding it is established" (Prov. 24:3).

A family is a natural and simple society of certain persons, having mutual relation to one another under the private government of one. These persons must be at the least three, because two cannot make a society. And above three under the same head, there may be a thousand in one family, as it is in the households of princes, and men of state in the world.

Chapter 2

The Household Service of God

A family, for the good estate of itself, is bound to the performance of two duties: one to God [and] the other to itself.

Duty 1

The duty unto God is the private worship and service of God, which must be established and settled in every family. And the reasons hereof are these.

First, this duty stands by the express commandment of God, who by His apostle wills men "to pray everywhere, lifting up pure hands, without wrath or doubting" (1 Tim. 2:8).

Second, it is confirmed by the custom and practice of holy men in their times. "I know," says the Lord touching Abraham, "that he will command his sons and his household after him, that they keep the way of the Lord to do righteousness and judgment, that the Lord may bring upon Abraham, that which he hath spoken to him" (Gen. 18:19). Joshua speaks to the same purpose: "If it seem evil unto you to serve the Lord, choose this day whom ye will serve, whether the gods whom your fathers served (who were beyond the flood) or the gods of the Amorites in whose land ye dwell: But I and my house will serve the Lord" (Josh. 24:15). And Cornelius is reported to have been "a devout man, and one that feared God with all his household" (Acts 10:2).

Third, common reason and equity show it to be a necessary duty for the happy and prosperous estate of the family, which consists in the mutual love and agreement of the man and wife, in the dutiful obedience of children to their parents, and in the faithful service of servants to their masters. [It] wholly depends upon the grace and blessing of God, and this blessing is annexed to His worship. "Godliness hath the promises of this life, and the life to come" (1 Tim. 4:8). "Except the Lord build the house, they labor in vain that build; except the Lord keep the city, the keeper watcheth in vain. It is in vain for you to rise early, and to lie down late, and eat the bread of sorrow, but he will surely give rest to his beloved. Behold, children are the inheritance of Jehovah, and the fruit of the womb his reward" (Ps. 127:1–3). "Blessed is everyone that feareth the Lord, and walketh in his ways. When thou eatest the labors of thy hands thou shalt be blessed, and it shall be well with thee. Thy wife shall be as the fruitful vine upon the sides of thy house, and thy children like olive plants round about thy table.... Yea, thou shalt see thy children's children, and peace upon Israel" (Ps. 128:1–2, 6). "I prayed," says Hannah, "for this child, and the Lord hath given me my desire which I asked of him" (1 Sam. 1:27).

The household service of God has two parts. The first is a conference upon the Word of God for the edification of all the members thereof to eternal life. The second is invocation of the name of God with giving of thanks for His benefits. Both [of] these are commended in the Scriptures. "These words which I command thee this day, shall be in thy heart. And thou shalt whet them upon thy children, and talk of them when thou tarriest in thine house, and as thou walkest by the way, and when thou liest down, and when thou risest up.... When thy son shall ask thee in time to come, saying, what mean these testimonies, and ordinances, and laws, which the Lord our God hath commanded you? Then thou shalt say unto thy son, we were Pharaoh's bondmen in Egypt, but the Lord brought us out of Egypt with a mighty hand.... Therefore, the Lord hath commanded us to do all these ordinances, and to fear the Lord our God" (Deut. 6:6–7, 20–21, 24). "The fool hath said in his heart, There is no God.... They call not upon God" (Ps. 14:1, 4).

The times of this service are these: the morning, in which the family, coming together in one place, is to call upon the name of the Lord before they begin the works of their callings. The evening also is another time to be used in prayer, because the family has seen the blessing of God upon their labors the day before, and now the time of rest draws on, in which everyone is to commend his body and soul into the protection of the Lord. For no man knows what shall befall him before he rises again, neither knows any whether he shall rise again or not. It is, therefore, a desperate boldness to go to rest without praying.

Besides this, there are other times wherein to perform this duty, as before and after meals. For meats and drinks are blessed to the receivers by the Word and prayer. "Whatsoever God hath created is good, neither is anything to be refused, if it be taken with thanksgiving, for it is sanctified by the word of God and prayer" (1 Tim. 4:4–5).

Now, the Word of God approves these times: "Thou shalt talk of them when thou liest down, and when thou risest up" (Deut. 6:6). "Evening and morning and at noon, I will pray and make a noise, and he will hear my voice" (Ps. 55:17). "It is in vain to rise early, and to lie down late, and eat the bread of sorrow," except the Lord vouchsafe a blessing, "who will surely give rest to his beloved" (Ps. 127:2).

To these may sometimes be added the exercise of fasting, which is (as occasion serves) to be used both publicly and privately, especially when they of the family are thereunto called by some present or imminent calamity. "Go and assemble all the Jews that are found in Shushan, and fast ye for me, and eat not, nor drink in three days, day nor night: I also and my maids will fast likewise, and so will I go in to the king, which is not according to the law; and if I perish, I perish" (Esth. 4:16). "And in that day shall there be a great mourning in Jerusalem, and the land shall bewail, every family apart, the family of the house of David apart, and their wives apart, the family of the house of Nathan apart, and their wives apart, etc." (Zech. 12:11).

Wherefore, those families, wherein this service of God is performed, are (as it were) little churches, yea even a kind of paradise upon earth. And for this purpose, Saint Paul, writing to Philemon, greets "the church that is in his house" (Philemon 1:2). And in like manner, he sends salutations to the church of Corinth from Aquila and Priscilla, and "the church which was in their house" (1 Cor. 16:19). On the other side, where this duty of God's service is not used, but either for the most part or altogether neglected, a man may term those families no better than companies of profane and graceless atheists, who as they deny God in their hearts, so they are known by this note, that "they do not call upon the name of the Lord" (Ps. 14:4). Yea, such families are fitly compared to a herd of swine, which are always feeding upon the mast with greediness, but never look up to the hand that beats it down nor to the tree from whence it falls.

Duty 2

The other duty concerning the house itself is that every member in the family, according to their ability, employ themselves in some honest and profitable business, to maintain the temporal estate and life of the whole. "In the sweat of thy face shalt thou eat bread, till thou return to the earth, for out of it wast thou taken; for dust thou art, and to dust shalt thou return" (Gen. 3:19). "Let every man abide in the same vocation wherein he was called" (1 Cor. 7:20). Now if anyone in the family starts aside out of his calling, and entices another to idolatry, he is to be revealed (Deut. 13:6). And again, their case is very fearful, who do nothing in their houses but go finely and fare daintily from day to day. This is the black mark that the Scripture sets upon the rich glutton. "There was a certain rich man, which was clothed in purple and fine linen, and fared deliciously every day" (Luke 16:19).

Chapter 3

Married Folks

A family is distinguished into sundry combinations (or couples) of persons. A couple is that whereby two persons, standing in mutual relation to each other, are combined together (as it were) in one. And of these two, the one is always higher and bears rule [while] the other is lower and yields subjection.

Couples are of two sorts: principal or less principal.

The principal is the combination of married folks, and these are so termed in respect of marriage.

Marriage is the lawful conjunction of the two married persons; that is, of one man and one woman into one flesh. So was the first institution of marriage (Gen. 2:21), which is expounded by our Savior Christ, "Therefore they are no more two, but one flesh" (Matt. 19:6), and also by Paul, "For this cause shall a man leave father and mother, and shall cleave[1] unto his wife (as two boards are joined together with glue), and they which were two, shall be one flesh" (Eph. 5:31). Wherefore, this is an eternal law of marriage, that two (and not three or four) shall be one flesh. And for this cause, the fathers, who had many wives and concubines, [though] it may be that (through custom) they sinned of ignorance, yet they are not in any way to be excused.

Marriage of itself is a thing indifferent, and the kingdom of God stands no more in it than in meats and drinks. And yet, it is a state in itself far more excellent than the condition of single life. For, first, it was ordained by God in Paradise, above and before all other states of life, in Adam's innocency before the fall. Second, it was instituted upon a most serious and solemn consultation among the three Persons in the Holy Trinity. "Let us make man in our image, according to our likeness, and let them rule over, etc." (Gen. 1:26). "Jehovah Elohim said, It is not good that the man should be himself alone, I will make him an help meet for him" (Gen. 2:18). Third, the manner of this conjunction was excellent, for God joined our first parents, Adam and Eve, together immediately. Fourth, God gave a large blessing unto the estate of marriage,

1. In the margin: Προσκελ. Ληθησετας.

saying, "Increase and multiply and fill the earth."[2] Lastly, marriage was made and appointed by God Himself to be the fountain and seminary of all other sorts and kinds of life in the commonwealth and in the church.

Now if mankind had continued in that uprightness and integrity which he had by creation, the state of single life had been of no price and estimation among men, neither should it have had any place in the world without great contempt of God's ordinance and blessing.

Nevertheless, since the fall, to some men, who have the gift of continency, it is in many respects far better than marriage, yet not simply, but only by accident in regard of sundry calamities which came into the world by sin. For, first, it frees a man from many and great cares of household affairs. Second, it makes him much more fit and disposed to meditate of heavenly things without distraction of mind. Besides that, when dangers are either present or imminent, in matters belonging to this life, the single person is in this case happy because he and his are more secure and safe than others who are in [a] married state. "Therefore, I say to the unmarried and widows, It is good for them if they abide even as I do" (1 Cor. 7:8). "I suppose then this to be good for the present necessity, I mean, that it is good for a man so to be" (v. 26). "But if thou takest a wife thou sinnest not, and if a virgin marry she sinneth not; nevertheless such shall have trouble in the flesh" (v. 28). "And I should have you without care" (v. 32).

The end of marriage is fourfold.

The first is procreation of children for the propagation and continuance of the seed and posterity of man upon the earth. "Bring forth fruit, multiply, fill the earth, and subdue it" (Gen. 1:28). [See] Gen. 9:1; 1 Tim. 5:14.

The second is the procreation of a holy seed whereby the church of God may be kept holy and chaste, and there may always be a holy company of men who may worship and serve God in the church from age to age. "And did not he make one? Yet had he abundance of spirit; and wherefore one? Because he sought a godly seed" (Mal. 2:15).

The third is that, after the fall of mankind, it might be a sovereign means to avoid fornication, and consequently to subdue and slake the burning lusts of the flesh. "Nevertheless for the avoiding of fornication, let every man have his wife, and every woman have her husband" (1 Cor. 7:2). "But if they cannot abstain, let them marry; for it is better to marry than to burn" (v. 9). And for this cause, some schoolmen do err, who hold that the secret coming together of man and wife cannot be without sin unless it is done for procreation of children.

2. Gen. 1:28.

Lombard, the master of the *Sentences*, says the contrary, namely, "that marriage before the fall was only a duty, but now since the fall it is also a remedy."

The fourth end is that the married parties may thereby perform the duties of their callings in [a] better and more comfortable manner. "The heart of her husband trusteth her, and he shall have no need of spoil" (Prov. 31:11). "She seeketh wool and flax, and laboreth cheerfully with her hands" (v. 13).

Marriage is free to all orders and sorts of men without exception, even to those who have the gift of continency. But for them who cannot abstain, it is, by the express commandment of God, necessary. "Marriage is honorable amongst all men, and the bed undefiled" (Heb. 13:4). "But if they cannot abstain, let them marry" (1 Cor. 7:9).

By which it appears to be a clear case that the commandment of the pope of Rome, whereby he forbids [the] marriage of certain persons (as namely, of clergymen), is merely diabolical, for so writes the apostle: "The spirit speaketh evidently, that in the latter times some shall depart from the faith, and shall give heed unto spirits of error, and doctrines of devils...forbidding to marry" (1 Tim. 4:1, 3).

But sundry things are alleged against this doctrine.

Objection 1. The apostle commands the married, among the Corinthians, "to abstain with consent for a time, that they might give themselves to fasting and prayer" (1 Cor. 7:5). *Answer.* Paul speaks not in that place of daily and common service of God in prayer, but of the solemn and extraordinary exercise thereof, which was joined with fasting and abstinence in common dangers and calamities.

Objection 2. "He that is unmarried careth for the things of the Lord, how he may please the Lord; but the married person careth for the things of the world" (1 Cor. 7:32). *Answer.* The place is not to be understood generally of all, but indefinitely of those married persons who are carnal and fleshly. And he who is married is to be so careful for the things of the world as that he also ought [to] (and may) have a special regard of those things that concern God and His kingdom.

Objection 3. "The younger widows will marry, having damnation because they have broken the first faith" (1 Tim. 5:11). *Answer.* By "the first faith," Paul understands that promise and vow which they made unto Christ when they were baptized. And they are there said "to begin to wax wanton against Christ" by denying or renouncing that faith, and not otherwise.

Objection 4. He who does earnestly, and from his heart, crave the gift of continency, God will give it to him, and therefore he need not marry. *Answer.* The gifts of God are of two sorts: some are general [and] some are proper. General gifts are such as God gives generally to all, and these may be obtained if they are asked lawfully according to God's Word. "If any of you lack wisdom, let him ask it of God, who giveth to all men liberally, and reproacheth no man, and it shall be given him. But let him ask in faith, and waver not" (James 1:5–6). Proper gifts are those which are given only to some certain men. Of this sort is the gift of continency and such like, which though they are often and earnestly asked, yet they are seldom or never granted unto some men. This appears in Paul's example, who, being "buffeted by Satan," says of himself: "For this thing I besought the Lord thrice, that it might depart from me; but he said unto me, My grace is sufficient for thee" (2 Cor. 12:8–9).

Chapter 4

The Contract

Marriage has two distinct parts: first, the beginning; [and,] second, the accomplishment or consummation thereof.

The beginning is the contract or espousals. The end (or accomplishment) is the solemn manifestation of the contract, by that which properly we call marriage. "What man is there that hath betrothed a wife, and hath not taken her? Let him go and return again unto his house, lest he die in battle and another man take her" (Deut. 20:7). "When his mother Mary was betrothed to Joseph, before they came together, she was found with child of the Holy Ghost" (Matt. 1:18).

Between the contract and marriage, there ought to be some certain space or distance of time. The reasons whereof may be these: First, a business of so great importance (as this is) should not be attempted rashly or unadvisedly, but should rather be done by degrees in process of time, according to that saying, not so ancient as true: "Actions of weight, before resolution, require mature deliberation."[1] Second, during such a space, inquiry may be made whether there is any just cause that may hinder the consummation of marriage. [We must] consider that, before the parties come and converse together, what is amiss may be remedied and amended. It will be too late to do this afterward. Third, in these cases, persons espoused must have regard of honesty as well as of necessity, not presently upon the contract seeking to satisfy their own fleshly desires after the manner of brute beasts, but proceeding therein upon mature deliberation.

The contract is a mention or mutual promise of future marriage before fit and competent judges and witnesses.

The best manner of giving this promise is to make it in words touching the present time,[2] and simply without any exception or condition expressed or conceived. For by this means it comes to pass that the bond is made the surer, and the ground or foundation of future marriage the better laid. And hence alone it is that the persons betrothed in Scripture are termed "man and wife." Jacob,

1. In the margin: *Diu deliberandum quod semel statuendum.*

2. In the margin: *In verbis de praesenti tempore.*

speaking of Rachel, who was only betrothed unto him, says to Laban: "Give me my wife" (Gen. 29:21). "If a maid be betrothed to a husband, and a man find her in the town, and lie with her, then shall ye bring them both out unto the gates of city, and shall stone them with stones to death, the maid, because she cried not, being in the city, and the man, because he hath humbled his neighbor's wife" (Deut. 22:23). "Joseph, fear not to take Mary thy wife" (Matt. 1:20).

Now if the promise is uttered in [the] words "for time to come,"[3] it does not precisely bind the parties to performance. For example, if one of them says to the other, "N. I will take you, etc." and not, "N. I do take you, etc.," by this form of speech the match is not made, but only promised to be made afterwards. But if on the other side it is said, "N. I do take you," and not, "N. I will take you," by these terms the marriage at that very instant is begun, though not in regard of fact,[4] yet in regard of right and interest which the parties have each in another in deed and truth. And this is the common opinion of the learned. Yet notwithstanding, if the contracting parties shall say to each other, "I will take you to, etc.," with intention to bind themselves at the present, the bond is in conscience precisely made before God, and so the contract is indeed made for the present time[5] before God. It is true that he who stands to his promise made, as much as in him lies, does well. Yet, if the promise has or conceives some just cause why he should afterward change his purpose, the contract expressed in terms for time to come, though it were formerly made and confirmed by oath, must notwithstanding give place to the contract made for time present.

Those espousals which are made upon condition, which is honest, possible, and belonging to marriage, do cease or depend, so far forth as the condition annexed ceases or depends. For example, if the one party promises to marry the other upon condition that his or her kinsman will yield consent to the match, or upon condition of a dowry that she shall bring unto him, suitable to her education and the family whereof she comes, these conditions, being kept or not kept, the promise does likewise stand or not stand.

But those conditions which are necessarily understood, or which may certainly be kept and come to pass, do neither hinder nor suspend marriage. As this: "I promise you marriage, if I live; or, I promise to marry you, if the sun rises tomorrow."

Again, conditions that are either impossible or dishonest are not to be accounted as promises annexed in way of marriage.[6] Of which sort are these:

---

3. In the margin: *In futurum.*
4. In the margin: *Non de facto, de juro.*
5. In the margin: *De praesenti.*
6. In the margin: *In favorem matrimonii.*

"I will be your wife, if you will take unto you wings and fly, or if you will bring an untimely birth."

Furthermore, if the betrothed parties do lie together before the condition (though honest and appertaining to marriage) is performed, then the contract for time to come is, without further controversy, sure and certain. For where there has been a carnal use of each other's body, it is always presupposed that a mutual consent, as touching marriage, has gone before.

Chapter 5

The Choice of Persons Fit for Marriage

For the making of a contract, two things are requisite: the choice and the consent of the parties. Choice is an enquiry after marriageable persons. Marriageable persons are such as are fit and able for the married state. This fitness (or ability) is known and discerned by certain signs, which are either essential or accidental to the contract.

Part 1: Essential Marks

An essential sign is that without which the contract in hand becomes a mere nullity. And of this sort there are principally five.

Mark 1

The first is the distinction of the sex, which is either male or female. The male is man of a superior sex, fit for procreation. The female is woman of an inferior sex, fit to conceive and bear children. "The man ought not to cover his head; for as much as he is the image and glory of God; but the woman is the glory of the man" (1 Cor. 11:7). "I permit not the woman to teach, neither to usurp authority over the man, but to be in silence" (1 Tim. 2:12). By this distinction is condemned that unnatural and monstrous sin of uncleanness between parties of the same sex [Rom. 1:26], commonly termed sodomy, as also the confusion of the kinds[1] of creatures, when one kind commits filthiness and abomination with another (Lev. 18:22–23).

Mark 2

The second sign is the just and lawful distance of blood.

Distance of blood is just and lawful when neither of the persons, who are to be married, do come near to the kindred of their flesh or to the flesh of their flesh, for so the Scripture speaks: "No man shall come near to any of the flesh of his flesh (or, to the kindred of his flesh)" (Lev. 18:6). Here it is to be observed that by a man's "flesh" is meant that substance which is of himself or whereof

1. In the margin: Species.

[he] himself consists. And by the "flesh of his flesh" [is meant] that which next and immediately issues out of that flesh whereof he consists. Whereupon it follows that the touching or coming near of flesh to flesh is not spoken of strangers but only of those who are of kindred.

Kindred is of two sorts: consanguinity or affinity.

Consanguinity

Kindred in consanguinity are those who issue from one and the same common blood or stock. And there are certain degrees whereby kinsmen of this sort are distinguished from one another.

A degree is a generation or descent between two persons who are of the same blood. For one person cannot make a degree unless he is considered relatively in regard of generation.

Now many degrees, continued or derived from one and the same head, do make a line. And a line is twofold: (1) the right line, or (2) the overthwart, commonly termed collateral.

In the right line, look how many persons there are, so many degrees there are, that only excepted which upon occasion offered is in question and from which we begin the account.

Abraham
|
Isaac
|
Jacob
|
Joseph

Here Joseph is distant three degrees from Abraham, two [from] Isaac, [and] one from Jacob.

This right line is either ascending or descending.

The right line ascending is the race of all the ancestors, and it has sundry degrees. The first is the father and the mother. The second [is] the grandfather (both by the father's and mother's side, that is, the father of my father and the father of my mother), and the grandmother (that is to say, my father's and my mother's mother). The third is the great grandfather (or the father of my grandfather), and the great grandmother (or the mother of my grandfather). The fourth is the great grandfather's father, and the great grandfather's or grandmother's mother. The fifth is the great grandfather's grandfather, and the great grandfather's or great grandmother's grandmother. The sixth is the great, great grandfather's grandfather, and the great, great grandfather's or great, great grandmother's grandmother.

The right line descending is the race of a man's own posterity. And it also has sundry degrees. The first is the son and the daughter. The second [is] the nephew and the niece. The third [is] the nephew's son and the niece's daughter. The fourth is the nephew's nephew (or the son in the fourth degree of lineal descent), and the niece's niece (or the daughter in the same degree of descent). The fifth is he and she who are three lineal descents from the child's child. And so are the rest in their order, by whatever names they are called and known.

Now in this right line, whether ascending or descending, the person of whom the case or question is moved, comes near to the kindred of his flesh. And, therefore, marriages in this line are prohibited infinitely without any limitation. So as, if Adam himself were now alive, he could not marry by the law of God because he should come near to the kindred of his own flesh (as Moses speaks). The reason hereof is because in the right line superiors and inferiors are to each other as parents and children, and the kindred between parents and children, being the first and nearest of all other, their conjunction in marriage must needs be most unclean and repugnant unto nature.

The collateral (or crooked) line is that which walks by the sides of the right line, whether ascending or descending, in the row of the kindred. And it is either unequal or equal.

The unequal is that whereby the person in question and his kinsman are unequally distant from the common stock or head of the kindred.

And in this line, look how many degrees the kinsman, who is furthest off from the common stock, is distant from the same, so many is he and his kinsman in question distant one from the other. For example:

Terah
|
Abraham -------------- Nahor
|
Bethuel
|
Laban

Here Laban, being removed further off, to wit, three degrees from the common stock, Terah, is likewise three degrees distant from Abraham, his great uncle, and Abraham so many from him.

Furthermore, kinsmen in this line are of two sorts: (1) some are superiors to the person in question, [and] (2) some are inferiors to him.

Superiors are such as are kin to his father and mother, of some side, and that either nearer or further off.

Those who are of near kin to them are these: (1) The uncle of the father's side (or the father's brother), the aunt of the father's side (or father's sister). The uncle of the mother's side (or the mother's brother), and the aunt of the mother's side (or the mother's sister). (2) The great uncle (or grandfather's brother), and the great aunt (or grandfather's sister). The great uncle (or grandmother's brother), and the great aunt (or grandmother's sister). (3) The great uncle by the father's side (or great grandfather's brother), and the great aunt by the father's side (or great grandfather's sister). (4) The great grand-uncle by the father's side (or great grandfather's father's brother), and the great grand-aunt by the same side (or the great grandfather's father's sister). The great grand-uncle by the mother's side (or great grandmother's mother's brother), and the great grand aunt by the same side (or the great grandmother's mother's sister).

Now these, in regard of their inferiors, are in [the] stead of parents, and therefore do come near to the kindred of their flesh.

Those superiors who are of kindred to parents on the one side, afar off, are these: (1) The son and daughter of the great uncle (or aunt by the father's side), or the great uncle or aunt by the mother's side. (2) The nephew and niece of the great uncle or aunt by the father's side, or of the great uncle or aunt by the mother's side, near to the cozen-german.[2]

And these, as they stand in comparison with their inferiors, do not come near to the kindred of their flesh.[3]

The equal collateral line is that whereby kinsmen are equally distant from their head.

Kinsmen of this line are [these]: (1) Whole brothers, that is brothers by the same father and mother, or half-brothers, that is brothers by the same father but not by the same mother. Again, whole sisters by the same father or mother, or half-sisters by one of them and not by both. (2) The brothers' children (or cozen-germans), that is, the uncle's sons or daughters, or the aunt's sons or daughters. The sisters' children (or cozen-germans), that is, the aunt's sons or daughters, which are the children of two sisters. (3) The cozen-german, the son of the great uncle by the father's or mother's side, and the cozen-german the son of the great aunt by the father's or mother's side. The cozen-german, the daughter of the great uncle by the father's or mother's side, and the cozen-german, the daughter of the great aunt by the same sides.

In this line, look how many degrees the party in question is removed from the common stock, by so many twice told, is he removed from his kinsman in question. Put the case between Bethuel and Isaac, as in this example:

2. *Cozen-german:* first cousin.

3. In the margin: *Sobrino propior.*

Terah

Abraham --------------- Nahor

Isaac Bethuel

Here, Bethuel, being two degrees removed from Terah, is four degrees distant from Isaac.

Now he who is in the second degree of this line comes near to the kindred of his flesh, and for that cause the marriages of brothers and sisters are unlawful and forbidden.

But sundry things are alleged against this.

Objection 1. The sons of Adam, who were the first brethren in the world, married their sisters. Marriages, therefore, in this degree may seem to be lawful. *Answer.* The case of those persons in those times was a case of necessity, which could not be avoided, and thereupon was warranted by divine dispensation. For God had given them His own express commandment in this behalf: "Bear fruit and multiply" (Gen. 1:28). Beside that, there were then no other women in the world by whom they might have issue and posterity, but only by their sisters. Whereupon it is manifest that God's will was to permit them to take even their sisters to [be] their wives. But now, out of this special dispensation from God, such matching is utterly unlawful, being an apparent breach of another express commandment given afterward by God Himself (Lev. 18:9–11). To this purpose Augustine says in way of an answer to the example propounded: "The practice of those first times, then backed by urgent necessity, the more ancient it was, the more damnable it proved afterward, when it was restrained by God's commandment."[4]

Objection 2. Sarah was Abraham's sister, and yet Abraham took her to [be his] wife. "Yet in very deed she is my sister, for she is the daughter of my father, but not the daughter of my mother, and she is my wife" (Gen. 20:12). "Abraham and Nahor took them wives, and the name of Abraham's wife was Sarah" (Gen. 11:29). *Answer.* Touching this instance, there are sundry opinions. The Jews do grant thus much, that she was called by a name common to all kinsfolk of the sex, to wit, a sister. Yet, indeed, she was Abraham's niece, the sister of Lot, and the daughter of Haran, Abraham's brother, who Moses elsewhere calls Iscah [Gen. 11:29]. Others think that she was daughter-in-law to Terah, Abraham's

4. In the margin: De civit. Dei. lib. 15. cap. 16.

father, because Abraham himself says, "She is the daughter of my father, not of my mother." Others are of [the] opinion that she was Haran's daughter-in-law, and after his death [she] was translated into the family of Terah, her grandfather, who was also in [the] stead of her father, being dead, and thence she was termed his daughter. Now, howsoever in this variety of judgments it is hard to find certainty of truth, yet this is out of doubt, that God in those days tolerated many things which notwithstanding He did not altogether approve.

Objection 3. Tamar says to her brother Amnon: "Speak I pray thee to the king, and he will not deny me unto thee" (2 Sam. 13:13). *Answer.* The speech of Tamar is not simply to be taken as if she desired that which she said, or as if it were lawful to be done, which she wished him to do, but only that she sought to put him off by giving him this counsel in respect of her own deliverance from that present danger wherein she was. Or, at least it may be said that she erroneously supposed it was lawful for the king to grant such a suit, if it had been made unto him by her brother Amnon. Whichever way this speech is taken, there can be no such thing gathered thence as is pretended.

Now out of the second degree of the equal collateral line, it should seem that those who are joined to one another in marriage do not touch the kindred of their flesh, and therefore the law of God forbids not consobrines or cozen-germans, that is, brothers' and sisters' children to marry.

Yea, if examples are of force for this purpose, the Scripture approves such marriages. For thus it is written that Jacob married Rachel, the daughter of Laban, his mother's brother (Gen. 28:2). Again, that "Mahlah, Tirzah, Hoglah, Milcah, and Noah, the daughters of Zelophehad, were married unto their father's brothers' sons" (Num. 36:11). And Othniel, the son of Kenaz, the cousin of Caleb, took Kirjathsepher, and he gave him Achsah his daughter to [be his] wife (Josh. 15:17).

Howbeit in this case, the rule of the apostle is to be followed: "That nothing be done, even in things that are otherwise lawful, whereby a man's brother may stumble, or be offended, or made weak" (Rom 14:21). Wherefore, it is convenient that such marriages should not be, because sometimes they may give offence in regard of the law of the magistrate, and because they come somewhat near to the bonds and terms of blood and stock, which God has set down in His Word. Augustine says to this purpose: *Expertiautem sumus*, etc., that is, "We have found by experience that in regard of this nearness of blood, which cozen-germans have unto the degrees of brothers and sisters, how rarely custom has admitted those marriages which were warrantable by laws, because the law of God has not forbidden them, nor as yet the law of man. Nevertheless, the practice lawful in itself was forborne the rather because it came near to that which was unlawful, and therefore marriage with the cozen-german seemed in a manner to be marriage with a man's own brother or sister, etc. Howbeit, there is no question, but [that] in these times, it has been well provided by laws that such marriages should not be undertaken. For as the multiplication of alliance is hindered thereby, so this in convenience also grows from them, that friendship and love which is procured by affinity, between men who are strangers, cannot be enlarged and increased, where men go not out of the limits, and terms of their own blood. Yea, there is naturally in man a commendable measure of shamefastness whereby, upon consideration of nearness in blood, he acknowledges a due debt of modesty and honor to his next [of] kindred, and consequently restrains himself in regard of them from the occasions and actions of concupiscence, whereunto he is inclinable in respect of others. And hence it is that generally the modesty that ought to be in those who intend marriage avoids, as much as may be, these and such like conjunctions."[5] The same is the judgment of Ambrose in one of his epistles to his friend, Paternus, wherein he dissuades him from marrying his son with his cozen-german, upon the grounds before alleged by Augustine, adding this withal, that though it were in itself lawful, being nowhere forbidden by God, yet in sundry respects being inexpedient, it ought not to be done, according to the saying of the apostle, "All things are lawful for me, but all things are not expedient" [1 Cor. 6:12].[6]

But it is avouched to the contrary that God by express law forbids marriage with the aunt, the father's sister (Lev. 18:12), and with the mother's sister (v. 13), and with the father's brother's wife, which is also the aunt (v. 14); therefore, by the law of proportion He forbids matching with the children of these persons. For in nature it is a ruled case: if a man may not marry the mother, much less may he marry the daughter. *Answer.* The argument is faulty, and concludes nothing to the purpose. For there is not the same reason of both. In the right line of consanguinity, those who are sisters to the father and mother stand in the place and stead of parents, and their nephews and nieces are to them as children, therefore marriages among them can stand by no law, either of God or nature or by the positive laws of nations. It is not so with cozen-germans. For, having no such relation, there is not in their marriages, by the Law of Moses, any discovery of shame or breach of civil honesty. The blessing of God upon some of them mentioned in Scripture, as upon Jacob and Rachel, and such like, do evidently show that they were lawful in themselves, and pleasing unto him.

And thus much touching kindred by blood or consanguinity.

5. In the text: De civitate Dei, book 15, chap. 16.

6. In the margin: Epist. lib. 8. Epist. 66.

Affinity

Kindred in affinity is that whereby the terms of two kindred are brought into the society of one and the same family, or whereby persons who are not of blood are by marriage allied to each other. Hence it is termed affinity because it makes a unity of terms in kindred, who before were distant.

Affinity or alliance grows by mixtion[7] or participation of blood in the coupling of man and wife together in lawful marriage. For a bare and simple contract makes not [an] alliance between party and party properly, but marriage after the contract finished and consummated.

Again, the same alliance ceases and determines upon the death of either party espoused or married, yet so as the prohibition of conjunction remains, and stands in force, for the preservation of public honesty.

Now there is a kind of resemblance and proportion between kindred of blood and kindred by marriage, not only in regard of degrees and line, but also in respect of the prohibition of degrees.

Those who are of alliance are commonly reduced to these heads: (1) The father-in-law (or the husband's or wife's father). The mother-in-law (or the husband's or wife's mother). (2) The mother's husband, or step-father to them who come by another man. The father's wife, or step-mother to those who come by another woman. (3) The wife's father's father (or grandfather), and the wife's mother's mother (or grandmother), or the grandfather and grandmother of the wife. (4) The son-in-law (or daughter's husband), and the daughter-in-law (or son's wife). (5) The niece's husband, and the nephew's wife. (6) The step-son or son-in-law, that is, the son of a man by another wife, or of a woman by another husband. The step-daughter or daughter-in-law, that is, the daughter of a man by another wife, or of a woman by another husband. (7) The step-son's son, or his son who comes of a man by another woman, or of a woman by another man. And the step-daughter's daughter, or her daughter, who comes of a man by another woman, or of the woman by another husband. (8) The husband's or wife's brother, and the husband's sister, or brother's wife. (9) The sister's husband, or the brother's wife.

Concerning affinity, I propound these rules.

Rule 1. Look in what degree a man is of consanguinity to one's wife, in the same degree of affinity he is to the wife's husband, and contrariwise. For example,

7. *Mixtion:* mixture.

Isaac				Samuel	
Esau	Jacob	Joseph	Aaron	Eli	Levi
	Joseph			Mary	

Here, if Mary, Joseph's wife, is distant from Esau, Joseph's uncle, by the father's side, two degrees, then also is Joseph himself distant from Aaron, the brother of Eli, his father-in-law, [by] two degrees. If Mary, the wife, is distant from her own father, Eli, [by] one degree, and from her grandfather Samuel [by] two, then her husband is also distant from Eli, his father-in-law, [by] one degree, and from Samuel, his wife's grandfather, [by] two. Another example,

Herod

Herod ----------------- Philip (whose wife is Herodias)

Here Herod, being in the first degree of consanguinity with his brother Philip, Herodias, his brother's wife, is in the first degree of affinity to him.

Rule 2. Cousins by marriage within the degrees, both of the right and collateral line, do come near to the kindred of their flesh, in the same manner that cousins by blood do in the same lines. And the like degrees in both are forbidden. Therefore, in the right line of affinity, it is as unlawful for the father-in-law to marry the daughter-in-law, or the son-in-law to marry the mother-in-law, as it is for the father to marry the daughter, or the son the mother. Again, in the collateral, it is as unlawful for the uncle by the mother's side to marry the wife of his sister's son, and so in other degrees, as it is for him to match in the same degrees of consanguinity. The reason is because in these lines, as well as in those of consanguinity, superiors and inferiors are each to [the] other as parents and children.

From hence, among other things, it may be gathered that it is in no sort lawful for a man, when his wife is dead, to marry her sister. "Thou shalt not discover the shame of thy brother's wife; for it is thy brother's shame" (Lev. 18:16). And, "The man that taketh his brother's wife, committeth filthiness, because he hath uncovered his brother's shame" (Lev. 20:21).

Against this doctrine it is objected:

Objection 1. God commands, not to take a wife with her sister during her life (Lev. 18:18). In this place, He does not simply forbid a man to marry two sisters, one after another, but to marry them both together, and therefore after the wife is dead a man may marry her sister. *Answer.* The place is a flat prohibition of the sin of polygamy. For to take a wife to her sister, in the Hebrew phrase, is nothing else but to take two wives one to another. The like form of speech is used elsewhere by Moses: "Five curtains shall be coupled together (the woman to her sister, that is, one to another), and the other five curtains shall be coupled (the woman to her sister, that is, the one to the other)" (Ex. 26:3). "The four beasts were joined with their wings (the woman to her sister, that is the one to the other)" (Ezek. 1:9). Again, Moses himself alleges two reasons against polygamy. The first is because the man is to love, cherish, and comfort his wife, whereas, if he should take unto him another besides her, he should greatly vex his first lawful wife. The second is because by that means he should uncover the shame of his wife; that is, he should play a very dishonest part with her, to whom he was before lawfully married.

Objection 2. The Lord commanded by a special law that the brother, in case his brother died without issue, should take his wife, and raise up seed unto him (Deut. 25:5). *Answer.* The words of Moses are a special exception of a general law propounded in Leviticus 18:16, "Thou shalt not discover the shame of thy brother's wife; for it is thy brother's shame." And they are peculiarly directed to the Israelites upon special cause, that when the elder brother died without seed, the name of the first born might not be extinct, but the family might be preserved in that name, by raising up of seed unto him, which, being a privilege proper to the Israelites, upon that special consideration, it must not be enlarged to any other sort of men whatsoever. Neither is the text to be understood of cousins removed only, as some think, but also of the next of kindred by blood, as appears plainly by the story of Ruth, in these words of Naomi to her daughters-in-law: "Turn again, my daughters; for what cause will you go with me? Are there any more sons in my womb, that they may be your husbands? Turn again, my daughters, go your way, for I am too old to have a husband" (Ruth 1:11).

Rule 3. The wife's kinsman by blood is of affinity to her husband alone, but unto his kindred by blood the said kinsman has no affinity at all. So, on the contrary it is true that, though the husband's kinsman by blood is allied to his wife, yet he has no alliance to those who are kinsmen of blood unto her. The reason is because between the kindred of blood on the man's side and the kindred of blood on the woman's side there is no affinity. For the prohibition of the degrees of affinity has force in only those who are the cause thereof, and goes no further. Now the cause, being only in the married persons themselves, the effect may not in reason be enlarged to them who are of the same blood with either of them.

From this rule it follows that the kindred of both married persons by blood may lawfully match together. The son-in-law may match with the daughter of his mother-in-law. The father and the son by another wife, may marry the mother and the daughter. Two brothers may lawfully match with two sisters.

Rule 4. Kindred of affinity to the wife are also kindred of affinity to her husband.[8] But how? Not properly, but only after a sort and (as it were) of affinity. So, on the contrary. Kindred of alliance to the husband are (as it were) of alliance to his wife. For example, the wife of my father-in-law, who is not my wife's own mother, but her step-mother, is (as it were) my mother-in-law, for she is (as it were) of affinity to me because she is indeed of affinity to my wife.

Those who are of affinity only after a sort cannot conveniently match one with another. And, therefore, the son-in-law may not marry with his wife's step-mother, because, being of affinity to his wife, she is in [the] stead of a mother-in-law to him. Neither may the daughter-in-law match with her husband's step-father, because he is (as it were) a step-father to her. Again, my sister's husband may not marry my brother's wife, for they are after a sort brother and sister to each other. The reason hereof is because the wife is held in law a part of her husband, and therefore if affinity hinders marriage with one of the married couples, it hinders as well in the like case and respect marriage with the other.[9]

And thus much touching the distance of blood which in the choice of persons fit for marriage is most necessarily to be observed. For in Leviticus 18, there are sixteen several sorts of persons with whom marriage is forbidden: (1) the mother; (2) the step-mother; (3) the sister by the same father and mother; (4) the half-sister by one of the parents only; (5) the niece by the son; (6) the niece by the daughter; (7) the father's sister; (8) the uncle's, that is the father's brother's, wife; (9) the mother's sister; (10) the daughter-in-law, or son's wife; (11) the brother's wife; (12) the wife's mother; (13) the step-daughter, or the wife's daughter by another husband, or husband's daughter by a former wife; (14) the step-son's daughter, that is, his daughter who was the wife's son by another husband; (15) the step-daughter's daughter; and (16) the wife's sister. And not only these, but all other answerable to them, either in the same or like degree, are by equal proportion forbidden to be had in marriage.

8. In the margin: Beza derepudijs. 82.

9. In the margin: *Cujus nuptias inire non licet, ejus nec conjugis licet.*

It is alleged that the prohibitions mentioned in that chapter are merely Mosaical (that is, ceremonial), and therefore do not bind us now in the New Testament. *Answer.* It is a flat untruth, as shall appear by these reasons:

First, the Canaanites, long before these laws were given by Moses to the Israelites, were grievously afflicted for the breach and contempt of the same, as may be gathered by that which is written in that same chapter. "According to the works of the land of Canaan, ye shall not do, neither walk in their ordinances" (Lev. 18:3). "You shall not defile yourselves in any of these things: for in all these the nations are defiled, which I will cast out before you. And the land is defiled; therefore I will visit the wickedness thereof upon it, and the land shall vomit out her inhabitants" (vv. 24–25).

Second, the prophets themselves after Moses are wont to account these prohibitions not ceremonial, but moral. "In thee, have they discovered their father's shame; in thee have they vexed her, that was polluted in her flowers" (Ezek. 22:10). "A man and his father will go in to a maid, to profane the name of my holiness" (Amos 2:7).

Third, the same laws are also urged in the New Testament, wherein legal ceremonies were determined, and had their end. John said to Herod, "it is not lawful for thee to have thy brother's wife" (Mark 6:18). "It is heard certainly, that there is fornication among you, and such fornication, as is not once named among the Gentiles, that one should have his father's wife" (1 Cor. 5:1).

Fourth, nature itself by proper instinct abhors such kind of conjunctions, and the prohibitions of them have sufficient ground even from its principles. For to this purpose it is that not only the laws of the Roman emperors, but also the civil canons and constitutions of men, very skillful in that kind, have in all ages expressly been made against such persons as have offended in those societies forbidden by the law of Moses.

Fifth, the Lord Himself has denounced many and great punishments to be inflicted upon the breach of the same laws. "The man that lieth with his father's wife, because he hath uncovered his father's shame, they shall both die; their blood shall be upon them. The man that lieth with his daughter-in-law, they both shall die the death; they have wrought abomination; their blood shall be upon them.... He that takes a wife and her mother, committeth wickedness; they shall burn him and them with fire.... The man that taketh his sister, his father's daughter, or his mother's daughter, and seeth her shame, and she seeth his shame; it is villainy; therefore they shall be cut off in the sight of their people.... The man that lieth with his father's brother's wife, and uncovereth his uncle's shame, they shall bear their iniquity, and shall die childless" (Lev. 20:11–12, 14, 16, 20). "A bastard shall not enter into the congregation of the

Lord, even to his tenth generation" (Deut. 23:2). "Cursed be he that lieth with his father's wife" (Deut. 27:20).

Mark 3

The third essential sign of a marriageable person is ability and fitness for procreation. And this in a holy and modest sort is always supposed to be in the party contracted, unless the contrary is manifestly known and discerned by some apparent infirmity in the body.

Hence, I gather that it is unlawful to make a contract with such a person as is unfit for the use of marriage, either by natural constitution of body or by accident. For example, in regard of sickness, or frigidity, or the incurable palsy, or lastly the deprivation of the parts belonging to generation. These, and such like impediments, are of force, though a contract should already be made, yet to make it a mere nullity, considering that God makes known His will in them, that He approves not of such espousals, but would have them to be dissolved.

Again, that which is made between two persons [who] are underage[10] is to be held and accounted as unlawful. And though it should be done by consent, or commandment of parents, yet it is of no moment. This always remembered: except it is ratified by a new consent of the parties after they come to age, or they in the meantime have had private and carnal copulation one with another.

Again, put the case [that] two be espoused, whereof the one is under age [and] the other [is] of full age. The party who is of full age ought to tarry and expect the time wherein the issue of the espousals formerly made, may be manifested. And the under-aged may not break off consent, either before or when they come to perfect years, but must rest in expectation of the accomplishment of the contract when he or she shall be out of their minority.

Mark 4

The fourth essential sign is a sound and healthy constitution of body, free from incurably contagious diseases.

Whereupon it follows that a promise of marriage made between those whereof the one has a disease so loathsome as that the other, upon good ground, cannot possibly endure familiar society and company with him, though it does not wholly hinder the use of the body, is utterly unlawful.

Of this sort is the leprosy, the French pox, and such like. For seeing there cannot be any matrimonial use of them who are tainted with such contagious diseases without apparent danger of infecting each other, and those also who have society with them and others (yea, and by this means the issue of their

10. In the margin: *Impuberes.*

bodies, growing from a corrupted seed, are even born to perpetual misery and to the great hurt and hindrance of the commonwealth), the case is plain that such marriages cannot be undertaken with good conscience.

Now if the one party has a disease, though not contagious, yet either incurable or so loathsome[11] as the other has just cause to abhor his company (for example, if he is sick of a lethargy, the falling sickness, or such like diseases), then, though it is lawful to match with him because such a contract is not expressly forbidden, neither is it apparently hurtful to the commonwealth), yet is it not expedient because the disease, being loathsome to the sound party, the marriage will also become unprofitable, and the party in danger of breaking the commandment of the moral law wherein God forbids to commit adultery.

Mark 5

The fifth essential sign of a marriageable person is freedom from marriage whereby both parties, who enter contract, are so at liberty that neither the man has at present another wife or is promised to another, nor the woman has another husband or is promised to another. The reason is because God Himself esteems that marriage only lawful wherein one man is joined to one woman, and they both into one flesh, and consequently [He] judges it unlawful, as for one man to have more wives, so for one woman at the same time to have more husbands.

Hence, it follows that it is against the law of God, and the first institution of marriage, that a contract should be made between such persons whereof the one is formerly betrothed to another. For so long as the first promise stands in force, the man can no more be betrothed to two women than he may be the husband of two wives, because the spouse by the bond of her promise to the man becomes a wife, and the man by the bond of his promise to the woman becomes a husband (Deut. 22:23–24).

Again, there can be no sure making and consequently no marriage with such a one as either has been divorced without a sufficient cause or has wrongfully forsaken and rejected a lawful mate before. To this purpose our Savior Christ says, "I say unto you, that whosoever shall put away his wife, except it be for whoredom, and marrieth another, committeth adultery; and whosoever marrieth her which is divorced, committeth adultery" (Matt. 19:9). And Saint Paul [says], "But and if she depart, let her remain unmarried, or be reconciled unto her husband, and let not the husband put away his wife" (1 Cor. 7:11).

---

11. In the margin: *Turpi.*

Part 2: Accidental Marks

Hitherto I have treated of essential marks which belong to the being of marriage. Now I come to those that are accidental.

An accidental mark of a person fit for marriage is that which belongs not to the being, but to the well-being (that is, to the holiness and purity) of that estate. And of this sort, there are three that are the principal.

Mark 1

The first is parity or equality in regard of Christian religion. For in marriage there is a special care to be had that believers are matched with believers and Christians with Christians, not believers with infidels or Christians with pagans. For only the former sort are always to be made and kept, and the latter [are] to be avoided, yea inhibited by positive laws and constitutions, the breach whereof in such cases is to be severely punished. The neglect of this point was one principal cause of the destruction of the old world by the flood. "The sons of God saw the daughters of men, that they were fair, and they took them wives of all that they liked" (Gen. 6:2). Abraham observed it in the marriage of Isaac his son, and for that purpose took an oath of his servant: "I will make thee swear by the Lord God of heaven, and God of the earth, that thou shalt not take a wife unto my son of the daughters of the Canaanites among whom I dwell" (Gen. 24:3). And in imitation of that holy example, Isaac also gives a charge unto Jacob his son, that he should "not take a wife of the daughters of Canaan" (Gen. 28:1). Afterwards there was an express law of God given by Moses touching the Gentiles who lived in that land: "Beware that thou make not a covenant with the inhabitants of the land.... And take of their daughters unto thy sons, and their daughters go a whoring after their gods; and make thy sons go a whoring after their gods" (Ex. 34:15–16). And the same law was urged by Ezra the priest in his time: "Separate yourselves from the people of the land, and from the strange wives" (Ezra 10:11). Lastly, Saint Paul exhorts the Corinthians: "Be not unequally yoked with the infidels" (2 Cor. 6:14). And [he says], "Reject him that is a heretic, after once or twice admonition" (Titus 3:10).

But suppose it falls out that the espousals are past, and that both parties at the first were believers (or only one of them), or that at first both were unbelievers, and yet afterwards one of them is converted to the faith, or further admit that both were believers at the contract, yet within sometime after, the one becomes an infidel (that is to say, a Jew, Turk, or obstinate heretic) who denies the faith and razes even the very foundation of religion. What is to be done in this case? Surely even such espousals, once made and ended, if there are no other impediments but these, are to stand and continue firm and unchangeable so long as the unbelieving party does willingly yield and submit himself or herself to the performance of marriage duties properly belonging to man and wife. My reason is the speech of Paul who says, "If any brother have a wife that believeth not, if she be content to dwell with him, let him not forsake her. The woman which hath a husband that believeth not, if he be content to dwell with her, let her not forsake him" (1 Cor. 7:12–13).

If it is here alleged that the sin of adultery dissolves the bond of both contract and marriage, and therefore much more does idolatry or infidelity, which is a sin far more detestable than adultery, I answer that the question is not which of these is the greater sin or more heinous in the sight of God, for infidelity in both respects far exceeds the other, but which of them is more repugnant to the nature and condition of wedlock. Now the sin of adultery alone is that which breaks the bond, and renounces the troth[12] plighted[13] in marriage, and is the proper cause of a divorce, and not idolatry or infidelity.

Mark 2

The second note is parity or equality in regard of age and condition.

First, of age. Though the marriage of persons whose years are far unequal is not expressly forbidden in the Word, yet it is agreeable to the rules of expediency and decency that the aged should match with the aged [and] the younger with the younger. [The] reasons are these: First, the comforts of this society in likelihood will by this means always be equal, and consequently bring the more contentment to either party. Second, these unequal marriages are oftentimes offensive to others. Third, they cannot but in some cases prove offensive even to themselves. For when a man of great years matches with a very young woman, or a young stripling marries an aged woman, the elder party, growing weak and impotent, may the sooner come to be unfit for marriage duties, and the younger, being of greater strength and ability, the more in danger of being exposed to incontinency, and that in the highest degree, unless he is restrained by God's special grace. For this cause, it was a great fault, wherewith one Apuleius was justly charged, that, being but a very young man, he was married to a wife of sixty years of age.

Second, of condition and estate. This also is answerable unto the apostle's rule. He exhorts men to think of (and to do) those things which are "true, just, commendable, and of good report (Phil. 4:8). Thus, it is a seemly and commendable practice that the prince, nobleman, freeman, gentleman, yeoman, etc. should be joined in society with them who are of the same or like condition with themselves, and not otherwise. For this cause, the ancient Romans

12. *Troth:* pledge.
13. *Plight:* promise.

are greatly to be commended. As we read in their stories, [they] had such a careful respect of their marriages in this behalf that they made laws and constitutions for the restraining of inequality of worldly estate in such societies, by this means preventing much confusion and disturbance in families and other orders of men. Whereunto agrees that of Tertullian, who says, "That if a free woman had affianced[14] herself to him who was a bond-man to another, and being thrice admonished thereof, by him who had authority over her, did notwithstanding persevere in her purpose, she should, according to the law, lose her freedom."[15]

Mark 3

The third note is public honesty and credit, whereby the contract made becomes a matter of good report, well thought and spoken of abroad. "Whatsoever things are of good report, think on them" (Phil. 4:8). From hence I gather:

First, it is an unseemly thing for a man to make [a] promise of marriage to such a woman as has been formerly deflowered, or has, or is, or may be, convicted of adultery and uncleanness. Nay, I add further that a contract made with such a one as has been before deflowered is by the law of God unlawful. For the adulterer and the adulteress, by divine law, should be put to death and be cut off from human society (Lev. 20:10).

Second, it is altogether inexpedient that a woman should be married to such a man as has a concubine, unless he formerly renounces her, and testifies the same by true and unfeigned repentance. The reason is plain. Such a marriage cannot be undertaken in the Lord. And the party himself, being before polluted with his concubine, becomes now by marriage to another, an adulterer, and she who is married unto him, by this act, yields consent unto his adultery.

Third, no man, professing Christian religion, much less a minister of the Word, ought to take to himself in marriage a harlot, defamed woman, or one who comes from infamous parents, though she is repentant. "The priest shall not take to wife one that is a whore, or profaned" (Lev. 21:7), that is to say, [one] who has an evil name or comes from ignominious parents. This law, though it was in part ceremonial and levitical, and so far forth abrogate, yet, having in it some morality, in as much as the reason thereof (to wit, because it is reproachful to a Christian, but especially to a minister), [it] is still in force, [and] it is to be held [as] perpetual. For Christian profession and the ecclesiastical ministry are principally to be respected, and whatsoever may prejudice the dignity and credit thereof [is] to be avoided.

---

14. *Affiance:* engage to be married.
15. In the margin: Tertull. adver. lib. 2.

Objection 1. The prophet Hosea was commanded to take unto him "a wife of fornication," that is, a harlot (Hosea 1:2). *Answer.* Hosea did it not in deed, but in type and resemblance. For God commanded him in his prophecy to take upon him (as it were) the person of a fornicator that by this means he might the more effectually charge and convince the Israelites of their unclean and unchaste conversation.

Objection 2. The Lord also forbids the priest to marry a widow (Lev. 21:14). It may seem, therefore, inexpedient for a minister so to do. *Answer.* The law concerning the marriage of a virgin, and not a widow, was not enjoined to all priests, but only to the chief priest (v. 10). And he also might marry a widow, but only such a one as had been the widow of a priest, and not any other (Ezek. 44:22). Now this was commanded them upon special consideration. For the high priest was a type of Christ, and Christ was in time to come to call His church, the elect, [from] among the Gentiles, and to marry them as a virgin espoused unto Himself. Yea, He was also to marry His church as a widow, but the widow of a priest only, because He was to gather to Himself the remnants of the church of the Jews; howbeit, not all of them, but only such as came from the holy fathers, and were Israelites, not according to the flesh, but according to the promise.

Fourth, it is not meet for a man to be contracted to the sister of her who is already affianced unto him.

And so much of the first point, required to the making of a contract, namely, the choice of a person fit for marriage.

Chapter 6

Consent in the Contract

The second thing required to the making of a contract is the free and full consent of the parties, which is indeed the very soul and life of the contract. And this consent stands in the approbation or (as we commonly call it) the sure-making of the contracted parties.

Consent in this case is twofold: (1) of the man and the woman, or (2) of their parents.

Point 1

Touching the first. That the man and the woman may yield free consent to each other, it is necessary that, in respect of understanding, their judgment should be sound, and in regard of [their] will, their choice should be free. And here sundry cases are to be resolved.

Case 1

When the contract flows not from the will and good liking of the parties, but is forced and compelled, what then is to be done?

Answer. If the espousals have been made through force or fear (I mean, such as may befall a constant and resolute man, and which has been wrought upon good knowledge and consideration), then they are of no moment, and in truth mere nullities, because there is wanting to them the free and voluntary accord and assent of both parties. Nevertheless, if afterwards they shall grow to a new consent, or both yield to an after acceptation of that which was formerly made, the espousals shall then stand in force, without further exception or contradiction.

Case 2

But what if consent is past and, in process of time, it appears to the espoused persons that they have erred either in choice or consent or both?

Answer. There is a three-fold error in consent: the first of the person; the second of the ability (or estate) of the person; [and] the third of the quality [of the person].

Error in respect of the person is when one person is taken for another, or when the contract is made between two whereof the one was taken to be such a party as afterwards he proved not to be. Now where this error is committed, it is a plain case, there was no consent, and therefore the contract, upon certain knowledge thereof, is quite frustrate. For the knowledge of the party is the ground of consent, and belongs consequently to the very substance of marriage.

Nevertheless, if, the error being once known, the parties have had secret society with one another, and have either consented or grown to an after-acceptation of the consent before made, the contract may and does stand in full force. For example, by the deceit of Laban, Jacob had taken Leah for Rachel to [be] his wife, so says the text: "When the evening was come, Laban took Leah his daughter, and brought her to him, and he went in unto her" (Gen. 29:23). "But when the morning was come, behold it was Leah" (v. 25). Now by the judgment of the best divines, Jacob might justly have renounced Leah, if he would, because Laban had given her unto him for Rachel, and so deceived him. Yet, he would not use extremity, but kept her as his wife.

If it is said [that] there was an error in the person, therefore no consent, and so Leah was not his lawful wife, but Rachel, I answer that Jacob did renew his consent afterward, and that renewed consent, following upon their knowing of one another, made her his wife, though in extremity and rigor she was not. Again, Rachel was indeed the party to whom he was espoused by the former contract. And, therefore, upon their mutual agreement afterward, she also became his wife. The Holy Spirit says so: "Fulfill seven years for her, and we will also give thee Rachel for thy service.... Then Jacob did so, and Laban give him Rachel his daughter to be his wife" (vv. 27–28).

Error of the ability (or estate) is when one of the parties, to whom consent was given by the other, being taken for rich and wealthy, in the issue proves to have been very poor, and not sufficient to maintain that state of life.

Touching this error, it is to be considered whether the contract was made absolute for the time present, and so forever afterward, or conditional only for time to come. If it were absolute (that is, conceived in terms of the present time), then (though the deceit is very offensive to the deluded party, and upon his complaint ought in equity to be punished by the magistrate) it is not of force to break off the contract, because the ability of either or both parties belongs not to the essence of marriage. But if it were for time to come and conditional, then he or she who made promise upon this condition is free and not bound in conscience to fulfill the promise, unless the condition expressed beforehand is kept and performed.

Error of the quality of the person is when she, who was in the espousals taken to be a virgin, is afterwards found to be with child by another before they come together. By this error the covenant is made void, and becomes a mere nullity, so as the man cannot be compelled, upon true and certain knowledge thereof, to marry the woman, but may renounce her, unless both parties come to a new agreement, or have privately known each other upon mutual consent. For, first, God did in express terms command the Jews that such a woman should be stoned to death, "If the maid (that was given to [be a] wife) is not found a virgin, then they shall bring the maid to the door of her father's house, and the men of her city shall stone her with stones to death, because she hath wrought folly in Israel by playing the whore in her father's house" (Deut. 22:20–21). Therefore, it was not the will of God that she should be retained as a wife, but utterly rejected and forsaken. Again, this was so usual a practice in Israel, upon God's commandment, that godly and righteous men, upon the discovery of this error, would not in conscience be persuaded to marry them to whom they had been betrothed. "Joseph her husband (having found, before Mary and he came together, that she was with child), being a just man, and not willing to make her a public example, was minded to put her away secretly" (Matt. 1:18).

Case 3

What shall we think of the espousals of such as are furious and frantic?

Answer. We must distinguish of these diseases. For madness is either perpetual or by fits only with intermission.

If it is perpetual, the case is clear that, whether one or both of the parties is frantic, the contract made between them is altogether unprofitable and vain. For such know not what they do when they make a promise, and the consent which passes between them cannot be free, full, and perfect, but must needs be hindered and prejudiced by the heat and violence of their disease.

Now although perpetual madness is a just impediment of marriage, and a sufficient cause to dissolve a contract, yet it is meet that there is a convenient space of time agreed upon, wherein all means may be used for the curing of this disease, to the end that God's will touching their amendment may be the more evidently known, and both the parties themselves, and their friends, may give testimony to the world that they have had a careful respect of the contract before made.

Again, if it is not continual, but by fits,[1] so as they have some good days and quiet intermission, the case is otherwise. For the contract shall be ratified and

1. In the margin: *Dilucida intervalla.*

stand in force, provided that it was manifestly known that the said parties were both in their right wits before they plighted their troth each to other, and [they] themselves are willing afterwards to confirm their promise formerly made by renewing their consent.

Point 2

Consent of the parents is that act whereby they give their word and promise to bestow their children in marriage, and in regard of right [they] do indeed presently bestow them.

Therefore, private contracts that are made without free and lawful consent of parents are not only unprofitable and unlawful, but even by the law of God mere nullities. *Reasons.* (1) They are contrary to the express will and commandment of God: "Honor thy father and thy mother" (Exodus 20). (2) They are flatly repugnant to natural equity which teaches that he who has not power nor right over himself cannot bind himself by promise to another. Now children have no power over themselves [Gal. 4:1], but are under the government and the disposition of their parents. Therefore, the covenants which they make are not made and appointed by God, and those which God makes not are in deed and truth none at all.

Chapter 7

Rejection or Refusal of the Contract

Contrary to a complete and lawful contract is rejection,[1] whereby the contract is dissolved or broken off.

A lawful contract is then dissolved when some great and heinous fault follows immediately upon it in either of the espoused parties. And from hence arise divers and sundry cases to be set down and resolved.

Case 1

The first is this. What is to be done when some disease befalls one of the parties immediately after the contract [is] made?

Answer. Those diseases which take away the use of the body and altogether disable the party from the performance of the promise made, in respect of marriage duties, are very just impediments of marriage, and consequently do break off the contract. Of which sort are incurable palsies, frigidity, and such like, whereof I have spoken before.

Nevertheless, a covenant once made is not suddenly to be renounced for fear of breeding offence. And, therefore, some longer respite is to be taken from the time of the contract, in which they are to rest in expectation of amendment, before the said diseases are publicly and solemnly declared to be incurable, and consequently that the covenant made is become void.

Now, if the disease does not for the present take away the use of the body, and yet in time proves incurably contagious, and so loathsome, that the one may justly fear to keep and confer with the other (as it falls out when one is tainted with leprosy), then the contract is utterly to be dissolved, as if God Himself should have commanded it, though the promise was formerly made, and the parties themselves should be unwilling. God has ordained matrimony to help, not to hurt, either the persons themselves or others. Where, therefore, these diseases are, which may infect, hurt, or destroy others, there God has (as it were) testified from heaven that the act done is not pleasing unto Him, and that presently it ought to be frustrate.

---

1. In the margin: *Repudium.*

The contract, being thus once dissolved, the sounder party shall be at his or her liberty to marry again. But the diseased is, by the magistrate's authority, to be forbidden society with any other in way of marriage, and commanded to lead his life where he may conveniently from company for fear of infection. And withal he is, for his own part, to sue unto God by prayer in faith for the gift of continency. For certain it is that he, to whom God has denied the power of using marriage with good conscience, is thereby even called to continency and single life.

But if the disease is not contagious, yet either incurable or so nasty that either of the espoused has just cause to be afraid of the other's company, then both are to be advised not to claim their right, but willingly to surrender it each to [the] other by mutual consent, that they may be free again, and not bound by any former promise to live together as man and wife. Considering that they have no hope mutually to converse together, with comfort and contentment, while they so remain.

Upon this advice given by their lawful pastor, or someone in his stead, if they both yield or one of them (at the least) desires to be at his own liberty, the espousals are forthwith to be broken off. But if neither will consent to a separation, but rather proceed as they have begun, and in probability the one has no just cause to hold the other in suspicion in respect of contagion, they are not to be hindered from the consummation of their marriage.

Furthermore, though one of them should have a disease which is continual without intermission, and yet curable, or any other inconvenience should befall either of them, after the sure-making, whereby they become lame, deaf, or dumb, etc., yet this is not a sufficient cause to move them to renounce and dissolve the contract.

Case 2

What if it falls out that, after the finishing of the contract, one of the espoused persons is long absent from the other so as the absence is prejudicial to the marriage that should ensue upon the contract?

Answer. Inquiry must be made whether this absence is voluntary or against the will of the party.

If it is voluntary, for example if the man upon an honest and just cause, the woman also being privy thereunto, shall go beyond seas, and being admonished of his duty beforehand, shall notwithstanding stay a whole year or more, and will not return, but further willfully absent himself, then it may be lawful to the woman to crave of the public magistrate a dissolution of the covenant made, and consequently marry another man, unless the former, to whom she was contracted, is heard of. If he is, then it shall be lawful for him to plead for himself, and rendering no just cause of his refusal, he shall be forced by the magistrate's authority to stand to his promise, and take the woman for his wife. And the same order is to be taken in the willful absence of the woman, after she is contracted.

If again, the man or woman shall upon an evil mind, and with purpose to deceive each other, absent themselves and depart, [then] means must be used that they may be admonished of their duty. That being done, or at least undertaken, and yet the party offending will not appear, if the other who is present, upon certain knowledge of his or her want in respect of continency, shall sue to the magistrate, after public and solemn notice given, the contract may be broken.

But if on the other side, either of them is absent against their will, and intends no fraud or deceit, but is violently detained by captivity, imprisonment, sickness, force, banishment, transportation, or such like, then the present party, being desirous of the consummation of the marriage, ought either to make means unto him and expect his return, or have certain notice of his death, before the promise, or have to do with any other in way of marriage.

Case 3

What if, after the contract, one of the parties becomes furious or mad?

Answer. If the disease is continual without intermission, in all equity and likelihood the espousals are to be dissolved, unless both parties, after knowledge and experience of the disease, have known one another. Yet in this, and all such like cases, it is fit that all good means are tried and used, and sufficient time is given for the restoring of the diseased to their former good estate, and for the accomplishment of the marriage lawfully begun, as before.

Chapter 8

Marriage

Marriage is that whereby the conjunction, formerly begun in the contract, is solemnly manifested and brought to perfection. Marriage is consummated by three sorts of actions: the first [is] of the parents of the bride and bridegroom; the second [is] of the minister in public; [and] the third [is] of the persons coupled together.

Action 1: The Parents

The action of the parents is upon the marriage day to bring the bride, and deliver her to the bridegroom, that the two may become actually man and wife, and perform to each other all matrimonial duties.

And where the marriage is complete in any other manner so as the parents, upon sound judgment and deliberation, shall deny their full and free consent, either in express words or by connivence and silence, and that upon just and lawful cause, there (though in the civil courts of men, it may stand, and the children born therein may be legitimate before men) yet the truth is [that] before God it is of no force, but a mere nullity.

And because this doctrine, touching consent of parents in these cases, is of great use and avails much to the supporting and maintaining of families, I will first open the truth thereof and then prove it by reasons.

Under the name of parents are comprehended, first, the father and mother; second, all tutors and guardians who have the proper and sole charge of wards or others under years of discretion; [and,] third, all such as are kindred of blood, who are in [the] stead of parents to children, as the uncle by the father's side, the uncle by the mother's side, and such like.

Now touching the consent of parents (that is, father and mother), I hold it requisite of necessity to marriage, for the authority of parents must not be resisted or violated. As for tutors, and such as have the place of parents, their consent is not required of necessity, but of honesty[1] at least, because the power and authority of the parent, though it is not taken away, is lessened

1. In the margin: *De honestate.*

when it is either transferred to another person or in part rests in the child already bestowed.

Second, by parents' consent I understand that which they give, not rashly, unadvisedly, or foolishly, but out of good and wise consideration, and upon true and sound judgment, of the business in hand. For otherwise, as much as in them lies, they make the marriage void and of none effect. And they are then thought to carry a right judgment of the thing when they are able to yield a just cause of yielding or denying their consent. For example, if a father denies to bestow his daughter Julia upon Sempronius because he knows him to be an Arian, Pelagian, or of any other sort of heretic, he withholds his consent upon a good ground, and he does that which he does of judgment.

Yet, further, I add that where the parents do dissent, and can yield no probable cause thereof, the marriage consummated without their consent ought to be confirmed and ratified by the authority of the magistrate, who is *Pater Patria*. And this seems to be the most equal course, both for the avoiding of greater scandals and for the preventing of wrong that may otherwise be done in some particular case, as to a woman that is deflowered and rejected.

Third, consent of parents is either expressed or implied: expressed, when it is given by words; [and,] implied, when it [is] yielded by silence. For it stands with most equity and indifference to think that those parents do give consent who do not by word expressly deny the same.

Fourth, children are either subject to the authority of their parents in the family or at their own liberty and out of their parents' subjection. Those who are at liberty are tied necessarily to subjection in respect of marriage, but the other, being still of the family and under jurisdiction, are bound to be ordered by their parents in the bestowing of themselves.

This is briefly the meaning of the question in hand. Now, for proof of this point, I will propound three sorts of arguments, whereof some are drawn from the law of God, some from the light of nature, and some from the judgment of the ancient church.

Argument 1

For the first sort. According to the law of God, marriage is not only a civil and political, but a divine and spiritual, conjunction. The author and ordainer whereof, upon special cause, was God Himself. Our Savior Christ witnesses this when He says, "Those whom God hath joined together, let no man separate" (Matt. 19:6). That, therefore, marriages may be soundly ratified and confirmed, the authority and power of God Himself is necessarily to be interposed.

If it is asked how God, who is in heaven, should bring and join together man and wife upon the earth, I answer that He does it not immediately by

Himself, as He brought Eve unto Adam, but in and by some solemn and lawful means. And this means is that great and ancient power and prerogative of parents. And the law of God has given them this power, not in civil contracts and compositions alone, but even in the beginning and accomplishing of marriages. "Thou shalt not give thy daughter unto his son, nor take his daughter unto thy son" (Deut. 7:3). "Take wives for your sons, and give your daughters unto husbands, that they may bear sons and daughters" (Jer. 29:6). "But if any man think that it is uncomely for his virgin, if she pass the flower of her age, and need so require, let him do what he will, he sinneth not, let them be married" (1 Cor. 7:36).

Hence it was that Abraham, by right of this authority, gave order what wife his servant should provide for his son: "Thou shalt not take a wife to my son of the daughters of the Canaanites; But thou shalt go unto my country, and to my kindred, and take a wife unto my son Isaac" (Gen. 24:3–4). Samson, though he was enflamed with the love of the woman in Timnath, whom he saw to be beautiful in his eyes, yet he durst not take her to [be] his wife, until she was given [to] him by his parents (Judges 14:1). It was an express law of God that if a man enticed a maid who was not betrothed, and lay with her, he should endow her and take her to [be] his wife. But how? Mark in what manner the Holy Spirit proceeds: "If her father refuse to give her to him, he shall pay money according to the dowry of virgins" (Ex. 22:16–17; Deut. 22:28–29). In this text, Moses plainly teaches that the consent of the two parties is not sufficient, no not though they have had society together, unless they also have the free consent of their parents. In like manner it was ordained by God that "if a woman vowed a vow unto the Lord, being in her father's house, and her father hearing it, holdeth his peace concerning her (that is, approves her vow by winking at it), her vow shall stand. But if her father disallow her (that is, gives no approbation or consent unto the vow made), it shall be of no value, and the Lord will forgive her, because her father consented not" (Num. 30:4–6). Now, if the vow of children made unto God, and pertaining to His worship, cannot be ratified without the parents' approbation, of how much less force shall any private contract or marriage be without their allowance?

Argument 2

The second argument is taken from the light of nature, and it is gathered by proportion in this manner. A son privily alienates and sells away his father's lands, either in whole or in part. The question is whether this alienation is good in law, yes or no? [The] answer is no. And why? Because the land did not belong to the son, but was part of his father's substance. In like manner, a son alienates himself, and is betrothed to a woman, to marry her without his parents' knowledge. Is this act of the son warrantable and sound? By no means, for the son, in respect of his body, is part of the father's goods, and may not be alienated from him without consent. A notable reason hereof we find in Job 1. For when God had given Satan power to destroy and spoil all Job's goods, and whatsoever he had, the devil does not only touch the wealth of Job, but his children also, as a part of his substance. In this respect the Jews were permitted by God to sell their children (Ex. 21:7).

Again, for the accomplishment of marriage, there must needs be a mutual donation between the spouse and the espoused. And what is that which is mutually given? Surely their persons, or rather their bodies, to each other, for so Paul says, "Let every man have his wife, and let every woman have her own husband" (1 Cor. 7:2). But by whom is this donation to be made? By sons and daughters who are in the family, under the jurisdiction of their parents? It may not be. For nature itself takes it for granted that he who is not at his own liberty cannot yield to the giving of himself. The donation, therefore, remains in the right of the parent, in as much as the will and consent of the child ought to depend upon his will and consent, to whom God has given power and authority in this behalf.

Argument 3

In the third place, let the judgment of the ancient church be observed. Ambrose, in his first book of the patriarch Abraham, chapter 9, requires this consent in marriages, which he says is so equal and agreeable to nature that even the poets acknowledged the same. For which purpose he recites two verses out of the Grecian poet, Euripides, in his tragedy called *Andromache*. When Orestes desired to marry Hermione, she framed him this answer: that the matter of her marriage wholly depended upon the pleasure and authority of her father, and was not in her own power or liberty. Innocentius, who was both a pope and martyr, in his decretal epistles, so strictly requires consent of parents, "as where it is wanting, he concludes the marriage to be void."[2] In the Council of Lateran, it was decreed that clandestine contracts and "secret marriages, made and undertaken between party and party, should be held as unlawful as marriage in those degrees of consanguinity and affinity, which are forbidden by God." Tertullian says that "in this world the son cannot rightly and lawfully[3] marry without the allowance of his father."[4] Basil; in an epistle to Amphilochius, bishop of Iconium, affirms, "Marriages which are made without them who have power over the parties are fornications, and therefore they who are joined together in

2. In the margin: Sub Innoc. 3. canon. 51.
3. In the margin: Rite & Jure.
4. In the margin: Tertul. lib. ad uxor. 2. ad sinem.

marriage, while their parents or masters live, are in no sort free from imputation of sin, until they have approbation from them, for the marriage is ratified and confirmed when they have yielded allowance thereunto."[5]

Action 2: The Minister

The second action touching the consummation of marriage is the action of the minister. And it is the blessing or sanctification thereof, which is a solemn work whereby the minister, pronouncing the contracted parties to be man and wife before the whole congregation, commands them and their estate unto God by solemn prayer.

This solemn sanctification is grounded upon the practice of God Himself, who, having given Eve to Adam, blessed them, saying, "Increase and multiply" (Gen. 2:22; 1:27). For that which God then gave, the minister, standing in His room, now prays may be given to the man and wife. Yea, it is agreeable to the general rule of the apostle: "Let all things be done decently and in order" (1 Cor. 14:40).

Now, that this action is to be approved and used in the church appears by these reasons. (1) Marriage, as it is a public action, so it is after a sort a spiritual and divine ordinance, whereby it differs from the contract. For the contract, being merely civil as it stands by consent of men, so by the same consent it may be broken and dissolved, but with marriage it is otherwise. (2) Marriage is the seminary of the church and commonwealth. (3) It was the practice of the primitive church. Tertullian, speaking of the marriage of Christian with Christian, acknowledges himself not to be able sufficiently to declare the happiness "of that conjunction which is made by the church, consecrated by prayers and solemn service,[6] witnessed by the angels, and ratified by God Himself."[7] Nicephorus reports of one Synecious, who avouched that "God and the laws, and the holy hand of Thesphylus had given him a wife."[8] Ambrose says, "Marriage ought to be sanctified with the veil wherewith the priest was wont to cover the bride and the bridegroom in the public congregation, and with his blessing."[9]

Action 3: The Couple

The third and last action belonging to the accomplishment of this estate is that of the parties themselves, whereby the bride is in decent and modest manner brought unto the house and home of the bridegroom. It is the law of this estate

---

5. In the margin: Basil Epist. 1. ad Amphil. can. 42.
6. In the margin: Oblationem sic exponit Beatus Rhenanus.
7. In the margin: Lib 2. ad uxorem.
8. In the margin: Nicephorus l. 14. c. 55.
9. In the margin: Ambrose epist. l. 9. epist. 70 ad Vigil.

published by God Himself in Paradise that the man, even in respect of habitation, "should leave father and mother and cleave to his wife" (Gen. 2:24).

Here question is moved whether marriage is to be solemnized with mirth and feasting? *Answer.* (1) It is lawful and warrantable to use feasting and mirth at marriages, because these are things indifferent, and we have examples thereof in the Scriptures. Laban made a feast at the wedding of Jacob and Rachel, and invited all the men of the place to it (Gen. 29:32). Christ Himself did approve the resort of people to marriage at Cana in Galilee, both by His presence and by that honorable gift of six water pots of the best wine (John 2:2, 7–8). (2) It is not only lawful but convenient and fit to be done, if there is ability, according to the commendable custom of the place and country wherein men do dwell [as long] as in the use thereof these cautions are observed. First, in mirth and merry-making, there is care had that nothing is done which is dishonest, profane, or of ill report. "Whatsoever things are honest, pure, of good report, think on these things" (Phil. 4:8). Second, joy in them is mixed and moderated with the fear of God, without which laughter and rejoicing is mere madness (Eccl. 2:2). Third, it is performed in a moderate and sober use of the creatures, without riot and excess. Thus, we read that at the great feast of Ahasuerus, it was appointed by the king himself, "that they should drink orderly, that none might compel another to drink more that he thought convenient" (Esther 1:8). And where weddings are kept contrary to these directions, they are not feasts celebrated unto God, but unto the devil, which also may be said of all other festival meetings.

And so much touching the point of marriage, in which this is to be remembered for a conclusion: that where there is generally a nullity in the contract, or a separation following upon it, there is also a nullity in regard of the consummation of marriage.

Chapter 9

The Duties of Married Persons: Cohabitation

We have proceeded thus far in the doctrine of marriage, and now we come to the duties which they who are married are to perform to each other. These are principally two: cohabitation and communion.

Cohabitation

Cohabitation is their quiet and comfortable dwelling together in one place for the better performance of mutual duties. "And to the married command I, not I but the Lord, let not the wife separate herself from her husband.... But to the remnant I say, not the Lord, if any brother have an unbelieving wife, and she be content to dwell with him, let him not forsake her. And the wife which hath an unbelieving husband, which is content to dwell with her, let her not forsake him" (1 Cor. 7:10, 12–13). "Likewise let the men dwell together, as becometh them that have knowledge, giving honor to the woman as to the weaker vessel, even as they which are heirs together of the grace of life, that your prayers be not interrupted" (1 Peter 3:7).

This duty must be kept especially the first year of marriage. "When a man taketh a wife, he shall not go on warfare; neither shall he be charged with any business, but shall be free at home one year, and rejoice with his wife which he hath taken" (Deut. 24:5). And the ground of this commandment, no doubt, is that they might learn to know one another's conditions, and that they might work a settled affection one toward another, which afterwards upon no occasion might be changed.

Yet they may be absent from each other in two cases. First, upon mutual consent for a time for the performing of some business that is requisite for the family. "For mine husband is not at home, he is gone a far journey: at the appointed time he will return again" (Prov. 7:19). Second, the like absence is allowed when some great and weighty affairs either in the church or commonwealth are in hand. "But Uriah slept at the door of the king's palace, with all the servants of his lord, and went not down to his house.... Then Uriah answered David, the ark, and Israel, and Judah dwell in tents, and my lord Joab, and the servants of my lord abide in the open field; shall I then go into my house to eat, and drink, and lie with my wife? By thy life, and by the life of my soul, I will not do this thing" (2 Sam. 11:9, 11–12).

Question. Hence arises a question. What if, after [the] marriage [is] consummated, there grows upon one of the parties a contagious disease that cannot be cured, but is so loathsome that the other party cannot endure cohabitation at all? *Answer*. Both the marriage itself, and the duty of dwelling together, ought to continue firm and sure notwithstanding, yet so as the sound party neither may, nor ought in good conscience, to desire conjunction with the other whereby he or she may bring infection upon themselves, and consequently hurt their children and endanger the commonwealth. But if either of the parties has not the gift of continence, nor cannot abstain, they must sue for it unto God in earnest prayer, who will give it unto them. For God has called a man or woman to continency when they are necessarily hindered from the use of the ordinary and lawful remedy of the contract.

Desertion

The contrary to cohabitation is desertion. Desertion is when one of the married folks, upon a willful and obstinate mind of their own head, departs from the other without a just and necessary cause. Touching this point, sundry cases are expounded.

Case 1

Suppose that a husband, who is an unbeliever or a heretic in the foundation, of his own accord, upon detestation of true religion, quite forsakes the believing wife, and denies to dwell with her any more. What is to be done?

Answer. All good means must be first used to bring the infected party to repentance. And when none will succeed, but the case remains desperate, then marriage is dissolved on his part, and the believing wife is free to marry another. The apostle says so: "If the unbelieving party depart, let him depart; a brother or a sister is not in subjection in such things; but God hath called us unto peace" (1 Cor. 7:15). Observe a twofold reason in these words. First, he who is at liberty may marry another. Now the believing party, [who is] forsaken, is at liberty because he is not in subjection in such things; therefore, he may marry another. Second, God has called us unto peace, says Paul, and this peace cannot be kept if the believing party, [who is] forsaken, cannot contain unless he marries.[1]

Ambrose says upon the place: "Marriage, which is separated from the worship and service of God, cannot stand firm. And, therefore, it is no sin in

1. This paragraph break is not in the original.

the party, who is forsaken for God's cause, to be married to another. And the departing unbeliever sins both against God and against the law of wedlock, because he denies to remain in that estate in regard of religion. Therefore, he breaks the covenant of marriage, and the other is not bound in this case to keep touch with him."[2] Lombard, the master of the *Sentences*, says, "The believing party in this case is not bound to follow the unbeliever when he departs, but while he lives may marry another."[3] Augustine affirms that "even the wife, who is joined to her husband in lawful society, if she will not abide with her Christian husband, because he is a Christian, may be forsaken and left without sin."[4] And it is far better that the covenant, which man and wife have made with each other, should be dissolved than the covenant which man has made with God. The people of Israel, being in affliction, were constrained to break the former made with strange women that they might keep the latter (Ezra 10:11, 19).

It is alleged that the unbelieving party may haply repent, and then to make a dissolution is in vain. But I say that it is as likely that he will never repent, and therefore there is cause that the knot should be dissolved.

Again, it is lawful (say some) to make a divorce out of the case of adultery. *Answer.* The believing party who is forsaken is not the cause of the divorce, but is a patient of the separation, wrongfully made by the unbeliever. And Christ, where He mentions the case of adultery (Matthew 19), speaks of an equal marriage, whereas Paul speaks of an unequal.

Case 2

What if there falls out a desertion between two married folks who are both believers?

Answer. The faulty person, who is the cause of this desertion, is to be forced by course of civil and ecclesiastical censure to perform his or her duty. Upon this proceeding, if he remains obstinate and perverse in will, the other must in patience and earnest prayer unto God wait the time until his mind may be changed and made to relent by the order of the magistrate. But if the one of them, by just occasion of fear, is compelled to depart from the other, and cannot return again without apparent danger of life, in this case they are not bound to return. But the delinquent party is to remain solitary, until they are instructed and made willing to do their duties. And in the meanwhile, the innocent party must be resolved that God has called him or her to [a] single life.

Again, what if the one is resolutely unwilling to dwell with the other, and thereupon flies away without any fault of the other? If after a long space the

2. In the margin: Ambrose in 1 Cor. 7:15.

3. In the margin: Lib. 4. dist. 39.

4. In the margin: Lib. de Fide & Oper. cap. 16.

thing is sufficiently known beforehand, and all possible means have been used to reclaim the guilty person, yea (being called) he does not personally appear before the judge to yield a reason of the fact, the minister upon such desertion may (after public and solemn declaration [is] made) pronounce the marriage to be dissolved. For he who upon malice flies away from his mate is to be held in the same terms with an unbeliever who departs upon detestation of religion and the service of God (1 Tim. 5:8).

Howbeit, if the place where he has fled is unknown, and upon his flight there is found some fault in the plaintiff, she is not to be heard or set at liberty by the judge in this case, though she pretends want of the gift of continency.

But suppose [that] he who fled comes again, unlooked for, and requires his spouse, then in case the former course has not been taken, nor judgment given against him, they may be reconciled and come together again. If it has, and matters are concluded, he is not upon his return to be heard, but rather severely punished.

Like unto desertion is malicious and spiteful dealing of married folks one with the other. Malicious dealing is when, dwelling together, they require of each other intolerable conditions, and when the one does not regard nor relieve the other, being in danger or extremity, as is meet. For this is as much as to betray one another's estate and life to their utter enemies.

Here it may be demanded what a believer should do, who is in certain and imminent danger, either of loss of life or breach of conscience, if they both abide together? *Answer*. (1) This certain danger has its original, either from one who is a stranger or from one of the parties. If from a stranger, then the husband either takes upon him the defense of his believing wife or not. If he does, then she ought to abide with him. If not, she may depart and provide for her own safety. (2) If the husband threatens hurt, the believing wife may flee in this case. And it is all one as if the unbelieving man should depart. For to depart from one and drive one away by threats are equivalent.

Neither may this seem strange unto any, that the believer in such case is allowed to depart. For a husband who is a Christian is married two ways: first, with Christ; and, second, with his wife. The former marriage is made in baptism, and is a more holy conjunction than the latter. Therefore, when these two cannot stand together, but one of them must needs be dissolved, the latter must rather be left than the former. Again, if the believer should remain with the unbeliever, she should haply be urged sometimes, in case of danger upon infirmity, to deny Christ and make shipwreck of faith and good conscience, which may in no sort be done by either party. And, therefore, separation is to be made in this society rather than that the conjunction with Christ should not stand firm and continue.

It is alleged that if this is so, then the believing wife forsakes the unbelieving husband, which she may not do. *Answer.* She forsakes him not finally, but leaves him for a time. Again, the desertion is not made by the person who gives place for the time, but by him in whom is the cause of the desertion, even as he is not to be termed a schismatic, who separates himself but he in whom is the cause of schism.

Again, it is objected that he who flies leaves his calling, and every man must abide in his calling, according to the rule of the apostle (1 Cor. 7:20). *Answer.* There is a double calling: (1) the general, standing in the worship of God; [and] (2) the particular, as the calling of marriage or single life. When these two callings cannot stand together, the latter must give place to the former. "If any man come to me, and hate not his father, and mother, and wife, and children, and brethren, and sisters; yea and his own life also, he cannot be my disciple" (Luke 14:26).

Case 3
When the husband is perpetually absent from the wife, what is to be done?

Answer. If he is absent because he is in captivity, or upon malice, or fear, or any such like cause, the wife must rest in expectation of his return, till she has notice of his death, either by sufficient testimony or by apparent likelihoods. Now in the want of testimonies and conjectures in this behalf, if the forsaken party cannot certainly determine that the absence was made upon an evil mind, some have thought that it behooves her to expect his coming again for the space of four years, others of five, some of seven, some of ten years. After this time, she is free, and may marry another man. And if the party does haply return again after some long space of time, who was probably thought to have been dead, the latter marriage, undertaken upon necessary ignorance of such an event, may be dissolved. And it shall not be imputed to either party, considering it fell out not by their fault, but only by accident.

Now if the question is of willful and affected absence, the same is to be determined concerning that which has been said before touching the point of desertion.

Chapter 10

The Duties of Married Persons: Communion

The communion of man and wife is that duty whereby they do mutually and willingly communicate both their persons and goods to each other, for their mutual help, necessity, and comfort. "So ought men to love their wives as their own bodies; he that loveth his wife, loveth himself" (Eph. 5:28).

This duty consists principally in the performance of special benevolence to one another, and that not of courtesy but of due debt. "Let the husband give unto the wife due benevolence, and likewise also the wife unto the husband" (1 Cor. 7:3).

Due benevolence must be shown with a singular and entire affection toward one another, and that [in] principally three ways.

Point 1

First, by the right and lawful use of their bodies (or of the marriage bed), which is indeed an essential duty of marriage.

The marriage bed signifies that solitary and secret society that is between man and wife alone. And it is a thing of its own nature indifferent, neither good nor bad. And so, Paul numbers it among indifferent things. "Art thou bound unto a wife? seek not to be loosed: art thou loosed from a wife? seek not a wife" (1 Cor. 7:27). Wherefore, the Church of Rome errs [in] two contrary ways. First, in that it makes marriage to be a sacrament, and so every action of it to be of its own nature good. Second, in that they prohibit marriage of certain parties, and the reason of the prohibition may seem to be this, that they think this secret coming together of man and wife to be filthiness. This was the sentence of Syricus, that filthy pope of Rome, who determined that marriage was the uncleanness of the flesh, and to that purpose abused the words of the apostle, affirming, that "they which are in the flesh (that is, in the estate of matrimony) cannot please God" (Rom. 8:8).[1] Yea, and after marriage was condemned by them, some began to detest and hate women, as Ephraim, the Syrian, of whom

1. In the margin: Canon. Proposuisti. Dist. 82.

ecclesiastical stories make mention.[2] And the Council of Trent is of the same judgment.[3] For whereas it opposes marriage and chastity, it plainly determines that there is no chastity in marriage.

This coming together of man and wife, although it is indifferent, yet by the holy usage thereof, it is made a holy and undefiled action. "Marriage is honorable among all, and the bed undefiled" (Heb. 13:4). And it is (as all other creatures and ordinances of God are) sanctified by the Word and prayer. "Forbidding to marry.... And nothing ought to be refused: for it is sanctified by the word of God and prayer" (1 Tim. 4:3–5). In this place, it is to be observed how the apostle applies the point of sanctification directly to marriage.

The Word of God gives direction to married folks two ways. First, by giving them warrant that they may lawfully do this action, because whatsoever is not done of faith (which faith must be grounded on God's Word) is a sin. Second, by prescribing the right and holy manner of doing the same.

The holy manner stands in these particulars.

First, that it is done in moderation. For even in wedlock excess in lusts is no better than plain adultery before God. This is the judgment of the ancient church, that intemperance (that is, immoderate desire even between man and wife) is fornication.[4]

Second, that it is used in a holy abstinence. Abstinence from this secret society must be used in two cases. First, while the woman is in her flowers: "Thou shalt not go to a woman to uncover her shame, as long as she is put apart for her disease" (Lev. 18:19). And it is made one of the properties of a good man not to lie with a menstruous woman (Ezek. 18:6). Second, in the time of a solemn fast when some grievous calamity is imminent, then they are to give themselves (by mutual consent) to fasting and prayer. "Defraud not one another, except it be with consent for a time, that you may give yourselves to fasting and prayer: and again come together, that Satan tempt you not for your incontinency" (1 Cor. 7:5). "Then Uriah answered David, the ark and Israel, and Judah dwell in tents: and my lord Joab, and the servants of my lord abide in the open fields: shall I then go into mine house to eat and drink, and lie with my wife? By thy life, and by the life of thy soul, I will not do this thing" (2 Sam. 11:11). "The family of the house of David shall mourn apart, and their wives apart; the family of the house of Nathan apart, and their wives apart, etc." (Zech. 12:12).

Next unto the Word, this action may be sanctified by prayer for a blessing upon it. Children are the gift of God, and therefore married folks are not only

---

2. In the margin: Sozom. l. 3. c. 16.
3. In the margin: Sess. 8. cap. 9. 10.
4. In the margin: Ambros. lib. de Philosop. citat. ab August. contr. Julian. lib. 2.

to use the means, but also to pray for the obtaining of them. "He maketh the barren woman to dwell with a family, and to be a joyful mother of children" (Ps. 113:9). "Behold children are the inheritance of the Lord, and the fruit of the womb his reward" (Ps. 127:3). Examples for this purpose are these: "Isaac prayed unto the Lord for his wife, because she was barren, and the Lord was entreated of him; and Rebekah his wife conceived" (Gen. 25:21). "And she said, Oh my lord, as thy soul liveth, my lord, I am the woman that stood with thee here, praying unto the Lord. I prayed for this child, and the Lord hath given me my desire, which I asked of him" (1 Sam. 1:26–27).

Now the fruits which are reaped and enjoyed by this holy usage of the marriage bed are three. (1) The having of a blessed seed. "If thou shalt obey diligently the voice of the Lord thy God.... Blessed shall be the fruit of thy body, and the fruit of thy ground" (Deut. 28:1, 4). This is also called "the seed of God," being begotten in a holy manner. "And did not he make one? Yet had he abundance of Spirit: And wherefore one? Because he sought a seed of God: therefore, keep yourselves in your spirit, and let none trespass against the wife of his youth" (Mal. 2:15). (2) The preservation of the body in cleanness, that it may be a fit temple for the Holy Spirit to dwell in. "This is the will of God, even your sanctification, that every one of you should know how to possess his vessel in holiness and honor, and not in the lust of concupiscence, even as the Gentiles that know not God" (1 Thess. 4:3–4). (3) The holy estate of marriage is a lively type of Christ and His church, and this communion of married persons is also a figure of the conjunction that is between Him and the faithful. "I will marry thee unto me, forever; yea I will marry thee unto me in righteousness, in judgment, in mercy, and in compassion: I will even marry thee unto me in faithfulness, and thou shalt know the Lord" (Hos. 2:19). "For the husband is the wife's head, even as Christ is the head of the church, and the same is the Savior of his body" (Eph. 5:23).

Here some questions are to be resolved.

Case 1

Whether marriage may be dissolved in the case of barrenness?

Answer. No, for barrenness is a hidden infirmity for the most part, and God has many times cured it, even when it seemed to be desperate, as in Sarah. Again, the fruit of the womb is God's blessing, and [it] wholly depends upon Him. He, therefore, who in want of children, rejects his wife whom he has received at the hands of God, offers wrong even to God Himself.

Case 2

What if either of the married folks commits fornication, or any sin of the same kind greater than fornication, as incest, sodomy, lying with beasts, or such like?

Answer. Adultery and fornication are most grievous and open crimes, which do break the very bond and covenant of marriage (Prov. 2:17). Therefore, when they are certainly known by such persons, they are at no hand to be winked at, but the magistrate is presently to be informed of them. Howbeit, if the innocent party is willing to receive the adulterer again, in regard of his repentance, lest he should seem to favor and maintain sin and to be himself a practicer of uncleanness, he is to repair to the congregation, and declare the whole matter to the minister, that he may understand the party's repentance and desire of forgiveness.

And if the adulteress has conceived and is in travail, the husband, to avoid the imputation of having an heir in bastardy, is to make relation to the church of the repentance of the adulteress, or to acquaint some certain persons therewith, not to the end that she should be punished for the act, but that they may take notice of a child conceived in adultery, whom afterward he may lawfully put off as none of his.

The matter being known, the innocent party may require a divorce. For adultery is such a sin as does quite break off, not only the use, but the bond and covenant of marriage. "I say therefore unto you, that whosoever shall put away his wife, except it be for whoredom, and marry another, committeth adultery, etc." (Matt. 19:9). And yet, the same bond may be continued, and grow up again by the good will and consent of the innocent party, and consequently they may be reconciled and dwell together still. "Now Saul had given Michal his daughter, David's wife, to Phalti the son of Laish, which was of Gallim" (1 Sam. 25:44). "Then David sent messengers to Ishbosheth, Saul's son, saying, Deliver me my wife Michal, which I married for a hundred foreskins of the Philistines" (2 Sam. 3:14). The same course may be taken in like cases by the innocent, especially upon the repentance of the guilty person. But yet, every man must be left to his own conscience, and none is to be compelled to take another from whom he may justly be separated against his will.

Now, in requiring a divorce, there is an equal right and power in both parties, so as the woman may require it as well as the man, and he as well as she. The reason is because they are equally bound to each other, and have also the same interest in one another's body, provided always that the man is to maintain his superiority and the woman to observe that modesty which beseems her toward the man.

After the divorce [is] made, it shall be lawful for the harmless party, not having the gift of continency, upon leave obtained of the church and the Christian magistrate, to marry again.

But what then shall become of the offending party? *Answer.* If upon the hazard of his conscience in want of the remedy, any liberty of second marriage is to be granted unto him by the church or civil magistrate (as indeed here in England there is not), divers restraints must be observed in this case.

First, no such liberty is to be granted so long as the matter remains uncertain whether they may be reconciled, especially while the innocent party lives in single life. Second, it must evidently appear that the said offending party has earnestly repented him of his sin, before he can either be received into the church or admitted to a second marriage. Third, this liberty is not to be granted him either presently or unadvisedly, but upon frequent and serious admonition, to give himself to mourning and lamentation, and still to remain alone rather than to desire again to enjoy the benefit of that state which he has already so shamefully abused.

So much of the first way of performance of due benevolence.

Point 2

The second way is by cherishing one another. "No man ever hated his own flesh, but nourisheth and cherisheth it, as Christ also doth the church" (Eph. 5:29). This cherishing is the performing of any duties that tend to the preserving of the lives of one another. Wherefore, they are freely to communicate their goods, counsel, [and] labors to each other, for the good of themselves and theirs.

Point 3

The third way is by a holy kind of rejoicing and solacing themselves with each other, in a mutual declaration of the signs and tokens of love and kindness. "Rejoice with the wife of thy youth. Let her be as the loving hind and pleasant wild goat: let her breasts satisfy thee at all times, and delight in her love continually" (Prov. 5:18–19). "Let him kiss me with the kisses of his mouth, for thy love is better than wine" (Cant. 1:1). "So after he had been there a long time, Abimelech, king of the Philistines, looked out at a window and lo, he saw Isaac sporting with Rebekah his wife: Then Abimelech called Isaac and said; Lo, she is of a surety thy wife" (Gen. 26:8). "As a young man marrieth a virgin, so shall thy sons marry thee; and as a bridegroom is glad of the bride, so shall thy God rejoice over thee" (Isa. 62:7).

This rejoicing and delight is more permitted to the man than to the woman, and to them both more in their young years than in their old age.

Chapter 11

The Husband

Married folks are either husband or wife. The husband is he who has authority over the wife. Hereupon in Scripture he is called the "guide of her youth" (Prov. 2:17). And being but one flesh, he is also the head over his wife. The duties of the husband toward the wife are these.

Duty 1

First, to love her as himself: "Let everyone love his wife even as himself" (Eph. 5:33). "Afterward Isaac brought her unto the tent of Sarah his mother; and he took Rebekah and she was his wife, and he loved her; so Isaac left mourning for his mother" (Gen. 24:67). Note, how the love of the husband to the wife mitigates sorrow for the death of the mother.

He is to show this love in two things. First, in protecting her from danger. "And unto Sarah he said, Behold I have given 1,000 shekels of silver unto thy brother: behold he is the covering of thine eyes amongst all that are with thee. Let it be known amongst all, and be thou instructed" (Gen. 20:16). "David's two wives were taken prisoners also, Ahinoam, the Jezreelite, and Abigail, the wife of Nabal the Carmelite.... Then David asked counsel of the Lord saying, Shall I follow after this company? Shall I overtake them? And he answered him, Follow, for thou shalt surely overtake them, and recover all" (1 Sam. 30:5, 8). Second, in regarding her estate as his own, and providing maintenance for her, both for his lifetime and (as much as he may) for time to come after his death. "So ought men to love their wives, as their own bodies: he that loveth his wife loveth himself. For no man yet hated his own flesh, but nourisheth it, etc." (Eph. 5:28–29). "If he take him another wife, he shall not diminish her food, her raiment, and recompense of her virginity" (Ex. 21:10). "Unto whom he said, who art thou? Which said; I am Ruth thine handmaid, spread therefore the wing of thy garment over thine handmaid; for thou art the kinsman" (Ruth 3:9).

Duty 2

Second, to honor his wife: "Giving honor to the woman" (1 Peter 3:7). This honor stands in three things.

First, in making account of her as his companion (or yoke-fellow). For this cause, the woman, when she was created, was not taken out of the man's head, because she was not made to rule over him, nor out of his feet, because God did not make her subject to him as a servant, but out of his side, to the end that man should take her as his mate.

Second, in a wise and patient bearing or covering of her infirmities, as anger, waywardness, and such like, in respect of the weakness of her sex. "Giving honor to the woman, as unto the weaker vessel, seeing ye are heirs together of the grace of life, that your prayers be not hindered" (1 Peter 3:7).

Third, by suffering himself sometimes to be admonished or advised by her. It was God's commandment to Abraham concerning Sarah his wife: "Let it not be grievous in thy sight for the child, and for thy bondwoman: in all that Sarah shall say unto thee, hear her voice; For in Isaac shall thy seed be called" (Gen. 21:12). Elkanah was willing to subscribe thus unto his wife Hannah's advice, for her tarrying at home till the child was weaned. "And Elkanah her husband said unto her, do what seemeth thee best: tarry until thou hast weaned him: only the Lord accomplish his word" (1 Sam. 1:23). Hereupon the heathen philosopher said, "The master of the family exercises (after a sort) a tyrannical power over his servants, a regal power over his children, because kings are fathers of their commonwealths; but, in respect of his wife, he exercises an aristocratical power, not after his own will, but agreeable to the honor and dignity of the married estate."[1] And consequently, that he ought not in modesty to challenge the privilege of prescribing and advertising his wife in all domestic matters, but in some to leave her to her own will and judgment.

Here [a] question is moved, whether the husband may correct the wife? *Answer.* Though the husband is the wife's head, yet it seems he has no power nor liberty granted him in this regard. For we read not in the Scriptures [of] any precept or example to warrant such practice of his authority. He may reprove and admonish her in word only, if he sees her in fault. For, thus we read that Jacob censured his wife, being impatient, even in anger: "Am I in God's stead, which hath withholden from thee, the fruit of the womb?" (Gen. 30:2). And Job reproved his wife: "Thou speakest like a foolish woman. What? Shall we receive good at the hand of God, and not receive evil?" (Job 2:10). But he may not chastise her either with stripes or strokes. The reason is plain. Wives are their husband's mates; and they, [though] two, are one flesh. And no man will hate, much less beat, his own flesh, but [he] nourishes and cherishes it (Eph. 5:29). Again, it is the commandment of God that man should not "trespass against the wife of his youth" (Mal. 2:15). Chrysostom says, "It is the greatest reproach

1. In the margin: Arist. Ethic. lib. 8.

for any man (that can be) to beat his wife."[2] Plutarch, in the life of Cato the Censor, affirms that "he who smites his wife does all one as if he should lay violent hands upon the sacred images of the gods," which was counted a high degree of offence among the heathen.

It is alleged [that] husbands are commanded so to love their wives as Christ does His church. Now Christ chastises His church with strokes. And, therefore, so may the husband his wife. *Answer.* As Christ does entirely love His church, so He may also chastise the same, because He is not only the husband, but also absolute Lord and King of His church. [But] so the husband is not absolute over the wife.

But his authority over the wife is after a sort civil, as is the authority of the magistrate over his people. *Answer.* It is not so. For the magistrate has in his hand the power of the sword, by which power he inflicts punishment in case of offence. But the husband can challenge to himself no such power; yea, it is flatly forbidden in the civil law that he should scourge or strike his wife.[3]

Nevertheless, if she grows to extremities and is desperately perverse so as there is no hope of amendment, then the magistrate may be informed, who, to prevent scandals and provide for public peace, both ought and may assign unto her necessary correction and punishment according to her desert. Now the husband who has a wife so stubborn and peevish must bear it (if it may be borne) as the portion of his cross laid upon him by God. And in this case, if he is impatient, he may in some sort be pardoned and pitied, but he is not wholly to be excused.

---

2. In the margin: In 1. Cor. 11. Hom. 26.
3. L. Consensu. C. Divortijs.

Chapter 12

The Wife

The wife is the other married person who, being subject to her husband, yields obedience unto him.

Touching the subjection of the wife, the Word of God mentions it in sundry places. "The woman which is in subjection to the man, is bound by the law to the man, while he liveth" (Rom. 7:2). "As the church is in subjection to Christ, even so let the wives be to their husbands in everything" (Eph. 5:24). "Wives submit yourselves unto your husbands, as it is comely in the Lord" (Col. 3:18). "I permit not a woman to usurp authority over the man" (1 Tim. 2:12). And it was a law established by God immediately after the fall: "Unto the woman he said, I will greatly increase...and thy desire shall be subject to thine husband, and he shall rule over thee" (Gen. 3:16). Indeed, the daughter, according to the civil law, even when she is married is "in the power of her father,"[1] and not of her husband. But this is directly against the law of Moses, and [it] crosses the law of nature (Lev. 22:12–13; Num. 30:13).

Now the duties of the wife are principally two.

Duty 1

The first is to submit herself to her husband, and to acknowledge and reverence him as her head in all things. "Likewise Abimelech said unto Sarah, Behold thy brother (that is, your husband, whom you call your brother) is the veil of thine eyes to all that are with thee" (Gen. 20:16). As if he should say: "Your husband is your head, and has power over you, and you ought to reverence him." For, of ancient times, the wife was covered with a veil in the presence of her husband in token of subjection to him. Thus, Rebekah at the sight of Isaac, took a veil "and covered her head therewith (Gen. 24:65). "The man is the woman's head" (1 Cor. 11:3). "Wives submit yourselves unto your husbands, as unto the Lord; for the husband is the wife's head, even as Christ is the head of his church" (Eph. 5:22). The reason hereof is good. For the wife enjoys the privileges of her husband, and is graced by his honor and estimation among men. His nobility

1. In the margin: *In potestate patris.*

makes her noble, though otherwise she is base and mean. As contrariwise, his baseness and low degree causes her, though she is by birth noble and honorable, to be by estate base and mean.

Duty 2

The second duty is to be obedient unto her husband in all things; that is, wholly to depend upon him, both in judgment and will. For look as the church yields obedience to Christ, her head, and yields herself to be commanded, governed, and directed by Him, so ought the woman to the man. So, Sarah is said "to obey Abraham," and to give him the terms of obedience: "she called him lord," or sir (1 Peter 3:6). Hence it follows that the woman is not to take liberty of wandering and straying abroad from her own house without the man's knowledge and consent. "Then she called to her husband and said, Send with me, I pray thee, one of the young men, and one of the asses; for I will haste to the man of God, and come again" (2 Kings 4:22). Again, she is to follow her husband when he flits or departs from place to place, unless he forsakes either her or Christ. To this purpose, Paul says he "had power to lead about a wife, being a sister, as well as the rest of the apostles" (1 Cor. 9:5). Thus, Sarah went with Abraham into Egypt (Gen. 12:11), and out of Egypt (Gen. 13:1), and to "Gerar to sojourn there" (Gen. 20:1–3). Thus, the wives of Jacob departed with him from their father Laban (Gen. 31:17).

Contrary to these duties are the sins of wives: to be proud, to be unwilling to bear the authority of their husbands, to chide and brawl with bitterness, to forsake their houses, etc. "A continual dropping in the day of rain and a contentious woman are alike. He that hideth her, hideth the wind, and she is as the oil in his right hand, that uttereth itself" (Prov. 27:15–16). "Then Zipporah said, O bloody husband; because of the circumcision..." (Ex. 4:26). It was the fault of the Levite's concubine, "Who played the whore, and went away from him unto her father's house to Bethlehem Judah, and there continued the space of four months" (Judges 19:2). It was the sin of Queen Vashti, "who refused to come at the king's word, which he had given in charge to the eunuchs: therefore, the king was very angry, and his wrath kindled in him" (Esther 1:12). Lastly, to be a cause of grief to their kindred; thus, the proud wives of Esau, the daughters of the Hittites, were a grief of mind to Isaac and Rebekah (Gen. 26:35; 27:46).

Chapter 13

The Parent

Hitherto the first couple, whereof the family consists, has been treated; namely, married folks. Now follow the others. And they are of two sorts: (1) such as whereby the family is increased and multiplied; and (2) such as are helps thereunto.

Those whereby the family is enlarged are also of two sorts: parents and children. Parents are they who have power and authority over children. The duties of parents are especially two: (1) to bring up their children; [and] (2) to bestow them when they have brought them up.

Duty 1

Touching education (or bringing up of children), the parents' care must be both, that they may live and that they may live well (Eph. 6:4).

Point 1

Touching the preservation of the life of the child, there are many duties required of the parents, especially four.

First, the mother is herself to give the infant suck, and to wrap it up in swaddling clothes. Paul commends it for a note of a good wife: "to nurse her own children" (1 Tim. 5:10). Thus, Sarah gave suck to Isaac (Gen. 21:7). Hannah nursed Samuel (1 Sam. 1:22). David in likelihood was nursed by his mother: "Thou gavest me hope even at my mother's breasts" (Ps. 22:9). And our Savior Christ was also nursed and swaddled by Mary His mother (Luke 11:27; 2:7). Now the reason hereof is plain. God has given milk to women who bear children, and so appointed that no meat is more natural to the child than the mother's milk. And nature itself teaches this in the course of other creatures. The earth nourishes that which it brings forth. The fruit, which the tree bears, is fed by the sap that comes from the root thereof. Yea, among the brute beasts, even those that are most savage, as the tigers, do give suck unto the young ones which they bring forth.

Yet, in case of want of health, or ability, or any other just impediment, the mother may in equity be forborne, and the child committed unto a nurse. And so, we read that Rebekah, the daughter of Bethuel, and afterward the wife of Isaac, had a nurse (Gen. 24:59) whose name was Deborah (Gen. 35:8). And Pharaoh's daughter, in a case of necessity, committed Moses to be nursed by a Hebrew woman, whom she took not to be his mother, but a stranger, and her act was allowed by God (Ex. 2:7–9).

The second duty of the parent is to provide meat, drink, and clothing for his child. Our Savior Christ says that parents, even by the light of nature, though they are evil, will not deny or withhold necessary food from their children. "What man is there among you, that if his son ask him bread, will give him a stone, or if he ask a fish, will give him a scorpion?" (Matt. 7:9–10). And Paul says, "If there be any that provideth not for his own, and namely for them of his household, he denieth the faith, and is worse than an infidel" (1 Tim. 5:8).

The third duty is, when God gives ability and means, to lay up something for the future maintenance of the child. "For the children ought not to lay up for the fathers, but the fathers for the children" (2 Cor. 12:14). "House and riches are the inheritance of the fathers" (Prov. 19:14).

The fourth is to observe both the inclination and natural gifts of body and mind that are in the child, and accordingly to bestow it in some honest calling and course of life. "A child is known by his actions, whether his work be pure and right" (Prov. 20:11). In the *Ecclesiastical History*, written by Ruffinus, it is recorded that Alexander, bishop of Alexandria, saw afar off, in a place near to the sea, a company of children playing together, and in their play imitating himself in sundry ministerial actions.[1] And when [he] had a while viewed them, he perceived that they examined and baptized one another according to the solemn order used in his congregation. When he had made some of his clergy acquainted with this thing, and withal taken order that the children should be sent for and brought before him, he demanded of them what sport they used, and in what manner they played with one another. The children at first, for fear, denied what they had done, yet upon further examination they confessed that they had made Athanasius (who afterward became bishop of the place) their bishop, and that he instructed and baptized sundry of their company. He further asked both Athanasius himself, and those who were said to have been baptized, what questions he asked them and what answers they gave. And perceiving by their speeches that they had framed themselves, though in sporting manner, to the church proceedings in those actions, upon conference had with his clergy, he determined that those who had first been asked, and had given answer fully, according to the form used in that church, and thereupon baptized, should not be re-baptized. And for Athanasius and the other

1. In the margin: Ruffin. Eccl. Hist. lib. 1. c. 14.

children, who had done the part of ministers in their kind, he sent for their parents, and gave them great charge that they should be brought up in learning and religion, so that they might in time be fit for the public ministry. We read the like course to have been taken by the heathen, for judgment of the inclination and towardness of their children. The Athenians made a law that before children were bestowed in any calling, they should be first brought into a public place where instruments, belonging to all sorts of trades were laid.[2] And look in what kind of instrument any of them took most delight, the child was thought to be most fit for the trade whereunto that instrument belonged, and afterward applied to the same with good success.

Now the parents' first and principal care must be for the church, that those of their children, who have the most pregnant wit and are endued with the best gifts, are consecrated unto God and brought up in the study of the Scriptures, to serve afterward in the ministry of the church. Thus, Hannah dedicated Samuel her son unto God by [a] vow: "And she vowed a vow, and said, O Lord of hosts, if thou wilt...give unto thine handmaid a man-child, then I will give him unto the Lord all the days of his life" (1 Sam. 1:11). And she did according to her vow, and the Lord blessed Samuel her son, who in process of time became a great prophet.

Point 2

The next point of education of children is to provide that they may live well and lead a godly life. To this purpose, parents must do three things.

First, they are to be careful that the child, as soon as may be, after it is born, is admitted into the true church of God by baptism, and have a fit name given unto it.

Second, they are to endeavor to sow the seeds of godliness and religion in the heart of the child, as soon as it comes to the use of reason and understanding. And, as it grows in years, so care must be had that it grows in knowledge and grace. To this purpose is the vow and promise made in baptism, which parents are bound to call upon the child to remember when it comes to years. It was the godly care of Timothy's parents: "But continue thou in the things which thou hast learned, knowing of whom thou hast learned them. And that thou hast known the Holy Scriptures of a child, which are able to make thee wise unto salvation, through the faith which is in Christ Jesus" (2 Tim. 3:14–15). This was the commandment of God to the parents of His people: "Thou shalt rehearse these words which I command thee continually to thy children, and shalt talk of them when thou tarriest in the house.... When thy son shall ask

2. In the margin: Nazian. Epist. ad Eudox.

thee in time to come, saying, What mean these testimonies, and ordinances, and laws, which the Lord our God hath commanded you? Then thou shalt say unto thy son, We were Pharaoh's bondmen in Egypt, etc." (Deut. 6:7, 20). This was observed by the Israelites in the succeeding ages: "We have heard with our ears, O God: our fathers have told us the works that thou hast done in their days in old time" (Ps. 44:1).

Third, the first instruction of children in learning and religion must be so ordered that they may take it with delight. For which purpose, they may be sometimes allowed in moderate manner to play and solace themselves in recreations fitting for their years. And if they do amiss in either, they are to be restrained by the bridle of discipline. First, by reproof in word, and when that will not help, by the rod of correction. "The streets of the city shall be full of boys and girls, playing in the streets thereof" (Zech. 8:5). "The rod and correction give wisdom, but a child set at liberty makes his mother ashamed.... Correct thy son, and he will give thee rest, and give pleasures to thy soul" (Prov. 29:15, 17). "We have had the fathers of our bodies which correct us, and we gave them reverence" (Heb. 12:9).

Yet, in this point, two extremes are carefully to be avoided. The parent [must] not be either too severe or too indulgent to the child. For severity, Paul gives this rule: "Parents, provoke not your children to anger" (Eph. 6:3); that is, by too much austerity in government. For leniency, we have old Eli's example: "And he said unto them, Why do ye such things? For of all this people, I hear evil reports of you. Do no more my sons, etc." (1 Sam. 2:23).

So much for education.

Duty 2

The second general duty of parents is the bestowing of their children. This bestowing is when they, knowing their children fit for marriage, not to have the gift of continency, do use their best endeavor to provide matches for them in time, or, at least, do advise them thereunto by themselves or by their friends. "If any man think it uncomely for his virgin to pass the flower of her age, and need so require...let them be married.... He that giveth her to marriage, doth well" (1 Cor. 7:36, 38). "Take ye wives...and take wives for your sons, and give your daughters to husbands, etc." (Jer. 26:6). "Isaac called Jacob and blessed him, and charged him and said unto him, Take not a wife of the daughters of Canaan. Arise, get thee to Padan Aram...and thence take thee a wife of the daughters of Laban thy mother's brother" (Gen. 28:1). "Samson came and told his father and his mother, and said, I have seen a woman of the daughters of the Philistines; now therefore give me her to wife" (Judges 14:2).

This duty is now-a-days carelessly neglected by parents. And the fruit thereof is dangerous. For hence it comes to pass that their children oftentimes do either commit whoredom or undertake wicked and ungodly marriages.

In the choice of a husband or wife, the parents ought to have a greater respect unto piety and wisdom than unto beauty and riches or any other outward blessings. Yet, where they all concur, the party so qualified is the more thankfully to be entertained. Upon these grounds the priest (or prince) of Midian gave his daughter Zipporah to Moses, and Moses agreed to take her. "A man of Egypt delivered us from the Philistines, and also drew us water enough, and watered the sheep.... And Moses agreed to dwell with the man, who gave unto Moses Zipporah his daughter" (Ex. 2:10). "Then Caleb said, He that smiteth Kiriath-sepher, and taketh it, even to him will I give Achsah my daughter to wife" (Josh. 15:16). Yea, it is a sin to marry only for beauty without consideration of the better things. The old world sinned thus when "the sons of God saw the daughters of men that they were fair, and took them wives of all that they liked" (Gen. 6:2). And Samson, who only upon the sight of the woman in Timnah, of the daughters of the Philistines, without further inquiry, desired that she might be given him for his wife (Judges 14:2).

Again, it is meet that parents should deal moderately with their children in this case, and not undertake at any hand to force and compel them to marry this or that party. This was the just commendation of Rebekah's parents, who, though they were idolaters, yet had that regard of equity that they first called her and asked her consent before they sent her away with Abraham's servant to be married to Isaac (Gen. 24:58). Now in [the] case [of] parents [who] fail in their duty in this regard, the son or daughter may lawfully declare the matter first to their kinsfolk, and afterward (if need be) to the minister or magistrate, and sue for redress by their means and direction.

Chapter 14

The Son

The son is he who is in subjection to his parents. The duties of a son to be performed to his parents are principally two.

Duty 1

First, to yield them obedience, whether they are his natural parents or otherwise, as his step-father and step-mother, and that while he lives. "Children obey your parents in the Lord; for this is right" (Eph. 6:1). "Then he went down with them, and came to Nazareth, and was subject to them" (Luke 2:51). Moses's father-in-law said unto him: "Hear now my voice, I will give thee counsel, and God shall be with thee" (Ex. 18:19). "And Ruth said unto Naomi her mother-in-law, All that thou biddest me, I will do" (Ruth 3:5). "And when the days of their banqueting were gone about, Job sent and sanctified them" (Job 1:5).

This obedience must show itself in two things. First, in the choice of a lawful calling, wherein the child is to be ordered and appointed at the discretion of the parent. Second, in marriage, for in that the parent is the principal agent and disposer of the child. Now, although his authority is not so great as that the child is to be forced and compelled by him, yet the reverent and dutiful respect which the child ought to bear toward him ought to be a strong inducement, not to dissent or renounce his advice without great and weighty cause. Yea, the child must endeavor by all manner of dutiful carriage to overcome or (at least) to mitigate his parents' severity in that behalf.

Now for the daughters, they must yield obedience to their parents in all domestic labors, that they may be skillful in household affairs. The seven daughters of the priest of Midian did thus accustom themselves to draw water, and fill the troughs to "water their father's sheep" (Ex. 2:16). Thus, Rebekah was seen to come out of her father's house, with her pitcher upon her shoulder, and to go down with it to the well to fill it, and "give drink to her father's camels" (Gen. 24:16–17).

Duty 2

The second duty of the son is to recompense his father's love and care over him by relieving him in case of want, if God gives ability, with food and raiment and other necessaries. Herein children must deal with their parents as the brood of the stork is reported to do with her, by feeding her when she is old, wherein they do no more but what she has done unto them. It is Paul's counsel that children and nephews should recompense the kindness of their kindred in the first place (1 Tim. 5:4), and therefore to their parents, the head and foundation of their kindred. When Joseph was in prosperity, and his father Jacob in want, he first gave him corn freely, and afterwards sent for him to Egypt, and there provided for him, insomuch as the text says of him that he nourished his father and his brethren and all his father's household with bread, "even as the mother puts meat into the child's mouth" (Gen. 47:12). When Naomi, the step-mother of Ruth, was of great years, and her strength spent, Ruth gathered corn in the harvest for relief of them both. Yea, when Boaz gave her to eat and to drink, she reserved part of her victuals, and brought it home with her gleanings to refresh her mother (Ruth 2:14, 18).

The necessity of the performance of these duties is so great that if the son neglects them, and does the contrary by ill usage of his parent either in word or deed, he is worthy of death, even by Moses's law: "He that smiteth his father or his mother, shall die the death" (Ex. 21:15).

The law of the first born of a man's children, that he should have a greater portion of his father's goods than any of the rest of his brethren, is perpetual, and [it] admits no exception but only in the case of notorious wickedness. "He shall acknowledge the son of the hated for the first born, and give him a double portion of all that he hath, for he is the first of his strength, and to him belongeth the right of the first born" (Deut. 21:17). This was the law. Yet, we read that Reuben lost this prerogative by reason of his incest, and Judah the fourth son of Jacob had the dignity of the first born. "Thou Judah, thy brethren shall praise thee...thy father's sons shall bow down unto thee" (Gen. 49:8).

In the church of the Old Testament, the privilege of the first born was three-fold: the first of government and royalty; the second of priesthood; [and] the third of the double portion. And it is probable that this was for the most part ceremonial, and was accomplished and determined in Christ, who "was the image of the invisible God, and the first born of every creature" (Col. 1:15).

Here two questions are propounded.

Question 1. Whether it is lawful for the son to make a vow belonging either to religion or to civil conversation without the consent of the parent? *Answer.* A vow so made is not of force to bind the child, but by the law of nature and common equity is to be made void. For it is a ruled case that he who is not his own man (that is to say, at his own liberty, but under the power of another) cannot bind himself. Again, the authority of the parent by the law of God is great, for it allows the father to make void the vow of the child pertaining to God's worship (Num. 30:6).

Question 2. Whether the consent of the parents is to be required in the second marriage of their children? *Answer.* Of ancient times, both by civil laws and imperial constitutions, it was provided that no widows, though made free by their former marriages, should make any contract again without the good will of their parents.[1] Consent in this case, though it is not absolutely necessary, yet it is to be thought fit and convenient, because children in some regards, exempted from [their] parents' authority, do owe notwithstanding the duty of honor unto them by God's express commandment (Ex. 20:12), and consequently ought to testify the same by being ordered and advised by them in some sort, even at the after-bestowing of themselves. Hence it is that later divines have held upon good ground that the espousals of widows, who have some more liberty than the child first married, being made without their parents' knowledge, cannot but incur just reprehension, howsoever they may stand in force without it.[2]

1. In the margin: C. de Nuptiis. L. vidua, & L. in conjunctione.
2. In the margin: Beza de repud. & divor. sect. de sponsalibus absq. consens. par. factis.

Chapter 15

The Master

Next unto parents and children, whereby the family is increased, is a second sort of couple who are helps thereunto. And they are masters and servants. The master is a member in the family who has power and bears rule over the servant. And his duty stands principally in three things.

First, to make a good choice of his servants, which is done when he inquires first after such as fear God and are willing to serve Him. Paul makes the service and fear of God the main ground of true obedience in servants (Eph. 6:5–7; Col. 3:22). It was the rule of David's choice: "He that walketh in the perfect way, he shall serve me" (Ps. 101:6). Abraham's chief servant of his house was a man who feared God, as appears in that he made conscience of his oath (Gen. 24:2–3), and [he] also prayed for success in the business whereabouts he was sent: "O Lord God of my master Abraham, I beseech thee send me good speed this day, and show mercy to my master Abraham" (Gen. 24:12). Cornelius of Caesarea, the captain of the Italian band, had a soldier who daily attended on him, who feared God, and also servants besides him, to whom he made known the heavenly vision which he saw (Acts 10:7).

Second, to enjoin them labor, and not to require more of them than their strength will bear. The master is to rule over the servant in justice, and his commandment is unjust when it will not stand with the course of nature, with the ability of his servant, or with the Word of God. Therefore, he is to require labor at their hands proportional to their strength, and yield them sometimes intercession and rest. "Over your brethren the children of Israel, ye shall not rule over one another with cruelty" (Lev. 25:46). "Be pitiful, be courteous, bear with one another" (1 Peter 3:8). And for the furtherance of business, it is convenient that the master is oftentimes present with the servants in their works. "Be diligent to know the state of thy flock, and take heed to thy herds" (Prov. 27:23). The good matron "overseeth the ways of her household (Prov. 31:27). A man of Libya, being asked what it was that might make a horse fat, answered, "the master's eye."[1]

---

1. In the margin: Arist. Oeco. 7.

Third, to recompense the diligence and pains of his servant, and that three ways. First, by giving him his due of meat and drink for the present. The good matron "giveth the portion to her household, and the ordinary to her maids" (Prov. 31:15).

Second, by paying him his hire in the end of his service. "The laborer is worthy of his wages" (Luke 10:7). "Well done, good servant and faithful; thou hast been faithful in little, I will make thee ruler over much; enter into thy master's joy" (Matt. 25:21). Here three caveats are to be observed. (1) The wages [must] be proportionate to the work. (2) It [must] be paid in due time, without deferring. So, the master of the vineyard, "when even was come," called his servants together, to "give them their hire" (Matt. 20:8). (3) The servant [must] not be defrauded of any part of his due. For this is a crying sin. "Thou shalt give him his hire for his day, neither shall the sun go down upon it…lest he cry against thee unto the Lord, and it be sin unto thee" (Deut. 24:15). "Behold, the hire of the laborers which have reaped your fields, which is kept back by fraud, crieth, and the cries of them which have reaped, are entered into the ears of the Lord of hosts" (Lam. 5:4).

Third, if the servant in [the] time of his service is sick, the master's care must be to procure his recovery by all possible means. Equity must be the rule in these cases. And masters are to "do to their servants that which is just and equal" (Col. 4:1). Now the servant haply falls sick by and in his service, and his health yields not only profit to his master, but encouragement also to himself. The good centurion, in [the] case of his servant's sickness, took the best course to have him restored (Matt. 8:6).

Chapter 16

The Servant

The servant is a person in the family subject unto his master. The duty of a servant is faithfully and diligently to demean himself in the affairs of his master, and to do service unto him as unto Christ, though he is froward and hard-hearted. "Let servants be subject to their masters, and please them in all things, not answering again" (Titus 2:9). "Servants, be obedient to them that are your masters according to the flesh, with fear and trembling, in singleness of your hearts, as unto Christ" (Eph. 6:5). [See] Col. 3:22. Thus Jacob served Laban. "These twenty years have I been with thee; thy ewes and thy goats have not cast their young, and the rams of the flock have I not eaten…" (Gen. 31:38).

Contrariwise, the servant must take heed that he does not his master's business negligently, or for fashion's sake, or with eye-service as a man-pleaser, [and] that in [the] case of rebuke or controlment he answers not again, [and,] lastly, that he is trustworthy and withholds his hands from picking and his heart from deceiving his master.

Servants are of two sorts: free or bond-servants.

A free servant is he whom his master hires for wages to do him service. To him belongs the just payment of his hire, and in case of offence the master has authority to censure and correct him, provided that in the execution thereof, respect is had unto his age, and the correction is used with moderation, as if he were his son.

A bond-servant is a servant bought for money, and is commonly called a slave. Touching this sort, a question is moved, whether a Christian may with safe conscience, have and use a man as his slave? *Answer.* The power and right of having bond-men in those countries, where it is established by positive laws, may stand with good conscience, if it is used with moderation. That authority in this behalf is moderate wherein these seven caveats are observed:

(1) The master has not over his servant the power of life and death, for this takes away the lawful power of the magistrate, to whom alone the Lord has committed the sword of justice.

(2) There is not liberty granted him to use his servant at his own will and pleasure in all things, for this was not granted by the law of God to His own

people. "If a man smite his servant or his maid in the eye, and hath perished it, he shall let him go free for his eye. Also, if he smite out his servant's or his maid's tooth, he shall let him go out free for his tooth" (Ex. 21:26).

(3) The power is not enlarged to the commanding of things against piety or justice; for in these cases a man must rather obey God than man (Acts. 4:19).

(4) Masters do not take liberty to make separation of their servants who are married, the one from the other, or of those who are parents from their children, considering that God Himself has made these societies, and joined such persons together, and therefore man may not separate them.

(5) Masters do not take liberty to put over their servants to ungodly and unbelieving masters, for that is an unkind and cruel liberty, and may be an apparent occasion to make the servant fall away from religion and renounce the true God.

(6) They do not bind them to perpetual slavery and never make them free. "But if the servant say thus, I love my master, my wife and my children, I will not go out free" (Ex. 21:5).

(7) The servitude is not procured and retained by force, for it is a more grievous crime to spoil a man of his liberty than of his riches.

Now, that the same power limited with these cautions is lawful and warrantable in conscience appears by these reasons.

(1) God has ordained and allowed it, even by warrant of His own law. The posterity of Canaan was cursed by Noah and condemned to slavery. "And he said, Cursed be Canaan, a servant of servants shall he be to his brethren" (Gen. 9:25). So were the Gibeonites by Joshua: "Now therefore ye are cursed, and there shall none of you be freed from being bondmen, and hewers of wood, and drawers of water, for the house of my God" (Joshua 9:23). So was the thief: "If he had not wherewith to make restitution, then he should be sold for his theft" (Ex. 22:3). Again, those who are overcome in war may be held captive, and it is lawful for the conqueror to kill them, and therefore to make them slaves. And if, being taken, they are saved from death, they owe all that they have to them by whom they are saved.

(2) The law of God gave liberty to any man that would, to make sale of himself to another. "Of the children of the strangers that are sojourners among you, of them shall ye buy, and of their families that are with you, which they begat in your land, these shall be your possession" (Lev. 25:45). "If thy brother a Hebrew sell himself to thee, or a Hebrewess, and serve thee six years, even in the seventh year thou shalt let him go free from thee.... Thou shalt take an awl, and pierce his ear through against the door, and he shall be thy servant forever" (Deut. 15:12, 17).

(3) The man who is ransomed from his enemy is bound to serve as a slave in lieu of thankfulness.

(4) The examples of the godly in the Scriptures. Abraham had servants whom he bought for silver. "Every man-child of eight days old among you, shall be circumcised in your generations, as well he that is born in thine house, as he that is bought with money of any stranger, which is not of thy seed" (Gen. 17:12). "The Lord hath blessed my master Abraham wonderfully—for he hath given him sheep and beefs, and silver and gold, and men-servants and maid-servants, and camels and asses" (Gen. 24:35).

(5) The apostles do not disallow of such servants, but command them, being servants, and called to the profession of Christianity in that state, not to change, but to abide in their calling. "Art thou called being a servant? Care not for it" (1 Cor. 7:21).

It is alleged that such servitude is against the law of nature. *Answer.* It is indeed against the law of entire nature as it was before the fall, but it is not against the law of corrupted nature since the fall.

But Christ has purchased liberty to believers (Col. 3:11). *Answer.* Only a spiritual liberty in this life, and a corporal only in the life to come. For though a servant in regard of faith and the inner man is equal to his master, because in Christ Jesus there is neither master nor servant, bond nor free, yet in regard of the outward man and civil order among men, the master is above the servant, and the servant is and must be subject to the master.[1] Nevertheless, where this kind of servitude is abolished, it is not to be again received or entertained among Christians, especially considering [that] it is a far more mild and moderate course to have hired servants.

If it is said again that the heathen philosopher holds servitude to be natural, whereby some are by birth bond and others free,[2] I answer that servitude proceeds not of nature, but has its original from the laws of nations, and is a consequence of the fall. For all men by nature are equally and indifferently free, none more or less than others.

1. In the margin: Theodor. Orat. 8.
2. In the margin: Arist. pol. lib.1.

Chapter 17

The Master of the Family, or Good-Man of the House

Thus much touching the divers and several combinations (or couples) belonging to the oeconomical state. From these arise two persons of a mixed (or compounded) nature and condition, commonly called the good-man and the good-wife of the house.

The good-man (or master) of the family is a person in whom rests the private and proper government of the whole household. And he comes not unto it by election, as it falls out in other states, but by the ordinance of God settled even in the order of nature. The husband, indeed, naturally bears rule over the wife, parents over their children, [and] masters over their servants. But that person who, by the providence of God, has the place of a husband, father, [and] master in his house, the same also, by the light of nature, has the principality and sovereignty therein. And he is *paterfamilias*, the father and chief head of the family. Therefore, the true right and power over all domestic matters appertains by right to him. The duties of the master of the family are especially five.

Duty 1

To bear the chief stroke, and to be the principal agent, director, and furtherer of the worship of God within his family. "I and my household will serve the Lord" (Joshua 24:15). And he does this partly by praying for and with his household, and partly by instructing them in the holy Scriptures and in the grounds of religion, so that they may grow in knowledge and reap benefit by the public ministry. God commanded the men of Israel to walk thus in their families. "Thou shalt rehearse them continually unto thy children, and shalt talk of them, when thou tarriest in thine house, and when thou liest down, and when thou risest up.... When thy son shall ask thee, What mean these testimonies, and ordinances, and laws, which the Lord our God commanded you? Then thou shalt say unto thy son, We were Pharaoh's bondmen in Egypt, but the Lord brought us out of Egypt, with a mighty hand" (Deut. 6:7, 20).[1]

1. This paragraph break is not in the original.

God gave this testimony of Abraham before the law was given: "For I know Abraham that he will command his sons, and his household after him, that they keep the way of the Lord" (Gen. 18:19). And this household of Abraham was very large, for the Holy Spirit says long before that he had "three hundred and eighteen, that were born and brought up in his house" (Gen. 14:14). It was in likelihood the course of Solomon, which he had learned of his father David, and given for a rule to all masters of families. "Hear, O children, the instruction of a father, and give ear to learn understanding.... For I was my father's son, dear and tender in the sight of my mother, when he taught me and said unto me, Let thine heart hold fast my words" (Prov. 4:1–4a). The company of the disciples were the household of Christ, and He Himself did administer all parts of the service of God with them and among them (Luke 22:15). To this purpose, Augustine says, "The master of the family does after a sort, and in his measure, perform the duty of a churchman or bishop within his house."[2]

Duty 2

To bring his family to the church or congregation on the Sabbath day, to look that they do there behave themselves religiously, and, after the public exercises [are] ended and the congregation is dismissed, to take account of that which they have heard, that they may profit in knowledge and obedience. "The day after, they entered into Caesarea. Now Cornelius waited for them, and had called together his kinsmen and special friends.... Now therefore (says Cornelius to Peter) are we all here present before God, to hear all things that are commanded thee of God" (Acts 10:24, 33). "And when the days of their banqueting were gone about, Job sent and sanctified them, and rose up early in the morning, and offered burnt offerings..." (Job 1:5). "And he said, Wherefore wilt thou go to him today? It is neither new moon nor Sabbath" (2 Kings 4:23). For this very cause, the fourth commandment is given first of all and principally to the master of the family, that he might see the Sabbath kept, and be a principal doer in all parts of God's worship therein. "In it thou shalt not do any work, thou nor thy son, nor thy daughter, thy man-servant, nor thy maid, nor thy cattle, nor thy stranger that is within thy gates" (Ex. 20:10).

Neither is his care tied only to the Sabbath, but upon other days besides it he ought to cause them of his household, as much as in him lies, to repair to places where the Word of God is preached. Commendable was the practice of Mary, the sister of Martha, in this case. When Christ came to her house, she is said "to sit at his feet and attend unto his preaching" (Luke 10:39).

---

2. In the margin: In Joan. tract. 51. in sine.

Duty 3

To provide meat, drink, and clothing for his family, and that they may live a quiet and peaceable life (1 Tim. 5:8). "The lambs are for thy clothing, and the goats for the price of thy field. And let the milk of thy goats be sufficient for thy food, for the food of thy family, and for the sustenance of thy maids" (Prov. 27:26–27). "Thou shalt not muzzle the mouth of the ox that treadeth out the corn: doth God care for oxen? either saith he it not altogether for our sakes?" (1 Cor. 9:9). "Every scribe which is taught unto the kingdom of heaven is like unto a householder, that brings forth out of his treasury, things both new and old" (Matt. 13:52).

Duty 4

To keep order, and to exercise discipline in his house, and that in this manner. In [the] case of offence, when a capital crime is committed, which incurs public censure, he is not to punish it himself, but to bring the offender to the civil magistrate, to inform of his fault, that he may have his desert. It was a course established by the judicial law, which God gave unto Moses for his direction in criminal cases among the Israelites. "If any man hath a son that is stubborn, and disobedient, which will not hearken unto the voice of his father, nor the voice of his mother, and they have chastened him; then shall his father and his mother take him, and bring him out, unto the elders of his city, and unto the gates of the place where he dwelleth, and shall say unto the elders of his city, This our son is stubborn, and disobedient, and he will not obey our admonition: he is a rioter, and a drunkard" (Deut. 21:18–20). Again, "If thy brother the son of thy mother, or thine own son, or thy daughter, or the wife that lieth in thy bosom, or thy friend which is as thine own soul, entice thee secretly saying, Let us go and serve other gods (which you have not known; you, I say, nor your fathers).... Thou shalt not consent unto him, nor hear, neither shall thine eye pity, nor show mercy, nor keep him secret" (Deut. 13:6, 8). "And when any shall yet prophesy, his father and his mother that begat him shall say unto him, Thou shalt not live: for thou speakest lies in the name of the Lord: and his father, and his mother that begat him, shall thrust him thorough when he prophesieth" (Zech. 13:3).

If the fault is of an inferior nature and lesser in comparison, the master of the family ought to proceed by private censure upon the delinquent party, sometimes by admonition, other times by correction and chastisement, according to the quality of the offence and the condition and state of the person. "Thou shalt plainly rebuke thy neighbor, and not suffer him to sin" (Lev. 19:17). "If thy brother sin against thee, go and tell him his fault between him and thee alone.

If he hear thee not, take yet with thee one or two" (Matt. 18:15). "Correct thy son, and he will give thee rest, and will give pleasures to thy soul" (Prov. 29:17).

When admonitions and corrections will not prevail, the party must be brought before the ministers and governors of the church, that they may censure him. "If he will not hear them, tell it unto the church" (Matt. 18:17). And the apostle James gives order that the ministers of the church should come to those who are sick, and pray for them (James 5:14). If they do this in [the] case of infirmity, then they are also to be sought unto in [the] case of error and offence committed for redress.

But when none of all these means will do good, if the party is a servant, his master may and ought to remove him. "There shall no deceitful person dwell within mine house; he that telleth lies shall not remain in my sight" (Ps. 101:7). "The servant abideth not in the house forever" (John 8:35).

Duty 5

To give entertainment to those who are strangers, and not of the family, if they are Christians and believers, but especially to the ministers of the Word. "Giving yourselves to hospitality" (Rom. 12:13). "Be not forgetful to lodge strangers: for hereby some have received angels into their houses unawares" (Heb. 13:2). The woman of Shunem and her husband performed this duty unto the prophet Elisha. "Let us make him a little chamber, I pray thee, with walls, and let us set him a bed there, and a table, and a stool, and a candlestick, that he may turn in hither, when he cometh to us" (2 Kings 4:10). These are the duties.

Here it may be demanded whether the master of a family is always and necessarily bound in his own person to do all these things? I answer that if there is just and necessary cause, either in respect of his own inability or in regard of public employment upon a lawful calling, whereby he is hindered so as he cannot do any of them himself at some times, it is lawful for him to have and use a deputy. Our Savior Christ teaches this in effect, when He says, "Who then is a faithful servant, and wise, whom his master hath made ruler over his household, to give them meat in season?" (Matt. 24:25). Abraham had a steward of his house, Eliezer of Damascus (Gen. 15:2), who performed the weightiest matters that concerned the establishment and continuance of a family, not by himself, but by his steward, as namely the choice of a wife for his son, Isaac. "Therefore, Abraham said unto his eldest servant of his house, which had the rule over all that he had, put now thine hand under my thigh…" (Gen. 24:2). Thus Pharaoh king of Egypt had Joseph. "So Joseph found favor in his sight, and served him, and he made him ruler of his house, and put all that he had in his hands" (Gen. 39:4).

Chapter 18

The Mistress of the Family, or Good-Wife of the House

The good-wife (or mistress) of the house is a person who yields help and assistance in government to the master of the family. For he is (as it were) the prince and chief ruler [and] she is the associate, not only in office and authority, but also in advice and counsel unto him. "And after these things, the son of the woman, which was wife, or mistress of the house, was sick" (1 Kings 17:17).

Her duty is twofold.

First, to govern the house as much as concerns her in her place. "I will therefore that the younger women marry, and govern the house" (1 Tim. 5:14). And she does [this in] three ways. (1) By exercising herself in some profitable employments for the good of her charge. "She seeketh wool, and flax, and laboreth cheerfully with her hands" (Prov. 31:13). (2) By appointing her maids' work, and overseeing them therein. "She riseth while it is yet night, and giveth the portion to her household and the ordinary to her maids" (v. 15). (3) By ordering her children and servants in wisdom, partly by instruction [and] partly by admonition, when there is need. "She openeth her mouth with wisdom, and the law of grace is in her tongue.... Her children rise up, and call her blessed..." (vv. 26, 28). "That they be discreet, chaste, keeping at home..." (Titus 2:5). Priscilla, in her house, with Aquila, instructed Apollos, in that wherein he was wanting, expounding unto him "the way of God more perfectly" (Acts 18:26). Gregory Nazianzen, in an oration made for his father, says that "his mother was not only a helper, but also a teacher or instructor, and guide unto his father in matters of religion and godliness."

The second duty is to give the portion of food unto her family, or cause it to be given in due season. "She riseth while it is yet night, and giveth the portion of meat to her household" (Prov. 31:15). Rebekah did thus in her house. "Get thee now to the flock, and bring me thence two good kids of the goats, that I may make pleasant meat of them for thy father, such as he loveth" (Gen. 27:9).

Question. Whether may the good-wife, without the consent of the good-man, give and bestow the goods belonging to the family? *Answer.* (1) There are some things which are proper to herself, and not part of her dowry which she brought unto her husband. And she may claim these as her own, because either they were reserved upon the match made between them, or else [they] are peculiar unto her by their mutual consent, and of them she may lawfully give without her husband's knowledge. (2) The goods which are common to them both are of another nature, and she may not bestow these without his allowance, either express or at least general and implicit, especially when the giving of them does (or may) grow in likelihood to the hindrance and prejudice of the state of the family.

Finis

The Calling of the Ministry

Two Treatises, Describing the Duties and Dignities of that Calling

Delivered publicly in the University of Cambridge
by Master Perkins.

Taken from his mouth, and now diligently perused
and published by a preacher of the Word.

With a preface prefixed touching the publishing of
Master Perkins's works, and a catalogue of all such particulars
thereof as are to be expected.

"Let a man so think of us as of the ministers of Christ,
And disposers of the secrets of God" (1 Cor. 4:1).

Imprinted at London by I. R. for William Welby,
and are to be sold at his shop in Paul's Churchyard,
at the sign of the Greyhound.

London
1605

The Epistle Dedicatory

To the Right Worshipful, Sir Edward Cooke, Knight,[1] his Majesty's Attorney General, and Sir Thomas Heskith, Knight,[2] Attorney of his Highness' Court of Wards and Liveries,[3] and one of his Majesty's honorable counsel in the north, two of God's principal attorneys in the cause of true religion, grace and peace from Jesus Christ.

Right Worshipful, give me leave to put you both in one epistle, whose one order and one religion have so nearly combined. As you are brethren [in] many ways, and especially in the profession and practice of one religion, so vouchsafe to be joint patrons of this little afterbirth, this *faetus posthumus* of that worthy man Master Perkins, now deceased. I send you here one of the shortest and one of the sweetest of his treatises. Had it been as well brought forth by me as it was begot by him, it had been a child not unworthy of so great a father. But, seeing it is now as a fatherless child, be you the tutors to this orphan, at whose hands orphans and wards have ever been well used. The father, while he lived, was a shining light in our church, and being dead, [he] is a shining star in heaven, for "he turned many to righteousness."[4] And his doctrine will shine in Christian churches while the sun shines upon the earth.[5]

The subject of this treatise is the ministry, whereof are laid down the duties and dignities. And well does he couple these two together, for some can challenge the dignities of the ministry and cunningly cast the duties from their shoulders. Others perform the duties, but are kept from the dignities duly belonging to that calling. But as he who will do the duties may justly challenge the dignities, so he who will expect the dignities must do the duties of a

1. Sir Edward Cooke (Coke), 1552–1634. Promoted ecclesiastical liberty and opposed Divine Right philosophy of the Stuarts. Worked with Puritans like Pym in Parliament. *DNB* 4:103.

2. Sir Thomas Hesketh, 1548–1605. Supporter of Puritans. From Yorkshire. Buried in Westminster Abbey, monument on north choir aisle.

3. The Court of Wards and Liveries handled matters of inheritance relating to lands, estates, and under-age heirs.

4. Deut. 12:3.

5. This paragraph break is not in the original.

minister. Therefore, in this building, these two beams are in great wisdom well set together by this wise master builder, and [they are] so closely coupled as the idle or ambitious man cannot look at the dignities but he must withal behold the duties, nor the painful and laborious man see his duty but withal shall see the dignity belonging thereto.

And surely (Right Worshipful), none might better have written on this subject than he. For who may more worthily describe the dignities of the ministry than he who neither by doctrine nor conversation was ever the least disgrace unto his ministry? Or, who may better challenge the honor of his calling than he who was ever an honor to his calling? And who might better teach the duties of the ministry than he who so discharged them as envy itself cannot justly reprove and the enemies themselves cannot but commend?[6] And who may better teach them to others than he who carefully practiced them in his own person? And as none could be a fitter author of this discourse than he, so not many fitter patrons than yourselves, not many in your profession better scholars, nor any that better love scholars than yourselves. And you are some of those few, in this wicked age, who willingly yield all dignities and due reverence to such ministers as you see willingly to discharge the duties of good ministers.[7]

Well would it be with the ministry of England (and the better with it, the better with England), if all (as great as you) were as great friends to it as you. And if the papists except, and say, how can this be, for you have been persecutors of their priests, let me answer once for you who often answer for many distressed men. They persecute you with slander, who say you persecuted them (but be content to bear your part in popish slanders, with our prince and state, our counselors and clergy, our parliaments and laws, for none of these have escaped these viperous tongues). For though you have executed the laws upon some of them in your several places, yet not with sharpness nor severity, but with merciful justice, and that also not as they were priests, but plotters, practicers, subverters, and seducers. And as they were priests, you sought their reformation, not their ruin. And if they, who can hardly discharge themselves from being priests of Baal, have had but justice, and that also tempered with mercy, it shows how good regard you have and how much you esteem all good and faithful ministers who are God's interpreters.[8]

In a word, if all our ministers were such as this treatise describes, or came but as near it as the author hereof did, and if all our great ones did use and esteem good ministers as you do, we should then soon pull the ministry from under that foot of contempt, with which this profane age does daily tread upon

6. In the margin: Answer to Perkins's *Reformed Catholic* by B. a priest.
7. This paragraph break is not in the original.
8. This paragraph break is not in the original.

it. [Those of] the Church of Rome, who are far wiser in their kind than the children of light, have taken other and strange courses to magnify the clergy. They teach that the ecclesiastical state is so far more excellent than the civil, as the sun is than the moon, and that not in spiritual only (for that we deny not), but in temporal power, pomp, and estate. And [they teach], therefore, that the chief of their clergy is as far above the mightiest emperor as the sun is above the moon, and as the moon borrows her light from the sun, so does the emperor his state and power from the pope.

They teach that the clergy is a state so distinct and so absolute of itself as it has not to do with the civil state, yea they exempt their clergy from being [in] any way subject to the temporal magistrate. And though their crimes are ever so many or monstrous, yet the prince (or civil authority) has nothing to do to take notice thereof, much less to punish them. And hereupon great volumes are written, and many acts and decrees are made in their Canon Law, *De Exemptione Clericorum*. They extol their clergy above the temporality, allowing the priests both bread and wine in the sacrament, but leaving the laity bread alone. They make them, in their mass, mediators between Christ and God the Father, and creators of their Creator and Redeemer, when and as often as [they] themselves list. And finally, they send for the most part all their clergy immediately to heaven without let, whereas all the temporality (except martyrs) must pass by purgatory. Here are great buildings, but on a sandy foundation; goodly castles, but built in the air. If these devices were of God, they would certainly stand, but their long tottering threatens a sudden fall.

Contrariwise, our church (or rather the corruption of our church), by avoiding this Scylla, have fallen into Charybdis,[9] by avoiding one extremity [they] have fallen into the other by taking too much dignity and authority from our ministry, and by laying too much poverty, contempt, and baseness upon it. It would be a work worth the labor of the wisest heads to put down the true mean between both extremes, and worth the labor of our noble king to take order that that mean be kept, without rising to the right hand or falling to the left. This short treatise may hap[10] to give form and light and directions therein, or at least may encourage and stir up their hearts in whose hands it is to do it.[11]

I would have it see the world under your worthy names, not so much because I am bound to you both in many private and particular respects (though that is much), as because I know you both to be of so right and reformed a judgment in this case as you would have no ministers but of sufficient gifts and unblameable lives, nor those ministers put to their pensions or uncertain

9. Scylla and Charybdis are monsters from Greek mythology.

10. *Hap:* by chance.

11. This paragraph break is not in the original.

salaries, but to have certain and sufficient maintenance proportionable to their charge and beseeming the honor of a Christian church. God continue you still in that mind, and make many more of the same with you, so we should have as flourishing a church as any [in] Christendom has seen. Go forward in that and your other religious resolutions. It is the true way to honor both here and in a better world. Stand firmly for the truth, and boldly against the popish enemies thereof, as hitherto you have done. Religion had never more cause to thank you (and all that do so) than now it has, for her enemies were never so insolent since they were our enemies. But if you and others hold on as in your several places you have well begun, and others take the like course, there is hope [that] their insolences will be easily (if timely) repressed, and [they] themselves nearest the fall when they imagine they are in the full. The Lord bless and assist you in your painful places, and make you on earth instruments of His glory, to the good of His church, so shall you be vessels of glory in the kingdom of heaven. And thus, commending this little treatise to your reading, and myself to your favor, I take leave, and will ever rest.

Your Worships' in the Lord,
W. Crashawe, 1605

To the Reader

To the Christian Reader, and especially to all such as have any copies of the works of Master Perkins, or intend to [bring] any of them [to] the press.

For as much as there has been lately signification made of divers of Master Perkins's works hereafter to be printed in an epistle to the reader promised before the treatise of *Callings*, and that signification, being but general, might peradventure give occasion to some to set out some particulars (without the consent of Master Perkins's assignees) as imperfectly as are these two books, entitled, *The Reformation of Covetousness* and *The Practice of Faith*, justly and truly (for ought that I see) censured in the aforesaid epistle. It is, therefore, now thought good to mention the particular treatises, and works of his, which shall hereafter (if God will) be published, for the benefit of God's church. I do, therefore, hereby make known to all, whom it any way may concern, that there were found in the study of the deceased, and are in the hands of his executors (or assignees) and preparing for the press:

1. His expositions on the Epistle to the Galatians.
2. On the Epistle of Jude.
3. His book of the Cases of Conscience.
4. His treatises: (1) Of Witchcraft. (2) Of Callings.

All these he had perused himself, and made them ready for the press, according to which copies by himself so corrected, some of them already are, and the rest will be published in due time. And hereupon we desire all men who have copies of them, not to offer that wrong to that worthy man of God, as to publish any of their own, seeing the copies hereof which are to be printed, are of his own correcting. But rather if they can help to make any of them more perfect by their copies, they may therein do a good work to the benefit of many and much comfort to themselves.

And further, I do hereby make known that I have in my hands at this present of his works, taken from his mouth with my own hand, hereafter (if God will) to be published, with the allowance of our church and for the benefit of his children, these particulars:

1. His expositions or Readings on Psalm 101.

2. On Psalm 32.
3. On Hebrews 11.
4. On Revelation 1–3.
5. On Matthew 5–7.
6. His confutation of Canisius, his little Popish Catechism.
7. His treatises: (1) Of Imaginations, out of Genesis 8:2. (2) Of Temptations, out of Matthew 4. (3) Of Christian Equity, out of Philippians 4:3. (4) Of the Callings of the Ministry, out of two places of Scripture. (5) Of Repentance, out of Zephaniah 2:1.

Besides many other particular sermons, and short discourses made upon several and special occasions, of all which some are already published by others and some by myself. And all the rest that remain, as they are the jewels of God's church, so did I willingly dedicate them to the public and general good, judging it were a foul sin in me, or any other, to impropriate to our sins or our own private use the labors of this or any other learned man, which are in my opinion parts of the treasury of the militant church. And as it were wrong to the church if I should conceal them, so doubtless were it to him and his children if I should publish them for mine own alone and not for their benefit. If I do, I think it may be justly said unto me, or whosoever does so, "Your money perish with you." And what herein I have said for myself, I know I may boldly and safely say for his executors or assignees, who have or had in their hands, any of those which were found in his study. In the publishing of all which, as we do intend to deal truly with the Christian reader, and not to commit anything to the press which has not either been written or corrected by the author himself, or faithfully penned according to the truest copies, taken from his own mouth, and since by others of sufficiency and integrity, diligently perused. Some purpose to refer them to the benefit of the author's wife and children, as much as may be, wishing that upon this caveat, men would not be so hasty (as some have been) to commend to the world their imperfect notes, upon a base desire of a little gain, both to hinder the common good of the church, and to defraud the said parties of their private benefit, to whom in all equity and conscience, it does principally appertain. And desiring all who have any perfect copies of such as are in my own hands, that they would either help me with theirs, or rather take mine to help them. That by our joint power and our forces laid together, the walls of this worthy building may go up the fairer and the faster. And so, I commend them all to God's blessing, who endeavor to commend themselves and their labors to God and to His church.

Your brother in the Lord,
W. C.

The Duties and Dignity of the Ministry

> "If there be with him a messenger, an interpreter, one of a thousand to declare unto man his righteousness: Then will he have mercy on him, and will say, Deliver him, that he go not down into the pit, for I have received a reconciliation" (Job 33:23–24).

In this chapter and the former, Elihu (a holy, learned, and wise young man) has conference with Job in matters of high and excellent divinity. The points of his conference are these: from verse 1 to verse 7, [there] is a preface to his speech; from there to verse 13, he repeats certain of Job's propositions and reproves them; [and] from there to these words, he instructs Job in certain points touching God's dealing with sinners. And those are two: (1) how God preserves a sinner from falling; [and] (2) how God restores a sinner being fallen.

The means whereby God preserves a sinner are principally two: (1) by admonitions in dreams and visions; [and] (2) by scourges and chastisements when the first will not prevail. And these are laid down from verse 13 to these words.

Then follows the second point; namely, the restoring of a sinner when both [of] the means, formerly spoken of, have not prevailed with him, but through his corruption he is fallen. And concerning this point, he handles these particulars: (1) the remedy and means of his restoring; [and] (2) the effect that follows thereupon.

The remedy is laid down in these words now read unto us; then follows the effect, which is that, when a sinner is restored by repentance, then the graces of God are plentifully poured upon him both for soul and body. [And this is found] from these words to the end of the chapter.

The intent, then, of this Scripture is that God uses means in His mercy to preserve sinners from falling into sin. But if they do [fall into sin], then He in much greater mercy affords them means and helps to rise again. And this is the sum and substance of the words. Now, that means and remedy is the matter I purpose to speak of out of these words. The means, then, to restore a sinner after a fall is to raise him by repentance into a better estate than he was in before, and that is inclusively and by implication taught in this text. But the instrument by whom that great work is to be wrought is here in plain terms laid down to be a minister of God, lawfully called and sent by God, and appointed by His church to that great duty. So that, these words contain a worthy description of a true minister, and he is here described,

(1) By his titles, which are two: "angel" [and] "interpreter."

(2) By his rarity: "one of a thousand."

(3) By his office: "to declare unto men his righteousness."

(4) By the blessing that God gives upon the labors of this true minister: "then God will have mercy upon the sinner."

(5) By His commission and authority in the last words: God will say, "Deliver him that he go not down into the pit, for I have received a reconciliation."

Let us speak of them in order as they lie in the text, and first of his titles.

Chapter 1

His Titles

Title 1: Messenger

The first title of a minister of God is "messenger" (or "angel"). And [it is found] not here alone, but elsewhere in the Scripture. "He is the messenger of the Lord of hosts" (Mal. 2:7). And in the Revelation, the ministers of the seven churches are called the "angels" of those churches.[1] So, it is apparent [that] a true minister is an angel of God in one place, and the angel of the church in the other place. He is an angel (or messenger) sent from God to His church.

This consideration affords matter of much use.

Use 1

Most of us in this place[2] are either prophets or sons of the prophets. If you are a prophet, you are God's angel. If [you] intend to be a son of the prophets, then mark your duty: prophets and ministers are angels in the very institution of their calling. Therefore, you must preach God's Word as God's Word, and deliver it as you receive it. For angels, ambassadors, and messengers, carry not their own message, but the message of their lords and masters who sent them. But ministers carry the message of the Lord of hosts; therefore, they are bound to deliver it as the Lord's and not their own.

In 1 Peter 4:11, we are bid, "If any man speak, let him speak," not only the Word of God, but "as the word of God." God's Word must be spoken, and [spoken] as God's Word. Then show your faithfulness to the Lord in discharging your hands sincerely of that message which He has honored you to carry. God's Word is pure, therefore purely to be thought upon and to be delivered. Then let all who are God's angels, and would be honored as His angels and ambassadors, think it no less reason to do the duty of God's angels, lest (as many men mar a good tale in the telling) so they take away the power and majesty of God's Word in the manner of delivering it.

---

1. In the margin: Rev. 2 & 3.

2. In the margin: This sermon was preached in the university church, to the body of the university.

Use 2

The second use also concerns the ministers. Are they God's angels? Therefore, they must preach God's Word in the evidence and demonstration of the Spirit of God. For he who is God's angel, the Spirit of that God must speak in him. Now to speak in the demonstration of God's Spirit is to speak in such a plain[ness], and yet such a powerfulness, as that the capacities of the simplest may perceive not man but God teaching them in that plainness, and the consciences of the mightiest may feel not man but God reprove them in that powerfulness. That this is so appears by Saint Paul: "If a man prophesy aright," says the Holy Spirit, "the unlearned or unbelieving man comes in, he thinks his secret faults are disclosed and laid open; he thinks all men see his nakedness, and do reprove him for it, he therefore falls down and saith, Surely God speaks in this man" [1 Cor. 14:24–25].

In these words, observe an admirable plainness and admirable powerfulness (which a man would think could not so well stand together). First, plainness, for whereas the unlearned man perceives his discovered faults, it follows necessarily he must needs understand, and if an unlearned man understands it, then consequently it must needs be plain. Second, powerfulness, in that his conscience is so convinced, his secret faults so disclosed, and his very heart so ripped up, that he says, "Certainly God speaks in this man." This is the evidence and demonstration of God's Spirit.[3]

It is thought good commendation before the world when men say of a preacher: "Surely this man has shown himself a proper scholar of good learning, great reading, strong memory, and good delivery." And so, it is. And such commendation (if just) is not to be condemned. But that which commends a man to the Lord his God and to his own conscience is when he preaches so plainly to the capacity, and so powerfully to the conscience of a wicked man, as that he thinks doubtless God is within him. Are you, therefore, an angel of God? Then magnify the Spirit of God, and not yourself, in your preaching of His Word.

Use 3

The next use is for the hearers. And they are here taught that if their ministers are angels sent [to] them from God, then they are to hear them gladly, willingly, reverently, and obediently. Gladly and willingly, because they are ambassadors. Reverently and obediently, because they are sent from the high God, the King of kings, and [they] do deliver His embassage. God says, "The people must seek the law at his mouth" [Mal. 2:7], and [for] good reason, for if

3. This paragraph break is not in the original.

the law is the revealed will of God, then where should they seek the will of God but at the mouth of His angel? The reason, therefore, follows well in that place: they should "seek the law at his mouth; for he is the messenger of the Lord of hosts." And all Christians must do this, not only if their doctrine is pleasing unto them, but [even] though it crosses their corruption and is quite contrary to their disposition, yea though it is ever so unfavorable and hard unto nature. Yet, in as much as it is a message from your God and King, and the teacher [is] the angel or messenger of that God; therefore, both he and it must be received with all reverence, and with the very obedience of the heart and soul.[4]

And this is the cause why a convenient reverence and honor is to be given by all good Christians even to the persons of God's ministers (especially when they adorn their high calling with a holy life), even because they are angels of God. Saint Paul teaches that women ought to be modestly attired in the congregation because of the angels [1 Cor. 11:14]. It is not only because the holy angels are present, and always beholders of our service of God, but even because the ministers, who are angels and ministers sent from God, are there, delivering their message and embassages received from God.

And thus, we have the first title given to the minister: he is an angel.

Title 2: Interpreter

Second, he is an interpreter; that is, one who is able to deliver aright the reconciliation made between God and man. I say not [that he is] the author of that reconciliation, for that is the Godhead Himself; nor [is he] the worker of this reconciliation, for that is the second person, Christ Jesus; nor [is he] the assurer or ratifier, for that is the Holy Spirit; nor [is he] the instrument of it, for that is the glad tidings of the gospel. But I say [that] he is the interpreter of it; that is, first, one charged to open and explain the covenant of grace, and rightly lay down the means how this reconciliation is wrought. Second, one who can rightly and justly apply those means for the working out of it. Third, one who has authority to publish and declare it when it is wrought. And by these three actions he is God's interpreter to the people.

Then he is also the people's interpreter to God by being able to speak to God for them, to lay open their wants and nakedness, to confess their sins, to crave pardon and forgiveness, to give thanks in their names for mercies received, and (in a word) to offer up all their spiritual sacrifices unto God for them. And so, every true minister is a double interpreter: God's to the people, and the people's to God. In these respects, he is properly called, God's mouth to the people, by preaching to them from God, and the people's mouth to God, by

4. This paragraph break is not in the original.

praying for them to God. And this title shows how great and glorious a calling this ministry is, if it is rightly conceived.

Now then for the use of it.

Use 1

First, if every true minister must be God's interpreter to the people, and the people's to God, then hence we learn that everyone, who either is or intends to be a minister, must have that tongue of the learned which is spoken of in Isaiah 50:4. Here the prophet says (first, in the name of Christ, as He is the great Prophet and Teacher of His church, and, second, in the name of himself and all true prophets while the world endures), "The Lord God hath given me a tongue of the learned, that I should know to speak a word in season to him that is weary." Here note [that] the weary soul (or troubled conscience) must have a word "in season" spoken to it for its comfort, and that [it] cannot be spoken without "the tongue of the learned," and lastly that the tongue of the learned must be given by God. Now, what is it to have this tongue of the learned, of which Isaiah speaks, but to be this interpreter which the Holy Spirit here says a minister must be? But to be able to speak with this tongue is, first, to be furnished with His learning, and, second, with divine knowledge, as far as it may by outward means be taught from man to man. But besides these, he who will speak this tongue aright must be inwardly learned and taught by the Spirit of God. He must learn the first two from men, but the third from God. A true minister must be inwardly taught by the spiritual scholar, the Holy Spirit.[5]

Saint John must take the book, that is the Scripture, and eat it. And when he has eaten it, then (says the angel) he must go "preach to nations, tongues, people, and kings" [Rev. 10:9, 11]. This was done, not that Saint John had not eaten that book in the coming down of the Holy Spirit (Acts 2), the very end of whose coming was to teach them spiritually, but that in him Christ might teach His church forever that no minister is fit to preach to nations and to kings, until they have eaten the book of God, that is, till after and besides all the learning that man can teach them, they are also taught by the Spirit of God Himself. And it is this teaching that makes a man a true interpreter, and without this he cannot be. For how can a man be God's interpreter to His people unless he knows the mind of God Himself, and how can he know the mind of God but by the teaching of the Spirit of God? Indeed, we may be man's interpreter by human teaching, and may interpret the Scriptures truly and soundly as a human book or story for the increase of knowledge, but the divine and spiritual

5. This paragraph break is not in the original.

interpretation, which shall pierce the heart and astonish the soul of man, must be taught by the inward teaching of the Holy Spirit.

Let no man think I here give the least allowance to Anabaptistical fancies and revelations, which are nothing but either dreams of their own or illusions of the devil. For they condemn both human learning and the study of the Scripture, and trust wholly to revelations of the Spirit. But God's Spirit works not but upon the foundation of the Word. I only teach this, that a minister must be a divine interpreter, an interpreter of God's meaning. And, therefore, he must not only read the book, but eat it, that is, not only have the knowledge of divine things flowing in his brain, but engraven in his heart and printed in his soul by the spiritual finger of God. And, therefore, for this end, after all his own study, meditation, commentaries, and after all human helps, he must pray with David: "Open thou mine eyes, that I may see the wonders of thy law" [Ps. 119:18]. The discerning of those wonders requires a spiritual illumination, and the opening of them requires the tongue of the learned. Therefore, after all the study which flesh and blood and human reason can yield, pray with the prophet: "Lord, give me the tongue of the learned, that I may be a right interpreter of Thy holy will."

Furthermore, inasmuch as ministers are interpreters, they must labor for sanctity and holiness of life. The king of Assyria is said to be sanctified (or set apart) to destroy God's enemies [Isaiah 13]. If there is a certain kind of sanctification necessary for the work of destruction, then how much more is true sanctification necessary for this great and glorious work of the edification of God's church? A minister is to declare the reconciliation between God and man, and is he himself not reconciled? Dare he present another man to God's mercy for pardon, and never yet [have] presented himself? Can he commend the state of grace to another, and never [have] felt the sweetness thereof in his own soul? Dare he come to preach sanctification with polluted lips, and out of an unsanctified heart? Moses might not stand upon the mount in God's presence, till he had put off his shoes from his feet (Exodus 3), and dare any man presume to come into this most high and holy presence of the Lord, until he has mortified his corruptions and cast off the unruliness of his affections?

The priests are bid to sanctify the people, and it is said that God will be sanctified in all who come near Him [Ex. 19:20; Lev. 10:3]. But who comes so near unto God as the ministers do? So, it is apparent that ministers do sanctify the people, and in some construction God Himself. Now, shall they one way be sanctifiers of the people, another way of God Himself, and no way of themselves? Surely, if it is so, they are but lame interpreters. And, doubtless, this is the reason why unsanctified ministers, and such as are of a loose conversation, bestow such fruitless labors in the church. Many want no learning, no ability to interpret, and yet how few souls do they bring to God? May it be [that] some are converted by their ministry, that God may show the efficacy is not in the person of man but in the ordinance of God! But few, doubtless (for aught that we can see), do teach us how God hates him who will take in hand to reconcile others, himself being unreconciled to God. Seeing, then, [that] ministers are God's interpreters to the people, to declare and publish their reconciliation with God, and that they cannot be reconciled unless they are sanctified, and can so hardly be sanctified by the ministry of an unsanctified man, let therefore all true ministers of God, first, be God's interpreters to their own consciences, and their own souls interpreters to God, then shall they know more perfectly how to discharge the office of true interpreters between God and His people.

And thus, we have the two titles of a true minister.

Chapter 2

His Rarity

Now it follows in the text: "one of a thousand." Here is the second part of this description, which is by the rareness (or scarceness) of good ministers. It is laid down in a very strange phrase, namely, that a true minister (one who is a right angel and a true interpreter) is no common or ordinary man, but thin sown, one of many, nay, "one of a thousand." The meaning hereof is to be conceived either properly or figuratively. In the figurative sense, it is spoken in relation to ministers themselves. In the proper sense, it has a comparison with all men. The figurative and hyperbolical sense is that of all the ministers in the world, not one of many is a right angel and a true interpreter. The plain and proper sense is that, among the men of this world, there is not one of a thousand who proves a true minister. For this point let us examine the truth of it, the reasons of it, and the use of it.

The Truth

The truth hereof is manifest by the experience of all ages, wherein it is strange to observe how few men of any sort, especially of the better sort, affect the calling of a minister. And what is stranger [is] how few of those who are ministers in name and title do deserve these honorable names of an angel and an interpreter.

The Reasons

And the truth is too manifest in common practice to insist much upon it, therefore let us see the reasons of it. And they are principally these:

[The] first [is] the contempt that lies on that calling. It [is] always hated by wicked and profane men because it discovers their filthiness and unmasks their hypocrisy, and its doctrine is oftentimes a fretting corrosive to their conscience, [so] that they cannot welter and wallow so quietly and secretly in their sins as otherwise they would. Therefore, it is that they spurn both against the calling and the men, and watch them narrowly, and take hold of their least infirmities, thereby to disgrace them, judging that to cast contempt on that calling is to remove shame from their own shameful courses. Nor is it possible but that they should thus hate this calling, inasmuch as they hate so deadly both that law and embassage which they bring and that God whose ambassadors they are.

This hatred and disgrace in the wicked world were that which caused Jeremiah to cry: "Woe is me" [Jer. 15:10]. And [it] made him in the seeming of his natural reason [to] "curse the time that ever he was a prophet." For he says, "I am a man of contention, every man is at strife and enmity with me."

The second reason is the difficulty of discharging the duties of his calling: to stand in God's presence; to enter into the holy of holies; to go between God and His people, to be God's mouth to the people, and the people's to God; to be the interpreter of the eternal laws of the Old Testament and the everlasting gospel of the New; to stand in the room and to bear the office of Christ Himself; [and] to take the care and charge of souls. These considerations are so many amazements to the consciences of such men who do with reverence approach (and not with rashness rush into) this sacred seat. This made Saint Paul cry out: "Who is sufficient for these things?" [2 Cor. 2:16]. And if Paul said "who is?" no marvel that many men say, "I am not sufficient," and do therefore draw their necks from this yoke and their hands from this plow, until God Himself or His church do press them to it.

The last reason is more peculiar to this age of the New Testament, namely, want of maintenance and preferment for those who labor in this calling. Men are flesh and blood, and in that respect must be allured and won to embrace this vocation by some arguments which may persuade flesh and blood. The world has in all ages been negligent herein, and therefore God in His law took such strict order for the maintenance of the Levites [Deut. 10:9; 28:2; Num. 18:26]. But especially, now under the gospel, this calling is unprovided for, when it deserves best of all to be rewarded. Certainly, it would be a worthy Christian policy to propound good preferments to this calling, that thereby men of the worthiest gifts might be won unto it. And the want hereof is [the] cause why so many young men of special parts and greatest hope turn to other vocations, and especially to the law, wherein at this day the greatest part of the finest wits of our kingdom are employed. And why? Because they have all the means to rise, whereas the ministry, for the most part, yields nothing but a plain way to beggary. This is a great blemish in our church, and surely, I wish the papists, those children of this world, were not wiser in their kind (in this point) than the church of God. The reformation hereof is a work worth the labor of prince and people, and special care is to be had in it, else it will not be reformed. For, doubtless, had not God Himself in the Old Testament taken such straight orders for the livings of the Levites, they had been put to no less extremities than is the ministry of this age. And this reason added to the other makes them perfect, and all put together make an infallible reason. For who will undergo so vile contempt, and undertake so great a charge, for no reward? And where there is so great contempt, so heavy a burden, and so mean a reward, what marvel if a good minister is one of a thousand?

The Use

Now let us make use of this doctrine. The use is manifold, and yields instructions to many sorts of people.

Use 1

First, rulers and magistrates are here taught [that], if good ministers are so scarce, therefore [they must] maintain and increase, and do all [the] good they can to the schools of the prophets, to universities, colleges, and schools of good learning, which are the seminaries of the ministry. Herein the example of Samuel is very worthy to be followed. In his days, the schools of the prophets flourished, and even Saul himself (though he did much hurt in Israel) when he came to the schools of the prophets, even his hard heart relented. He could do them no hurt, nay he "put off his robes, and prophesied amongst them" [1 Sam. 19:24].[1]

All Christian princes and magistrates should so advance these schools, and see them both well maintained and well stored. The reason is evident and forcible: a good minister is one of a thousand. If, therefore, they would have the number increased, let them maintain the seminaries. And again, if antichrist is so careful to uphold his kingdom, the kingdom of Satan, to erect colleges and endow them with living, and to use so great means to sow his tares in the hearts of young men, so that they may sow them in the hearts of the people abroad, shall not Christian princes be as careful (or rather, much more zealous) for the increasing of the number of godly ministers? Shall Baal have his four hundred prophets, and God have only His Elijah (1 Kings 18:22)? It must be a great shame to Ahab, or any king, whose kingdom is in that estate!

The Jesuits' diligence is such in teaching and the readiness of some of their novices [is] such in learning (doubtless, the devil himself putting his help withal) that in three years (as some of them say of themselves) they proceed in human learning, and in the fourth in divinity. If it be so, then it may be a good lesson for our schools of learning, and an inducement to move all who have the government thereof to labor to advance learning by all good means, and to give it more speedy passage. And it may shame some who spend so many years in the university, and yet, alas for all that, prove not [to be] one of a thousand.[2]

1. This paragraph break is not in the original.
2. This paragraph break is not in the original.

In our schools, there are, by God's mercy, many young trees planted by the river side of this goodly orchard, who by good ordering and dressing may prove goodly trees in the temple of God and strong pillars in the church. But they are like tender plants, and must be cherished. Princes and great men, by allowing maintenance, and the governors, by establishing good orders and looking carefully to their execution, must see that these plants have sufficient moisture to grow speedily to perfect ripeness, and that then they are transplanted in due time into the church and commonwealth. These are the trees spoken of in Ezekiel, "which grow by the sides of that river, which floweth out of the sanctuary" [Ezek. 47:1]. Waters out of the sanctuary must nourish them, and so they grow unto their perfection. But take away these waters, take away the liberality of princes and good discipline from the universities, and these trees must needs decay and wither. If they do, then the small number of good ministers will be fewer and fewer, and of one of a thousand, there will not be one of two thousand.

Use 2

In the next place, ministers themselves are here taught, first, [that] if good ministers are so scarce, then let every man fear to make them fewer than they are. Every man, therefore, labor (for himself) first for ability, [and] then for conscience to discharge his duty, namely to be an angel to deliver faithfully God's embassage, and a true interpreter between God and His people. If you do thus, then, howsoever the number of good ministers is small, it shall be nothing smaller for you.

Second, if they are so few, labor to increase them, for the more they are, the less burden lies upon each particular man. Therefore, let every minister, by his teaching and by his conversation, labor to honor his calling so that he may thereby allure and draw others to a love and liking thereof.

Third, are good ministers sown too thin[ly]? Are there so few of them? Then, let all good and godly ministers "give the right hand of fellowship" to one another [Gal. 2:9], and join together in love, and by that means arm themselves against the scorn and contempt of the world. We see them who are of a kindred or brotherhood (or any kind of society), [that] the fewer they are, the more closely do they combine [and] the more firmly do they hold together against all foreign force. God's ministers ought to do [the same] because their number is so small. If they were many, [there would be] less danger in their disunion. But, seeing they are so few, the more it concerns them to cut off contentions and all occasions of debate, and to join hand in hand against these common adversaries.

Use 3

In the third place, young students are here taught, seeing a true minister is but one of a thousand, that they [should] therefore bend their studies and their thoughts to the ministry. For they well know it is an old proverb: "The best things are hard to come by." And, certainly, there are so few good ministers because the holy ministry in itself is so high and excellent a calling. And as it is a shame to the men that there are so few good ministers, so it is a commendation to the calling whose honor and excellency is such that (as we see here) scarce one of a thousand attains unto it. Therefore, men of the most excellent gifts are here invited to dedicate themselves unto the most excellent vocation, yea, very reason itself would urge a man to be one of a thousand.

And further, as they are to intend this calling as the most rare and excellent, so this must teach them likewise to hasten to furnish themselves with all good helps and means that they may become true ministers and able interpreters, and not to stick too long in those studies which keep a man from the practice of this high function. For it is not to live in the university or in the college, and to study, though a man devours up learning ever so fast, but to be a good minister is that which makes a man one of a thousand.

Use 4

In the last place, hearers are here taught their duty. First, to respect with reverence the person, and to receive with reverence the message, of every true messenger, seeing it is so rare a thing to find a true minister. For as nothing is more vile or base than an evil and lewd minister (whom Christ compares to "salt which hath lost its savor, which is good for nothing, but to be cast out, and trodden down of men" [Matt. 5:13]), so is there none worthy of more love and reverence than a holy minister. For as Isaiah says, "The very feet are beautiful which bring glad tidings." And we should kiss their feet, who bring news of peace. Therefore, all good Christians are to receive and use a good minister as Saint Paul says the Galatians did him, "even as an angel of God" [Gal. 4:14]. Have you then a godly pastor? Run to him for conference, comfort, [and] counsel. Use his company, frequent his sermons, account him worthy of double honor, think it no small or ordinary blessing, for you have one of a thousand. And bless God for bestowing His mercy to you, which He has denied to so many others. For some have no minister, [and] some have a minister, and yet alas he is not one of a thousand.

In a word, to conclude this point, all men must here learn, seeing good ministers are so scarce, to pray the Lord of the harvest to thrust out more laborers into His harvest. And for those who are called already, [we must pray] that

God would make them faithful in that high function, and as Elisha craved of Elijah, that the good "spirit may be doubled, and trebled upon them" [2 Kings 2:9], so that the number may be increased.

And thus, we have the truth, the reason, and the use of this, that a good minister is one of a thousand.

Chapter 3

His Office

It follows: "to declare unto man his righteousness." Here is the third part of the description of a minister (by his office): "to declare unto man his righteousness." When a poor sinner is brought down by his sins, seeing their foulness and feeling their burden, (as it were) to the very gates of hell, when this sinner is brought to a true sight of his misery by the preaching of the law and brought to lay hold on Jesus Christ by the preaching of the gospel, then it is the proper office of a minister to declare unto that man "his righteousness"; namely, that though in himself he is as ill and foul as sin can make him and as the law can discover him to be, yet in Christ he is righteous and just, and by Christ so justified as he is no more a sinner in the presence and account of God. This is the righteousness of a Christian man. This is the justification of a sinner. And to declare this righteousness to him who repents and believes is the proper duty of a true minister.

Paul says of himself that he "witnessed to the Jews and to the Gentiles, the repentance toward God, and faith toward our Lord Jesus Christ" [Acts 20:21]. The complete duty of a minister (as he is a public angel or interpreter) is laid down in these words. First, [he is] to preach repentance, which a man must perform to God, whom he has grievously offended by his sins. Second, [he is] to preach faith in Christ, and free forgiveness, and perfect salvation through that faith in Christ, to all who shall truly believe in Him. And after both [of] these follows that which is here spoken of. It comprehends both [of] the former, namely, "to declare unto man his righteousness." So that, in these words, these points of a minister's calling are inclusively laid down.[1]

First, a true minister may and must declare unto a sinful man where righteousness is to be found, namely, in "Jesus Christ the righteous" [1 John 2:1].

Second, [he must declare] how that righteousness may be obtained, namely, by doing two duties: (1) by denying and disclaiming his own righteousness, and that is done by repentance; [and] (2) by claiming and cleaving to Christ's righteousness, and that is done by faith.

1. This paragraph break is not in the original.

Third, a true minister may and must "declare this righteousness to him." (1) [He must] first publish and proclaim that it is ready to be bestowed on every sinner who will thus apprehend it, and that it is able to justify and save him. (2) Besides a bare publication of this justification, he must (as Paul did) witness and testify it to the conscience of the sinner, that it is as certainly true as God is true. For as a witness in doubtful cases is called that by his testimony he may clear the truth, so when the consciences of poor sinners are wavering and doubtful what to believe, when they doubt of this righteousness, then a true minister is as a faithful witness of God to aver and testify this truth from his own conscience, knowledge, and feeling, of the infallible certainty of God's promises unto the doubtful and distressed conscience of the sinner. (3) Besides declaration and testification, he is to maintain this truth and this righteousness (if the sinner's conscience is yet not quiet) against all gainsayers, against the power of darkness and all the gates of hell, that this is true and perfect righteousness to him who apprehends it, as afore is laid down. And this is so infallible to every soul who repents and believes. The minister may assure it to the conscience of the sinner in the Word of truth and in the name of God, and may call to witness all God's saints and all His holy angels, and may pawn unto Him his own soul upon it, that it is most true, that this is true, perfect, and all-sufficient righteousness.

Thus, we see in some measure what it is to declare unto a man his righteousness. And this is the peculiar office of a minister of God, and this is the height and excellency of his office. In the want of godly ministers, I confess that godly Christian men may help one another in the performance of these duties, and that with profit. But it is the proper function of a godly minister to do it, and the promise and blessing belongs properly to him, as the consciences of all penitent sinners will testify in this case. Let David's [conscience] serve for many. When he was cast down, even to the mouth of hell, by that fearful discovery of his two hideous sins by Nathan's preaching, and when the faith of his soul began to wrestle against hell and strive against despair and to apprehend the mercy of God in Christ, then, I say [that] not the testimony of all the men in the world could have given him that joy, comfort, and assurance, that Nathan did when he said in the word of a prophet and of a true minister: "God hath taken away thy sin; thou shalt not die" [2 Sam. 12:13]. What did Nathan here but declare unto a man his righteousness? What did Nathan here but the duty of every true minister?

If this is the office and duty of a minister, and if such is the height and excellency of his office, let us then see what use we make of it.

Use 1

First, concerning the ministry, it first discovers how nakedly, weakly, and inefficiently the popish church does declare unto man his righteousness. It will let a man see it in himself, where alas it is not. For Paul himself testifies that his desire is that he may be found "out of himself, and in Christ" [Phil. 3:8–9]. And yet, certainly, if ever [a] man had [a] righteousness of his own (worth trusting in), Paul had [it]. This is the cause why so many of that religion find not that righteousness which will pacify and satisfy their consciences when they come to die. And [it is] why so many of them, when it comes to the pinch, do then go out of themselves, and with us do seek for this righteousness in Christ, where both assuredly and sufficiently it is to be found.

Use 2

Then for our own ministry, here they are taught, first, the true manner of teaching and declaring righteousness, namely this, not to preach the law alone or the gospel alone as some unadvisedly do (but both without profit), but both the law and the gospel. [We preach] the law to breed repentance [and] the gospel to work faith, but in order: first, the law to breed repentance; and then the gospel to work faith and forgiveness, but never before.

Second, they are taught to be holy, to be sanctified and reconciled themselves. For it is your office to declare unto man his righteousness, and not your own to yourself. And how can you be a true witness to testify between God and the soul of a sinner when your own soul knows not, nor feels, the truth of it? Certainly, such men are but lame witnesses between God and the sinner's soul. David says to the sinner: "I will instruct thee in the way wherein thou shalt go" [Ps. 32:8]. But, first of all, in the same, he sets down his own experience in a large story of his own repentance and of God's mercy on him. And though God sometimes does satisfy and save the poor distressed soul of a sinner by the testimony of such men to teach us that the virtue is not in the men but in the truth of God's covenant, yet alas, how few they are, to teach us how pleasing it is unto Him, when a minister is a declarer of that righteousness to others, which he first has himself, and is a witness of truth to others, which he first knows in his own experience.

Third, the consideration of this high excellency of their calling must arm all true ministers against the scorn and contempt of the world, which by wicked men is cast like dust and mire into the face of ministers. Let this suffice them, they are the men who must declare unto man his righteousness, even he who scorns and condemns the ministry. He has no righteousness in him, unless it is by the means of a poor minister. Then, do you your duty. And he who mocks you has cause to honor you.

Use 3

And let this encourage students to consecrate themselves to the ministry. For what calling has so high an office as this, to declare unto man his righteousness? And assuredly, however in this wicked world you are little accounted of (for, if it did not so, it would not be wicked), yet you are honored in the hearts of all God's children, and even in the consciences of some whose tongues do smite you, and the souls of thousands when they shall bless you, who in their lives cared not for you. And the devil himself does envy, and the holy angels themselves do wonder at the excellency of your calling, in that you have power to declare unto man his righteousness.

Use 4

In the next place, hearers may here learn, first, if their righteousness is that to be declared as afore, then if they will have it, they must seek it as it may be found, namely both in the law and in the gospel, and not in the gospel alone, and first in the law, then in the gospel. For he must never look to taste the sweetness of the gospel, who has not first swallowed the bitter pills of the law. If, therefore, you would be declared righteous by the gospel, be content first to be pronounced miserable by the law. If you would be declared righteous in Christ, then be content first to be pronounced sinful and unrighteous in yourself.[2]

Second, all men may here learn how they are to esteem God's ministers, and what reverence and obedience are due to their persons and their doctrine. These are they who must declare unto you your righteousness, if you have any. Are you beholden to him who, when you have lost a jewel (which was all your wealth), can tell you where it is, and help you to it again? Or to him who, when your cause is in trial at the bar, will plead it for you? Or to him who, when your health is lost, can tell you how to get it again? Then, behold how you are beholden to a godly minister who, when Adam had lost both himself and you, that jewel of righteousness which was and is the whole wealth of your soul, can truly tell you where it is, and how it is to be had again; and who, when the devil hauls you to the bar of God's justice to receive trial for your sins, can draw you there such a declaration as the devil himself shall not be able to answer; and who, when your soul is sick to death and even to damnation, can heal the deadly wounds thereof. A good minister, therefore, is worthy (as the apostle says) "of double honor," whose duty we see is "to declare unto man his righteousness."[3]

2. This paragraph break is not in the original.

3. This paragraph break is not in the original.

And to conclude this point, the consideration of the height of this office of a minister may encourage fathers to dedicate their sons to this holy calling. For the physician's care for the body or the lawyer's [care] for your cause are both inferior duties to this of the minister. A good lawyer may be one of ten, a good physician one of twenty, a good man one of a hundred, but a good minister is one of a thousand. A good lawyer may declare the true state of your cause, a good physician may declare the true state of your body. No calling [and] no man can declare unto you your righteousness but a true minister.

And thus, we see the office or function of a minister.

Chapter 4

His Blessing

Now follows the blessing: "then will he have mercy upon him." The fourth general part of this description is the blessing which God gives to the labors and function of a true minister. When a man, by the preaching of the law, is brought to true humiliation and repentance, and by the preaching of the gospel [is brought] to true faith in the Messiah, then will He (that is, God) have mercy on him (that is, on the penitent and believing sinner). Behold here the admirable sympathy and the cooperation of God and the minister's office. Man preaches and God blesses. Man works on the heart and God gives grace. A minister declares unto man his righteousness, and God says so be it, he shall be righteous. A minister pronounces mercy to a penitent sinner, and forthwith God has mercy on him.[1]

Here we see the great and glorious account which God makes of the word of His ministers, truly taught and rightly applied by them, namely, that He (as it were) ties His blessing unto it. For, ordinarily, till a man knows his righteousness by the means of an interpreter, God has not mercy on him. But, as soon as he does know it, then (as we see here) God will have mercy on him, and will say, "Deliver him, etc." This is no small honor to ministers and to their ministry, that God Himself gives a blessing unto it, and works when they work, and (as it were) stays waiting when they declare unto a man his righteousness, and then He has mercy on him. So powerful and so effectual is the word spoken by a minister of God. This is that which Christ avouches: "Whatsoever you bind in earth, shall be bound in heaven, and whatsoever you loose in earth, shall be loosed in heaven" [Matt. 16:16]. Will you know the meaning hereof? Read John 20:23, "Whosesoever sins you remit, they are remitted, whose you retain they are retained." Will you have the meaning of both? Read Isaiah 44:25–26, "God destroyeth the tokens of soothsayers, and makes wizards and astrologers fools, turneth worldly wisemen backward, and makes their knowledge foolishness: but he confirmeth the word of his servants, and performeth the counsel of his

1. This paragraph break is not in the original.

messengers." Thus, God binds and looses with them, remits and retains with them, by confirming their word and performing their counsel.

For example, a true minister sees a sinner burdened in his sins, and still rebelling against the will of God. He, therefore, declares unto him his unrighteousness and his sin, and denounces unto him the miseries and curses of God's justice as [are] due unto him for the same. Here he binds on earth, here he retains on earth. This man's sins are likewise bound and retained in heaven. On the other side, he sees a penitent and believing man. He pronounces forgiveness of sins and happiness unto him for the same. He looses him from the band of his sins by declaring unto him his righteousness. This man's sins are likewise loosed and remitted in heaven, and God Himself does pronounce him clear in heaven when the minister does on earth. Thus, God confirms the word of His servants, and performs the counsel of His messengers.

Use 1

The use of this doctrine is, first, for rulers and great men of this world. This may teach them to be nursing fathers and nursing mothers unto the church, whose authority they see is so great over them as that their decree stands ratified in heaven. Therefore, though their place is great, and they are gods upon earth, yet they must withal acknowledge that in justifying a sinner, in interpretation, in declaring unto man his righteousness, in binding and loosing, their power also is immediate from God, and above theirs. And they themselves, as they are men, must submit themselves to this powerful word of the ministers, to be taught by it, and to be reconciled by means of it. And they must highly receive it, for though a man speaks it, yet it is the Word of God. This is to "lick the dust of Christ's feet," of which the prophet speaks [Isa. 49:23], not as the pope would have it, to hold the stirrup and lead the horse, and hold the water to the pope, to kiss his toes, to hold their kingdoms by him as tenants at will or by courtesy, but reverently to acknowledge the ordinance to be God's, the function and duty to be high and excellent, to acknowledge the power of their keys and censures (being rightly applied), their promises and their threatenings to be as from God, and to submit to them accordingly.

Use 2

Second, ministers themselves here must learn [that], when they take the word of reconciliation into their hands and mouths, to call to mind whose it is, even the Lord's, and that He works with them, and has the greatest hand in the work, and that therefore they must use it in [a] holy manner with much fear and reverence. It is not their own. They may not use it as they list.

Use 3

And, lastly, hearers are here taught, first, to see how mad such men are who carelessly and seldom hear sermons, but upon any occasion fly to wizards and charmers, who are the devil's prophets. For see the difference between those two: the wizard and charmer has society with the devil, [but] the preacher with God; the charmer has his calling from the devil, [but] the preacher [has] his [calling] from God; the charmer's charm is the devil's watchword, [and] when he charms, the devil does the feat, [but] the preacher's doctrine is God's watchword, [and] when he truly applies it, God Himself ratifies and makes it good. Therefore, let all men fear to have thus to do with the devil by seeking to his slaves, and let them draw near to God by entering into fellowship with His holy prophets and godly ministers.

And further, if when they preach and God blesses, then God has mercy on you, then learn what reverence they and their word (which is thus accompanied with God's mercy and forgiveness) is worthy of. And then learn to hear the word with fear and trembling for it is God's Word and not theirs. And when a true minister says unto you, on a true ground, "I denounce you a sinful man or under the curse," or "I declare you to be righteous and a child of grace," it is all one as though God from heaven had said so unto you. If any man asks, but is it not as good if another man pronounce forgiveness unto me upon my repentance, I answer, yes undoubtedly, if it is in extraordinary times or places when there are no ministers. For otherwise, certainly this blessing is principally tied unto the minister's calling. For it is not said of any private men's calling anywhere in the Scripture, as it is here said of the minister's.

If an angel (an interpreter) comes to a man and declares unto him his righteousness, then (mark the connection) God will have mercy on him. And [He] will say, "Deliver him, etc." Whence comes this blessing? From this promise of God. If then other callings will challenge ordinarily the same blessing, then they must have the same promise besides. Other Christians, being private men, though they are sanctified, and have a good measure of knowledge, yet they have not the same spirit of discerning that godly ministers have. Nor can [they] so fully and truly judge when a man has repented [and] when not. And, therefore, [they] cannot so truly pronounce the sentence of the law or gospel, nor have the ability ordinarily by their good conference and Christian counsel to convert a soul, but to confirm one converted. But that power ordinarily belongs to the public ministry of the Word. Therefore, it follows that ordinarily they have not the power to pronounce the sentence of binding or loosing upon any man.[2]

2. This paragraph break is not in the original.

I confess [that] in times or places where no minister can be had, God blesses the labors of private men who have knowledge, sometimes even for the converting of a man to God, and for comforting him at the hour of death. And [He] gives a virtue and power to that sentence which they shall pronounce upon one another's repentance. But as this is extraordinary, and in the want of ordinary ministers, so in that case a private man of knowledge and godliness is made a minister for that time to himself, or to another, even as a private man in cases of extreme danger, when no magistrate is present, is made a magistrate himself to defend his own life. So then, as in want of a magistrate, the sword of the magistracy is put into the hand of a private man, so in the want of ministers, the keys of the ministry are committed and put into the hands of private men (as in days of persecution), that then they may with comfort admonish and advise, and with power pronounce mercy and forgiveness unto one another upon their true repentance. Yet, always remember that in so doing, a private man is as a minister for that time and in that case. But, ordinarily (and always in settled churches), this power pertains to the ministry, and [it] is theirs alone by ordination. And to them belong the promise and the blessing, that when he has declared to a man his righteousness, then God will have mercy on him.

And thus, we see the blessing of God upon the function of the ministry, and connected thereunto by the merciful dispensation of God.

Chapter 5

His Authority

It follows: "And will say, Deliver him that he go not down into the pit: for I have received a reconciliation." The fifth and last part of this description is the commission and authority given unto him. It is as great as ever was given to any creature, and [it] is thus: when a minister of God has declared unto man his righteousness, [and] has brought him to the state of grace, and God in His favor has had mercy on him, then God says to the minister, "Deliver that soul from hell, for I have pardoned him in Christ. I am reconciled to him."

In these words, authority is given to a minister of God to redeem a penitent man from hell and damnation, not that he is the means of working out this redemption, for that wholly and only is Christ Himself, but he is God's instrument and Christ's instrument: first, to apply those means unto him; [and,] second, to pronounce his safety and deliverance when these means are used. Here is the principal honor of all belonging to that calling. And it is the greatest that ever was vouchsafed to any creature, man or angel, for it is a plain commission to go and deliver such a man from the power of hell, and to redeem him into the state of God's children, and to make him [an] heir of heaven. Angels never had this commission. They are messengers sent out for the good of those whom ministers have redeemed [Heb. 1:14], and they have brought many comfortable messages unto them. But it was never said to any angel, "Deliver that man, that he goes not down into the pit," as it is here said unto a minister. No men but ministers have this commission. To some callings God says, "Work you for man, build him houses, provide him sustenance." To the physician, "heal that man." To the lawyer, "do that man justice." To the soldier, "fight for him." To the magistrate, "defend him." To the king, "govern him, and see that everyone does his duty." To none but to the minister does He say, "Deliver him that he goes not down into the pit."

If this is so, then for the use.

Use 1

First, ministers must learn here that if they will have the honor of redeemers, then they must do the duty of redeemers. They must pray earnestly for the people, for that is one means whereby they redeem men. They must say with Samuel, "God forbid that I should cease to pray for you" [1 Sam. 12:23]. They must mourn for the impenitent, when they will not turn to God. David did so. His eyes "gushed out with rivers of waters, because men kept not God's law" [Ps. 119:136]. And Jeremiah who "wished a fountain of water in his eyes, that he might weep for the sins of the people."[1] They must privately confer, visit, admonish, and rebuke, and principally they must preach, and that in such good manner, and in so diligent measure, as that they may redeem and win souls, and the end that they must aim at must be to win souls. Some preach for fear of the law, to avoid censure or punishment, some for fashion sake, that they may be like others, some for ostentation sake, to win credit and praise, some for ambition, to rise in the world. All these forget their commission, which is, "Deliver him from hell."

This should be the end of their preaching, to deliver a soul from hell, and what should commissioners do but execute their commission? High commissioners are worthy to be low commissioners, or rather no commissioners, if they will not put it in execution. It is, therefore, lamentable to see that some by not preaching, some by vain preaching, show that they intend anything rather than the winning of souls to God. Let then all good ministers so preach as they may say with Isaiah, "Behold, Lord, here am I, and the children whom thou hast given me,"[2] and as they may return their commission thus: "Whereas Thou, Lord, hast given me this people, and had me deliver them that they go not down into hell, Lord, I have done it. It is the thing my soul aimed at, with all my desire and endeavor. And by Thy mercy I have effected it accordingly."

And all Christian ministers must seriously intend the saving of souls, inasmuch as antichrist does so earnestly seek the destruction of souls by winning them to his synagogue. The Turk spares no labor, no cost, to infect young children of Christians with his impure and blasphemous superstition. The pope and his vassals (especially Jesuits) use all means, devise many stratagems, spare no cost nor labor, to seduce and inveigle[3] young men and the best wits. Surely, their care and policy are admirable, and yet alas, when (like the Pharisees) they have compassed sea and land to make a proselyte, they make him like themselves, the child of hell. And they are so far from having any commission from God to do this, or any blessing promised, as contrariwise God forbids them, and His curse lies upon them for so doing.

Shall they be so diligent to destroy souls without a commission, and incur God's curse for their labor, and shall not Christian ministers be much more

1. Cf. Jer. 9:1; Lam. 3:48.

2. Isa. 8:18.

3. *Inveigle:* entice or deceive.

diligent to win and redeem souls, having so large a commission for the purpose, and so great a blessing promised thereunto?

Use 2

In the next place, this doctrine has use for the hearers. First, to let them see the excellency of this calling, which has a commission and power to redeem them from hell and damnation, and what honor is due unto it. And to let the wicked man see (who abuses either the persons or the function) how base and unthankful they are, to recompense evil for so great a good, and therefore no marvel that evil does never depart from the houses and families of such men. And further, to encourage all men to give themselves to God in this great calling, for see here what they are, even the high commissioners of God.[4]

We have in our state a power delegated to certain men of worth, and it is called the high commission, because they have power to do great things. And that man thinks himself happy, who can bring his son to this, to be thought fit to be one of this commission. But, behold here a higher commission, a commission from God to redeem souls from the power of hell and the devil's claws. This is indeed a high commission, and so high as this was never granted out of the court of heaven to any creature but to ministers. They, therefore, are the high commissioners of the high God. Is it not then an honor and happiness unto you to bring your son to this estate?

Use 3

And, lastly, this must teach all hearers their duty to God's Word, namely, to submit themselves unto it. For if the minister has a commission to redeem your soul, it must be by the Word and holy discipline. Therefore, your duty is to hear God's Word patiently, to submit yourself unto it, to be taught and instructed, nay to be checked and rebuked, and to have your sins discovered and your corruptions ripped up. If you would have your cause succeed well, your lawyer must discover the weakness of it. If your body [is] to be cured, your physician must purge the corruption of it. So, if your soul is to be redeemed, your minister must see the weakness and purge the corruptions of it. And though his doctrine is harsh and hard unto your nature, and the discipline of the gospel seems rough unto you, yet you must not rage and rebel against it, nor hate nor rail at his person, but submit yourself unto it, for it is the message and ministry of your salvation. If otherwise, you do indeed a great wrong to the minister, for you frustrate his commission; but alas, [you do] a far greater to yourself, for you frustrate your own salvation.

Finis

4. This paragraph break is not in the original.

The Second Treatise of the Duties and Dignities of that Calling

By that late and reverend divine,
M. W. Perkins

"They that turn many to righteousness, shall shine as the stars, forever and ever" (Dan. 12:3).

The Epistle Dedicatory

To the Right Worshipful and Reverend Judges, Sir John Savile,[1] Knight,
one of the Barons of his Majesty's Exchequer, and Sir Christopher Yelverton,[2]
Knight, one of the Judges of his Majesty's Court of King's Bench, and
Sir Edward Philips, Knight, his Majesty's Sergeant at Law,
now, or late, the worthy Judges of our Northern Circuit,
the spirit of wisdom, zeal, and courage be multiplied.

Right Worshipful, it is said in other nations, and written in some of their books, that there are three disgraces of the English nation: the ignorance or (what I may so call it) the unlearnedness of our gentry and nobility; the beggary of our poor; and the baseness of the body of our ministry.[3]

The first blot has been well wiped away by our nobility and gentry, since the first days of blessed Queen Elizabeth, partly by study at home [and] partly by travel abroad. And I hope they will do it more and more.[4]

The second [blot] has been well lessened by good laws of late, and would be more if the execution were as good as our laws are. And it would be much honor to our nation and more to our religion, if it were quite taken away. For He who tells us there shall be poor ever with us [Matt. 26:11] also says there shall not be a beggar among us [Deuteronomy 15]. If there were no poor, what should become of charity? For it is charity to relieve poverty [and] not to maintain beggary. Poverty may be a cross, but it is no curse. But beggary is a fearful curse, threatened on the enemies of God. And David says not [that] he never saw a righteous man's child poor, but that he never saw him beg [for] his bread [Pss. 109:10; 37:25). The daily cries in our streets cry for yet further reformation hereof, that the impotent poor may be sufficiently provided for, that he need

1. Sir John Savile, 1545–1607. Was a judge; in 1599, placed on commission for suppressing heresy, *DNB* 17:860.

2. Sir Christopher Yelverton (1534?–1612). A judge prominent in reign of Elizabeth and James 1. Speaker of the house in parliament, *DNB* 21:1230.

3. This paragraph break is not in the original.

4. This paragraph break is not in the original.

not, and the sturdy beggar compelled to work, that he may not be suffered to beg. Happy you, or whosoever can have a hand in effecting this blessed work. We, who can do little else, shall pray for it and for them who labor in it.[5]

But now for the third [blot]. I fear none but the very hand of God can wipe out this stain from our church. The baseness of the general body of our ministry is either from the unworthiness or poverty thereof. And the unworthiness thereof is from the poverty and base maintenance of our ministry, which was once robbed by the abbeys, and after worse by some in our own state, which was then popish. And popery, that stands so much upon *non dimittitur peccatum nisi restituatur ablatum*,[6] yet for all that could not restore unto the church her tenths again. But as popish abbeys stole them, so a popish state kept them. And to their shame, some of these good professors of our religion have restored such as were in their hands, and there is hope that all our professors (whether they care not to be accounted hypocrites) will make some conscionable restitution. We do not crave that they would with Zacchaeus restore fourfold [Luke 19:8], though it is apparent that the tenths were got from us in old time by most false and forged cavillations. We only crave our own. We would ask no more, nor willingly take less, for our whole duty is still required, then why should not our whole due be paid. And yet, that the world may learn of us contentedness, as well by our practice as our doctrine, we would for the present take in good part, and rest contented, with a part of our own. And some competent portions out of the impropriations[7] (proportioned to the quantity of the charge imposed, and the gifts and pains required) would for a time be a reasonable satisfaction to our ministry, until our state found itself either better enabled or more straightly tied in conscience to full restitution.[8]

But, as I said, this is a work of God Himself, for if man could do it, so many parliaments would not have slipped it, but one of them would have eternalized itself with this honorable name to all posterities: the parliament that restored impropriations. But till that, or some other course (as good) is taken, it is both unseasonable and unreasonable to complain of the ignorant or to crave a learned ministry. For shall the ox's mouth be muzzled, which treads out the corn, or shall a man go to war at his own cost [1 Cor. 9:7, 9, 14]? And has not God ordained (mark it is His ordinance) that those who teach the gospel shall live by the gospel?[9]

5. This paragraph break is not in the original.
6. A sin is not forgiven, until the damage is restored.
7. "Impropriations," to put church property income into hands of laymen.
8. This paragraph break is not in the original.
9. This paragraph break is not in the original.

But alas, how shall the ministry of England live by the gospel, when my small experience can show that in one corner of one county of this kingdom, wherein there are some 105 parishes or parochial chapels (the East Riding of the county of York), almost 100 of them (if not a full 100) are impropriate, and among them I can show that most parishes have but ten pounds or thereabouts, some eight pounds, some four pounds, some not four pounds yearly living for the minister, and these impropriations [are] worth some 300 pounds, many 200 pounds, almost all 100 pounds per year; yea, there is one worth 400 pounds per year, where there are but eight pounds left for the minister. Until of late, with much ado, ten more pounds was obtained for a preacher, and so there is out of 400 pounds eight pounds shared for a minister and ten pounds earned for a preacher in that parish where there are 2,000 communicants. Of all the rest, the crown has some 100 pounds rent (or not so much), and the remaining 280 pounds (being a rich living for a worthy learned minister, a competent living for two, and more than some seven painful and able ministers have). I know not what becomes of it, unless it goes to the feeding of kites and cormorants.[10]

Are not these goodly livings for learned men, and may not we expect a learned ministry where there is such maintenance? And I heartily wish that other countries are not able to show the like precedent I have the rather made relation hereof, [and] that our high court of parliament may see what great cause they have to go forward with that motion, already by them made, for the establishing of a learned ministry. But if they bring it not to pass, what then remains but to hope that the great God of heaven will put into the heart of the god on earth, our noble king (into whose hands He has put the sword of sovereign authority) an irrevocable and irresistible resolution to execute his supreme power for the reformation of this evil, which (as Master Perkins says in this treatise) may well be called the king's evil, for it will hardly be healed but by the will and power of a king.[11]

In the meantime, this treatise, of that worthy man, may be a motive to our zealous professors who have any impropriations in their own hands, to excite and provoke them to a conscionable restitution in whole or in part, as their estates may bear or their conscience shall move them. For herein are laid down and mixed together both the duties to be done by faithful ministers and the dignities due unto them for their duties. And so, seeing the dignities of that calling to be most honorable and the duties so chargeable, it cannot but grieve their Christian hearts to see the maintenance so miserable.

---

10. These terms refer to birds.

11. This paragraph break is not in the original.

This treatise I, first of all, send to you, and under your names to the world, and to you first for, as I am sure you loved the author and honored those excellent gifts of God in him, so you cannot but accept this afterbirth of his (as a fatherless child for the father's sake). And for myself (to conceal all personal and private respects), in the name of many thousands in the northern countries, I praise God for the good done in those parts by your painful courses and religious care, not doubting, but if yourselves, or the like are employed there to assist our honorable and religious Lord President, that the multitude of popish priests (there lurking) will be daily lessened, the number of painful preachers augmented, popery put down, and the gospel maintained more and more. God grant this blessing to that and all other countries of this kingdom, for His mercy's sake, and give unto you and all others in your place the spirit of courage and constancy in these declining days, that, being faithful in your great charges unto the end, you may receive the crown of life, for which he heartily prays, who will ever rest, yours to command,

W. Crashawe

The Second Treatise of the Dignity and Duty of the Ministry

"Then I said, Woe is me, I am undone, for I am a man of polluted lips and dwell in the midst of a people of polluted lips: for my eyes have seen the King and Lord of hosts. Then flew one of the Seraphim unto me, with a hot coal in his hand, which he had taken from the altar with the tongs: And he touched my mouth, and said, Lo, this hath touched thy lips, and thine iniquity shall be taken away, and thy sin shall be purged. Also I heard the voice of the Lord, saying, Whom shall I send? and who shall go for Us?

Then said I, Here am I, send me. And he said, Go" (Isa. 6:5–8).

The five former chapters contain such sermons as the prophet had made under Uzziah, king of Judah. At this chapter begin such [sermons] as he preached in the reign of Jotham, and so forward. But before he either preaches or prophesies of anything in king Jotham's days (or his successors'), the Lord in this chapter gives a new commission to the prophet, and a new confirmation to this calling. The old king (being now dead), in whose days Isaiah was first called, and another succeeding him, God with the new king renews the calling and commission of the prophet. Wherein God does not give him another calling, for one calling to the office of the ministry is sufficient, but He confirms the calling formerly given by repeating and ratifying it. And this God did to Isaiah, not as he was an ordinary but an extraordinary prophet. For ordinary ministers need no renovation of their calling, nor any new signs of confirmation, but extraordinary prophets, who come in extraordinary manner, and to do many extraordinary works, God in His wisdom will have their calling confirmed again and again, and that by very extraordinary means.[1]

Out of this practice of the Lord we learn what great cause we have to doubt those men, to be either fantastical or worse, who pretend extraordinary callings in these days, and yet scarce can show us any good signs of an ordinary, much less of an extraordinary, motion. For if in those days, when such courses were

1. This paragraph break is not in the original.

more common, God will have his extraordinary prophets' calling to be renewed and confirmed again and again, then certainly in these days we may justly require more and more wonderful signs of an extraordinary calling before we believe it. And if God Himself was so careful to satisfy His church in those days of the vocation of His prophet, surely the church in these days has much more cause to doubt in such cases, and to require many and extraordinary signs, before it acknowledges any such extraordinary calling. These men, therefore, offer much wrong to the church, and deserve both the censure thereof and the sword of the magistrate, who dare so boldly offer and obtrude to the church their own fancies and dreams as extraordinary motions of God's Spirit.

This is the occasion and coherence.

This chapter has two parts: first, the means of his confirmation, from the beginning to these words; [and,] second, the confirmation itself, from these words to the end.

The means of his confirmation is a vision he saw from heaven of certain holy angels appearing and speaking to him (vv. 1–4). In the confirmation, which follows in these words, are three points: (1) the effect of the vision, which is wrought in the prophet, [in that] it caused him fear, astonished him, and cast him down (v. 5); (2) his consolation and raising up again after his fear (vv. 6–7); and (3) the renewing of his commission again (vv. 8–13).

Part 1: The Vision

The fear and astonishment of the prophet is described by [two things]. The first is its signs: (1) a note of exclamation, "Woe is me"; [and] (2) a note of extreme dejection in himself, "I am undone." The second is its causes: (1) he was a man "polluted, and dwelt amongst people polluted"; [and] (2) he had seen the Lord, "Then said I, Woe is me, I am undone."

Point 1: The Signs of His Fear

The first point in order is the fear and ecstasy into which the Lord drove this holy prophet. And the Lord did [it] not in His anger, but in His love unto him, not for a punishment for sin, but as an evidence of His further love. For the intent and purpose of God in striking this fear into him was to make him to be a true prophet and a fit messenger for Himself. It may seem a strange course which God takes to confirm and raise up His servant in zeal and courage, to strike him into an extreme fear, even to astonish and amaze him. And yet, we see it is the course which the Lord takes.

The Doctrine

Out of this practice of the Lord, we learn this doctrine: that all true ministers, especially such as are deputed to the greatest works in His church, must be first of all stricken into a great fear in consideration of the greatness of their function, yea into an amazement and astonishment in the admiration of God's glory and greatness, whose room they occupy and whose message they bring. And the more they are afraid and shrink, so it is under the contemplation of God's majesty and their own weakness, the more likely it is that they are truly called by God, and appointed for worthy purposes in His church. But he who steps [in]to this function without fear, he may trust in himself, but it is doubtful whether he is called by God, as here the prophet was.[2]

Nor is it so here alone, but everywhere, when God called any of His servants to any great work, He first drove them into these fears and amazements. [This] is evident in Moses [Ex. 3:11; 4:10, 13], Jeremiah [Jer. 1:6–7], Paul [Acts 9:6, etc.], and others. The reason of this dealing of the Lord is plain; namely, because man's nature is always ready to take enough and too much upon itself. God, therefore, in His wisdom puts a bridle unto the corrupt nature of man, and astonishes it, lest it presumes too much and takes too much upon itself. Again, a minister is to preach unto the people fear and reverence of the Lord, but how can he do so to others when he has not tied that bond in his own conscience, nor was ever cast down in admiration of God's glory and majesty?[3]

And, lastly, the ministry is a high and excellent calling (especially the office of extraordinary prophets in the Old Testament), and [it] is, therefore, subject to pride and to be puffed up with self-conceits. And, therefore, the apostle preaches to Timothy, that "a minister may not be a young scholar, lest he be puffed up, and fall into the condemnation of the wicked" [1 Tim. 3:6]. [He] gives us to understand that it is the peculiar danger of the calling to have high conceits of themselves, because of the height and dignity of their function. Therefore, to prevent this inconvenience, God in mercy appoints that all His true ministers shall have some means or other to be cast down, even to nothing in themselves, and shall be [so] driven into such fears and amazements at [the] sight of their own wickedness as they shall throw down themselves at Christ's feet, and denying themselves wholly, shall acknowledge that they are in Him whatsoever they are, and do rely and trust only on His grace and help.

---

2. This paragraph break is not in the original.

3. This paragraph break is not in the original.

Use 1

The use of this doctrine, as it is for all ministers, so [it is] especially for us who live in the university. We live (as it were) in a seminary, and many of us are hereafter by God's grace to be framed to the ministry, and some of us already are. Now here we have many occasions to be puffed up in self-conceits: we see ourselves grow in time, in degrees, in learning, in honor, in name and estimation, and God gives good portions of His gifts to many of us. What are all these but so many baits to allure us to pride and vain opinions of our own worth? But let us remember [that] the end at which we aim is not human or carnal. Our purpose is to save souls. Then "the weapons of our war must not be carnal" [2 Cor. 10:4], as pride, vainglory, and self-conceit. If, therefore, we ever look to be made instruments of God's glory in [the] saving of souls, then, at the first, we [must] not set before our eyes the honor, but the danger, of our calling, and we [must] humble ourselves under the mighty hand of our God, so that He may exalt us in His due time.[4]

And let us be content that God gives any occasion or means to pull us down, either by outward cross or inward temptation. And let us rejoice when we are thereby so far cast down that we cry out in the astonishment of our spirits, as the prophet here, "Woe is me, I am undone!" But, otherwise, if we will needs follow the swing of our proud natures, and trust in our own ability, gifts, and learning, let us know [that] we use carnal weapons in a spiritual warfare. And let us be assured the Lord will work no great work in His church by our ministry. We may raise ourselves in worldly estimation, and work out our own purposes, but we shall do little in the salvation of souls. For those men do pronounce the most powerful blessings on other men's souls, and speak the best words of comfort to other men's consciences, who most often say unto themselves, "Woe is me, I am undone!"

Use 2

Furthermore, whereas the prophet, at this vision and revelation of God's glory unto him, cries out of himself, "Woe is me, I am undone," being words of extreme fear and astonishment and of so low a dejection as [it] is a degree toward desperation (if it had gone forward), let us learn that the prophet held not in his judgment the doctrine of intercession of angels and saints for particular men. For if he had, he need not at the sight of God's majesty forthwith to have cried out, "Woe is me, I am undone." But he might have stayed himself a while in this cogitation: "I will desire Moses, Samuel, or David, to pray to this glorious God for me." Or, "The holy angels of the seraphim are here present,

4. This paragraph break is not in the original.

and they see in what fearful case I am. I will pray to them to speak to this glorious and mighty Lord for me, that I perish not in this fear." But, instantly, he, seeing the Lord appear in majesty, and fearing His just wrath (being guilty of his own corruptions) without any hope or expectation (or, as it seems, without the least cogitation of help or assistance from any creature), cries out, "I am undone."

Use 3

Lastly, whereas he exclaims, "Woe is me, I am done," being words of a soul humbled and dejected, and hereby showing himself to be in that case which a poor sinner is when the preaching of the law has humbled him by showing him his sins and his extreme danger by them, we may learn that to be called to the ministry is to be (as it were) converted and regenerate. And [we may learn] that when a man is called thereunto, it is a work little less than that whereby God calls a sinner from his sin to the state of repentance. For as God first casts down the sinner before He gives him grace, or any feeling of His love in Christ, so here He first abases and casts down the prophet in the sight of God's majesty and his own misery before He honors him with a commission to preach peace unto His people.[5]

I note this against those men who hold it so ordinary a matter to enter into the ministry as many do. They take it upon themselves in worldly and political purposes, and some of a better rank, who think [that] if a man has learning, degrees, and age, he is sufficiently qualified for that calling. But alas, this is not all. There is a greater work to be wrought than this. He must be humbled and cast down in [the] sight of the greatness of that calling, of the majesty of that God whose room he is to execute, and of the unworthiness of himself to so great a work. He must be resolved that to call a man to the ministry is the greatest work that God works in His church, [except for] converting a sinner and calling him to the state of grace. Nay, it is a work even like unto it. For as a sinner in his conversion, so he at his vocation to that place, is often to cry out in the amazement of his soul, "Woe is me, I am undone." As, therefore, they are foully deceived who think any holiness or sanctification can sufficiently qualify a man without learning, so are they no less who think all outward complements to be sufficient without this work which here was wrought in the holy prophet.

Thus, we see the fear and astonishment of the prophet.

5. This paragraph break is not in the original.

Point 2: The Causes of His Fear

It follows: "For I am a man of polluted lips." Now follow the causes of his fear, which are two.

Cause 1: Man's Misery

The first is his own pollution and sinfulness, and the sinfulness of his people.[6]

The Prophet's Pollution

He freely confesses his own in these words: "I am a man of polluted lips," that is, I am a miserable and sinful man, and therefore I fear and tremble to stand in God's presence, nay I dare not look upon the Lord, for my sins.[7]

General Pollution

But it may be demanded, how could the prophet truly say this, for he was a holy man, and justified in God's presence by his true faith in the Messiah, and sanctified by repentance? Can a man, who is justified and sanctified, say [that] he is a polluted man? I answer, it is doubtless [that] he was so. Here, therefore, he complains not of any great and enormous sins which he had committed to the public scandal of the church. But, first, [he complains] of the corruption of his nature. [It was] in him (as in all men) a very sea of iniquity, and [it] always appears more, the nearer a man comes to God, and therefore [it] did now most apparently discover itself in the prophet when he was in the presence of the Lord Himself.[8] Second, he complains of some actual sins of his life, and it is more likely of some sins of omission than of commission. For we find not that the prophet was ever touched with any great sin, and where we know it not, we are in charity not to imagine it. So, it is most probable [that] he complains of some smaller faults, or negligence, in his ministry, as not preaching to the people at some time when he ought, or not preaching so willingly or cheerfully as he should, or desiring to leave preaching because the people were stubborn and disobedient, or [demonstrating] some impatience in his ministry when the people were rebellious and resisted his doctrine. This passion might the rather vex him (as we read it did Jeremiah), [because] the Jews were such a stubborn and stiff-necked people. Or, it may be [he complains of] some want of zeal or forwardness. These, or some such, were the cause of his fear. And the conscience of these makes him cry out that he cannot stand in the sight of God.[9]

---

6. This paragraph break is not in the original.
7. This paragraph break is not in the original.
8. This paragraph break is not in the original.
9. This paragraph break is not in the original.

Use 1

Where we learn, first, what a tender conscience godly ministers must have above all men; namely, that they must make conscience, not only of the great and gross sins, but even of the lowest and least sins. And he must endeavor in his calling, not only to be clear of great crimes, but, as far as may be, to be free from the least appearance of evil and from the least negligence in his place. For a small fault in other men is great in them, and that which may be some ways pardonable in other men is no way in them. They must, therefore, watch over themselves most carefully, and take heed to all their ways. And for this end it is that a minister in godly wisdom must often deprive himself even of many things (which, it may be, lawfully he might use) lest his liberty is an occasion of evil to others. And [he] must abstain from the least sins, lest even they are blemishes to his calling and burdens to his conscience.[10]

And hence it is that a minister cannot be too careful in his calling, words, diet, company, recreation, apparel, gestures, and in his whole carriage, because little sins are so great in him. Here ministers especially learn the apostle's lesson to be "instant in season and out of season, to preach and exhort, to comfort and rebuke publicly and privately" [2 Tim. 4:2], to good [and] to bad, when it is well taken [and] when it is ill taken, when they willingly receive it and when they stubbornly resist it, when they commend him and reward him and when they rail at him and persecute him for it. He must thus be diligent in season and out of season, for the least negligence in his duty, or omitting the least opportunity of doing good, will, when God visits his conscience, be a burden and vexation to him, as it was here to the prophet.

Use 2

And furthermore, if these small sins thus afflicted the prophet, then alas what is to be thought of those ministers who make no conscience of foul and scandalous sins? How shall simony, incontinency, usury, inhospitality, covetousness, ignorance, idleness, careless non-residency, and other like grievous crimes, oppress and burden the soul when as the smallest sins do so affright this holy man? Surely, when God shall visit them, their states will be most fearful, nor shall any man's case be so miserable as an unconscionable minister's. And though such loose and licentious ministers seem to live now in jollity, and without any fear, yet when God shall appear unto their consciences, then they will cry out in fearful anguish: "Woe is me, I am undone!"[11]

---

10. This paragraph break is not in the original.
11. This paragraph break is not in the original.

Use 3

And again, if these small faults so affrighted this holy prophet and burdened his conscience, then what pitiful consciences have those ministers whose daily negligence and unconscionable carelessness in their places is such as all men speak of, and yet they are not touched. Surely, these men are not of so tender consciences as the prophet was. And either the prophet was here much nicer[12] than needed, or else these men will prove to be in a miserable estate.

Use 4

Lastly, let ministers of care and conscience be here comforted in the example of the prophet. Who is there but may find imperfections and blemishes in himself, which will often make him cry out, "Woe is me"? But let not that discomfort them, but rather rejoice that they can see their own weakness as the prophet did here. If they have cause to exclaim against themselves, they are not alone. It was this prophet's case, and that of all other holy prophets before him. In having imperfections in themselves, they are no more miserable than the prophet was. But let them labor to be as blessed in seeing and complaining of themselves as he was. And let every minister assure himself that the more he makes conscience, even of the least sins of all, the more he resembles the ancient holy prophets, and the more likely he is to work effectually in his ministry. For his duty is to work in his people a conscience, not of great sins only, but even of all. But how can he do that to them, if he has not first of all done it in himself? Hence it is, therefore, that godly ministers find fault with themselves when other men cannot, and cry out against themselves for their pollution (with the prophet here) when no other man can accuse them of the least crime. Nay, when others do magnify God for His graces on them, and praise their gifts, and commend their good lives, even then do they condemn themselves, and exclaim against their own corruptions. And their own smallest negligences or omissions are great wounds to their consciences, and their least sins and their most pardonable infirmities are sore burdens unto them, for, of all men in the world, a godly minister is a man of the most tender conscience.

Particular Pollution

Hitherto has the prophet complained generally of his pollution. Particularly he exclaims against the pollution of his lips rather than of his heart or his hands or any other part of him. Were they not all polluted? Yes, all in some measure. And was he not grieved at them all? Yes, assuredly, we must grant that also. But the reason is he was a prophet. His duty was to use his tongue. The practice of

12. *Nice:* finicky.

his calling consisted in the use of his tongue. For a minister is an interpreter, as he is called, that is, the people's to God by prayer, and God's to the people by preaching (Job 33:23). He is God's mouth, and the people's mouths, so that the tongue of a minister is that part of his body which is to be used as a principal instrument of God's glory, and more to the setting forth of His honor than any other. Now every man is to be tried what he is by his calling rather than by any other accidental or collateral courses. Therefore, the honor or dishonor of a minister is the use or the abuse of his tongue. And his comfort or discomfort is the well using or not using of it. The prophet, therefore, here affrighted at God's presence, and therefore retiring into himself, presently his conscience checks him for his most proper sins; namely, for some fault or negligence in his ministry (which is the proper sin of that calling). And hence it is that he exclaims against the pollution of his lips.

Use 1

Out of his practice, we may learn, first, of the vanity of the papists who magnify the merits of holy men's works. For if this holy prophet, a man truly justified and extraordinarily sanctified, durst not stand before God in this little appearance of His glory, notwithstanding all his zeal, courage, conscience, pains, and sufferings in his function, but was cast down so far, from a conceit of his own worth, that he cried out, "Woe is me, I am undone," how then can we (who are no better, but rather worse than he) stand before God in the Day of Judgment in the great appearing of His infinite justice and glory? Rather, doubtless, as here the smallest pollution of his lips and negligence in his calling drove him out of all conceit of merit when once he came into the presence of God, so the due consideration of our many and foul pollutions (above his) should beat down all proud conceits of our own goodness when we appear before God. It is, therefore, to be feared that the papists, who thus magnify their own merits, do seldom or never enter into earnest consideration of their own infirmities, and do seldom present themselves in the presence of God's majesty. For if they did, then doubtless the least sight of their least pollution would make them far from ever thinking of their own merits.

They also tell us of works of supererogation, but it seems here [that] this holy prophet had none of them. And they teach [that] a man may in this life perfectly fulfill the law, but who can do it if not ministers? And what ministers if not extraordinary prophets? And yet Isaiah (the first and chief of them) here exclaims, in pitiful manner, against his pollutions. Doubtless, if the papists would cease flattering themselves, and not examine their consciences by their own pleasing corruption, but present themselves in the face and presence of God's majesty, they would be far from these conceits.

Use 2

In the next place, whereas the prophet complains of the pollution of his lips as the peculiar sin of his place, ministers are here taught to avoid that sin above all others, and to labor in that duty above any other. For the doing of it is his most comfort. The want of it is his most vexation. His tongue is the instrument given him to honor God. If he uses it well, it yields him comfort more than any other duties.

But if he uses not (or abuses) his tongue, the pollution of his lips will be the heaviest burden of all. They, therefore, are greatly deceived, who think a minister to discharge sufficiently his duty, though he preaches not, if he keeps good hospitality, makes peace amongst his neighbors, and performs other works of charity and good life. For if a minister has not this virtue, he has none. If he preaches not, if he abuses his lips, or if he opens them not, he has no conscience, nor can [he] have any comfort, for that is the principal duty of a minister (though all the others are required to make him complete). The want of these may condemn him before men, but it is the pollution of his lips which presently checks him before God, as we see here in this holy prophet.[13]

The conclusion, then, to every minister, is that if he has all the virtues and good properties that can commend a man in the world, yet if his lips are polluted either by not preaching or by negligent, idle, or careless preaching, this pollution will so stain his conscience, and so burden him in the presence of God, that the time will come (notwithstanding all his other good qualities) [that] he will cry out in far more pitiful manner than the prophet does here: "Woe is me, I am undone, because I am a man of polluted lips."

The People's Pollution

It follows: "And I dwell in the midst of a people of polluted lips." The prophet not only complains of his own pollution but of his people's, among whom he lived. And this he does for these causes.

Cause 1

First, to teach us that it is the minister's duty to confess, not only his own sins, but the sins of his people, and to complain of them to God. For as he is the people's interpreter to God, he must not think it enough to put up their petitions, to unfold their wants, and to crave relief for them at God's hand, but he must further take knowledge of the sins of his people, and make both public and private confession of them to God. And the more particularly he can do this, the better. And this he is to do both for the people's good and for his own

13. This paragraph break is not in the original.

also, because it cannot be but that the sins of his people are in some sort his. For this is the peculiar danger of the magistrate's and minister's calling, that generally the sins of their people are theirs. I mean, that they are accessory to the sins of their people, either by provoking them by their evil examples or by suffering, winking, covering, and concealing them, or by not reproving or not hindering or not punishing or not carefully enough using means to prevent them. By all these means (and many more), it comes to pass that the people's sins are the minister's by communication, so that he is to confess to God their sins as well as his own, for his own sake as well as theirs.

Now if a minister must confess his people's sins, then it follows consequently that he must know them and take notice of them, for else he cannot confess them. And this is one cause why the Holy Spirit commands a pastor to "know his flock" [Prov. 27:23]. He must not only have a flock, and know which is his flock, or have a general eye over it, but he must have a particular and distinct knowledge of the state of it, and the more particular the better.

Use 1

And if the minister ought to know his people's sins, then it follows, first, that it is best for a minister to be present with his people, so that he may better know them and their state. And, certainly, if it is a minister's duty to confess to God the pollutions of his people, then willful and careless non-residency and all absence, without just and conscionable causes, must needs be a foul and fearful sin. For how could Isaiah have confessed he dwelt in the midst of a people of polluted lips, but that he dwelt among them? Nay, the prophet says [that] he dwelt in the "midst" among them. Indeed, he, who dwells in the midst among them, may well know and confess his people's pollutions.

Use 2

Again, if the minister is to confess his people's sins, and therefore must needs know them, then it also follows that they must discover and confess them unto him, or else it is not possible he should perfectly know their estate. The want of this is a great fault in our churches, for however we condemn auricular confession as a very policy in the devisers, and as a rack to the consciences of poor Christians, yet we not only allow but call and cry for that confession whereby a Christian voluntarily at all times may resort to his pastor, open his estate, disburden his conscience of such sins as disquiet him, and crave his godly assistance and holy prayers. Great blessing and comfort do doubtless follow them who use this godly practice. And the want of it is cause that a minister cannot discern the state even of his own flock, nor can complain to God of their pollutions and confess their sins so particularly as would be good both for him and them.

Cause 2

Second, the prophet couples together his own pollution and the pollutions of his people, as the *adjuvant* (or helping cause) and the effect. For the pollution of a people helps forward the pollution of a minister, and the worse people they are, the worse do they make him, though he is otherwise ever so good. For even the prophet, though called of God Himself, and justified and sanctified, and a man of extraordinary grace, yet dwelling in the midst of a people so stubborn and disobedient, as the Jews were, he was something touched with their pollutions. Ministers (even the best) are men, and this comes to pass by reason of the corruption of their nature, as they are men. The nature of this corruption is to apprehend any evil wherever it can be found, and to partake with it. Regeneration qualifies and abates this corruption, but takes it not away perfectly in this life. Whereby it comes to pass that a minister, living among evil people, cannot but be somewhat stained with their pollutions, of whatsoever sort they are. Insomuch as it is often seen that one known to be otherwise disposed of himself is found to be disposed to this or that evil by living among a people so disposed. And again, that a minister in such a place and among such people, free from such and such sins, removed to another place, is there found more or less tainted with them, because they abound among the people. And yet further, that a minister, known to be faithful, painful, and zealous, and coming to a disobedient, stubborn, froward, profane, and dissolute people, his faith is weakened, his zeal and courage abated, God's graces in him dulled, and much decayed. Godly ministers do daily complain hereof, and experience everywhere shows it to be true.

Out of this, we may learn something both for our instruction and our conversation.

Use 1

For our instruction, it here appears how wicked and wretched the corruption of our nature is. It cannot but receive some contagion from the pollution of those with whom we live. For this is so, not only in them who carry a loose hand over themselves, but even in such as look most narrowly unto their steps, as we see here in this holy prophet who was a man of more than ordinary sanctification. How little cause, therefore, has any man to extol nature. And how much less cause [have] the schoolmen and some other papists to give the least commendation to our "pure naturals." For if nature, rectified by grace, is so hardly kept within compass, alas how outrageous and perverse it is when it reigns without controlment!

And for our further instruction, here we may see of what a creeping and encroaching nature sin is. Like a secret venom in the natural body, so in the politic body it rests not in the place or party poisoned, but closely creeps and diffuses itself into every part and member of the whole. It creeps from man to man, yea from an evil man to a good, from the worst man to the best, from profane men to godly ministers. And as from public persons (as magistrates and ministers) it descends visibly, and the example of their evil life is palpably scandalous, so it creeps closely from the people to the magistrate or minister, and [it] ascends in more secret and insensible manner, yet in the effect is too sensible. For it is always seen that they are something touched with their people's pollutions. Sin is not only as a poison spreading from the heart to all parts, from the minister to the people, but as a gangrene, if it begins in the foot, [it] will without speedy prevention spread privily to the heart. Sin shows itself so, even from the people to the ministers. So, there is great cause for all men to stop sin in the beginning, to break it in the egg, to give water no passage, no not a little, for let this gangrene begin at the feet, it will not rest till it is in the heart.

Use 2

For our conversation we are here taught, first, if a minister, by reason of the corruption of his own nature and the creeping nature of sin, is in such danger to be stained with the people's pollutions, then let all ministers desire, and use all good means, to dwell with a people as little polluted as may be. Otherwise, let him assure himself to be polluted with them, which is both a great discomfort to his own conscience (as here it was to the prophet) and disgrace to his profession. For if it is a duty of every good professor of religion to "keep himself unspotted of the world" [James 1:27], then how much more is it the minister's duty so to do, and how foul a stain is it to the honor of his calling to be polluted in the common pollutions of his people?

It may be, therefore, good counsel to all godly ministers in the placing and disposing of themselves, not to inquire only how good a living such and such a place is, how well seated, how healthful and beneficial it will be (which are alas the common and almost the only questions nowadays), but principally to regard what a people they are, and how affected, among whom they are to live. If godly and well disposed, or at least tractable and gentle, and willing to be taught, then less to regard other incommodities. But if wicked and profane, or (which is worse) stubborn, froward, and intractable, then less to regard the greatest commodities. And, certainly, if this point is well considered, and how bitter it has been in the end to many who have not regarded it, it will appear that this is the best encouragement or discouragement, the greatest commodity or discommodity, and the best reason either to win a man to a place or to draw him from it, howsoever good it is otherwise. They who neglect this duty and are led (or misled rather) with carnal and worldly respects, how just it is upon them when they are made to cry in the sorrow of their soul: "Woe is me, I dwell in the midst of a people of polluted lips"?

And here such ministers as have poor livings but good people, let them not faint nor be discouraged. They have more cause to bless God than to be grieved, for doubtless they are far better than those who have great livings and an evil people.

But as for those to whom God has been so good as to bestow upon them competent livings and a willing and well-disposed people, let them think themselves doubly blessed by God, and trebly bound to honor God, and to do good in His church. And if such men go not before their brethren in all ministerial care and duty, their fault is above all men's, and they make themselves unworthy of so great mercies.

Second, if a polluted people pollutes their minister, here is a good warning for all ministers to be wary and choice of their company with whom they will most privately converse. For, as on the one side they may not retire themselves into solitariness nor sequester themselves from all society with their people (which is rather a cynical and fantastical [practice] than [in] any way a religious practice), so of all men are they to be most careful, that they do not loosely and lavishly bestow themselves on all companies, as too many do in our church, to the great scandal thereof. They care not with whom they converse, but all companies, all places, all times, all sports and recreations, all meetings, all occasions, are one with them. But alas, what marvel, though such men keep not themselves unspotted from the world, but prove too offensive to their calling. For, seeing the best men cannot live with the best people but they shall receive some contagion from them, how carefully ought ordinary ministers to make difference of men and meetings, times and places, and not diffusedly and carelessly to thrust themselves into all. So doing, they shall keep their calling from much reproach and preserve themselves from much pollution, which otherwise they are sure to receive from their polluted people.

And here people are to be admonished to censure not their minister too sharply, though he is not so sociable with them all as it may be many would expect. For it concerns no man to be so wary of his company and his sports as it does the minister. And if they would have comfort and honor by their minister, let them be careful into what recreations and company they draw or desire him. For the more polluted the people are among whom he lives, the more careful must he be to keep himself clear from their pollutions.

Lastly, here people are taught not to be too sharp condemners of those ministers whose conversations are not so unblameable as were to be wished. For if they live ill, generally the cause is because they live among an ill people.

Why then should they so much condemn them for such faults as wherein [they] themselves have made them faultier. I say not but our church, state, and ministry, are to censure such men (and it were good they did it more), but it is against all reason the people should do so when [they] themselves are the cause of it. For alas, if this holy prophet was a man of polluted lips because he dwelt with a people of polluted lips, what marvel then that ordinary ministers are polluted with the common and universal pollutions of their people? People, therefore, are first of all to see that [they] themselves are well ordered and godly, and then justly they may complain if the lives of their ministers are not agreeable. But, otherwise, it is not possible, without very special grace from God, but that a minister shall be more or less touched with those crimes which are the common faults of his people. And lamentable experience daily lets us see that where a people in a town is given to drunkenness, there the minister is either so for company or at least too good a fellow; where a people are given to contention, there the minister has too many suits; where the people are popish, there the minister is too superstitious; where the people are ignorant, there the minister is no great clerk; where the people are given to any great sin, there the minister generally is not clear from the same pollution.[14]

And it is seen that the best ministers, and most careful of all, do complain bitterly of the pollutions of their people. For howsoever it may be [that] they escape partaking with their sins, yet they always find, at the least, a dulling and decaying of God's graces in themselves where the people are untoward and disobedient. If, therefore, a minister lives with such a people, his case is pitiful and dangerous, for he walks in the midst of nets and snares, which are laid for him on every side. And if he escapes them (I mean, if he keeps himself unspotted in the midst of a spotted and polluted people), his care and his conscience is worthy both admiration and imitation, and [he] himself is worthy [of] double honor, as being both a zealous minister and a holy man. But he whom God has blessed with a good and tractable people, and well affected to the Word, and yet [he] himself lives loosely and scandalously among them, a heavy burden and a hard account lies on that minister, and no rebuke is too rough, no punishment too great, no censure too sharp for him. And if this holy prophet fears so much the presence of God for his small pollutions, and yet lived among so wicked and polluted a people, then what heaviness and horror shall be heaped on his

14. This paragraph break is not in the original.

soul, who cares not with what foul pollutions his life is stained, and yet lives among a godly and well-disposed people.

And thus, we have the first cause of his fear: his own and his people's pollutions.

Cause 2: God's Glory

It follows: "And mine eyes have seen the King, and Lord of hosts." The second cause of the prophet's fear and astonishment is [that] he saw the Lord, who then appeared in glory unto him; not that he saw the substance of God (for that is invisible and incomprehensible), but His glory; not the fullness of His glory, for that cannot be endured, but a glimpse of it; not with the eyes of his body in [an] ordinary manner, but in a vision. The prophet neither expresses nor can we well conceive how far the eyes of his body were used. The meaning then is [that] he saw in a vision such glory and majesty as he knew there was an extraordinary presence of the Lord of hosts, who is the King of glory. At the sight and thought of His presence, his conscience is instantly smitten with fear for his own infirmities and the pollutions of his people.

Wherein let us, first of all, observe the connection and dependence of these two causes one upon another. For as they are both jointly the cause of his fear, so one of them is in a sort the cause of another. He fears because of his own and his people's sins, and because he saw the Lord. But why is he afraid to see the Lord? The cause thereof is his own and their sins, without which he would never have been afraid, but rather [would] have gloried to see the Lord. But his conscience checking him for some defect of duty in his calling, he trembles therefore at the least glimpse of God's glory. Here let us mark the ground of his reason, which is this: that man, who is in his sins, is not able to stand in the presence of God. This is a general and certain truth, and the reasons of it are these:[15]

The first is the contrariety [that exists] between God and the nature of sin, it being the only thing which offends Him and provokes His wrath and just displeasure. Therefore, as a subject cannot but be much amazed if he happens to come into the king's presence with anything about him which the king hates or cannot abide to see, so a man cannot but be extremely astonished if he knows himself to be in God's presence with his sins, which God's soul hates.

Second, sin makes a man indebted to God, for as the law ties him first to obedience, so if he sins and fails in that, it binds him to punishment. And the more a man sins, the deeper he is in God's debt. If then in this world a man willingly endures not the sight of him in whose debt he is, what marvel that

15. This paragraph break is not in the original.

a poor sinner trembles at the presence of God, to whom he has forfeited soul and all.

Third, sin is that which provokes God to wrath. Therefore, a sinful man fears the presence of God, as a traitor the face of the prince or a malefactor of the judge.

For these causes, a wicked man endures not God's presence.

God's Ordinary Presence

Now God's presence has divers degrees. First, God is present to our conscience when we think of Him. Second, He is present when we name Him, or hear Him named or mentioned by others, and these are the farthest off. Third, God is nearer unto us in the presence of His ordinances, as His Word and sacraments, and public service in the congregation. Fourth, there is a most apparent and sensible presence of God, which shall be at the last judgment, when all men shall stand before Him in His immediate presence, to receive their judgment.[16]

Now all these presences of God are hateful to a wicked man.

For the first, a wicked man by his good will never thinks of God, and if sometimes a thought of God (like lightning) flashes in his mind, presently he quenches it as being a most unwelcome and burdensome thought unto him. Therefore, David says, "The wicked is so proud, he careth not for God; neither is God in all his thoughts" [Ps. 10:4]. Nay, God Himself is so little thought on by them that they will willingly think of nothing that might bring God into their thoughts, as namely, God's great works of His wonderful judgments, of which the same prophet says in the same place: "Thy judgments are far above, out of his sight" [Ps. 10:5]. As if he had said [that] he labors to set them far from the eye of his mind, so that he may never have occasion to think of them nor on God by them. That this is true for his thoughts, I have endeavored thus to prove by God's own testimonies because thoughts cannot be discerned by man.

But alas, for the second, that is, for his words, that is too apparent in the sight of all men. For observe it, and you shall never see a wicked man by his good will have God in his mouth (unless it is to abuse His name by swearing or blasphemy), nor does he willingly hear any other man talk or discourse largely of God or of His greatness and His justice. But such talk is tedious and cumbersome unto him. And if he cannot break it off with other discourse, then he sits as mute as a fish, and inwardly either frets with anger or is tormented with fear. All this is true in Felix the governor. While Paul "discoursed of righteousness, temperance, and judgment to come" [Acts 24:25], the text says [that] "he trembled" in the meantime.

16. This paragraph break is not in the original.

And, for the third, we see daily [that] wicked men endure not God's presence in the church. For nothing is more troublesome unto them than many sermons, often praying, and much receiving of the sacrament. And, therefore, they never come to the church, nor receive more often than the law lays upon them. But further than that, as the psalmist says, "They never call upon God" [Ps. 14:4].

But, as for the last, they fear and abhor it above all. They wish in their heart it may never be. And, therefore, Saint Paul makes it a token of a true believer, and a holy man, "to love, and look for the appearing of Jesus Christ" [2 Tim. 4:8]. Thereupon it follows that, even so, it is a sign of a wicked man to fear the last judgment and to wish it might never be. And when it comes indeed, and they see they cannot escape it, what then do they? Even "cry to the mountains, Fall upon us; and to the hills, Cover us and hide us." From what? "From the presence of God" [Rev. 6:16]. So fearful and so hateful is God's presence to a sinful man.

God's Extraordinary Presence

Besides these, there is another way whereby God shows His presence. And it is immediately by [an] extraordinary revelation of His glory. It was usual in the Old Testament, as here to the prophet, but now [it] is not to be expected. But how terrible it is to the sinful nature of man appears in this place. For if the prophet, a most holy man, whose conscience accused him but of a few and small sins, yet thus cries out, amazed and affrighted, at the revelation of some part of God's glory, alas, how would they be terrified with it, whose consciences are burdened with great and grievous sins, and that without repentance?

Thus, we see the ground of his reason, how true it is that a man in his sin cannot cheerfully come, nor boldly stand, in God's presence.

The use of this doctrine.[17]

Use 1

First of all, let us see the monstrous presumption of such ministers as dare venture rashly into the ministry, to tread upon the holy ground of God with unclean feet [and] to handle the holy things of God with unwashed hands. For what is it to enter into the ministry but to enter into the chamber of presence of the great King? And should not a man look about him before he comes there? Therefore, if God rebuked Moses for stepping too hastily toward the bush (where His presence was), and said, "Come not too near, for the place where thou standest is holy ground" [Ex. 3:5], then how will God rebuke and check

17. This paragraph break is not in the original.

the consciences of such carnal men as carelessly and carnally rush into the pulpit and to God's holy table, where God is present in a far more excellent manner than He was in the bush? And if they, who enter into this calling without fear and reverence, are to be blamed so, then how much faultier are they who, being ministers, dare venture to preach or minister the holy sacraments without holy and private preparation and sanctification of themselves, but rush upon them as upon common and profane actions? Whereas God is present there in a most holy and glorious manner, these men surely will say [that] the prophet here was of too nice a conscience. But, at last, God shall appear fearfully and terribly unto such men as care not how they appear in His holy presence.

Second, this shows the reason for the practice of all Christian churches which pray before and after the sermon; namely, not only for decorum, and to grace the action, but to sanctify and humble ourselves because then we come before God's presence. They, therefore, do not think reverently enough of God, and His presence, who do by their practice in any sort make way to the contrary.

Third, we may here learn the pitiful case of those ministers who are so presumptuous as to exercise that holy function, and yet remain in their sins without repentance. What do these men [do]? They approach to the burning bush with their shoes on their feet; that is, unto God's presence in their sins. What shall come of it in the end? Surely, that burning fire shall consume them. The least sin and smallest negligence affrighted this holy prophet when he should go into God's presence. But these men dare come into the sanctuary of God, yea dare take God's Word in their mouths [Ps. 50:16], and yet hate to be reformed, and do cast the glorious Word of God (which they preach to others with their mouths) behind their backs. These men may wonder at this holy prophet's niceness, or else all the world may wonder at their profaneness. A little pollution of his lips frightened him from coming into God's presence. But these [men] dare do it with eyes, ears, lips, feet, hands, heart, and all polluted. Their eyes [are] polluted with careless looking at all vanities, their ears with hearing [and] their lips with speaking wanton and wicked talk, their feet with running into wicked company, their hands with practicing, and their hearts with devising and consenting to all wickedness.

This is the cause why the labors of such men are most unprofitable: because they dare come into God's presence in their sins. In many places of our land, there is by God's blessing much teaching, yet there is little reformation in the lives of the most, but contrariwise some fall to atheism, some to papism, [and] some into soul sins not to be named among Christians.

Where is the cause? Surely not in the gospel, nor in our doctrine, nor in the teaching of it, but one very principal cause is [that] many ministers come into God's presence unsanctified, and in their sins, not caring how loosely they live in the face of their people. And, therefore, God in justice, though He instantly smites them not with visible vengeance for their presumption, yet He smites the people with spiritual blindness, that they regard not their doctrine, but look at their lives, and do rather follow the profaneness of the one than the holiness of the other. Ministers are such in whom God will be sanctified. Because they do not so, but dishonor Him by coming into His presence in their sins, He cannot abide them nor give any blessing to their labors.

All ministers, therefore, as they would see any fruit of their ministry, let them first sanctify themselves, and cleanse their hearts by repentance, before they presume to stand up to rebuke sin in others. Else, let them not think that their golden words shall do so much good as their leaden lives shall do hurt. And they may hap to confirm men who are already converted, but any such men shall hardly convert any souls from popery or profaneness. And it is a vain conceit for men to imagine [that] there is any force in eloquence or human learning to overthrow that sin in others which rules and reigns in themselves. Our church, and all reformed churches, may make use of this doctrine. For it is the glory of a church to have their doctrine powerful and effectual for the winning of souls; therefore, it concerns them to take order that their ministers be godly men as well as good scholars, and their lives inoffensive as well as their doctrine sound, or else they will find in woeful experience that they pull down as much with the one hand as they build up with the other.

But most nearly this doctrine touches ministers themselves. They must know [that] their case is most fearful of all men's, if they come into God's presence in their profaneness. For as no man is more honorable than a learned and holy minister, so none more contemptible in this world, none more miserable for that to come, than he who (by his loose and lewd life) does scandalize his doctrine. And let him assure himself that, for his presumption in rushing into God's presence in his sins, he shall in this world be cast out as "unsavory salt, and trodden down of men" [Matt. 5:13] with the foot of contempt. And in the world to come, he shall above all men cry out in most extreme torment of conscience: "Woe is me, that my eyes must see the King and Lord of hosts." And so, because he would not, in this world, come into God's presence in sanctification and holiness, he shall therefore in fear and horror be hauled into the presence of God's glory at the last day, there to receive the just sentence of his condemnation.

Lastly, all painful and godly ministers may receive comfort not to be discouraged or driven from God's presence because of their corruptions or infirmities, for we see it was the prophet's case. But let them still approach in fear and reverence, and be so far from being driven from their duty, because they, being sinful men, dare not come into God's presence without much fear, as let them contrariwise be assured that the more they tremble at God's presence here, the less shall they fear it at the last day. And when profane and ungodly men, who in this world feared not to stand in God's presence in their horrible sins, shall cry to the "mountains, fall upon us, and to the hills, cover us and hide us from the presence of God" [Rev. 6:16], then such ministers as in this world, in fear and trembling and always in repentance, did approach into God's presence shall then look up and lift up their heads, and shall say to the holy angels, and all the powers of heaven, help us and hasten us to come into the glorious presence of our God and Savior.

And thus, we see the manifold use of this doctrine to our church and ministry.

Use 2

Second, inasmuch as here the prophet, in a conscience of his corruptions, fears and cries out at the least apparition of God's glory, the vanity and false dealing of the Church of Rome is here discovered. In [their] legends and stories of their saints, nothing is more common than apparitions from heaven of departed saints, glorious angels, the Virgin Mary (and so familiarly that sometimes she sang with them in their cell, kissed them, and let them suck her breasts), nay, God Himself, and especially our Savior Christ Jesus. They say [Christ] appeared (I know not how often) to one man (namely, Saint Francis), and appeared as He was crucified with His wounds, and imprinted His wounds in Francis's body (which, they say, he bore all his life). [These wounds] bled whenever he would suffer them, which he always did on Good Friday, that he might be like Christ. This, and many more such, you may see in that fabulous and blasphemous book, *The Conformities of St. Francis.*

But for the matter: Are apparitions from heaven so ordinary in the popish church? How then came it to pass that the greatest and holiest men in the Old Testament were so amazed at the very apparition but of an angel (as we may see in the whole course of the story)? Some ran away and hid themselves. Some covered their faces. Some fell down flat on the ground. And the prophet here cried out, "Woe is me, I am undone; my eyes have seen the King and Lord of hosts." But in the Church of Rome, look [at] the stories! That saint or monk, who has not had some apparition of the Virgin Mary, some of the apostles, an angel, or Christ Jesus, appearing and talking with him, is nobody. And yet, alas, Peter, James and John, those three great pillars [Gal. 2:9], were as good "as beside themselves" at the appearing of a "little part of the glory of Christ" in His transfiguration [Matt. 17:6; Luke 9:33].

It must, therefore, follow that either these men (who dare, and can, behold God's glory so easily and so ordinarily) have no sin in them (which is impossible) or rather (which indeed is truth) it appears that these are but deceitful fancies and forgeries of their own device to deceive the world and to magnify themselves before the eyes of the common people. For it is, first of all, most false that apparitions are so common as they make them. For if they were, then they are more ordinary in the New Testament than in the Old. For whereas the Scripture has one, their legends have twenty, and whereas one (namely, St. Paul) was once "rapt into heaven" [2 Cor. 12:2], they have twenty who were rapt thither. And as that is false, so it is impossible that any man clothed with flesh can endure an extraordinary apparition of God's glory without extreme amazement, as is plain here in the prophet. I hope [he] was as holy a man as the holiest monk who ever was. I have noted this, that young divines may be occasioned to look a little into their fabulous legends, so that they may discover the false tricks and juggling casts of that religion, which needed not evil shifts if it were of God.

Use 3

Third, the people may here learn, first, in that God's presence is so glorious and fearful to man's nature, how mercifully God has dealt with them in teaching them not by Himself or by His angels from heaven (which they could never endure), but by men who are like themselves, and how vain and fond these men are who would be taught from heaven and not by men who are so full of wants. In the Old Testament, when the people received the law from God's own mouth, it is said they ran away and cried out, "Why should we die? if we hear the voice of God anymore, we shall die; for what flesh ever heard the voice of the living God and lived?" Therefore, they said to Moses: "Go thou near and hear all that the Lord shall say, and declare thou unto us what God saith to thee, and we will hear it and do it." And then says the text that "the Lord said, I heard the words of this people, they have said well in all that they have spoken" [Deut. 5:25–28]. And so, from that day forward, God ordinarily taught His church by men like themselves. And we see that the beginning of it was not in judgment, but in mercy unto them. It is, therefore, the duty of all men both to acknowledge this mercy of God in due thankfulness, and withal to remember, when they see infirmities in ministers, that they are but men, and that, if they had not the ministry of men, how hard it would go with them, considering that the least measure of God's own presence cannot be endured by any man.

Second, inasmuch as God's presence is so glorious in itself and fearful to our nature, all men are taught to prepare themselves by holy prayer, humiliation, and confession of their sins and unworthiness, before they come to God's Word or sacraments. For they come at that time into God's presence. They, therefore, are not to come in their security nor in their ordinary sins unrepented of, lest

God strike their consciences with a sense of His fearful displeasure, and make them cry out, upon far greater cause, than here the prophet did.

Third, and lastly, we learn here the different natures and properties of sin and holiness. Sin, even the least sin, nay a very sinfulness of nature, makes a man afraid of God's presence. That sin unrepented of does so appears in Adam, who, in his integrity, spoke and conversed even in a familiar sort with God. So, no sooner had he sinned but he ran from God and hid himself. And that even the least sins not repented of do so also appears in this prophet, who, being a holy man, yet his conscience being privy to itself of some small omissions or negligences in his calling, he cries out [that] he is undone because he sees the Lord of hosts. But contrariwise the state of perfect holiness, and the want of all sin, makes a man bold in God's presence, and desirous rather than afraid to behold God's glory, which shall be most apparent at the last day. For when the wicked shall desire to be "covered with the hills, and ground to dust by the mountains" [Rev. 6:16] rather than to appear before the face of God, then shall the godly (whose holiness shall then be perfect) "look up and lift up their heads, because their redemption is so nigh" [Luke 21:28]. And Job testifies of himself that "he knoweth his redeemer liveth" and that he shall "stand before him and look upon him with his eyes" [Job 19:25–27]. Thus, as guiltiness drives a man from the king's presence but innocency makes him bold before him, so sinfulness makes a man avoid God's presence but holiness makes him draw near unto God and to rejoice in His presence.

Then for a conclusion of this point, let all men here learn the way to true courage and boldness before God; namely, to repent daily of their sins, and labor to grow in true holiness. Wealth or wit, learning or authority, cannot do this for you, but only a good conscience, which must be made good by grace and by repentance. Then, you shall rejoice in God's presence in this world, and delight to think of God, to speak of God, to pray unto Him, to meet Him in His Word and sacraments, and at the last day you shall stand with confidence before the throne of His glory.

Hitherto of the fear and astonishment of the prophet, and of the causes thereof. Now follows his consolation.

Part 2: The Consolation

"Then flew one of the Seraphim...." In these two verses is laid down the second general point; namely, the consolation of the prophet. Concerning this, there are two points in the text. The first [is] the ground and matter of his consolation; that is, the forgiveness of his sins. The second [is] the divers circumstances of that consolation. (1) The time: "then." (2) The minister by whom it was done:

an angel, "one of the Seraphim." (3) The manner how he did it: speedily, "he flew." (4) The instrument or outward sign: "a coal from the altar." (5) The outward action or application of it: "he touched his lips."

Point 1: The Circumstances of His Consolation

The matter of the consolation is last in order. Let us, therefore, first speak of the circumstances.

Circumstance 1

The first circumstance is the time when this prophet was comforted and raised from his fear. "Then," says the text; that is, after his fear and astonishment, but not before. God always deals thus with all His saints. He bestows no graces on them pertaining to salvation but after He has by some means or other brought them to true humiliation in themselves and to sorrow for their sins. Humiliation is the preparative for grace. For when by sight and sense of their sins, and their own misery by sin, He has even driven them quite out of themselves, finding nothing in themselves but cause of fear and astonishment, then He pours the oil of grace and of sweet comfort into their hearts, and refreshes their weary souls with the dew of His mercy. This point needs no further proof, for look into the Scriptures and we shall find [that] God never called any man to the state of grace or to any notable work or function in His church, but He first humbled them, and then brought them out of all conceit with themselves, and then wrought in them, and by them, His wonderful works.

Use 1

The use of this doctrine is, first of all, to teach all men to esteem aright of the afflictions that God lays upon them in this world. Commonly, men take them impatiently, and our nature grudges against them. But let a Christian man consider with[in] himself how God has always dealt with His children, and he has cause not to think so. For does God lay some great affliction on you? It may be [that] He has some mighty work of His grace to work in you, or some great work of mercy to be wrought by you in His church, and hereby [He] prepares you for the same. Say, therefore, with the holy prophet: "I held my tongue, O Lord, and spoke nothing, because it was thy doing" [Ps. 39:9]. And what God may intend in His so doing to you, you cannot tell. And, therefore, possess your soul in silence and patience.

Use 2

Again, here is a comfort to all such as are distressed in mind in sense of their sins and sight of God's wrath. Their state is not miserable, much less desperate, for they are in the high way to grace and favor. God justifies not but him who repents, God exalts not but him who is humbled, God comforts not but him who is distressed, God has mercy on none but such as both know and feel they want it, and know also that they know not where to have it but at His hands. Happy, therefore, is that soul who feels the weight and burden of sin, for to him Christ will bring most ease and comfort. God's ministers, therefore, are hereby to comfort distressed consciences, to assure them that if with this prophet they are so deeply touched with [the] sight of their sins and God's justice as that they cry, "Woe is me, I am undone," then, even then, they are most capable of comfort, and best prepared to receive it, as here it fell out to the holy prophet.[18]

Use 3

Third, here the way is taught us how to attain to any excellent graces from God, either for our own salvation or the good of the church; namely, to labor for a sensible feeling of the want of them in ourselves. For God usually bestows no gifts on any man but such as do in humility and lowliness confess to God and acknowledge in themselves the want of them. So, the blessed Virgin sings, "God filleth the hungry with good things, but the rich he sends empty away" [Luke 1:53]. And so, the psalmist [says], "God satisfieth the hungry soul, and filleth the empty soul with goodness" (Ps. 107:9). So then, if you are rich in your conceits, God has nothing for you. But if you are hungry, He is ready to fill you with good things. And do you acknowledge your empty soul? Then, behold treasures of goodness to feed and fill you. And are you cast down with the prophet, and is your soul empty of hope and fraught with fear? Then, behold even then God and His angels ready to raise you up, and to fill you with consolation.

Thus much for the time of his consolation. Now for the minister by whom it was.

Circumstance 2

"One of the Seraphim." The second circumstance of his consolation is the minister by whom it was done: an angel, [or] one of the Seraphim, that is, an angel of that order so called. From this we learn:

First, there are divers degrees and several orders of angels, though we know not the true distinction thereof. [We do not] think it lawful to imagine them to be nine, nor to set them down particularly, as the Church of Rome does. They make many of their own devices (which they call traditions) of equal authority with the Scriptures.

18. This paragraph break is not in the original.

Second, these holy angels are the glorious guard of God, and do continually stand about the throne of His glory, and attend His holy will, both in heaven and in earth.

Third, they are also by the merciful appointment of God the guard of God's children [Psalm 34], and ministering spirits sent out (as it were) for a commission, for the good of the elect [Hebrews 1]. Because they are plain in the Scripture, and do less concern our general scope, which is concerning the ministry, I pass over all of these points.

Fourth, here it is apparent that the angels are sent out for the help and service of the elect [but] especially of God's ministers, as is plain in this place where the prophet, being affrighted, a holy angel is ready to give him comfort. And so, over the whole course of the prophets, and at this day, their protection and comfortable assistance is no less present to the godly ministers of the New Testament, though not in such sensible signs and such visible manner as in the old. For if they are ministering spirits sent out for the good of them who shall be saved, how much more for their good [of those who] shall both be saved themselves and save others also.

[This is] a doctrine of great comfort and much good use to all ministers. First of all, [they] may here learn contentment in their calling. For howsoever no calling has more crosses, so none again has more comforts. And howsoever none is more disgraced by evil men, yet none is more honored by the holy angels. And howsoever they (above any calling) are servants to all men in this world, yet none has the service and attendance of angels so much as they. For though we have them not to help us to do the outward actions of our ministry with us or for us (as some popish doctors teach that in their mass "amen" is not said to one collect because the angels say "amen" to it), yet doubtless they are present always at all holy exercises and lawful actions but especially at the public service of God, performed by the ministers. And besides that, they are witnesses thereto and of the pains and diligence and faithfulness of a good minister. They also do minister unto them oftentimes bodily strength and assistance and many comforts in their troublesome travels, which they know not how by any natural means they come unto them.[19]

And as this doctrine does thus yield them contentment against the contempt, so also courage against the danger of this calling. For what though you have mighty men of this world against you when you have angels for you? And what though you fight against principalities and powers when you have Cherubim and Seraphim on your side? Godly ministers have many enemies, but if by the eye of faith they can see who are with them as well as with the eye of

19. This paragraph break is not in the original.

reason who are against them, they will confess with Elisha [that] there are more with us than against us. The stories of all ages do affirm, and the comfortable experience of these days of ours does verify, the truth hereof. Ministers who live in places very profane or very popish, it is admirable to see how many dangers they have escaped and plots they have avoided, which by their enemies (or rather the enemies of their doctrine) have been laid for their lives. From whence are their deliverance and many other comforts in their ministries but from God's protection by the ministry of His angels?

Before we leave this point, two questions may be asked, not amiss, briefly to be resolved.

Question 1. First, if any asks whence it comes that angels perform more service to good ministers than to other men, I answer [that] the reason is partly from God [and] partly from the angels. First, God has a principal care of them above other men because they work His work above all other callings, for their labors immediately concern the good of men's souls. Whereas others do first concern the body and consequently the soul. Therefore, whereas "he hath given his angels charge over all his elect, to keep them in all their good ways" [Ps. 91:11–12], they have a special charge doubtless over all godly and faithful ministers, whose ways are God's in a special manner. Second, angels themselves, as they willingly perform any service to the church (or to any part thereof), so most willingly of all they are employed for the good of godly ministers, and that for two causes.

First, they are their fellow-laborers. The angels and good ministers are both called God's ambassadors and God's own servants (or officers) in a more peculiar manner than any other calling (1 Cor. 4:2; Heb. 1:14; Mal. 2:7; Revelation 2; 3). And their service is so alike that their names are common one to the other, angels being called ministers, and ministers angels, as though they were almost all one.

Second, the minister's duty is to convert and save souls, being a work which (next to the glorifying of God and doing His will) the angels do take most delight in, above any other. For if they "be sent out for the good of them which shall be saved" [Heb. 1:14], how much more willingly for their good by whom they are saved? And if the angels "rejoice at the conversion of a sinner" [Luke 15:10], surely, they much love him, and desire to do him good, by whom the sinner is converted. And in these respects, angels and ministers have the same names and are both employed in the same great work, namely doing good to the elect. Therefore it is that the angel calls himself the evangelist's fellow in Revelation 19:10; 22:9. If then they are fellows, even fellow-servants and fellow-laborers, in a more special manner than any other, what marvel that the angels are most willingly employed in doing any service of help or comfort to godly ministers.

Question 2. In the second place, if any asks if it is so, then what duties are ministers to perform to angels for their so careful service and special attendance upon them above other men? A papist would answer [that] ministers must therefore worship them, and keep their fasting and holy days, and say their service, and pray unto them as to their keepers and mediators. But alas, cannot the king's messenger or officer be honored unless he is set upon the king's throne? Will nothing serve him but the crown and scepter? So, cannot angels be honored unless they are made gods or saviors or mediators? I answer, therefore, [that] we dare not go so far, lest we remember the servant so much that we forget the master. But, rather, we answer thus: seeing angels are thus serviceable to God's ministers, it should first of all teach all men to honor that calling with all due reverence. For they cannot but please the angels in honoring good ministers whom they esteem their fellows.

Second, it should teach all ministers not to content themselves with the name and title, but to labor to be good and faithful. For so doing, they are fellows to the angels, and it is a disgrace to the angels when those who are their fellows are unfaithful.

And it should further teach them to adorn their calling with a holy life, for as sin is that which grieves the angels and drives them away, so it is grace and holiness which makes them delight in the fellowship of men.

And it may also encourage any man to take pains in that holy calling wherein he is sure to have God's angels in a special manner to attend him, assist him, protect him, and be a witness of his faithfulness. And who would not work cheerfully in that labor wherein he has the angels to be (in a sort) fellow-workers with him?

To do these three duties is to honor good angels. And that minister who conscionably performs them, the angels will take themselves sufficiently honored by that man.

And if besides this honor, we would rejoice God's angels and minister matter of joy unto them, then, in the fourth place, let all ministers propound to themselves above all things the conversion of souls rather than their own praise, or living, or pleasing of men, and so endeavor it both in teaching and all their other courses that the angels may see it and be witness of it. For if they rejoice at the conversion of a sinner (as Christ says they do), then those men, who do most seriously aim at the conversion of sinners, make them most often rejoice.

And thus, we see both the service of angels to God's ministers and the duties they are to perform to them in that regard. The due consideration of this point may raise the world to a better conceit of this calling and persuade fathers to dedicate their sons to it, and stir up young students to consecrate themselves thereto, and turn their studies to that end. For no man in no calling has so special attendance and assistance of God's angels as godly ministers have. At least, if it works not this in the world, yet it may yield comfort and contentment to all faithful ministers in their painful calling.

Circumstance 3

But let us see how the angel performed his service to the prophet: not unwillingly or lingeringly, but speedily. The text says so: "he flew." This is not so to be understood as though the angels had wings. For they have no corporal nor sensible bodies, but spiritual and insensible substances, the actions whereof are performed with such nimbleness and agility as cannot fall within the compass of outward sense. But the phrase is used for our capacities, to show how readily and speedily the angel went about to minister comfort to the prophet. For as nothing moves so quickly to our sense as does the creature that flies, and as we say, that man does fly about his business, who does it quickly and diligently, so here the Holy Spirit sets down the willingness of the angel to comfort this holy prophet and to do the will of God. Where we learn:

First, what excellent servants of God the holy angels are, who so readily, willingly, and speedily execute the will of their Lord. This must teach all God's servants to do the like, and to imitate them in this excellent obedience. And the rather because we pray daily to God, "Thy will be done in earth as it is in heaven"; [that is,] in earth (of us) as it is in heaven (of the holy angels). But they do it most cheerfully and without all lingering, therefore so ought we. Magistrates in their places, and ministers in theirs, and every man in his function, is to apply this to himself, and to be stirred up thereby to a cheerfulness and quickness in their duties. For therein they resemble the blessed angels, and then their deeds accord with their prayer; but contrariwise, he who does his duty unwillingly and unreadily is like the devil who indeed does God's will, and yet against his will. And surely, unto such obedience there belongs no reward. But as "God loveth a cheerful giver" [2 Cor. 9:7], so doubtless He loves a cheerful worker.

Second, we see here how great love angels bear unto God's children, especially unto godly ministers, how willingly they are employed to do them good. Willingness and readiness to do good to any man must needs come from love. And yet, alas, all men, even the best, and all ministers, even the best, are creatures far inferior to the angels.

Here magistrates and ministers must learn to be far from contempt of their inferiors, and to do their duties of ruling and teaching carefully, though the people are far their inferiors. It is the nature of love to make any man do service most willingly to him whom he loves though he is far meaner than himself.

If, therefore, princes love their subjects, they will not spare any care, cost, nor pains, nay they will rejoice to do them good, and they will labor to be like the angels, who are as far greater than men as they are than their subjects.

And if ministers love their people, they will forget their own dignity, which often times they might stand upon, and will make themselves even servants to all, that they may win some [1 Cor. 9:19].

And seeing angels do fly so fast to give help and comfort to good ministers, this must teach them further:

First, everyone to labor to be a good minister, for then they are sure of the love of angels, and then most willingly do the angels any service to them.

Again, let it teach them to fly as fast to the discharge of their duties to God's church as the angels fly to do them service, so shall God's angels think their diligence and careful service well bestowed upon them.

Lastly, this diligence of the angels, and their willingness proceeding from love, must stir up all Christians to perform all duties of godliness to God, and of love unto His church, with alacrity and cheerfulness. God's angels do so. We look to be like the angels in glory in the world to come. Then, be like the angels in diligence, love, and faithfulness in this world. The wise man says, "He that is slothful in his business is good for nothing: but the diligent man shall stand before the king" [Prov. 22:29]. And surely, he who is willing and diligent in the duties of Christianity shall stand before the King of kings in heaven.

And let this suffice for the angel's service, and his diligence in his service. Now let us see what instrument the angel used.

Circumstance 4

"A coal from the altar." The fourth circumstance of this consolation is the instrument which (it pleased God) the angel should use to minister comfort to the prophet, a strange instrument for so great a work: a coal of fire. Here let human reason hide itself, and worldly wisdom be confounded, to see the wonderful works of the Lord. God could have healed the prophet's infirmities, and given him comfort against his fear and courage in his calling, without means. But He will use means. And what? A weak means; nay, a means that seems contrary: a coal of fire must touch his lips. That which in all reason would have made him speak worse, by God's appointment and the power of His word, shall make him speak better. From this practice of God, we learn many points.

First, see how God magnifies means. He can work without them, and so He did in the creation, giving light to the world divers days before there was sun [Gen. 1:4–17]. But since the order of nature was established, He generally uses means, not only in His ordinary but even in His miraculous actions. And though He uses not always the ordinary and direct means, yet means He generally uses, though they seem contrary, as here in this place. And the same will be found true in almost all the miracles, both of the Old and New Testament.

This, therefore, commends unto all men the use of such good means as God's providence has ordained of any duties, or effecting of anything that does belong unto us to do, and not to depend upon immediate helps from heaven, as many fond and fantastical men do, who are therefore oftentimes justly forsaken of God, and left destitute of all help, and so exposed to shame and reproach.

Second, see here the mighty power of God's ordinance, how it appears in weakness. Such are all His great works. In the creation, He brought light out of darkness. In our redemption, He brought us life out of death. In our conversion, He works upon us by His Word, and by it He draws us to Him, which in all reason would drive us from Him, and by it [He] confounds the wisdom of the world, which is stark foolishness to the wisdom of the Lord.

And so here, He cleanses the prophet by a coal of fire, which would rather defile him, and [He] seasons his mouth with it, which in reason should have burned him. So great, so admirable, and so powerful are the ordinances of God, though they seem ever so contrary, or so weak in themselves, or in their means.

Let this teach all men not to condemn the sacraments, though the outward elements (bread, wine, and water) are weak and common, and dead creatures in themselves, nor the ministry of the Word, though it is exercised by a weak man, mortal and miserable as others are. For that God which can season the prophet's mouth and cleanse his heart by a coal of fire, no marvel that He works upon the consciences of men by His Word and sacraments.

And again, when we see grace and holiness conveyed into men's hearts by the Word and sacraments, let us learn not to ascribe it to the dignity, either of the minister or the elements, but to the supreme power of the mighty God who can purge the prophet by a coal from the altar.

Neither is it altogether without mystery that God here sanctifies the prophet by touching his lips with a fiery coal. For it signifies that the apt and sufficient teacher must have a fiery tongue, and to that same purpose the Holy Spirit came down upon the apostles in fiery tongues [Acts 2]. And it may be that the one is a type of the other. Certain it is that they both teach us thus much, that all true and able ministers must pray and endeavor to have a tongue full of power and force, even like fire, to eat up the sins and corruptions of the world. For though it is a worthy gift of God to speak mildly and moderately, so that his speech shall fall like dew upon the grass, yet it is the fiery tongue that beats down sin, and works sound grace in the heart. It may be there are some who need the fiery tongue.

This shows apparently that those ministers never had their lips touched with a coal from God's altar (that is, their consciences never touched nor their souls seasoned with the sanctifying grace of God's Spirit) who sit still and see great and grievous stains in a church and corruptions in a state, and can be content never to reprove them, as though ministers were persuaders only and not reprovers.

But when this comes to be weighed in the balance of a good conscience, it will be found that not the pleasing tongue, but the fiery tongue, is the principal grace of a good minister.

But to go further: whence came this coal? "Taken from the altar." This coal of fire was taken by the angel from the altar of God, where [there] was a fire which never went out. And this fire was that which came from heaven, sent down by God, at the dedication of the temple by Solomon. And this fire kindled by God never went out. For no man could kindle the like, but all other was counted strange fire, as Nadab and Abihu tried in woeful experience when they would needs offer with it [Lev. 10:1–2].

Now the prophet must be cleansed with the fire which came from heaven, teaching us that the minister must have his fiery tongue from the Holy Spirit, as the apostles were said to be baptized "with the Holy Ghost and with fire" [Acts 1:5; Matt. 3:11]. A fiery tongue is a special ornament of a minister, but that fire must come from heaven; that is, his zeal must be a godly and heavenly zeal. But he who has a railing, lying, slanderous, malicious, or contentious tongue, has a fiery tongue indeed, but it is kindled by the fire of hell, as Saint James says, "the unbridled tongue is a world of wickedness, and defileth the whole body, setteth on fire the whole course of nature, and is set on fire of hell" [James 3:6].

So then, we see [that] a spiteful and malicious tongue is a fiery tongue, but that fire is taken from hell and not from God's altar. And he who stands up to preach with this tongue, God will never suffer any great work to be done by him in His church, though his tongue is ever so fiery and his speech ever so powerful.

As, therefore, ministers must abhor the flattering and pleasing tongue, and must have a fiery tongue, so on the other side this fire must be from God's altar, that is, the fire of their zeal must be built by God's Spirit, and not by the spirit of discord and dissension. Ambitious humors, turbulent and proud humors, new opinions, private quarrels, all these, nor any of these, are for the pulpit.

These may make a man fiery tongued, but this fire was never taken from God's altar, as the prophet's was. This fiery tongue never came from heaven, as the apostles' did.

Circumstance 5

It follows: "And touched my lips." This fifth and last circumstance is the application of the remedy. The coal, which is the medicine, is applied by this angel to his lips, that is, to that part which was polluted. And as he formerly complained of the pollution of his lips, so the medicine is applied to his lips. Here the angel, who in this case is made God's minister, does teach all God's ministers a great point of wisdom in heavenly divinity, namely, to apply their doctrine to their audience in such manner as the circumstances of place, times, or persons do require. Some ministers come to an ignorant and unhumbled people, who never knew the law, and teach them the gospel. Here the fiery coal is used, but the lips are not touched; that is, good doctrine [is] taught but not well applied. For the law should first be laid to their consciences.

Others beat all upon the law, when it may be their hearers are a people sufficiently cast down, and have more need to be raised up with the sweet comforts of the gospel. Others lay open the nakedness of the court in the country, and reprove the faults of princes and great magistrates before the common people, who have more need of the catechism. Others bring the catechism or points of ordinary instruction into the court, where the duties of kings and counselors should be taught in all plainness and sincerity. Others bring their new opinions or controversial points unto popular audiences, who indeed are fit for the schools. Others busy themselves about ceremonies when the substance is in danger to be lost. All these have (it may be) the coal of fire, but it is misapplied, and not applied to the polluted lips. Let all ministers, therefore, learn this point of wisdom of the angel, to apply the medicines of their doctrine to the times, persons, and places, which are infected, so shall they be sure not to take pains in vain.

And thus much of the circumstances of his consolation.

Point 2: The Ground of His Consolation

It follows in the text: "Lo thine iniquity shall be taken away, and thy sin shall be purged." After the circumstances, the ground and matter of his consolation follows. And [it] is the forgiveness of his sins.[20]

Observation 1

First, here let us mark how it and the instrument are annexed together. Lo, says the angel, this coal has touched your lips, and your iniquities shall be forgiven, and your sins purged, as though he had been cleansed by the coal. Here we may note how greatly God magnifies the means which [He] Himself ordains, even true remission and salvation to the right and holy using of them, though

20. This paragraph break is not in the original.

it comes not from them, but from His own mercy, and power of His ordinance. It is, therefore, no marvel that God sanctifies the child by the ministry of water in baptism, and feeds our souls in the Lord's Supper by feeding our bodies with bread and wine. And no marvel that the careless neglect of either of them is damnation to him who despises them, seeing they are God's instruments, ordained by Him to convey His grace unto us. And yet, for all this, we are to know that remission (or salvation) is no more tied to the very elements or the actions than here the prophet's forgiveness is to the coal of fire.

But the main point is that, for the prophet's consolation, the angel tells him his iniquities shall be taken away, and his sins purged, as thereby he had said your sins were the cause of your fear, therefore that your fear may be taken away, your sins shall be forgiven.

Here we learn that as fear comes by sin, so all true comfort comes from the forgiveness of sins. This is that which alone pacifies the conscience and satisfies the soul. When David had sinned against the Lord in his two great sins, and thereby provoked God's wrath against him, and wounded his own conscience, if the prophet had told him [that] he had made him king of ten more kingdoms, he had not so rejoiced his heart, as when he told him, after his repentance, "thy sins are forgiven thee, thou shalt not die" [2 Sam. 12:13]. So, when this prophet was extremely affrighted at God's presence because of some sins and negligences in his calling, it had been no comfort to his poor soul to have been told, "you shall have a more eloquent tongue and a more powerful speech, you shall have better access to the court and audience before the king." All these, and all such like, would have been no better than gilded poison unto him, being in this case. But the happy answer, that refreshes his weary soul more than all the world, was this, "Lo thy iniquities are forgiven, and thy sins purged."

All faithful ministers must here learn the true way of comforting troubled and distressed consciences, namely, first to draw him unto a sight of some particular sins, then to summon him into God's presence, and there to arraign him for those sins until the view of the foulness of his sins and the glory of God's justice have sufficiently humbled him, and then to labor to persuade his conscience upon good grounds of the pardon of those sins by Christ Jesus. This is the way that God used and devised. This is the sure way that cannot fail.

Some think that all trouble of mind is nothing but melancholy, and therefore think [it] needs nothing but physic and outward comforts. But he who considers in what case the prophet was here, or David [was] when he made Psalms 6, 32, or 51, will be of another mind, and will find that nothing can properly trouble the mind but sin. Therefore, as the wise physician, in his cure, first searches out the cause, and then endeavors to take it away, so the good physician of the soul must first of all search into the cause of his sickness (that is, his sins), and must take them away. If they do not, then all their labor is lost. For all the company, music, recreation, wit, diet, nay all worldly comforts and delights, if it were the advancement to a kingdom, cannot so much comfort the distressed soul of a sinner as this voice of a minister spoken from God upon good grounds: "Thy sins are forgiven thee." Now, to lay down what are those true and good grounds whereupon a minister may safely and comfortably pronounce pardon of sins to a sinner belongs properly to another place.

Observation 2

In the next place, let us here observe how the Lord, before He renews the prophet's commission or sends him to preach to the people, first humbles him for his sins, and then upon his repentance, gives him pardon. [This] teaches us that no minister is well qualified to the holy duties of the ministry unless he has truly repented of his sins, and has obtained pardon and mercy in the Messiah.

Ministers labor for qualifications, but the true minister of God will labor for this qualification above all others. For, doubtless, he (to whose conscience God has pronounced pardon of his own sin) shall pronounce most powerfully the pardon of sins to others.

Observation 3

In the last place, let us observe how the preacher is comforted before he goes [to] this new embassage. The Lord is so careful for him: rather than he not be comforted (if there is no man to do it), an angel shall be sent to be his comforter, and (if there is not another prophet to do it) an angel shall pronounce unto him the pardon of his sins.

Let this be an encouragement for all pastors and ministers of God's church to labor painfully and faithfully in their places, for the goodness of the Lord will never fail them, nor shall they want comfort whenever they stand in need thereof. Yea, angels from heaven shall be their helps and comforters rather than faithful ministers shall be left destitute.

Hitherto of the second general point; namely, of the prophet's consolation.

Part 3: The Commission

The third and last general point is the renovation of the prophet's commission (vv. 8–9). And it contains three parts. (1) A question (or inquiry) made by God: "Whom shall I send, and who shall go for us?" (2) The answer of the prophet: "Here am I, send me." (3) The commission renewed unto him: "The Lord said, Go and speak unto this people."

Point 1: The Question

The first part is a question made by God (by way of proclamation), wherein He inquires who shall go preach unto this people. "Also, I heard the voice of the Lord, saying, Whom shall I send, and who shall go for us?"

In this proclamation and inquiry of the Lord, we are not to imagine that the Lord was either unprovided of such as should execute His will, or knew not who were able or who were willing to go preach His Word. For as the apostle says, in the matter of election, "The Lord knoweth who are his" [2 Tim. 2:19], so much more in particular vocations, the Lord knows who are His, and [He] needs not to ask, "Whom shall I send, or who shall go?" But then, it may be demanded why the Lord says so? I answer, not for His own sake, but for ours, whom He would instruct hereby in divers points of holy doctrine.

Doctrine 1

First, He would hereby give us to understand how hard a thing it is to find an able and godly minister, for if there were not a great scarcity of such men, the Lord needed not ask this question. But some will object against this, that there are in many Christian churches so many ministers as they cannot all be maintained, but some go up and down, undisposed, and unprovided for. I answer [that] this is too true in all ages. There were wandering Levites in the Old Testament, who went up and down and offered their service, and served for "ten shekels of silver, and a suit of apparel, and meat and drink" [Judg. 17:10; 18:4]. But this calamity was upon the church of the Jews (never but then) when there was no king in Israel, and everyone did that which was good in his own eyes. If, therefore, there are any in our church and in Christian nations, who go up and down, and offer their service at such rates, it is much more miserable, seeing now there are kings in Israel [Judg. 17:6]. And, therefore, it is no reason that every man robs the church as it shall please his covetous mind. But ceasing to inquire whether this is so or not, and if it is so, leaving the reformation thereof to those churches and states which it may concern, I answer, for the matter in hand, that this may be so, and yet the Lord may complain as here He does, "Whom shall I send?" For the Lord means not such as bear the name of Levites or priests in the old, or of ministers in the new, for there were always some of them who (some for preferment's sake, some for their ease, and some for a refuge how to live) are willing to enter that function, and accordingly in that calling seek not the Lord but themselves and their own ends.

But here the Lord inquires for such men as, first, purely do seek and undertake that function therein to honor God and to gather His church, and then in all their labors and ministerial duties truly and faithfully endeavor to the same ends, preaching God's Word, and as God's Word, diligently proving, exhorting, and admonishing, and shining before their people in good works. It is no marvel that the Lord lights a candle at noon day and makes open proclamation to seek for such men, saying, "Whom shall I send?" For such a man is as Job says, "one of a thousand" [Job 33:23]. For some want ability to discharge their duties, as Saint Paul says, "Who are sufficient for those things?" [2 Cor. 2:16]. And some want willingness to undertake the labor, as God here complains: "Who shall go for us?"

The Use

Now to make use of this doctrine to our church. It is to be wished that in these days, and for our Christian churches, the Lord had not as great cause to cry out in the want of able, faithful, and godly ministers: "Whom shall I send, and who shall go for us?" But alas, this want is too apparent, and this blemish is too notorious, and it is a work worthy [of] the labor of kings and princes to reform it. And [it] is a king's evil, not to be healed but by the power of a king, for as long as there are so few and mean preferments for painful ministers, there will never want abundance of such ministers as do want either conscience or ability to discharge their duties. In the meantime, till God puts into the hearts of parliaments and princes to look to this great and needful work, let us ministers learn our duties.

And, first, we who are in the universities are here admonished to look to ourselves. By God's blessing we are many and daily grow more and more. Let us, therefore, so furnish ourselves as that, when God or His church shall say, "Who shall go for us, and whom shall I send?" then He may find many among us whom He may send to that great work of the ministry. And let us fear to be such that God may affirm of us, as in the days of Job, that He cannot find one of a thousand.

Second, all ministers learn here not to content themselves with the name and title of ministers, but labor for the substantial ornaments thereof, nor to be willing to take the honor and livings, and to refuse the burden and duties of the ministry. For else, let them know [that] God has no need of them. For had the Lord pleased or contented Himself with such kind of men as seek to be ministers for themselves and not for His sake, or being ministers, do feed themselves and not their flock, or preach themselves and not Christ, then He had not needed to have made this proclamation. For all ages have yielded store of such. But, contrariwise, he who is painful and faithful in this function, let him know that God and His church have need of him.

Lastly, here the Romish clergy are justly to be taxed. Their number is infinite, but it is lamentable to see how few among them are such as the Lord here seeks for. Their orders of regulars are exceedingly many, beside all their secular priests. And it is almost incredible how many thousands there are of Dominicans or Franciscans, or in some one of their orders, and yet among the many millions of their monks there is scarce to be found one of many who for his learning and other gifts is fit to be sent to the work of God. Nay, their ignorance was palpable and ridiculous to the world, until of late, being (by Luther and others of our church) made ashamed thereof, they have labored (especially the Jesuits) to become learned. How foul a thing it is that, among so many, the Lord should have cause to complain, "Whom shall we send?" Many of the Jesuits are indeed learned, but for other qualities, they are fitter to be plotters and practicers in state matters, spies or intelligencers, reconcilers, seducers, and subverters, than ministers. And [they are] fitter to be instruments of policy to evil kings than ministers of the gospel unto God. But take them away, and some few selected monks (and those but few out of many millions) and then even for learning God may cry, and call, and proclaim in their monasteries: "Whom shall I send?" And if it is a shame and misery to a church to want such as God may send, or to have but a few, then the Romish church is shameless, which shames not to have so many, and yet among them all almost none whom God may send.

Doctrine 2

In the next place, by this inquiry and question made by God, "Whom shall I send, and who shall go for us?" the Lord would teach us that no man is to undertake this function unless God calls and sends him. Therefore, here are condemned the profane fancies of the Anabaptists, and all like them, who think that any man upon a private motion may step forth and undertake the duties of a prophet, to preach and expound, etc. Oh, but they say [that] these motions are from God's Spirit. Surely, they can say little for themselves, who cannot say so much. But that cannot serve their turn. For if we say, contrariwise, [that], nay, they are but from the devil, or at the least from your own vanity and pride, how can they disprove it? Again, might not the prophet have alleged that with a better pretense and color than they? Yet he stays till God here calls him. Even so, all good ministers are to stay God's calling.

If any asks how he shall know when God calls him, I answer [that] God calls ordinarily by His church. Her voice is His. Therefore, whenever the church of God says unto you, "you shall be sent, and you shall go for us," even then does the Lord call us out to this holy function.

Doctrine 3

Third, let us observe how the Lord says, "Who shall *I* send, and who shall go for *us*?" Some interpreters gather out of this chapter an argument for the Trinity of persons, as namely, out of the third verse where the angels sing, "Holy,

Holy, Holy, Lord God..." But it is not sound enough to overthrow our stubborn enemies the Jews, and therefore it seems those divines are of a sounder and wiser judgment who, seeing we have other places pregnant and plain enough, therefore think it no good discretion to urge this or any such place which may probably admit another interpretation, lest that the Jews, finding the weakness of the argument, do judge all our proofs to be as weak, and so take occasion to persist the rather in their blindness, by that which we brought to have converted them. And as for that song of the angels in the third verse, where they ascribe holiness to the Lord three times, their repetition signifies nothing else but the continual joy and delight which the holy angels take in praising of God, who cannot satisfy themselves in honoring His name. [They] teach us in their example never to be weary of praising God by prayers and holy hymns, and of honoring Him in our lives and callings.

But to prove the three persons in Trinity out of the words, "Holy, Holy, Holy," seems to be no fit nor sound collection. Rather, in my opinion, we may safely collect and conclude out of these words ("I" and "us") that there are more persons in the Trinity than one. For first God the Father, or the whole deity, says, "Whom shall I send?" And then, changing the number, He says, "Who shall go for us?" For howsoever God may imply in the word "us" that he who is sent to preach is sent as well for the good of the church as for His own glory, yet it cannot be denied but that the plural number here, and elsewhere ascribed to the deity, must needs argue a certain plurality of persons in that deity, as in Genesis it is written that God said, "Let us make man" [Gen. 1:26], and here, "Who shall go for us?"

Out of the evidence of these places, seeing the enemies of this doctrine must needs grant a plurality, namely, that there are more than one, then we shall sufficiently prove out of other places, and by other arguments, that there are three.

Doctrine 4

In the last place, let us mark what God says: "Whom shall I send, and who shall go for us?" God sends a minister to preach, and he goes for God. Then, behold here what is the trade and profession of a minister. He is the servant of God. God says so here: "He goes for me." And the apostle says so of himself and all other good ministers, that they are God's laborers.

And in another place, the angel of God appeared: "whose I am, and whom I serve" [Acts 27:23]. But if any man thinks that either God speaks so favorably of them, or Saint Paul too partially of themselves, then let the devil himself be judge in this case, who plainly and freely confesses (though he did it not in love to the truth or them), "These men are the servants of the most high God, which teach unto us the way of salvation" [Acts 16:16–17]. Let, therefore, either God (who is for them) or the devil (who is against them) be believed. But what kind of servants are they? What place or office have they? They are His messengers or ambassadors [Job 33:23]. This is their profession and their place.

The Use

Now then for the use thereof. If they are God's servants, then they are not their own masters. They have a master, even God, whose they are, and for whom and from whom they come. They may not, therefore, please themselves nor serve their own pleasures, nor seek the satisfying of their own carnal lusts either in matter of pleasure, credit, or profit. If then they do evil, He calls them to a heavy account, whose servants they are.

Second, if they are God's servants, then let them do their service to God, and expect their reward from God. Some ministers will expect the reward and honor of God's servants, but will do no service. That beseems not servants. Let such men remember from whom they come, even from that God who, as He can give reward, so He will expect service.

And as for such men as painfully do their service, but are not regarded nor rewarded of men as they deserve, let them be content and continue in their faithfulness. For they are God's ambassadors. And we know ambassadors may have gifts given them by those to whom they are sent, but they expect their maintenance from the kings (their own masters). So, the maintenance which the world should give ministers is like gifts given to ambassadors. If it comes, it is no more than they deserve. If it comes not, yet will faithful ministers do their duty, and expect their payment from their King and Master, God, whose they are and whom they serve.

Third, if they are God's ambassadors, sent by Him, and come from and for Him, then let all such as either condemn or any way injure them, be assured that as God is mighty and powerful so He will mightily revenge it.

There was never king so poor or weak but thought himself strong enough to revenge any wrong offered to his ambassador. And shall God suffer so foul a wickedness to lie unpunished? Nay, they and their posterities shall smart for it. Let Ahab, Jezebel, and Julian,[21] say if it is not so [1 Kings 22:26–28, 34; 2 Kings 9:33; Acts 12:1–2, 23). And all ages or stories show the contrary if they can, that any condemner and abuser of godly ministers ever escaped the visible vengeance of God's revenging hands on him or his.

Fourth, seeing they are God's messengers and servants, they must not be the servants of men, to please or flatter or satisfy humors. This is not for them

21. Julian writing about Herod Antipas.

who are God's servants. They, therefore, who will be slaves to the persons, pleasures, and humors of men, forget that they are God's servants, and came for Him. Yea, they must not endeavor the pleasing of themselves nor the bringing of their own purposes to pass, but in every motion (either made to them by others or suggested from their own hearts) they must forthwith call to mind, "Who sent me higher, and for whom am I come?" Even from and for God. Therefore, they are to yield to nothing nor aim at anything but which may be both to the will and for the glory of Him who sent them.

And if the great men of this world do think it wrong that any man should command their servant against their will, or expect any service from them against their own honor, then let them think it reason that God's ministers should not be commanded anything contrary to God's will or against His honor.

And further, if ministers are God's servants, then let them regard their master's glory, and be ashamed to do anything, whether in their doctrine or lives, which may dishonor Him. That servant is unworthy of a good master, who seeks not his master's credit in all his courses.

Lastly, if they are God's ambassadors, then they must not deliver their own fancies or inventions, but that message they received. And as they received it, so they must deliver it. And if they do their duties faithfully, this doctrine is comfortable to them. They may take pains with joy [that] they have a Master [who] will reward them. They may speak freely (so it is with discretion), [for] they have a Master [who] will make it good. They may stand boldly in the face of their enemies, [for] they have a Master who will defend them. And every faithful minister may say to himself: "I will do my duty, and deliver my embassage. He whom I serve and whose I am, He who sent me and for whom I come, will bear me out."

And thus much of the inquiry which God makes, and the means of it.

Point 2: The Answer

Now let us see the answer which the prophet makes in these words: "Then I said, Here am I, send me."

Doctrine 1

After he was comforted by God, and had his sins forgiven, the prophet then answers, "Here am I, send me." First, mark here what a great change is wrought on the sudden. He, who a little before feared and shrunk at the least appearance of God's glory, now stands forth boldly, as soon as he is called, and answers, "Here am I, send me." So great a matter is it for a minister to have his sins forgiven, and to feel the favor of God to his soul and conscience. Here, therefore, we have an answer to two great questions often moved in the world.

First, many would have quietness of mind and peace of conscience, and cannot attain unto it. If they ask how they might, I answer [that] here is the way. Seek it not in worldly wealth, carnal pleasures, human learning, company, or recreations. But seek it in the favor of God and pardon of your sins, and you shall not miss of it. Thus, you shall have comfort in your own conscience, courage before men, and boldness toward God.

Second, many students in divinity would gladly be ministers, and do much honor the calling, but they find a fear and shrinking in themselves, and thereby an unwillingness to venture upon it. If they ask how they may amend this, I answer (or rather the example of this prophet answers for me): let that man set himself in God's presence, enter into himself, search his conscience, find out his sins, confess and bewail them to God, crave pardon in Christ's blood, and grace to leave them, and cease not till he hears the voice of God's Spirit sounding in his conscience: "Thy sins are forgiven thee." Then, when God shall ask, "Whom shall I send?" you will answer readily and with joy, "Here am I, send me."

And again, many are driven from this calling, beholding the contempt, reproach, and dangers which belong unto it. But let those men mark here the phrase of this holy prophet. When God asked, "Whom shall I send?" he might have answered, "Lord, I would go, but such disgraces and discouragements do accompany this function, as I desire to be excused." But he, casting aside all such conceits, answers peremptorily, "Here am I, send me." How came this to pass, for certainly the prophet was as sensible of these wrongs as any of us, for he was nobly born and brought up, and was of the royal blood? Surely, [it was] because he saw he was in God's favor. He had Him and His commission on his side. And he held this for a sure ground: if God is on my side, who can be against me?

Therefore, doubtless, those men who are driven back by these discouragements were never settled in assurance that their sins were forgiven, nor satisfied sufficiently that God is on the side of all good ministers and that that calling, as it has its authority from God, so likewise allowance, blessing, assistance, and defense of God, above any other calling. For if they were, they would scorn the scorn and contemn the contempt of the profane world, and with much courage and comfort set their hand to God's plough, and say with the prophet: "Here I am, send me."

Doctrine 2

Second, let us observe how the prophet, when God asks the question, sends Him not to others, nor commends others to that service, as is to be thought he might have done many in the church of the Jews. But [he] offers himself: "Here am I."

It controls the carnal courses of many among us in the university, who think it sufficient to live there, and send out other men, and give testimonies and letters of commendation to other men, but [they] themselves stir not. When question is made, "Who shall go to such a place?" or "Who shall be sent to such a parish?" they say not, "Here am I," but that it is too little a living, or too great a charge, or ill suited, or it has some fault. They will not be sent to it, but will answer God and His church [that] there is such a man, and give him letters of testimony or commendation, and so all is well. But for [they] themselves, they live too sweet and easy lives, unwilling to undertake the contempt and burden of the ministry.

Let such men, therefore, learn, when God and His church give them a calling, to answer with the prophet, "Here am I, send me."

And let all such as are students of divinity in the universities mark here the prophet's answer. [It is] not "I will be ready," but "Here I am." Why takes he no longer time? [It is] because he was now sufficiently qualified. Where let them learn not to linger and lie loitering too long in their speculative courses, but when they are competently furnished with learning and other qualities befitting that calling, let them show themselves willing and ready to yield their service to the church when they shall be called. For as an apple may hang too long on the tree, as well as be pulled too soon, and both make it unfit for use, so many men stay too long as go out too soon. And both ways are made unprofitable, or at least less profitable, in the church.

Doctrine 3

And to conclude this second point, it is not unworthy to be noted that the prophet says not, "Here I am, and I run on my own head," but "Send me." He wills the Lord to send him. Then, where are they who dare brag of their private motions, and will run when they are not sent?

The prophet might have said, "Oh, now I feel a motion from the Spirit, therefore I will go and preach." But he stays till he is sent in express terms. Let no man, therefore, presume to press into this function, till he is fully resolved in his conscience that God and His church have said unto him, "Go."

And though a man is ever so well qualified with all manner of sufficiency, yet let him sit still and stay God's leisure, and let him say, "Here I am, send me," and so rest contented until he is sent. If any man says it is unfit that a man should say so of himself, I answer, let him not say so in words but in deeds. Let him, therefore, make proof of himself, and give the church trial of his gifts. Upon this experience of his gifts, if he is found sufficient, that practice of his is all one, and much more, [as] if he had said, "Here I am, send me."

Point 3: The Commission

Thus, we see the prophet would not stir till he was sent. And, therefore, in the next words, he is bid to go. "And he said, Go and speak unto this people." Here is the third and last promise, namely, the essential words of his commission. Wherein (after God had sought for one to go, and the prophet had presented himself and offered his service) God both gives him leave to go and further does furnish him with authority both to go and speak.

The Doctrine

Wherein the principal point is that the authority of the prophet's calling is derived from God Himself, in plain and evident words: "Go and speak." And till then the prophet went not. So, in the New Testament, the apostles went not into the world to preach till they had their commission: "Go and teach all nations" [Matt. 28:19]. And after them, Saint Paul preached not till it was said unto him: "Arise, and go" [Acts 9:6].

In all this is discovered and condemned the pride and presumption of those who dare run on their own heads, and will not stay till the Lord says unto them: "Go, and speak." These men are bolder than either the extraordinary prophets of the Old Testament or the apostles, who are the extraordinary ministers of the New, who always had their warrant with them when they went. And if any man asks why it is necessary they should have [it] so, I answer [that] the reasons are many.

First, all prophets and ministers are God's deputies and commissioners. It is, therefore, reason that they have authority from their Lord and Master.

Second, their words and deeds bear no credit, nor have any power in them, unless they are spoken by virtue of a commission. Nor have their labors any blessing unless God gives it.

Third, these persons have no protection nor safety unless they are God's ambassadors. And how are they so unless they are called and sent by God, and have authority given by God? For these causes no man is to thrust himself into the ministry without a calling from God, and therefore no marvel that those men who will be choosers and callers of themselves, and run when they are not sent, are in their persons subject to all dangers. They are out of God's protection, and their labors without profit because no blessing nor promise of God was given unto them. For God may justly say unto them: "Let him who sent you, protect your persons. Let him who sent you, bless your labors."

But it will then be demanded, how may I know if God bid me go? God speaks not now from heaven as in old time and as to this prophet. I answer, it is true [that] we are to look for no such visions nor apparitions from heaven, for ordinarily there are none such. And the popish church does but deceive themselves and cozen the world, when [they] tell us of so many apparitions that happen to their monks and friars. For now, ordinarily, God speaks in another manner to His church. For in general duties God speaks to us out of His Word and holy Scriptures, and in particular and personal duties (where the Word in plain terms serves not) He speaks to a man by his own conscience and by the voice of His church.

Out of His Word, God shows you the dignity and excellency of this calling, to be a minister of the Word; namely, they are His messengers and ambassadors, etc., [1 Cor. 4:1; Job 33:23; Acts 16:17; Prov. 29:18], so that He may win them to love and affect it. And again, the necessity of it, that it teaches the way to salvation, that without it ordinarily God's church is not gathered nor men's souls saved, that this may stir you up to undertake the burden. This is general. But now particularly for yourself, would you know whether God would have you to go or not, then you must ask your own conscience, and ask the church, for if you are heartily willing, and are fully and worthily qualified, then God bids you, "Go."[22]

Now your conscience must judge of your willingness, and the church of your ability. And as you may not trust other men to judge of your inclination or affection, so you may not trust your own judgment to judge of your worthiness or sufficiency. If, therefore, your own conscience tells you, upon true examination, that you do not love and affect this calling above another, then God sends you not. And if you enter with such a testimony, not God, but some worldly and sinister respect does send you, and put you forward. For though you do desire it, yet if the church of God gives not allowance of your sufficiency, God does not send you. But if, contrariwise, your conscience does truly testify unto you that you desire to do service to God and His church in this calling above any other, and if withal, upon signification hereof to the church and upon trial made of your gifts and sufficiency, the church (that is, many learned, wise, and godly, and such as the church has publicly appointed for that purpose) do approve of your desire and of your sufficiency to do God service in His ministry, and thereupon by a public calling bid you go, then assuredly God Himself has bid you go. And it is as effectual a calling as if you heard the voice of God from heaven. For as in repentance, if your conscience tells you [that] you have truly repented, and if you can make that known to the church by so good evidence as thereupon a minister of God pronounces the pardon of your sins unto yourself, if you rest herein and know it to be as effectual as if God from heaven had told you [that] your sins are pardoned. So is it here, if you have the testimony, first of your conscience, and then of the church, you are to rest therein as in the voice of God. And this is the calling that we are to look for in these days.

22. This paragraph break is not in the original.

The Use

By this doctrine, those who dare run upon private motions and carnal respects are justly condemned of foul presumption, and are justly left without blessing or protection. And those, on the other side, do offer great wrong to God and to His church, who when they cannot deny, but they affect the ministry above any calling, and have approbation of their gifts from the good church, yet will not believe the testimony of the church herein, but their own private judgments, which in this case is no way a competent judge either for or against. Let such men know that they oppose themselves even against God Himself, it being certain that where the inward calling of the conscience and the outward calling of the church do concur, there God Himself calls and bids that man: "Go, and speak."

Now then (to draw to an end), let us observe in the last place with what authority a minister of God comes unto us and executes his function, even with an immediate authority and commission from God, whereby he is bid, "Go, and speak." If it is so, let it persuade the world to fear to do any wrong, either to that calling or to those persons who come with so fair a commission from God Himself. But if it does not persuade the profane world, at least let this be a comfort and encouragement to all true ministers, for if God bids them go, He will go with them Himself. If He sends them, He will not forsake them, but assist them, bless them, open their mouths, enlarge their hearts, harden their foreheads, and give power unto their words to convert His children and to confound and astonish the hearts of His enemies. If He sends them, He will defend and protect them, so that one hair of their heads shall not fall to the earth without His providence. If He sends them, He will provide for them, sufficiently reward them, honor them in the hearts of His own people, and magnify them in the faces of their enemies. And, lastly, if He sends them, He will pay them their wage, even an eternal weight of comfort here and of glory in heaven. And as they are here bid "Go," so once they shall be bid "Come." And that not only with the general call of all the elect, "Come ye blessed of my Father, inherit the kingdom prepared for you" [Matt. 25:34], but even with that particular call which especially belongs to them who are faithful in this service, "Come thou good and faithful servant, enter into thy master's joy" [Matt. 25:21].

"Blessed be he that cometh in the name of the Lord" (Ps. 118:16).

"They that turn many to righteousness,
shall shine as the stars for ever and ever" (Dan. 12:3).

Finis

The Art of Prophesying

or

A Treatise Concerning the Sacred and Only True Manner and Method of Preaching

First written in Latin by Master William Perkins,
and now faithfully translated into English
(because it contains many worthy things fit for the
knowledge of men of all degrees) by Thomas Tuke

"And Ezra the scribe stood upon a pulpit of wood, which he had made for the preaching.... And Ezra opened the book before all the people: for he was above all the people: and when he opened it, all the people stood up. Moreover, Ezra praised the Lord the great God, and all the people answered, Amen, Amen. In like manner Jeshua and Bani.... And they read in the book of the law of God distinctly: and gave the sense, and caused them to understand the reading" (Neh. 8:4–8).

Imprinted at London by Felix Kingston for E. E.

And are to be sold in Paul's Churchyard
at the Sign of the Swan.

1607

The Epistle Dedicatory

To the Right Worshipful, Sir William Armin, Knight.[1]

Sir, the Lord in mercy has vouchsafed many excellent benefits to us these past forty-eight years together, of which this is not the least, if not the greatest, that He has dispelled the dusky clouds of popish darkness as palpable as that of Egypt [Ex. 10:21], and has caused the sunlight of the gospel to shine clearly on all our coasts. He shows His Word unto us as He did unto Jacob [Ps. 147:19], His statutes and His judgments as He did sometimes to Israel. He has given us His prophets and ambassadors who do serve like that cloud and pillar of fire [Ex. 13:22] to direct us in our pilgrimage through the wilderness of this wicked world into celestial Canaan. He has thrust forth many faithful and industrious laborers into His vineyard to prune and to dress the vines of our souls, that we may bring forth the grapes of piety and the clusters of justice (unless we will needs be like the cypress, which, as Pliny says, can endure no husbanding, but makes that which is a medicine to other trees her malady), among whom the author of this learned tractate did show himself with the foremost. [He] always carried with him a light of learning and a lamp of godly living. And, *qualis vita, finis ita*,[2] as he was a lamp while he lived, so like a lamp, *aliis inserviens seipsum consumpsit.*[3] His whole life was labor, *scribenda dicens & legenda scribens.*[4] One whereof was this present discourse and platform concerning the true understanding and using of the Scriptures, written in his younger years. I am bold to present and dedicate [it] to your Worship in this plight you see, partly because it is a thesaurus and storehouse of excellent precepts (as Domitius Piso says that books should be such), having in it κρεας αμαλθειας,[5] sufficient furniture

1. Sir William Armine, d.1620/21, from Yorkshire; member of Parliament; friend of Puritans. *DNB* 1:559.

2. "As in life, so in death."

3. "He gave himself completely for others." I would translate this, He gave himself to be consumed for others.

4. "Writing, saying and reading, writing."

5. This dictum arises from a Greek myth involving Amalthea, the nurse of baby Zeus. It means "horn of plenty."

to further perfection in that sacred science, and partly to demonstrate my gratitude and devoted affection to you who have always been a constant patron (*etiam minitante fortuna*)[6] to my nearest and dearest friends.

Thus, I take my humble leave, desiring your kind acceptance, and so commend your Worship with your whole progeny to the protection of the Lord.

Your Worship's in all duty,
Thomas Tuke

London, January 1, 1606

6. "Even in adverse times."

To the faithful ministers of the gospel and all who are desirous of, and do labor for, the knowledge of holy learning

That common place of divinity, which concerns the framing of sermons, is both weighty and difficult, if there is any other throughout all that sacred science. For the matter, which it is to explicate and treat on, is prophecy, an excellent gift indeed, whether we consider it in respect of dignity or use. The dignity thereof appears in that like a lady it is highly mounted and carried aloft in a chariot, whereas all other gifts (both of tongues and arts) attend on this like handmaids aloof. Answerable to this dignity there is also a twofold use: (1) in that it serves to collect the church and to accomplish the number of the elect; [and] (2) in that it drives away the wolves from the folds of the Lord. For this is indeed that flexanima (that allurer of the soul) whereby men's froward minds are mitigated and moved from an ungodly and barbarous life unto Christian faith and repentance. This also is that engine which, as it has shaken (the foundation of) ancient heresies, so it has in these few past years cut asunder the sinews of that great antichrist.[1]

Wherefore, if it is demanded what is the most excellent gift of all, doubtless the praise must be given to prophesying. Now by how much the more excellent anything is, by so much the more diligently it ought to be adorned with variety and plenty of precepts. Therefore, when I saw this handled as common place by so many as that it would remain naked and poor, if all other arts should call for those things which are their own, I perused the writings of divines, and having gathered some rules out of them, I have couched them in that method which I have deemed most commodious, that they might be better for use and fitter for the memory. I do also publish them that they might be approved if they bring with them that which is good; if any evil, that they may receive their deserved punishment. And whosoever you are who pleases to read them, where you are persuaded of this order of preaching, which I handle here, walk on with me; where you stand at a stay, inquire with me; where you perceive your own errors, return to me; where you see mine, call me back to you. For the one who now

1. This paragraph break is not in the original.

likes me shall dislike me if one likes not godly and moderate minded men. But if any man shall carp at my travail, though very small, let him know that my only meaning is to benefit the church of God, and that the conscience of my act is a sufficient movement against all calumnies. I do now betake you to God, and this (tractate of the) art of prophesying both to you and to God.

William Perkins

December 12, 1592[2]

---

2. This work was originally published in Latin in 1592, and translated into English in 1606.

The Analysis of the Whole Book

The Art of Prophesying, the parts thereof are two:

1. Preaching, in which consider:
    1. The object, which is the Word of God. In it, note:
        1. The excellency thereof.
        2. The parts, which are the two Testaments:
            1. The Old, whose books are historical, dogmatical, prophetical.
            2. The New.
    2. The parts, which are:
        1. The preparation (or provision) of the sermon, consisting of:
            1. Interpretation of the text:
                1. Analogical and plain.
                2. Cryptic and dark.
            2. The cutting (or dividing) of it aright, consisting of:
                1. The resolving or untwisting of it.
                2. The applying of it:
                    - Seven ways of applying it.
                    - The parts which concern the understanding:
                        - Doctrine
                        - Redarguation (or improving)
                    - The parts which concern the practice
                        - Instructing
                        - Correcting
        2. The uttering of the sermon:
            1. The hiding of human wisdom.
            2. The demonstration of the Spirit in:
                1. The speech, which must be:
                    - Spiritual
                    - Gracious

Grace is of the person (to wit, holiness):
- An inward feeling
- A good conscience
- The fear of God
- A love for the people

Grace is of the ministry:
- Authority
- Zeal

2. The gesture and action of:
   - The voice
   - The body

2. Conceiving of public prayer, in which note:
   1. The Matter
   2. The Form
   3. The Parts
      - Meditation
      - Ordering
      - Uttering

Chapter 1

The Art of Prophesying

The art or faculty of prophesying is a sacred doctrine of exercising prophecy rightly.

Prophecy (or prophesying) is a public and solemn speech of the prophet, pertaining to the worship of God and to the salvation of our neighbor. "But he that prophesieth speaketh unto men to edification, to exhortation and to consolation.... But if all prophesy, and there come in one that believeth not, or one unlearned, he is rebuked of all men, and is judged[1] of all men" (1 Cor. 14:3, 24). "God is my witness, whom I serve (or worship, λατρευω) in my spirit in the gospel of his Son" (Rom. 1:9).

---

1. In the margin: ανακρινεται.

Chapter 2

The Preaching of the Word

There are two parts of prophecy: (1) preaching of the Word, and (2) conceiving of prayers. For in speaking there are only two duties of the prophet (that is, of the minister of the Word), to wit, preaching of the Word and praying unto God in the name of the people. "Having prophecy, let us prophesy according to the proportion[1] of faith" (Rom. 12:6). "Deliver the man his wife again, for he is a prophet: and when he shall pray for thee, thou shalt live" (Gen. 20:7). For this cause the word *prophecy* is given also to prayers. "The sons of Asaph, and Heman and Jeduthun, who were singers, prophesied with harps, with vials, and with cymbals" (1 Chron. 25:1). "The prophets of Baal called upon the name of Baal from morning to noon.... And when midday was passed, and they had prophesied until the offering of the evening sacrifice" (1 Kings 18:26, 29).

And every prophet is partly the voice of God (to wit, in preaching) and partly the voice of the people in the act of praying. "If thou take away the precious from the vile, thou shalt be as it were my mouth" (Jer. 15:19). "And Ezra blessed the Lord the great God, and all the people answered, Amen" (Neh. 8:6).

Preaching of the Word is prophesying in the name and room of Christ, whereby men are called to the state of grace, and conserved in it. "And hath committed to us the word of reconciliation. Therefore, we are ambassadors for Christ: as though God did beseech you by us, we pray you in the name of Christ, that ye be reconciled to God" (2 Cor. 5:19–20). "God hath from the beginning elected you to salvation, through sanctification of the Spirit, and faith embracing the truth: whereunto he called you by our gospel" (2 Thess. 2:13–14). "The gospel is the power of God to salvation to everyone that believeth" (Rom. 1:16). "When there is no vision the people are naked" (Prov. 29:18; Rom. 10:19).

---

1. In the margin: αναλογιαν.

Chapter 3

The Word of God

The perfect and equal object[1] of preaching is the Word of God. "They have Moses and the prophets, let them hear them" (Luke 16:29). "The scribes and Pharisees sit in Moses' chair (that is, they teach the doctrine of Moses, which they do profess). All therefore whatsoever they bid you observe, that observe and do" (Matt. 23:2–3).

The Word of God is the wisdom of God concerning the truth which is according unto godliness, descending from above. James 3:17, "But the wisdom, which is from above[2] is first pure…." "Paul a servant of God—according to the acknowledging of the truth, which is according unto godliness" (Titus 1:1).

Admirable is the excellency of the Word, which is evident partly by the nature thereof, partly by the operation.

The excellency of the nature is either the perfection thereof or the eternity.

The perfection is either the sufficiency or the purity. The sufficiency is that whereby the Word of God is so complete that nothing may be either put to it or taken from it, which appertains to the proper end thereof. "The law of the Lord is perfect, converting the soul" (Ps. 19:7). "Whatsoever I command you, take heed ye do it: thou shalt put nothing thereto, nor take ought therefrom" (Deut. 12:32; Rev. 22:18–19).

The purity thereof is whereby it remains entire in itself, void of deceit and error. "The words of the Lord are pure words, as silver tried in a furnace of earth fined seven times" (Ps. 12:6).

The eternity of the Word is that whereby it abides inviolable, and cannot pass until all that which it commands is fully accomplished (Matt. 5:18).

The excellency of operation is that whereby it is endowed with virtue. (1) To discern the spirit of man. "For the word of God is lively, and mighty in operation, and sharper than any two-edged sword, and entereth through even

1. In the margin: Or, the Word of God is the whole and only matter about which preaching is exercised. It is the field in which the preacher must contain himself.

2. In the margin: ανωθεν.

to the dividing asunder of the soul and spirit, and of the joints and marrow, and discerneth the thoughts and intents of the heart" (Heb. 4:12). (2) To bind the conscience. "There is one law-giver, who is able to save and to destroy" (James 4:12). "The Lord is our Judge, the Lord is our Law-giver, the Lord is our King, he will save us" (Isa. 33:22). To bind the conscience is to constrain it either to accuse us or to excuse us of sin before God.

The Word is in the Holy Scripture.

The Scripture is the Word of God written in a language fit for the church by men immediately called to be the clerks (or secretaries) of the Holy Spirit. "For prophecy came not in old time by the will of man, but the holy men of God spoke as they were carried[3] and moved by the Holy Ghost" (2 Peter 1:21).

It is called canonical because it is (as it were) a canon, that is to say, a rule (or line) of the master workman, by the help whereof the truth is both first to be found out and also afterwards to be examined. "And as many as walk according to this canon[4] or rule" (Gal. 6:16). Therefore, the supreme and absolute determination and judgment of the controversies of the church ought to be given unto it.

The sum of the Scripture is contained in such a syllogism (or form of reasoning) as this which follows. The true Messiah shall be both God and man of the seed of David; He shall be born of a virgin; He shall bring the gospel forth of His Father's bosom; He shall satisfy the law; He shall offer up Himself a sacrifice for the sins of the faithful; He shall conquer death by dying and rising again; He shall ascend into heaven; and in His due time He shall return unto judgment.[5] But Jesus of Nazareth the Son of Mary is such a one.[6] He, therefore, is the true Messiah.[7]

In this syllogism the major is the scope or principal drift in all the writings of the prophets, and the minor in the writings of the evangelists and apostles.

The Scripture is either the New or Old Testament.

Old Testament

The Old Testament is the first part of the Scripture, written by the prophets in the Hebrew tongue, or at least in the Chaldea, unfolding chiefly that old covenant of works. "And he began at Moses, and at all the prophets, and interpreted unto them in all the scriptures the things which were written of him" (Luke 24:27; 16:19).

3. In the margin: φερομενοι.
4. In the margin: κανονι.
5. In the margin: The major, or proposition.
6. In the margin: The minor, or assumption.
7. In the margin: The conclusion.

It is distinguished by books which are either historical, dogmatical, or prophetical.

Historical

The historical books are stories of things done, for the illustration and confirmation of that doctrine which is propounded in other books. "Now all these things came upon them for ensamples:[8] and were written to admonish us" (1 Cor. 10:11). "For whatsoever things were written aforetime, are written for our learning" (Rom. 15:4).

These books are fifteen in number.

1. Genesis, which is a history of the creation, fall, promise, and of the state of the church conserved (and shut up) in private families.
2. Exodus, which is a history of the deliverance of the Israelites from the Egyptians, of their going out of Egypt, of the promulgation of the law, and of the tabernacle.
3. Leviticus, which contains a story of the ceremonial worship.
4. Numbers, which is a history of their martial marching into the land of Canaan.
5. Deuteronomy, which is a commentary repeating and explicating the laws out of the foresaid books.
6. The book of Joshua, which declares their entrance into, and possession of, the land of Canaan under Joshua.
7. The book of the Judges, which comprehends a history of the corrupt and miserable condition of the church and commonwealth of Israel from Joshua to Eli.
8. The book of Ruth, which is a history concerning the marriages and posterity of Ruth.
9. The first and second books of Samuel, which are a story of things done under priests, Eli and Samuel, and under kings, Saul and David.
10. The first and second books of Kings, which make a narration of things achieved in the days of the kings of Israel and Judah.
11. The first and second books of Chronicles, which are a methodical history of the beginning, increase, and ruin of the people of Israel, serving to explain and show the line or lineage of Christ.

---

8. In the margin: τυποι.

12. The book of Ezra, which contains a history of their return from captivity in Babylon, and of the beginning of the restoring of the city.
13. The book of Nehemiah, which speaks of the restoring of the city which was to be finished.
14. The book of Esther, which is a history of the preservation of the church of the Jews in Persia by Esther.
15. The book of Job, which is a history treating of the causes of his temptations, as also of his manifold conflicts, and lastly of his happy issue.

Dogmatical
The dogmatical books are those which teach and prescribe the doctrine of divinity. These are four in number.

1. The book of Psalms, which contains sacred songs to be fitted for every condition, both of the church and the particular members thereof, and also to be sung with grace in the heart (Col. 3:16).
2. The book of Proverbs, which is a treatise of Christian manners, teaching piety towards God and justice towards our neighbor.
3. The book of the Preacher,[9] which discloses the vanity of all human things so far forth as they are used without the fear of God.
4. The Song of Songs,[10] which speaks of the mutual communion of Christ with the church under an allegory of a bridegroom and his bride.[11]

Prophetical
The prophetical books are predictions, either of the judgments of God for the sins of the people or of the deliverance of the church, which is to be perfected at the coming of Christ.

But with these predictions they do mingle the doctrine of repentance, and do almost always use consolations in Christ to them that do repent.

It is their custom also, for the helping of their hearers' memory and understanding, to propound their sermons briefly, which they made at large. "Moreover, the Lord said unto me, take thee a great roll, and write in it with a

9. In the margin: Ecclesiastes.
10. In the margin: The book of Canticles.
11. In the margin: Or husband and spouse.

man's pen" (Isa. 8:1). "Write the vision, and make it plain upon tables, that he may run that readeth it" (Hab. 2:2).

Prophecies are either greater or lesser.

Greater are such as do more plentifully deliver all those things that are foretold, as the prophecy of Isaiah, Jeremiah, Ezekiel, [and] Daniel.

Hitherto belong the Lamentations of Jeremiah, touching the misery of the people of the Jews about the time of the death of Josiah.

Lesser prophecies are those which intreat more sparingly or briefly of all those things that are foretold, or at least of some of them, as the prophecy of Hosea, Joel, Amos, Obadiah, Jonas, Micah, Nahum, Habakkuk, Zephaniah, Haggai, Zechariah, [and] Malachi.

Thus much for the Old Testament.

The New Testament

The New Testament is the second part of the Scripture written in the Greek tongue by the apostles, or at least approved of them, propounding plainly the doctrine of the new covenant. "And are built upon the foundations of the prophets and apostles" (Eph. 2:20).

Peter approved the Gospel of Mark, at whose motion and appointment it was written by Mark, as it pleases Nicephorus to aver.[12] And John, who wrote the Gospel, approved the Gospel of Luke. It is of small moment what is reported by Eusebius, to wit, that it is apparent by two places (2 Tim. 2:8; Rom. 2:16) that Paul was the author of that Gospel which is called Luke's. For Paul does not here speak of any one book, but of his whole ministry, for he adds, "In which[13] I suffer trouble as an evil doer even unto bonds" (2 Tim. 2:9).

The New Testament contains partly histories and partly epistles.

Histories

The histories are:

1. The four Gospels of Matthew, Mark, Luke, and John. They are a history of the life, deeds, and doctrine of Christ exhibited unto the world, continuing from His conception even until His ascension into heaven.

And here are four writers: two who were hearers, and two who were eyewitnesses, that they might give greater assurance of the truth of the history.

The difference between the evangelists is in this way: Matthew lays open the doctrines which Christ delivered. Mark sets down the history briefly. Yet, he did not make an abridgement of the Gospel which Matthew wrote (as Jerome supposes), for he begins his discourse in a diverse manner, and proceeds in

12. In the text: Lib. 2. Cap. 45.

13. In the margin: εν ω.

another order, partly treating of things more largely, and partly interlacing of new matters. Luke aims at (or frames) a perfect history, and describes in a certain order. John is almost wholly taken up in laying open the Godhead and benefit of Christ, which is derived from His Godhead unto us.

Jerome distinguishes the evangelists by their beginnings or entrance. He says Matthew is like a man, because he begins with the manhood of Christ. He likens Mark to a lion, because he begins with the preaching of John, which was like the roaring of a lion. He compares Luke to an ox, because he begins with Zechariah the priest offering his sacrifice. He compares John to an eagle, because he does (as it were) soar up aloft and begin with the Godhead of Christ.

2. The Acts of the Apostles is an orderly history, especially relating the deeds of Peter and Paul, that there might be an extant example of governing the church (2 Tim. 3:10–11).

3. The Revelation is a prophetical history concerning the condition of the church from the age in which John the apostle lived unto the end of the world.

Epistles

The epistles follow.

Thirteen epistles of Paul. (1) To the Romans, of justification, sanctification, and the duties of Christian life. (2) The first to the Corinthians, concerning the reforming of the abuses of the church of Corinth. (3) The second to the Corinthians, containing chiefly the defense of himself and of his apostleship against his adversaries. (4) To the Galatians about justification by faith without the works of the law. (5) To the Colossians. (6) To the Philippians. (7) To the Ephesians. (8) The first to the Thessalonians. (9) The second to the Thessalonians. These confirm the churches in doctrine and in the duties of Christian life. (10) The first to Timothy. (11) The second to Timothy. These prescribe the form of ordering the church aright. (12) The Epistle to Titus, of ordering the church of the Cretans. (13) To Philemon, of receiving Onesimus.

The epistle to the Hebrews, concerning the person and offices of Christ, and of faith bringing forth fruit in good works.

The epistle of James, concerning works to be joined with faith.

The first and second epistles of Peter, touching sanctification and the works of new obedience.

The first epistle of John, concerning the signs of fellowship with God.

The second epistle of John to the elect lady, about perseverance in the truth.

The third epistle of John to Gaius, concerning hospitality and constancy in that which is good.

The epistle of Jude, of constancy in the faith against false prophets.

And thus, the canonical Scripture is distinguished by her books.

The Proof

Now there are very strong proofs which show that it alone is the Word of God, and no other besides. Of these proofs one does make a man certainly to know the same,[14] the others do but declare or testify it.

The Testimony of the Holy Spirit

Of the former kind there is only one, namely the inward testimony of the Holy Spirit speaking in the Scriptures, and not only telling a man within in his heart but also effectually persuading him that these books of the Scripture are the Word of God. "My Spirit that is upon thee and my words which I have put in thy mouth, shall not depart out of thy mouth,—from henceforth even forever" (Isa. 59:21).

The manner of persuading is in this way: the elect, having the Spirit of God, do first discern the voice of Christ speaking in the Scriptures. Moreover, that voice which they do discern, they do approve, and that which they do approve, they do believe. Lastly, believing they are (as it were) sealed with the seal of the Spirit. "Wherein also after that ye believed, ye were sealed with the holy Spirit of promise" (Eph. 1:13).

The church may also bear witness of the canon, [but] she cannot persuade. For by this means the voice of the church should be of greater force than the voice of God, and the whole state of man's salvation should depend upon men. What can be said to be more miserable than this?

Objection 1. The Scripture is the Word of God by itself, but it is not so to us but by the judgment of the church. *Answer.* (1) The distinction is vain. For the first part thereof shows the manner whereby the Scripture is the Word of God. The latter part shows not the manner how, but the person to whom. (2) The Scripture does also testify the same thing with that kind of testimony which is surer even than all the oaths of men. For we have the voice of the Holy Spirit speaking in the Scripture. He does also work in our hearts a certain (πληροφοριαν) full persuasion of the Scriptures, when we are exercised in hearing, reading, and meditating of them. Neither do we believe a thing because the church says it is to believed, but therefore we do believe a thing because that which the church speaks the Scripture did first speak. Yea, the church cannot stand, nor yet be imagined, without faith. Faith is not without the Word, which Word is the rule or object of faith, and not the judgment, though it is of most holy men. (3) He who doubts of the Scriptures will doubt as well of the testimony of the church.

14. In the margin: Προβατιο οπισημονιχη, ενδειχδεχη.

Objection 2. The church has a judgment to determine of matters. "It seemeth good to the Holy Ghost and to us" (Acts 15:28). *Answer.* (1) The sovereign or supreme judgment concerning matters of faith belongs to the Holy Spirit speaking in the Scriptures. The ministry of judgment (or a ministerial judgment) is only given unto the church because she must judge according to the Scriptures and because she does not this always but sometimes fails. (2) The apostles were present at that council which was held at Jerusalem. They were men who had authority which was of itself to be believed,[15] which authority the ecclesiastical ministry now has not.

The Confirmation of the Holy Spirit's Testimony

The proof of declaration or testification is that which does not demonstrate or persuade, but only testifies and (by certain tokens) approves the true canon. This proof is manifold.

First, the perpetual consent of the church.

Of the ancient church of the Jews: "For chiefly, because unto them were of credit committed the oracles of God" (Rom. 3:2).

Of the new and latter church. First, from Christ and the apostles, who cited testimonies forth of those books. Second, from the fathers. (1) Origen, as Eusebius testifies (Lib. 6.18, 23). (2) Meliton, as the same Eusebius witnesses (Lib. 4). (3) Athanasius. (4) Cyril (Serm. 4). (5) Cyprian, or rather Ruffine, in his exposition of the Creed. (6) Hilary, in his preface upon Psalm 1. (7) Jerome, in *Prologo Galeaio* and in his preface upon the books of Solomon. (8) Epiphanius, in his book of weights and measures. (9) Damascene in his fourth book of faith (chap. 18). (10) Gregory, Moral. on John lib. 9. chap. 27. Third, in councils: the Nicene and Laodicean (can. 59).

With these agree Hugo de Sancto Victore in his first book of sacraments (chap. 7); N. Lyra in his prologue upon the books of Apocrypha; [and] Hugo Cardinalis in *Prologo in Josuam*.

Second, the consent in part made by the Gentiles and enemies, affirming the same things which are delivered in holy Scriptures.

Of the creation: Homer and Plato (in *Timao*).

Of Christ: Josephus (in *Antiquities*, lib. 20., chap. 6, 8; and in *The War of the Jews*, book 6, chap. 8, 25, 27, 28, 47).

Of the Redeemer of the world, who was to be exhibited in the last times: the Sibyls, as recorded by Lactantius (lib. 4, chap. 6), Cicero (*de Divinat.*, lib. 2), and Virgil (fourth Eclogue).

Of the miracles of Christ: Suetonius (in *Nero*) and Tacitus (lib. 5, 20).

15. In the margin: αυτο πισον.

Of the wise men's star: Pliny (lib. 2, 25).

Of the slaughtering of the infants: Macrobus (in *Satur.*).

Of the death of Herod Agrippa: Josephus (in *Antiquities*, book 19, chap. 7).

Of the flood: Berosus (in those fragments which are extant), Josephus (in *Antiquities*, book 1, chap. 3), and the poets.

Of the tower of Babel: Eupolemus, as Eusebius testifies (*De Præparat. Evangel.*).

Of the dove which Noah sent out: Plutarch (*Lib. quod bruta sunt rationalia*).

Of Japheth, the son of Noah: the poets fable many things.

Of Abraham's sacrifice: Alexander (in *Polyhist*).

Of the miracles of Moses: Pliny speaks, though he does ill in calling him a magician.

Third, the antiquity of the Word, for it contains in it a narration of things done from the beginning of the world. But the most ancient human history whatsoever was not written by any before the days of Ezra and Nehemiah, who were about 3,500 years from the world's creation.

Fourth, the most certain accomplishment of the prophecies: as are these, of the calling of the Gentiles, of antichrist, of the apostasy of the Jews, etc.

Fifth, the matter thereof, which is of one true God, the true worship of God, and that God is the Savior.

Sixth, the consent of all the parts of the Scripture.

Seventh, the miraculous preservation of the Scriptures in the perils of the church, and in the time of general revolting.

Eighth, the operation thereof, for it converts men, and though it is flatly contrary to the reason and affections of men, yet it wins them unto itself.

Ninth, it is full of majesty in the simplicity of the words.

Lastly, the holy penmen set down their own corruptions, and Moses commends himself, saying that he was the meekest of all men, which argues that they were led by the Holy Spirit. And Christ, who is described in the Gospel, affirms very plainly that He is the Son of God, and that He is one with God the Father, and challenges all the glory of God unto Himself. If this had not been right and true, He would have felt the wrath of God with Adam and with Herod, who would needs be like unto God. But on the contrary, God has avenged His death upon Herod, upon the Jews, upon Pilate, and upon those emperors who persecuted the church.

And thus, we have seen the tokens of the Scriptures. Whereby it appears that the book of Tobit, the Prayer of Manassas, the book of Judith, the book of Baruch, the epistle of Jeremiah, the additions to Daniel, the third and fourth books of Ezra, the additions to the book of Esther, the two books of Maccabees, the book of Wisdom, and Ecclesiasticus are not to be reckoned in the canon.

Reasons. (1) They are not written by the prophets. (2) They are not written in Hebrew. (3) Christ and His apostles alleged in the New Testament no testimonies out of those books. (4) They contain some feigned things, and contrary to the Scriptures.

Chapter 4

The Interpretation of the Scriptures

Hitherto has been spoken of the object of preaching. The parts thereof are two: (1) the preparation for the sermon; and (2) the promulgation (or uttering) of it. "Then said he unto them, therefore every scribe, which is taught unto the kingdom of heaven, is like unto a householder, which bringeth forth out of his treasure both new and old" (Matt. 13:52).

In preparation, private study is with diligence to be used. "Till I come give attendance to reading, to exhortation, and to doctrine" (1 Tim. 4:13). "Of the which salvation the prophets have inquired and searched, which prophesied of the grace that should come unto you" (1 Peter 1:10). "In the first year of his reign, I Daniel understood by books the number of the years" (Dan. 9:2).

Concerning the study of divinity, take this advice.

First, diligently imprint both in your mind and memory the substance of divinity described with definitions, divisions, and explications of the properties.

Second, proceed to the reading of the Scriptures in this order: Using a grammatical, rhetorical, and logical analysis,[1] and the help of the rest of the arts, read first the epistle of Paul to the Romans [and], after that, the Gospel of John (as being indeed the keys of the New Testament). And then the other books of the New Testament will be easier when they are read. When all this is done, learn first the dogmatical books of the Old Testament, especially the Psalms; then the prophetical, especially Isaiah; lastly the historical, but chiefly Genesis. For it is likely that the apostles and evangelists read Isaiah and the Psalms very much. For there are no books of the Old Testament out of which we can read more testimonies to be cited than out of these. There are about threescore[2] places alleged out of Isaiah and threescore and four out of the Psalms.

Third, we must get aid out of orthodox writings,[3] not only from the latter but also from the more ancient church, because Satan has raised up from the dead the old heretics that he might hinder the restoration of the church, which

---

1. In the margin: Opening of the text.
2. *Threescore:* sixty.
3. In the margin: Of sound judgment, or sound, judicious, and consonant to God's Word.

is begun to be made in our time. For the anti-Trinitarians have newly varnished that opinion of Arius and Sabellius. The Anabaptists renew the doctrines or sects of the Essenes, Catharists, Enthusiasts, and Donatists. The Swenkfeldians revive the opinions of the Eutychians, Enthusiasts, etc. Menon follows Ebion. And the papists resemble the Pharisees, Encratites, Tatians, [and] Pelagians. The Libertines renew the opinions of the Gnostics and Carpocratians. Servetus has revived the heresies of Samosatenus, Arius, Eutyches, Marcion, and Apollinaris. Lastly, the Schismatics, who separate themselves from evangelical churches, receive the opinions, facts, and fashions of Pupianus in Cyprian, of the Audians and Donatists. Therefore, in like manner, we must not so much seek for new repealing and confutations of these heresies as we are (for our use) to fetch those ancient ones out of councils and fathers, and to account them as approved and firm.

Fourth, those things, which in studying you meet with, that are necessary and worthy to be observed, you must put in your tables or common-place books, that you may always have in a readiness both old and new.

Fifth, before all these things God must earnestly be sued unto by prayer, that He would bless these means, and that He would open the meaning of the Scriptures to us who are blind. "Open mine eyes, that I may see the wonderful things of thy law" (Ps. 119:18). "I advise thee to buy gold for thee—and to anoint thine eyes with eye-salve, that thou mayest see" (Rev. 3:18).

Hitherto pertains the framing of common-place books. Concerning which, observe this slender counsel. (1) Have in readiness common-place heads of every point of divinity. (2) Distinguish the foremost pages of your paper book into two columns (or equal parts) lengthwise. In every one of those pages set in the top the title of one head or chief point, the contrary side remaining in the meanwhile empty, that fresh paper may be put to. (3) All things, which you read, are not to be written in your book, but those things that are worthy to be remembered, and are seldom met with. Neither must you put the words of the author in your common places, but briefly note down the principal points of stories and of things, that you may know from what author to fetch them when you shall have use. And make a point in the author himself, that you may know that the thing is there handled which you wrote in your common-place book. (4) Because some things do very often offer themselves with a doubtful signification, so as that you cannot tell, if you write them in your common places, from whence to fetch them, therefore to your common places you must join an alphabetical table. (5) Always provide that you trust not too much to your places. For it is not sufficient to have a thing written in your book, unless it is also diligently laid and locked up in your memory.

Preparation has two parts: interpretation, and right division (or cutting).[4] Interpretation is the opening[5] of the words and sentences of the Scripture, that one entire and natural sense may appear.

The Church of Rome makes four senses of the Scriptures (literal, allegorical, tropological, and anagogical) as in this example: "Melchizedek offered bread and wine." The literal sense is that the king of Salem refreshed the soldiers of Abraham, being tired with travel, with meat which he brought. The allegorical is that the priest does offer up Christ in the mass. The tropological is, therefore, [that] something is to be given to the poor. The anagogical is that Christ in like manner, being in heaven, shall be the bread of life to the faithful. But her device of the fourfold meaning of the Scripture must be exploded and rejected.

There is one only sense, and the same is the literal. An allegory is only a certain manner of uttering the same sense. The anagoge and tropology are ways whereby the sense may be applied.

The principal interpreter of the Scripture is the Holy Spirit. "So that ye first know this, that no prophecy in the Scripture is of any private interpretation"[6] (2 Peter 1:20). Moreover, He who makes the law is the best and the highest interpreter of the law.

The supreme and absolute means of interpretation is the Scripture itself. "And they read in the book of the law of God distinctly, and gave the sense, and caused them to understand by the Scripture itself (*per Scripturam ipsam*)" (Neh. 8:8).

The means subordinated to the Scripture are three: (1) the analogy of faith; (2) the circumstances of the place propounded; and (3) the comparing of places together.

The analogy of faith is a certain abridgement (or sum of the Scriptures) collected out of [the] most manifest and familiar places. The parts thereof are two. The first concerns faith, which is handled in the Apostles' Creed. The second concerns charity or love, which is explicated in the Ten Commandments. "Keep the true pattern[7] of the wholesome words, which thou hast heard of me, with faith and love which is in Christ Jesus" (2 Tim. 1:13).

The circumstances of the place propounded are these: Who? To whom? Upon what occasion? At what time? In what place? For what end? What goes before? What follows?

The collation (or comparing of places together) is that whereby places are set like parallels one beside another, that the meaning of them may more

4. In the margin: ορθοτομια.
5. In the margin: επιλισις.
6. In the margin: επιλυσεως.
7. In the margin: υποτυπωσιν.

evidently appear. "But Saul increased the more in strength, and confounded the Jews, which dwelt at Damascus, confirming (συμβιβαζων, that is, conferring or conjoining places of Scriptures, as artificers, being about to compact or join a thing together, are wont to fit all the parts among themselves, that each of them may perfectly agree with each other) that this was that Christ" (Acts 9:22).

Collation of places is twofold. The first is the comparing of the place propounded with itself cited and repeated elsewhere in holy writ. "Make the heart of this people fat, make their ears heavy, and shut their eyes, lest they see with their eyes, and hear with their ears, and understand with their hearts, and convert, and he heal them" (Isa. 6:10). This place is repeated six times in the New Testament (Matt. 13:14; Mark 4:12; Luke 8:10; John 12:40; Acts 28:27; Rom. 11:8).

Places repeated often have alterations for sundry causes. These causes are, first, exegetical (that is, for exposition sake) as:

Psalm 78:2 "I will open my mouth in a parable: I will declare things hidden[8] from of old."	Matthew 13:35 "I will open my mouth in parables, and will utter the things which have been kept secret from the foundation of the world."
Psalm 78:24 "He gave them of the wheat of heaven."	John 6:31 "He gave them bread from heaven to eat."
Isaiah 28:16 "Behold I will lay in Sion a stone, a tried stone, a precious corner stone, a sure foundation. He that believeth shall not make haste."	Romans 9:33 "Behold, I lay in Sion a stumbling block, and a rock to make men fall, and every one that believeth in him shall not be ashamed."
Psalm 110:1 "Sit thou at my right hand until I make thine enemies thy foot stool."	1 Corinthians 15:25 "He must reign till he have put all his enemies under his feet."
Psalm 116:10 "I believed, because[9] I did speak."	2 Corinthians 4:13 "I believed, and therefore have I spoken."

8. In the margin: *occulta*.
9. In the margin: *quia*.

Genesis 13:15	Galatians 3:16
"All the land which thou seest, will I give unto thee, and to thy seed forever."	"Now to Abraham and to his seed were the promises made. He saith not unto the seeds, as speaking of many: but, and to thy seed, as of one, which is Christ."

A second cause is diacritical (or for discerning sake), that places, times, and persons might be mutually distinguished.

Micah 5:2	Matthew 2:6
"And thou Bethlehem Ephrathah art little to be among the princes of Judah: out of thee shall he come forth to me, that shall be the ruler of Israel."	"And thou Bethlehem in the land of Judah art not the least among the princes of Judah: for out of thee shall come the governor, that shall feed my people Israel."

Third, these causes are circumscriptive (or for limitation sake), that the sense and sentence of the place might be truly restrained, according as the mind and meaning of the Holy Spirit was.

Deuteronomy 6:13	Matthew 4:10
"Thou shalt worship the Lord thy God, and shalt serve him."	"Thou shalt worship the Lord thy God, and him only shalt thou serve."

Isaiah 29:13	Matthew 15:8–9
"This people draweth near with their mouth and honor me with their lips: but their heart they remove far from me: and their reverence towards me is by the commandment of men."	"When this people draweth near unto me, they honor me with their mouth and with their lips, but they remove their heart far from me. In vain do they worship me, teaching for doctrines the commandments of men."

Genesis 2:24	Matthew 19:5
"Wherefore a man shall leave his father and his mother, and shall cleave unto his wife, and they shall be one flesh."	"Wherefore a man shall leave father and mother, and shall cleave unto his wife, and they which were two shall be one flesh."

Isaiah 59:20	Romans 11:26
"And the Redeemer shall come unto Sion, and unto them that turn from iniquity in Jacob, saith the Lord."	"The Deliverer shall come out of Sion, and shall turn away the ungodliness from Jacob."

A fourth cause is for application sake, that the type might be fitted unto the truth, and the general to a certain special, and so contrariwise.

Jonah 1:17	Matthew 12:39–40
"Now the Lord had prepared a great fish to swallow up Jonah. And Jonah was in the belly of the fish three days, and three nights."	"An evil and adulterous generation seeketh a sign, but no sign shall be given unto it, save the sign of the prophet Jonah. For as Jonah was three days and three nights in the whale's belly, so shall the Son of Man be..."

Isaiah 61:1–2	Luke 4:18
"The Spirit of the Lord God is upon me: therefore hath the Lord anointed me: he hath sent me to preach good tidings unto the poor, to bind up the broken hearted, to preach liberty to the captives, and to them that are bound the opening of the prison: To preach the acceptable year of the Lord, and the day of vengeance of our God."	"The Spirit of the Lord is upon me, therefore he hath anointed me that I should preach good tidings to the poor, he hath sent me to heal the broken in heart, that I should preach deliverance to the captives ..."

Psalm 69:27	John 19:28–29
"They gave me gall for my meat, and in my thirst they gave me vinegar to drink."	"That the Scripture might be fulfilled he said, I thirst. Therefore there was set a vessel full of vinegar: and they filled a sponge with vinegar, and put it about a hyssop stalk, and put it to his mouth."

Exodus 12:46	John 19:36
"Neither shall ye break a bone thereof."	"These things were done, that the Scripture might be fulfilled, which saith, there shall not a bone of him be broken."

Psalm 69:25	Acts 1:20
"Let their habitations be void, and let none dwell in their tents."	"It is written in the book of the Psalms; let his habitation be void, and let no man dwell therein."

Fifth, some things are omitted for brevity sake: or because they do not agree with the matter in hand.

Zechariah 9:9	Matthew 21:5
"Rejoice greatly O daughter Sion: shout for joy O daughter Jerusalem: behold thy King cometh unto thee: He is just, and saved himself, poor and riding upon an ass, and upon a colt the foal of an ass."	"Tell ye the daughter of Sion, behold thy King cometh unto thee, meek and sitting upon an ass, and a colt the foal of an ass used to the yoke."

The second collation is of the place propounded with other places, and those again are either like or unlike. Places that are alike are such, as by certain ways or in some sort, agree one with another. And places do agree either in their phrase and manner of speech, or in sense.

Places that agree as concerning the phrase, are such as these:

Genesis 28:12	John 1:51
"Then he dreamed, and behold there stood a ladder upon the earth, and the top of it reached up to heaven, and lo, the angels of God went up and down by it."	"And he said unto him, Verily, verily, I say unto you, hereafter shall ye see the heaven open, and the angels of God ascending and descending upon the Son of man."

Genesis 3:15 "I will also put enmity between thee and the woman, and between thy seed and her seed. He shall break thine head, and thou shalt bruise his heel."	Romans 16:20 "The God of peace shall break (συντριψει) Satan under your feet."
Genesis 8:20–21 "Then Noah built an altar to the Lord, and took of every clean beast, and of every clean fowl, and offered burnt offerings upon the altar. And the Lord smelled a savor of rest, and said."	Ephesians 5:2 "Christ hath loved us, and given himself for us an offering and a sacrifice of a sweet smelling savor to God."

For the finding out of these places the Greek and Hebrew concordances serve very fitly.

Places which agree in sense are those that have the same meaning. Here excels the comparing of a general place with a special example in the same kind, as:

Proverbs 28:13 "He that hideth his sins, shall not prosper, but he that confesseth and forsaketh them, shall find mercy."	Psalm 32:3–5 "When I held my tongue my bones consumed … I acknowledged my sin unto thee, neither hid I mine iniquity. I said, I will confess against myself my wickedness unto the Lord, and thou forgavest the punishment of my sin."
2 Samuel 15:25–26 "The king charged Zadok saying, carry the ark of God again into the city. If I shall find favor in the eyes of the Lord, he will bring me again, and shew me both it, and the tabernacle thereof. But if he thus say, I have no delight in thee, Behold, here am I, let him do to me, as seemeth good in his eyes."	1 Peter 5:6 "Humble yourselves therefore under the mighty hand of God, that he may exalt you in due time."

You shall have ready very many places of this kind in the common places of Marlorate[10] gathered together with diligence.

And thus much for places that are alike.

Places that are unlike are those which in show do not agree, either in respect of the phrase or in regard of the meaning, as:

Romans 3:28 "Therefore we conclude that a man is justified by faith without the works of the law."	James 2:24 "Ye see therefore how that of works a man is justified; and not of faith only."
1 Kings 9:28 "And they came to Ophir, and they fetched from thence four hundred and twenty talents of gold, and brought it to king Solomon."	2 Chronicles 8:18 "And they went with the servants of Solomon to Ophir, and brought from thence four hundred and fifty talents of gold, and brought them to king Solomon."
Acts 7:14 "Then sent Joseph and caused his father to be brought, and all his kindred, even threescore and fifteen souls."	Genesis 46:27 "All the souls of the house of Jacob, which came unto Egypt are threescore and ten."
Acts 7:16 "And were removed into Shechem and were put in the sepulcher, that Abraham had bought for money of the sons of Hamor, son of Shechem."	Genesis 48:22 "I" (that is Jacob) "have given unto thee one portion above thy brethren, which I got out of the hand of the Amorite by my sword and by my bow."
Zechariah 11:13 "And I took the thirty pieces of silver, and cast them to the potter in the house of the Lord."	Matthew 27:9 "Then was fulfilled that which was spoken by Jeremy the prophet, saying, and they took thirty silver pieces ..."

10. Augustine Marlorate, 1506–62. French, Calvinistic pastor. Executed for his faith, Oct. 31, 1562.

Chapter 5

The Ways of Expounding

The manner or ways of interpreting are according to the places of Scripture which are to be handled. Places are either analogical and plain or cryptical and dark.

Rule 1

Analogical places are such as have an apparent meaning agreeable to the analogy of faith, and that at the first view. Concerning these places receive this rule: if the natural signification of the words of the place propounded do agree with the circumstances of the same place, it is the proper meaning of the place.

For example: "To him also give all the prophets witness, that through his name, all that believe in him, shall receive remission of sins" (Acts 10:43). The signification of the words of this place is very manifest, to wit, that Jesus Christ does give righteousness and everlasting life to those who do believe in Him. And we do presently admit this sense without any delay, because we see that it does agree with the analogy of faith and with the holy Scriptures.

We must further know that every article and doctrine concerning faith and manners, which is necessary unto salvation, is very plainly delivered in the Scriptures.

Rule 2

Cryptical or hidden places are those which are difficult and dark. For the expounding of them, let this be your rule and leader: if the native (or natural) signification of the words do manifestly disagree with either the analogy of faith or very perspicuous places of the Scripture, then the other meaning, which is given of the place propounded, is natural and proper if it agrees with contrary and like places, with the circumstances and words of the place, and with the nature of that thing which is intreated of.

For example: "This is my body, which is broken for you" (1 Cor. 11:24).

The sense that is given by some: this bread is indeed and properly the body of Christ (namely, by conversion) or the body of Christ is in, under, or with the bread.

The unfitness of this sense: the letter (or words)[1] used in this place, being retained (or expounded accordingly without any alteration), does disagree with an article of the faith (He ascended into heaven) and with the nature of a sacrament (which ought to be a memorial[2] of the absent body of Christ). Therefore, a new exposition is to be sought for.

A new or second sense: in this place the bread is a sign of "my body" by a metonymy of the subject for the adjunct.

The fitness of this exposition:

First, it agrees with the analogy of faith. (1) He ascended truly into heaven, that is, He was taken up out of the earth into heaven locally and visibly. Therefore, His body is not to be received with the mouth at the communion, but by faith apprehending it in the heaven. (2) [He was] born of the Virgin Mary, etc. Therefore, He had a true and natural body, being long, broad, thick, seated, and circumscribed in some place. Whereby it appears that the bread in the Supper cannot properly be His very body, but only a sign or pledge thereof.

Second, this sense consents with the circumstances of the place propounded. (1) "He took." "He broke it." Here it is not likely that Christ, sitting among His disciples, did take and break His own body with His hands. Therefore, the bread is no more than a sign and seal. (2) "Delivered (or given) for you." The bread can in no way be said to be given for us, but the body of Christ [can]. Therefore, the bread is not properly the body, but symbolically or by way of signification. (3) "The cup is the new testament," not properly, but by a metonymy. Therefore, nothing hinders but that a metonymy may be as well in these words: "This is my body." (4) Christ Himself did eat of the bread, but He did not eat Himself. (5) "Do ye this in remembrance of me." Therefore, Christ is not corporally present to the mouth, but spiritually to the faith of the heart. (6) "Until he come." Therefore, Christ is absent in His body. (7) Christ said not, "under the form of bread," or "in the bread." But He said, "This (that is, this bread) is my body."

Third, this sense accords with the nature of a sacrament, in which we must make a proportion and resemblance between the sign and the thing signified, which here can be none if the bread is properly the body.

Fourth, it agrees with like places. "This is my covenant, which ye shall keep betwixt you and me… Ye shall circumcise the foreskin of your flesh, and it shall be a sign of the covenant between me and you" (Gen. 17:10–11). "They drank of the spiritual Rock, that followed them: and the Rock was Christ" (1 Cor. 10:4). "He received the sign of circumcision, which might seal the righteousness of

---

1. Το ρητον.
2. μνημοσυνον.

faith" (Rom. 4:11). "The lamb is the Lord's Passover.... It is a sign of his passing over" (Exod. 12:1, 13). "Be baptized for the remission of sins" (Acts 2:38). "And Jesus said unto them, I am the bread of life: he that cometh unto me shall not hunger, and he that believeth in me shall never thirst" (John 6:35). "The cup of blessing which we bless, is it not the communion of the blood of Christ? The bread which we break, is it not the communion of the body of Christ (that is, a sign of the communion)?" (1 Cor. 10:16).

Fifth, it agrees with the laws of logic. For one disparate is not spoken or predicated of another but by a borrowed speech.

Sixth, it is agreeable to the common custom of speaking. So, we put the fasces (or bundle of rods), usually carried before magistrates, for government itself. We put the gown for peace, and the laurel garland for a triumph, as in Tully, *Cedent armatogæ, concedat laurea lingua.*

Therefore, this other sense is proper.

Now from this fruitful *rule* do arise many consectaries[3] (or conclusions) necessary for the understanding of the Scriptures.

Consectary 1

The supply of every word, which is wanting, is fitting for the place propounded, if it agrees with the analogy (or squire) of faith and with the circumstances and words of the same place.

For example: "For which cause, I Paul the prisoner of Jesus Christ for you Gentiles" (Eph. 3:1). The sentence is defective. Therefore, a supply must be made. And let this be the supply: "I will be an ambassador for you Gentiles." This is not fit because Paul was not an ambassador for the Gentiles, but for Christ. Let another be given: "I have boasted for you Gentiles." But this seems to be something too bold. Neither is any such like speech to be met with in any part of the Scriptures. Therefore, the sentence may be fitly supplied after this manner: "For which cause I Paul am the prisoner of Jesus Christ for you Gentiles."

The same may be said of the rest.

3. *Consectary:* consequence.

Defective Speeches:	*Their Supply:*
Isaiah 1:13 "I cannot iniquity."	"I cannot (bear) iniquity."
Luke 13:9 "And if it bear fruit: if not, then after thou shalt cut it down."	"And if it bear fruit (thou shalt let it stand): if not, then after thou shalt cut it down."
Exodus 4:25 "Then Zipporah took a sharp, and cut away the foreskin of her son."	"Then Zipporah took a sharp (knife) and cut …"
2 Samuel 21:16 "Ishbi-benob, which of the sons of a certain giant, the weight of whose sword the weight of three hundred shekels of steel: and he girded with a new."	"Ishbi-benob, who (was) of the sons of a certain giant, the weight of whose sword (or spears head) (was) the weight of three hundred shekels, of steel: and he girded with a new (sword)."
1 Corinthians 9:25 "And every man, that proveth masteries, is continent in all things: and they to obtain a corruptible crown, but we for an incorruptible."	"And they (are continent) to obtain a corruptible crown…"
Exodus 19:4 "You have seen how I have carried you upon eagle's wings."	"(As it were) upon eagle's wings."

Consectary 2

If that other exposition given of the place propounded does change one noun (or name) for another, then the words of the place contain in them a trope (or borrowed speech).

Hence arise many cautions concerning sacred tropes.

First, an *anthropopathia* is a sacred metaphor whereby those things that are properly spoken of man are by a similitude attributed unto God. Hence it is that the soul of God is put for His life or essence. "Or shall not my soul be avenged of such a nation as this?" (Jer. 5:29). Head is used for prince (or above). "God is the head of Christ" (1 Cor. 11:3). His face is put for favor or anger. "Thou didst hide thy face, and I was troubled" (Ps. 30:7). "The face of the Lord is angry[4] at those that do evil" (Ps. 34:16). His eyes are used for grace and providence. "The eyes of the Lord are upon the just" (Ps. 34:15). The apple of His eye signifies a thing very dear. "He that toucheth you, toucheth the apple of mine eye" (Zech. 2:8). His ears are put for His accepting of men's prayers; His nostrils for indignation; His hands for power and protection; His arm for strength and fortitude; His right hand for authority and power; His finger for virtue; His foot for government and might. His smelling [is put] for His acceptation of something (Ps. 110:3). "He smelled the savor of the rest" (Gen. 8:21). Repentance is used for the alteration of things and actions made by God.

Second, a sacramental *metonymy* is that whereby the name of the adjunct, as also of the helping cause, is put for the thing represented in the sacrament, or [it is that] whereby the sign is put for the thing signified, or contrarily. "The tree of life…the tree of the knowledge of good and evil" (Gen. 2:9); that is, the tree which is a sign of these. Abraham called the name of that place, "the Lord will see or provide" (Gen. 22:14); that is, it is a sign that the Lord will do so. The stone is called "God's house" (Gen. 28:22). The paschal lamb is the passing over (Exodus 12). The altar is called, "the Lord is my standard (or banner)" (Exod. 17:15). Jerusalem is named, "the Lord is there" (Ezek. 48:35). The priest is termed a satisfier (Leviticus 16). Christ is called a lamb: "Behold the Lamb of God which taketh away the sins of the world" (John 1). The paschal lamb is called Christ: "Our Passover Christ is sacrificed for us" (1 Cor. 5:7). And in the same place Christians are said to be "unleavened." Christ is termed the propitiatory (ιλαστηριον) or the cover of the ark of the covenant (Rom. 3:25). Christians are said to be "one bread"[5] (1 Corinthians 10). And the Rock is called Christ. Baptism is named the "washing of the new birth" (Titus 3:5). The cup is called "the new testament," and the bread is said to be "the body of Christ" (1 Corinthians 11).

Third, the communication of the properties is a *synecdoche*, by the which by reason of the personal union, that is spoken of the whole person of Christ, which does properly belong to one of His two natures. "To feed the church of God, which he hath purchased with his own blood" (Acts 20:28). "For no man

4. In the margin: *Irata*.
5. In the margin: loaf.

ascendeth up to heaven, but he that hath descended from heaven, the Son of man which is in heaven" (John 3:13). "For had they known it, they would not have crucified the Lord of glory" (1 Cor. 2:8). "Jesus said unto them, Verily, verily I say unto you, before Abraham was I am" (John 8:58). "And Jesus increased in wisdom, and in stature, and in favor with God and man" (Luke 2:52).

This communication of the properties has place only in the concrete, and not in the abstract. Concrete is the name of the whole person, as God, man, Christ, etc. Abstract is the name of either of the two natures considered apart, as the Godhead, manhood, etc.

Fourth, things spoken of God, which carry with them the show of evil, must be understood in regard of His operative or working permission. "And it yieldeth much fruit unto the kings, whom thou hast set over us because of our sins: and they have dominion over our bodies, and over our cattle at their pleasure, and we are in great affliction" (Neh. 9:37). "The Lord hath mingled among them the spirit of errors: and they have caused Egypt to err in every work thereof" (Isa. 19:14). "God doth harden the heart of Pharaoh" (Exodus 4, 9, 11, 14). "The Lord thy God hath hardened his spirit, and made his heart obstinate, because he would deliver him into thine hand, as appeareth this day" (Deut. 2:30). "It came of the Lord, that their heart was hardened, that they might come against Israel in battle, to the intent that they should destroy them utterly, and shew them no mercy, but bring them to naught" (Josh. 11:20). "They hearkened not to the voice of their father, because the Lord meant to destroy them" (1 Sam. 2:25). "The destruction of Ahaziah came from God" (2 Chron. 22:7). "He turned their heart to hate his people, and to work craftily against his servants" (Ps. 105:25). "God delivered them up to a reprobate mind" (Rom. 1:28). "God will send them strong delusions, that they may believe lies" (2 Thess. 2:11). "And when that prophet shall be enticed to speak a prophecy, I the Lord will entice that prophet, and stretching out mine hand against him, I will destroy him out of the midst of my people" (Ezek. 14:9).

Fifth, things spoken (*completive*) as if they were already finished, if they are not as yet finished, they are to be understood (*inchoative*) as being begun, and in the way to be fulfilled. "And when Noah was five hundred years old, he begat Shem, Ham, and Japheth" (Gen. 5:32); that is, he began to beget them. "Terah lived seventy years, when he begat Abram, Nahor, and Haran" (Gen. 11:26). See 1 Kings 6:2, 37. "I will observe thy statutes, do not forsake me" (Ps. 119:8). It is to be understood of his endeavor to do so, as in Philippians 3:12, "Not as though I had already attained to it, or were already perfect: but I follow on, if that I may comprehend that for whose sake also I am comprehended of Jesus Christ." "Let us therefore as many as be perfect be thus minded" (v. 15). "And they were both just in the sight of God, walking in all his commandments and ordinances without blame" (Luke 1:6).

Sixth, moral commandments (or laws), expressed by name under one sin, do signify and mean all the sins of that kind, their causes, occasions, and allurements to them, and command the contrary virtues. For so Christ expounded moral laws [from] Matthew 5:2 to the end of the chapter. "He that hateth his brother is a manslayer" (1 John 3:15).

Seventh, threats and promises are to be understood with their conditions. Those are to be conceived with the condition of faith and repentance, and these especially if they are corporal, with the exception of chastisement and the cross. "When I shall say unto the wicked, Thou shalt die the death: if he turn from his sin, and do that which is lawful and right, he shall surely live, and not die" (Ezek. 33:14–15). "But the fearful and unbelievers...shall have their portion in the lake, which burneth with fire and brimstone, which is the second death" (Rev. 21:8). But He annexes a promise, saying, "I will give unto him that is athirst of the well of the water of life freely" (v. 6). "Yet forty days, and Nineveh shall be subverted" (Jonah 3:4). By those things which follow it appears that a condition is to be understood (Jer. 18:9–10).

Like to these there are particular examples. [The Lord says to] Hezekiah: "Give commandments to thy family, for thou shalt shortly die, and shalt not live" (Isa. 38:1). The condition of God's will is [here] to be understood. The Lord says to Abimelech, because he had taken Abraham's wife to himself: "Behold, thou shalt die for the woman which thou hast taken," except, "unless thou restore her" (Gen. 20:3).

Hence arose the distinction in the schools of the signifying will[6] and the will of God's good-pleasure. The will of good-pleasure is that whereby God does will something absolutely and simply without any condition, as the creation and regiment of the world, and the sending of His Son. The signifying will is that whereby He wills some things for some other thing and with condition. And so, we say, because the condition annexed is a sign of the will, that God does so will.

Eighth, superlative (or exclusive) speech used of one person does not exclude the other persons of the Deity, but only creatures and feigned gods, to which the true God, whether in one person or in more, is opposed. "This is life eternal to know thee to be the only true God, and Jesus Christ whom thou hast sent" (John 17:3). He calls the Father the only true God, that He might oppose Him to all false gods. "To the only wise God be glory by Jesus Christ" (Rom. 16:27). See 1 Timothy 1:17. "The Father is greater than all"

6. In the margin: *Signi. Beneplaciti.*

(John 10:29), not [greater] than the rest of the persons but the creatures. "The Father alone knoweth the day of judgment" (Mark 13:37). All the outward works of the Trinity, and all attributes, are to be understood inclusively, that is, without exception of any of the persons.

Ninth, when God is considered absolutely, or by Himself, the three persons are comprehended. When the word "God" is conferred (or set) with a person of the Trinity, it signifies the Father. "The grace of our Lord Jesus Christ, and the love of God, and the fellowship of the Holy Ghost be with you all" (2 Cor. 13:13).

Tenth, a general word is taken specially, and so on the contrary, as "all" (says August. lib. 6. *cont. Julian.* cap. 12), for "many" and "many" for "all" are oftentimes used in the Scriptures. "God hath had mercy on me, therefore I have all things" (Gen. 33:11). "All are turned to their own race" (Jer. 8:6), that is, the greater part. "All men counted John as a prophet" (Matt. 21:26), that is, the most. "All seek their own things, and not the things of Christ" (Phil. 2:21). "And God shall scatter thee among all people" (Deut. 28:64), that is, many. "And all the Israelites stoned him" (1 Kings 12:18), that is, all who were present. "All the living creatures of Egypt died" (Exod. 9:6). "Then was gathered together all the people against Jeremiah in the house of the Lord" (Jer. 26:9), that is, all wicked people. "Healing every disease" (Matt. 4:23), to wit, that was offered to Him. "Whatsoever ye shall ask the Father in my name" (John 14:13), that is, whatsoever you shall ask according to His Word. "All things are lawful for me" (1 Cor. 6:12), that is, all (*adiaphora*) things that are indifferent and not simply evil.

"Nothing" is put for little or small. "I have spoken nothing in secret" (John 18:20), that is, little. See Acts 27:33.

"None" is used for few. "There is none that repenteth of his wickedness" (Jer. 8:6), that is, but a few. "Which wisdom none of the rulers of this world knew" (1 Cor. 2:8), that is, very few.

"Always" is taken for often or long. "Amongst the proud there is always contention" (Prov. 13:10), that is, often. "He spoke unto them a parable that they ought to pray alway" (Luke 18:1). "And they were always in the temple lauding and praising of God" (Luke 24:53). "I alway taught in the synagogue, and in the temple" (John 18:20).

"Eternal" is used for a long time, agreeing with the matter in hand. "All the land of Canaan is given unto Abraham for an everlasting possession" (Gen. 17:8). "Ye shall use their labors forever" (Lev. 25:46). "If thy servant be thy brother a Hebrew, and will not go from thee, then shalt thou take an awl, and pierce his ear through against the door, and he shall be thy servant forever (*in* æternum)" (Deut. 15:17). "God hath chosen the Levites, that they might minister for ever unto him" (1 Chron. 15:2). "And beasts shall possess Edom and Bozra eternally" (Isa. 34:6). "O king live forever" (Dan. 2:4). "I will make Judea and the regions bordering upon it an amazement, a hissing, and a perpetual desolation" (Jer. 25:9).

"Everywhere"[7] is used for here and there, without respect of place. "And they went out and preached everywhere, the Lord co-working" (Mark 16:2). "The Lord admonisheth all men everywhere to repent" (Acts 17:30).

"Not"[8] is restrained to some special matter. "Iniquity is not in mine hands" (Ps. 7:4), that is, in my cause against the accomplices of Saul. "Neither have his parents sinned" (John 9:3), that is, that this man should be born blind for his sins. "I will have mercy, not sacrifice" [Matt. 9:13]. "Not" is put for seldom, scarcely, or hardly. "David declined not from any of the things which the Lord had commanded unto him, saving in the matter of Uriah" (1 Kings 15:5), that is, seldom. "She was a widow, and went not out of the temple" (Luke 2:37).

Consectary 3

Grammatical and rhetorical proprieties of words signify diversely with those words. As:

An ellipsis[9] signifies either brevity or the swiftness of the affections. "Let us build us a city and a tower, whose top [may reach] unto heaven, that we may get us a name" (Gen. 11:4). "But if it be of God ye cannot destroy it, [*ac nescio*, and I know not] whether ye shall be found fighters also with God" (Acts 5:39). "And thou O Lord how long?" (Psalm 6). "He that sacrificeth to strange gods, let him be destroyed as a thing execrable: saving him [who sacrificeth] to Jehovah" (Exod. 22:20). "Now therefore [we must look] lest that stretching out his hand, he take of the tree of life" (Gen. 3:22). "If thou wilt bless me effectually [I will do this or that]. If thou vex the fatherless child [I will vex thee]" (1 Chron. 4:10).

The enallage of the preterperfect tense, whereby the time past is put for the time to come, signifies in the oracles of the prophets the certainty of the thing that is to come. "Thou hast died because of the woman" (Gen. 20:3), that is, "thou shalt die." "Unto us a child is born, unto us a son is given" (Isa. 9:6). "It is fallen, it is fallen Babylon…" (Isa. 21:9).

A pleonasm,[10] which is manifold. When it is of the substantive repeated in the same case, it does signify [the following]. (1) A force and emphasis.[11] "As the ointment which descended unto the beard, the beard of Aaron" (Ps. 133:2). "Why call ye me Lord, Lord?" (Luke 6:46). (2) A multitude. "He gave into the hands of his servants droves, droves" (Gen. 32:16), that is, many droves.

7. In the margin: *Ubique passim*.
8. In the margin: Non.
9. In the margin: That is, when one or more words are wanting.
10. In the margin: When some words abound.
11. In the margin: It is when words signify more than they show for or seem.

"Troupes, troupes in the valley of concision" (Joel 3:14), that is, many troupes or multitudes. (3) Distribution. "At the gate and gate" (1 Chron. 26:13), that is, in every gate. "A man and a man" (Lev. 17:3), that is, every man. "Thou shalt appoint judges in a city and in a city" (2 Chron. 19:5), that is, in every city. (4) Diversity and variety. "They speak with a heart, and a heart" (Ps. 12:2), that is, with divers or a double heart. "A weight and a weight are abominable unto the Lord" (Prov. 20:20).

There is a pleonasm of the substantive when one is governed by another. (1) In the singular number it is very significant and argues certainty. "On the seventh day is the Sabbath of Sabbath" (Ex. 31:15). "And they shall lament the lamentation of lamentation" (Micah 2:4). (2) In the plural number it signifies excellency. "The God of gods," that is, "the most high God" (Ps. 136:2). "The King of kings" (Daniel 3). "Vanity of vanities" (Eccl. 1:2). A song of songs. A servant of servants.

The pleonasm of the adjective, and sometimes also of the substantive repeated, signifies exaggeration or increasing. "I see good figs, good" (Jer. 24:3). "Holy, holy, holy the Lord God of hosts" (Isa. 6:3). "The Lord passing before his face cried, Jehovah, Jehovah, the strong God" (Ex. 34:6). "Trust not in lying words saying, the temple of the Lord, the temple of the Lord, this is the temple of the Lord" (Jer. 7:4). "O earth, earth, earth, hear the word of the Lord" (Jer. 22:9). "Say thou the sword, the sword is drawn, and furbished for the slaughter" (Ezek. 21:28). See Prov. 6:10.

The pleonasm of the verb does either make the speech more emphatical and significant, or else signifies and shows vehemency, certainty, or speediness. "In dying thou shalt die" (Gen. 2:17). "Is mine hand shortened in shortening?" (Isa. 50:2). "By separating God hath separated me from his people" (Isa. 56:3). "Thou thinkest me by being to be like thee" (Ps. 50:21). "Let his children in wandering be wanderers (or vagabonds) and let them beg" (Ps. 109:10). "And it shall come to pass if in learning they shall learn the ways of my people…" (Jer. 12:16). See 2 Kings 5:11; 8:10; Prov. 27:23; Ex. 13:17; Isa. 6:9; 55:2; Gen. 46:4; 2 Sam. 15:30; Jer. 23:29.

The pleonasm of the conjunction sometimes argues earnestness. "Therefore, therefore because they have made my people to err" (Ezek. 13:10). Wherefore, a conjunction doubled (otherwise than it is in Latin) increases the denial. "Hast thou brought us to die in the wilderness, is it because there were no no graves in Egypt?" that is, none at all (Ex. 14:11). "By seeing ye shall see and shall not not (ου μη) perceive" (Matt. 13:14).

The pleonasm of the sentence signifies, first, distribution. "A court was in the corner of the court: a court was in the corner of the court: a court was in the corner of the court" (Ezek. 46:21); that is, there was one court in every corner of the court. Second, it makes an emphasis. "The Israelites did as Moses and Aaron commanded, so did they" (Ex. 12:50). "The Lord is near unto all that call upon him: to all that call upon him in truth" (Ps. 145:18). "Unless the Lord had been on our side may Israel now say: unless the Lord had been on our side" (Ps. 124:1). Third, the repetition of the sentence, which is done in other words, is for exposition's sake. "I beseech thee, O Lord, remember now how I have walked before thee in truth and with a perfect heart, and have done that which is good in thy sight" (2 Kings 20:3). "The Lord hath heard the voice of my weeping, the Lord hath heard my prayer: the Lord hath received my supplication" (Ps. 6:9–10). "They have declared their sin, and have not hidden it" (Isa. 3:9). "All things were made by him, and without him nothing was made" (John 1:3).

All tropes are emphatical,[12] and besides delight and ornament they do also afford matter for the nourishment of faith, as when "Christ" is put for a Christian man or for the church of God (Matt. 25:35). "As the body is one, and hath many members: and all the members of one body, though they be many, are yet but one body: so also Christ (that is, the church)" (1 Corinthians 12). See Acts 9:4. This trope does comfort a faithful soul, and [it] nourishes faith.

An irony[13] signifies a just reprehension of sin. "And the Lord said to the children of Israel: Go ye, and cry out to your gods, whom ye have chosen: let them save you in the time of trouble" (Judges 10:14). "And he said unto them, Well ye abrogate the commandment of God, and observe your own traditions" (Mark 7:9). "The king said unto him, Micaiah, shall we go against Ramoth Gilead to battle? or shall we not? and he answered, Go up and prosper: doubtless the Lord shall deliver it into the hand of the king" (1 Kings 22:15). "And at noon Elijah mocked them, and said, Cry aloud, for he is a god: either he talketh, or pursueth his enemies, or is in his journey: or it may be he sleepeth, and must be awaked" (1 Kings 18:27). "Now are ye full, now are ye enriched, without us ye have gotten a kingdom" (1 Cor. 4:8).

Figures of a word in the repetition of a word or sound have for the most part an emphasis in them. "Let God, even our God bless us" (Ps. 66:7). "For mine own sake, for mine own sake will I do it" (Isa. 48:11). "Verily, verily I say unto you" (John 1:51). "The people shall praise thee, O God; all the people shall praise thee" (Ps. 67:6). In Psalm 136, there is a repetition made in every verse for this cause.

An interrogation signifies, first, an earnest affirmation or asseveration. "Is there not remission, if thou shalt do well?" (Gen. 4:7). "Is not this written in the book of the just?" (Josh. 10:13). "Do ye not say that it is yet four months

12. In the margin: They enlarge the sense.

13. In the margin: It is when the contrary to that which was spoken is meant. It is used in flouting sometimes.

to harvest?" (John 4:35). See Josh. 1:9; Gen. 37:13; 1 Kings 20:27; Mark 12:24; John 6:7. Second, it signifies a denial. "Shall any word be hard unto God?" (Gen. 18:4). "Shall their incredulity make the faith of God of none effect?" (Rom. 3:3). "If Satan shall vanquish Satan, how shall his kingdom continue?" (Matt. 12:26). Third, it signifies a forbidding. "Help us, O God, why shall the Gentiles say, where is their God?" (Ps. 79:10). "And Abner said to Asahel, depart from me: wherefore should I smite thee to the ground?" (2 Sam. 2:22). Fourthly, it argues sundry affections, as admiration, compassion, complaining, and finding of fault. "O Lord, how admirable is thy name in all the earth!" (Ps. 8:10). "How is the faithful city become a harlot!" (Isa. 1:21). "My GOD, my GOD, why hast thou forsaken me?" (Ps. 22:1).

Concession (or yielding) signifies a denial and reprehension. "But be it, that I charged you not, but because I was crafty, I took you with guile. Did I pill[14] you by any of them, whom I sent?" (2 Cor. 12:16–17).

Consectary 4

If the opposition of unlike places shall be taught to be, either not of the same matter, but of name only, or not according to the same part, or not in the same respect, or not in the same manner, or not at the same time, a reconciliation or agreement is made. Examples:

Psalm 7:8	Isaiah 64:6
"Judge me, O Lord, according to my righteousness."	"We have all been as an unclean thing, and all our righteousness is as filthy cloths."

The reconciliation: It appears by the scope and circumstances of both the places that this contradiction is not in the same respect. Distinguish therefore. There is one righteousness of the cause or action, and another of the person. The first place speaks of the former, and the second of the latter.

Matthew 10:10	Mark 6:8–9
"Not a scrip for the journey, neither two coats, neither shoes, nor a staff."	"And commanded them, to take nothing for their journey, save a staff only, neither scrip, neither bread, nor money in their girdles, but that they should be shod with sandals."

14. *Pill*: plunder.

The reconciliation: Distinguish the respects. Matthew means such a staff as may be a burden to the bearers thereof. Mark understands such a one as may sustain and ease those who travel. Jacob used such a one (Gen. 32:10). Moreover, the shoes that Matthew mentions are new, such as are with care and diligence prepared for to travel in. The sandals in Mark are not new, but such as are daily worn on the feet.

From this fourth consectary many provisos or cautions arise meet to be observed in the reconciling of places.

First, the holy writers, speaking of things and persons that are past, do anticipate, that is, they speak of them according to the custom of that place and time in which they wrote. "Afterward removing thence unto a mountain eastward from Bethel" (Gen. 12:8). The place was so called in the days of Moses, but in Abraham's time it was not called Bethel, but Luz (Gen. 28:19). "Abram went up out of Egypt—towards the south" (Gen. 13:1), not in respect of Egypt, but of that place wherein Moses was. "Christ in his Spirit preached to them that are in prison" (1 Peter 3:19). They are said to be in prison in regard of the time in which Peter wrote this epistle, and not of that wherein Noah lived. "Touch not mine anointed" (Ps. 105:15). Abraham, Isaac, and Jacob are said to be anointed in respect of the manner and fashion of the time wherein David lived. For they had no external anointing.

Second, allegories are to be expounded according to the scope or intent of the place. So, Chrysostom says upon Matthew 8, "Parables must not be expounded according to the letter, lest many absurdities do follow." Augustine, upon Psalm 8, speaks in this sort: "In every allegory this rule is to be retained, that it is considered according to the purpose of the present place which is there spoken of under a similitude."

Third, places and persons in the Scriptures have very often two names: Gideon was called Jerubbaal and Jerubbesheth, (Judges 6:32; 2 Sam. 11:21). Abimelech and Abiathar (1 Sam. 21:3; Mark 2:26). Solomon and Jedidiah (1 Sam. 12:24–25). Zimri and Zabdi (1 Chron. 2:6; Josh. 7:1). Hazariah, Ahaziah, and Jehoahaz (2 Chron. 22:6; 1 Chron. 3:11; 2 Chron. 21:17). Johanan and Jehoahaz (1 Chron. 3:15; 2 Kings 23:30). Shallum, Jehoiachin, Jeconiah, and Coniah (Jer. 22:11; 2 Kings 24:6; 1 Chron. 3:17; Jer. 32:24). Mephibosheth and Meribbaal (2 Samuel 4; 1 Chron. 8:34). Abinadab and Ishvi (1 Chron. 10:2; 1 Sam. 14:49). Eliakim and Jehoiakim (2 Kings 23:34). Uzziah and Azariah (2 Kings 15:1; 2 Chron. 26:1). Esther and Hadassah (Esther 2:7). Simon and Peter (John 1:42) and Cephas and Barjona. Joseph and Barnabas (Acts 4:36). Saul and Paul (Acts 13:6, 8). Matthew and Levi. Jerusalem is called Jebus and Salem.

Moreover, the name, which is indeed one, receives many times changes and differences. As Salmon (Ruth 4:21) is called Salma (2 Chron. 2:11). Abigal

(2 Sam. 17:25) is named Abigail (1 Chron. 2:16). Tiglath-pilezer (2 Kings 15:19) is termed Tiglath-pilneezer (1 Chron. 5:6). Aram (Matt. 1:3) is the same with Ram (1 Chron. 2:9).

Again, on the contrary, distinct persons and divers places have one name. "Josiah begat Jechoniah and his brethren about the time they were carried away into Babylon. And after they were carried away into Babylon Jechoniah begat Shealtiel" (Matt. 1:11–12). Here now, because Jechoniah does both finish the second tesseradecade,[15] and begin the third, one of them will be wanting to one of those tesseradecades, unless we say that there were two Jechoniahs, both father and son. Succoth is a name of three places. The first is in Egypt (Exod. 12:37). The second [is] in the tribe of Gad (Josh. 13:27). The third [is] in the tribe of Manasseh (1 Kings 7:46).

Fourth, in sacred accounts, by reason of the wickedness of the prince, either his name or the number of years in which he reigned wickedly are omitted and left out. "Saul reigned two years over Israel" (1 Sam. 13:1), that is, lawfully, or (as Lyra speaks) rightly;[16] but otherwise he reigned longer. "Joram begat Uzziah" (Matt. 1:8). Here three are left out for their wickedness, to wit, Ahaziah, Joash, and Amaziah.

Fifth, the time spoken of is taken either completely[17] or incompletely, and the parts thereof are understood either inclusively or exclusively. "And in the twentieth year of Jeroboam Asa reigned over Judah" (1 Kings 15:9).

1 Kings 15:25	1 Kings 15:28
"Nadab the son of Jeroboam [began to reign over Israel the second year] of Asa king of Judah: and reigned over Israel [two years]."	"Even in the [third year of Asa king of Judah] did Baasha slay Nadab, and reigned in his stead."

The reconcilement: Nadab, who began to reign in the second year of Asa, might reign two years, although Baasha succeed him in the third year of Asa, because the last years of the kings of Israel and Judah are not fully expired, but some of them (as in this place) do scarcely contain months in them, the rest of the years being put completely.

15. In the margin: That is, the second fourteenth generation mentioned in Matthew 1:17, in which place three fourteen generations are set down.

16. In the margin: *De jure*, according to law or equity.

17. In the margin: That is, as fully finished, or as but in the finishing.

Matthew 17:1	Luke 9:28
"And the sixth day after Jesus took Peter, and James, and John his brother, and brought them up unto a high mountain."	"And it came to pass about eight days after, that having taken to him Peter, and James, and John, he went up into a mountain."

The reconcilement: Matthew puts exclusively only the days that were between, which were altogether accomplished. Luke puts the two outermost days also in the reckoning.

The parts of time are put sometimes inclusively and sometimes exclusively. (1) That the number may be more perfect. Augustine says (qu. 47) on Exodus: "In a perfect number oftentimes that which is either wanting or abounding is not counted." "Israel dwelt in Heshbon and Aroer and their towns three hundred years" (Judges 11:26). These years are to be reckoned from the departure of the Israelites out of Egypt, after this manner. The time of their abode in the wilderness was forty years. The time of the government of Joshua was seventeen years; of Othniel, forty years (Judges 3:11); of Ehud and Shamgar, eighty years (Judges 3:30); of Barak, forty years (Judges 5:31); of Gideon, forty years (Judges 8:28); of Abimelech, three years (Judges 9:22); of Tolah, twenty-three years (Judges 10:2); of Jair, twenty-two years (Judges 10:3). The whole in all is 305 years. Here, therefore, the five odd years are not named. It may be because this even number of three hundred is fitter both for the computation and the speech. (2) For brevity sake. "There were slain of the Benjamites twenty-five thousand" (Judges 20:46). Here a hundred are not counted, as appears [in] verse 35, "The Israelites slew that day of the tribe of Benjamin five and twenty thousand and a hundred men."

Fifth, the king, being hindered either with foreign war or with old age or by reason of some disease, does (while he yet lives) appoint his son to be king in his stead. And, therefore, with the computation of years of father and son reigning at one time, the years of the reign are reckoned sometimes jointly and sometimes apart.

2 Kings 1:17	2 Kings 3:1
"Ahaziah died, and Jehoram reigned in his stead [in the second year of Jehoram the son of Jehoshaphat] king of Judah."	"Jehoram the son of Ahab reigned in the eighteenth year of Jehoshaphat." Chapter 8:16, "In the [fifth year of Joram the son of Ahab] Jehoram the son of Jehoshaphat began to reign, and reigned eight years."

The reconciliation: Jehoshaphat, determining in the seventeenth year of his reign to help king Ahab against the Syrians, appoints his son Joram to be viceroy. In the eighteenth year of his own reign, and in the second of his son's, Joram the son of Ahab reigned. Afterwards, in the fifth year of this Joram the son of Ahab, Jehoshaphat (being stricken in age) confirms his kingdom to his son Joram, who is said to have reigned eight years, four while his father was alive and four alone by himself after the death of his father.

2 Kings 15:30	2 Kings 15:33
"And Hoshea the son of Elah wrought treason against Pekah the son of Remaliah, and smote him, and slew him, and reigned in his room [in the twentieth year of Jotham] the son of Uzziah."	"Jotham the son of Uzziah was five and twenty years old when he began to reign [and he reigned sixteen years] in Jerusalem."

The reconciliation: He reigned sixteen years alone after his father's death. He also reigned twenty [years] with his father, for he governed the kingdom for his father who was diseased with leprosy.

Sixth, the east country men do diversely distinguish their artificial day, both into twelve equal hours (commonly called planetary hours) and into quadrants, having their name of the hour going next before.[18]

The eastern men's counting:

1	2	3	4
(1 2 3)	(4 5 6)	(7 8 9)	(10 11 12)

The manner of our counting:

7 8 9 10 11 12 1 2 3 4 5 6

Mark 15:25	John 19:14
"And it was [the third hour] when they crucified him."	"And it was the preparation of the Passover, [and about the sixth hour] and he said unto the Jews, Behold your King."

The reconciliation: The opposition is not in the same respect. Therefore, distinguish the manners of accompting the hours of the day, and then it will appear that Christ might be crucified at the third hour and about the sixth.

18. In the text: *Beroald. Chronol.*

Seventh, the lesser number is to be counted under the greater and the more complete. "The land had rest forty years when Othniel died" (Judges 3:11). Under this number are all the years comprehended from the death of Joshua to the death of Othniel, as also the eight years of servitude under the Syrians. Judges 3:30, "The land had rest eighty years" (Judges 3:30). Here from the death of Othniel are numbered also the years of Ehud and Shamgar. For Ehud could not be judge eighty years, for when these years are expired the whole time of [the] man is run out. The like we meet with in Judges 5:31; 8:28; 9:22; 10:2–3; 11:26. Here, the forty years of their tarrying in the desert are included in the three hundred years.

Eighth, filiation (or sonship) is either natural or legal. Natural is by generation; legal is by adoption, which is to be testified by education and bringing up, and by succession in the kingdom, and in leviration[19] by the law of redemption.[20]

2 Samuel 21:8	1 Samuel 18:19
"And the king took the five sons of Michal, the daughter of Saul, whom she bore to Adriel the son of Barzillai the Mehalothite."	"When Merab Saul's daughter should have been given to David, she was given unto Adriel a Mehalothite to wife."

The reconciliation: They are the natural sons of Merab, and the legal sons of Michal, and therefore ("to bear") does only signify to bring up, to feed, and to nourish. For thus the sons of Machir are said to be "borne" (*nati*) "on Joseph's knees," that is, brought up (Gen. 50:23).

Matthew 1:12	Luke 3:27
"Jechoniah begat Shealtiel."	"Shealtiel the son of Neri."

The reconciliation: Shealtiel was the son of Neri by nature, and the son of Jechoniah legally in regard of succession in the same kingdom. After this manner, Zedekiah is the brother of Jechoniah or Jehoiachin (2 Chron. 36:10) and uncle (2 Kings 14:17) and son (1 Chron. 3:16). [He was] his brother by generation, and his son by the right of succession. In this manner, Matthew and Luke are reconciled in the genealogy of Christ, for the one follows the natural order (as Luke) and the other the legal.

---

19. *Leviration*: a type of marriage in which the brother of a deceased man is obliged to marry his brother's widow.

20. In the margin: To understand this, read Deut. 25:5.

Consectary 5

When the natural sense of the place (propounded) is given by the fore-said helps, a signification of a word, signifying divers things (πολυσημα) shall be given, which is fitting to the place.

Thus, the significations of *vau* (the prefix or copulative) are (as Brunerus has observed in his Hebrew Grammar) distinguished according to the diversity of the places. It signifies:[21] (1) *at* (Isa. 9:10; Gen. 42:10); (2) *quoniam* (Isa. 53:11); (3) *quin* (Isa. 9:11; Ps. 73:4); (4) *id est* (Isa. 9:14; 1 Sam. 17:40); (5) *idcirco* (Prov. 1:18); (6) *ita ut* (Ps. 18:39; Isa. 24:20); (7) *sic etiam* (Isa. 10:10; 51:11); (8) *et tamen* (1 Chron. 5:2; Neh. 9:19); (9) *atqui* (Pss. 73:2; 19:6); (10) *posteà tunc* (Isa. 16:12; Gen. 3:5); (11) *autem* (Isa. 1:21; Neh. 2:9); (12) *etiam* (2 Kings 3:8); (13) *num* (Isa. 37:11); (14) *sicut, sic* (Ps. 125:2; Dan. 7:2); (15) *qui, quæ, quod* (Isa. 43:8); (16) *quum* (Ps. 50:17); (17) *ut* (Isa. 49:6); (18) *quamuis* (Jer. 31:35); (19) *inquam* (Isa. 55:1); (20) *idque* (Ps. 105:12); (21) *atq ita* (Prov. 3:4); (22) *et ut* (Isa. 58:5–6); (23) *quoniam, ideo* (Ps. 109:17); (24) *imò* (Ps. 109:18); (25) *nec non* (Ps. 72:16); (26) *uerùm* (Ps. 73:23); (27) *etiam si* (Job 19:26); (28) *aut* (Ps. 139:7); (29) *quòd, idq* (Ps. 139:14); (30) *et vero* (Ps. 139:17); (31) *tum* (Neh. 12:27); (32) *simulatq* (Jer. 50:43); (33) *si sin* (2 Kings 5:17); (34) *nec* (Isa. 41:8); (35) *hoc igitur* (Prov. 17:33); (36) *unà cùm* (Prov. 8:18); (37) *quòd* (Gen. 47:6).

Thus it appears that *berech* signifies contrary things, as to bless and to curse (Job 1:5; 1 Kings 21:10; 11:29).

To conclude, hence it is evident that *huchal* does not signify "profaned," but "begun" (Gen. 4:26). *Reason 1.* When *chalal* signifies to profane, it ought to be joined with a noun, and to govern it. But here it does immediately follow *kara* (an infinitive verb). *Reason 2.* Moses reckons not the profanation of God's worship among the many causes of the deluge, which notwithstanding should have been chiefly noted if it had reigned among the people of God.

Consectary 6

If a word given in the Bible, whether it is a Hebrew or Greek word, does agree with grammatical construction and with other approved copies, [and] if it also does agree in respect of the sense with the circumstances and drift of the place and with the analogy of faith, it is proper and natural.

I lay down this rule, not because I think that the Hebrew and Greek text is in all copies corrupted through the malice of the Jews, as Lindanus[22] does wickedly calumniate (and after him all papists), but that the divers readings which

21. In the margin: I do not translate these adverbs and conjunctions on purpose, as being fittest in Latin.

22. William Damasus Lindanus (1525–88) was a priest, professor, and staunch defender of the Roman Catholic Church.

in some places have crept in, either by reason of the unskillfulness or negligence and oversight of the notaries, might be scanned and determined. [For example:] Psalm 22:16. In ordinary copies, the words run thus, *caari*, that is, "as a lion mine hands and my feet." In other copies, the reading is diverse after this manner: *caaru*, "They have digged (or pierced) mine hands and my feet." Now the rule propounded does teach that this latter reading is to be followed, for it agrees (1) with grammatical construction, (2) with the circumstances of the psalm, and (3) with some ancient copies, yea even by the testimony of the Jews.

Chapter 6

The Right Dividing of the Word

Hitherto we have spoken of interpreting the Word. We are now come to speak of the "right cutting"[1] (or right dividing) of it.

[The] "right cutting" of the Word is that whereby the Word is made fit to edify the people of God. "Study to show thyself approved unto God, a workman that need not to be ashamed, dividing (or cutting) the word of truth aright" (2 Tim. 2:15). It is a metaphor taken (it may be) from the Levites who might not cut the members of the sacrifices without due consideration. "The Lord hath given me the tongue of the learned, that I might know to minister a word in due season to him that is weary" (Isa. 50:4). The parts thereof are two: resolution (or partition) and application.

Resolution[2] is that whereby the place propounded is (as a weaver's web) resolved (or untwisted and unloosed) into sundry doctrines. "Mightily he confuted the Jews, with great vehemency publicly showing by Scriptures that Jesus was that Christ" (Acts 18:28). Resolution is either notation or collection.

Notation is when the doctrine is expressed in the place propounded. "We have already proved that all, both Jews and Gentiles, are under sin. As it is written, There is none righteous, no not one. There is none that understandeth, none that seeketh God. All are gone out of the way: they have been made altogether unprofitable: there is none that doth good, no not one" (Rom. 3:9–12). "Whom God hath raised up, and loosed the sorrows of death, because it was impossible that he should be held of it. For David saith concerning him, I beheld the Lord always before me: for he is at my right hand, that I should not be shaken. Therefore did mine heart rejoice, and my tongue was glad, and moreover also my flesh shall rest in hope. Because thou wilt not leave my soul with the dead, neither wilt suffer thine holy one to see corruption" (Acts 2:24–27).

Collection is when the doctrine [is] not expressed [but] is soundly gathered out of the text. This is done by the help of the nine arguments, that is,

---

1. In the margin: ορθοτομια.
2. In the margin: διαλυσις.

of the causes, effects, subjects, adjuncts, dissentanies,[3] comparatives, names, distribution, and definition. For example:

A place	The collection from the comparison of the lesser
John 10:34, "Jesus answered them, Is it not written in your law, I said ye are gods?"	Verses 35–36, "If he called them gods, unto whom the word of God was given, and the Scripture cannot be broken: … Say ye of me, whom the Father hath sanctified and sent into the world, thou blasphemest, because I said I am the Son of God?"
A place	The collection from the lesser
1 Corinthians 9:9, "For it is written in the law of Moses, thou shalt not muzzle the mouth of the ox that treadeth out the corn. What, hath God care of oxen?"	Verse 4, "Have we not power to eat, and to drink?"
A place	The collection from the contrary
Galatians 3:10, "For so many as are of the works of the law are under a curse: for it is written, Cursed is everyone that continueth not in all things which are in the book of the law to do them."	Verse 9, "Therefore those which are of faith are blessed with faithful Abraham."
Verse 11, "For the just shall live by faith."	Verse 11, "And that no man is justified by the law before God, it is evident."
A place	The collection from the adjunct
Hebrews 8:8, "For in rebuking them he saith, Behold, the days will come, saith the Lord, when I shall make with the house of Israel and with the house of Judah a new testament."	Verse 13, "In that he saith a new testament, he hath disannulled the old: now that which is disannulled and waxed old is ready to vanish away."

3. *Dissentanies:* differences.

In [the] gathering of doctrines, we must especially remember that an example in its own kind (that is, an ethic, economic, politic, ordinary, and extraordinary example) has the virtue of a general rule in ethic, economic, politic, ordinary, and extraordinary matters. The examples of the fathers are patterns for us (1 Cor. 10:11). "And whatsoever is written, is written for our learning" (Rom. 15:4). And it is a principle in logic that the *genus*[4] is actually in all the *species*,[5] and [it is] a rule in the optics that the general species of things are perceived before the particular.

A place	The collection from the species
Romans 9:7, "Neither are they all children, because they are the seed of Abraham: but in Isaac shall thy seed be called." Verse 10, "Neither he only felt this, but also Rebecca, when she had conceived by one, even by our father Isaac."	Verse 8, "That is, they which are the children of the flesh, are not the children of God: but the children of the promise are counted for the seed."
Romans 4:18, "Which Abraham against hope, believed under hope…" Verse 21, "Being fully assured that he which had promised was also able to do it." Verse 22, "And therefore it was imputed to him for righteousness."	Romans 4:23–24, "Now it is not written for him only, that it was imputed to him for righteousness. But for us also, to whom it shall be imputed for righteousness, which believe in him, that raised up Jesus our Lord from the dead."

This also I add, that collections ought to be right and sound, that is to say, derived from the genuine and proper meaning of the Scripture. If otherwise, we shall draw any[6] doctrine from any place. Proverbs 8:22, the Greek translation of the seventy interpreters is: (κυριος εκτισεν με) "The Lord hath created me." It is the speech of wisdom, that is, of Christ speaking of Himself. Whence the Arians collect (very wickedly) that the Son was created. But in the Hebrew, it is *Jehovah kanneni* ("The Lord hath possessed me"). Now the Father possesses the Son because He begat Him from eternity, and because the Father is in the Son and the Son in the Father. And so, when a son was born unto Adam, he says, "I have possessed a man from the Lord" (Gen. 4:1). The error perhaps

4. In the margin: Or general.
5. In the margin: Or specials and particulars of that kind or general.
6. In the margin: *Ad verb.* Anything out of anything, *quid libet è quo libet.*

came from this, that *ectise*[7] was either through ignorance or malice put for *ectese*.[8]

Augustine reads Psalm 39:10 in this way: "I held my peace because thou hast made me (*fecisti me*)." From whence he does wittily gather that it is a marvel that he who has received a mouth to speak should hold his tongue; whereas "me" is neither in the Hebrew nor in the Greek. And, upon Psalm 72:14, he disputes much about usuries, and proves that usuries are sins; whereas there is no such matter in that text. For the words are: "He shall deliver their soul from deceit and violence, so precious is their blood in his eyes."

It shall be lawful also to gather allegories, for they are arguments taken from things that are like. And Paul uses them often in his teaching (1 Cor. 9:9). But they are to be used with these cautions: (1) Let them be used sparingly and soberly. (2) Let them not be far-fetched, but fitting to the matter in hand. (3) They must be quickly dispatched. (4) They are to be used for instruction of the life, and not to prove any point of faith.

Any point of doctrine collected by just consequence is simply[9] of itself to be believed, and does demonstrate.[10] "And a certain Jew, named Apollos, born at Alexandria, came to Ephesus, an eloquent man and mighty (δυνατος) in the scriptures.... For mightily he confuted the Jews publicly with great vehemency, demonstrating (επιδεικνυς) by the Scriptures that Jesus was the Christ" (Acts 18:24, 28).

From hence it follows:

First, that human testimonies, whether of the philosophers or the fathers, are not to be alleged. Augustine, upon Psalm 66, says thus: "If I speak, let no man hear. If Christ speaks, woe be to him who does not hear." So again, he says, "Let us not hear, 'These things I say. These things he says.' But let us hear, 'These things the Lord says.'"[11] Yet, with this exception, "Unless they convince the conscience of the hearer." Thus, Paul alleged the testimony of Aratus: "For by him we live, and move, and have our being, as one of your own poets hath said; For we are all his progeny (γενος). Forasmuch then, as we are the progeny of God..." (Acts 17:28–29). [He] also [alleged] a saying of Menander: "Be not deceived, evil conversations[12] corrupt good manners" (1 Cor. 15:33). And of Epimenides: "As one of their prophets hath said, The Cretans are always liars,

7. In the margin: εκτισε, He has created.
8. In the margin: εκτησε, He has possessed.
9. In the margin: αυτοπισ.
10. In the margin: επιδεικτικοσ.
11. In the text: *De unitat. Ecclesia.*
12. In the margin: ομιλιαι.

evil beasts, and slow-bellies" (Titus 1:12). And then also it must be done sparingly, and with leaving out the name of the profane writer.

Second, that a few testimonies of Scripture are to be used for the proof of the doctrine, and that sometimes there is need of none.

Lastly, hence it follows that the prophets, delivering their doctrine thus, are not to be reproved by other prophets. "And the spirits of the prophets are subject unto the prophets" (1 Cor. 14:32). Yet afterwards, he adds, "If any one seem to be a prophet or spiritual, let him acknowledge that those things, which I write unto you, are the commandments of God" (v. 37).

Chapter 7

The Ways to Use and Apply Doctrines

Application is that whereby the doctrine rightly collected is diversely fitted according as place, time, and person do require. "I will feed my sheep, and bring them to their rest, saith the Lord. I will seek that which is lost, and bring again that which was driven away, and will bind up that which was broken, and will strengthen the sick" (Ezek. 34:15–16). "And having compassion of some in putting difference. And save others with terror, pulling them out of the flame" (Jude 22–23).

The foundation of application is to know whether the place propounded is a sentence of the law or the gospel. For when the Word is preached there is one operation of the law and another of the gospel. For the law is thus far forth effectual as to declare unto us the disease of sin, and by accident to exasperate and stir it up. But it affords no remedy. Now, the gospel, as it teaches what is to be done, so it has also the efficacy of the Holy Spirit adjoined with it, by whom we, being regenerated, have strength both to believe the gospel and to perform those things which it commands. The law, therefore, is the first in the order of teaching, and the gospel [is] second.

It is a sentence of the law which speaks of perfect inherent righteousness, of eternal life given through the works of the law, of the contrary sins, and of the curse that is due unto them. "So many as are of the works of the law, are under the curse; for it is written, Cursed is he whosoever abideth not in all things which are written in the book of the law to do them" (Gal. 3:10). "O generation of vipers, who hath forewarned you to flee from the anger to come?… And now also is the axe put to the root of the trees: therefore every tree which bringeth not forth good fruit is cut up (εκκοπτεται) and cast into the fire" (Matt. 3:7, 10).

A sentence of the gospel is that which speaks of Christ and His benefits, and of faith being fruitful in good works. "So God loved the world, that he gave his only begotten Son, that whosoever believeth in him should not perish, but have everlasting life" (John 3:16).

Hence it is that many sentences, which seem to belong to the law, are by reason of Christ to be understood not legally (νομικως) but with the qualification of the gospel.[1] "Blessed are those which hear the word of God and keep it" (Luke 11:28). "This commandment which I command thee this day, is not hidden, nor set afar off.... But it is by thee in thy mouth and in thine heart" (Deut. 30:11, 14). This sentence (which is legal in Moses) is evangelical in Paul (Rom. 10:8). "Blessed are those that are perfect in the way, who walk in the law of Jehovah. Blessed are they that keep his testimonies and seek him with their whole heart" (Ps. 119:1–2). "He that hath my commandments, and keepeth them, is he that loveth me: he that loveth me shall be loved of my Father.... If any man do love me, he will keep my word: and my Father doth love him, and we will come unto him, and we will dwell with him" (John 14:21, 23). "Noah was a just and upright man in his time: Noah walked with God continually"[2] (Gen. 6:9). "I am the strong God, omnipotent, walk alway before me and be upright" (Gen. 17:1).

The ways of application are chiefly seven, according to the divers conditions of men and people, which are sevenfold.

Condition 1

Unbelievers who are both ignorant and unteachable.

These men, in the first place, are to be prepared to receive the doctrine of the Word. Jehoshaphat sent Levites throughout the cities of Judah to teach the people and to bring them from idols (2 Chronicles 17).

This preparation is to be made partly by disputing or reasoning with them, so that you may thoroughly discern their manners and disposition, and partly by reproving some notorious sin in them, so that (being pricked in heart and terrified) they may become teachable. "He disputed in the synagogue with the Jews, and with them that were religious, and in the market place with whosoever he met" (Acts 17:17). "Now as he journeyed it came to pass that, as he was come near to Damascus, suddenly there shined round about him a light from heaven. And he fell to the earth and heard a voice saying to him, Saul, Saul, why persecutest thou me? And he said, Who art thou Lord? And the Lord answered, I am Jesus of Nazareth, whom thou dost persecute: it is hard for thee to kick against the pricks" (Acts 9:3–5). "Then the keeper of the prison awoke out of his sleep: and when he saw the prison doors open, he drew out his sword, and would have killed himself, supposing the prisoners had been fled. Then Paul cried with a loud voice, saying, Do thyself no harm, for we are all here. Then he called for a light, and leaped in, and came trembling, and fell down before Paul and Silas. And brought them out, and said, Sirs, what must I do to be saved? And they said, Believe in the Lord Jesus and thou shalt be saved, and thine

1. In the margin: *Evangelicè*.
2. In the margin: indefinenter.

household" (Acts 16:27–31). "And Paul stood in the midst of Mars-street, and said, Ye men of Athens, I see that in all things ye are too superstitious.[3] For as I passed by and beheld your devotions, I found an altar, wherein was written, Unto the unknown god; whom ye then ignorantly worship, him show I unto you. God, that made the world and all things in it, seeing that he is Lord of heaven and earth, dwelleth not in temples made with hands" (Acts 17:22–24).

When now there is hope that they are become teachable and prepared, the doctrine of God's Word is to be declared to them generally in some common terms or ordinary points. "And the time of this ignorance God regarded not, but now he commandeth (απαγγελλει) all men everywhere to repent. Because he hath appointed a day, in which he will judge the world in righteousness by that Man whom he hath appointed, whereof he hath assured all men, in that he hath raised him from the dead" (Acts 17:30–31).

If they shall approve this doctrine, then it is to be opened to them distinctly and in every particular. But if they shall remain unteachable without hope of winning them, they are to be left. "Give not that which is holy unto dogs: neither cast your pearls before swine, lest they tread them under their feet, and turning again all to rend you" (Matt. 7:6). "Reprove not a scorner, lest he hate thee" (Prov. 9:8). "But when certain men were hardened, and would not obey, speaking evil of the way of the Lord before the multitude, he departed from them, and separated the disciples from them" (Acts 19:9).

Condition 2

Some are teachable, but yet ignorant.

To these men the catechism must be delivered. "Apollos was catechized (κατηχημενος) in the way of the Lord. And he spoke fervently in the spirit, and taught diligently the things of the Lord, knowing only the baptism of John. And he began to speak boldly in the synagogue. Whom when Aquila and Priscilla had heard, they took him unto them, and expounded unto him the way of God more perfectly" (Acts 18:25–26). "That thou mayest know the truth of those things, whereof thou hast been catechized (κατηχηθης) (or instructed)" (Luke 1:4).

The catechism is the doctrine of the foundation of Christian religion briefly propounded for the help of the understanding and memory in questions and answers made by the lively voice.

The matter, therefore, of the catechism is the foundation of religion.

3. In the margin: δεισιδαιμονεστερους.

The foundation is a certain sum of the principles of Christianity. "For when as concerning the time ye ought to be teachers, yet have ye need again that we teach you the first principles of the word of God" (Heb. 5:12).

A principle is that which does directly and immediately serve both for the salvation of men and for the glory of God, which being also denied and overturned no salvation can be hoped for.

There are especially six principles: repentance, faith, baptism (that is, the sacraments), imposition of hands (that is, the ministry of the Word by a synecdoche), the resurrection, and the last judgment (Heb. 6:1–3).

The form of the catechism is to handle the elements or grounds plainly by asking and answering. "To the which also the figure that now saveth us, even baptism agreeth (not the putting away of the filthiness of the flesh, but the stipulation or interrogation[4] of a good conscience)" (1 Peter 3:21). "What doth let me to be baptized? And Philip said unto him, If thou believest with all thine heart, thou mayest. Then he answered saying, I believe that Jesus Christ is the Son of God" (Acts 8:37). Tertullian says, "The soul is not purged with washing, but with answering."[5]

And here we must hold a difference between "milk" and "strong meat," which are the same indeed, but do differ in the manner and fashion of delivering.

"Milk" is a certain brief, plain, and general explication of the principles of the faith, as when a man does teach that we must believe one God and three persons (Father, Son, and Holy Spirit), and that we must rely only upon the grace of God in Christ, and that we ought to believe the remission of sins; and when we are taught this, we ought to repent, abstain from evil, and do that which is good.

"Strong meat" is a special, copious, luculent, and clear handling of the doctrine of faith, as when the condition of man before the fall, his fall, original and actual sin, man's guiltiness, free-will, the mysteries of the Trinity, the two natures of Christ, the personal union, the office of Christ, the imputation of righteousness, faith, grace, and the use of the law, are delivered out of the Word of God distinctly and exactly.

Moreover, milk must be set before babes, that is, those who are rude (or weak) in knowledge. Strong meat must be given to such as are of ripe years, that is, to them who are better instructed. "Moreover, brethren, I could not speak unto you as to spiritual: but I have spoken unto you as to carnal, that is, to infants in Christ. I have fed you with milk, and not with meat" (1 Cor. 3:1–2). See Hebrews 5:13.

---

4. In the margin: επερωτημα.

5. In the text: De resur. car.

Condition 3

Some have knowledge, but are not as yet humbled.

In such men the foundation of repentance ought to be stirred up, that is to say, a certain sorrow which is according to God. "For though I made you sorry with a letter, I repent not, though I did repent: for I perceive that the same epistle made you sorry, though it were but for a season. I now rejoice, not that ye were sorry, but that ye sorrowed to repentance: for ye sorrowed according to God (κατα θεον) so that in nothing ye were hurt by us. For sorrow, which is according to God (or godly) causeth repentance unto salvation not to be repented of: but worldly sorrow causeth death" (2 Cor. 7:8–10).

Sorrow according to God is a grief for sin, even because it is sin.

To the stirring up of this affection, in the first place a man must use the ministry of the law, which may beget contrition of heart or the horrors of conscience, which, though it is not a thing wholesome and profitable of its own nature, yet it is a remedy necessary for the subduing of a sinner's stubbornness and for the preparing of his mind to become teachable.

Now, that this legal sorrow may be wrought, it is fit to use some choice parcel of the law, which may reprove some notable sin in men who are not as yet humbled. For sorrow for, and repentance, even of one sin is for substance sorrow for and repentance of all. "Repent therefore of this thy wickedness, and pray God, that if it be possible, the thought of thine heart may be forgiven thee" (Acts 8:22). "Him have ye taken by the hands of the wicked, being delivered by the determinate counsel, and foreknowledge of God, and have crucified and slain" (Acts 2:23). See Psalm 32:5.

Yea, further, if any man, being afflicted with the cross and with outward calamities, has only a worldly sorrow (that is, if he mourns not for sin as it is sin, but for the punishment of sin), he is not by and by to be comforted, but first this sorrow is to be turned into that other sorrow which is according to God. As it is the counsel of physicians in the like case. For if a man's life is in danger by reason of blood gushing out of his nose, they command that blood also be let out of his arm or some other place (as the case requires), that they might stay the course of the blood which rushes out of the nostrils, so that they might save his life, who was ready to yield up the ghost.

Then let the gospel be preached, in the preaching whereof the Holy Spirit works effectually unto salvation. For while He renews men that they may begin to will and to work those things that are pleasing to God, He does truly and properly bring forth in them that sorrow which is according to God and repentance unto salvation.

To the hard-hearted the law must be urged, and the curse of the law must be denounced with threatening, together with the difficulty of obtaining deliverance until they are purified in the heart. "And when he saw many of the Pharisees and of the Sadducees come to his baptism, he said unto them, O progeny[6] of vipers, who hath forewarned you to flee from the wrath to come?" (Matt. 3:7). "Good Master, what shall I do that I may have eternal life? And he said unto him—if thou wilt enter into life, keep the commandments" (Matt. 19:16–17). "Woe unto you scribes and Pharisees, hypocrites, because ye shut up the kingdom of heaven before men: for ye yourselves go not in, neither suffer ye those that are entering in (εισερχομενους) to go in.... O serpents, and progeny of vipers, how shall ye escape the damnation of hell?" (Matt. 23:13, 33).

But when the beginning of compunction does appear, they are presently to be comforted with the gospel.

Condition 4

Some are humbled.

Here we must very diligently consider whether their humiliation is complete and sound or but begun and but light or slight, lest he or they, receiving comfort sooner than is meet, should afterwards wax harder like iron which, being cast into the furnace, becomes exceeding hard after it is once cold.

Let your proceeding be after this manner with those who are humbled in part. Let the law be propounded, yet so discreetly tempered with the gospel that (being terrified with their sins and with the meditation of God's judgment) they may together also at the same instant receive solace by the gospel. "Then Peter said unto him, thy money perish with thee, because thou thinkest that the gift of God may be obtained by money. Thou hast neither part, nor fellowship in this business, for thine heart is not right in the sight of God. Repent therefore of this thy wickedness, and pray God, that if it be possible the cogitation of thine heart may be remitted. For I see that thou art in the gall of bitterness, and in the bond of iniquity" (Acts 8:20–23). "And the Lord God cried unto Adam, and said unto him, where art thou? And God said, who hath shewed thee that thou art naked? What, hast thou eaten of the fruit of that tree, of which I forbad thee to eat?... And the Lord God said to the woman, what is this which thou hast done? And the woman said, this serpent hath seduced me, and I have eaten.... Moreover, I will put enmity betwixt thee and this woman, and likewise between thy seed and her seed: this shall break thine head, and thou shalt bruise his heel" (Gen. 3:9, 13, 15). Being sent from God, Nathan (by a parable which he does propound) recalls David to the conscience of his act, and pronounces pardon to him being penitent (2 Samuel 12).

---

6. In the margin: γεννηματα.

The doctrine of faith and repentance and the comforts of the gospel ought to be promulgated and tendered to those who are fully humbled. "The Spirit of the Lord is upon me, therefore he hath anointed me to preach glad tidings to the poor: he hath sent me to heal the contrite in heart, to preach deliverance to the captives, and to the blind the recovery of their sight, and to set at liberty those that were broken" (Luke 4:18). "When they heard these things, they were pricked in heart, and said unto Peter, and the rest of the apostles, Men and brethren, what shall we do? And Peter said unto them: Repent and be baptized every one of you in the name of Jesus Christ for the remission of sins" (Acts 2:37–38). "I came not to call the just, but sinners unto repentance" (Matt. 9:13).

Condition 5

Some do believe.

To these must be propounded [the following]: (1) The gospel of justification, sanctification, and perseverance. (2) The law without the curse, whereby they may be taught to bring forth fruits of new obedience beseeming repentance. "There is no condemnation to those that are in Christ Jesus" (Rom. 8:1). "The law is not appointed for the righteous…" (1 Tim. 1:9). Let the epistle of Paul to the Romans be the example. (3) Howsoever the curse of the law is not to be urged against the person who is righteous and holy in the sight of God, yet it is to be urged against the sins of the person, which are remaining. And as a father does oftentimes set his iron rods, that are appointed for the servants, before the eyes of his sons that they may be afraid, so the meditation of the curse is to be stirred up very often in the faithful themselves, lest they should abuse the mercy of God to licentious living, and that they may be more fully humbled. For sanctification is but in part. Therefore, that the remainders of sin may be abolished, we must always begin with the meditation of the law and with the feeling of sin, and make an end in the gospel.

Condition 6

Some are fallen.

Those who are fallen are they who do in part fall from the state of grace. Falling is either in faith or in manners.

Falling in faith is either in the knowledge of the doctrine of the gospel or in the apprehending of Christ.

Falling in knowledge is a declining into error, whether lighter or fundamental.

Now unto those who fall thus, that doctrine which does cross their error is to be demonstrated and inculcated (or beaten upon them) together with the doctrine of repentance, and that with a brotherly affection. Take for example the epistle of Paul to the Galatians. "Instructing them with meekness that are contrarily affected (τους αντιδιατιθεμενους): if God at any time will give them repentance that they may know the truth" (2 Tim. 2:25).

The fall which is in apprehending Christ is desperation.

For the restoring of those who do despair, a trial and a remedy are to be used.

The trial (or search) is either of the cause of the temptation or of their estate.

The trial of the cause is made fitly by private confession. "Confess your sins one to another, and pray for one another that ye may be healed" (James 5:17). But lest that confession should be made a kind of rack or torture, it must be limited with these provisos. (1) It ought to be free and not compelled, because salvation depends not upon it. (2) It must not be of all sins, but of those only which wring the conscience. Unless they do reveal them, greater danger may hang over their heads. (3) Let it chiefly be made to pastors, yet so as that we must know that it may be safely made to other faithful men in the church.

The trial of their estate is whereby we make diligent inquiry whether they are under the law or under grace.

That this may manifestly appear, we must by asking of questions first draw out of them whether they are displeased with themselves because they have displeased God, that is to say, whether they hate sin as it is sin, which is the foundation of repentance unto salvation. Second, we must demand of them whether they have or do feel in their heart a desire to be reconciled with God, which is the ground of a lively faith.

When trial is made, the remedy must be applied unto them out of the gospel, which is double.

First, some evangelical meditations are to be often inculcated and pressed upon them. (1) That their sin is pardonable. (2) That the promises are general in respect of believers, and that they are indefinite in respect of particular men, and do exclude no man. (3) That the will to believe is faith (Ps. 145:19; Rev. 2:6). (4) That sin does not abolish grace, but rather (God turning all things unto the good of those who are His) does illustrate it. (5) That all the works of God are done by contrary means.

Second, they must be entreated to stir up in them (in the very bitterness of the temptation) their faith which has lain in a swoon and been covered[7] (as it were) with ashes, and that they would certainly set down with themselves that their sins are forgiven them, and that it would please them to struggle manfully in prayer either alone or with others against carnal sense and human hope. And

7. In the margin: *Sopitam fidem.*

that they may perform these things, they must be earnestly beaten upon, and those who are unwilling must in a manner be constrained. "Out of the depths have I called to thee, O Lord. Lord, listen unto my voice: let thine ears attend to the voice of my prayers" (Ps. 130:1–2). "My voice came to God when I prayed, my voice went to God, that he would turn his ear (*ut advertat aurem*) unto me. In the day of my distress I besought the Lord" (Ps. 77:1–2). "Who (Abraham) against (παρα) hope believed under hope, that he should be the father of many nations" (Rom. 4:18).

Now that these medicines may be of force, that ministerial power of binding and loosing is to be used according to the form prescribed in the Word. "Then David said to Nathan, I have sinned against the Lord: Wherefore Nathan said to David, God hath also forgiven thy sin: thou shalt not die" (2 Sam. 12:13). "Therefore we are ambassadors in the name of Christ, God as it were beseeching you by us: we pray you in the name of Christ that ye would be reconciled to God" (2 Cor. 5:20). And if perhaps melancholy troubles the mind, the help of the medicine must be sought for in private.

Falling in manners is when any faithful man falls to the committing of some actual sin in life, as Noah's drunkenness, David's adultery, Peter's denial, etc.

To those who are fallen thus, for as much as grace remaining in respect of her virtue and habit may be lost for a time in respect of sense and working, the law must be propounded, being mixed with the gospel, because a new act of sin requires a new act (or work) of faith and repentance. "Ah, sinful nation, a people laden with iniquity, a seed of the wicked, corrupt children: they have forsaken the Lord: they have provoked the holy one of Israel to anger, they are gone backward.... Wash you, make you clean, take away the evil of your works from before mine eyes... Come now, and let us reason together, saith the Lord; Though your sins were as crimson, they shall be made white as snow: though they were red like scarlet, they shall be as wool" (Isa. 1:4, 16, 18).

Condition 7

There is a mingled people.

A mixed people are the assemblies of our churches. To these any doctrine may be propounded, whether of the law or of the gospel, if the limitation[8] and circumscription of the doctrine is made to those persons for whom it is convenient. "Now in the last and great day of the feast, Jesus stood and cried, saying, If any man thirst let him come unto me and drink" (John 7:37). And this was the manner of the prophets in their sermons, to denounce judgments and destruction to the wicked: and to promise deliverance in the Messiah to those

8. In the margin: If it is limited and meant to them.

who do repent. *A doubt.* If any man shall despair in the public congregation, when the rest are hardened, what ought to be done? *Answer.* Let those who are hardened, hear the law circumscribed within the limits of the persons and of the vices, and let the afflicted conscience hear the voice of the gospel applied in special manner unto it.

Chapter 8

The Kinds of Application

Application is either mental or practical.

Mental

Mental is that which respects the mind, and it is either doctrine or redargution.[1] "The whole scripture is given by God's inspiration, and is profitable for doctrine (προς διδασκαλιαν), for redargution (or improving) (προς ελεγμον), for correction (προς επανορθωσιν) and for instruction (προς παιδειαν) in righteousness. That the man of God may be perfect, being perfectly instructed unto every good work" (2 Tim. 3:16–17).

Doctrine is that whereby doctrine (or teaching) is used for the information of the mind to a right judgment concerning things to be believed.

Redargution is that whereby teaching is used for the reformation of the mind from error.

In confutations, which are made publicly before the assembly, these cautions must be used. (1) The thing that is determined (or the state of the question that is to be discussed) must be thoroughly understood. (2) Let those errors only be reproved which trouble the church in which we live. All others, which do either lie dead or are external, [are to be] let alone, unless some danger is ready to ensue from them. "Beware of the leaven of the Pharisees and Sadducees" (Matthew 16). "Take heed, and beware of the leaven of Herod" (Mark 9). The men of Pergamum are warned to beware of the Nicolaitans, to whom some of them did assent (Revelation 2). (3) If the error is out of the foundation of faith, the confutation must not only be Christian-like (as it should ever be), but also a friendly, gentle, and brotherly dissension.

Practical

Practical application is that which respects the life and behavior. And it is instruction (παιδεια) and correction (επανορθωσις).

1. In the margin: Improving, confuting.

Instruction is that whereby doctrine is applied to frame a man to live well in the family,[2] commonwealth, and church. To this place belong consolation and exhortation (Rom. 15:4).

Correction is that whereby the doctrine is applied to reform the life from ungodliness and unrighteous dealing. Hitherto belongs admonition. This must be done, first, generally, the circumstances of the persons being omitted. Nathan brings David to the knowledge of his sin by the help of a general parable (2 Samuel 12). "Ye see and hear, that not only at Ephesus, but almost throughout all Asia, this Paul hath persuaded and turned away much people (because he saith that those are not gods which are made with hands).... Then the town clerk, when he had stayed the people, said, Ye men of Ephesus,... Ye have brought hither these men, which have neither committed sacrilege, neither [do blaspheme] your goddess" (Acts 19:26, 35, 37).

Afterwards, if the former reproof prevails not, it must be urged after a more special manner. "Them that sin, rebuke openly, that the rest may also fear" (1 Tim. 5:20). But always, in the very hatred of sin, let the love of the person appear in the speeches, and let the minister include himself (if he may) in his reprehension, that it may be mild and gentle. "Then Daniel said, My lord, the dream be to them that hate thee, and the interpretation thereof to thine enemies. ... The tree, which thou sawest...it is thou" (Dan. 4:19, 20, 22). "We that are Jews by nature, and not sinners of the Gentiles" (Gal. 2:15). "These things, brethren, I have by a kind of figure translated to myself, and to Apollo for you, that ye might learn by us not to be wise above that which is written" (1 Cor. 4:6).

Now these four kinds of application do offer themselves in every sentence of the Scripture. I will also set down that example which Illyricus has propounded.[3]

"Fear ye not them which kill the body, but are not able to kill the soul: but rather fear him, which is able to destroy both soul and body in hell. Are not two sparrows sold for a farthing, and one of them shall not fall on the ground without your Father? Yea, and all the hairs of your head are numbered. Fear ye not therefore, ye are of more value than many sparrows" (Matt. 10:28–31).

Doctrine. It would be easy to draw from hence many doctrines, partly of the confession of the faith, and partly concerning (God's) providence. (1) That it is needful for us to profess publicly the doctrine[4] which we know, so often as there is need. (2) That we must make confession also with the hazard of goods and life. (3) That our life should be condemned in comparison of Christ

2. In the margin: Or government of the family, *oeconomia*.

3. In the text: Illyricus in his book of the way to understand the Scriptures, Tract. 1.

4. In the margin: Διδασκαλια.

and His truth. (4) That eternal punishments to be suffered both in soul and body are prepared for those who are not afraid to deny Christ and His truth. (5) That God is intent and ready to govern us, that we might make our confession aright. (6) That the providence of God is not only general, but also special, which is diligently occupied about all our smallest matters, yea even the hairs of our head.

Redargution.[5] (1) Those do err, who think it to be sufficient if in heart they do embrace the faith and a right opinion concerning religion, and that it is at a man's choice in the meantime to grant or affirm anything before men, as the condition of the place, time, and persons requires, especially when the life seems to be in imminent danger to be lost. (2) The Epicures err, in that they deny the divine providence, because they think it too base for the majesty of God to take care of human affairs. (3) The Stoics do err, who imagine that all things are governed by the fate (or an irresistible and violent necessity). (4) They do err who make chance and fortune, without any wise ordination of the divine providence. (5) The Pelagians do err in giving more than is due to man's strength, as if it were put in men's power to embrace the faith at their pleasure, to continue constant in the same, and to confess it to the end without fear. (6) They do err, who do lean more upon outward things and inconstant riches than upon the power and goodness of God.

Instruction.[6] (1) You must to the utmost of your power labor to have the true fear of God before your eyes, because you now hear that one God is to be feared above all men. (2) You must learn such a contempt of human things, as that you may always desire, having forsaken them, to depart hence, and to be joined together with Christ in the heavens. (3) The consideration of (God's) special providence does cause you to think of the presence of God, that Beholder, to crave His help, and also to believe that you are helped in all things, and finally that there is no danger so terrible but He both can and will deliver you, when it is fit.

Correction.[7] (1) These words of Christ correct their negligence, who in their prayers do not crave of God sincere love, that being inflamed with it they may not refuse to lay down their life for His name. (2) The negligence of those men is also taxed, who do not acknowledge and behold the providence of God showing itself in all things. (3) Those are reproved, who give not God thanks

5. In the margin: Ελεγχος.
6. In the margin: Παιδεια.
7. In the margin: Επανοθωσις.

for vouchsafing to govern and defend us and all things that belong unto us by His providence. (4) Those are reproved, who abuse the good creatures of God, seeing that it is manifest that God has care of all things.

Thus, any place of Scripture ought to be handled, yet so as that all the doctrines are not propounded to the people, but those only which may be fitly applied to our times and to the present condition of the church. And they must not only be choice ones, but also few, lest the hearers are overcharged with their multitude.

Chapter 9

The Memory in Preaching[1]

Because it is the received custom for preachers to speak by heart[2] before the people, something must be here annexed concerning memory.

Artificial memory, which stands upon places and images, will very easily without labor teach how to commit sermons to the memory. But it is not to be approved. (1) The animation of the image, which is the key of memory, is impious, because it requires absurd, insolent, and prodigious cogitations, and those especially which set an edge upon and kindle the most corrupt affections of the flesh. (2) It dulls wit and memory because it requires a threefold memory for one: the first of the places; the second of the images; [and] the third of the thing that is to be declared.

It is not, therefore, an unprofitable advice, if he who is to preach does diligently imprint in his mind by the help of disposition (either axiomatical, or syllogistical, or methodical) the several doctrines of the place he means to handle, the several proofs and applications of the doctrines, the illustrations of the applications, and the order of them all, in the meantime nothing careful for the words, which (as Horace speaks) "will not unwillingly follow the matter that is premeditated." *Verbaque provisam rem non invita sequentur.*

Their study has many discommodities, who do con their written sermons word for word. (1) It asks great labor. (2) He who through fear does stumble at one word, does both trouble the congregation and confound his memory. (3) Pronunciation, action, and the holy motions of affections are hindered, because the mind is wholly bent on this, to wit, that the memory fainting now under her burden may not fail.

---

1. See Volume 6, *On Memory.*
2. In the margin: *Memoriter.*

Chapter 10

The Uttering of the Sermon

The preparation (or provision) of the sermon has been spoken of hitherto. The promulgation (or uttering) of it follows. In the promulgation two things are required: the hiding of human wisdom, and the demonstration (or showing) of the Spirit.

Requirement 1

Human wisdom must be concealed, whether it is in the matter of the sermon or in the setting forth of the words, because the preaching of the Word is the testimony of God and the profession of the knowledge of Christ and not of human skill, and again because the hearers ought not to ascribe their faith to the gifts of men but to the power of God's Word. "When I came unto you, brethren, I came not with the eminency of eloquence or of wisdom, declaring unto you the testimony of God. For I did not decree to know anything among you but Jesus Christ, and him crucified.... That your faith should not consist in the wisdom of men, but in the power of God" (1 Cor. 2:1–2, 5).

If any man thinks that by this means barbarism should be brought into pulpits, he must understand that the minister may, yea and must, privately use at his liberty the arts, philosophy, and variety of reading, while he is framing his sermon. But he ought in public to conceal all these from the people, and not to make the least ostentation. *Artis etiam est celare artem*; it is also a point of art to conceal art.

Requirement 2

The demonstration of the Spirit is when the minister of the Word does in the time of preaching so behave himself that all, even ignorant persons and unbelievers, may judge that it is not so much he who speaks as the Spirit of God in him and by him. "Neither was my speech and my preaching in the persuasive words of man's wisdom, but in the demonstration of the Spirit and of power" (1 Cor. 2:4). "If all prophesy, and there enter in an unbeliever, or one that is ignorant, he is reproved of all, he is judged of all. And so the secrets of his heart are disclosed, and so falling upon his face, he will worship God, returning word that God indeed is among you" (1 Cor. 14:24–25). "I will come unto you shortly—and I will know not their words[1] that are puffed up, but their power. For the kingdom of God is not in words but in power" (1 Cor. 4:19–20). "I am filled with power by the Spirit of the Lord, and with judgment and might to shew to Jacob his defection, and to Israel his sin" (Micah 3:8). This makes the ministry to be lively and powerful. "And it came to pass, when he had spoken these things, that a certain woman of the multitude lifting up her voice said unto him, Blessed is the womb that bare thee, and the breasts that gave thee suck" (Luke 11:27).

This demonstration is either in speech or in gesture.

Speech

The speech must be spiritual and gracious.

Spiritual

That speech is spiritual which the Holy Spirit does teach. "Which things also we speak, not in the words, which man's wisdom teacheth, but which the Holy Ghost teacheth, comparing spiritual things with spiritual things" (1 Cor. 2:13). And it is a speech both simple and perspicuous, fit both for the people's understanding and to express the majesty of the Spirit. "Paul disputed with them three Sabbath days out of the scriptures. Opening (διανοιγων) and showing that Christ must suffer and rise again" (Acts 17:2–3). "O ye foolish Galatians:—to whom Jesus Christ before was described in your sight, and among you crucified" (Gal. 3:1). "But we have cast from us the cloaks of shame, and walk not in craftiness, neither handle we the word of God deceitfully: but in declaration of the truth we approve ourselves to every man's conscience in the sight of God. If our gospel be then hid, it is hid to them that perish. In whom the god of this world hath blinded the minds, that is, of the infidels…" (2 Cor. 4:2–4).

Wherefore, neither the words of arts nor Greek and Latin phrases and quirks must be intermingled in the sermon. (1) They disturb the minds of the auditors, that they cannot fit those things which went afore with those that follow. (2) A strange word hinders the understanding of those things that are spoken. (3) It draws the mind away from the purpose to some other matter.

Here also the telling of tales and all profane and ridiculous speeches must be omitted.

1. In the margin: *Non verba sed virtutem.*

Gracious

The speech is gracious wherein the grace of the heart is expressed. "And all bare witness of him, and wondered at the gracious words, which proceeded out of his mouth" (Luke 4:22). "The officers answered, never man spoke like this man" (John 7:46).

Grace is either of the person or of the ministry.

Grace of the person is the holiness of the heart and an unblameable life. Howsoever it makes not a minister, yet it is very necessary.

First, the doctrine of the Word is hard both to be understood and to be practiced, therefore the minister ought to express that by his example which he teaches (as it were) by a type. "Not as though ye were lords over God's heritage, but that ye may be examples (τυποι types) to the flock" (1 Peter 5:3). "Be an example to the faithful, both in word and conversation" (1 Tim. 4:12). "Furthermore, brethren, whatsoever things are true, whatsoever things are honest—think on these things. Which ye have both learned, and received, and heard, and seen in me, those things do, and the God of peace shall be with you" (Phil. 4:8–9).[2]

Second, he who is not godly, howsoever he may understand the Scriptures, yet he does not perceive the inward sense and experience of the Word in his heart. "The Lord is good and right, therefore he teacheth sinners his way. He maketh the meek to walk in the law, and teacheth the meek his way" (Ps. 25:8–9). "Surely the Lord God will do nothing, but he revealeth his secret to his servants the prophets" (Amos 3:7). "And the Lord said, Shall I hide from Abraham the thing which I am about to do? Seeing that Abraham shall be indeed the father of a great and mighty nation.... For I know him that he will command his sons and his household after him, that they keep the way of the Lord to do righteousness and judgment" (Gen. 18:17–18, 29).[3]

Third, it is a thing execrable in the sight of God that godly speech should be conjoined with an ungodly life. "Unto the wicked God saith, what hast thou to do to declare mine ordinances, and to take my covenant into thy mouth, seeing thou hatest to be reformed" (Ps. 50:16–17). It is a strange sight to see him who is the guide of the way to others to wander out of the way himself, and to see a physician of others to be full of botches himself in the meanwhile, as [Gregory of] Nazianzen speaks.[4]

2. This paragraph break is not in the original.
3. This paragraph break is not in the original.
4. This paragraph break is not in the original.

Fourth, it is an ecclesiastical secret: that the minister ought to cover his infirmities so that they are not seen. For the simple people behold not the ministry but the person of the minister. Herod heard John [the] Baptist willingly, not because he was a good minister, but because he was a good man (Mark 6:20). Well saith Nazianzens: "He who teaches sound doctrine, and lives wickedly, reaches that with one hand which he clicks away with the other." Chrysostom, upon Matthew 25, says, "The doctor of the church by teaching well and by living well instructs the people how they ought to live well. But by living ill he does instruct God how to condemn him." And in Homily 30 in Acts, he says, "It is an easy matter to show wisdom in words. Teach me to live by your life. This is the best teaching." For words make not such an impression in the soul as works do.[5]

Fifth, a minister who is wicked either openly or secretly is not worthy to stand before the face of the most holy and the almighty God. "Therefore thus saith the Lord, If thou return, then will I bring thee again and thou shalt stand before me" (Jer. 15:19). "Then flew one of the seraphim unto me with a hot coal in his hand, which he had taken from the altar with the tongs. And he touched my mouth and said, Lo, this hath touched thy lips, and thine iniquity shall be taken away, and thy sin shall be purged. Also, I heard the voice of the Lord, saying, Whom shall I send? and who shall go for us? Then I said, Here am I, send me" (Isa. 6:6–8). "Then Moses said to Aaron, This is that which the Lord said, I will be sanctified in them that come near unto me, and I will be glorified before the sight of all the people" (Lev. 10:3). And hence it is that the judgments of God remain for wicked ministers to tremble at. "Therefore the sin of the young men was very great before the Lord: for men abhorred the offering of the Lord.... They obeyed not the voice of their father, because the Lord meant to slay them" (1 Sam. 2:17, 25).

The parts of sanctity are especially [these]: (1) A good conscience. "For our rejoicing is this, the testimony of our conscience, that in simplicity and godly sincerity, and not in fleshly wisdom, but by the grace of God, we have had our conversation in the world" (2 Cor. 1:12). "Keeping faith and a good conscience, which some having put away as concerning the faith have made shipwreck" (1 Tim. 1:19). "And herein I endeavor myself to have alway a clear conscience towards God, and towards men" (Acts 24:16). If this is wanting, the mouth of the speaker is shut. "Their watchmen are all blind: they have no knowledge, they are all dumb dogs, they cannot bark, they lie and sleep, and delight in sleeping" (Isa. 56:10). (2) An inward feeling of the doctrine to be delivered. Wood, that is capable of fire, does not burn unless fire is put to it. And he

5. This paragraph break is not in the original.

must first be godly affected himself, who would stir up godly affections in other men. Therefore, what motions a sermon does require, such the preacher shall stir up privately in his own mind, that he may kindle up the same in his hearers. (3) The fear of God, whereby, being thoroughly stricken with a reverent regard of God's majesty, he speaks soberly and moderately. (4) The love of the people. "But were gentle amongst you, as a nurse that cherisheth her children" (1 Thess. 2:7). And that this affection may appear, the minister's duty is to pray seriously and fervently for the people of God. "God forbid that I should sin against the Lord and cease praying for you" (1 Sam. 12:23). (5) The minister must also be venerable, that is, such a one as is to be reverenced for constancy, integrity, gravity, and truth-speaking, who also knows how to perform reverence to others either privately or publicly, as is befitting the persons of all his hearers. (6) He must be temperate, who restrains inwardly his over vehement affections, and has his outward fashions and gestures moderate and plain, by the which dignity and authority may be procured and preserved. Therefore, he must be neither covetous (αφιλαργυρον, a lover of silver) nor a follower of wine (παροινον), nor litigious, nor a striker, nor wrathful. And let the young men exercise themselves to godliness, and flee the lusts of youth (1 Tim. 4:7).

The grace of the ministry is [the following]: (1) To be apt to teach (διδακτικον ειναι) (1 Tim. 3:2). Now Paul's meaning is that it is not only decent and laudable if this gift is had, but also that it is so necessary as that it may not be wanting. For this consideration Nazianzen refused a bishopric, and Theophylact upon this place says that "this duty of teaching is especially of all others necessary to be found in bishops." In the Nicene and Miletian Councils, this was imposed instead of a punishment, to hold the name of a minister but not to preach the gospel. (2) Authority, whereby he speaks as the ambassador of the great Jehovah. "These things speak and exhort, and rebuke with all authority" (Titus 2:15). "If any man speak, let him speak as the oracles of God" (1 Peter 4:11). (3) Zeal, whereby being most desirous of God's glory he does endeavor to fulfill and execute the decree of election concerning the salvation of men by his ministry. "I am full of matter, and the spirit within me compelleth me. Behold, my belly is as the wine which hath no vent, and like the new bottles that blast" (Job 32:18–19). "Instructing them—proving if God at any time will give them repentance, that they may know the truth" (2 Tim. 2:25). "Admonishing every man—that we may present every man perfect in Christ Jesus" (Col. 1:28–29).

Gesture

Gesture is either in the action of the voice or of the body.

The voice ought to be so high that all may hear. "Cry aloud, and spare not: lift up thy voice like a trumpet" (Isa. 58:1). "In that last and great day of the feast

Jesus stood up and cried" (John 7:37). "And Peter standing with the eleven lift up his voice and said" (Acts 2:14).

In the doctrine he ought to be more moderate, in the exhortation more fervent and vehement.

Let there be that gravity in the gesture of the body which may grace the messenger of God. It is fit, therefore, that the trunk or stalk of the body, being erect and quiet, all the other parts (as the arms, hands, face, and eyes) have such motions as may express and (as it were) utter the godly affections of the heart. The lifting up of the eye and the hand signifies confidence. "Solomon made a brazen scaffold, and set it in the midst of the court—and upon it he stood, and kneeled down upon his knees before all the congregation of Israel, and stretched out his hands toward heaven. And said, O Lord God of Israel..." (2 Chron. 6:13–14). "And Stephen being full of the Holy Ghost, bending his eyes up to heaven beheld the glory of God" (Acts 7:55). The casting down of the eyes signifies sorrow and heaviness. "But the publican standing afar off would not so much as lift up his eyes unto heaven, but he smote his breasts, saying, God be merciful to me a sinner" (Luke 18:13).

Concerning the gesture other precepts cannot be delivered; only, let the example of the gravest ministers in this kind be in [the] stead of a rule.

Chapter 11

The Conceiving of Prayer

Hitherto has been spoken concerning [the] preaching of the Word. It remains now to speak of the conceiving of prayers. This is the second part of prophesying, whereby the minister is the voice of the people in calling upon God. "One of his disciples said unto him, Lord, teach us to pray, as John also taught his disciples" (Luke 11:1). See 1 Sam. 14:24. Here are to be considered:

First, the matter of prayer. First, the wants and sins of the people, and then the graces of God and the blessings they stand in need of. "I exhort therefore above all things, that supplications…be made for all men. For kings and those that are in authority…" (1 Tim. 2:1–2). Tertullian says, "We do all pray for all emperors that they may obtain a long life, a quiet reign, a safe family, courageous armies, a faithful counsel, loyal subjects, a peaceable world, and whatsoever things are desired of a man and of Caesar." Again, "We pray for emperors, for their ministers and powers, for the state of the time, for the quietness of their affairs, and for the delaying of their death."[1] The Lord's prayer reduces this matter to six heads, which are God's glory, kingdom, obedience, the preservation of the life, the remission of sins, and the strengthening of the spirit.

Second, the form of prayer. (1) Let there be one voice, and that the minister's alone, the people being in the meanwhile silent, and showing their assent at the end by saying "Amen." "Who when they had heard these things, they lift up their voice with one accord unto God, and said…" (Acts 4:24). "And Ezra praised the Lord the great God, and all the people answered, Amen, Amen" (Neh. 8:6). "Else, when thou blessest with the spirit, how shall he that supplieth the place of the unlearned say Amen at thy giving of thanks" (1 Cor. 14:16). Justin says, "When the president has finished his prayers and thanksgivings, all the people who are present cry out with a favorable approbation, saying, Amen."[2] (2) Let the voice be understood. "I will pray with the spirit, I will pray also with the understanding: I will sing with the spirit, I will sing with the understanding

1. In the text: *Apolog.*

2. In the text: In his second apology to Antoninus. Athanasius, Apolog. ad Constant. Imp. Euseb. lib. 7. cap. 8; Jerome, Proœm. 2, in Galatians.

also" (1 Cor. 14:15). (3) Let the voice be continued, not jagged and abrupt, that idle repetitions (βαττολογησητε) may be avoided (Matt. 6:7).

Third, the parts [of prayer], which are three: consideration, ordering, and uttering of it. Consideration is that whereby fit matter for the framing of prayers is diligently searched for. Ordering is that whereby the matter being found out is disposed in the mind in a certain order. Prolation (or uttering) of it is that whereby it is orderly pronounced in public to the edifying of the people.

Trin-uni Deo gloria

The order and sum of the sacred and only method of preaching:

1. To read the text distinctly out of the canonical Scriptures.
2. To give the sense and understanding of it, being read, by the Scripture itself.
3. To collect a few and profitable points of doctrine out of the natural sense.
4. To apply (if he has the gift) the doctrines rightly collected to the life and manners of men in a simple and plain speech.

The sum of the sum:

Preach one Christ
by Christ
to the praise of Christ.

The writers who lent their help to the framing of this *Art of Prophesying* are Augustine, Hemingius, Hyperius, Erasmus, Illyricus, Wigandus, Jacobus Matthias, Theodorus Beza, Franciscus Junius.

Soli Deo Gloria

Epieikeia

or

A Treatise of Christian Equity and Moderation

Delivered publicly in lectures by M. W. Perkins,
and now published by the consent of his
assignees in Cambridge, by a preacher of the Word.

"Forgive one another, as God for Christ's sake
doth forgive you" (Eph. 4:31).

Printed by John Legate,
printer to the University of Cambridge.

1604

The Epistle Dedicatory

To the Right Honorable, the Lord Sheffield, Lord Lieutenant and Lord President[1]; Sir Thomas Heskith,[2] Sir John Benet,[3] Knights; Charles Hales, R. William, Cutbert Pepper,[4] John Ferne[5], Esquires; and the rest of his Majesty's Honorable Council[6]; established in the north parts, and under his Highness, the highest patrons of equity, grace and peace from Jesus Christ.

Right honorable and worshipful, how famous in all writers [was] the year eighty-eight, and how fatal it was made by all the old and later conjecturers, is not unknown to any of you.[7] But how the issue answered the expectation, I see not, save only in that notable overthrow of the enemies of God, the papists, whereupon our reverend countryman, and Christ's champion for England,[8] said very well: *Octogesimus octavus, mirabilis annus, Clade Papistarum, faustus ubiq pijs.*

But if ever [a] year deserved to be famous in English chronicles, it is this year. I cannot tell whether I should say 1602 or 1603, whether God's anger was more in taking from us such a queen (as for ought I [have] read) the world never had, or His mercy [was more] in giving us such a king as England never had. I leave it to better heads to be determined. How is the name of our God to

1. Lord Sheffield, 1565?–1646. Fought under Leicester in Netherlands; commanded one of the ships that defeated Spanish Armada. He was lord-lieutenant of Yorkshire and president of the council of the North. *DNB* 18:11.

2. Sir Thomas Hesketh, 1548–1605. Supporter of Puritans. From Yorkshire. Buried in Westminster Abbey, monument on north choir aisle.

3. Perhaps Sir John Bennet, c. 1553–1627. Member of the council of the North and member of Parliament.

4. Cuthbert Pepper, d. 1608. Member of the council of the North and member of Parliament. A very godly man. *History of Parliament, 1558–1603.*

5. Sir John Ferne (c. 1609). In 1595, the queen appointed him deputy-secretary of the council of the North at York. *DNB* 6:1237.

6. Dedicated to them because they were in the office of executing judgment.

7. 1588, the defeat of the Spanish Armada.

8. In the margin: Fulk. in Pref. in Test. Rhem.

be magnified, by whose mercy so great a loss is made no loss, but a gain unto us? For who sees not that all her princely virtues do not only live in him, but [are] also in him (being a man) more perfect and accomplished? She is dead, but her heroic zeal and love to religion is alive. She bequeathed it with her kingdom to his Highness, who doubtless will make both her religion and her kingdom to flourish as much as a man does excel a woman. And who knows not that the enemies of our religion and our peace (notwithstanding all their political dissembled brags to the contrary) do find his Majesty so little for their purpose that now they would sing a thousand masses to have her alive again, against whom they thundered out so many curses and excommunications,[9] and after whose blood they so thirsted while she lived? What straits are they driven into? Who would wish her alive again, at whose hands (though a woman) they never gained, nor got one inch of ground in forty-four years, though nine or ten popes, and ten thousand of their slaves,[10] wrestled with her all the while, with all the power, policy, craft, and treachery, which the devil could lend them.[11]

Nay, her end was as glorious as her beginning, and her last proclamation against them was more to their shame and less to their comfort than ever any in her life before. And she was so far from allowing them a toleration of their intolerable religion in her old and, therefore, weakest age, as that it never entered into her royal heart, nor did she ever think it worthy to be made a question, whether it should be or not. No, she halted not between two religions; but to her Baal was Belial and, therefore, she banished him, and God was the Lord and, therefore, she served Him [1 Kings 18:21]. She was resolved that Dagon must [come] down if God's ark [would] stand, or else, if Dagon [would] stand, [then] the ark must [be taken] away (1 Sam. 5:2–4). For both together cannot stand upright. She held that as Dagon fell down when the enemies themselves brought the ark into Dagon's temple, so if the Israelites should have admitted Dagon into God's temple, that the Lord Himself would have removed His ark from them.[12]

Blessed was she in her life, and twice blessed [was she] in her end. She lost not her first love, and her works were more at the last than at the first. And blessed are we who enjoyed her [for] so long, and more blessed [are we] who under her enjoyed such forty-four years as all the books in the world cannot show under a woman. But most blessed of all in that, after such a David, God has sent us such a Solomon, after such a woman, such a man, after such

9. In the margin: Pius 5. Gregorius 13. Sixtus 5.

10. In the margin: Paulus 4. Pius 4. Pius 5. Gregorius 13. Sixtus 5. Urbanus 7. Gregorius 14. Innocent 6. Clement. 9.

11. This paragraph break is not in the original.

12. This paragraph break is not in the original.

a queen, such a king, who will make an end of many a Joab, and many a Shimei, which she could not so well do, and [he will] finish that temple which she so well began. And [he] (I doubt not to affirm it), do the devil and the crafty papist all they can, is the chief champion of Christ Jesus upon the face of the earth.

And how happy a year shall this be, if the losses which learning has sustained are as well recompensed. Junius of Leiden, Tossaine of Heidelberg, Perkins of Cambridge, besides many others of inferior note, have been taken from us this year. Happy should those three famous universities be, if the like were seated in their rooms. Let us leave the first to the lower [Germany] [and] the second to the higher Germany, to praise them, to lament them, and to make supply for them. It is the third who especially concerns us. What loss the church of God, and in the church, England, and in the Church of England, the ministry, and in the ministry, the universities, and in the universities, the younger students, have sustained by the untimely death of that reverend man! I think [it] is not unknown to any of you. For how should he be unknown to any (of any note) in England, whose name and estimation is such in other nations as that at one mart[13, 14] we find that in one half year two of his books[15] were translated into Latin and four were printed beyond the seas. The best recompense of this loss is the fruit of his labors, which he has left behind him, whereof some were written by himself and others taken by other men from his mouth. All [of these], at least as many of them as may be perfected, there is hope we shall in time enjoy. Had not Johannes Budæus and Carolus Jonvillaus done so to Calvin,[16] [and] Vitus Theodorus, Johannes Frederus, and Justus Jonas done so to Luther,[17] many worthy works of those two great instruments of God [would have] utterly perished. And had not some done so to this worthy man, no doubt many sweet blasts of that silver trumpet of God [would have] vanished away.[18]

For my part, though time is precious unto me other ways, yet I think that time well spent which I may bestow in preparing anything of his for the press. This discourse of *Equity* now made ready, as a child born after his father's death, I present to your honorable view and patronage. If any asks why I dare

13. *Mart*: major trade fair/market.
14. In the margin: Nund. Frank. ver. 603.
15. In the margin: Catholicus Reformatus, de Morte, de Vita, Prophetia.
16. In the margin: Calvin in Dan.
17. In the margin: Luther in Genes. in Hos., etc.
18. This paragraph break is not in the original.

tender so small a gift to so great personages, my only answer is [that] I make the judges of equity the patrons of equity. God grant you a long and honorable state under our worthy Solomon. Amen. From my study, September 10, 1603.

Your honors' and worships' in the Lord,
W. Crashawe

To the Christian Reader

I do here present unto you (Christian brother) a small discourse of *Equity*, delivered by that faithful laborer in the harvest of God, M. William Perkins, in a few lectures. The discourse is little and brief, but the matter is pithy and the use [is] profitable. Equity and Christian moderation, whether public or private, is the true badge of Christianity. Without public equity, what is the court of justice but turned into the seat of iniquity? And without private equity, what is man's life, human society, neighborhood, nay friendship, nay kindred, nay marriage itself, but even a potion of poison in a golden cup? Are you, therefore, a magistrate? Here you are taught how to discharge your place in the execution of the laws as shall neither be unbecoming the lenity[1] of a Christian nor the severity of a magistrate. Are you a private man? Here you are taught how to carry yourself in all dealing and bargaining with another, how to demean yourself toward your wife, servant, child, friend, [and] neighbor, in such [a] manner as if you had all the comforts and contentments of this earth, yet the practice hereof shall make them all ten times more comfortable, and the want hereof shall turn all their sweetness into gall and wormwood. When, therefore, you read this little book, and withal (laying it to your life) do find the truth of it in your course and conversation, then acknowledge the Spirit of God in this holy man (who now sleeps in peace), praise God for him, bewail his loss, and help me and others with your holy prayers, that we may still go forward in this good work of publishing his godly labors and in delivering out to the church of God these jewels, which the Lord from his mouth gave us to keep, not for our own, but for the common good.

Your brother in Christ Jesus,
W. C.

1. *Lenity:* kindness.

"Let your moderation of mind be known to all men; the Lord is at hand" (Phil. 4:5).

In this chapter, the apostle gives sundry exhortations to many Christian duties. In the first verse, [he exhorts] to perseverance in faith and true religion. In the second and third verses, [he exhorts] to mutual concord. In the fourth verse, [he exhorts] to a spiritual joy in the Lord. In the fifth verse, he exhorts to the virtue of equity (or moderation of mind). Our English translations commonly read it thus: "Let your patient mind be known to all men." Though it is truly and well said, yet the translated words have a larger and fuller significance. Therefore, according to the nature and force of the words, I rather choose to read it thus: "Let your equity or moderation of mind be known to all men." The words contain two parts.

Part 1: An Exhortation

"Let your equity be known to all men." The drift and scope of the exhortation is to persuade the Philippians, and in them the whole church, to the practice of equity.

Now this equity, whereunto the holy apostle so earnestly exhorts, is a worthy Christian virtue, so excellent as the careful practice thereof is the marrow and strength of a commonwealth, and where it is there cannot but be peace and contentment in all estates. And [it is] so necessary [that] without the practice of it, no house, family, society, city, commonwealth, kingdom, or church, can stand or continue. Indeed, a kingdom may be established by force and arms, by violence and cruelty, but it cannot stand or continue without this equity and Christian moderation between man and man. Nay, civil society and common dealing between man and man cannot continue, unless one man yields to another. In a word, there can be no peace in families, no sound nor lasting love between man and wife, nor any comfortable quietness, where one does not yield to the other and one [does not] bear with another in many things. And if it is so in marriage, which is the nearest conjunction and the most excellent and perfect society which is in this world, then it is much truer in all other societies of men, that there can be no peace, no Christian neighborhood, no true friendship, unless one bears with another and one carries himself toward another in an even and moderate course.

Seeing, therefore, this is [such] a necessary and excellent virtue, I have purposed to speak of it at large. Let us then examine these two points: (1) the nature of it; and (2) the kinds of it.

Point 1: The Nature of Christian Equity

For the first, Christian equity is a rare and excellent virtue whereby men use a true mean and an equal moderation in all their affairs and dealings with men for the maintaining of justice and preservation of peace. I take this to be the true description of the general nature of this virtue.

And herein, first, I say it is a virtue which is conversant about practicing a moderation in all our courses and dealings with men. For we (men) can use no mean nor moderation with God, but if we do evil, it is all too much, and if we do good, it is all too little. Again, equity (or moderation) is to be performed by God toward men, and not by men toward God. For if men deal not equally toward God, the fault is theirs and not His. God is not the worse for it. But if God dealt not moderately with men, the world would not last one hour. And, lastly, where there are no faults, there is no forgiveness [and] where [there are] no infirmities, there needs [be] no moderation. But in God there is no want, no error, no imperfection. But His love, His mercy, and His works of love and mercy toward mankind, and to His church especially, are most perfect. Therefore, there needs [be] no moderation, nor forbearance toward God, but toward men, who, being flesh and blood and full of infirmities (from which regeneration itself does not fully free us) do therefore stand in need of this virtue to be practiced among them. Else, their society and fellowship cannot endure. And further, all men in this case are alike, and therefore one has good cause to bear with another. The prince is flesh and blood as well as his subjects. The husband is flesh and blood as well as the wife. The pastor is a man as his people and hearers are. Hence, it follows that one is subject to infirmities as well as another. And, therefore, I conclude that in all our courses and dealings of man with man in this world, there must be practiced a Christian moderation.

Second, I say in the description that the end of this virtue is to maintain justice and preserve peace. These two are the very sinews and strength of a Christian kingdom. For where we do not to other men as we would others should do to us, there is no justice. And where we will not pass by small faults and forbear infirmities, there can be no peace. Such is the excellency of this virtue [that] it serves to maintain two other such great and principal virtues as are even the heart and the brain of the commonwealth, namely justice and peace.

Point 2: The Kinds of Christian Equity

But for the more exact and particular knowledge of the nature of this necessary virtue, let us descend to the particular branches and kinds of it. Christian equity, therefore, is either public or private.

Public Equity

Public equity is that which is practiced in public meetings and assemblies of men, as in courts of justice, assizes, sessions, councils, parliaments, and such like. The matter, whereabout this public equity is conversant, is the right and convenient, and the moderate and discrete, execution of the laws of men.

Branch 1: The Law of Man

Laws of men, made by lawful authority according to God's law, and for the common good, are (and are to be esteemed as) bones and sinews to hold together, props and pillars to uphold, the commonwealth and all societies. God, therefore, has given to kings, and to their lawful deputies, power and authority, not only to command and execute His own laws, commanded in His Word, but also to ordain and enact other good and profitable laws of their own for the more particular government of their people, and to be helps for the better executing of the laws of God; and also to annex a punishment and penalty to the said laws, which penalty is to be according to the quality of the fault, greater or less, insomuch that they may in many cases (if the common good so requires) inflict even death itself. And, further, God has given [to] these gods upon earth a power as to make these laws and annex these punishments, so also, upon men's defaults and breaches, He has given them authority to execute the law so made, and to inflict upon the offender the punishment annexed.

Now, because this point is of great moment in a commonwealth, and the true knowledge and due practice thereof is the glory and beauty of a kingdom, therefore for the better direction herein, both of prince and people, magistrate and people governed, let us enter further into the consideration thereof.

In the laws of commonwealths, two things are to be considered, the sight whereof will give great light to know more perfectly what this public equity is. These are (1) the extremity of the law, and (2) the mitigation of the law. Both [of] these are put into the hand of the magistrate by God Himself, to be ordered according to his discretion and as the circumstances require. And of them in order.

First, the extremity of the law is when any law of man is urged and executed straightly and precisely, according to the literal sense and strict form of the words and the most exact meaning that can be made out of the words, without any manner of relaxation, at that time when there is good and convenient cause of mitigation in regard of the offending person. This point cannot be well expressed in fewer words.

The principal and most material clause in this description of extremity is in these words: "at that time when there is just cause of mitigation in regard of the offending person." For if there is no good cause of mitigation, then it is not called "extremity," but "justice of the law." But when there is [a] good cause why, in a Christian consideration of some circumstances, this justice should be mitigated, and yet [it] is not, but contrariwise [it] is extremely urged and pressed to the furthest, then it is extremity. Now, this extremity of the law is in this case so far from justice as indeed it is flat injustice. And herein is the proverb true: *summum jus, summa injuria*; that is, the extremity of the law is extreme injury. And [this is what] the Holy Spirit means in Ecclesiastes 7:16, "Be not over just"; that is, press not justice too far, nor urge it too extremely in all cases, lest sometimes you make the name of justice a cover for cruelty.

Now, besides this, there is a second thing in the hand of the magistrate, namely the moderation, relaxation, or mitigation of this extremity. And that is when the proper form of the words and the strictest meaning of the law is not urged, and the punishment prescribed in the law is moderated, lessened, deferred, or (it may be) remitted, upon good and sufficient reason, and in such cases as whereof the law speaks not directly nor the law-maker did purposely aim at. The ground of this mitigation is because no law-makers (being men) can foresee or set down all cases that may fall out. Therefore, when the case alters, then the discretion of the law-maker must show itself, and [he must] do that which the law cannot do.

This mitigation, as well as the extremity, is in the hand of the magistrate. Nay, it, as well as the former, is a part of his duty. And he who neglects to mitigate the extremity when [there] is just occasion offends, as does he who neglects to execute the extremity when there is need. Therefore, as he who has no knowledge or care to execute the law is [in] no way fit to be a judge, so he who can do nothing but urge the law and the plain words of the law, and is not able also to mitigate the rigor of the law when need so requires, is but half a judge. Therefore, every magistrate is to practice this with the other, and not to separate those things which God has joined.

But now, lest this moderation and mitigation of man's laws (which is the practice of public equity) should turn to the maintenance of malefactors, the abolishing of laws, the despising or weakening of authority (which in these days little needs), we must therefore remember this caution: there must be no mitigation but [that which is] honest, profitable, and convenient. If any man asks when it is so, I answer, in three cases: first, when the mitigation stands with the law of nature; second, when it agrees with the moral law or any part of the written Word; [and,] third, when an inferior law is overruled or countermanded by a higher law. In these three cases, the moderation of men's laws and the mitigation of the punishment due by the extremity of these laws is honest and good, and may (and ought to) be practiced. But if it is contrary and not warranted by some of these, then that mitigation is flat injustice and a manifest wrong unto the law.

That the difference of these two, the extremity and mitigation, may be better discerned, let us consider it in some examples. It is the law of England, and many other countries, that the thief shall die. Now though the Word of God has not the same punishment in plain terms, yet the law is good and warrantable, as shall appear in the sequel, and I think [it] is doubted of by none. The drift of this law is to repress that common and general sin of thievery, a prevailing sin, as any other, and [it is] so far prevailing [that] the rigor of good laws is necessarily required for the repressing of it, so that this law was made for the cutting off of such rotten members as do but corrupt others, and of whose amendment there is no hope.

Now, suppose a young boy, pinched with hunger, cold, and poverty, steals meat, apparel, and other things for relief, being pressed to it by want, and not having knowledge or grace to use better means. To put this person to death for this act is the extremity of the law in respect of the circumstances of the person who did it, being a child, and of the end for which he did it, to relieve his wants.

Now the moderation in this case is [based] upon these considerations: (1) he is not an old or practiced thief, but young and corrigible, one who (being reformed) may live long and prove [to be] a good member in the commonwealth; (2) his theft was not heinous, but the things he stole were of small value; and (3) he did it not upon a malicious, cruel, and injurious intent, but to relieve his hunger and want. The equity (or moderation) in this case, I say, is not to inflict death (for that would be extremity), but to determine a punishment less than death, yet such a one as shall be sufficient to reform the party from his sin, to punish the fault, to terrify others, and to satisfy the law.

Thus, it manifestly appears in this example what moderation is and what extremity is (which is contrary to it). And we might see the same in many more [examples].

Now, having thus considered these two together, hereupon we may see what this public equity is, namely, nothing else but a moderation and mitigation of the extremity of a law upon honest and convenient reasons, and in such cases as were not directly intended in the law. The observation and due practice of this equity is the glory, credit, and honor of all public assemblies, as assizes, sessions, and courts of justice. And without the observation of this (when need be), all that they do is flat injustice in that case. For they lame and maim the law; they fulfill but the one part of the law. For in every law there are these two things: the extremity in plain terms, and the implied mitigation. And these two together make the law perfect. And the glory of the law stands in [the] practicing of mitigation as well as in the execution of extremity, nay sometimes it stands in the mitigation and not in the extremity, insomuch as the moderation is then the equity of the law and the extremity is more injustice.

And as this is the glory of the law, so it is the glory of judges and magistrates thus to execute the laws and to temper them with such discretion as neither too much mitigation does abolish the law nor too much extremity leaves no place for mitigation. Therefore (to make an end of this point), two sorts of men are here reproveable.

First, such men as, by a certain foolish kind of pity, are so carried away that [they] would have nothing but "mercy, mercy," and would have all punishments, forfeitures, penalties, either quite taken away and remitted, or at least lessened and moderated. They would also have the extremity of the law executed on no man. This is the high way to abolish laws, and consequently to pull down authority, and so in the end to open a door to all confusion, disorder, and to all licentiousness of life. But I need not say much herein, for there are but few who offend in this kind, man's nature being generally inclined rather to cruelty than to mercy. This fault proceeds either from a weakness of wit and an effeminateness of mind, and then a man is unfit to be a judge, or else from vain glory and a base and affected popularity, and such a man is unworthy to be a judge.

But in the second place, this doctrine, and the very scope of this text, condemns another sort of men who are more cumbersome, that is to say, such men as have nothing in their mouths, but "the law, the law" and "justice, justice." In the meantime, [they] forget that justice always shakes hands with her sister mercy, and that all laws allow a mitigation. The causes of this evil are two.

[The first is] the general corruption of man's nature, which is always ready to deal too hardly with other men, as also too mildly with themselves and partially in their own causes.

And, second, for the most part, such men do gain more by law than by equity, more by extremity than by mitigation. As the soldier lives better by war than by peace, and as the flesh-fly (that cannot feed on the sound flesh) feeds on the wound, so these men gain by law that which they can never get by equity. For equity and moderation breed unity, and if all men were at unity, what should become of them? But extremity breeds variance, for (in reason) one extremity draws on another, and so in men's variances they are set on work, and the more the better for them. These men, therefore, stick so precisely on their points and on the very tricks and trifles of the law, as (so the law is kept, and that in the very extremity of it) they care not, though equity is trodden underfoot [as long as] law may reign upon the earth and they by it. They care not, though mercy takes her to her wings, and flies to heaven. These men (for all their goodly shows) are the decayers of our estate and enemies to all good government. For though they have nothing in their mouths but "justice, justice," and have banished mercy, yet let them know that justice will not stay where mercy is not. They are sisters, and [they] always go hand in hand. They are the two pillars that uphold the throne of the prince. As you cannot hold mercy where justice is banished, so you cannot keep justice where mercy is exiled. And as mercy without justice is foolish pity, so justice without mercy is cruelty. So that, as these men have banished mercy, so within a short time they will send justice after her, and cruelty and oppression will come in their rooms, which are the very overthrow of all estates.

These men (when they are made practicers of the law, judges or magistrates), are to learn this lesson, which the Holy Spirit here teaches: "Let your equity be known to all men." And let all magistrates think it their honor to be counted [as] merciful judges. Let them rejoice to show mercy when there is cause, as well as to execute extremity when there is desert. And let them labor for that Christian wisdom and discretion whereby they may be able to discern when mercy and mitigation should take place, and when extremity should be executed. If inferior judges or magistrates are negligent herein, then we must have recourse to the prince, the highest judge on earth, and under God the first fountain of justice and mercy, whose care must be that as justice and mercy (not one of them, but both together) do uphold his throne and fasten the crown upon his head, so he likewise sees them both maintained, and takes order that in the execution of his own laws there is always room for mercy and mitigation as well as for justice and extremity. He must do this because his laws cannot be as God's laws are. God's laws are perfect and absolute, and of such a universal righteousness that, at all times and in all places, they are of equal strength and of the same equity in all cases. And, therefore, [they] are to be executed without dispensation, relaxation, or any mitigation, which cannot be offered unto them but with injury and violation. But men's laws, coming from their own wits, are imperfect, and so in all cases they do not hold the same equity, and therefore [they] must needs be executed with a discreet and wise moderation. This moderation is public equity, and this public equity is the scope of this text, and the due practice of it in the execution of man's laws is the glory of all Christian commonwealths.

Hitherto of the first and principal branch of public equity.

Branch 2: The Life of Man

To proceed further. As this public equity principally stands in the moderation of the laws of men, so it descends more especially even to all the public actions of a man's life. So that, by the rule and direction of this equity, thus described, men may know how to guide themselves in suing bonds and taking forfeitures, and how men may with good conscience carry themselves in suretyships, in taking of fines, in letting of leases, and in all manner of mutual bargains between man and man. By virtue of this, a man may see how to frame all these and such like actions in such sort as [he] himself shall reap enough credit and gain, and his neighbor help and succor by him.

For in forfeitures of bonds, lands, or leases, in suretyships, rents, or fines, and [in] all other dealings of men together, there are these two things: first, the extremity, that is, that which the law will afford a man in that case; and, second, the moderation of the extremity upon good and convenient reasons. Let us consider them in a few examples.

A man is bound to another in a hundred pound, to pay fifty a day. The same man, not by negligence, but by some necessity, breaks his day, and afterwards brings the principal debt. Now, it is extremity to take the forfeiture in this case, though the law does yield it. And if a man stands upon this extremity, he deals not honestly and equally, but hardly and extremely, with his neighbor. And the law cannot free him in this case from manifest injustice.

What then is the moderation in this case? Even this, to take your own and remit the forfeiture. The reason is because the cause and ground of appointing a forfeiture was not for advantage, but only for the better security of the principal, which, seeing you have, you have that which the law did intend [for] you.

Again, his breach was not willful or with purpose to hurt you, but against his will. If, therefore, you are directly damnified by his missing your day (without all equivocation), then take your reasonable damages out of his forfeiture. If not, then remit the whole forfeiture. And this moderation is public equity. And without this, there can be no buying or selling, borrowing or lending, between man and man.[1]

See another example. One takes a lease from you for years, to pay you such a rent, and for [his lack of] payment of that rent, his lease [is] to be void. The poor man misses his rent day. Now what says the law? His lease is forfeited. But to take this advantage is the extremity of the law. The moderation is to remit the same forfeiture in part or in whole, as you shall see reason in equity and

1. This paragraph break is not in the original.

conscience. This moderation is in this case public equity, and without this there can be no letting of lands between man and man.

[The same is so] for fines and rents. The law says that you may make the most of your own. If you stretch this law as far as the very words will bear, then you may make such fines and rents as may grind the faces of the poor so as no man shall live under you. But to do thus is extremity, and beyond the purpose of the law.

The moderation in this case is not to take all you may get, but so to fine and rent your lands as he who takes them may live by them. The reason of this mitigation is because envy and hatred may often make many men offer more for a farm than it is worth, to cross and hurt their neighbor, or to get all into their own hand. Here, therefore, though the law does yield you all that which a man does willingly offer, yet your own conscience must be a law unto you, to make you a moderator of that extremity.

Let these three examples serve for many. Now in these and all other public dealings between men in the world, a man observes public equity when he deals not with his neighbor according to that extremity which the strict words of the law will bear, but according to that moderation which good conscience requires and which the law itself in some cases does admit. By the knowledge of these two, a man who has any conscience may see how to carry himself, in all these civil affairs, in an even, upright, and equal course, and warrantable, not only by the law of the land, but even by the law and Word of God.

And I make this distinction [between] the law of the land and the Word of God, because we are to know this for a rule: that every extremity, which a law in the strictest acceptation does afford, is not warrantable to be urged by the Word of God, and yet notwithstanding it is good, convenient, and requisite that the extremity is warranted by the law because in some cases it must needs be executed. The laws of men may ordain and appoint extremities, but the law of God must tell us when to urge them and when to moderate them. So then, when a man takes the extremity, he does that which is always warrantable by the law, but in some cases is not warrantable by God's Word which commands a mitigation when there is good reason for it. But he who takes the extremity when there is no just cause of mitigating it, and again does mitigate it when there is cause, his course is not only warrantable by the laws of men, but even by the laws of God also. For it is the duty of every Christian man to remember, in all his bargains and dealings, that his manner of dealing must not only be warranted by the laws of the land, but even by God's Word also. And this is to be known and taken for a general rule in all this treatise. And he who will duly consider the true difference [between] extremity and moderation, as they are here described, may see how to carry himself in all his dealings so as they may be warrantable, both by our own laws and by the Word of God.

To return then to the matter, and to end this point of public equity, if any man shall object that this moderation is a wrong to the law, I answer [that] it is not, for it is neither against the law nor altogether beside the law, but only beside the strictest meaning of the law. Nay, it is included in the law, as the extremity is, though not in the same manner. For the extremity is warranted by the law; mitigation is but tolerated. The law allows extremity, but it only admits a mitigation. So then, both extremity and mitigation are within the law, but it is principally in the hand of the magistrate, and in some cases of other men, to discern the several circumstances when the one is to be executed and when the other. For sometimes one is the justice of the law, and sometimes the other. And according as these two are justly and wisely executed or neglected, so is the justice of the law executed or neglected.

The want of this equity in men's public actions is the cause of much cruelty, oppression, and inequality in dealings between man and man, because extremity is for the most part only regarded, and mitigation is banished out of all bargains. And it is impossible to keep good conscience in forfeitures of bonds, and in forfeiture of lands, suretyships, fines, rents, and such kinds of actions, unless there is due regard to the practice of this public equity. Men, therefore, must consider that they are Christians, and live in a Christian commonwealth, and they must not stand only upon the law and the advantage that the law gives. As they are men, they have a law of the country which may allow extremity, but as they are Christians, they live under a law of God, the eternal law, which must judge them at the last day – the righteous law, which no creature shall ever be able to blame of injustice or of extremity. And men must know that God Himself commands this equity of one man to another.

But if men, for the fear of God, will not deal equally and moderately with them who are in their power, but stand strictly upon forfeitures and other extremities, then the godly magistrate must exercise his power, and by the force of his authority cause them to mitigate their extremity, and to put in practice that equity which becomes Christians. And let every judge and magistrate know that by the law of the everlasting God, he not only may, but is bound thus, to do to them who will not do it of themselves. It may be, therefore, good counsel to all men to practice this Christian equity of themselves rather than to be compelled to it by authority. For every virtue and good work, the freer and more voluntary it is, the more acceptable it is to God and [the] more commendable before men. And let all men remember that whereas the strict words of men's laws seem to give them leave to urge the extremity, yet that cannot excuse them nor free them from the danger of God's law, which commands them to practice Christian equity and moderation.

Now before we make an end of this public equity, one point is necessary to be handled in [a] few words. Some may object, if moderation is intended and included in our law as well as extremity, why then is extremity only mentioned in the law, and not this mitigation which they so much do urge unto us? The answer is ready. The law expresses and urges the extremity to fray[2] men thereby from coming within the danger of the extremity, and [it] conceals the mitigation lest it should be an encouragement to offend, yet, intending it as well as the extremity, and leaving it in the hands of the magistrate to put in practice when just occasion is offered, as well as the extremity. Herein appears the great wisdom of the law-makers, our ancient forefathers, who well and wisely foresaw that though mitigation is as necessary as extremity, and oftentimes more, yet because of the ill consciences of most men, and the readiness of all men to offend, it [is] fitter to express the extremity in plain terms thereby to keep ill men within the compass of obedience, and closely to leave the mitigation to the discretion of the magistrate. So then, our lawgivers concealed the mitigation, and expressed it not in their laws, in good policy and to good purpose. If we, therefore, do only take the extremity, we take only one part of their intent, and show ourselves unwise and shallow witted, who cannot see the wisdom which they closely concealed in wise and Christian policy.

He is not worthy [of] the name of a lawyer, at least of a Christian lawyer, much less worthy [of] the place and seat of a judge, who knows not this. For if the law contained not both [of] these, it would be unrighteous, and so no law. For mitigation is for the good man, and extremity for the evil, careless, and unconscionable man. If there were no extremity, how could the evil man be kept within compass? And how could the poor honest man live, if there were no mitigation? So then, it is warrantable by the Word of God and good conscience that extremity should be in force, and should stand by the law, but so as it always admits of mitigation (when need be).

Let, therefore, our conclusion be to exhort every man, into whose hands is put the execution of laws, to show himself as wise in executing them as our forefathers were in making them; that is, to regard the mitigation, which is concealed, as well as the extremity, which is expressed. So shall the lawmaker's wise intent be performed, public equity preserved, and much injustice and hard dealing prevented.

Now in regard of what has been delivered touching public equity, lawyers must not think that I have gone beyond the compass of my calling and

2. *Fray:* frighten.

encroached upon their liberties. For they are to know that the laws of men are policy, but equity is Christianity. Now Christianity was before there were any laws of men. And, therefore, they must be ordered according to the rules of Christianity. Again, divines must take lawyers' advice concerning extremity and the letter of the law. Good reason then that lawyers take divines' advice touching equity which is the intent of the law. Moreover, their law is but the minister of equity, but our law, the Word of God, is the fountain of equity. Therefore, they must fetch the principal rules of equity from our law, considering that law without equity is plain tyranny. Lastly, in the first Christian commonwealth that ever was, namely, the Jews, the divines (that is, the priests of those days) were the only lawyers. For their positive laws were the judicial laws, given by God Himself, whose interpreters were the priests and Levites. If, therefore, the divines had [at one time] so much to do with positive laws, it may not now be thought amiss if they give advice out of the Word of God touching the equal execution of the laws of men.

Private Equity

And so much touching the doctrine of public equity, grounded upon the Word of God.

Now follows the second kind of equity, called private, namely that which is to be exercised between man and man in their private actions.

But before we go further, some may demand the difference between public and private actions. Private actions of men are such as are practiced among men without any help of the law. As contrariwise, public actions are such as cannot be performed but by the help of the law and the hand of the magistrate. Whereupon it follows that public actions may be between private men, and private actions between public persons. There is a publicness and a privateness (as I may term it) both of men and actions. A man is private until he is exalted unto some authority in church or commonwealth. Then he is a public person. An action is private as long as it is begun and handled between two men, and does not need the public voice nor censure of the law to determine it. [But when it needs these things,] then it is public.[3]

For example, a magistrate may have dealings with another man, or two magistrates together. If they determine it together between themselves, it is a private action because they do it, not as they are magistrates, but as they are men. And so, there is a private action between public persons. So, a private man, no magistrate, may have a trespass, debt, forfeiture, or any other action or

3. This paragraph break is not in the original.

demand against another man, wherein (because he cannot come to a reasonable and equal end by private means) he craves the help of the law and the voice of the magistrate. And so, here is a public action between private men. Now this virtue of equity respects not the publicness or privateness of the persons, but of the actions. Therefore, as that is public equity which is exercised in the determining of public actions, which come to the judgment of the law, so that is private equity which is practiced in the managing of private actions, which are begun and concluded privately between man and man, and never come to public hearing nor trial of the law.

Now let us come to search more nearly[4] into the nature of this virtue. Private equity is a moderate, even, and equal carriage of a man's self in all his private words and deeds, toward all other men and all their words and deeds. First, I say, it is a moderate carriage of a man's self, that is, between both extremes, neither bearing all things nor revenging everything. Second, I say, toward all other men, wherein I comprehend all men and all sorts of men: husbands, wives, magistrates, subjects, teachers, hearers, masters, servants, parents, children, men, women, neighbors in towns, fellows in societies, in service, in labor, etc. In a word, none are excepted, who [in] any way live or converse together. But it is true of all of them that if there is not a moderation and a forbearance one of another, there can be no peace among them, but their lives shall be all (as it were) a hell upon the earth.

Seeing, therefore, the necessity and excellency of this virtue is such that the due practice of it is the ornament of families and societies, and the comfort of a man's life in this world, let us enter into a more particular consideration thereof. Private equity has four degrees (or principal duties): (1) to bear with natural infirmities; (2) to interpret doubtful things in the better part; (3) to depart from our own right sometimes; [and] (4) to forgive private and personal wrongs. Of all these briefly and in order.

Duty 1

The first duty of private equity is to bear with the defects and infirmities of men's natures, with whom we live, as long as they break not out into any great inconvenience or enormity. These infirmities are manifold, as for example: frowardness (or morosity) of nature; hastiness; slowness of conceit; dullness of wit; suspiciousness; desire of praise; and such like. A Christian man must patiently bear and tolerate these, and many other natural infirmities, in those with whom he converses, as with his wife, child, servant, friend, neighbor, etc.

4. *Nearly*: closely.

And he must bear with them so long as they are kept within a mean, and break not out into extremity.[5]

The Holy Spirit speaks of these in Proverbs 19:11, "It is the glory of a man to pass by an infirmity"; that is, if he sees in his brother weaknesses of nature which do not arise from settled malice or cankered corruption. It is always a man's glory and praise so far to moderate himself as not to see them nor to take notice of them, at least not to be moved nor disquieted at them, and oftentimes so little to regard them as though they were not done. To this end the apostle says, "Love suffereth all things" (1 Cor. 13:7); that is, all things that may be borne with good conscience, and are done by them whom we love. Now anything may be borne with good conscience, which is either so private or so small that the wrong is only ours, and no dishonor ensues thereby to God's glory nor ill example to the church. Love suffers all such things. And, indeed, it is the property of true love to pass by many wants. And the more that a Christian is rooted in true love, the more infirmities will he pass by in them whom he loves. He sets no limits to himself, how many or how long to bear, but even all that are infirmities of nature. He will put up with many hard words, many angry fits, many needless surmises, many unkindnesses, and (as it were) not see them, [for their] hearts [are] possessed with true love, wisdom, and the fear of God. And everyone who will practice Christian equity must do thus. For this is a man's glory and commendation. Let us lay this doctrine nearer to our consciences by considering the nature of this virtue in [a] few examples.

A man has a wife, or a woman [has] a husband, in whom there is the fear of God, and honest and faithful love. But he or she is subject to anger, or to hastiness, or to an austerity in their behavior, or it may be [that] it is not in their nature to practice those outward complements of kindness which others can do with great facility. These, and such like, are but weaknesses of nature in them who fear God. Therefore, love must cover them, bear them, and oftentimes not take notice of them, and the rather because he or she, who has not such, has either the like or greater weaknesses. If one forebears [them] not in another, it is not possible to live in peace and comfort. But if this part of equity were practiced, it is scarce credible how much it would augment the happiness and add to the comfort of them who are married.

Again, a man has a servant, careful and willing enough to obey and please his master, also trustworthy and faithful, but he is slow in his business, and does not dispatch things appointed him, to the mind of his master, not so speedily, not so readily, nor with that facility as his master requires. What is to be done in this case? To see it, and always to check him for it, and to gall and gird him

5. This paragraph break is not in the original.

with it, and ever to be casting it in his teeth, and threatening him for it, is the extremity which the apostle here condemns. The equity then, in this case to be performed, is in consideration that it is not a fault of malice, but of nature, not of idleness nor carelessness, but of a natural weakness, the master must gently tell him of it, and privately and seldom, and advise him what are the best helps for nature in this case. And though he sees not that speedy amendment which he desires, yet he is to bear with him as long as he is trustworthy, diligent, dutiful, and willing. And for those so many good properties, he must bear with his wants, and not be too sharp either in reproving or in correcting him for them.

In the third place, a man has occasion to confer often with another man by reason that they are neighbors, or special friends, or of the same calling and course of life. But one of them is hasty and soon angry. And it may be [that] in his talk, either for the matter or the manner of it, he cannot but show his anger. Extremity in this case is for a man to deal roughly with him, to contradict and cross him, to deny what he says, to stand stiffly to our own opinion, and to be angry again with him. But on the other side, Christian equity teaches a man not to see it, nor take notice of it, nor to be angry again, nor to check him for it, but to put it off by gentle words, soft demands, and other talk, and to yield to him as far as a man may do in good conscience without betraying the truth. And by the way, in conference hold it always for a rule of Christian wisdom and private equity never to stick stiffly to any opinion, unless it is in a plain truth and of great moment. Now, thus doing to our brother, and sparing his weakness, and continuing on our speech, as though we saw not that he was angry, hereby the conference holds on, and love is continued as afore. But if contrariwise, we take the advantage of his infirmity, and display it, and rub him for it, if we are as short as he, and stand stiffly upon points, then the conference is broken off without edification, and heart-burning rises between them instead of true love.

Thus, we see in these examples how in Christian moderation we are to bear and forbear the natural weaknesses of our brethren, if we purpose to live in any comfort with them in this world.

Yet, this forbearance must be with two conditions. First, these wants [must] be wants of nature, not of malice, nor of old, rooted, settled, and cankered corruption. Second, they whom we forbear [must] contain themselves within convenient bounds, and not exceed nor break out into any outrage or extremity. For then they are not to be forborne, but to be told and reproved for them. And a man's duty is not to wink at them, but to take notice of them, and to show open dislike of them. But in as much as these are wants of nature, as it is infirmity in the one to show them, so it is the glory and praise of the other to pardon them. Yea, it is a token of wisdom, and good government, and a sign that a man is a lover of peace, and consequently of religion, and of God Himself, to pass by them. The practice of this duty maintains peace in kingdoms, countries, states, cities, colleges, families, and all societies of men.

Thus much for the first duty.

Duty 2

The second duty of private equity is to construe and interpret men's sayings, which are doubtful, in the better part (if possibly it may be). This is to be understood of all men, [even] though they are our enemies. And a man must do this if he will live in peace in this world.

Our nature is given to take men at the worst, to deprave men's deeds and words, and to pervert them to the worst sense that may be. And this is commonly the cause of debate and dissension in the world.

But the duty of Christian equity is contrary hereunto; namely, to think the best they can of all men, to construe all doubtful actions in the better part, and to make the best sense of all doubtful speeches if we have any probable reason to induce us to it. The apostle makes this the property of love: "Love thinks not evil" (1 Cor. 13:5); that is, not only when there is manifest and good cause to think well, but when it is doubtful, if it may by any means have a good meaning, if by any means it may be well thought of, love will make a man think well of it. And the more specially a man loves another, the more equally, indifferently, and Christianly, will he interpret all his sayings and doings. The want of this duty and the practice of the contrary is the cause of more troubles, tumults, garboils,[6] fallings out, and heart-burnings, in kingdoms, countries, societies, and families, between man and man, than any other thing in the world besides.[7]

Dealing thus with the words of Christ cost Him His life. For when Christ said, "Destroy this temple and I will build it in three days," they interpreted it as the temple of Jerusalem, when He meant the temple of His body. And the wrong and sinister interpretation of David's embassage by his neighbor, king Hanun, was the cause of that great war between two mighty kingdoms, the Israelites and the Ammonites, which cost so many thousands their lives.[8] For when David sent ambassadors to comfort him after his father's death, he and his wicked counselors interpreted it that he sent spies and intelligencers to find out the weakness of the land. It cannot be spoken what broils, hurly-burlies, and confusions in kingdoms, what contentions in commonwealths, what factions and divisions in colleges and societies, what disquietness in families, what unkindness and falling out among old friends, and what separation even among them who should be nearest, are daily in the world, by reason of

6. *Garboil:* uproar.
7. This paragraph break is not in the original.
8. 2 Sam. 10.

this sinister interpretation of men's words and deeds. We, therefore, who do profess ourselves the children of peace must learn to make conscience of this, the due practice whereof is the conservation of peace.

And further in this duty, one more thing is to be remembered, namely, that we must not give too sharp a censure of even the open and manifest evil sayings or doings of our brother. We must not judge them to be done carelessly when it may be they are done ignorantly, nor deliberately when it may be they are done rashly, nor presumptuously when it may be they are done upon infirmity, nor to be done upon hatred or malice to us when it may be they are done for another cause, nor may we judge an evil thing to be done for want of conscience, when it may be it is done for want of heedfulness. But we must always remember to make the best we can, even of another man's infirmities. And, if our brother does well, we are to acknowledge it, and commend him for it; so, if he does amiss, we must not make it worse than it is.

But the world is far[9] to blame herein, for they can extol their own well doing, and twenty ways excuse their evil doing, but, as for other men, they can debase their well doing, and advance their evil doing. Nay, it is a common thing to make a bad man worse than he is, and to speak of an evil action and of men's faults worse than they are; yea, to speak worse (even of ill men) than they deserve. But it is flat injustice, not only to speak evil of that which is good, but even to make an evil thing worse than it is. There are many cases wherein a man is bound to make the best he can of a bad action. But to make it worse than it is, there is no case wherein a man may do it without plain injury to his brother.[10]

If any man replies, and says, "I am not to spare myself nor excuse my own faults, but to judge as hardly of my own sayings and doings as they deserve, why then should I not also do so to another?" The answer is ready. Because a man knows not another man so well as himself. Words and deeds are known to other men, but a man's heart is known to himself alone. Therefore, for your own sayings and doings, you are able to judge of your own heart and of your purpose and intent in so speaking and doing. But of another man, you can say he spoke or did thus or thus, but you cannot judge his heart, purpose, and intent, in so doing. And, therefore, you may not judge so sharply of another man's sayings and doings as of your own.[11]

To make an end of this point, two cautions must be remembered in the performance of this duty. First, we speak not of continued courses in doing or speaking evil, but of particular speeches and actions. For not an action or a speech, but the course of life, shows what a man is. One evil speech or action

9. *Far*: much.

10. This paragraph break is not in the original.

11. This paragraph break is not in the original.

may be excused, but a continued course in doing or speaking evil may be by no means colored or excused. Second, we speak not of manifest and public enormities, as of treasons against the prince or state. For therein it may be dangerous to the prince, and hurtful to the state, to have anything colored, concealed, or excused. In such cases, we must set aside our duty to our brother, and remember our duty to the head and whole body. And better it is that one member is cut off than that the whole body perish. But we speak of private evil words or deeds, the evil and hurt whereof redounds to private men. And in them we speak not of manifest, gross, and palpable crimes, wherein not only the action is plainly evil, but the intent also. For to excuse or conceal, or to extenuate such, is to make ourselves accessory to the evil of them. But we speak of doubtful words or deeds, wherein either the action itself or (at the least) the intent of it may receive a likely excuse and a probable interpretation of good.

And, unto these two cautions, add thus much further: that the practice of this duty for the most part ceases when the minister is to work upon the conscience of an impenitent or a presumptuous sinner. For then he is not to moderate or mitigate, to color or excuse, to lessen or extenuate his sins, but to speak of sin as it deserves, and to lay out his sins in their own colors, so that he may humble him and cast him down.

But out of these three cases, this duty lies upon all men at all times to interpret everything in the better part. So then, the conclusion of this second duty is this: apparently good actions are to be commended, [and] doubtful are to be construed in the best sense; apparently evil [actions] are to be made no worse than they are, but rather to be excused. And let a man always speak too well rather than too evil of another man, and speak better rather than worse than he deserves, and judge too mildly and mercifully rather than too sharply. For if a man is deceived either way, that is the safer way wherein to be deceived. To do thus is to perform that Christian equity which is here commanded, and to maintain peace which is the comfort of a Christian life.

And thus much of the second duty.

Duty 3

The third duty and degree of private equity is, in sundry cases, to depart from a man's own right; that is, to yield oftentimes in such things wherein by law he might stand, and oftentimes to forgo such things which by law he might require. Without this equity, justice and peace cannot stand. Christ, our Savior, gave a notable example hereof in paying [the] toll (Matt. 17:27). Christ needed not to have done it, nor could any law have compelled Him to it, yet because He would not trouble the public peace, nor give them occasion of contention, He yields from His right and pays them [a] toll. All Christian men must learn by His example not to stand always upon their right, if they will continue peace in the church of God. It is not sufficient in Christianity, nay, it is a very wicked speech which we often hear men speak: "It is my right and, therefore, I will not lose it." Christ might have said so. And if you look [at] the place, you shall find that He first of all argues the case and concludes that He is free and not bound to pay, and yet He says, "Rather than I will offend them, or give them cause to think worse of me or my doctrine, I will pay it." Even so, a Christian man must, in many cases, go from his right, and that for the maintenance of public peace in the commonwealth and of private peace one man with another.

For the maintenance of public peace, men must do thus in public conferences, as in parliaments and councils, and such like general assemblies, wherein the several opinions of men are to be delivered. And men must do thus in bonds, forfeitures, borrowing, lending, losing, finding, buying, selling, in leases, fines, rents, and all manner of bargains.

And for the maintenance of private peace, men must in their most private actions yield one to another in such things wherein they might stand, and oftentimes be contented to lose that which is their own. And in conferences a man must oftentimes suffer himself to be crossed and over-thwarted in that which he is often certain of. And [he must] grant that to be which is not, and that not to be which he knows to be, if the matter is of small moment and concerns not religion nor the state. A Christian man must put up daily many such things at the hands of his brother, for the maintenance of peace and love among them.[12]

This is a doctrine [that is] little known and less regarded in the world, for it is a general opinion that a man may take his own and may lawfully stand upon his own right (which, if it is meant generally in all cases, [it] is most false). Nay, this is a common speech of all men: "I demand but my right, and I will not lose my right." And this is thought a reasonable speech, and he is esteemed a good man who takes no more than his right. For oftentimes men stand so strictly upon their right that they go further than their right reaches. But this is a very carnal practice, and [it is] controlled by the Scripture and by the example of Christ, as we heard afore. But if any man objects that the example of Christ is not to bind us because He is the Mediator and, therefore, was to perform extraordinary obedience, I then answer that, not only Christ, but other holy men, have practiced this duty, for He pays [the] toll, not only for Himself, but for Peter also. And there is a notable example of this duty in Abraham, who, when his brother Lot and his shepherds could not agree, was content to depart from his right. For whereas he (being the elder) might have chosen first, he

12. This paragraph break is not in the original.

notwithstanding stands not upon that, but bids his brother, Lot, [to] choose whither he will, and he will take what he leaves. A most equal, Christian, brotherly part of that holy Abraham, whose faith is so much commended in the Scriptures. If we, therefore, will be called the children of Abraham, then we must be followers of him in his works, and namely in this, we must oftentimes depart from our own right.

In the practice of this duty, one caution only must be remembered, namely, we must distinguish between another's right and our own. In your own right you may yield, but when you are to deal for another man, you must not yield too much, nor be too lavish of another man's right. But this caution holds especially when the cause is not ours, but God's or His church's. For when it is such a truth which directly concerns the honor of God or the good of His church, then a man must take heed he yields not without warrant from God's Word. For as it is equity often to yield your right, so to yield in God's causes is to betray the truth. If, therefore, you may not give another man's right from him without his consent, much less may you without warrant from God yield anything at all of His right from Him. This duty, therefore, is to be performed in actions that concern ourselves, and wherein the loss is not God's or His church's, but our own.[13]

But it is lamentable to see many men, how lavish they are in giving from God, and care not how much they lose of His glory, but [they] stand most strictly upon their own points, and will not yield one inch nor lose one foot of their own right. And from hence come so many suits in law, and other brabbling[14] contentions in the world, all [of] which (or many of them) might be stayed if men had but conscience to practice this Christian equity, to yield one to another in matters of their own and of small moment. And it is certain that, if men in the world were not persuaded, some by religion and conscience, some by natural reason and policy, to practice this duty, it would not be possible for the society of men to continue long upon the earth.

So much for the third degree.

Duty 4

The fourth and last degree of private equity is to forbear and to forgive wrongs and injuries done unto us in word or deed. The Scripture is plain for this, and so is natural reason which teaches that everyone who bears the name of a man should forgive another because he (being a man) may deserve and stand in need of the same himself. And, therefore, [he] is to do as he would be done

13. This paragraph break is not in the original.

14. *Brabbling*: wrangling.

unto. But especially a Christian man, who looks for forgiveness at God's hand for his own sins, must needs forgive his brother. So that, to a Christian man, there is a double bond or reason to tie him to this duty. The first is [that], since he is a man, he must forgive him who offends him, so that another man may also forgive him when he offends. For there is none but, being a man and living among men, he must needs offend. Another more forcible reason is [that], since he is a Christian, he must forgive because how else can he in reason demand or pray for forgiveness at God's hand for many thousands [of] offences of his own, and those exceedingly great, when another man cannot obtain forgiveness at his hands for a few small offences?[15]

This duty is of greater necessity than all the former, for upon the practice of this depends the preservation of peace. But where this is not practiced, there is no religion, conscience, or salvation, for where there is no forgiving of another man, that man is not forgiven at God's hands. And he whose sins are not in Christ forgiven and taken away, that man is in the state of damnation, and till he is forgiven, he can never be saved. But he can never be forgiven, till he forgives his brother. And so, it is plain that even salvation itself, in some sort, depends upon the practice of this duty, yet not as a cause but as a sign (or an effect) of salvation. For it is not true that everyone who forgives is forgiven of God, but it is true that whoever is forgiven of God will forgive his brother. So then, neither in reason nor in religion can a man look for forgiveness himself, unless he makes conscience to forgive another. Yea, God has made every man a judge in this case to condemn himself, if he does it not when he prays every day, [asking] that God would forgive him even as he does forgive others.

Yet, in this duty of forgiving outward injuries, two cautions are to be remembered.

First, there is a time when a man is not to forbear and suffer, but may stand upon his guard, and defend himself from the injury. And that is when his life is endangered, as when a man is assaulted by a thief or by his deadly enemy who seeks his life, and [he] has no help. He is in that case to help himself. When he must either kill or be killed, then reason and religion bids him defend himself. And, being in that case that a man cannot have the magistrate's help, who bears the sword for his defense, God puts for that time the sword into a man's own hand, and makes him a magistrate for that time and occasion. For in cases of such extremity, God allows every man to be a magistrate, not only to defend himself, but even to kill his enemy, if it is impossible any way else to save his own life. And this defense of a man's [own] self hinders not the duty

15. This paragraph break is not in the original.

of forgiving, for so far must a man forbear and forgive that he is sure to defend his own life.

In the second place, though a man forgives the injury and wrong done unto him, yet he may safely in some cases go to law for recompense of that wrong. It is a devilish opinion in the world that a man cannot go to law and yet be in charity. We must know that a man may go to law and yet be in charity, for to forgive the malice and to sue for recompense are things indifferent. It is not so much charity to forbear the recompense as it is to forgive the malice. If, therefore, a man forgives not the malice, he is out of charity; but he may sue for satisfaction and yet be in charity. The Scripture forbids not men's going to law, but tells them how they should do it. Law is not evil, though contentious men and unconscionable lawyers have vilely abused it. But it is God's ordinance, and [it] may lawfully be used, [as long as] it is in this manner.

First, it must not be [used] for every trifle, every trespass, [or] every ill word; but, in these cases, a man is both to forgive the malice and to remit the recompense because he is little or nothing at all hurt by it. For example, a poor man steals a little meat from you in his hunger. Let the law take hold on him. But you pursue him no more for it than you must by the law. Again, your neighbor's cattle do trespass you. You must not go to law for it, the malice be it more or less, you must forgive in Christianity and for conscience's sake. And the damage is so small as that, therefore, you may not go to law for it. For the law is abused in being executed upon trifles. And those lawyers shame themselves and dishonor their profession, who are willing that every trespass of sixpence damages is an action in the law. This is one of the causes of the base and vile names that are given to the law and lawyers in these days, because the law is employed upon such trifles. And it is to be wished that the supreme magistrate would take order to restrain this general evil: that contentious men and unconscionable lawyers might not conspire together to pester the law with these trifles. And though men are so unconscionable as to run to the law for every trespass, yet lawyers should be so conscionable and so wise as they should drive them from the law again. Third, your neighbor gives you ill words, raises or carries evil tales of you. Equity is not to go to law for every evil word, but to consider that you are to forgive the malice. The damage cannot be great because many men's tongues are not slanderers. Neither are you anything worse for it, especially when he dares not stand to what he has said, as for the most part they do not.

The second caution in going to law is that it must not be the first but the last means of public peace. Law is a kind of war; therefore, as war is to be the last means of public peace, so should the law be the last means to be used for the attaining of private peace. All means must be tried, ere you go to law, and if none will serve, then is the law ordained for you, whereby to recover your right and to maintain equity. For as to go to law for a trifle (or at the first) is extremity, and so injury, so to go to the law for a cause sufficient, and after other means [are] used in vain, is justice and equity, and no extremity.

Here, therefore, let all Christians learn how to go to law. And the rather I do urge this point because the law is notoriously abused. And it is almost incredible what infinite sums and masses of money are daily spent most unnecessarily in it, insomuch as the lawyers do exceed in wealth any other sort or calling of men in this whole realm.

For [the] reformation whereof, let men but learn and practice the two former rules. First, law is not ordained to be a judge of every trifle. It is a shame to our law that men be suffered in the commonwealth to arrest each other for debts of small value, so as ten times and [even] twenty times as much is spent for the recovery of them as the principal is. Are not we a Christian commonwealth? Why then have we not the wisdom to appoint another, an easier, and a more direct way for the recovery of such debts? And if there is no other way, why does not a Christian man stay for it, or lose it, rather than go to law for it? It is a shame for our nation that there should be at one assize in England so many hundreds [of] actions of trespasses, wherein the damage is little or nothing. To reform these is a work worthy of a prince, and every man should put his helping hand to it.

Second, let law be your last remedy. This rule controls another foul disorder in our land. Men are sued when they would gladly compound. When they would willingly satisfy by private order, they are compelled to answer by law. And yet there is a worse thing than this: the law, which should be the last, is not only made the first means, but whereas it should be open and public, it is used as a closed and secret means. It steals upon men (as the phrase is). For men are sued before they know [it], and great charges come upon them ere they are told of it, by them who sue them. Is this equity? Yea, is it not rather extremity? And yet (alas) how common it is in most places! Let, therefore, every Christian man remember his lesson here taught by the apostle: "Let your equity be known to all men."[16]

But it seems, then, some will say that men may not go to law. I answer, you may go to law, though not for trifles, yet for things of weight, as for the pursuit of a notorious thief to his due and just trial, for the title of your lands, for the recovery of your just and due debts of value and of your child's portion, for the making straight of great accounts, for the trial of your good name when you are so slandered (and by such as that your credit is publicly endangered). For these and such like causes, you may go to law, when by other easier means you

16. This paragraph break is not in the original.

cannot procure a reasonable satisfaction. For then it is unlawful to sue for the greatest cause in the world.

Paul teaches the truth of all this doctrine to the Corinthians, whom he reproves for three faults: (1) they went to law before heathen judges; (2) [they went to law] for every cause; and (3) they used no private means of satisfaction, but ran to the law at the first.

The first of these cannot be our sin, for we have no heathen judges in as much as our state and government, by the mercy of God, is not heathenish, but we have a Christian commonwealth. But the other two are the general sores of this land. Let us, therefore, labor to heal them and to cover our shame. Let us remember that not extremity but equity becomes a Christian. And let every man take heed of this, as he would be known to be a Christian, for the known badge of Christianity is mercifulness. The better Christian [is] the more merciful, for he has tasted deeper of God's mercies to himself, and therefore he is merciful to his brother. And the worse Christian [is] the less merciful, for he never felt God's mercies to himself, therefore he cannot be merciful to his brother. Now, to go to law for every trifle, or to steal law upon your brother, or to sue him before you offer him peace, it argues a hard and unmerciful heart, and [it is] far from this duty of forgiving. But to be loath to go to law, and to put it off as long as may be, and first to give warning and to offer peace, and not to do it but in matters of weight, it argues a merciful heart, and such a one as is ready to forgive and such a one in whom the Spirit of God does dwell.

And thus, I hope I have opened this duty of forgiving and forbearing in such sort as a Christian may see how to practice it with comfort to his conscience, also without any great loss in this world or hurt to his estate.

And thus much for the four several duties and degrees of private equity.

Point 3: The Practice of Christian Equity

Now, having opened the nature and kinds of Christian equity, let us proceed further in the text. "Let your equity," says the apostle, "be known to all men." The words import that it is our duty, not only to know this virtue and the nature of it, and to be able to talk of it, but in all our affairs (public and private), and in all our dealings with men, so to put it in practice that men may see it, and that it may be known to other men, and that they may be able to avouch for us that our dealing is upright, equal, and indifferent, joined with equity and moderation, and free from extremity and oppression. This is the meaning of that which we are here commanded by the apostle.[17]

17. This paragraph break is not in the original.

And the reason why the apostle urges us to make it known is because there is a privy hypocrisy in our natures, whereby we are given to make show of more than is in us. We do truly labor against this vice when we labor to make our virtues manifest and known to the world, so that the tree may be known by its fruits. He is a holy and religious man, not who knows and talks well, but whose religion and holiness are known in the world, and seen by men. He is a merciful man, of whose mercy men do taste. So, he is an equal and upright man, whose equity is felt and found by them who deal with him. Let, therefore, our actions with men testify the virtues of our heart, that men who live with us and deal with us may be able to say for us that we are possessed with those virtues. For this is to be truly good, not when a man can speak well or tell of his own goodness, but when other men see it, feel it, and speak of it.

Hitherto of the meaning of the words.

Part 2: A Reason

Now that which was Paul's exhortation to the Philippians shall be mine to all true Christians: "Let your equity be known to all men." You have learned what it is and how it is to be practiced. It now remains that we content not ourselves with the bare knowledge [of it], but take notice of it as of a doctrine belonging to us, and put it in practice [in] all our dealings, public and private, yea and make it manifest to the consciences of all men, good and bad, so that every man, with whom we deal, may taste and feel of our equity, and be able to testify of us that equity bears rule in all our actions. If we do thus, we are Christians, not in name and profession only, but in deed and truth.

And to persuade us all to this holy duty, let us use [a] few reasons to enforce it. And among all the reasons that might be brought, there is none better than this here used in the text: "The Lord is at hand."

But before we come to speak of it, let us consider of one another what does most naturally enforce this exhortation. And it is this: God shows most admirable equity and moderation toward us, therefore we ought to show it one toward another. It is the reason of the Holy Spirit: "Be ye merciful, as your heavenly Father is merciful."[18] Wonderful is the moderation that God shows to man, and it appears especially in four things, whereof two belong to all men and the other two concern His church.

18. Luke 6:36.

God's Moderation toward the World

The first action of God wherein He shows great moderation toward all men is this. A law was given to our first parents: "Eat not of this tree; if you do, you die for it." And that [death was] a double death, both of body and soul. But they ate, and so broke the law, and thereby did undergo the annexed penalty. By force and virtue whereof, they should have died presently, the death both of body and soul. And this [would have] been no extremity but justice, for this was due unto them by the justice of that law which was given them. But now, behold God's equity and moderation of the justice of that law. He strikes them not presently, as the tenor of the law and their desert required, neither with the first nor second death, but defers the full execution, laying upon them (for the present) a lesser punishment, namely a subjection to the first death, and a guiltiness of the second, that is, of damnation. Behold a marvelous mitigation. By the tenor of that law, their bodies and souls should both have presently died and been cast into hell, but God in mercy suspends and defers the execution of it, and only strikes Adam's body with mortality whereby he was subject to the first death, and his soul with guiltiness whereby he was subject to the second death. By this mitigation it came to pass that as Adam by his repentance afterwards quite escaped the second death, so he tasted not of the first death till nine hundred years after. If a prisoner counts it a merciful favor of the prince, or the judge, when after his judgment to die, he is reprieved but one year, then what a merciful mitigation was this in God, to reprieve our first parents for so many hundreds [of] years? This was the first action of God's mercy to man, and this concerns all mankind generally, but especially Adam and Eve.

But the second does more nearly concern all men. So soon as man commits any sin, even then he is guilty of eternal damnation because he has broken the law. For the curse of the law is not only a guiltiness, but a subjection to the wrath of God, presently to be inflicted upon the sin committed, without any intermission, so that as often as a man sins so often does he deserve to be plunged (soul and body) into hell, without being spared one hour. If, therefore, the Lord did cast ten thousand into hell in one hour, He did but justice, for so the law requires. But see the merciful moderation of the Lord. Though we deserve every hour to be cast into hell, yet every hour and minute of our lives is full of the mercy and moderation of the Lord, so as though our sins cry for damnation presently, yet God stays His hand, and does not execute the sentence of damnation upon the sinner instantly after his sin, no not in one of ten thousand, but spares every man many years, some more, some less, but all more than their sins deserve or the law requires. We often read, and always find, that God hears the cry of sinners. But we seldom read that God hears the cry of sin, for if He always heard it, when sin cries for vengeance to Him, He should turn us all into hell in one hour. This is a wonderful patience and moderation in God, and yet behold a greater.

For we by our sins do every hour plunge ourselves into hell, as a man who violently casts himself into a gaping gulf. See God's wonderful mercy. We thrust ourselves in, and He pulls us back. He stays us with His own hand, and so keeps us out. See what a sea of mercies the Lord does pour upon man. For how can that but be an infinite sea of mercies which is shown to so many thousands of men, so many thousands [of] times in one hour. If His mercy did not moderate the extremity of His law, there should not be one man left upon earth, but all in one hour [would be] cast into hell. But God stays His justice, and stays His law, yea stays us, who would execute the law upon ourselves and so cast ourselves into hell. He keeps us out, and gives unto us a longer time to repent. And this is true in all men. To some He gives longer, to some [He gives] shorter, but to everyone [He gives] some [time]. The law gives not one hour to any man, nay the law is so far from giving time to repent that it admits no repentance at all. Though a man should sin but once, and instantly after that one sin humble himself in repentance and crave forgiveness, the law will not accept him to favor nor yield forgiveness nor allow his repentance. For the law can do nothing but this: either justify and reward him who fulfills it, or condemn and punish him who breaks it. Further than this the law by itself goes not.

It is the gospel that commands us and teaches us to believe and repent. And we are beholden to the gospel for accepting our repentance, which the law would never do. Indeed, [it] is so far from accepting repentance as it never intends nor aims at repentance directly in itself. And, therefore, in itself it is worthily called "the ministry of condemnation."[19] So then, behold a most straight law and a most merciful God: so straight a law as (if mercy were not) it would never give us one hour to repent nor receive us to favor though we repented presently, but presently upon our sin [it would] cast us into hell. O, therefore, taste and see how good and gracious the Lord is.[20]

The law cannot have its extremity, nor can the devil (who is the jailer of the law, and is malicious though the law is just) have his will upon us. By the extremity of the justice of the one, and the extremity of the malice of the other, no man should live one hour in the world, were it not for the wonderful mercy and mitigation of God, who, contrary to the course of the law, both accepts men when they repent and gives also time to repent. And God has done thus, as in the beginning with Adam, so in all ages. To the old world, after many preachers [were] sent, and many hundreds [of] years [of] patience, and many thousands

19. 2 Cor. 3:9.

20. This paragraph break is not in the original.

of sins [were] ripe for vengeance, yet God gives one hundred and twenty years more. O how many millions of sins did they commit against Him in that time? And yet, [if] they had repented at the last, they [would have] been saved. But all was in vain, and therefore in the end God sent a flood and swept them all away. Even so, and more patiently, God has suffered us in these latter days. But how comes it to pass then, some will say, that we have not a flood as well as they? Surely because His mercy was great to them, but wonderful to us. We are as evil as they, yea if we judge aright, and consider duly all circumstances, our sins are far more, yea far more heinous than theirs were, so that we deserve a flood ten times more than they did. And if God dealt but justly with us, where He brought one upon them, He should bring a hundred upon us. And if justice bore the sway, it should sweep us away, one generation after another, with a continual flood. But mark the moderation of God more to us than to them, who deserve worse than they. He gave us not a hundred and twenty [years], but many hundreds [of] years, and [He] brings no floods of judgments, but spares us from year to year and from age to age, so that we may either repent and escape hell, or (when our time is come) drown ourselves in damnation, and so be the principal cause of our own destruction.

It may not unfitly be noted in this place that sometimes God may be said to cast a man into hell, and sometimes man himself. God throws a man into hell when, for some monstrous and contagious sin, He takes away a wicked man in the midst of his wickedness by some sudden judgment, and so sends him to hell. But a man plunges himself into hell when God gives him leave to live, and liberty and time to repent, but he continues carelessly in his sins till he dies, and so [he] casts himself violently into damnation. Now, such is the merciful moderation of God that for one man whom He casts into hell (as He did Judas presently upon his sin) a hundred wicked men cast themselves into hell, abusing that time and liberty which He gave them to repent in, and so bringing upon themselves swift damnation. Let every man, therefore, every day of his life, when he considers the thousands of sins that are committed that day, and sees no flood of water, fire, nor brimstone to come upon us, let him wonder at God's mercy, and say with the prophet: "It is the Lord's mercy that we are not consumed."[21]

Furthermore, this moderation of God to all men has another branch. Every man's ill conscience is to him like the fire of hell, and doubtless the torment of conscience is a part of the very real torment of hell. Now, if every man had but justice, he should feel presently, after every sin, the very torment of hell, namely the sting and torment of a guilty, accusing conscience. But see the mercy and

21. Lam. 3:22.

moderation of God. He inflicts it not presently, but only gives the sinner a prick, or a little pang (as it were), when he has sinned. But He defers the raging fury of the conscience (which is the greatest hell that is upon earth) till the hour of death or the day of judgment. When, therefore, you have done evil, and feel a prick in your conscience, and a check, but no more, remember that even then, if God did not moderate His justice, you should feel the extreme horror of your conscience, which would overwhelm you as a burden, which is too heavy for you to bear.

Thus then, we see the marvelous mercy of God. Wicked men are His sworn enemies, for sin is that which offends Him above all things in the world, yet so great is His mercy, and so large is His moderation, that even His enemies taste of it every day and hour.

Thus much of God's equity and moderation to all men.

God's Moderation toward the Church

Now, second, this moderate and mild dealing of the Lord is more special to His church and children. And it also shows itself in two actions.[22]

First of all, justice requires that every man should pay his debt. And common reason tells us that words and promises cannot pass for payment, but due debt must be satisfied. Now every Christian man is in a great debt to God. This debt is obedience to His law, for Christ came to save us from the rigor of the law, not to free us from obedience to it. But how do we pay that debt? Even as he does, who owes ten thousand pounds, and craves to pay it by a penny a year, for so we, owing perfect obedience in thought, word, and deed, and also purity of nature (the root of all), we (I mean the best and holiest men of all) have nothing to tender to God but a few good desires and groans of the heart, and a silly, poor endeavor. All this is, [in comparison to] what the law requires, like unto one penny to ten thousand pounds. Yet, behold the mercy of God and His compassion to His children. He accepts our desires and our endeavor, coming from the truth of our hearts, for perfect payment, and [He accepts] that man who has a heart fearing God, and a care and desire to please God in all things, and in his place and calling endeavors it accordingly. [This] is the man whom God loves and embraces in the arms of His mercy, though he is far from that which in debt and duty he owes to God.[23]

God does thus testify of Himself in Malachi: "I will spare you, even as a father spareth his own son that serveth him."[24] Now we know there is no sparing nor forbearance like unto that. A father bids his little son do this or that

22. This paragraph break is not in the original.
23. This paragraph break is not in the original.
24. Mal. 3:17.

which is far above his strength. The child, not considering the difficulty, but looking at his duty, and desiring only to please his father, goes about it, and does his best. And yet, when all is done, he can do nothing to it at all. Now the father rejoices in this willing obedience of his son, and approves in his child the will and endeavor, though he cannot do the thing he bids him. Even so, the Lord does spare His children. He commands us to keep His law, and it is no more than our duty, which notwithstanding of ourselves we can do no more than a little child is able to carry a millstone. Yet, if we willingly go when God commands us, and do our endeavor, and all we can, and groan under the burden, and desire to do more, our desire and endeavor, proceeding from faith and from a son-like willingness, the Lord accepts for the perfect deed. This is no small moderation, but great and wonderful. For whereas we owe perfect obedience, and He might justly challenge it, and for want of it, make us pay it with soul and all, He is content to take a will, a desire and endeavor, which is all we can, and is in effect nothing at all. In this world, the man who will take from his debtor (who owes him 100 pounds) a penny a week, or who takes all he can pay and accepts his good mind for the rest, would be extolled for his mercy. Oh then, how merciful is our God, who, for so great offences and so huge a debt as ours is to His majesty, is content to accept of our endeavor and hearty desire? The heart and tongue of man cannot sufficiently magnify so great a mercy.

Thus much for the first.

Second, the mercy and moderation of God toward His children appears thus: There is not the best man but he sins, and there is not a sin so little but in justice it deserves a whole world of punishments, yea all those curses denounced in the law, even all those plagues threatened (Deuteronomy 28). All this in justice should overwhelm him, press him down, and crush him to nothing. But behold the merciful moderation of God. He is content to lay no more crosses on His children, than by His own grace (which He also gives them) they shall be able to undergo, and in the end to overcome also. When His children sin (and when do they not?), does He punish them according to the proportion of their sin? No. For then all the curses of His law should be heaped on them for one sin. And if He did so, He did but justice. Nay, He deals so with them as it is not to be called a punishment at all, but rather a chastisement. For a punishment must be in some sort proportionable to the offence, but that which He lays on His children is nothing at all to their sin. And, therefore, it is no punishment properly, but (as it were) the chastisement or correction of a father, to teach his son his duty, and to reform him, and bring him home from his evil ways. And, therefore, not in the rigor of a judge, but in the love and wisdom of a father, He first considers what we are able to bear, and then lays no more on us than we may well bear. And what is most wonderful of all [is that] He gives us strength to bear them.[25]

To this end the apostle speaks to the Corinthians: "There hath no temptation taken you, but that which befalls the nature of man" (1 Cor. 10:13). Whereby he imports thus much, that there are temptations and crosses in God's justice due for sin, and which He has in store, ready at His pleasure, which are so great, so heavy, and so fearful, as the nature of man could not possibly bear them, but should sink under them and perish, as did Cain and Judas and such like. An evil conscience is among these. [It] is so intolerable, as the wise man says, "A wounded spirit, who can bear it?" (Prov. 18:14). But the crosses He lays on His children are always such as they bear with comfort for a time, and at last with joy do overcome them. We have a notable example hereof in Solomon, of whom God says to David: "If he sin, I will chastise him with the rod of men."[26] [It is] as if He should have said, "I could in My justice, for Solomon's great sins, beat him with scorpions and bring him to nothing by My heavy hand, but I will consider [that] he is My child and but a man. Therefore, I will lay upon him no more than the nature of man is able to bear." As God dealt with His son, Solomon, so this is God's voice to all His sons: "Unto all My church and children, I will use such lenity and moderation, and in My chastising of them I will so abate the rigor of My justice, that by My hand and rod they shall not be pressed down, but rather raised up in new obedience, and learn thereby to fear and love Me more than before."

Every Christian man should seriously consider this, and think with[in] himself how much this binds a man to deal moderately with his brother when the Lord deals so moderately with him. You sin, and God chastises you most mildly, and lays not on you the thousandth part of these crosses, which in justice He might do. Shall the Lord deal thus moderately with you for your many and so great sins, and will you deal so hardly with your brother in his few and small offences against you? Remember, therefore, in your dealing with your brother, this dealing of God with you, and certainly you cannot forget the one if you have tasted of the other. Show yourself, therefore, that you have been [a] partaker of God's favor, and that you have felt in your soul the sweetness of His mercies by being mild and merciful to your brethren. Out of that great sea of mercies, which God lets flow over you all your life long, let fall some drops of mercy on your brother, and remembering how God deals with you, deal not you with your brother always so hardly nor so straightly as you may or he deserves. Let these four merciful actions of God toward you be four strong

25. This paragraph break is not in the original.

26. 2 Sam. 7:14.

bonds to tie you to the obedience of this duty, to be mild and merciful to your brethren, remembering every day how moderately God deals with you, and how far from that extremity which you deserve. And to move us hereunto, let every man be well assured that the more he has tasted of God's mercy, the more shall men taste of his mercy, and the more sins that a man has forgiven him at God's hands, the more will he remit and forgive in his brother, and the more he feels in his own soul God's love and mercy to him, and the more near he is to God by his faith and repentance, the more careful will he be to deal gently with his brethren. And the reasons hereof are these.

First, God forgives not a man his faults but upon condition that he shall forgive his brother. God is not merciful to a man but upon condition he shall be so to all men with whom he deals. Second, the mercy of God to us, in forgiving our sins, is not made known to the world by any means more than this, when a man is not hard and extreme, but equal and merciful in his dealing with men. Whereupon, therefore, it follows that the further a man is from God, and the less that he has felt of God's love to him, the less moderation will he perform to his brother. Let every man then be ashamed by these extreme courses with his brethren, to make it known to the world that he is an impenitent sinner, unreconciled to God, and his sins unpardoned. And let no man think he shall escape that censure, if he is an unmerciful man. For certainly it is imprinted in men's dealings, whether they are in God's favor and their sins are pardoned, or not. Let, therefore, every man, when his own crooked nature (or the devil) makes him boil against his brother in anger, and urges him to use him hardly and extremely, consider with[in] himself, and say, "I live under God. I am more in God's hand than this man [is] in mine. I have offended God more than he [has] me. And if I had my desert, I had now been in hell for my sins. But yet, I live, and by His mercy I am spared, and [I] am still here. But has God spared me that I should pinch others? Has He been merciful to me that I should be cruel to others? Surely, therefore, I will be merciful and moderate to my brethren, more than they deserve, lest God take His mercy from me. And then what shall become of me, but to be thrown suddenly into hell, which I deserved long ago? Nay, I will by my equity and moderation toward my brethren, move the Lord to be still more merciful to me, without which mercy I cannot live one day in the world."

The Reason: The Lord Is at Hand

Hitherto of the exhortation of the apostle, and of the great moderation of God to man. Now follows the apostle's reason: "the Lord is at hand." These words bear two senses or meanings: the first [is] of the last judgment; [and] the second [is] of God's presence. The first is thus framed: if the Holy Spirit meant of the last judgment, be you equal and moderate one toward another, for God is ready in His great and general judgment to judge all men, and then happy is he who finds not justice but tastes of mercy. And who shall taste of mercy then but he who showed mercy in this world? But if, second, the Holy Spirit meant of God's presence, then is the argument framed thus: God is present with every man and at every action to testify and judge of it, and either to approve it and reward it (if it is upright, equal, and merciful) or to correct and punish it (if it is extreme and void of equity). Therefore, "let your equity be known to all men." Both senses are good, but we will cleave unto the latter. It is then all one as if the Holy Spirit had said, "Use equity and moderation in your dealings, and remember [that He] who is at your elbow stands by and looks on, ready to judge you for it."

Surely, there can be no better reason than this, if it is settled in a man's heart, for a thief or a cut-purse, if he saw the judge stand at his elbow, and look upon him, he would not do evil, he would stay his hand, even because he sees that the judge (who can presently hang him) sees him. [This is] a strong reason with men, and it keeps even bad men from lewd practices. Consider, therefore, when the Judge of judges, the Lord of heaven and earth, stands by and sees and marks all your actions, whether they are toward your brother as His are toward you. This ought to make the greatest man on earth fear how he deals cruelly or hardly with his brother.[27]

But worldly men will not be persuaded of this. But when they are laying their plots to deceive their brother, and when by injustice and extremity they pinch and wring him, they think in their hearts [that] God sees them not. Nor do they ever think of God, but labor that God may be out of all their thoughts. This is the cause of all sin in the world. For thence it is that men's hearts are hardened, and that they care not how extremely they deal with men, because they think God sees them not, nor will [He] call them to account for it, and do with them as they have done with their brother. Hence comes all injustice, cruelty, extremity, suits in law for trifles, taking forfeitures of leases and of bonds, and taking all advantages. Hence it comes that one man will not spare another one day, nor forgive one fault, nor pass by any infirmity, nor put up [with] the least injury, nor yield one inch from his right. But if his brother offends ever so little, upon ever so apparent weakness, he shall hear of it on both sides (as they say). And if he deserves ill, he shall have his deserts to the full. Thus, hearts are hardened, affections are immoderate, bowels of compassion are shut up, love and pity are banished, and in their rooms reign cruelty and injustice.[28]

27. This paragraph break is not in the original.

28. This paragraph break is not in the original.

Moderation dwells in corners, but extremity is that which bears sway over all the world. What is the cause of all this? Surely, first, because men are unsanctified, and have not repented of their sins, and so they feel not that God is moderate and merciful to them. Second, they persuade not themselves that God sees them. Therefore, arm yourself against this blasphemous thought, the root of all evil and cause of all sin, with this reason of the apostle, and resolve of it that this is the eternal truth of God and shall stand forever. "The Lord is at hand." And [He] sees and observes you and all your doings. Therefore, as you will escape His mighty and fearful hand, season your doings and dealings with moderation. And if you had no conscience, nor no mercy in you, yet be merciful, remembering who sees you. And deal moderately and equally in the sight and presence of so moderate, so mild, and so merciful a God, so merciful a Rewarder of him who deals moderately, and so powerful an Avenger of him who deals hardly and extremely with his brother.

Let us then end with the apostle as we began: "Let your equity and moderation be known to all men, for God is at hand."

And thus much out of God's Word of public and private equity, wherein I have not spoken all I might, but given occasion to others to enter into further consideration thereof.

Trin-uni Deo Gloria.

A Salve for a Sick Man

or

A Treatise Containing the Nature, Differences, and Kinds of Death, as also the Right Manner of Dying Well

And it may serve for spiritual instruction to:

1. Mariners when they go to sea
2. Soldiers when they go to battle
3. Women when they travail with child

Printed by John Legate,
Printer to the University of Cambridge

1597

The Epistle Dedicatory

Right honorable and worshipful, how famous in all writers [was] the year
To the Right Honorable and Virtuous Lady,
the Lady Lucy, Countess of Bedford.[1]

The death of the righteous (that is, of every believing and repentant sinner) is a most excellent blessing of God, and brings with it many worthy benefits. I prove it in this manner: First, God, both in the beginning and in the continuance of His grace, does greater things unto His servants than they do commonly ask or think. And because He has promised aid and strength unto them, therefore in wonderful wisdom He casts upon them this heavy burden of death, that they might make experience what is the exceeding might and power of His grace in their weakness. Second, judgment begins at God's house. And the righteous are laden with afflictions and temptations in this life, and therefore in this world they have their deaths and hells, that in death they might not feel the torment of hell and death. Third, when Lazarus was dead, Christ said, "He is not dead but sleepeth."[2] Hence, it follows that the Christian man can say, "My grave is my bed; my death is my sleep. In death I die not, but only sleep." It is thought that death is [the] most terrible of all terrible things. But it is false to them who are in Christ, to whom many things happen, [which are] far heavier and more bitter than death. Fourth, death at the first brought forth sin, but death in the righteous (by means of Christ's death) abolishes sin because it is the accomplishment of mortification. And death is so far from destroying such as are in Christ that there can be no better refuge for them against death, for presently after the death of the body follows the perfect freedom of the spirit and the resurrection of the body. Lastly, death is a means of a Christian man's perfection, as Christ in His own example shows, saying, "Behold I will cast out devils, and will heal still today and tomorrow, and the third day I will be perfected" (Luke 13:32). Now this perfection in the members of Christ is nothing else but

1. 1627. Best known as patroness of the poets: Johnson and Donne. *DNB* 17:467. Also supported Calvinistic authors. *Wikipedia, accessed November 28, 2019.*

2. John 11:11.

the blessing of God, the Author of peace, sanctifying them throughout, so that their whole spirits and souls and bodies may be preserved without blame to the coming of our Lord Jesus Christ.

Now, having often thus considered with[in] myself of the excellency of death, I thought [it] good to draw the sum and chief heads thereof into this small treatise, the protection and consideration whereof I commend to your Ladyship, desiring you to accept it and read it at your leisure. If I am blamed for writing unto you of death, whereas by the course of nature you are not yet near death, Solomon will excuse me. [He] says that we must remember our Creator in the days of our youth.[3] Thus, hoping of your Honor's good acceptance, I pray God to bless my little labor to your comfort and salvation.

September 7, 1595

Your Honor's in the Lord,
William Perkins

3. Eccl. 12:1.

"The day of death is better than the day that one is born" (Eccl. 7:1).[1]

These words are a rule (or precept) laid down by Solomon for weighty causes. For, in the chapters going before, he sets forth the vanity of all creatures under heaven, and that at large in the very particulars. Now men hereupon might take occasion of discontentment in respect of their estate in this life. Therefore, Solomon in great wisdom here takes a new course, and in this chapter begins to lay down certain rules of direction and comfort, so that men might have somewhat wherewith to arm themselves against the troubles and the miseries of this life. The first rule is in this first [or third][2] verse: "a good name is better than a precious ointment"; that is, a name gotten and maintained by godly conversation is a special blessing of God, which, in the midst of the vanities of this life, ministers greater matter of rejoicing and comfort to the heart of man than the most precious ointment can do to the outward senses. Now some men, having heard this first rule concerning a good name, might object and say that renown and good report in this life affords slender comfort, considering that death follows after it, which is the miserable end of all men. But the wise man removes this objection by a second rule in the words which I have in hand, saying, "the day of death is better than the day that one is born."

That we may come to the true and proper sense of this precept (or rule), three points are to be considered: first, what is the death here mentioned; second, how it can be truly said that "the day of death is better than the day of birth"; [and,] third, in what respect it is better.

Point 1

For the first, death is a deprivation of life as a punishment ordained by God and imposed on man for his sin. First, I say it is a deprivation of life because the very nature of death is the absence or defect of that life which God vouchsafed man by his creation. I add further that death is a punishment, more

1. Perkins gives the reference in the original as Eccl. 7:3. He is following the versification of the Geneva Bible, which places the last two verses of chapter 6 at the beginning of chapter 7.

2. Third in modern translations.

especially to intimate the nature and quality of death, and to show that it was ordained as a means of execution of God's justice and judgement. And Paul plainly avouches that death is a punishment when he says that "by one man sin entered into the world, and death by sin" [Rom. 5:12]. And again, [he says] that "death is the stipend (wages or allowance) of sin" (Rom. 6:23). Furthermore, in every punishment there are three workers: the ordainer, the procurer, and the executioner.[3]

The Ordainer

The ordainer of this punishment is God in the estate of man's innocency by a solemn law then made in these very words: "In the day that thou eatest thereof, thou shalt die the death" (Gen. 2:17).[4]

But it may be alleged to the contrary, that the Lord says by the prophet Ezekiel that He "wills not the death of a sinner" (Ezek. 33:11), and therefore that He is no ordainer of death. The answer may easily be made, and that sundry ways. First, the Lord speaks not this to all men or of all men, but to His own people, the church of the Jews, as appears by the clause prefixed: "Son of man, say unto the house of Israel…" (v. 10). Second, the words are not spoken absolutely but only in way of comparison, in that of the two He rather wills the conversion and repentance of a sinner than his death and destruction. Third, the very proper meaning of the words imports thus much, that God does take no delight or pleasure in the death of a sinner, as it is the ruin and destruction of the creature. And yet all this hinders not but that God in a new regard and consideration may both will and ordain death, namely, as it is a due and deserved punishment, tending to the execution of justice, in which justice God is as good as in His mercy.[5]

Again, it may be objected that if death indeed had been ordained by God, then Adam should have been destroyed, and that presently upon his fall. For the very words are thus: "Whensoever thou shalt eat of the forbidden fruit, thou shalt certainly die" (Gen. 2:17). *Answer.* [First,] sentences of Scripture are either legal or evangelical: the law and the gospel being two several and distinct parts of God's Word. Now this former sentence is legal and must be understood with an exception borrowed from the gospel or the covenant of grace made with Adam, and revealed to him after his fall. The exception is this: "You will certainly die whenever you eat the forbidden fruit, except I do further give you [the] means of deliverance from death, namely the seed of the woman to bruise the serpent's head." Second, it may be answered that Adam and all his posterity

3. This paragraph break is not in the original.
4. This paragraph break is not in the original.
5. This paragraph break is not in the original.

died, and that presently after his fall, in that his body was made mortal and his soul became subject to the curse of the law. And whereas God would not utterly destroy Adam at the very first, but only impose on him the beginnings of the first and second death, He did the same in great wisdom, so that in the midst of His justice He might make a way to mercy. This thing could not have been if Adam had perished.

The Executioner

The executioner of this punishment is He who does impose and inflict the same on man, and that also is God Himself, as He testifies of Himself in the prophet Isaiah: "I make peace and create evil" (Isa. 45:7). Now evil is of three sorts: natural, moral, [and] material. Natural evil is the destruction of that order which God set in every creature by creation. Moral evil is the want of righteousness and virtue which the law requires at man's hand, and that is called sin. Material evil is any matter or thing which in itself is a good creature of God, yet so, as by reason of man's fall, it is hurtful to the health and life of man, as henbane, wolfsbane, hemlock,[6] and all other poisons are. Now this saying of Isaiah must not be understood of moral evils, but of such as are either material or natural. Death is to be referred to the latter of these. [It] is the destruction (or abolishment) of man's created nature.

The Procurer

The procurer of death is man, not God, in that man by his sin and disobedience did pull upon himself this punishment. Therefore, the Lord says, "O Israel, one hath destroyed thee, but in me is thine help" (Hos. 13:9). Against this it may be objected that man was mortal in the estate of innocency before the fall. *Answer*. The frame and composition of man's body considered in itself was mortal, because it was made of water and earth and other elements which are of themselves alterable and changeable. Yet, if we respect that grace and blessing which God did vouchsafe man's body in his creation, it was unchangeable and immortal, and so by the same blessing should have continued if man had not fallen. And man, by his fall, depriving himself of this gift and blessing, became every way mortal.

How Man's Death Differs from That of an Animal

Thus, it appears in part what death is. Yet, for the better clearing of this point, we are to consider the difference between the death of a man and a beast. The death of a beast is the total and final abolishment of the whole creature, for the

6. Poisonous plants, often associated with witchcraft.

body is resolved to its first matter, and the soul arising from the temperature of the body vanishes to nothing. But it is otherwise in the death of man. For though the body for a time is resolved to dust, yet it must rise again in the last judgment and become immortal. And as for the soul, it subsists by itself out of the body and is immortal. And this being so, it may be demanded how the soul can die the second death? *Answer*. The soul dies, not because it is utterly abolished, but because it is as though it were not, and it ceases to be in respect of righteousness and fellowship with God. And indeed, this is the death of all deaths, when the creature has subsisting and being, and yet for all that [it] is deprived of all comfortable fellowship with God.

The reason for this difference is because the soul of a man is a spirit or spiritual substance, whereas the soul of a beast is no substance, but a natural vigor or quality, and [it] has no being in itself without the body on which it wholly depends. Contrariwise, the soul of man is created from nothing and breathed into the body, and subsists forth of it as well as in it.

The Kinds of Death

The kinds of death are two (as are the kinds of life): bodily and spiritual. Bodily death is nothing else but the separation of the soul from the body, as bodily life is the conjunction of body and soul. And this death is called "the first" because in respect of time it goes before the second. Spiritual death is the separation of the whole man, both in body and soul, from the gracious fellowship of God. Of these two, the first is but an entrance to death, and the second is the accomplishment of it. For as the soul is the life of the body, so God is the life of the soul, and His Spirit is the soul of our souls, and the want of fellowship with Him brings nothing but the endless and unspeakable horrors and pangs of death.

Again, spiritual death has three distinct and several degrees. The first is when a man, who is alive in respect of temporal life, lies dead in sin. Paul speaks of this degree when he says, "But she that liveth in pleasure is dead while she liveth" (1 Tim. 5:6). And this is the case of all men by nature, who are children of wrath and "dead in sins and trespasses" (Eph. 2:1). The second degree is the very end of this life when the body is laid in the earth, and the soul descends to the place of torment. The third degree is in the day of judgment, when the body and soul meet again and go both to the place of the damned, there to be tormented forever and ever.

Having thus found the nature and differences and kinds of death, it is more than manifest that the text in hand is to be understood, not of the spiritual, but of the bodily death, because it is opposed to the birth or nativity of man. The words then must carry this sense: the time of bodily death, in which the body and soul of man are severed asunder, is better than the time in which one is brought into the world.

Point 2

Thus much of the first point; now follows the second. And that is: How can what Solomon says, "the day of death is better than the day of birth," be true? I ask not this question to call the Scriptures (which are truth itself) into controversy, but I do it for this end: that we might without wavering be resolved of what Solomon avouches. For there may be sundry reasons brought to the contrary. Therefore, let us handle the question. The reasons or objections, which may be alleged to the contrary, may all be reduced to six heads.[7]

Objection 1

The first is taken from the opinion of wise men who think it [is] the best thing of all never to be born, and the next best [thing is] to die quickly. Now, if it is the best thing in the world not to be born at all, then it is the worst thing (that can be) to die after a man is born.[8]

Answer. There are two sorts of men: first, [those who] live and die in their sins without repentance; [and,] second, [those who] unfeignedly repent and believe in Christ. Now this sentence may be truly avouched of the first, of whom we may say as Christ said to Judas: "It had been good for him that he had never been born" (Matt. 26:24). But the saying, applied to the second sort of men, is false. For to them, who in this life turn to God by repentance, the best thing of all is to be born because their birth is a degree of preparation to happiness, and the next best [thing] is to die quickly because by death they enter into possession of their happiness. For this cause Balaam desired to die the death of the righteous.[9] And Solomon, in this place, prefers the day of death before the day of birth, understanding that death which is joined with [a] godly life (or the death of the righteous).

Objection 2

The second objection is taken from the testimonies of Scripture. Death is the "wages of sin" (Rom. 6:23). It is an "enemy of Christ" (1 Cor. 15:26) and "the curse of the law."[10] Hence, it seems to follow that in and by death men receive

7. This paragraph break is not in the original.
8. This paragraph break is not in the original.
9. Num. 23:10.
10. Gal. 3:13.

their wages and payment for their sins, that the day of death is the doleful day in which the enemy prevails against us, [and] that he who dies is cursed.[11]

Answer. We must distinguish of death. It must be considered [in] two ways: first, as it is by itself in its own nature; [and,] second, as it is altered and changed by Christ. Now death, considered by itself, is indeed the wages of sin, an enemy of Christ and of all His members, and the curse of the law, yea the very suburbs and the gates of hell. Yet, in the second respect, it is not so. For by the virtue of the death of Christ, it ceases to be a plague or punishment, and of a curse it is made a blessing, and [it] is become unto us a passage (or midway) between this life and eternal life, and (as it were) a new wicket (or door) whereby we pass out of this world and enter into heaven. And in this respect the saying of Solomon is most true. For in the day of birth men are born and brought forth into the vale of misery, but afterwards, when they go hence, having death altered unto them by the death of Christ, they enter into eternal joy and happiness with all the saints of God forever.

Objection 3

The third objection is taken from the examples of [the] most worthy men who have made their prayers against death. As our Savior Christ, who prayed in this manner: "Father if it be thy will, let this cup pass from me, yet not my will but thy will be done" (Luke 22:42). And David prayed, "Return, O Lord, deliver my soul, save me for thy mercy's sake: for in death there is no remembrance of thee: in the grave who shall praise thee?" (Ps. 6:4–5). And Hezekiah, when the prophet Isaiah bade him set his house in order, and told him that he must die, wept sore[ly], and that in respect of death (Isa. 38:1–3). Now by the examples of these most worthy men, yea by the example of the Son of God Himself, it may seem that the day of death is the most terrible and doleful day of all.[12]

Answer. When our Savior Christ prayed thus to His Father, He was in His agony, and He then stood as our Redeemer in our room and stead to suffer all things that we should have suffered in our own persons for our sins. And, therefore, He prayed not simply against death, but against the cursed death of the cross, and He feared not death itself, which is the separation of the body and the soul, but the curse of the law which went with death, namely the unspeakable wrath and indignation of God. The first death troubled Him not, but the first and second [deaths] joined together [did].[13]

Touching David, when he made Psalm 6, he was not only sick in body, but also perplexed with the greatest temptation of all, in that he wrestled in

11. This paragraph break is not in the original.
12. This paragraph break is not in the original.
13. This paragraph break is not in the original.

conscience with the wrath of God, as appears by the words of the text, where he says, "Lord, rebuke me not in thy wrath."[14] And by this we see that he prayed not simply against death, but against death at that instant when he was in that grievous temptation. For at other times he had no such fear of death, as he himself testifies, saying, "Though I should walk through the valley of the shadow of death, I will fear no evil" (Ps. 23:4). Therefore, he prayed against death only as it was joined with the apprehension of God's wrath.[15]

Lastly, Hezekiah prayed against death, not only because he desired to live and do service to God in His kingdom, but upon a further and more special regard: because when the prophet brought the message of death, he was without issue,[16] and [he] had none of his own body to succeed him in his kingdom. It will be said, what warrant had Hezekiah to pray against death for this cause? *Answer.* His warrant was good, for God had made a particular promise to David and his posterity after him that so long as they feared God and walked in His commandments, they should not want issue to sit upon the throne of the kingdom after them (1 Kings 8:25). Now Hezekiah, at the time of the prophet's message, remembering what promise God had made, and how he for his part had kept the condition thereof, in that he had walked before God with an upright heart, and had done that which was acceptable in His sight, he prayed against death, not so much because he feared the danger of it, but because he wanted issue. God accepted and heard this prayer, and He added fifteen years unto his days, and two years after [He] gave him Manasseh.

Objection 4

The fourth objection is that those who have been reputed to be of the better sort of men oftentimes have miserable ends, for some end their days despairing, some raving and blaspheming, some strangely tormented. It may seem, therefore, that the day of death is the day of greatest woe and misery.

Answer. To this I answer, first of all, generally, that we must not judge of the estate of any man before God by outward things, whether they are blessings or judgments, whether they fall in life or death. For, as Solomon says, "All things come alike to all: and the same condition is to the just and the wicked, to the good and to the pure and to the polluted, and to him that sacrificeth and to him that sacrificeth not: as is the good so is the sinner, he that sweareth, as he that feareth an oath" [Eccl. 9:2].[17]

14. Ps. 6:1.
15. This paragraph break is not in the original.
16. *Issue:* posterity.
17. This paragraph break is not in the original.

Second, I answer the particulars which are alleged in this manner. And, first of all, touching despair, it is true that not only wicked and loose persons despair in death, but also repentant sinners, who oftentimes in their sickness testify of themselves that, being alive and lying in their beds, they feel themselves (as it were) to be in hell, and to apprehend the very pangs and torments thereof. And I doubt not for all this but that the child of God, most dear unto Him, may through the gulf of desperation attain to everlasting happiness. This appears by the manner of God's dealing in the matter of our salvation. All the works of God are done in and by their contraries. In the creation, all things were made, not of something, but of nothing, clean contrary to the course of nature. In the work of redemption, God gives life, not by life, but by death. And if we consider aright of Christ upon the cross, we shall see our paradise out of paradise in the midst of hell, for out of His own cursed death He does bring us life and eternal happiness. Likewise, in effectual vocation, when it pleases God to convert and turn men unto Him, He does it by the means of the gospel preached, which in reason should drive all men from God. For it is as contrary to the nature of man as fire to water and light to darkness, and yet for all this, though it is thus against the disposition and heart of man, it prevails with him and turns him to God. Furthermore, when God will send His own servants to heaven, He sends them a contrary way, even by the gates of hell. And when it is His pleasure to make men depend on His favor and providence, He makes them feel His anger and to be nothing in themselves, so that they may wholly depend upon Him, and be whatsoever they are in Him. This point being well considered, it is manifest that the child of God may pass to heaven by the gulfs of hell. The love of God is like a sea into which when a man is cast, he neither feels bottom nor sees bank. I conclude, therefore, that despair, whether it arises from weakness of nature or from conscience of sin, though it falls out about the time of death, cannot prejudice the salvation of them who are effectually called.[18]

As for other strange events which fall out in death, they are the effects of diseases. Raving and blaspheming arise from the disease of melancholy and of frenzies, which often happen at the end of burning fevers, the choler shooting up to the brain. The writhing of the lips, the turning of the neck, the buckling of the joints and the whole body, proceed from cramps and convulsions, which follow after much evacuation. And whereas some in sickness are of that strength that three or four men cannot hold them without bonds, it comes not from witchcraft and possessions, as people commonly think, but of choler in the veins. And whereas some, when they are dead, become as black as pitch

18. This paragraph break is not in the original.

(as Bonner was)[19] it may arise by a bruise, or an impostume,[20] or by the black jaundice, or by the putrefaction of the liver. And it does not always argue some extraordinary judgment of God.[21]

Now these and the like diseases, with their symptoms and strange effects, though they shall deprive man of his health, and of the right use of the parts of his body, and of the use of reason too, yet they cannot deprive his soul of eternal life. And all sins, procured by violent diseases, and proceeding from repentant sinners, are sins of infirmity. If they know them, and come again to the use of reason, they will further repent of these [sins]. If not, [these sins] are pardoned and buried in the death of Christ. And we ought not so much to stand upon the strangeness of any man's end when we know the goodness of his life. For we must judge a man, not by his death, but by his life. And if this is true, that strange diseases, and thereupon strange behaviors in death, may befall the best man that is, we must learn to reform our judgments of such as lie at the point of death. The common opinion is that if a man dies quietly and goes away like a lamb (which in some diseases, as consumptions and such like, any man may do), then he goes straight to heaven. But if the violence of the disease stirs up impatience, and causes frantic behaviors in the party, then men usually say [that] there is a judgment of God serving either to discover a hypocrite or to plague a wicked man. But the truth is otherwise. For, indeed, a man may die like a lamb and yet go to hell. And one, dying in exceeding torments and strange behaviors of the body, may go to heaven. And by the outward condition of any man, either in life or death, we are not to judge of his estate before God.

Objection 5

The fifth objection is this: when a man is most near death, then the devil is most busy in temptation, and the more men are assaulted by Satan, the more dangerous and troublesome is their case. And, therefore, it may seem that the day of death is the worst day of all.[22]

Answer. The condition of God's children in death is twofold: some are not tempted, and some are. Some, I say, are not tempted, as Simeon who, when he had seen Christ, broke forth and said, "Lord, now lettest thou thy servant depart in peace, etc."[23] [This] signified, no doubt, that he should end his days in all manner of peace. As for them who are tempted, though their case is very

---

19. Possibly a reference to Edmund Bonner (1500–1569), bishop of London, who was known as "bloody" Bonner for his persecution of Protestants during the reign of Mary I.

20. *Impostume:* abscess.

21. This paragraph break is not in the original.

22. This paragraph break is not in the original.

23. Luke 2:29.

troublesome and perplexed, yet their salvation is not further off by reason of the violence and extremity of temptation. For God is then present by the unspeakable comfort of His Spirit. And when we are most weak, He is most strong in us, because His manner is to show His power in weakness. And for this cause, even in the time of death, the devil receives the greatest foil when he looks for the greatest victory.

Objection 6

The sixth objection is this: violent and sudden death is a grievous curse, and of all [the] evils which befall man in this life none is so terrible. Therefore, it may seem that the day of sudden death is most miserable.[24]

Answer. It is true indeed that sudden death is a curse and a grievous judgment of God and, therefore, [it is] not without cause [to be] feared by men in the world. Yet, all things considered, we ought to be more afraid of an impenitent and evil life than of sudden death. For though it is evil as death itself is in its own nature, yet we must not think it to be simply evil, because it is not evil to all men nor evil in all respects. I say it is not evil to all men, considering that no kind of death is evil or a curse unto them who are in Christ, who are freed from the whole curse of the law. And, therefore, the Holy Spirit says, "Blessed are they that die in the Lord, for they rest from their labor" (Rev. 14:13). Whereby is signified that they who depart this life, being members of Christ, enter into everlasting happiness, of whatsoever death they die, yea though it is sudden death. Again, I say that sudden death is not evil in all respects. For it is not evil because it is sudden, but because it commonly takes men unprepared, and by that means makes the day of death a black day, and (as it were) a very speedy downfall to the gulf of hell. Otherwise, if a man is ready and prepared to die, sudden death is in effect no death, but a quick and speedy entrance to eternal life.

These objections being thus answered, it appears to be a manifest truth which Solomon says, "the day of death is better indeed than the day of birth."[25]

Point 3

Now I come to the third point, in which the reasons and respects, which make the day of death to surpass the day of a man's birth, are to be considered. And they may all be reduced to this one, namely, that the day [of] birth is an entrance into all woe and misery, whereas the day of death, joined with [a] godly and reformed life, is an entrance (or degree) to eternal life. I make this

---

24. This paragraph break is not in the original.
25. This paragraph break is not in the original.

manifest thus: Eternal life has three degrees. [The first is] in this life, when a man can truly say that he lives not, but that Christ lives in him. And all men can say this, who repent and believe, and are justified and sanctified, and have peace of conscience with [the] other gifts of God's Spirit, which are the earnest of their salvation. The second degree is in this life, when the body goes to the earth, and the soul is carried by the angels into heaven. The third [degree] is in the end of the world at the last judgment, when body and soul [are] reunited, [and] do jointly enter into eternal happiness in heaven.

Now, of these three degrees, death itself, being joined with the fear of God, is the second. It also contains in it two worthy steps to life.[26]

Step 1

The first is a freedom from all miseries, which have their end in death. For though men in this life are subject to manifold dangers by sea and land, as also to sundry aches, pains, and diseases (as fevers, consumptions, etc.), yet when death comes, there is an end of all.[27]

Second, so long as men live in this world, whatsoever they are, they do in some part lie in bondage under original corruption and the remnants thereof (which are doubting of God's providence, unbelief, pride of heart, ignorance, covetousness, ambition, envy, hatred, lust, and such like sins), which bring forth fruits unto death. And to be in subjection to sin in this manner is a misery of all miseries. Therefore, when Paul was tempted unto sin by his corruption, [he] calls the very temptation "the buffets of Satan" and (as it were) a prick (or thorn) wounding his flesh and paining him at the very heart [2 Cor. 12:7]. Again, in another place, wearied with his own corruptions, he complains that he is sold under sin, and he cries out, "O miserable man that I am, who shall deliver me from this body of death?" (Rom. 7:24). David says that his eyes "gushed out with rivers of tears when other men sinned against God" (Ps. 119:136). How much more then was he grieved for the sins wherewith he himself was overtaken in this life? And, indeed, it is a very hell for a man, who has but a spark of grace, to be exercised, turmoiled, and tempted with the inborn corruptions and rebellions of his own heart. And if a man would devise a torment for such as fear God and desire to walk in newness of life, he cannot devise a greater than this. For this cause, blessed is the day of death, which brings with it a freedom from all sin whatsoever. For when we die, the corruption of nature is quite abolished and sanctification is accomplished.[28]

26. This paragraph break is not in the original.
27. This paragraph break is not in the original.
28. This paragraph break is not in the original.

Lastly, it is a great misery that the people of God are constrained in this world to live and converse in the company of the wicked, as sheep are mingled with goats which strike them, annoy their pasture, and muddy their water. Hereupon David cried out, "Woe is me that I remain in Mesech, and dwell in the tents of Kedar" (Ps. 120:5). When Elijah saw that Ahab and Jezebel had planted idolatry in Israel, and that they also sought his life, he went apart into the wilderness and desired to die [1 Kings 19:4]. But this misery is also ended in the day of death, in as much as death is (as it were) the hand of God to sort and single out those who are the servants of God from all ungodly men in this most wretched world.

Furthermore, this exceeding benefit comes by death: that it does not only abolish the miseries which presently are upon us, but also prevents those which are to come. "The righteous perisheth, and no man considereth it in his heart: and merciful men are taken away, and no man understandeth that the righteous is taken away from the evil to come" (Isa. 57:1). We have an example of this in Josiah. "Because thine heart did melt, and thou hast humbled thyself before the Lord, when thou heardest what I spoke against this place…behold therefore I will gather thee to thy fathers, and thou shalt be put in thy grave in peace, and thine eyes shall not see all the evil which I will bring upon this place" (2 Kings 22:19–20). And Paul says that among the Corinthians "some were asleep (that is, dead) that they might not be condemned with the world" (1 Cor. 11:32).

Step 2

Thus much of freedom from misery, which is the first benefit that comes by death, and the first step to life. Now follows the second, which is that death gives an entrance to the soul, that it may come into the presence of the everlasting God, of Christ, and of all the angels and saints in heaven. The worthiness of this benefit makes the death of the righteous to be no death, but rather a blessing to be wished by all men. The consideration of this made Paul to say, "I desire to be dissolved" (Phil. 1:23). But what is the cause of this desire? It follows in the next words, namely that by this dissolution he might "come to be with Christ." When the Queen of Sheba saw all of Solomon's wisdom, and the house that he had built, and the meat of his table, and the sitting of his servants, and the order of his ministers, and their apparel, etc., she said, "Happy are thy men, happy are these thy servants which stand ever before thee and hear thy wisdom" (1 Kings 10:8). Much more then may we say that they, who stand not in the presence of an earthly king but before the King of kings, the Lord of heaven and earth, and enjoy at His right-hand pleasures forevermore, are ten thousand-fold happier. Moses has been renowned in all ages for this, that God vouchsafed him but so much favor as to see His hinder parts at his request.[29] O then, what happiness is this, to see the glory and majesty of God face to face, and to have eternal fellowship with God our Father, Christ our Redeemer, and the Holy Spirit our Comforter, and to live with the blessed saints and angels in heaven forever.

Thus, the third point is now manifest, namely in what respects death is more excellent than life.

Objection

It may be here [that] the mind of [the] unsatisfied man will yet further reply and say that howsoever the souls of men enter into heaven at death, yet their bodies, though they have been tenderly kept for meat, drink, and apparel, and have slept many a night in beds of down, must lie in dark and loathsome graves, and there be wasted and consumed by worms.[30]

Answer. All this is true indeed, but all is nothing, if (so be it) we will but consider aright of our graves as we ought. We must not judge of our graves as they appear to the bodily eye, but we must look upon them by the eye of faith, and consider them as they are altered and changed by the death and burial of Christ, who, having vanquished death upon the cross, pursued it afterwards to its own den, and foiled it there, and deprived it of its power. And by this means Christ has buried our death in His own death, and by the virtue of His burial, as sweet incense, [He] has sweetened and perfumed our graves, and made them of stinking and loathsome cabins to become princely palaces and beds of most sweet and happy rest, far more excellent than beds of down [Isa. 57:2].

And though the body rots in the grave, or is eaten by worms or by fish in the sea, or [is] burned to ashes, yet that will not be unto us a matter of discomfort, if we do well consider the ground of all grace, namely our conjunction with Christ. It is indeed a spiritual and yet a most real conjunction. And we must not imagine that our souls alone are joined to the body or soul of Christ, but the whole person of man, both in body and soul, is joined and united to [a] whole Christ. And when we are once joined to Christ in this mortal life by the bond of the Spirit, we shall remain and continue eternally joined with Him. And this union, once truly made, shall never be dissolved. Hence, it follows that, although the body is severed from the soul in death, yet neither body nor soul are severed from Christ, but the very body, rotting in the grave, drowned in the sea, burned to ashes, abides still united to Him, and is as truly a member of Christ then as before.[31]

29. Exod. 33:23.

30. This paragraph break is not in the original.

31. This paragraph break is not in the original.

We must remember this point as the foundation of all our comfort, and hold it forever as a truth. For look [at] what was the condition of Christ in death, the same or the like is the condition of all His members. Now the condition of Christ was this: though His body and soul were severed from each other as far as heaven and the grave, yet neither of them was severed from the Godhead of the Son, but both did in death subsist in His person. And, therefore, though our bodies and souls are pulled asunder by natural or violent death, yet neither of them (no not the body itself) shall be severed and disjoined from Christ. It will be alleged that if the body were then united to Christ, it should live and be quickened in the grave. *Answer*. Not so. When a man's arm or leg is taken with the dead palsy, it receives little or no heat, life, sense, or motion from the body. And yet, notwithstanding, it still remains a member of the body because its flesh and bone remain joined to the body's flesh and bone. Even so, the body remains a member of Christ, though for some space of time it receives neither sense nor motion nor life from the soul or from the Spirit of Christ.

Furthermore, we must remember that by the virtue of this conjunction, the dead body (be it rotten, burned, devoured, or howsoever consumed) shall rise to eternal glory at the day of judgment. In the winter season, trees remain without fruit or leaves and, being beaten with wind and weather, appear (to the eye) as if they were rotten trees. Yet, when the spring time comes again, they bring forth (as before) buds, blossoms, leaves, and fruit. The reason is because the body, grains, and arms of trees are all joined to the root, where the sap lies in the winter season, and whence by means of this conjunction it is derived to all the parts of the tree in the spring time. Even so, the bodies of men have their winter also, in which they are turned to dust, and so remain for the space of many thousands [of] years. Yet, in the day of judgment, by means of that mystical conjunction with Christ, divine and quickening virtue shall stream thence to all the bodies of the elect to cause them to live again, and that to life eternal.[32]

But some will say that the wicked also rise again. *Answer*. They do so indeed, but not by the same cause, for they rise by the power of Christ as He is a judge to condemn them, whereas the godly rise again by the virtue of Christ's resurrection, whereof they are partakers by means of that blessed and indissoluble conjunction which they have with Christ. And the bodies of the elect, though they putrefy and consume ever so much in the grave, yet they are still in the favor of God and in the covenant of grace. Because they have [a] right and title to [this covenant], they (being dead) shall not remain so forever, but shall rise to glory at the last judgment. Therefore, the rotting of the body is nothing in respect, and the death of the body is no death. And, therefore, death in the

32. This paragraph break is not in the original.

Old and New Testaments is also made but a sleep, and the grave a bed, whereof the like was never seen, wherein a man may rest, nothing at all troubled with dreams or fantasies, and whence he shall rise no more subject to weakness or sickness, but presently be translated to eternal glory. By this then, which has been said, it appears that the death of the righteous is a second degree to everlasting happiness.

Now then, considering our conjunction with Christ is the foundation of all our joy and comfort in life and death, we are in the fear of God to learn this one lesson, namely, that while we have time in this world, we must labor to be united unto Christ, so that we may be bone of His bone and flesh of His flesh. This very point is (as it were) a flagon of wine to revive our souls when they are in a swoon at any instant. And that we may be assured that we are certainly joined to Christ, we must show ourselves to be members of His mystical body by the daily fruits of righteousness and true repentance. And being once certainly assured in conscience of our being in Christ, let death come when it will, and let it cruelly part asunder both body and soul, yet they shall both remain in the covenant, and by means thereof be reunited and taken up to eternal life. Whereas, on the contrary, if men are out of the covenant and die out of Christ, their souls go to hell, and their bodies rot for a time in the grave, but afterwards they rise to endless perdition. Wherefore, I say, again and again, labor that your consciences by the Holy Spirit may testify that you are living stones in the temple of God, and branches bearing fruit in the true vine. And then you shall feel by experience that the pangs of death shall be a further degree of happiness than ever you found in your lives, even then when you are gasping and panting for breath.

Thus much of the meaning of the text; now follows the uses, and they are manifold.

DOCTRINE 1:
We Must Seek to Die Well

The first and principal is this: in that Solomon prefers the day of death before the day of birth, he does therein give us to understand that there is a direct and certain way whereby a man may die well. If it had been otherwise, he could not have said that "the day of death is better." And whereas he avouches this, he shows withal that there is an infallible way whereby a man may make a blessed end. Therefore, let us now come to search out this way. The knowledge and true understanding of it must not be fetched from the writings of men, but from the Word of God, who has the power of life and death in His own hand.

Now that a man may die well, God's Word requires two things: a preparation before death, and a right behavior and disposition in death.

Requirement 1: Our Preparation for Death

The preparation unto death is an action of a repentant sinner whereby he makes himself fit and ready to die, and [it] is a very necessary duty to which we are bound by God's commandment. For there are sundry places of Scripture which do straightly enjoin us to watch and pray, and to make ourselves ready every day against the second coming of Christ to judgment. Now the same places do withal bind us to make preparation against death, at which time God comes to judgment unto us particularly. Again, look, as death leaves a man, so shall the last judgment find him, and so shall he abide eternally. There may be changes and conversions from evil to good in this life, but after death there is no change at all. Therefore, a preparation to death can in no way be omitted by him who desires to make a happy and blessed end. This preparation is twofold: general and particular.

Part 1: General Preparation

General preparation is that whereby a man prepares himself to die through the whole course of his life.[33]

The Need for General Preparation

[This is] a duty most needful, which must in no way be omitted. The reasons are these:

First of all, death which is certain is most uncertain. I say it is certain, because no man can eschew death. And it is uncertain three ways. (1) In regard of time, for no man knows when he shall die. (2) In regard of place, for no man knows where he shall die, whether in his bed or in the field, whether by sea or by land. (3) In respect of the kind of death, for no man knows whether he shall die of a lingering or sudden, of a violent or natural, death. Hence, it follows that men should every day prepare themselves for death. Indeed, if we could know when, where, and how we will die, the case would be otherwise. But, seeing we know none of these, it stands us in hand to look about us.[34]

A second reason, serving further to persuade us, is this: the most dangerous thing of all in this world is to neglect all preparation. To make this point more manifest, I will use this comparison. A certain man, pursued by a unicorn, in his flight falls into a dungeon, and in his fall takes hold and hangs by the arm

33. This paragraph break is not in the original.
34. This paragraph break is not in the original.

of a tree. Now, as he thus hangs, looking downward, he sees two worms gnawing at the root of the tree, and as he looks upward he sees a hive of most sweet honey. Whereupon he climbs up to it and, sitting by it, [he] feeds thereon. In the meantime, while he is thus sitting, the two worms gnaw in pieces the root of the tree. Once done, [the] tree and [the] man and all fall into the bottom of the dungeon. Now this unicorn is death. The man, who flees, is each one of us and every living man. The pit, over which he hangs, is hell. The arm of the tree is life itself. The two worms are day and night. The continuance whereof is the whole life of man. The hive of honey is the pleasures and profits and honors of this world. When men wholly give themselves to these, not considering their ends till the tree root (that is, this temporal life) is cut off, they plunge themselves quite into the gulf of hell. By this, we see that there is good cause that men should not defer their preparation till the time of sickness, but rather every day make themselves ready against the day of death.[35]

But some will say [that] it shall suffice if I prepare myself to pray when I begin to be sick. *Answer.* These men greatly deceive themselves, for the time then is most unfit to begin a preparation, because all the senses and powers of the body are occupied about the pains and troubles of the disease. And the sick party is exercised partly in conference with the physician, partly with the minister about his soul's health and matters of conscience, and partly with friends who come to visit. Therefore, some preparation must go before in the time of health, when the whole man with all the powers of body and soul are at liberty.[36]

Second, there are some others who imagine and say that a man may repent when he will, even in the time of death, and that such repentance is sufficient. *Answer.* It is false what they say, for it is not in the power of man to repent when he himself wills. When God wills, he may. It is not in him who wills or runs, but in God who has mercy. And Christ says that many shall seek to enter into heaven and shall not be able. But why so? Because they seek when it is too late, namely when the time of grace is past. Therefore, it is exceeding folly for men to dream (so much as once) that they may have repentance at command. Nay, it is a just judgment that they who did condemn God in their life should be condemned by God in death, and that they who did forget God in their health should quite be forgotten by God in sickness. Again, I answer that this late repentance is seldom or never true repentance. It is sick, like the party himself, commonly languishing and dying together with him. Repentance should be voluntary (as all obedience to God ought) but repentance taken up in sickness

35. This paragraph break is not in the original.
36. This paragraph break is not in the original.

is usually constrained and extorted by the fear of hell and other judgments of God. For crosses, afflictions, and sickness will cause the grossest hypocrite (that ever was) to stoop and buckle under the hand of God, and to dissemble faith and repentance and every grace of God as though he had them as fully as any of the true servants of God, whereas indeed he wants them altogether. Wherefore, such repentance is commonly but counterfeit. For in true and sound repentance men must forsake their sins. But in this [repentance] the sin forsakes the man, who leaves all his evil ways only upon this, that he is constrained to leave the world. Wherefore, it is a thing greatly to be wished that men would repent and prepare themselves to die in the time of health before the day of death or sickness comes.[37]

Lastly, it is alleged that one of the thieves repented upon the cross. *Answer.* The thief was called after the eleventh hour at the point of the twelfth, when he was now dying and drawing on. Therefore, his conversion was altogether miraculous and extraordinary. And there was a special reason why Christ would have him to be called then: that while He was suffering He might show forth the virtue of His passion, so that all who saw the one might also acknowledge the other. Now it is not good for men to make an ordinary rule [out] of an extraordinary example.

The Manner of General Preparation

Thus then, this point being manifest, that a general preparation must be made, let us now see in what manner it must be done. And for the right doing of it, five duties must be practiced in the course of our lives.[38]

Duty 1. The first is the meditation of death in the time of life. For the life of a Christian is nothing else but a meditation of death. A notable practice hereof we have in the example of Joseph of Arimathea, who made his tomb in his life time in the midst of his garden. No doubt [he did so] for this end: to put himself in mind of death, and that in the midst of his delight and pleasures. Heathen philosophers, who never knew Christ, had many excellent meditations of death though not comfortable in regard of everlasting life. Now we, who have known and believed in Christ, must go beyond them in this point, considering with[in] ourselves such things as they never thought of, namely, the cause of death, our sin, [and] the remedy thereof, the cursed death of Christ. I say "cursed" in regard of the kind of death and punishment laid upon Him, but "blessed" in regard of us. Third, we must often meditate of the presence of death. We do this

37. This paragraph break is not in the original.
38. This paragraph break is not in the original.

when, by God's grace, we make an account of every present day as if it were the present day of our death, and reckon with ourselves, when we go to bed, as though we should never rise again, and when we rise, as though we should never lie down again.

This meditation of death is of special use and brings forth many fruits in the life of man. First of all, it serves to humble us under the hand of God. We have an example in Abraham, who said, "Behold I have begun now to speak to my Lord, and I am but dust and ashes" (Gen. 18:27). Mark here, how the consideration of his mortality made him to abase and cast down himself in the sight of God. And thus, if we could reckon of every day as of the last day, it would straightway pull down our peacock's feathers, and make us with Job abhor ourselves in dust and ashes.

Second, this meditation is a means to further repentance. When Jonah came to Nineveh and cried, "Yet forty days and Nineveh shall be destroyed," the whole city repented in sackcloth and ashes (Jonah 3:4–5). When Elijah came to Ahab and told him that the dogs should eat Jezebel by the wall of Jezreel, and him also of Ahab's stock who died in the city, etc., it made him to humble himself so as the Lord says to Elijah: "Seest thou how Ahab is humbled before me" (1 Kings 21:29). Now if the remembrance of death was of such force in him who was but a hypocrite, how excellent a means of grace will it be in them who truly repent.

Third, this meditation seems to stir up contentation in every estate and condition of life that shall befall us. Righteous Job, in the very midst of his afflictions, comforts himself with this consideration: "Naked came I forth of my mother's womb, and naked shall I return again...blessed be the name of the Lord" (Job 1:21). And surely, the often meditation of this, that a man can carry nothing with him from all his abundance but a coffin or a winding sheet or both, should be a forcible means to repress the insatiable desire of riches and the love of this world.

Thus, we see what an effectual means this meditation is to increase and further the grace of God in the hearts of men. Now I commend this first duty to your Christian consideration, desiring the practice of it in your lives. That it may take place, two things must be performed.[39]

First, labor to pluck out of your hearts a wicked and erroneous imagination, whereby every man naturally blesses himself and thinks highly of himself, and though he has one foot in the grave, yet he persuades himself that he shall not yet die. There is almost no man so old but, by the corruption of his heart, he thinks that he shall live one year longer. Cruel and unmerciful death makes

39. This paragraph break is not in the original.

league with no man. And yet, the prophet Isaiah says that "the wicked man makes a league with death" (Isa. 28:15). How can this be? There is no league made indeed, but only in the wicked imagination of man, who falsely thinks that death will not come near him, though all the world should be destroyed. See an example in the parable of the rich man, who having stored up abundance of wealth for many years, said unto his own soul: "Soul, thou hast much goods laid up for many years, live at ease, eat, drink, and take thy pastime" (Luke 12:19), whereas his soul was fetched away presently. And seeing this natural corruption is in every man's heart, we must daily fight against it, and labor by all might and main that it takes no place in us. For so long as it shall prevail, we shall be utterly unfit to make any preparation to death. We ought rather to endeavor to attain to the mind and meditation of Saint Jerome, who testifies of himself in this manner: "Whether I wake or sleep, or whatsoever I do, I think I hear the sound of the trumpet, 'Rise ye dead, and come to judgment.'"[40]

The second thing which we are to practice, so that we may come to a serious meditation of our own end, is to make prayer unto God that we might be enabled to resolve ourselves of death continually. Thus, David prayed, "Lord, make me to know mine end, and the measure of my days, let me know how long I have to live" (Ps. 39:4). And Moses, "Lord, teach me to number my days, that I may apply mine heart unto wisdom" (Ps. 90:12). It may be said, what need men pray to God that they might be able to number their days? Cannot they of themselves reckon a few years and days, who are able by art to measure the globe of the earth, and the spheres of heaven, and the quantities of the stars, with their longitudes, latitudes, altitudes, motions, and distances from the earth? No verily. For howsoever by a general speculation we think something of our end, yet unless the Spirit of God is our schoolmaster to teach us our duty, we shall never be able soundly to resolve ourselves of the presence and speediness of death. And, therefore, let us pray with David and Moses that God would enlighten our minds with knowledge, and fill our hearts with His grace, that we might rightly consider of death, and esteem of it every day and hour as if it were the day and hour of death.

Duty 2. The second duty in this general preparation is that every man must daily endeavor to take away from his own death the power and strength thereof. And I pray you mark this point. The Philistines saw by experience that Samson was of great strength and, therefore, they used means to know in what part of his body it lay. And when they found it to be in the hair of his head, they ceased not until it was cut off [Judges 16]. In like manner, the time will come when we

40. In the margin: In epist.

must encounter hand to hand with tyrannous and cruel death. The best, therefore, is beforehand, now while we have time, to search where the strength of death lies, which being once known, we must with speed cut off its (Samson's) locks, and bereave it of its power, disarm it, and make it altogether unable to prevail against us. Now to find out this matter, we need not use the counsel of any Delilah, for we have the Word of God which teaches us plainly where the strength of death consists, namely in our sins. As Paul says, "The sting of death is sin" (1 Cor. 15:56).[41]

Well then, knowing certainly that the power and force of every man's particular death lies in his own sins, we must spend our time and study in using good means that our sins may be removed and pardoned. And, therefore, we must daily inure ourselves in the practice of two duties. The first is to humble ourselves for all our past sins, partly [in] confessing them against ourselves, [and] partly in prayer crying to heaven for the pardon of them. The second is for time to come to turn unto God, and to carry a purpose, resolution, and endeavor in all things to reform both heart and life according to God's Word. These are the very principal and proper duties whereby the strength of death is much rebated, and it is made of a mighty and bloody enemy so far forth friendly and tractable that we may with comfort encounter with it and prevail too. Therefore, I commend these duties to your Christian considerations and careful practice, desiring that you would spend your days ever hereafter in doing them.[42]

If a man were to deal with a mighty dragon or serpent hand to hand in such [a] way as he must either kill or be killed, the best thing would be to bereave it of its sting or of that part of its body where its poison lies. Now death itself is a serpent, dragon, or scorpion, and sin is the sting or poison whereby he wounds and kills us. Wherefore, without any more delay, see that you pull out its sting. The practice of the foresaid duties is (as it were) a fit and worthy instrument to do the deed. Have you been a person ignorant of God's will, a contemner of His Word and worship, a blasphemer of His name, a breaker of His sabbaths, disobedient to parents and magistrates, a murderer, a fornicator, a railer, a slanderer, a covetous person, etc. Reform these sins and all others like them, pull them out by the roots from your heart, and cast them off. As many sins as are in you, so many stings of death are also in you to wound your soul to eternal death. Therefore, let not one sin remain, for which you have not humbled yourself and repented seriously. When death hurts any man, it takes the weapons whereby he is hurt from his own hand. It cannot do us the least

41. This paragraph break is not in the original.
42. This paragraph break is not in the original.

hurt but by the force of our own sins. Wherefore, I say again and again, lay this point to your hearts, and spend your strength, life, and health, that you may, before you die, abolish the strength of death. A man may put a serpent in his bosom when the sting is out. And we may let death creep into our bosoms, and grip us with its legs, and stab us at the heart, so long as it brings not its venom and poison with it.

And because the former duties are so necessary, as none can be more, I will use some further reasons to enforce them. Whatsoever a man would do when he is dying, he ought to do the same every day while he is living. Now the most notorious and wicked person who ever was, when he is dying, [he] will pray and desire others to pray for him, and [he will] promise amendment of life, protesting that if he might live, he would become a practitioner in all the good duties of faith, repentance, and reformation of life. Oh, therefore, be careful to do this every day. Again, the saying is true, [that] he who would live when he is dead must die while he is alive, namely to his sins. Would you then live eternally? Sue to heaven for your pardon, and see that now in your lifetime you die to your own sins. Lastly, wicked Balaam would fain die the death of the righteous. But, alas, it was to small purpose, for he would by no means live the life of the righteous. For his continual purpose and meaning was to follow his old ways in sorceries and covetousness. Now the life of a righteous man stands in the humbling of himself for his past sins, and in a careful reformation of life to come. Would you then die the death of the righteous? Then look unto it, that your life is the life of the righteous. If you will needs live the life of the unrighteous, you must look to die the death of the unrighteous. Remember this, and content not yourselves to hear the Word, but be doers of it.[43] For you learn no more indeed, whatever measure of knowledge you have, than [what] you practice [Eph. 4:21–22].

Duty 3. The third duty in our general preparation is, in this life, to enter into the first degree of eternal life. For, as I have said, there are three degrees of everlasting life, and the first of them is in this present life. For he who would live forever in eternal happiness must begin in this world to rise out of the grave of his own sins (in which by nature he lies buried), and live in newness of life, as it is said in the Revelation: "He that will escape the second death, must be made partaker of the first resurrection" (Rev. 20:6). And Paul says to the Colossians that they were in this life delivered from the power of darkness "and translated into the kingdom of Christ" (Col. 1:13). And Christ says to the church of the

43. James 1:22.

Jews: "The kingdom of heaven is amongst you."[44] Now this first degree of life is when a man can say with Paul, "I live not, but Christ lives in me" (Gal. 2:20); that is, "I find, partly by the testimony of my sanctified conscience and partly by experience, that Christ my Redeemer by His Spirit guides and governs my thoughts, will, affections, and all the powers of body and soul, according to the blessed direction of His holy will."[45]

Now that we might be able to say this, we must have three gifts and graces of God, wherein especially this first degree of life consists. The first is saving knowledge whereby we do truly resolve ourselves that God, the Father of Christ, is our Father, Christ His Son [is] our Redeemer, and the Holy Spirit [is] our Comforter. That this knowledge is one part of eternal life appears by the saying of Christ: "This is life eternal (that is, the beginning and entrance into life eternal), to know thee the only God, and whom thou hast sent, Jesus Christ" (John 17:3).[46]

The second grace is peace of conscience which "passeth all understanding" (Phil. 4:7). And, therefore, Paul says that the kingdom of heaven is "righteousness, peace of conscience, and joy in the Holy Spirit" (Rom. 14:17). The horror of a guilty conscience is the beginning of death and destruction. Therefore, peace of conscience, derived from the death of Christ, is life and happiness.[47]

The third [grace] is the regiment of the Spirit whereby the heart and life of man is ordered according to the Word of God. For Paul says that they who are the children of God "are led by the Spirit of Christ" (Rom. 8:14). Now seeing this is so (that if we would live eternally, we must begin to live that blessed and eternal life before we die), here we must be careful to reform two common errors.[48]

The first is that a man enters into eternal life when he dies and not before, which is a flat untruth. Our Savior Christ said to Zacchaeus: "This day is salvation come to thy house" (Luke 19:9). [He] gives us to understand that a man then begins to be saved when God does effectually call him by the ministry of the gospel. Whosoever then will be saved, when he is dying and dead, must begin to be saved while he is now living. His salvation must begin in this life, [if he] would come to salvation after this life. "Verily, verily," says Christ, "he that heareth my word, and believeth in him that sent me, hath eternal life" [John 5:24], namely in this present life.[49]

---

44. Luke 17:21.
45. This paragraph break is not in the original.
46. This paragraph break is not in the original.
47. This paragraph break is not in the original.
48. This paragraph break is not in the original.
49. This paragraph break is not in the original.

The second error is that howsoever a man lives, if, when he is dying he can lift up his eyes and say, "Lord, have mercy on me," he is certainly saved. Behold a very dangerous and foolish conceit, that deceives many a man! It is all one as if an arrant[50] thief should thus reason with himself, and say, "I will spend my days in robbing and stealing. I fear neither arraignment nor execution. For at the very time when I am to be turned off the ladder, if I do but call upon the judge, I know I shall have my pardon." Behold a most dangerous and desperate course! And the very same is the practice of careless men in the matter of their salvation. For a man may die with "Lord have mercy" in his mouth, and perish eternally, unless in this world he enters into the first degree of eternal life. "For not everyone that saith Lord, Lord, shall enter into heaven: but he that doth the will of the Father which is in heaven" (Matt. 7:21).

Duty 4. The fourth duty is to exercise and inure ourselves in dying by little and little so long as we live here upon earth, before we come to die indeed. And as men, who are appointed to run a race, exercise themselves in running so that they may get the victory, so we should begin to die now while we are living so that we might die well in the end. But some may say, how should this be done? Paul gives us direction in his own example when he says, "By the rejoicing which I have in Christ I die daily" (1 Cor. 15:31). And he died daily, not only because he was often in danger of death by reason of his calling, but also because in all his dangers and troubles he inured himself to die. For when men do make the right use of their afflictions, whether they are in body or mind or both, and do with all their might endeavor to bear them patiently, humbling themselves as under the correction of God, then they begin to die well. And to do this indeed is to take an excellent course. He who would mortify his greatest sins must begin to do it with small sins, which, when they are once reformed, a man shall be able more easily to overcome his master sins. So likewise, he who would be able to bear the cross of all crosses, namely death itself, must first of all learn to bear small crosses (as sickness in body, and troubles in mind, with losses of goods and of friends, and of a good name), which I may fitly term little deaths, and the beginnings of death itself. And we must first of all acquaint ourselves with these little deaths, before we can well be able to bear the greatest death of all.[51]

Again, the afflictions and calamities of this life are (as it were) the harbingers and purveyors of death. And we are first to learn how to entertain these messengers, so that when death, the Lord himself, shall come, we may in better

---

50. *Arrant:* utter, total, absolute.

51. In the margin: *Mors post crucem minor est* (Death is after small difficulties).

manner entertain him. Bilney,[52] the martyr, well considered this point. Oftentimes, before he was burned, [he] put his finger into the flame of the candle, not only to make trial of his ability in suffering, but also to arm and strengthen himself against greater torments in death. Thus, you see the fourth duty, which you must in anywise learn and remember, because we will not be able to bear the pangs of death well, unless we are first well-schooled and nurtured by sundry trials in this life.

Duty 5. The fifth and last duty is set down by Solomon: "All that thine hand shall find to do, do it with all thy power" (Eccl. 9:10). And mark the reason: "for there is neither work, nor invention, nor knowledge, nor wisdom in the grave whither thou goest." To the same purpose, Paul says, "Do good to all men while ye have time" (Gal. 6:10). Therefore, if any man is able to do any good service, either to God's church or to the commonwealth or to any private man, let him do it with all speed and with all his might, lest death itself prevents him. He who has care to spend his days thus shall end his life with much comfort and peace of conscience.

Part 2: Particular Preparation

Thus much of general preparation; now follows the particular, which is in the time of sickness. And here, first of all, I will show what is the doctrine of the papists, and then afterwards the truth.

By the popish order and practice, when a man is about to die, he is enjoined [to do] three things: first, to make sacramental confession, especially if it is in any mortal sin; second, to receive the eucharist; [and,] third, to require his anoiling,[53] that is, the sacrament (as they call it) of extreme unction.

They term sacramental confession a rehearsal or enumeration of all man's sins to a priest, that he may receive absolution. But sundry reasons may be alleged against this kind of confession.[54]

First of all, it has no warrant either by commandment or example in the whole Word of God. They say [it does,] and they endeavor to prove it thus: he who lies in any mortal sin is by God's law bound to do penance and to seek reconciliation with God; now the necessary means after baptism to obtain reconciliation is the confession of all our sins to a priest. Because Christ has appointed priests to be judges upon earth, with such measure of authority that no man, falling after baptism, can without their sentence and determination be reconciled. And they cannot rightly judge unless they know all [of] a man's

52. Thomas Bilney (1495–1531).
53. *Annoil:* anoint.
54. This paragraph break is not in the original.

sins. Therefore, all who fall after baptism are bound by God's Word to open all their sins to a priest. *Answer*. What they say is false, namely that priests are judges, having [the] power to examine and take knowledge of men's sins, and jurisdiction whereby they can properly absolve, pardon, or retain them. For God's Word has given no more to man but a "ministry of reconciliation" (2 Cor. 5:18) whereby in the name of God, and according to His Word, he does preach, declare, and pronounce that God does pardon or not pardon his sins. Again, pardon may truly be pronounced, and right judgment of the estate of any man, without a particular rehearsal of his sins. For he who soundly and truly repents of one or some few sins, repents of all.[55]

Second, this confession is overturned by the practice of the prophets and apostles, who not only absolved particular persons, but also whole churches without exaction of auricular confession. When Nathan, the prophet, had rebuked David for his two great and horrible crimes, David, touched with remorse, said, "I have sinned" (2 Sam. 12:13), and Nathan presently, without further examination, declared unto him in the name of God that his sins were forgiven him.[56]

Third, it cannot be proved by any good and sufficient proofs that this confession was used in the church of God till after five or six hundred years were expired. For the confession which was then in use was either public before the church or the opening of a public fault to some private person in secret. Therefore, to urge sick men unto it, lying at the point of death, is to lay more burdens on them than ever God appointed.

And whereas they make it a necessary thing to receive the eucharist in the time of sickness toward death, and that privately by the sick party alone, they have no warrant for their practice and opinion. For in the want of the sacrament there is no danger, but in the contempt. And the very contempt itself is a sin which may be pardoned, if we repent. And there is no reason why we should think that sick men should be deprived of the comfort of the Lord's Supper, if they receive it not in death, because the fruit and efficacy of the sacraments, once received, is not to be restrained to the time of receiving, but it extends itself to the whole time of man's life afterward. Again, the Supper of the Lord is no private action, but merely ecclesiastical. And, therefore, [it is] to be celebrated in the meeting and assembly of God's people, as our Savior Christ prescribes, when He says, "Do ye this" [Luke 22:19], and Paul in saying, "When ye come together" [1 Cor. 11:20].[57]

55. This paragraph break is not in the original.
56. This paragraph break is not in the original.
57. This paragraph break is not in the original.

But it is alleged that the Israelites did eat the Paschal lamb in their houses when they were in Egypt. *Answer.* The Israelites had then no liberty to make any public meeting for that end, and God commanded that the Paschal lamb should be eaten in all the houses of the Israelites at one and the same instant, and that in effect was as much as if it had been public.[58]

Second, they allege a canon of the Council of Nicea, which decrees that men, being about to die, must receive the eucharist, and not be deprived of the provision of food necessary for their journey.[59] *Answer.* The Council made no decree touching the administration of the sacrament to all men who die, but to such only as fell away from the faith in persecution, or fell into any other notorious crime, and were thereupon excommunicated, and so remained till death, and either then or somewhat before [they] testified their repentance for their offenses. And the canon was made for this end, that such persons might be assured that they were again received into the church, and by this means depart with more comfort.[60]

Third, it is objected that in the primitive church part of the eucharist was carried by a lad to Serapion, an aged man, lying sick in his bed.[61] *Answer.* It was indeed the custom of the ancient church, from the beginning, that the elements of the bread and wine should be sent by some of the deacons to the sick, who were absent from the assembly. And yet, nevertheless, here is no footing for private communions. For the eucharist was only sent when the rest of the church did openly communicate, and such as were then absent, only by reason of sickness, and desired to be partakers of that blessed communion, were to be reputed as present.[62]

Lastly, it is objected that it was the manner of men and women in former times to carry part of the sacrament home to their houses, and to reserve it till the time of necessity, as the time of sickness and such like.[63] *Answer.* The reservation of the sacrament was but a superstitious practice, though it is ancient. For out of the administration (that is, before it begins and after it is ended), the sacrament ceases to be a sacrament, and the elements to be elements. As for the practice of them who cram the eucharist into the mouth of them who were deceased, it is not only superstitious but also very absurd.[64]

---

58. This paragraph break is not in the original.
59. In the margin: Frauda. riviatico.
60. This paragraph break is not in the original.
61. In the margin: Euseb. l. 6. c. 36.
62. This paragraph break is not in the original.
63. In the margin: Basil. ep. ad Caes. Tertul. l. 2. ad uxorem. Heir. in Apol. prol. in lob.
64. In the margin: Concil. Carth. 3. can. 6.

As for the anoiling of the sick (that is, the anointing of the body, especially the organs or instruments of the senses) that the party may obtain the remission of his sins, comfort against all [the] temptations of the devil in the hour of death, and strength more easily to bear the pains of sickness and the pangs of death, and be again restored to his corporal health, if it is expedient for the salvation of his soul, it is but a dotage of man's brain, and has not so much as a show of reason to justify it. The fifth chapter of James is commonly alleged to this purpose, but the anointing there mentioned is not of the same kind with this greasy sacrament of the papists. For that anointing of the body was a ceremony used by the apostles and others, when they put in practice the miraculous gift of healing, which gift is now ceased. Second, that anointing had a promise that the party should recover his health [James 5:16]. But this popish anointing has no such promise, because for the most part the persons thus anointed in the primitive church always recovered. Third, the ancient anointing served only for the procuring of health, but this tends further to the procuring of remission of sins and strength in temptation.

Having thus seen the doctrine of the papists, I come now to speak of the true and right manner of making particular preparation before death, which contains three sorts of duties: one concerning God; the other concerning a man's own self; [and] the third concerning our neighbor.[65]

Concerning God

The first [duty] concerning God is to seek to be reconciled unto Him in Christ, though we have been long assured of His favor. All other duties must come after in the second place, and they are of little or no effect without this. Now this reconciliation must be sought for and is obtained by a renewing of our former faith and repentance. And they must be renewed in this manner. So soon as a man shall feel any manner of sickness to seize upon his body, he must consider with[in] himself whence it arises. And after serious consideration, he shall find that it comes not by chance or fortune, but by the special providence of God. This done, he must go yet further and consider for what cause the Lord should afflict his body with any sickness or disease. And he shall find by God's Word that sickness comes ordinarily and usually for sin. "Wherefore is the living man sorrowful? Man suffereth for his sin" (Lam. 3:39).[66]

It is true indeed [that] there are other causes of the wants of the body and of sickness beside sin. And though they are not known to us, yet they are known to the Lord. Hereupon Christ, when He saw a certain blind man, and

65. This paragraph break is not in the original.
66. This paragraph break is not in the original.

was demanded what was the cause of the blindness, answered, "Neither hath this man sinned nor his parents, but that the work of God should be showed on him" (John 9:2–3). Yet we, for our parts, who are to go not by the secret but the revealed will of God, must make this use of our sickness, that it is sent unto us for our sins. When Christ healed the man sick of the palsy, He said, "Be of good comfort, thy sins are forgiven thee" (Matt. 9:2). And when He had healed the man by the pool of Bethesda, who had been sick thirty-eight years, He bids him "sin no more lest a worse thing happen unto him" [John 5:14]. [He] gave them both to understand that their sickness came by reason of their sins. And every sick man should resolve himself thus.[67]

Now when we have proceeded thus far, and have (as it were) laid our finger upon the right and proper cause of our sickness, three things concerning our sins must be performed by us in sickness. First, we must make a new examination of our hearts and lives, and say as the Israelites said in affliction, "Let us search and try our ways, and turn again to the Lord" (Lam. 3:40). Second, we must make a new confession to God of our new and particular sins, as God sends new corrections and chastisements. When David had the hand of God very heavy upon him for his sins, so as his very bones and moisture consumed within him, he made confession of them unto God, and thereupon obtained his pardon, and was healed (Ps. 32:3–5). The third thing is to make new prayer and more earnest than ever before, with sighs and groans of the Spirit, and that for pardon of the same sins, and for reconciliation with God in Christ. In the exercise of these three duties stands the renovation of our faith and repentance whereby they are increased, quickened, and revived. And the more sickness prevails and takes place in the body, the more should we be careful to put them in use, so that spiritual life might increase as temporal life is decayed.[68]

When King Hezekiah lay sick, as he thought upon his death bed, he wept as for some other causes so also for his sins, and withal he prayed God to cast them behind His back. David made certain psalms when he was sick (or, at the least, upon the occasion of his sickness), as namely Psalms 6, 32, 38, 39, etc. And they all are psalms of repentance, in which we may see how in distress of body and mind he renewed his faith and repentance, heartily bewailing his sins and entreating the Lord for the pardon of them. Manasseh, one who fell from God and gave himself to many horrible sins, when he was taken captive and imprisoned in Babylon, "he prayed to the Lord his God, and humbled himself greatly before the God of his fathers, and prayed unto him: and God was entreated of him, and heard his prayer, and brought him again into Jerusalem

67. This paragraph break is not in the original.

68. This paragraph break is not in the original.

into his kingdom, and then Manasseh knew that the Lord was God" (2 Chron. 33:12–13). Now, look what Manasseh did in his tribulation, we must do the same thing in the time of our bodily sickness.

Here I have occasion to mention a notorious fault that is very common in this age, even among such as have long lived in the bosom of the church. And it is this: men nowadays are so far from renewing their faith and repentance that, when they lie sick and are drawing toward death, they must be catechized in the doctrine of faith and repentance, as if they had been but of late received into the church. Whosoever will, but as occasion is offered, visit the sick, shall find what I say to be true. What a shame is this, that when a man has spent his life and days in the church for the space of twenty or thirty or forty years, he should at the very end of all, and not before, begin to inquire [as to] what faith and repentance [are], and how his soul might be saved. This one sin argues the great security of this age, and the great contempt of God and His Word. Well, let all men hereafter, in time to come, be warned to take heed of this exceeding negligence in matters of salvation, and to use all good means beforehand, that they may be able in sickness and in the time of death to put in practice the spiritual exercises of invocation and repentance.

Now, if (so be) it falls out that the sick party cannot of himself renew his own faith and repentance, he must seek the help of others. When the man who was sick of the dead palsy could not go to Christ, he got others to bear him in his bed. And when they could not come near [because of] the multitude, they uncovered the roof of the house and let the bed down before Christ (Mark 2:4). Even so, when sick men cannot alone by themselves do the good duties to which they are bound, they must borrow help from their fellow members, who are partly by their counsel to put to their helping hand, and partly by their prayers to present them unto God and bring them into the presence of Christ.

And touching help in this case, sundry duties are to be performed. Saint James sets down four: two concerning the sick patient, and two concerning such as are helpers.[69]

The first duty of the sick man is to send for help. Here two circumstances must be considered: first, who must be sent for; and, second, when [they must be sent for].[70]

For the first, Saint James says, "Is any sick among you? Let him call for the elders of the church" (James 5:14). Whereby are meant, not only apostles and all ministers of the gospel, but others also (as I take it) who were men, ancient for years, endued with the spirit of understanding and prayer, and had withal

69. This paragraph break is not in the original.
70. This paragraph break is not in the original.

the gift of working miracles and of healing the sick. For in the primitive church this gift was for a time so plentifully bestowed on them who believed in Christ that soldiers cast out devils and parents wrought miracles on their children.[71] Hence we may learn that howsoever it is principally the duty of the ministers of the Word to visit and comfort the sick, yet it is not their duty alone, for it belongs to them also who have [a] knowledge of God's Word and the gift of prayer. "Exhort one another," says the Holy Spirit, "while it is called today" (Heb. 3:13). And again, "Admonish them that are disordered, and comfort those that are weak" (1 Thess. 5:11, 14). And indeed, in equity it should be the duty of every Christian man to comfort his brother in sickness. Here we must needs take knowledge of the common fault of men and women [who,] when they come to visit their neighbors and friends, cannot speak a word of instruction and comfort, but spend the time in silence, gazing and looking on, or in uttering words to little or no purpose. [They] say to the sick party that they are sorry to see him in that case, that they would have him to be of good comfort, but wherein and by what means they cannot tell, that they doubt not but that he shall recover his health and live with them still and be merry as in former times, that they will pray for him, whereas all their prayers are nothing else but the Apostles' Creed, the Ten Commandments, and the Lord's Prayer, uttered without understanding. And this is the common comfort that sick men get at the hands of their neighbors when they come unto them. And all this comes either because men live in ignorance of God's Word or because they falsely think that the whole burden of this duty lies upon the shoulders of the minister.

The second circumstance is when the sick party must send for the elders to instruct him and pray for him. And that is in the very first place of all before any other help is sought for. Where the divine ends, there the physician must begin. And it is a very preposterous course that the divine should there begin where the physician makes an end. For till helps are had for the soul, and sin (which is the root of sickness) is cured, physic for the body is nothing. Therefore, it is a thing much to be disliked that in almost all places the physician is first sent for, and [he] comes in the beginning of the sickness, and the minister comes when a man is half dead. And [he] is then sent for oftentimes when the sick party lies drawing on and gasping for breath, as though ministers of the gospel in these days were able to work miracles.

The second duty of the sick party is to confess his sins, as Saint James says, "Confess your sins one to another, and pray one for another" [James 5:16]. It will be said that this is to bring in again popish shrift. *Answer*. Confession of our sins, and that unto men, was never denied by any. The question only is of

71. In the margin: Tert. de corona milit. c. 11 & de Idol. c. 11.

the manner and order of making confession. And for this cause, we must put a great difference between popish shrift and the confession of which Saint James speaks. For he requires only a confession of that or those sins which lie upon a man's conscience when he is sick. But the popish doctrine requires a particular enumeration of all [a] man's sins. Again, Saint James enjoins confession only as a thing necessary, meet, and convenient, but papists as a thing necessary to the remission of sins. Third, Saint James permits that confession be made to any man, and by one man to another mutually, whereas popish shrift is made only to the priest. The second duty then is that the sick party, troubled in mind with the memory and consideration of any of his past sins, or any manner of way tempted by the devil, shall freely of his own accord open his case to such as are both able and willing to help him, that he may receive comfort and die in peace of conscience.

Thus much of the sick man's duty: now follow the duties of helpers. The first is to pray over him, that is, in his presence to pray with him and for him, and by prayer to present his very person and his whole estate unto God. The prophet Elisha, the apostle Paul, and our Savior Christ used this manner of praying when they would miraculously restore temporal life [2 Kings 4:33; Acts 20:10; John 11:41]. And, therefore, it is very meet that the same should also be used by us, that we might the better stir up our affection in prayer and our compassion to the sick, when we are about to entreat the Lord for the remission of their sins and for the salvation of their souls.

The second duty of him who comes as a helper is to anoint the sick party with oil. Now this anointing was an outward ceremony which was used with the gift of healing which is now ceased. And, therefore, I omit to speak further of it.

Concerning Ourselves

Thus much of the duty which the sick man owes to God; now follow the duties which he is to perform unto himself. And they are twofold: one concerns his soul [and] the other his body.[72]

Duty 1. The duty concerning his soul is that he must arm and furnish himself against the immoderate fear of present death. And the reason hereof is plain: because howsoever naturally men fear through the course of their lives more or less, yet in the time of sickness, when death approaches, this natural fear bred in the bone will most of all show itself, even in such sort, as it will astonish the senses of the sick party and sometimes cause desperation. Therefore, it is

72. This paragraph break is not in the original.

necessary that we use means to strengthen ourselves against the fear of death. The means are of two sorts: practices and meditations.[73]

Practices are two especially. The first is that the sick man must not so much regard death itself as the benefits of God which are obtained after death. He must not fix his mind upon the consideration of the pangs and torments of death, but all his thoughts and affections must be set upon that blessed estate that is enjoined after death. He who is to pass over some great and deep river must not look downward to the stream of the water. But if he would prevent fear, he must set his foot sure and cast his eye to the bank on the farther side. And so, he who draws near death must (as it were) look over the waves of death and directly fix the eye of his faith upon eternal life. The second practice is to look upon death in the glass of the gospel, and not in the glass of the law; that is, we must consider death, not as it is propounded in the law, and look upon that terrible face which the law gives unto it, but as it is set forth in the gospel. Death in the law is a curse and the downfall to the pit of destruction, [but] in the gospel it is the entrance to heaven. The law sets forth death as death, [but] the gospel sets death as no death but only as a sleep because it speaks of death as it is altered and changed by the death of Christ. By the virtue of [His death,] death is properly no death to the servants of God. When men shall have care in this manner to consider of death, it will be a notable means to strengthen and establish them against all immoderate fears and terrors that usually rise in sickness.

The meditations which serve for this purpose are innumerable, but I will touch only those which are the most principal and the grounds of the rest. And they are four in number.[74]

The first is borrowed from the special providence of God, namely that the death of every man, much more of every child of God, is not only foreseen but also fore-appointed by God. Yea, the death of every man, deserved and procured by his sins, is laid upon him by God, who in that respect may be said to be the cause of every man's death. So says Hannah: "The Lord killeth and maketh alive" (1 Sam. 2:6). The church of Jerusalem confessed that nothing came to pass in the death of Christ but that which the foreknowledge and eternal counsel of God had appointed (Acts 4:28). And, therefore, the death of every member of Christ is also foreseen and ordained by the special decree and providence of God. I add further that the very circumstances of death (as the time when, the place where, the manner how, the beginning of sickness, the continuance, and the end, every fit in the sickness and the pangs of death) are

73. This paragraph break is not in the original.
74. This paragraph break is not in the original.

particularly set down in the counsel of God. "The very hairs of our heads are numbered," as our Savior Christ says, "and a sparrow lights not on the ground without the will of our heavenly Father" (Matt. 10:29–30). David says excellently, "My bones are not hid from thee, though I was made in a secret place, and fashioned beneath in the earth: thine eyes did see me when I was without form, for in thy book were all things written, which in continuance were fashioned, when there was none of them before" (Ps. 139:15–16). And he prays to God "to put his tears into his bottle" [Ps. 56:8]. Now if this is true, that God has bottles for the very tears of His servants, much more has He bottles for their blood, and much more does He respect and regard their pains and miseries with all circumstances of sickness and death. The careful meditation of this one point is a notable means to arm us against fear and distrust and impatience in the time of death, as some examples in this case will easily manifest. "I held my tongue and said nothing," says David (Ps. 39:9). But what was it that caused this patience in him? The cause follows in the next words: "Because thou Lord didst it." And Joseph saith to his brethren: "Fear not, for it was the Lord that sent me before you" [Gen. 45:5]. Mark here how Joseph is armed against impatience and grief and discontentment by the very consideration of God's providence. And so, in the same manner we shall be confirmed against all fears and sorrows, and say with David, "Precious in the sight of the Lord is the death of his saints" (Ps. 116:15), if this persuasion is once settled in our hearts, that all things in sickness and death come to pass unto us by the providence of God, who turns all things to the good of them who love Him.

The second meditation is to be borrowed from the excellent promise that God has made to the death of the righteous: "Blessed are they that die in the Lord, for they rest from their labors, and their works follow them" [Rev. 14:13]. The Author of truth, who cannot lie, has spoken it. Now then, let a man but thoroughly consider this, that death joined with [a] reformed life has a promise of blessedness adjoined unto it, and it alone will be a sufficient means to stay the rage of our affections and all inordinate fear of death, and the rather if we mark wherein this blessedness consists. In death we are indeed thrust out of our old dwelling places, namely these houses of clay and earthly tabernacles of our bodies, wherein we have made long abode. But what is the end? Surely, that living and dying in Christ, we might have a building given by God, that is, a house not made with hands, but eternal in the heavens, which is unspeakable and immortal glory [2 Cor. 5:1]. If a poor man should be commanded by a prince to put off his torn and beggarly garments, and instead thereof to put on royal and costly robes, it would be a great rejoicing to his heart. Oh then, what joyful news must this be unto all repentant and sorrowful sinners, when the King of heaven and earth comes unto them by death and bids them lay down their bodies as ragged and patched garments, and prepare themselves to put on the princely robe of immortality? No tongue is able to express the excellency of this most blessed and happy estate.

The third meditation is borrowed from the estate of all them who are in Christ, whether living or dying. He who dies, believing in Christ, dies not forth of Christ but in Him, having both His body and soul really coupled to Christ according to the tenor of the covenant of grace. And though after death body and soul are severed one from another, yet neither of them is severed or disjoined from Christ. The conjunction which is once begun in this life remains eternally. And, therefore, though the soul goes from the body, and the body itself rots in the grave, yet both are still in Christ, both in the covenant, both in the favor of God as before death, and both shall again be joined together; the body by the virtue of the former conjunction being raised to eternal life. Indeed, if this union with Christ were dissolved as the conjunction of body and soul is, it might be some matter of discomfort and fear, but the foundation and substance of our mystical conjunction with Christ, both in respect of our bodies and souls enduring forever, must needs be a matter of exceeding joy and comfort.

The fourth meditation is that God has promised His special, blessed, and comfortable presence unto His servants when they are sick or dying, or any way distressed. "When thou passest through the waters, I will be with thee," says the Lord, "and through the floods that they do not overflow thee: when thou walkest through the very fire, thou shalt not be burnt, neither shall the flame kindle upon thee" (Isa. 43:2). Now the Lord does manifest His presence [in] three ways. The first is by moderating and lessening the pains and torments of sickness and death, as the very words of the former promise do plainly import. Hence, it comes to pass that to many men the sorrows and pangs of death are nothing so grievous and troublesome as the afflictions and crosses which are laid on them in the course of their lives. The second way of God's presence is by an inward and unspeakable comfort of the Spirit, as Paul says, "We rejoice in tribulations, knowing that tribulation bringeth forth patience, etc." But why is this rejoicing? "Because," says he in the next words, "the love of God is shed abroad in our hearts by the Holy Ghost" (Rom. 5:3, 5). Again, Paul, having in some grievous sickness received the sentence of death, says of himself that "as the sufferings of Christ did abound in him, so his consolation did abound through Christ" (2 Cor. 1:5). Here then we see that when earthly comforts fail, the Lord Himself draws near the bed of the sick (as it were), visiting them in His own person, and ministering unto them refreshing for their souls: "With his right hand he holds up their heads, and with his left hand he embraceth them" (Song 2:6). The third means of God's presence is the ministry of His good angels, whom the Lord has appointed as keepers and nurses unto His servants to hold them up and to bear them in their arms as nurses do young children, and to be as a guard unto them against the devil and his angels [Ps. 91:11–12]. And all this is verified especially in sickness, at which time the holy angels are not only present with such as fear God, but ready also to receive and to carry their souls into heaven, as appears by the example of Lazarus.

And thus much of the first duty which a sick man is to perform unto himself, namely that he must by all means possible arm and strengthen himself against the fear of death.[75]

Duty 2. Now follows the second duty which concerns the body, and it is that all sick persons must be careful to preserve health and life till God does wholly take it away. For Paul says, "None of us liveth to himself, neither doth any die to himself: for whether we live, we live unto the Lord, or whether we die, we die unto the Lord: whether we live therefore or die we are the Lord's" [Rom. 14:7–8]. For this cause, we may not do with our lives as we will, but we must reserve the whole disposition thereof unto God, for whose glory we are to live and die. And this temporal life is a most precious jewel, and as the common saying is, "Life is very sweet," because it is given man for this end, that he might have some space of time wherein he might use all good means to attain to everlasting life. Life is not bestowed on us that we should spend our days in our lusts and vain pleasures, but that we might have liberty to come out of the kingdom of darkness into the kingdom of grace, and from the bondage of sin into the glorious liberty of the sons of God. And in this respect special care must be had of preservation of life, till God does call us hence.

In the preserving of life, two things must be considered: the means and the right use of the means. The means is [a] good and wholesome physic, which, though it is despised by many as an unprofitable and needless thing, yet must it be esteemed as an ordinance and blessing of God. This appears because the Spirit of God has given approbation unto it in the Scriptures. When it was the good pleasure of God to restore life unto King Hezekiah, a lump of dry figs by the prophet's appointment was laid to his boil and he was healed. Indeed, this cure was in some sort miraculous, because he was made whole in the space of two or three days, and "the third day he went up to the temple" [2 Kings 20:7]. Yet, the bunch of figs was a natural and ordinary medicine or plaster, serving to soften and ripen tumors or swelling of the flesh.[76] And the Samaritan is commended for the binding up and for the pouring of wine and oil into the wounds

75. This paragraph break is not in the original.

76. In the margin: Gal. 1. de art curat. cap. 6.

of the man who lay wounded between Jerusalem and Jericho [Luke 10:34]. Now this dealing of his was a right practice of physic, for the wine served to cleanse the wound and to ease the pain within, and the oil served to supple the flesh and to assuage the pain without.[77] And the prophet Isaiah seems to commend this physic when he says, "From the sole of the foot there is nothing whole therein, but wounds and swellings, and sores full of corruption: they have not been wrapped nor bound up, nor mollified with oil" (Isa. 1:6). And whereas God did not command circumcision of children before the eighth day, he followed a rule of physic observed in all ages, that the life of the child is very uncertain till the first seven days are expired, as we may see by the example of the child, who David had by Bathsheba, which died the seventh day. And upon the very same ground heathen men would not name their children before the eighth day.[78] Thus then, it is manifest that the use of physic is lawful and commendable.

Furthermore, that physic may be well applied to the maintenance of health, special care must be had to make choice of such physicians as are known to be well learned, and men of experience, as also of good conscience and good religion. For as in other callings, so in this also, there are sundry abuses which may endanger the lives and health of men. Some venture upon the bare inspection of the urine, without further direction or knowledge of the estate of the sick, to prescribe and minister as shall seem best unto them. But the learned in this faculty do plainly avouch that this kind of dealing tends rather to kill than to cure, and that sundry men are indeed killed thereby.[79] For judgment by the urine is most deceitful. The water of him who is sick of a pestilent fever, even unto death, looks for substance and color as the water of a whole man; and so does the water of them who are sick of a quartan[80] (or any other intermitting fever), especially if they have used good diet from the beginning, as also of them who have the pleurisy[81] (or the inflammation of the lungs) or the squinancy,[82] oftentimes when they are near death. Now then, considering the waters of such as are at the point of death appear as the urine of whole and sound men, one and the same urine may fore-signify both life and death, and be a sign of divers, nay of contrary, diseases. A thin, crude, and pale urine in them who are in health is a token of want of digestion, but in them who are sick of a sharp or burning ague it betokens the frenzy and is a certain sign of death.

---

77. In the margin: Valla de sacra. phil. c. 8.
78. In the margin: Arist. de hist. anim. l. 7. cap. 1.
79. In the margin: Forrest. de urin. judiciis lib. 3. Lang. 1. 2. epist. 41.
80. *Quartan:* a malarial fever recurring every 72 hours.
81. *Pleurisy:* an inflammation of the pleura of the lungs.
82. *Squinancy:* a peritonsillar abscess.

Second, there are others who think it [is] a small matter to make experiments of their devised medicines upon the bodies of their patients whereby the health, which they hoped for, is either much hindered or much decayed.

Third, there are others who minister no physic at any time, or use phlebotomy[83] without the direction of judicial astrology. But if they shall follow always this course, they must needs kill many a man. Put the case that a full-bodied man is taken with a pleurisy, the moon being in Leo, what must be done? The learned in this art say [that] he must presently be let blood, but by astrology a stay must be made till the moon is removed from Leo, the house of the sun. But by that time the impostume will be so much increased by the gathering together of the humors that it can neither be dissolved nor ripened. And by this means the sick party, wanting help in time, shall die either by inflammation or by the consumption of the lungs. Again, when a man is sick of the squinancy, or of the fever called Synochus,[84] the moon then being in malignant aspects with any of the unfortunate planets (as astrologers speak), if letting of blood is deferred till the moon is free from the foresaid aspects, the party dies in the meantime.[85] Therefore, they who minister purgations and let blood [in no other way] than they are counselled by the constitution of the stars are far wide. It is a far better course to consider the matter of the disease, with the disposition and ripening of it, as also the courses and symptoms and crisis thereof. This being so, there is good cause that sick men should be as careful to make choice of meet physicians, to whom they might commend the care of their health, as they are careful to make choice of lawyers for their worldly suits, and divines for cases of conscience.

Furthermore, all men must here be warned to take heed that they use not such means as have no warrant. Of this kind are all charms or spells, of whatsoever words they consist; characters and figures, either in paper, wood, or wax; all amulets and ligatures, which serve to hang about the neck or other parts of the body, except they are grounded upon some good natural reason, as white peony hung about the neck is good against the falling sickness, and wolf dung tied to the body is good against the colic, not by any enchantment, but by inward virtue.[86] Otherwise they are all vain and superstitious because neither by creation nor by any ordinance in God's Word have they any power to cure bodily disease. For words can do no more but signify, and figures can do no more but represent. And yet, nevertheless, these unlawful and absurd means are more used and sought for by common people than good physic.

83. *Phlebotomy:* bloodletting.

84. *Synochus:* a continuous fever.

85. In the margin: Lang. l. 1. epist. 35. See Ganiuettus called Amicus medicorum.

86. In the margin: Gal. l. 6 & 10. de simp. medic.

But it stands all men greatly in hand in no way to seek forth to enchanters and sorcerers, who indeed are but witches and wizards, though they are commonly called cunning men and women. It would be better for a man to die of his sickness than to seek recovery by such wicked persons. "For if any turn after such as work with spirits, and after soothsayers, to go a whoring after them, the Lord will set his face against them, and cut them off from among his people" (Lev. 20:6). When Ahaziah was sick, he sent to Baalzebub, the god of Ekron, to know whether he should recover or not. As the messengers were going, the prophet Elijah met them, and said, "Go and return to the king which sent you, and say unto him, Thus saith the Lord, Is it not because there is no God in Israel that thou sendest to inquire of Baalzebub the god of Ekron? Therefore thou shalt not come down from thy bed on which thou art gone up, but shalt die the death" (2 Kings 1:6). Therefore, such kind of help is so far from curing any pain or sickness that it rather doubles them and fastens them upon us.

Thus much of the means of health; now follows the manner of using the means, concerning which three rules must be followed. First of all, he who is to take the physic must not only prepare his body, as physicians prescribe, but he must also prepare his soul by humbling himself under the hand of God in his sickness for his sins, and make earnest prayer to God for the pardon of them before any medicine come to his body. Now that this order ought to be used appears plainly in this, that sickness springs from our sins as from a root, which should first of all be stocked up that the branches might more easily die. And, therefore, Asa, commended for many other things, is blamed for this by the Holy Spirit, that he sought not the Lord, but to physicians, and put his trust in them (2 Chron. 16:12). Oftentimes, it comes to pass that diseases, curable in themselves, are made incurable by the sins and impenitency of the party. And, therefore, the best way is for them who would have ease when God begins to correct them by sickness, then also to begin to humble themselves for all their sins and turn unto God.

The second rule is that when we have prepared ourselves, and are about to use physic, we must sanctify it by the Word of God and prayer, as we do our meat and drink (1 Tim. 4:3). For by the Word we must have our warrant that the medicines prescribed are lawful and good, and by prayer we must entreat the Lord for a blessing upon them in restoring of health, if it is the good will of God.

The third rule is that we must carry in mind the right and proper end of physic, lest we deceive ourselves. We must not, therefore, think that physic serves to prevent old age or death itself. For that is not possible, because God has set down that all men shall die and be changed. And life consists in a temperature and proportion of natural heat and radical moisture. This moisture, being once consumed by the former heat, is by art unrepairable; and, therefore, death must needs follow. But the true end of physic is to continue and lengthen the life of man to its natural period, which is when nature, that has been long preserved by all possible means, is now wholly spent. Now this period, though it cannot be lengthened by any skill of man, yet it may easily be shortened by intemperance in diet, by drunkenness, and by violent diseases.[87] But care must be had to avoid all such evils, that the little lamp of corporal life may burn till it goes out of itself. For this very space of time is the very day of grace and salvation. And whereas God in justice might have cut us off and have utterly destroyed us, yet in great mercy He gives us thus much time that we might prepare ourselves to His kingdom. When this time is once spent, if a man would redeem it with the price of ten thousand worlds, he cannot have it.

And to conclude this point touching physic, I will here set down two special duties of the physician himself. The first is that in the want and defect of such as are to put sick men in mind of their sins, it is a duty especially concerning him, he being a member of Christ, to advertise his patients that they must truly humble themselves, and pray fervently to God for the pardon of all their sins. And surely this duty would be more commonly practiced than it is, if all physicians did consider that oftentimes they want good success in their dealings, not because there is any want in art or good will, but because the party with whom they deal is impenitent. The second duty is [that] when he sees manifest signs of death in his patient, [he is] not to depart concealing them, but first of all to certify the patient thereof. There may be (and is) too much niceness[88] in such concealments, and the plain truth in this known case is very profitable. For when the party is certain of his end, it bereaves him of all confidence in earthly things, and makes him put all his affiance in the mere mercy of God. When Hezekiah was sick, the prophet speaks plainly to him, and says, "Set thine house in order: for thou must die" (Isa. 38:1). And Paul shows what good we may reap by knowing certainly that we have received the sentence of death, when he says, "We received the sentence of death in ourselves, because we should not trust in ourselves, but in God which raiseth the dead" (2 Cor. 1:9).

Concerning Our Neighbors

Having thus seen what are the duties of the sick man to himself, let us now see what are the duties which he owes to his neighbor. And there are two.

The first is the duty of reconciliation whereby he is freely to forgive all men, and to desire to be forgiven by all. In the Old Testament, when a man was

87. In the margin: *Intercia aeneus carnifex.*

88. *Niceness:* foolishness.

to offer a bullock or lamb in sacrifice to God, he must leave his offering at the altar, and first go and be reconciled to his brethren, if they had aught against him. Much more then must this be done when we are in death: to offer up ourselves, our bodies and souls, as an acceptable sacrifice unto God. *Question.* What if a man cannot come to the speech of them with whom he would be reconciled? Or, if he does, what if they will not be reconciled? *Answer.* When they shall in their sickness seek and desire reconciliation, and cannot obtain it, either because the parties are absent or because they will not relent, they have discharged their conscience, and God will accept their will for their deed. [Imagine this] case: a man, lying sick on his death bed, is at enmity with one who is then beyond the sea so as he cannot possibly have any speech with him. If he were ever so fain,[89] how shall he stay his mind? He must remember that in this case a will and desire to be reconciled is reconciliation itself.

The second duty is that those who are rulers and governors of others must have care and take order that their charges, committed to them by God, are left in good estate after their death. And here come three duties to be handled: the first of the magistrate, the second of the minister, [and] the third of the master of the family.

Magistrate. The magistrate's duty is to provide as much as he can, before he dies, for the godly and peaceable estate of the town, city, or commonwealth. And that is done partly by procuring the maintenance of sound religion and virtue, and partly by establishing the execution of civil justice and outward peace. Examples of this practice in God's Word are these: When Moses was 120 years old, and was no longer able to go in and out before the people of Israel, he called them before him, and signified that the time of his departure was at hand, and thereupon took order for their welfare after his death [Deuteronomy 31]. And first of all, he places Joshua over them in his stead to be their guide to the Promised Land. Second, he gives special charge to all the people to be valiant and courageous against their enemies, and to obey the commandments of God. And Joshua follows the same course (Joshua 23). For he calls the people together, and shows them that the time of his death is at hand, and [he] gives them a charge to be courageous, and to worship the true God. Once done, he ends his days as a worthy captain. When King David was to go the way of all flesh, and lay sick on his death bed, he placed his own son Solomon upon his throne, and gives him charge, both for maintenance of religion and execution of justice (1 Kings 2).

89. *Fain:* willing.

Minister. The duty of ministers, when they are dying, is (as much as they can) to cast and provide for the continuance of the good estate of the church over which they are placed. Consider the example of Peter: "I will endeavor always, that ye also may be able to have remembrance of these things after my departure" (2 Peter 1:15). If this had been well observed, there could not have been such abundance of schisms, errors, and heresies as have been, and the church of God could not have suffered so great havoc. But because men have had more care to maintain personal succession than the right succession (which stands in the doctrine of the prophets and apostles), therefore wolves have come into the rooms of faithful teachers, and the apostasy (of which Paul speaks) has overspread the face of the church [Acts 20:28; 2 Thess. 2:2].

Master. Third, householders must set their families in order before they die, as the prophet Isaiah says to Hezekiah: "Set thine house in order: for thou must die" [Isa. 38:1]. For the procuring of good order in the family after death, two things are to be done.[90]

Duty 1. The first concerns this life, and it is to dispose of lands and goods. And that this may be well and wisely done (if the will is unmade), it is with godly advice and counsel to be made in the time of sickness according to the practice of ancient and worthy men. Before his death, Abraham makes his will, and gives legacies [Gen. 25:5–6]; so did Isaac and Jacob, in whose last will and testament are contained many worthy blessings and prophesies of the estate of his children [Genesis 27 and 49]. And Christ, our Savior, when He was upon the cross, provided for His mother, especially commending her to His disciple, John, whom He loved. And, indeed, this duty of making a will is a matter of great weight and importance, for it cuts off much hatred and contention in families, and stays many suits in law. It is not, therefore, always a matter of indifference, which may be done or not done, as many falsely think, who upon blind and sinister respects abstain from making wills, either because their wealth should not be known, or because they would have their decayed estate to be concealed, or because they fear they shall die the sooner if the will is once made.

Now though the making of wills belongs to another place and profession, yet so much may be spoken here as the Holy Spirit has uttered in the Word. And I will reduce it to certain rules.

The first is that the will must be made according to the law of nature, the written Word of God, and the good and wholesome positive laws of that

90. This paragraph break is not in the original.

kingdom or country whereof a man is a member. The will of God must be the rule of man's will. And, therefore, the will that is made against any of these is faulty.

The second [rule] is that, if goods evil gotten are not restored before, they must even then be restored by will or by some other way. It is the practice of covetous men, when they die, to bequeath their souls to God, and their goods (evil gotten) to their children and friends, which in all equity should be restored to them to whom they belong. *Question*. What if a man's conscience tells him that his goods are evil gotten, and he knows not where or to whom to make restitution? *Answer*. The case is common, and the answer is this. When the party is known (whom you have wronged), restore to him particularly. If the party is unknown, or dead, restore to his executors and assigns, or to his next [of] kin. If there is none, yet keep not goods evil gotten to yourself, but restore to God, that is, in way of recompense and civil satisfaction. Bestow them on the church or commonwealth.

The third rule is that heads of families must principally bestow their goods upon their own children, and them that are of their own kindred. "This man," says God to Abraham of Eleazar (a stranger), "shall not be thine heir, but the son which shall come of thy loins" [Gen. 15:4]. And this was God's commandment to the Israelites, that when any man dies, his son should be his heir; and if he had no son, then his daughter; and if he had no daughter, then his brethren; and if he had no brethren, then his father's brethren; and if there were none, then the next of his kin whosoever [Num. 27:8–11]. And Paul says, "If ye be sons, then also heirs" [Rom. 8:17]. And again, "He that provides not for his own, and namely for them of his own household, is worse than an infidel" [1 Tim. 5:8]. Therefore, it is a fault for any man to alienate his goods or lands wholly and finally from his blood and posterity. It is a thing which the very law of nature itself has condemned.[91] Again, it is a fault to give all to the eldest and nothing in respect to the rest, as though the eldest were born to be gentlemen and the younger brethren born to bear the wallet. Yet in equity the eldest must have more than any, even because he is the eldest, and because stocks and families in their persons are to be maintained, and because there must always be some that must be fit to do special service in the peace of the commonwealth or in the time of war. This could not be if goods should be equally parted to all.

The fourth and last rule is that no will is of force till the testator is dead, for so long as he is alive he may alter and change it [Heb. 9:16]. These rules must be remembered because they are recorded in Scripture. The opening of other points and circumstances belongs to the profession of the law.

---

91. In the margin: Plato de Rep. lib. 2. Arist. pol. l. 5. cap. 8.

Duty 2. The second duty of the master of the family concerns the souls of such as are under his government. And it is to give charge to them, that they learn, believe, and obey the true religion, that is, the doctrine of salvation set down in the writings of the prophets and apostles. The Lord Himself commends Abraham for this: "I know Abraham, that he will command his sons, and his household after him, that they keep the way of the Lord to do righteousness and judgment" [Gen. 18:19]. And David, on his deathbed, gives Solomon a most notable and solemn charge, the sum and substance whereof is to know the God of his fathers and to serve Him [1 Kings 2]. This being done, he further commends him to God by prayer. Psalm 72 was made for this purpose. His practice is to be followed by all. Thus governors, when they shall carefully dispose of their goods, and give charge to their posterity touching the worship of God, shall greatly honor God [in] dying as well as living.

Requirement 2: Our Disposition in Death

Hitherto I have entreated of the twofold preparation which is to go before death; now follows the second part of dying well, namely the disposition in death. This disposition is nothing else but a religious and holy behavior, especially toward God, when we are in or near the agony and pang of death. This behavior contains three special duties.

Duty 1

The first is to die in or by faith. To die by faith is when a man in the time of death does with all his heart rely himself wholly on God's special love and favor and mercy in Christ, as it is revealed in the Word. And though there is no part of man's life void of just occasions whereby we may put faith in practice, yet the special time of all is the pang of death, when friends, riches, pleasures, outward senses, temporal life, and all earthly helps forsake us. For then true faith makes us to go wholly out of ourselves, and to despair of comfort and salvation in respect of any earthly things, and with all the power and strength of the heart to rest on the pure mercy of God. This made Luther both think and say that men were best Christians in death.[92]

We have an example of this faith in David, who when he saw nothing before his eyes but present death, the people intending to stone him, "comforted himself at the very instant," as the very text says, "in the Lord his God" [1 Sam. 30:6]. And he reaped this comfort, in that by faith he applied unto his own soul the merciful promises of God, as he testifies of himself: "Remember the promise made to thy servant, wherein thou hast caused me to trust. It is

92. This paragraph break is not in the original.

my comfort in trouble: for thy promise hath quickened me" [Ps. 119:49–50]. Again, "My flesh failed and my heart also, but God is the strength of my heart, and my portion forever" [Ps. 73:26]. Now look what David here did. Every one of us must do the same in the like case. When the Israelites in the wilderness were stung with fiery serpents, and lay at the point of death, they looked up to the brazen serpent, which was erected by the appointment of God, and were presently healed. Even so, when any man feels death to draw near, and his fiery sting to pierce the heart, he must fix the eye of a true and lively faith upon Christ, exalted and crucified on the cross, which being done, he shall by death enter into eternal life [John 3:14].

Now because true faith is no dead thing, it must be expressed by special actions, the principal whereof is invocation whereby either prayer or thanksgiving is directed unto God. When death had seized upon the body of Jacob, he raised up himself, and turning his face toward the bed's head, leaned on the top of his staff by reason of his feebleness, and prayed unto God. His prayer was an excellent fruit of his faith [Heb. 11:21]. Job's wife, in the midst of his affliction, said unto him to very good purpose: "Bless God and die" [Job 2:9]. I know and grant that the words are commonly translated otherwise: "Curse God and die." But (as I take it) the former is the best, for it is not likely that in so excellent a family any person (much less a matron and principal governor thereof) would give such lewd and wretched counsel, which the most wicked man upon earth, having no more but the light of nature, would not once give but rather much abhor and condemn. And though Job calls her a "foolish woman," yet he does it not because she went about to persuade him to blaspheme God, but because she was in the mind of Job's friends, and thought that he stood too much in a conceit of his own righteousness.[93] Now the effect and meaning of her counsel is this: "Bless God," that is, husband, no doubt you are by the extremity of your affliction at death's door, therefore begin now at length to lay aside the great overweening which you have of your own righteousness, acknowledge the hand of God upon you for your sins, confess them unto Him, giving Him the glory, pray for the pardon of them, and end your days. This counsel is very good and to be followed by all, though it may be the applying of it (as Job well perceived) is mixed with folly.

Here it may be alleged that men, in the pangs of death, want their senses and convenient utterance, and therefore they are unable to pray. *Answer.* The very sighs, sobs, and groans of a repentant and believing heart are prayers before God, even as effectual as if they were uttered by the best voice in the world. Prayer stands in the affection of the heart. The voice is but an outward

93. In the margin: "Dost thou continue yet in thine uprightness?" (v. 9).

messenger thereof. God looks not upon the speech, but upon the heart. David says, "God hears the desires of the poor" [Ps. 10:17]. Again, "He will fulfill the desires of them that fear him" [Ps. 145:19]. Yea, their very tears are loud and sounding prayers in His ears.

Again, faith may otherwise be expressed by the last words, which, for the most part in them who have truly served God, are very excellent and comfortable and full of grace. Some choice examples whereof I will rehearse for instruction's sake and for imitation.[94]

The last words of Jacob were those whereby as a prophet he foretold blessings and curses upon his children [Genesis 49]. And the principal among the rest were these: "The scepter shall not depart from Judah, and the lawgiver from between his feet till Shiloh come…O Lord, I have waited for thy salvation" [vv. 10, 18]. The last words of Moses are his most excellent song set down in Deuteronomy 32. And the last words of David were these: "The Spirit of the Lord spoke by me, and his word was in my tongue; the God of Israel spoke to me, the strength of Israel said, Bear rule over men, etc." [2 Sam. 23:2–3]. The words of Zachariah, the son of Jehoiada, when he was stoned, were [these:] "The Lord look upon it and require it" [2 Chron. 24:22].[95]

The last words of our Savior Christ, when He was dying upon the cross, are most admirable, and stored with abundance of spiritual grace. (1) He says to His Father: "Father, forgive them, they know not what they do" [Luke 23:34]. (2) To the thief: "Verily I say unto thee, this night shalt thou be with me in paradise" [v. 43]. (3) To His mother: "Mother, behold thy son." And to John: "Behold thy mother" [John 19:26–27]. (4) In His agony: "My God, my God, why hast thou forsaken me?" [Matt. 27:46]. (5) Earnestly desiring our salvation: "I thirst" [John 19:28]. (6) When He had made perfect satisfaction: "It is finished" [v. 30]. (7) When body and soul were parting: "Father, into thy hands I commend my spirit" [Luke 23:46].[96]

The last words of Stephen were: (1) "Behold I see the heavens open and the Son of Man standing at the right hand of God" [Acts 7:56]; (2) "Lord Jesus, receive my spirit" [v. 59]; and (3) "Lord, lay not this sin to their charge" [v. 60].

Of Polycarp: "You are a true God without lying, therefore in all things I praise You, and bless You, and glorify You by the eternal God and High Priest Jesus

94. This paragraph break is not in the original.
95. This paragraph break is not in the original.
96. The following paragraph breaks are not in the original.

Christ, Your only beloved Son, by whom and with whom to You and the Holy Spirit be all glory now and forever."[97]

Of Ignatius: "I care not what kind of death I die. I am the bread of the Lord and must be ground with the teeth of lions, that I may be clean bread for Christ who is the bread of life for me."

Of Ambrose: "I have not so led my life among you as if I were ashamed to live; neither do I fear death, because we have a good Lord."[98]

Of Augustine: (1) "He is no great man that thinks it a great matter that trees and stones fall and mortal men die." (2) "Just are You, O Lord, and righteous is Your judgment."[99]

Of Bernard. An admonition to his brethren that they would ground the anchor of their faith and hope in the safe and sure port of God's mercy: "Because as I suppose I cannot leave unto you any choice example of religion, I commend three things to be imitated by you, which I remember that I have observed in the race which I have run as much as I possibly could. (1) I gave less heed to my own sense and reason than to the sense and reason of other men. (2) When I was hurt I sought not revenge on him who did the hurt. (3) I had care to give offence to no man, and if it fell out otherwise, I took it away as I could."

Of Zwingli. When in the field he was wounded under the chin with a spear: "O what happe[100] is this? Go to, they may kill my body but my soul they cannot."[101]

Of Oecolampadius. (1) An exhortation to the ministers of the church to maintain the purity of doctrine, to show forth an example of honest and godly conversation, to be constant and patient under the cross. (2) Of himself: "Whereas I am charged to be a corrupter of the truth, I weigh it not. I am going now to the tribunal of Christ and that with good conscience by the grace of God, and there it shall be manifest that I have not seduced the church. Of this my saying and contestation, I leave you as witnesses, and I confirm it with this my last breath." (3) To his children: "Love God the Father." And turning himself to his kinsfolk: "I have bound you with this contestation: you (which they here and I have desired) shall do your endeavor, that these my children may be godly, and peaceable, and true." (4) To his friend coming unto him: "What

97. In the margin: Euseb. l. 3. c. 30.
98. In the margin: Paulinus in vita eius.
99. In the margin: Possid. in vita Aug. cap. 8.
100. *Happe:* luck or fortune.
101. In the margin: Oswald. Mycon.

shall I say unto you? News, I shall shortly be with Christ my Lord." (5) Being asked whether the light did not trouble him, touching his breast: "There is light enough." (6) He rehearsed the whole [of] Psalm 51 with deep sighs from the bottom of his breast. (7) A little after: "Save me, Lord Jesus."

Of Luther: "My heavenly Father, God and Father of our Lord Jesus Christ and God of all comfort, I give You thanks that You have revealed unto me Your Son Jesus Christ, whom I have believed, whom I have professed, whom I have loved, whom I have praised, whom the bishop of Rome and the whole company of the wicked persecutes and reviles. I pray You, my Lord Jesus Christ, receive my poor soul. My heavenly Father, though I am taken from this life, and this body of mine is to be laid down, yet I know certainly that I shall remain with You forever, neither shall any be able to pull me out of Your hand."

Of Hooper: "O Lord Jesus, Son of David, have mercy on me and receive my soul."

Of Annas Burgius: "Forsake me not, O Lord, lest I forsake Thee."

Of Melanchthon: "If it is the will of God, I am willing to die, and I beseech Him that He will grant me a joyful departure."

Of Calvin: (1) "I held my tongue, because You, Lord, have done it." (2) "I mourned as a dove." (3) "Lord, You grind me to powder, but it suffices me because it is Your hand."

Of Peter Martyr. That his body was weak, but his mind was well; that he acknowledged no life or salvation but only in Christ who was given by the Father to be a Redeemer of mankind. And when he had confirmed this by testimony of Scripture, he added, "This is my faith in which I will die. And God will destroy them who teach otherwise." This done, he shook hands with all and said, "Farewell my brethren and dear friends."

It would be easy to quote more examples, but these few may be in [the] stead of many, and this is the sum of what all godly men speak. Some enlightened with a prophetical spirit foretell things to come, as the patriarchs Jacob and Joseph did [Gen. 49; 50:24–25]. And there have been some who by name have testified who should very shortly come after them, and who should remain alive, and what should be their condition. Some have shown a wonderful memory of things past, as of their former life, and of the benefits of God. And no doubt it was given to them to stir up holy affections and thanksgiving to God. Again, some, rightly judging of the change of their present estate for a better, do rejoice exceedingly that they must be translated from earth to paradise, as Babylas, Martyr of Antioch, when his head was chopped off. He says, "Return O my soul unto thy rest, because the Lord hath blessed thee: because thou hast delivered my soul from death, mine eyes from tears, and my feet from falling, I shall walk before thee, Jehovah, in the land of the living" [Ps. 116:7–9]. And some others spoke of the vanity of this life, of the imagination of the sorrows of death, of the beginning of eternal life, of the comfort of the Holy Spirit, which they feel, [and] of their departure unto Christ.

Question. What must we think if in the time of death such speeches are wanting, and in the stead thereof idle talk is used? *Answer.* We must consider the kind of sickness whereof men die, whether it is more easy or violent. For violent sickness is usually accompanied with frenzies and with unseemly motions and gestures, which we are to take in good part even in this regard, because we ourselves may be in the like case.

Duty 2

Thus much of the first duty, which is to die in faith. The second is to die in obedience, otherwise our death cannot be acceptable to God, because we seem to come unto God of fear and constraint as slaves to a master, and not of love as children to a father. Now to die in obedience is when a man is willing and ready and desirous to go out of this world whenever God shall call him, and that without murmuring or repining, at what time, where, and when it shall please God. Whether we live or die, says Paul, we do it not to ourselves but unto God [Rom. 14:7–8]. And, therefore, man's duty is to be obedient to God in death as in life. Christ is our example in this case. In His agony, [He] prayed, "Father, let this cup pass from me (yet with submission), not my will but thy will be done." [This] teaches us in the very pangs of death to resign ourselves to the good pleasure of God. When the prophet told King Hezekiah of death, presently without all manner of grudging or repining he addressed himself to prayer. We are commanded to present ourselves unto God as free-will offerings, without any limitation of time, and therefore in death as well as in life. I conclude, then, that we are to make as much conscience in performing obedience to God in suffering death as we do of any thing in the course of our lives.

Duty 3

The third duty is to render up our souls into the hands of God as the most faithful Keeper of all. This is the last duty of the Christian, and it is prescribed unto us in the example of Christ upon the cross, who in the very pangs of death, when the dissolution of the body and soul drew on, said, "Father, into thine hands I commend my spirit" (Luke 23:46), and so gave up the ghost. The like was done by Stephen, who when he was stoned to death, said, "Lord Jesus, receive my spirit" (Acts 7:59). And David in his lifetime, being in danger of death, used the very same words Christ uttered (Ps. 31:5).

Thus, we see what are the duties which we are to perform in the very pangs of death, that we may come to eternal life. Some men will haply[102] say, If this is all, to die in faith and obedience and to surrender our souls into God's hand, we will not greatly care for any preparation beforehand, nor trouble ourselves much about the right manner of dying well, for we doubt not but that when death shall come we shall be able to perform all the former duties with ease. *Answer*. Let no man deceive himself by any false persuasion, thinking with[in] himself that the practice of the aforesaid duties is a matter of ease, for ordinarily they are not, neither can they be performed in death unless there is much preparation in the life before.[103]

He who will die in faith must, first of all, live by faith. And there is but one example in all the Bible of a man dying in faith who lived without faith; namely, the thief upon the cross. The servants of God, who are endued with great measure of grace, do very hardly believe in the time of affliction. Indeed, when Job was afflicted, he said, "Though the Lord kill me, yet will I trust in him."[104] Yet, afterward, his faith, being overcast with a cloud, he says that God was "become his enemy," and that He had set him "as a mark to shoot at." And sundry times his faith was oppressed with doubting and distrust. How then shall they, who never lived by faith nor inured themselves to believe, be able in the pangs of death to rest upon the mercy of God?[105]

Second, he who would die in obedience must first of all lead his life in obedience. He who has lived in disobedience cannot willingly and in obedience appear before the judge when he is cited by death, the sergeant of the Lord. He dies indeed, but that is upon necessity, because he must yield to the order and course of nature as other creatures do.

Third, he who would surrender his soul into the hands of God must be resolved of two things. The one is that God can; the other is that God will receive his soul into heaven and there preserve it till the last judgment. And none can be resolved of this except he has the Spirit of God to certify his conscience that he is redeemed, justified, sanctified by Christ, and shall be glorified. He who is not thus persuaded dare not render up and present his soul unto God. When David said, "Lord, into thy hands I commend my spirit" (Ps. 31:5), what was the reason of this boldness in him? Surely, nothing else but

102. *Haply:* perhaps.
103. This paragraph break is not in the original.
104. Job 13:15.
105. This paragraph break is not in the original.

the persuasion of faith, as the next words import: "For thou hast redeemed me, O Lord, God of truth." And thus, it is manifest that no man can ordinarily perform these duties [when] dying [if he has] not performed them [while] living.

This being so, I do again renew my former exhortation, beseeching you that you would practice the duties of preparation in the course of your lives, leading them daily in faith and obedience, and from time to time commending your souls into the hand of God, and casting all your works upon His providence. They who have done this have made most happy and blessed ends. Enoch, by faith, walked with God as one who was always in His presence, leading an upright and godly life. "And the Lord took him away that he should not see death" [Heb. 11:5]. And this which befell Enoch shall also, after a sort, befall them who live in faith and obedience, because death shall be no death but a sleep unto them, and no enemy but a friend to body and soul.[106]

On the contrary, let us consider the wretched and miserable ends of them who have spent their days in their sins without keeping faith and good conscience. The people of the old world were drowned in the flood. The filthy Sodomites and Gomorrheans were destroyed with fire from heaven. Dathan and Abiram, with the company of Korah, [were] swallowed up of the earth. Korah himself (as it seems by the text) was burnt with fire [Num. 16:32; Ps. 106:17–18]. Wicked Saul and Ahithophel and Judas destroyed themselves. Herod was eaten up by worms and gave up the ghost.[107]

Julian, the apostate, smitten with a dart in the field, died casting up his blood into the air and blaspheming the name of Christ. Arius, the heretic, died upon the stool, scouring forth his very entrails. And this very age affords store of like examples. Hoffmeister, a great papist, as he was going to the council of Ratisbon to dispute against the defenders of the gospel, was suddenly prevented in his journey by the hand of God, and died miserably with horrible roaring and crying out. In the university of Louvain,[108] when Guarlacus, a learned papist, falling sick, perceived no way with him but death, he fell into a miserable agony and perturbation of spirit, crying out of his sins, how miserably he had lived, and that he was not able to abide the judgment of God, and so casting out words of miserable desperation [he] said [that] his sins were greater than they could be pardoned, and in that desperation ended his days.[109] Jacobus Latomus of the same university of Louvain, after he had been at Brussels, and there thinking to do a great act against Luther and his fellows, made an oration before the emperor so foolishly and ridiculously that he was laughed

106. This paragraph break is not in the original.
107. This paragraph break is not in the original.
108. In the margin: Illyric. de fide.
109. In the margin: Foxe book of Acts and Mon.

to scorn by almost the whole court. Then, returning from thence to Louvain, [he] fell into open madness in his public lecture, uttering such words of desperation and blasphemous impiety that other divines, who were present, were fain to carry him away as he was raving, and to shut him into a closed chamber. From that time to his very last breath, he had never anything else in his mouth but that he was damned and rejected by God, and that there was no hope of salvation for him because he withstood wittingly and against his knowledge the manifest truth of God's Word.[110]

Crescentius,[111] the pope's legate and vicegerent in the Council of Trent, was sitting all the day long until dark night in writing of letters to the pope. After his labor, when night was come, thinking to refresh himself, he began to rise, and, at his rising, behold there appeared to him a mighty black dog of a huge bigness, his eyes flaming with fire, and his ears hanging low down well near the ground, which began to enter in and to come straight toward him, and so to crouch under the board. The cardinal, not a little amazed at the sight thereof, somewhat recovering himself, called to his servants, who were in the outward chamber close by, to bring in a candle and to seek for the dog. But when the dog could not be found there, nor in any other chamber about, the cardinal, thereupon stricken with a sudden conceit of mind, immediately fell into such a sickness whereof his physicians, which he had about him, could not with all their industry and cunning cure him. And thereupon he died.[112]

When a certain bishop came unto Stephen Gardiner, and put him in mind of Peter's denial [of] his Master, [he] answered again that he had denied with Peter, but [that he had] never repented with Peter. And so, (to use Master Foxe's words) [he] stinkingly and unrepentantly died.

More examples might be added, but these shall suffice. Again, that we may be further induced to the practice of these duties, let us call to mind the uncertainty of our days. Though we now live, yet who can say that he shall be alive the next day or the next hour? No man has a lease of his life. Now mark, as death leaves a man, so shall the last judgment find him. And, therefore, if death takes him away unprepared, eternal damnation follows without recovery. If a thief is brought from prison, either to the bar to be arraigned before the judge or to the place of execution, he will bewail his past misdemeanor and promise all reformation of life, so be it he might be delivered, though he is the most arrant thief that ever was. In this case, we are as felons or thieves, for we are every day going to the bar of God's judgment. There is no stay or standing in the way, even as the ship in the sea continues on its course day and night whether the mariners

110. This paragraph break is not in the original.

111. Sleid 1.23.

112. This paragraph break is not in the original.

are sleeping or waking. Therefore, let us all prepare ourselves and amend our lives betimes, so that in death we may make a blessed end.[113]

Ministers of the gospel do daily call for the performance of this duty. But where shall we find the practice and obedience of it in men's lives and conversation? Alas, alas, to lend our ears for the space of an hour to hear the will of God is common. But to give heart and hand to do the same is rare. And the reason hereof is at hand. We are all most grievous sinners, and every sinner in the terms of Scripture is a fool. And a principal part of this folly is to care for the things of this world and to neglect the kingdom of heaven, to provide for the body and not for the soul, to cast and forecast how we may live in wealth and honor and ease, and not to use the least forecast to die well. Our Savior Christ noted this folly in the rich man who was careful to enlarge his barns, and had no care at all for his end or for the salvation of his soul [Luke 12:17–18]. Such a one was Ahithophel, who (as the Scripture terms him) was as the very oracle of God for counsel, being a man of great wisdom and forecast in the matters of the commonwealth and in his own private worldly affairs. And yet, for all this he had not so much as common sense and reason to consider how he might die the death of the righteous and come to everlasting life. And the Holy Spirit has noted this folly in him, for the text says [that], when he saw that his counsel was despised, "he saddled his ass, and arose: and went home into his city, and put his household in order, and went and hanged himself" (2 Sam. 17:23). And the five foolish virgins contented themselves with the blazing lamps of bare profession, never seeking for the horn of lasting oil of true and lively faith, that might furnish and trim the lamp both in life and death. But let us in the fear of God, cast off this damnable folly, first of all seeking the kingdom of God and His righteousness, and leading our lives in faith and obedience, that we may die accordingly.

DOCTRINE 2:
We Must Not Fear Death

And thus much of the first point of doctrine, namely that there is a certain way whereby a man may die well. Now, I come to the second. Whereas, therefore, Solomon says that "the day of death is better than the day of birth" (Eccl. 7:1), we are further taught that such as truly believe themselves to be the children of God are not to fear death overmuch. I say overmuch, because they must partly fear it and partly not.

113. This paragraph break is not in the original.

They must fear it for two causes. The first [is] because death is the destruction of human nature in a man's own self and others. And in this respect Christ feared it without sin. And we must not fear it otherwise than we fear sickness and poverty and famine, with other sorrows of body and mind, which God will not have us to despise or lightly to regard, but to feel with some pain, because they are corrections and punishments for sin. And He does, therefore, lay upon us pains and torments that they may be feared and eschewed, and that by eschewing them we might further learn to eschew the cause of them, which is sin, and by experience in feeling of pain, acknowledge that God is a judge and enemy of sin, and is exceedingly angry with it. The second cause of the fear of death is the loss of the church or commonwealth, when we or others are deprived of them which were indeed or might have been a help, stay, and comfort to either of them, and whose death has procured some public or private loss.

Second, we are not to fear death, but to be glad of it, and that for many causes. First of all, in it we have occasion to show our subjection and obedience which we owe unto God when He calls us out of this world, as Christ said, "Father, not my will but thy will be done." Second, all sin is abolished by death, and we then cease to offend God anymore as we have done. Third, the dead body is brought into a better condition than ever it was in this life, for by death it is made insensible, and by that means it is freed from all the miseries and calamities of this life, and it ceases to be either an active or passive instrument of sin, whereas in the lifetime it is both. Fourth, it gives the soul passage to rest, life, and celestial glory, in which we shall see God as He is, perfectly know Him, and praise His name forever, keeping without intermission an eternal Sabbath. Therefore, Paul says, "I desire to be dissolved and be with Christ, for that is best of all." Fifth, God executes His judgments upon the wicked, and purges His church by death. Now in all these respects godly men have cause not to fear and sorrow, but to rejoice in their own death and the death of others.

Third, if the day of death is so excellent, yea a day of happiness, then it is lawful to desire death, and men do not always sin in wishing for death. Paul says, "I desire to be dissolved" (Phil. 1:23). And again, "O miserable man that I am, who shall deliver me from this body of death?" (Rom. 7:24). Yet, this desire must not be simple, but restrained with certain respects, which are these: First, death must be desired so far forth as it is a means to free us from the corruption of our nature. Second, [it may be desired] as it is a means to bring us to the immediate fellowship of Christ and God Himself in heaven. Third, death may be lawfully desired in respect of the troubles and miseries of this life, two caveats being observed: (1) that this desire must not be immoderate; and (2) that it must be joined with submission and subjection to the good pleasure of God. If either of these is wanting, the desire is faulty. And, therefore, Job, Jeremiah, and Jonah failed herein, because they desired death, being carried away with impatience.

On the contrary, a man may also desire a continuance of life. Hezekiah prayed and desired to live when he heard the message of present death, so that he might do service to God [Isa. 38:3]. And Paul desired to live in regard of the Philippians, so that he might further their faith, though in regard of himself to die was [an] advantage to him [Phil. 1:24–25].

Lastly, if death joined with reformation of life is so blessed, then the death of the unbelieving and unrepentant sinner is every way cursed and most horrible. [The] reasons are these: First, it is the destruction of nature, and the wages of sin. Second, there is no comfort of the spirit to be found in it, no mitigation of pain, and no good thing that may countervail the miseries thereof. Third, that which is the most fearful thing of all, bodily death is the beginning of eternal death, desperation, and infernal torment, without hope of deliverance. Therefore, as I began so I end: Have care to live well and die well.

FINIS

An addition of things that came to my mind afterward.

First, the last combat with the devil in the pang of death is oftentimes [the] most dangerous of all. For he will not then urge men to desperation, knowing that by this means he shall stir them up to resist him. But he labors with them that they would not resist him when he assaults them, and by this means he endeavors to extinguish hope. And this is not done in any other temptation in which faith or hope alone are impugned, whereas in this they are both impugned together. This must be thought upon, for when the devil's temptation is not to resist his temptation, it is most deceitful of all. And it is easier to overcome the enemy who compels us to fight than him who dissuades us from it.

Second, the temptation of Master John Knox, in the time of his death, is worth the marking.[114] He lay silent on his death bed for the space of four hours, very often giving great sighs, sobs, and groans, so as the bystanders well perceived that he was troubled with some grievous temptation. And when at length he was raised in his bed, they asked him how he did. He answered them thus: that in his life he had endured many combats and conflicts with Satan, but that now most mightily the roaring lion had assaulted him. "Often," said he, "he set my sins before my eyes, often he urged me to desperation, often he labored to entangle me with the delights of the world, but being vanquished by the sword of the Spirit, which is the Word of God, he could not prevail. But now he assaults me another way. For the wily serpent would persuade me that I shall merit eternal life for my fidelity in my ministry. But blessed be God who brought to my mind such Scriptures whereby I might quench the fiery darts of the devil, which were: 'What hast thou that thou hast not received?' 'By the grace of God, I am that I am.' 'Not I but the grace of God in me.' And being thus vanquished, he departed."

Third, when you are tempted by Satan and see no way to escape, even plainly close your eyes, and answer nothing, but commend yourself to God. This is a principal point of Christian wisdom which we must follow in the hour of death.

Fourth, if your flesh trembles and fears to enter into another life, and doubts of salvation, if you yield to these things, you hurt yourself. Therefore, close your eyes as before, and say with Saint Stephen: "Lord Jesus, into thy hands I commend my spirit." And then, certainly Christ will come unto you with all His angels and be the guider of your way. Luther.

114. In the margin: Li. de obitu. Knoxi.

Scripture Index

OLD TESTAMENT

Genesis

1–2 xxivn66, xxv
1:1 33
1:4–17 264
1:26 123, 273
1:27 159
1:28 124, 134
2:9 314
2:15 45
2:17 319, 404
2:18 123
2:21 xxvin72, 123
2:22 159
2:24 160, 305
3:5 327
3:9 339
3:13 339
3:15 308, 339
3:16 174
3:19 33, 54, 122
3:22 318
4:1 331
4:5 57
4:7 320
4:7–8 57
4:26 327
5:22 14
5:32 315
6:2 144, 180
6:9 5, 335
6:12 112
8:2 202
8:20–21 308
8:21 314
9:1 124
9:25 187
11:4 318
11:26 315
11:29 134
12:4 9
12:8 322
12:11 175
13:1 175, 322
13:15 305
14:14 190
15:2 192
15:4 445
17:1 335
17:8 317
17:10–11 311
17:12 188
18:4 321
18:17–18 351
18:19 120, 190, 446
18:27 421
18:29 351
19:14 19
20:1–3 175
20:3 316, 318
20:7 290
20:12 134
20:16 171, 174
21:7 176
21:12 172
22:14 314

Genesis (*continued*)
24:2 192
24:2–3 184
24:3 144
24:3–4 157
24:12 184
24:16–17 181
24:35 188
24:58 180
24:59 177
24:65 174
24:67 171
25:5–6 444
25:21 168
26:8 170
26:35 175
27 444
27:9 193
27:46 175
28:1 144, 179
28:2 135
28:12 307
28:19 322
28:22 314
29:21 128
29:23 149
29:25 149
29:27–28 149
29:32 160
30:2 172
31:17 175
31:38 186
32:10 322
32:16 318
33:11 317
35:8 177
37:13 321
39:2–3 78
39:4 192
39:9 9
42:10 327
45:5 436
46:4 319
46:27 309
47:6 327
47:12 182
48:22 309
49 444, 448, 450
49:8 182
49:10 448
49:18 448
50:23 326
50:24–25 450

Exodus
2:7–9 177
2:10 180
2:16 181
3 209
3:5 252
3:11 237
4 315
4:10 237
4:13 237
4:25 313
4:26 175
9 315
9:6 317
10:21 283
11 315
12 314
12:1 312
12:13 312
12:37 323
12:46 307
12:50 320
13:17 319
13:22 283
14 315
14:11 319
17:15 314
18:19 181
19:4 313
19:20 209
20 151
20:10 190
20:12 813
21:5 187
21:7 158
21:10 171

21:15 182
21:19 48
21:26 187
22:3 187
22:16–17 157
22:20 318
26:3 139
31:15 319
33:23 415n29
34:6 319
34:15–16 144

Leviticus
10:1–2 266
10:3 209, 352
16 314
17:3 319
18:3 141
18:6 130
18:9–11 134
18:12–14 136
18:16 138–39
18:18 138
18:19 167
18:22–23 130
18:24–25 141
19:17 191
20:6 441
20:10 146
20:11–12 141
20:14 141
20:16 141
20:20 141
20:21 138
21:7 146
21:10 147
21:14 147
22:12–13 174
25:35 98
25:45 187
25:46 184, 317

Numbers
8 101
16:32 453
18:26 212
20:12 22–23
23:10 407n9
27:8–11 445
30 65
30:4–6 157
30:6 183
30:13 174
36:11 135

Deuteronomy
2:30 315
5:25–28 256
6:6–7 121
6:7 179, 189
6:13 305
6:20 179, 189
6:20–21 121
6:24 121
7:3 157
10:9 212
12:3 197n4
12:32 291
13:2 69
13:3 67
13:6 122, 191
13:8 191
15 231
15:7 96
15:12 187
15:17 187, 317
17:16–17 84
17:19 80
20:7 127
21:17 182
21:18–20 191
22:20–21 150
22:23 128
22:23–24 143
22:28–29 157
23:2 142
24:5 161
24:15 185
25:5 139, 326n20
25:16 90

Deuteronomy (*continued*)
27:20 142
28 394
28:1 168
28:2 212
28:4 168
28:64 317
30:11 335
30:14 335
31 443
31:2–7 102
32 448

Joshua
1:9 321
7:1 322
9:23 187
10:13 320
11:20 315
13:27 323
15:16 180
15:17 135
23 443
24:15 120, 189

Judges
3:11 324, 326
3:30 324, 326
5:31 324, 326
6:32 322
8:28 324, 326
9:22 324, 326
10:2–3 324, 326
10:14 320
11:26 324, 326
13:5 47
14:1 157
14:2 179–80
16 422
17:6 270
17:10 270
18:4 270
19:2 175
20:35 324
20:46 324

Ruth
1:11 139
2:14 182
2:18 182
3:5 181
3:9 171
4:21 322

1 Samuel
1:11 178
1:22 176
1:23 172
1:26–27 168
1:27 121
2:6 435
2:12 112
2:17 352
2:23 179
2:23–25 112
2:25 352
5:2–4 360
6:19 74n49
12:3 103
12:23 227, 353
12:24–25 322
13:1 323
14–15 112
14:24 355
14:49 322
15:23 47
17:40 327
18–21 47
18:19 326
19:24 213
21:3 322
25–26 47
25:44 169
30:5 171
30:6 446
30:8 171

2 Samuel
2:22 321
3:14 169
4 322

7:14 395n26
10 380n8
11:9 162
11:11 167
11:11–12 162
11:21 322
12 339, 345
12:13 218, 268, 342, 428
13:13 135
15:4 56
15:25–26 308
15:26 15
15:30 319
17:23 455
17:25 323
21:8 326
21:16 313
23:2–3 448

1 Kings
1 112
2 443, 446
5 112
6:2–3 315
7:46 323
8:25 409
9:28 309
10:8 414
11:29 327
12:18 317
13:2 24
15:5 318
15:9 323
15:25 323
15:28 323
17:17 193
18:21 360
18:22 213
18:26 190
18:27 320
18:29 190
19 66
19:4 414
20:27 321
21:10 327
21:29 421
22:15 320
22:26–28 274
22:34 274

2 Kings
1:6 441
1:17 324
2:9 216
3:1 324
3:8 327
4:10 192
4:22 175
4:23 190
4:33 434
5:11 319
5:17 327
6:15 15
7:12 22
7:17 22
8:10 319
8:16 324
9:33 274
11:15 71
14:17 326
15:1 322
15:19 323
15:30 325
15:33 325
20:3 320
20:7 438
22:19–20 414
23:30 322
23:34 322
24:6 322

1 Chronicles
2:6 322
2:9 323
2:16 323
3:11 322
3:15 322
3:16 326
3:17 322
3:25 322

1 Chronicles (*continued*)

4:10	318
5:2	327
5:6	323
8:34	322
10:2	322
15:2	317
25:1	290
26:13	319

2 Chronicles

2:11	322
6:13–14	354
8:18	309
16:12	441
17	335
19:5	319
20:20	12, 78
21:17	322
22:6	322
22:7	315
24:22	448
26:1	322
33:12–13	432
36:10	326

Ezra

9:6	105
10:11	144, 163
10:19	163

Nehemiah

2:9	327
8:6	190, 355
8:8	303
9:19	327
9:37	315
12:27	327

Esther

1:8	160
1:12	175
2:7	322
4:16	122

Job

1:1	5
1:5	181, 190, 327
1:21	83, 421
2:9	447
2:10	172
9:3	105
13:15	14, 452n104
19:25–27	257
19:26	327
32:18–19	353
33:1–7	203
33:13	203
33:23	243, 271, 274, 279
33:23–24	xiii, 203

Psalms

1:3	78
3:5	12
6	268, 318, 408, 431
6:1	409n14
6:4–5	408
6:9–10	320
7:4	318
7:8	22, 321
8	322
8:10	321
10:4–5	251
10:6	22
10:11	22
10:13–14	22
10:17	448
12:2	319
12:6	291
14:1	49, 121
14:4	121–22, 252
16:6	83
16:8	15
18:39	327
19:6	327
19:7	291
19:12	105
22:1	321
22:9	176
22:16	328

23:4 409
25:8–9 351
30:7 314
31:5 452
32 202, 268, 431
32:3–5 308, 431
32:5 338
32:8 219
34 260
34:9 17
34:15–16 314
37:25 231
38–39 431
39:4 422
39:9 258, 436
39:10 332
40:6 10
42:1 88
44:1 179
50:16 253
50:16–17 351
50:17 327
50:21 319
51 23, 268, 450
51:18 50
55:17 121
55:22 17
56:4 6
56:8 436
66 332
66:7 320
67:6 320
69:25 307
69:27 306
72 446
72:14 332
72:16 327
73:2 327
73:4 327
73:12–13 23
73:23 327
73:26 447
77:1–2 342
78:2 304
78:24 304
79:10 321
90:12 422
91:11 46
91:11–12 261, 438
101 201
101:2 119
101:6 184
101:7 192
103:20 55
105:12 327
105:15 322
105:25 315
106:17–18 453
107:9 259
109:10 231, 319
109:17–18 327
110:1 304
110:3 314
112:3 85
113:9 168
116:7–9 451
116:10 14, 304
116:15 436
118:16 280
119:1–2 335
119:8 315
119:11 9, 23
119:18 209, 302
119:24 80
119:39 53
119:49–50 26, 447
119:98–99 13
119:136 227, 413
120:5 414
122:6 50
124:1 320
125:2 327
127:1 93
127:1–3 120
127:2 121
127:3 168
128:1 113
128:1–2 121
128:3 115
128:6 121

Psalms (*continued*)
130:1–2 342
133:2 318
136 320
136:2 319
139:7 327
139:14 327
139:15–16 436
139:17 327
145:18 320
145:19 341, 448
147:19 283

Proverbs
1:18 327
2:17 169, 171
3:4 327
3:9 51
4:1–4 190
5:18–19 170
6:10 319
7:19 161
8:18 327
8:22 331
9:8 336
13:10 317
16:4 33
17:33 327
18:14 395
19:11 378
19:14 177
19:17 20
20:11 177
20:20 319
22:29 264
24:3 xxivn64, 119
26:6 37
27:15–16 175
27:23 184, 245, 319
27:26–27 191
28:13 308
29:15 179
29:17 179, 192
29:18 279, 290
30:8 83
31 xxivn66
31:11 125
31:13 125, 193
31:15 185, 193
31:26 193
31:27 184
31:28 193

Ecclesiastes
1:2 319
2:2 160
7:1 xxxii, 403–57, 455
7:16 368
9:2 409
9:10 xxxiv, 47, 427
11:9 103
12:1 402n3
12:14 104

Song of Solomon
1:1 170
2:6 437

Isaiah
1:4 342
1:6 439
1:13 90, 313
1:16 342
1:18 342
1:19 24
1:21 321, 327
3:9 320
6:1–13 236
6:3 319
6:5–8 xiii, 235
6:6–8 70, 352
6:8–9 269
6:9 319
6:10 304
7:9 22
8:1 295
8:15 23
8:18 227n2
9:6 318
9:10–11 327
9:14 327

10:10 327
13 209
16:12 327
19:14 315
21:9 318
24:20 327
26:3 11
28:15 19, 422
28:16 14, 304
29:13 305
33:22 202
34:6 317
37:11 327
38:1 316, 442, 444
38:1–3 408
38:3 100, 457
41:8 327
43:2 437
43:8 327
44:25–26 222
44:28 24
45:7 405
48:11 320
49:4 96
49:6 327
49:23 223
50:2 319
50:4 208, 329
51:11 327
53:11 327
55:1 327
55:2 319
56:3 319
56:10 352
57:1 414
57:2 415
58:1 353
58:5–6 327
59:20 306
59:21 297
61:1–2 306
61:3 52n11
62:7 170
64:6 321
66:3 90

Jeremiah
1:6–7 237
5:29 314
7:4 319
8:6 317
9:1 227n1
12:16 319
15:10 212
15:19 190, 352
18:9–10 316
22:9 319
22:11 322
23:29 319
24:3 319
25:9 318
26:6 179
26:9 317
29:6 157
31:35 327
32:24 322
48:10 47
50:43 327

Lamentations
3:22 392n21
3:39 430
3:40 431
3:48 227n1
5:4 185

Ezekiel
1:9 139
13:10 319
14:9 315
18:6 167
21:28 319
22:10 141
33:10–11 404
33:14–15 316
34:15–16 334
44:13 102
44:22 147
46:21 319
47:1 214
48:35 314

Daniel
2:4 317
3 319
4:19–20 345
4:22 345
7:2 327
7:9–10 104
9:2 14, 301
12:3 280

Hosea
1:2 147
2:19 168
13:9 405

Joel
3:14 319

Amos
2:7 141
3:7 351

Jonah
1:17 306
3:4 316
3:4–5 421

Micah
2:4 319
3:8 350
5:2 305
7:2 89

Habakkuk
2:2 295
2:4 xxxii, 5–29

Zephaniah
2:1 202

Zechariah
2:8 314
8:5 179
9:9 307
11:13 309
12:11 122
12:12 167
13:3 191

Malachi
2:7 205–6, 261
2:15 125, 168, 172
3:17 393n24

NEW TESTAMENT

Matthew
1:3 323
1:8 323
1:11–12 323
1:12 326
1:17 323n15
1:18 127, 150
1:20 128
2:6 305
3:7 334, 339
3:10 107, 334
3:11 266
4 202
4:3 7
4:10 305
4:23 317
5–7 202
5:2 316
5:13 215, 254
5:18 291
5:20 20
5:32 114
6:7 356
6:11 83
6:12 106
6:30 20
6:32 17
6:33 88
7:6 336
7:9–10 177
7:15 68
7:21 426
8 322
8:6 185

9:2 431
9:13 318, 340
9:38 50
10:10 321
10:28–31 345
10:29–30 436
11:30 24
12:14 22
12:26 321
12:36 106
12:39–40 306
13:14 304, 319
13:35 304
13:52 191, 301
15:8–9 305
16 344
16:16 222
17:1 324
17:6 255
17:27 382
18:6 26
18:7 53
18:15 191
18:17 192
19 163
19:5 305
19:6 xxvin72, 123, 156
19:9 143, 169
19:16–17 339
20:6 48
20:8 185
21:3 90
21:5 307
21:26 317
23:2–3 291
23:13 339
23:33 339
24:25 192
24:37–39 19
25 352
25:20–21 104
25:21 185, 280
25:26 48
25:34 280
25:35 320
26:11 231
26:24 407
27:9 309
27:46 448
28:19 278

Mark
2:4 432
2:5 26
2:26 322
2:27 82n61
4:12 304
6:3 55
6:5 22
6:8–9 321
6:18 141
6:20 352
7:9 320
9 344
12:24 321
12:30–31 xxii
13:37 317
15:25 325
16:2 318
16:16 27

Luke
1:4 336
1:6 5, 316
1:20–21 22
1:53 88, 259
2:7 176
2:29 13, 411n23
2:37 318
2:51 181
2:52 315
3:27 326
4:18 306, 340
4:22 351
5:5 80
6:36 389n18
6:46 318
7:47 13
8:10 304
8:13 8

Luke (*continued*)
8:15 8
9:28 324
9:33 255
10:7 185
10:34 439
10:39 190
11:1 355
11:13 24
11:27 176, 350
11:28 335
12:13–14 72
12:14 46
12:17–18 455
12:19 422
12:45 23
13:9 313
13:32 401
14:26 165
15:10 261
16:2 101n106
16:19 122, 292
16:29 291
17:2 53
17:21 425n44
18:1 317
18:10 79
18:11–12 22
18:13 354
19:8 232
19:9 425
20:4 67
21:19 95n95
21:28 257
22:15 190
22:19 428
22:42 408
23:34 448
23:43 448
23:46 448, 451
24:27 292
24:53 317

John
1 314
1:3 320
1:42 322
1:51 307, 320
2:2 160
2:7–8 160
3:13 315
3:14 447
3:16 334
3:33 9
4:34 48
4:35 321
5:14 431
5:24 425
5:35 8
6:7 321
6:31 304
6:35 312
7:17 12
7:37 342, 354
7:46 351
8:35 192
8:56 14
8:58 315
9:2–3 431
9:3 318
9:4 48n8
10:29 317
10:34–36 330
11:11 401n2
11:41 434
12:35 48n7
12:40 304
14:13 317
14:21 335
14:23 335
17:3 316, 425
18:20 317
19:14 325
19:26–27 448
19:28 448
19:28–29 306
19:30 448
19:36 307
20:23 222
20:29 14
21:22 73

Acts

1:5 266
1:20 307
2 208, 265
2:14 354
2:23 338
2:24–27 329
2:37–38 340
4:19 187
4:24 355
4:28 435
4:36 322
5:39 318
6:2 72
7:14 309
7:16 309
7:55 354
7:56 448
7:59 452
7:59–60 448
8:14 67
8:20–23 339
8:22 338
8:26 45, 66
8:37 337
9:3–5 335
9:4 320
9:6 237, 278
9:14 49
9:22 304
10:2 120
10:7 56, 184
10:43 310
11:20 67
12:1–2 274
12:23 274
13:6 322
13:8 322
15:9 13
15:28 298
16:14 9
16:16–17 274
16:17 279
16:27–31 336
17:2–3 350
17:17 335
17:22–24 336
17:28–29 332
17:30 318
17:30–31 336
18:3 72
18:24 332
18:25–26 336
18:26 193
18:28 329, 332
19:9 336
19:16 47
19:26 345
19:31 99
19:35 345
19:37 345
20:10 434
20:21 217
20:28 16n16, 45, 314, 444
20:32 115
24:16 352
24:25 251
27:23 273
27:33 317
28:27 304

Romans

1:5 xxxii, 7
1:9 289
1:16 290
1:17 5
1:26 130
1:28 315
2:16 295
3:2 298
3:3 321
3:9–12 329
3:25 314
3:28 309
3:31 9
4:11 312
4:18 7, 331, 342
4:21–24 331
5:1 12
5:3 13, 437

Romans (*continued*)
5:5 437
5:12 404
6:23 404, 407
7:2 174
7:24 413, 456
8:1 340
8:8 xxviii, 166
8:14 425
8:15 10
8:17 445
9:7–8 331
9:10 331
9:33 304
10:8 335
10:19 290
11:8 304
11:16 27
11:26 306
11:36 33
12:6 xiv, 290
12:8 47
12:13 192
13:7 54
14:7–8 438, 451
14:10 103
14:12 103
14:17 12, 425
14:21 135
14:23 14, 16n14, 46n2
15:4 293, 331, 345
16:20 308
16:27 316

1 Corinthians
1:2 49
2:1–2 349
2:4–5 349
2:8 315, 317
2:13 350
2:14 20, 22
2:15 12
3:1–2 337
4:1 279
4:2 261
4:6 345
4:8 320
4:19–20 350
5:1 141
5:7 314
6:9 90
6:12 136, 317
7 xxivn66
7:1–2 113
7:2 124, 158
7:3 166
7:5 125, 167
7:8 124
7:8–9 113
7:9 124–25
7:10 161
7:11 143
7:12–13 145, 161
7:14 27
7:15 162
7:17 44
7:17–25 43
7:20 xix, 43–107, 122, 165
7:21 63, 188
7:25–35 xxvn70
7:26 124
7:27 166
7:28 124
7:32 124–25
7:36 157, 179
7:38 179
9:2 70
9:4 330
9:5 175
9:7 232
9:9 191, 232, 330, 332
9:14 232
9:19 52, 264
9:25 313
10–11 314
10:4 311
10:11 293, 331
10:13 395
10:16 312
10:31 xxviii

10:33 51
11:3 174, 314
11:7 130
11:14 207
11:20 428
11:24 310
11:32 414
12 54, 320
13:5 380
13:7 378
14:1 64, 100
14:3 289
14:15–16 355
14:24 289
14:24–25 206, 350
14:32 333
14:37 333
14:40 159
15:24 102
15:25 304
15:26 407
15:31 426
15:33 332
15:56 423
16:19 122

2 Corinthians
1:5 437
1:9 442
1:12 352
1:20 24
2:16 212, 271
3:9 391n19
4:2–4 350
4:4 19
4:13 304
5:1 436
5:11 91
5:14 92
5:18 16, 428
5:19–20 290
5:20 342
6:14 144
7:8–10 338
9:7 263
10:4 238
10:4–5 9
10:5 23
12:2 256
12:7 413
12:8–9 126
12:14 177
12:15 29
12:16–17 321
13:13 317

Galatians
2:9 214, 255
2:15 345
2:20 6, 425
3:1 350
3:9–11 330
3:10 334
3:11 5
3:11–12 6, 18
3:13 407n10
3:16 305
4:1 151
4:14 215
5:13 52, 93
6:10 427
6:16 292

Ephesians
1:13 297
1:18 87
2:1 406
2:2 22
2:10 xxii
2:20 6, 295
3:1 312
4:1 52
4:21–22 424
4:28 55, 61
5:2 308
5–6 xxivn66
5:16 48n6
5:22 174
5:22–6:9 xxx
5:23 168

Ephesians (*continued*)
5:24 174
5:28 166
5:28–29 171
5:29 170, 172
5:31 xxvin72, 123
5:33 171
6:1 181
6:3 179
6:4 176
6:5 186
6:5–7 184
6:16 15

Philippians
1:23 414, 456
1:24–25 457
2:15 89
2:21 317
3:1 13
3:8 88
3:8–9 219
3:12 315
3:15 315
4:3 202
4:5 xxii, 96n96, 365–98
4:6 17
4:7 12, 425
4:8 145–46, 160
4:8–9 351
4:11 56
4:11–12 82

Colossians
1:13 424
1:15 182
1:24 29
1:28–29 353
2:14 106
3–4 xxivn66
3:11 188
3:14 53
3:16 25, 294
3:17 93
3:18 174
3:18–4:1 xxx
3:22 184, 186
3:24 58
4:1 185

1 Thessalonians
2:7 353
4:3–4 168
4:6 90
4:11 73
5:8 15
5:11 50, 433
5:14 433
5:20 50

2 Thessalonians
2:2 444
2:11 315
2:13–14 290
3:1 50
3:10 48
3:14 48

1 Timothy
1:9 340
1:13 23
1:17 316
1:19 8, 352
2:1–2 355
2:8 120
2:12 130, 174
3–4 xxivn66
3:1 70
3:2 353
3:5 112
3:6 237
3:10 65
4:1 125
4:3 125, 441
4:3–5 167
4:4–5 121
4:5 80
4:7 353
4:8 113, 120
4:12 351

4:13 301
4:14 16
5:4 182
5:6 406
5:8 164, 177, 191, 445
5:10 176
5:11 125
5:14 124, 193
6:10 83
6:20 81

2 Timothy
1:13 303
2:8–9 295
2:10 29
2:15 329
2:19 270
2:25 341, 353
3:10–11 296
3:14–15 178
3:16–17 344
4:2 241
4:7 100
4:7–8 103
4:8 252

Titus
1:1 291
1:12 333
1:15 22, 78
2:5 193
2:9 186
2:10 52
2:12 90
2:15 353
3:5 314
3:10 144

Philemon
1:2 122

Hebrews
1:14 226, 261
3:12 8, 19
3:13 433
4:12 23, 292
4:16 10
5:12 337
5:13 337
6:1–3 337
6:4 21
7:1 71
8:8 330
8:13 330
9:16 445
10:34 13
10:38 8
11 202
11:3 6
11:5 453
11:6 27, 46
11:7 9, 16, 91
11:21 447
11:26 87
11:27 15
11:37 25, 86
12:9 179
13:2 192
13:4 125, 167
13:5 82

James
1:5–6 126
1:21 8
1:22 424n43
1:27 247
2:24 309
3:6 266
3:17 291
4:12 292
5:14 192, 432
5:16 26, 430, 433
5:17 341

1 Peter
1:8 13
1:10 301
1:20 303
1:22–23 13
2:13–14 54

1 Peter (*continued*)
3 xxivn66
3:6 175
3:7 161, 171–72
3:8 184
3:19 322
3:21 337
4:11 205, 353
4:15 73
5:3 351
5:6 308
5:7 17

2 Peter
1:15 444
1:21 292

1 John
1:9 10
2:1 217
2:16 21
3:3 13
3:9 9
3:15 316
3:23 24
5:4 11

Jude
22–23 335

Revelation
1–3 202
2 344
2–3 205n1, 261
2:6 341
3:18 302
6:16 252, 255, 257
10:9 208
10:11 208
14:13 412, 436
18:7 22
19:10 261
20:6 424
21:6 316
21:8 316
22:9 261
22:18–19 291

Subject Index

Aaron, calling of, 66
Abiram, 453
Abraham
admonished by Sarah, 172
calling of, 45, 66
household service of, 120
marriage to Sarah, 134–35
as master of the household, 190
sacrifice of, 299
yielded rights to Lot, 384
Absalom, 56, 94, 112
abstinence, in marriage, 167
abundance, 83–86
account of calling, 103–7
Acts of the Apostles, 296
Adam, personal calling of, 54
Adam and Eve, God's mercy toward, 390
Additions to Daniel (apocrypha), 299
Additions to Esther (apocrypha), 299
adiaphora, 317
admonition, 345
Adonijah, 112
adultery, and divorce, 114, 163, 169
affections, restraining from the world, 82–86
affections of the world, turning from, 86–88
affinity (marriage), 131, 137–41
afflictions, 14
preparation for the pangs of death, 426–27
age (parity in marriage), 145
Ahab, 421
Ahithophel, 453
alchemists, 74
Alexander of Alexandria, 177
Alexander Polyhistor, 299
Alexander Severus, emperor, 65
allegory, 303, 322, 332
allowance from men, and calling, 64–65
"always," used for "often" or "long," 317
ambition, xx, 94–95
Ambrose, 136, 158, 159, 162, 449
Amnon, 135
Amos, 295
Anabaptists, 209, 272, 302
anagogical sense of Scripture, 303
analogical places, 310
analogy of faith, 303, 311, 312
angels, 259–64
bear love to God's children, 263–64
comfort to ministers, 260–61, 264
execute the will of God, 263
as fellow-laborers, 261
honoring of, 262
ministers as, 207–9
particular callings of, 55
rejoice at the conversion of a sinner, 261
animal death, 405–6
anointed preaching, xvii–xviii
anointing the sick, 430, 434

anthropopathia, 314
anti-Trinitarians, 302
apocrypha, not in the canon, 299–300
Apollinaris, 302
apostasy, 19
apostles, extraordinary calling of, 67, 70
Apostles' Creed, 433
application, kinds, 344–47
application of doctrine, 267, 334–43
"apt to teach," 353
Aratus, 332
Arius, 302, 453
Armine, William, 283
artificial memory, 348
Art of Prophesying (1607), xiv–xix, 281–356
assurance of God's presence, 15, 16
astrology, 74, 440
Athanasius, 63, 177–78, 298
atheism, 8, 19, 22, 29
Audians, 302
Augustine, xxin51, xxviin82, 135–36, 163, 317, 324, 332, 356, 449
auricular confession, 245, 427–28
avocations, 44

baptism, 337
  of children, 178
  valid and invalid, 76, 77
barrenness, 168
Basil, 158
Baxter, Richard, xxxn98
Beale, P. J., xxin53
beatific vision, xxxiiin118
beggars, 55, 96
benefits of God, obtained after death, 435
Benet, John, 359
Bernard, 449
Berosus, 299
betrothal, xxiv
Beza, Theodorus, 356
Bilney, Thomas, 427
binding and loosing, 342
birth, as entrance into sin and misery, 412
blessing of God, upon true minister, 222–25
bodily death, 406
body
  freed from all miseries in death, 456
  united to Christ, 416
body of Christ, 310
bond-servant, xxxn98, 186–87
Bonner, Edmund, 411
Breward, Ian, xii–xiii, xiin5
broken relationships, xxv
brotherhood, of good ministers, 214
Brunerus, 327
Budæus, Johannes, 361
Burgius, Annas, 450

Caiaphas, 76
Cain, 57, 395
calling, 15–17, 33
  change of, 99–100
  choice of, xx, 61–64
  constancy in, 94–100
  continuance in, xx, 73–100
  diligence in duties of, 47–48
  efficient cause of, 44–45
  end of, xx, 101–7
  entrance into, 64–72
  final cause of, 45–46
  fitness of, 61–62
  general rules of, 46–48
  giving account of, 103–7
  holiness in, 78–93
  imposition of, 45
  labor and work of, 16–17
  limits of, 46–47
  must be necessary, 74–77
  must be profitable, 74
  nature of, 43–47
  ordination of, 44–45
  preserving in, 17
  principal work of, 74–75
  proper works of, 73–74

resignment from, 101–3
use of, 60–107
see also general calling; particular calling
Calling of the Ministry (1605), xiii–xiv, 195–280
calling on the name of the Lord Jesus, 49
Calvin, John, xiv, xxxiiin120, 361, 450
Canaan, cursed by Noah, 187
Canaanites, wickedness of, 141
Canisius, 202
Canticles, 294
carding, 44
carnal security, 19
Carpocratians, 302
cases, in marriage, xxv
cases of conscience, xvii
casting down of the eye, 354
catechism
as foundation of religion, 336–37
as preparation for death, 432
Catharists, 302
celibacy, xxviin82
censure, of evil sayings or doings of a brother, 381
Chadwick, Henry, xxviin82
chance, 44, 346
charms, 224, 440
children
baptism of, 178
bestowing of, 179–80
consent of parents in second marriage, 183
education of, 176–79
fit callings for, 62–63
as gift from God, 167–68
natural gifts of, 62–63
preservation of life of, 176–77
Christian
live under the law, 374
must deal moderately with his brother, 395
Christian commonwealth, England as, 388
Christian equity, xxii, 366–89
Christian lawyer, 375
Christian liberty, 188
Christian life, as meditation on death, 420
Christian moderation, 365
Christian Oeconomie, or a Short Survey of the Right Manner of Erecting and Ordering a Family, According to the Scriptures (1609), xxiv–xxx, 109–94
Christians, as merciful, 388
Chronicles, First and Second, 293
Chrysostom, 172–73, 352
church
as a body, 45
civility within, xi
endowed with riches from God, 51
estate upheld by honest calling, 61
furthering the good estate of, 50–52
makes trial of gifts of a student of divinity, 277
ministry of judgment according to Scriptures, 298
voice in calling a minister, 277, 279
Church of England
calling of ministers, 77
spiritual condition of, xi, 232
Cicero, 298
civil government, 111
civil society, equity of, 365
coal of fire, 264–67
cohabitation, as duty of married persons, 161–63
collection (“right cutting” of the Word), 329–32
Colossians, 296
comfort, from forgiveness of sins, 268
commandments of the Word, 7
common good, xxii, 43, 45, 52
common-place books, 302
commonwealth
as a body, 45
equity of, 365

commonwealth (*continued*)
estate upheld by honest calling, 61
communication of properties (synecdoche), 314–15
communion, as duty of married persons, 166–70
completive things, understood as having begun, 315
conceiving of prayers, 290
concession (grammar), 321
concordances, 308
condition and estate (parity in marriage), 145–46
conditions, of hearers of the Word, 335–43
conference upon the Word of God, 121
confession of sin, voluntary, 245–46
confutations of errors (mental application), 344
consanguinity, 131–36
conscience, xvii, 251
consent, in marriage, 148–51
consolation, 345
consolation of the prophet, 257–59
circumstances of, 258–67
ground of, 267–69
contagious disease, and marriage, 142–43, 153, 162
contempt for God and His Word, 432
contentation, 17, 56, 82–83, 95, 421
continency, gift of, xxvn70, 113, 124, 125, 126, 162, 169
Cooke, Edward, 297
Corinthians, First and Second, 296
Cornelius, 120, 190
correction, 345, 346–47
corruption of nature, 246–47
Council of Lateran, 158
Council of Nicaea, 429
Council of Trent, 167, 454
counterfeit repentance, 420
couple, and consummation of marriage, 159–60
couples, principal sort, 123
cousins by marriage, 138
covenant of grace, 404, 416, 437
covetousness, xx, 81–88
Cradock, Timothye (Perkins's wife), xxivn64
Crashawe, W., 200, 202, 234, 362, 363
creation, testimony of Gentiles, 298
creation account, and male and female, xxv–xxvi
Crescentius, Marcellus, 454
crucified with Christ, xxxiv
cruelty, 368, 370, 371, 374, 397
cryptical or hidden places, 310
curiosity, of other callings, 73–74
Cyprian, 298
Cyril, 298

Damascene, 298
danger, faith in times of, 26
Daniel (book), 295
Dathan, 453
daughters, duties of, 181
David
faith in dying, 446–47
forgiveness of sins, 268
prayer against death, 408–9
within compass of calling, 46–47
Davies, Kathleen, xxivn67
Day of Judgment, 102, 103–7, 406
deacons, 65
dead in sin, 406
death
as deprivation of life, 403–4
from disease, 410–11
disposition toward, 446–55
and doubts, 458
and end of all miseries, 413–14
as end of calling, 102
as entrance to eternal life, 412
fear of, 455–57
immediate fellowship with Christ in heaven, 456
immoderate fear of, 434–38
as last combat with the devil, 458
meditation on, 420–22

preparation for, 418–46
and providence of God, 435–36
purges the church of wicked, 456
removal of power and strength of, xxxiii, 422–24
right behavior and disposition in, 417–18
of the righteous, 424
as second degree to eternal life, 413, 417
uncertainties of, 418
violent and sudden, 412
as wages of sin, 407–8
weakening the power of, xxxiii
death of a believer
as blessing, 407, 408, 436
excellency of, 399–400
death of Christ
altered death, 408
meditation on, 420
declaring the righteousness of Christ, 217–19
defective speeches (supply wanting), 312–13
Democritus, 63
deposition, from calling, 102
desertion of marriage, 162–65
desperation (falling in apprehending Christ), 341
Deuteronomy, 293
devil, temptations at death, 458
dicing, 44
diligence, in calling, 47–48
Directory for Public Worship (Westminster Assembly), xixn45
disabled, and calling, 98, 102
discontentment, in calling, 56–57
disease, and rejection of marriage contract, 152–53, 154
diseases, 411
disobedience, 7
divinity, study of, 301–2
divorce, and remarriage, 114, 143, 169–70
doctrine, application of, 267, 334–43
doctrine (mental application), 344
doctrine (practical application), 345–46
dogmatical books (Old Testament), 294
Dominicans, 272
Donatists, 302
doubtful sayings of men, interpreting in the better part, 380–82
doubtful things of men, interpreting in the better part, 377
doubts, and death, 458
dowry, 128, 193
dying by faith, 446–51
dying little by little each day, xxxiv, 426
dying in obedience, 451, 452
dying well, xxxiii, 417–55
dying while uncatechized, 432

Ebion, 302
Ecclesiasticus (apocrypha), 299
edification of the church, 50–51
effectual call, 410
Eli, 112
Elihu, 203
Elisha, 261
Elizabeth, Queen, xi, 231, 359
Elkanah, 172
ellipsis, 318
emperors and princes, injustices practiced by, 88
enallage of the preterperfect tense, 318
enchanters, 441
Encratites, 302
engagement, xxv
England, preaching in, xvn23
English Reformation, xi
Enthusiasts, 302
envy, xx, 95
Eopolemus, 299
Ephesians, 296
Ephraim the Syrian, 166–67
Epicures, 346

Epieikeia, or A Treatise of Christian Equity and Moderation (1604), xxii–xxiii, 357–98
Epimenides, 332
Epiphanius, 298
epistles (New Testament), 297
equity, 362, 365–89
  among masters and servants, 185
  nature of, 366–67
  practice of, 388–89
  private, 363, 376–88
  public, 363, 367–76
Erasmus, 356
error in respect to ability or estate (marriage consent), 149
error in respect to person (marriage consent), 149
error in the quality of the person (marriage consent), 150
Esau, proud wives of, 175
espousals. *See* marriage contract
Essenes, 302
estate, not judged by outward things, 409
Esther, 294
"eternal," as use for long time, 317
eternal life, 5, 6
  eye of faith fixed upon, 435
  first degree of, 413, 424–25
  in this life, 413
  three degrees of, xxxii, 413
eucharist, in the time of sickness, 427, 428–29
Euripides, 158
Eusebius, xxin51, 298, 299
Eutyches, 302
evangelists (early church), extraordinary calling of, 67
evangelists (Gospels), 295–96
evening household service of God, 121
"everywhere," used for here and there, 318
evil, 405
  God's permission of, 315
examination of heart, 431
examination of lives, 18–21
exhortation, 345
as fervent and vehement, 354
Exodus, 293
extraordinary callings, 60, 66–69
extreme unction, 427, 430
extremity in life of man, 372–75
extremity of law, 367–71
eyes, enlightened by Spirit of God, 87
Ezekiel, 295
Ezra, 294

faith, 337
  and calling, 16–17, 91–92
  cultivation of, 26–29
  cuts off worldly sorrows and cares, 3
  depends on God's promises, 14–15
  gives direction and stays the mind, 3–4
  and good conscience, 29
  of one's own, 26–29
  reigns in the heart, 9–10
falling in faith, 340–42
falling in knowledge, 340–42
falling in manners, 342
false faith, 21
false prophets, 67–68
false rules to order life, 20–21
false weights and measures, 89
family
  authority in, xxxi
  biblical view of, xxv
  as a body, 45
  definition of, 119
  equity of, 365
  estate upheld by honest calling, 61
  as first society in nature, 111–12
  as little churches, 122
family worship, xxxin104
famine, 25, 456
fashions of attire, 74
fasting, in families, 121–22

fathers, dedicating sons to holy calling of minister, 221
fear, of death, 455–57
fear of God, in the minister, 353
Felix (governor), 251
female, of an inferior sex, 130
Ferguson, Sinclair, xvin28
Ferne, John, 359–61
fever, 440
fiery tongues, 265–66
figure-casting, 74
filiation, 326
fines and rents, 372, 373
first born, greater portion of father's goods, 182
first death, 406
flood, 299
food and raiment, 17, 84, 86, 182
forfeitures of bonds, lands, or leases, 372, 397
forgiveness of sins, 267–69
forgiving and forbearing wrongs, 377, 384–88, 396, 397, 442
form of prayer, 355
fornication
  avoided by marriage, xxviii, 124–25
  in marriage, 167, 168–69
forthtelling, xiv
fortune, 346
"four last things," xxxiiin120
Fourth Book of Ezra, 299
Foxe, John, 454
Francis, Saint, wounds of, 255
Franciscans, 272
Frederus, Johannes, 361
free servant, 186
free servants, xxxn98
French pox, 142
friars, 55
fruits of new obedience, 340

Galatians, 296
gaming, 44
Gardiner, Stephen, 454
general calling, xix–xx, xxiin56, 49–53, 57–60, 100
general pollution of prophet, 240–42
general preparation for death, 418–27
general providence, 346
Genesis, 293
Gibeonites, 187
gifts from God
  and calling, 64–65
  general and proper, 126
glory of God, and fear of the prophet, 250–57
Gnostics, xxviin82, 302
God
  chastises but does not punish his children, 394
  efficient cause of every calling, 44–45
  exalts the humble, 259
  execution of death, 405
  mercy to Adam and Eve, 390
  mercy to sinners, 390–91
  moderation to the church, 393–96
  moderation toward men, 366, 389
  moderation toward the world, 390–93
  ordainer of death, 404
  as our portion, 83
  permission of evil, 315
  power in the weakness of dying, 412
  signifying the Father, 317
  and sin, 250–51
  uses means, 264–65
  will provide for his ministers, 280
  see also presence of God
godliness, xxix, xxxi, 113
godly minister, 351–52
godly sorrow, 338
good affections, 13
good conscience, 29
of minister, 352
good-man of the house. *See* master of the family, 189–92

goods evil gotten, to be restored before death, 445
good service, 427
good-wife of the house. *See* mistress of the family
good works, xxi–xxii, 13–14
gospel, comforts of, 340
Gospels, 295–96
grace, state of, xiv, 243, 226, 239, 258, 290
grace of the ministry, 353
grace of the person, 351–53
gracious speech, sermon as, 351
Great Commission, 278
greater prophecies (Old Testament), 295
Gregory of Nazianzen, 351–52
Gregory the Great, 298
Guarlacus, 453

Habakkuk, 295
Haggai, 295
Hales, Charles, 359
Hannah, 52, 121, 172, 178
heads of families, bestow goods on heirs, 445
hearers of the Word, 206–7
  divers conditions of, 335–43
  humbled, 339–40
  ignorant and unteachable, 335–36
  with knowledge but not humbled, 338–39
  as mixed people, 342–43
  must learn law and gospel, 220
  must submit to authority of minister, 228
  to receive with reverence the message, 215
  teachable yet ignorant, 336–37
  who are fallen, 240–42
  who believe, 340
heathen judges, 388
heaven, xxxiiin120
heavenly mindedness, xxxiiin119
Hebrews, epistle to, 296
hell, xxxiiin120, 392
  sins plunge ourselves into, 391–92
helps in callings, 96
Hemingius, 356
"Here I am, send me," 275–77
heresy, heretics, 19, 67, 301
Herod Agrippa, 299, 453
Herr, A. F., xvii–xviii
Heskith, Thomas, 297, 359
Hezekiah
  desired to live, 457
  prayer against death, 408, 409
  prayer on death bed, 431
high priests, calling of, 71
Hilary, 28, 298
Hill, Christopher, xxiiin63
historical books (Old Testament), 293–94
histories (New Testament), 295–96
Hoffmeister, 453
holiness
  in calling, 78–93
  nature and properties of, 257
  in a preacher, xix
holy abstinence, 167
holy seed, xxviii, 124, 168
Holy Spirit
  anoints preaching, xvii
  and preaching, 206
  testimony about Scripture, 297–300
home, xxiii–xxxi
Homer, 298
honest and lawful callings, 61
Hooper, John, 450
Hophni and Phineas, 112
Horace, 348
Hosea, marriage to harlot, 147
Hosea (book), 295
household, xxiiin63
household service of God, 120–22
How to Live, and That Well (1601), xxxii, 1–29
Hugo Cardinalis, 298
Hugo de Sancto Victore, 298

human testimonies, 332–33
human wisdom, concealed in sermons, 349
humble, exalting of, 259
humbling ourselves for past sins, 423
husband, xxix
  admonished and advised by wife, 172
  cannot strike wife, 172
  duties of, 171–73
  honor of wife, 171–72
  love for wife, 171
Huss, John, 66
Hyperius, 356
hypocrisy, 19, 389

"I am undone," 236
idleness, 48
Ignatius, 449
ignorance, of Word of God, 19–20, 433
Illyricus, 356
impatience, xx, 95–96
implicit faith, xi
imposition, of calling, 45
imposition of hands, 337
infants, faith of, 26–27
infirmities of men's natures, patience with, 377–81
injustice, xx, 88–91, 397
Innocentius, Pope, 158
instruction, 346
intermediate state, 413
interpreter, minister as, 207–10
interrogation, 320–21
invocation of the name of God, 121
inward gifts, and calling, 54
irony, 320
Isaiah (book), 295, 301

Jacob
  death of, 447
  last words of, 448
  marriage to Rachel, 135
James, letter of, 296
Japheth, 299
Jehoiada, 71
Jeremiah, desired death, with impatience, 457
Jeremiah (book), 295
Jerome, 28, 298, 422
Jerome of Prague, 66
Jerusalem council, 298
Jesuits, 227, 272
Jesus Christ
  calling as carpenter, 55
  last words of, 448
  love of, 92
  miracles of, 298
  prayer against death, 408
  righteousness of, 217–18
  temptation of, 7
Jews, false faith of, 21
Job, 421, 447, 457
Job (book), 294
Joel, 295
John the Baptist, 68
John, first, second and third letters of, 296
John, Gospel of, 295–96, 301
Jonah, desired death with impatience, 457
Jonah (book), 295
Jonas, Justus, 361
Jonvillaus, Carolus, 361
Joseph, sanctification in Egypt, 78
Joseph of Arimathea, 420
Josephus, 298, 299
Joshua, household service of, 120
Joshua (book), 293
joy of the Holy Spirit, 13
Judas, 395, 453
Jude, letter of, 296
Judges, 293
judgment, xxxiiin120, 18
  of heart of others, 381
  of own heart, 381
judicial astrology, 440
Judith, book of, 299
Junius, Franciscus, 356, 361

justice, 370–71
  of the gospel, 5
  of the law, 5, 390
  maintenance of, 366–67
justification, 5–6, 18, 340
"just and lawful distance of blood" (marriage), xxiv, 130–42

kindred of affinity. *See* affinity
kindred of alliance, 140
Kings, First and Second, 293
kinsmen, 132–34
knowledge of the will and Word of God, 25
knowledge of the Word of God, 6
knowledge without repentance, 338–39
Knox, John, death of, 458
Korah, 453

Lactantius, 298
Lamentations, 295
Laodicean Council, 298
last judgment, 251, 252, 337, 396–97
last will and testament, 444–45
  enforced when testator is dead, 445
Latomus, Jacobus, 453–54
law
  going to for recompense, 386
  as last remedy, 387
  as ministry of condemnation, 391
  notoriously abused, 387
  without equity becomes tyranny, 376
law and gospel, 404
law of man, 367–71
law without the curse, 340
lawyers, 375
legal sorrow, 338
Leites, Edmund, xxvin78
lending freely, 96
Leo, 28
leprosy, 142
lesser prophecies (Old Testament), 295
less principal promises, 7
lethargy, 143
Levites, 71
Leviticus, 293
Libertines, 302
life of the righteous, 424
lifting of the eye, 354
Lindanus, William Damascus, 327
lips, coal applied to, 267
literal sense of Scripture, 303
living by faith, 6, 25
living by works, 6
living in obedience, 452
living in peace, 73
logic, laws of, 312
Lombard, Peter, 125, 163
"Lord is at hand," 396–98
Lord's Prayer, 355, 433
Lord's Supper, not a private action, 428
love
  in calling, 92–93
  for inferiors, 263–64
  for neighbor, xxii, 52
  suffers all things, 378
  thinks not evil, 380
Lovelace, R. C., xin1
Luke, Gospel of, 295–96
lust of the heart, 21
lusts of the flesh, xxviii
Luther, Martin, xxi, xxixn91, 66, 272, 361, 446, 450, 458
Lyra, N., 298

Maccabees, books of (apocrypha), 299
Machiavelli, 95
Macrobus, 299
madness, as impediment of marriage, 150, 154
magistrate
  calling of, 53, 75
  duty at death, 443

and equity, 363
as merciful judge, 371
must advance schools of the prophets, 213–14
tributes paid to, 96
Malachi, 295
male, of a superior sex, 130
malicious dealing in marriage, 164
man
became mortal by way of the fall, 405
as procurer of death, 405
Manasseh, humble prayer of, 431–32
Manichaeism, xxviin82
manna, twelve wonders of, 84
Marcion, 302
Mark, Gospel of, 295–96
Marlorate, Augustine, 309
marriage, xxiv–xxv, 123–26
absence in, 165
cherishing one another in, 170
choice and consent of the parties, 130–48
consent in, 148–51
consummation of, xxiv, 127, 153, 155–60
as divine ordinance, 159
duties and callings in, 125
end of, 124–25
equity of, 365
first year of, 161
four ends of, xxviii
to a harlot, 146–47
intimacy of, xxvii
rejoicing in, 170
as seminary of church and commonwealth, 159
as type of Christ and His church, 168
to a widow, 147
marriageable persons
accidental marks of, 144–47
essential marks of, 130–43
marriage bed, xxvin75, 166–68
marriage contract, xxiv, 127–29
rejection or refusal of, 152–54
marriage feasts, 160
master, xxx, 184–85, 188
calling of, 53
duties of, 184–85
master of the family
charge of souls under him, 446
duties of, 189–92
to exercise discipline, 191–92
hospitality of, 192
to provide meat, drink and clothing, 191
setting house in order before death, 444–46
material evil, 405
Matthew, Gospel of, 295–96
Matthias, Jacobus, 356
meals, blessed to receivers by Word and prayer, 121
medicine. *See* physic
meditation
on death, xxxiii, 420–22, 435–36
on the future life, xxxiiin120
on union with Christ in life and death, 437
Melanchthon, Philip, 450
Melchizedek, 71, 303
Meliton, 298
members in the family, employed in honest and profitable business, 122
Menander, 332
Menon, 302
mental application, 344
mercy, 370–71
as badge of a Christian, 388
messenger, minister as, 207–9
metonymy, 314
Micah, 295
Michaelson, Robert, xxiin56
milk (principles of the faith), 337
minister
as angel, 207–9
authority of, 226–28, 280, 353

minister (*continued*)
blessed to have poor living and good people, 248
calling of, xiii–xiv, 69–70, 277, 279
comfort from angels, 260–61
comforts troubled and distressed consciences, 268
commission of, 228, 280
confesses the sins of his people, 244–45
and consummation of marriage, 159
double honor of, 220
duty while dying, 444
esteem for, 220
as example of his teaching, 351
fear of God, 353
fleeing persecution, 99
as godly, 351–52
as God's ambassador, 274
good conscience of, 352
holiness of life, 209
as interpreter, 207–10
inward feeling of doctrine, 352–53
knows his flock, 245
lawfully called and sent by God, 204
love for his people, 264, 353
as messenger, 207–9
must have fiery tongue, 265–66
need for faithful and godly, 270–71
not a servant of men, 274–75
not to be censured too sharply, 248–49
not to inquire of a good living, 247
office to declare the righteousness of Christ, 217–21
polluted by his people, 246, 248–49
present with his people, 245
profaneness of, 252–54
reconciliation of, 209, 219, 223
as reprover, 266
reverence and honor to, 207
sanctification of, 209–10, 219, 254
as servant of God, 273–75
stipends due to, 96
unsanctified, 253–54
as temperate, 353
too little a living, 277
as venerable, 353
visit and comfort the sick, 433
wicked, 352
works upon conscience of impenitent sinner, 382
ministry
duties and dignities of, 197–98
high and excellent calling, 237
miracles, of prophets, 23
mistress of the family
duties of, 193–94
to give a portion of food to her family, 193
to govern the house, 193
mitigation of law, 367–71, 374
moderation, xxii–xxiii, xxixn90, 363
of care, 17
with God, 266
in life of man, 372–75
of mind, 365
in wedlock, 167
monks, xxix, 55, 272
moral commandments, 316
moral evil, 405
Morgan, Edmund, xxixn93
morning household service of God, 121
mortification of sin, 426
Moses
calling of, 45, 66
miracles of, 299
nursed by Hebrew woman, 177
Muller, Richard A., xvn24

Nahum, 295
name of Christ, 49
name of God, 251
Nathan, 218
natural atheism, 22
natural delights, xxviii, xxviii–xxixn90

natural evil, 405
natural gifts, of children, 62–63
natural infirmities, and private equity, 377–80
natural life, 5. *See also* temporal life
natural reason, 20
Nazarite vow, 47
Nehemiah, 294
newness of life, 13–14, 424
new obedience, 340
New Testament, 295–96
Nicene Council, 298
Nicephorus, 159
Nineveh, repentance of, 421
Noah, 91, 111
"none" as used for few, 317
"not," restrained for special matter in Scripture, 318
notation ("right cutting" of the Word), 329
Numbers, 293

Obadiah, 295
obedience, 7–8
  must be absolute, 7
  must be sincere, 8
  must be stable and consistent, 8
Oecolampadius, 66, 449–50
Oeconomie. See *Christian Oeconomie*
office
  buying and selling of, 65
  desiring of, 70
Old Testament, 292–95
one flesh, xxvi–xxvii, xxxi, 123, 143, 171, 172
ordinances of God, 80, 167, 251, 265
ordination, of calling, 44–45
Origen, 63, 298
"ornate" style of preaching, xviii
orthodox writings, 301–2

papists, 29
  false faith of, 21
  vanity of, 243
parent and child, xxix–xxx
parents
  consent in marriage, 151
  and consummation of marriage, 155–59
  duties of, 176–80
  judging fit callings for children, 62–63
parity and equality in age and condition (marriage), 145–46
parity and equality in Christian religion (marriage), 144–45
particular calling, xix–xxii, 53–60
  in the commonwealth, xx
  in the family, xx
  gives place to general calling, 59–60
  and good works, xxii
  joined with general calling, 57–59
  and outward calling of men, 65, 66
  rules of, 54–60
particular pollution of a prophet, 242–44
particular preparation for death, 427–46
pastor. *See* minister
paterfamilias, 189
Paul
  in Athens, 336
  calling as apostle, 70, 71
  calling as tent maker, 72, 100
  desired death, 456
  desired to live, 457
  epistles of, 296
  temptation of, 413
  use of allegories, 332
  use of human testimonies, 332–33
peace
  of conscience, 12–13, 276, 425
  and forgiving wrongs, 385
  preservation of, 366–67
Pelagians, 302, 346
people, pollution of, 244–50
Pepper, Cutbert, 359
Perkins, William, 197, 361, 363
  exegesis of, xvn24
  growth in holiness, xix

Perkins, William (*continued*)
practical instruction of, xii
on slavery, xxxn98
persecution, fleeing of, 99
perseverance, 340
persons in Scripture, with two names, 322
Peter
curiosity of, 73
denied Christ, 47
first and second letters of, 296
Pharisees, 302
Philemon, 296
Philip, calling as evangelist, 45, 67
Philippians, 296
Philips, Edward, 231
phlebotomy (bloodletting), 440
physic
right practice of, 438–39
sanctified by Word and prayer, 441
physician
calling of, 53
duties of, 442
Pickering, Thomas, 115
place of death, 418
places in Scripture, 303–9, 322
plague, 25, 99
Plato, 298
pleonasm, 318–20
Pliny, 299
Plutarch, 173, 299
Polycarp, 448–49
polygamy, 139
poor, poverty, 231–32, 456
practical application, 344–45
practical syllogism, 11
Practice of Faith, 37–38, 201
prayer
before and after the sermon, 253
for blessing of means, 302
conceiving of, 355–56
for the good estate of the church, 50
and holy use of callings, 93–100
to resolve ourselves of death, 422
See also conceiving of prayers
Prayer of Manassas, 299
preacher, as God's mouthpiece, xii
preacher's life, grace evident in, xviii–xix
preaching
consistency in, xviii–xix
demonstration of the Spirit in, xvii, xviii, 349–50
doctrine in, xvi
eloquence in, 349
freedom in, xviii
gesture in, xviii, 353–54
and Holy Spirit, 206
of law and gospel, 219, 220, 338–39
memory in, xv, 348
ostentation in, 349
plainness in, xvii, 206
power in, 206
as prophesying, xiv, 290
sacred and only method of, xv, 356
simplicity in, xvii–xviii, 356
voice in, xviii
presence of death, meditation on, 420–21
presence of God, 396, 397–98
extraordinary presence, 252–57
glory of, 256
ordinary presence, 251–52
sensible presence at last judgment, 251
with the sick and dying, 437–38
preservation, in calling, 17
preservation of life, 438–42
princes, love for subjects, 264
principal promises, 7
principles of Christianity, 337
private actions, 276
private communions, 428–29
private confession, 341
private equity, 363, 376–88
private evil, 382
private necessity, and change in calling, 100
private worship, 120–22

procreation of children, xxvii, xxviii, 124, 142
profane and ridiculous speech, to be omitted in sermons, 350
profitable callings, 74
promises of God, 7, 14–15
prophecies, accomplishment of, 299
prophesying, 285, 289
  as forthtelling, xiv
  as preaching as, xiv, 290
prophet
  abased before he is commissioned, 239, 269
  comforted and raised from his fear, 258–59
  commission of, 269–80
  conscience of, 241
  consolation of, 257–69
  fear of, 236–57
  pollution of, 240–44
  touched by the pollution of his people, 246
  as voice of God, 290
  as voice of the people, 290
  as voice of the people calling unto God, 355
prophetical books (Old Testament), 294–95, 301
prophets
  miracles of, 23
  predictions of, 23
Proverbs, 294
providence of God, 82–83, 345–46
  and death, 435–36
Psalms, 294, 301
public actions, 276
publican and the Pharisee, parable of, 79
public calling, and reforming self in private, 59
public equity, 363, 367–76
  in laws of men, 367–71
  in life of man, 372–76
public evil, 382
public good, and change in calling, 100
public honesty and credit (in marriage contract), 146–47
public peace, and yielding rights, 382–84
Pupianus, 302
Puritan prudery, xxviiin87
Puritans, on calling, xxiin56

quietness of mind, 276

Rebekah, 174, 177, 180, 181, 193
rebuke, 345
receipts and expenses, 105
reconciliation, 207, 443
  with God, 10–12, 430
  as preparation for death, 430
  by the sick, 442–43
reconciliation (differences in Scripture), 321–26
recreation, 97–98
redargution, 344, 346
redeemers, duties of, 226–27
Reformation, calling of ministers, 66–67
Reformation of Covetousness, 37–38, 201
reformation of life, 18–25, 59, 423–24, 457
regiment of the Spirit, 425
relationships, xxiii
remarriage, after desertion, 162
remedy, for falling, 241–42
repentance, 203, 337, 338–40, 391
  of Nineveh, 421
  at time of death, 419–20
repetition of word, 320
resolution ("right cutting" of the Word), 329
resurrection, 337, 413, 416–17
Revelation (book), 296
reward, 104
rich, personal calling of, 55–56
Rich, Robert Lord, 111

riches. *See* abundance
"right cutting of the Word," xvi
rights, departing from, 377, 382–84
rogues, 55
Roman Catholic Church
apostate and heretical church, 67
baptism, 77
on celibacy of clergy, 125–26
clergy, 199, 271–72
on double justification, 18
on the family, 113–15
on four senses of Scripture, 304
on marriage as sacrament, 166
on orders of angels, 259
on preparation for death, 427–30
on separation of sacred and secular, xxi
vanity of, 255
Romans, epistle to, 296, 301
Roper, Lyndal, xxiiin63
Ruffinus, 177
rulers, as nursing fathers and mothers unto the church, 223
rulers and governors, to see that charges are left in good estate after death, 443
Russell, Lucy (Countess of Bedford), 399
Ruth, 293

Sabbath, 190
Sabellius, 302
sacrament, 311
sacramental confession, 427
sacraments, must not condemn in their commonness, 265
sacred-secular distinction, xx–xxi
Salve for a Sick Man (1597), xxxii–xxxiv, 399–458
Samosatenus, 302
Samson, 47, 180, 422–23
Samuel, and schools of the prophets, 213–14
Samuel, First and Second, 293
sanctification, 340
accomplished at death, 413
in marriage, 168
of marriage, 159
of the work, 79–80
of the worker, 78–79
Sarah, as Abraham's sister, 134–35
Saul, 47, 453
saving faith, 6
saving knowledge, 425
saving of souls, 227
Sayvile, John, 231
Schismatics, 302
schools of the prophets, 213–14
Schucking, Levin, xxiiin63
scribes and Pharisees, 76
Scripture
canon, 292, 296
consent of all the parts, 299
corruption of copies, 327–28
evidence of truth, 23
expounding of, 310–28
interpretation of, 301–9
meaning of, 302
miraculous preservation of, 299
places in, 303–9
reading of, xv, 301
right division of, 303
sum of, 292
tokens of, 299
as Word of God, 292, 297
Second Chronicles, 293
second death, 406
Second Kings, 293
Second Samuel, 293
secret marriages, 158
self-defense, 385–86
Seneca, 65
sense (seeing and feeling), 20–21
Seraphim, 257–58, 259
Serapion, 429
sermon
ancient and modern structures of, xviiin37
committed to memory, 348
preparation for, 301–3

promulgation of, 301
as spiritual and gracious speech, 350–51
uttering of, 349–54
servant, xxx, 184–85
duties of, 186–88
particular calling of, 56
servanthood, in the duties of love, 52
Servetus, 302
serving God and man, in calling, 58–59
Sheffield, Lord, 359
sick
and calling of the elders of the church, 432–33
care to preserve life and health, 438
confession of sins, 433–34
duties toward neighbor, 442–46
duties toward self, 434–42
humbling under hand of God for sins, 441
visiting of, 98–99
sickness, 25, 456
confession of new and particular sins, 431
and examination of heart, 431
and reconciliation with God, 431, 432
signification of a word, 327
signifying will of God, 316
Simeon, 411
Simon Magus, 65
sin
abolished by death, 456
creeping and encroaching nature of, 247
nature and properties of, 257
single life, 122, 123
sinner
preserved by God, 203
restoration of, 203
slaughtering of the infants, 299
slothfulness, 48
Sodomites and Gomorrheans, 453
sodomy, 130
Somerville, C. John, xxn47
Song of Songs, 294
sons
duties of, 181–83
obedience to parents in choice of lawful calling, 181
obedience to parents in marriage, 181
sons of Adam, marriage to sisters, 134
sons of the church, dedicating to ministry, 51–52
sons of Zebedee, discontentment of, 56
sorcerers, 441
soul
immortality of, 406
passage to rest in death, 456
special providence, 346
spells, 440
spiritual death, three degrees of, 406
spiritual household, xxiiin63, xxivn67, xxix–xxx
"spiritualization" of Puritan household, xxiiin63
spiritual liberty, 188
spiritual life, xxxiin111, 5, 10–15
spiritual speech, sermon as, 350
Stephen, last words of, 448
Stoics, 346
strong meat (doctrines of the faith), 337
students, must consecrate themselves to the ministry, 215, 220
students in divinity, 12, 276–77
Suetonius, 298
suits for trifles, 397
supererogation, works of, 243
superlative speech, for persons of the Deity, 316–17
synecdoche, 314–15
Synochus (fever), 440
Syricius, Pope, xxvii, 166

Tacitus, 298
taking up the cross, 29
Tatians, 302
Taylor, Robert, 33
telling of tales, to be omitted in sermons, 350
temporal life, xxxiin111, 10, 15–29, 419, 431, 438
temptation from Satan near death, 411–12
Ten Commandments, 433
Tertullian, 146, 158, 159, 337, 355
text
  doctrines in, xvi
  sense and understanding of, xv
Theodorus, Vitus, 361
Thessalonians, First and Second, 296
thief on the cross, repentance of, 420
thievery, 369
thinking the best of all men, 380–82
Third Book of Ezra, 299
thorn in the flesh, 413
threatenings of the Word, 7
threats and promises of Scripture, conditions of, 316
"three-couple" paradigm, xxix–xxx
Tiberius Caesar, 76
time of death, 418
Timothy, First and Second, 296
Titus, 296
Tobit, 299
Todd, Margo, xxivn67
tongue, minister's use of, 242–44
tongue of the learned, 208
Tossaine, Daniel, 361
tower of Babel, 299
treason, 382
Treatise of Christian Equity and Moderation. See Epieikeia, or A Treatise of Christian Equity and Moderation
Treatise of the Vocations (1603), xix–xxii, 31–107
trees of righteousness, 52
trial of the cause, 341
trial of the estate, 341
Trinity
  argument for, 272–73
  and marriage, xxvi
  outward works understood inclusively, 317
tropes, 313–18
tropological sense of Scripture, 303
true faith, xxxiv
true minister, xiii, 204, 210
  blessing from God upon, 222–25
  as double interpreter, 207–8
  rarity of, 211–16, 270
  stricken with great fear, 237
true and sound Christians, 49
trust, with whole heart, 8
trusting God, 7–9
Tuke, Thomas, xivn17, 284
Tully, 312
Turks, 21, 227
two callings, 71–72
two trades, 72
tyranny, of law without equity, 376

unbelief
  bewailing of, 12, 21–22
  and covetousness, 81
  fruits of, 20
unbelievers, 335–36
understanding, active and passive, 63
union with Christ
  in life and death, 415–17, 437
  as positional, xxxiv
  as transformational, xxxiv
universities, puffed up in self-conceits, 238
university students, 238
urine, inspection of, 439
usury, 44
Uzzah, 74

vacations, 97–99
vagabonds, 55, 96
Vashti, Queen, 175
Vermigli, Peter Martyr, 66, 450

vice, eschewing in calling, 81–91
Virgil, 298
Virgin Mary, apparitions of, 255
virtue, in practice of callings, 91–93
vocation. *See* calling

walking worthy of calling, 52–53
Wallace, Dewey, xxxiiin119
Walsham, Alexandria, xxiii–xxivn63
war, 25
weaknesses of brethren, forbearance with, 377–80
Weber, Max, xix–xxn47
"Whom shall I send and who shall go for us?" 270–75
widows, espousals of, 183
wife, xxix
  to avoid pride and bitterness of, 175
  duties of, 174–75
  obedience to husband, 174, 175
  reverence of husband, 174–75
will of God, xx
  as rule for last will and testament, 444
will of God's good pleasure, 316
William the Conqueror, 69
William, R., 359
Wingandus, 356
wisdom, 13
Wisdom (apocrypha), 299
wise and foolish virgins, 28–29
wise men's star, 299
witches, 441
wizards, 224, 441
"woe is me, I am undone," 212, 236, 238–39, 255, 259
Word of God, 291–300
antiquity of, 299
  certainty of, 22–24
  as directory for holy use of calling, 80
  eternity of, 291
  as fountain of equity, 376
  perfection of, 291
  purity of, 291
  rightly dividing, 329–33
  subjecting whole man to, 25
  substance and scope of, 24
  sufficiency of, 291
  trusting in, 8
  see also Scripture
words, grammatical and rhetorical proprieties of, 318–21
work. *See* particular calling
works of the law, 18
world, scorn and contempt against ministry, 219
worldliness, 20
worldlings, 29
worldly sorrow, 338
wrath of God, 250–51
Wycliffe, John, 66

Yelverton, Christopher, 231

Zacchaeus, 88, 232, 425
zeal, in the ministry, 353
Zechariah, 295
Zephaniah, 295
Zipporah, 175, 180
Zwingli, Huldrych, 449